ASIAN-
AMERICAN
LITERATURE

ASIAN-AMERICAN LITERATURE

An Anthology

Shirley Geok-lin Lim
University of California, Santa Barbara

McGraw-Hill

A Division of The McGraw-Hill Companies

McGraw-Hill

A Division of The McGraw-Hill Companies

Acknowledgments for literary selections begin on page 555, which is to be considered an extension of this copyright page.

Executive Editor: Marisa L. L'Heureux
Marketing Manager: Judy Rudnick
Design Manager: Ophelia M. Chambliss
Production Coordinator: Denise M. Duffy-Fieldman
Cover: Raging Sea, a quilt by Kumiko Sudo, 1986. Courtesy of Kumiko Sudo.

ISBN: 0-8442-1729-8 (student text)
ISBN: 0-8442-1744-1 (instructor's edition)

Published by NTC/Contemporary Publishing Group, Inc.
4255 West Touhy Avenue, Lincolnwood (Chicago), Illinois 60646-1975 U.S.A.
©2000 NTC/Contemporary Publishing Group, Inc.

3 4 5 6 7 8 9 0 QSR/QSR 0 9 8 7 6 5

Library of Congress Cataloging in Publication Data
Asian-American literature : an anthology / [edited by] Shirley
   Geok-lin Lim
      p. cm.
   Includes index.
   ISBN 0-8442-1729-8 (softbound)
      1. American literature—Asian American authors. 2. Asian
   Americans—Literary collections. I. Lim, Shirley.
   PS508.A8A83   2000
   810.8'0895—dc21   99-16872

For the Asian-American authors and scholars whose work has made this anthology possible.

CONTENTS

CHAPTER TWO

ASIAN AFFILIATIONS   65

CHAPTER THREE
STRUGGLES AND RECOGNITIONS

123

CHAPTER FOUR
THE INDIVIDUAL INSIDE/ AGAINST THE ETHNIC COMMUNITY

229

CHAPTER FIVE

GENDER IDENTITIES, GENDER RELATIONSHIPS

303

CHAPTER SIX
PARENTS AND FAMILIES

CHAPTER SEVEN

AMERICAN PLACE AND DISPLACEMENT

419

CHAPTER EIGHT

LANGUAGE AND VISION

513

PREFACE

There are few broad anthologies of Asian-American writing available to teachers, students, and the general reader today. A number of anthologies focus on specific ethnic communities within the larger Asian-American category; thus, anthologies of Filipino-American, South-Asian-American, and Vietnamese-American literature have recently been published. Other collections have concentrated on particular genres—for example, poetry or prose narratives—or on contemporary literary productions. This anthology is broadly structured. Its major goal is to offer teachers, students, and the general public an inclusive introduction to Asian-American writing. It seeks to place in a volume of about 550 pages a broad sampler of works whose critical reception has already marked them as belonging to an Asian-American canon or which represent emergent voices, communities, and concerns.

As an introduction to Asian-American literature, the anthology seeks to provide satisfactory access to some of the more provocative, challenging, and original of the literary works produced by Asian-American authors in the last century. The emphasis is on both well-known and acclaimed works and newer writing. The selections are made from considerations of literary quality—a criterion that is more often contested than agreed upon—and of historical and thematic significance.

The volume includes the writing of communities from different national origins: Chinese, Japanese, Filipino, Korean, Hawaiian-Asian, Vietnamese, Malaysian, Burmese, Indian, Pakistani, and other national origins. The anthology also seeks representation of different genres. Although most of it is composed of short stories, novel excerpts, and poetry, it also includes drama, nonfiction memoirs, and oral narratives. This range underlines the diversity of literary achievements and thematic concerns in Asian-American literature, a rich diversity that parallels the heterogeneity of Asian-American communities.

The anthology does not attempt to demonstrate that Asian-American works come from or contribute to a cohesive and united tradition. Rather, certain cultural elements appear to be shared by many of the authors who are marked by different histories and origins. Some of these shared cultural elements, for example, may be seen to arise from an East Asian Confucianist worldview, from common patriarchal constructions of kinship and gender, and from common histories of social and political struggles and racialization in the United States. Nonetheless, there is no single tradition that can contain the varied concerns expressed through such different literary strategies and techniques as are manifested in the selections.

The anthology is not organized by national origins of the authors or by genres or even by chronology. It is organized into eight chapters, each possessing a thematic core: the immigration experience; Asian affiliations; struggles and recognition; the individual inside/against the ethnic community; gender identities, gender relationships; parents and families; American place and displacement; and language and vision. Together, the chapters compose a kind of narrative and chronological progression, beginning with immigration and Asian histories and moving on to social conflicts and reconstructions in the United States, to focus on individual, community, and national identities, gender and family concerns, and aesthetic values and cultural practices.

ACKNOWLEDGMENTS

This book could not have been composed without the inspiring work produced by writers of Asian ancestry over at least a century, beginning with the work of Sui Sin Far at the end of the nineteenth century. I thank all these authors, including those whose works do not appear in these pages because of space restrictions but whose writings contribute to that confluence of culture and expression that enriches us all.

I also thank all the scholars and editors whose pioneering work and critical labor have helped the development of this literature, including, to mention just a few, Carol Bruchac, Nick Carbo, Frank Chin, Jeffery Paul Chan, King-Kok Cheung, Lawson Inada, Elaine H. Kim, Garrett Hongo, Luu Truong Khoi, Walter Lew, Amy Ling, Stephen Sumida, Barbara Tran, Monique T. D. Truong, Mayumi Tsutakawa, Sylvia Watanabe, Sau-ling Wong, Shawn Wong, and others.

In the completion of the anthology I pay particular tribute to Marisa L. L'Heureux, whose enthusiasm and support made the project possible, and to John Inouye, who wrote almost half of the headnotes that accompany the selections (as indicated by the use of his initials at the end of those headnotes he wrote). I also thank my colleagues who answered many of the bilingual and bicultural questions raised in specific texts: Jay Chan, Kip Fulbeck, Karen Gundersen, Susan Koshy, Hyung Il Pai, Joanne Rondilla, Xiaojin Zhao, and others. I am grateful to the Department of English and the Women's Studies Program at the University of California, Santa Barbara, for their support.

As always, my greatest debt is to my family, Charles Bazerman and Gershom Kean Bazerman, who keep me grounded.

INTRODUCTION TO ASIAN-AMERICAN LITERATURE

Asian-American literature has usually been presented primarily from the standpoint of "race." That is, the literature is read as being centered solely on the identity position of Americans of Asian descent and is read in the context of Asian-American immigration histories and legislative struggles against unjust policies and racial violence. Carlos Bulosan's *America Is in the Heart* (1946) is one such classical representation, following Bulosan, a Filipino immigrant, as he and other migrant workers struggle for social justice and acceptance during a time of nativist American hostility to Asian immigration.

In reality, the varying immigration histories of authors from different national-origin communities give rise to writings that reflect distinctive cross-generational concerns and styles. This diversity is obvious even in very early works, such as translations of Chinese-language poems written by immigrant Chinese on the walls at the Angel Island detention barracks and Issei (first-generation Japanese-American) tankas, works that add to the archival canon of Asian-American literature. Such heterogeneous representations help to overturn stereotypes of inscrutable Asian-Americans.

Three early Asian-American anthologies, *Asian-American Authors* (1972), *Asian-American Heritage* (1974), and *Aiiieeeee!* (1975), suggested that the melting pot paradigm was inadequate to an understanding of Asian-American cultural identity. Influenced by the civil rights movement of the 1960s, the editors of *Aiiieeeee!* looked beyond the melting pot to argue that Asian-American "sensibility" was an American phenomenon distinctively different from and unrelated to Asian cultural sources.

Drawn from different national-origin communities, memoirs were the favored genre with immigrant and first-generation writers. Younghill Kang's

The Grass Roof (1931), Pardee Lowe's *Father and Glorious Descendant* (1949), and Jade Snow Wong's *Fifth Chinese Daughter* (1950) sought to satisfy an American audience's curiosity about the strangers in their midst. Japanese-American internment history has also been a major source for memoirs, poetry, and other literary works, including Monica Sone's *Nisei Daughter* (1956); Jeanne Wakatsuki Houston and James D. Houston's *Farewell to Manzanar* (1973); and Mitsuye Yamada's poems in *Desert Run* (1988). Chinese- and Japanese-Americans began publishing imaginative literature in the 1950s (for example, Diana Chang's *The Frontiers of Love* received critical notice in 1956), but South Asian, Vietnamese, Hmong, and other, newer Asian-American groups are also now actively publishing in multiple genres. These range from Wendy Law-Yone's narration of a Burmese-American's initiation into the United States in *The Coffin Tree* (1983) to poetry and memoirs by Indonesian Chinese-American Li-Young Lee and Malaysian-American Shirley Geok-lin Lim.

After the awards garnered by Maxine Hong Kingston's memoir *The Woman Warrior* (1976), much Asian-American writing has also received critical acclaim. Among the most well-received collections of poetry have been Cathy Song's *Picture Bride* (1983) and Garrett Hongo's *The River of Heaven* (1988). Critically acclaimed novels include Amy Tan's *The Joy Luck Club* (1989), Bharati Mukherjee's *Jasmine* (1989), and Gish Jen's *Typical American* (1991). Among the short story collections that have been hailed are Hisaye Yamamoto's *Seventeen Syllables* (1988), David Wong Louie's *Pangs of Love* (1992), Wakako Yamauchi's *Songs My Mother Taught Me* (1994), and Lan Samantha Chang's *Hunger* (1999). David Henry Hwang's plays, including *M. Butterfly* (1989), have been successful on Broadway.

In works that treat Asian-American women's struggles against Asian and American patriarchal attitudes, issues of race and gender are intertwined. Maxine Hong Kingston's *The Woman Warrior* is a complex series of narratives about growing up in ethnic and national communities that are both racist and sexist. The anthologies *The Forbidden Stitch* (1989), *Making Waves* (1989), *Home to Stay* (1990), *Our Feet Walk the Sky* (1993), and others contain writing protesting female subordination and male privilege.

Many Asian-American works center on questions of individual identity and ethnic community conflicts, among them widely taught works like *Toshio Mori's Yokohama, California* (1949), John Okada's *No-No Boy* (1957), Louis Chu's *Eat a Bowl of Tea* (1961), Bienvenido Santos's *Scent of Apples* (1979), Kingston's *China Men* (1980), and Kim Ronyoung's *Clay Walls* (1987). Many of these works are also regionally identified. For example, Okada's, Mori's, Kingston's, and Kim's narratives are set in ethnic-specific enclaves on the West Coast, while Chu's novel is set in New York's Chinatown. Works written out of Hawaii, such as Milton Murayama's novel *All I Asking for Is My Body* (1975) and Lois-Ann Yamanaka's poems in

Saturday Night at the Pahala Theatre (1993), express a strong island identity.

Younger contemporary writers, such as novelist Cynthia Kadohata (*In the Valley of the Heart,* 1993) and playwright Philip K. Gotanda (*Yankee Dawg You Die,* 1991), following on Kingston's tour-de-force novel *Tripmaster Monkey* (1989), experiment with postmodernist techniques of parody, irony, pastiche, and bricolage; challenge the interlocking categories of race, class, and gender; and include sexual identity as central to the themes of identity. Using similar techniques, Jessica Hagedorn's *Dogeaters* (1990), set in the Philippines, critiques United States colonialism and the Marcos military regime, while celebrating the hybrid nature of Filipino culture.

Single-genre anthologies have been a useful means of exploring the cultural diversity of Asian-American writing. Among the best poetry anthologies are *Breaking Silence* (1983) and *The Open Boat* (1993), while short fiction has been the focus of *Charlie Chan Is Dead* (1993) and drama the focus of *Between Worlds* (1990), *The Politics of Life* (1993), and *Unbroken Threads* (1993). These anthologies testify to the diversity of styles, genres, and voices underlying Asian-American writing. This diversity—so multiple and heterogeneous—is also evident in recent anthologies that focus on specific groups of Asian-American authors and genres, as with the publication of the Filipino and Filipino-American poetry anthology *Returning a Borrowed Tongue* (1995) and the Vietnamese-American collection *Watermark* (1998).

Together these anthologies make emphatic the phenomenon of rapid publication and the continuous reinvention of Asian-American cultural identity. The visibility of such writing owes much to the success of the civil rights movement of the 1950s and 1960s, and particularly to the success of African-American writing, as seen, for example, in the works of Toni Morrison, who received the Nobel Prize for Literature in 1994.

This interest in Asian-American literature, however, brings both opportunities and a crisis of representation. One aspect of this crisis is that any attempts at defining and fixing a canon of texts—that is, a list of the best or the most significant (which are not the same categories) works—face internal debate as well as provisionality and temporality. Hence, Asian-American literature is a particularly shifting, slippery, contested field.

This anthology leaves open the question of how interpretation of texts should take into consideration the different literary formations of writers who now publish under an Asian-American rubric. Migrants, refugees, exiles, and immigrants have been coming continuously to the United States and have continued to write and publish while in the U.S., but until recently most of them had maintained their identities of origin and eventually returned to their national territories. For example, Lin Yutang returned to Taiwan after his retirement as professor at Columbia University; despite his publishing *Chinatown Family* (1948), a novel about a United States Chinatown community, he has never been claimed as Asian American. Today, however, these constructed borders have become more porous, a consequence of and resulting in further globalization of cultures and a transnational construction of American identity. In deliberately placing American-born, migrant, and transnational Asian-American writers together, this anthology seeks to suggest a collective set of new American identities now emerging as Asian American.

ASIAN-AMERICAN LITERATURE

CHAPTER ONE

THE IMMIGRATION EXPERIENCE

It is fitting that an anthology of Asian American literature should begin with expressions of the immigration experience. Like many other Americans, Asian Americans, despite the seemingly homogeneous sense of this ethnic identity label, come to the United States from a wide range of different national territories and bring with them very different social and cultural histories. There is no single immigration story that can be said to represent all Asian Americans. Instead, the narratives that describe the journey from an Asian territory to an American space, the crossing over and settling in, must be contextualized within the histories and cultures of a number of different Asian nations.

Filipino sailors working on the Spanish galleons jumped ship on the American continent in the 1600s, and sailors and traders from China were arriving in New York by the 1830s. The first recorded major influx of Asians to the United States occurred in 1848, after the news of the discovery of gold in California reached China. Anti-Asian sentiment began as early as 1850, with the onset of legislation to tax, contain, discriminate against, and exclude first the Chinese, then all Asians from U.S. soil.

Japanese and Koreans arrived as contract workers for the sugar plantations established in the new territory of Hawaii at the beginning of the twentieth century, and Filipinos entered the United States in sizeable numbers after the United States took control of the Philippines from the Spanish at the conclusion of the Spanish-American War in 1898. Southeast Asians began immigrating to the United States only after the revision of immigration laws in 1968, and Vietnamese and Cambodians began arriving in 1975 after Communist governments came to power in their countries.

While Asian American immigration narratives share common themes with other coming-to-America stories told by Italian or Central and Eastern

European authors, for example, they also reflect, express, and constitute social practices, beliefs, values, and experiences that are different from those portrayed in Euro-American literature. Authors who have immigrated from China, Japan, Korea, the Philippines, Vietnam and the rest of Southeast Asia, or India and other South Asian countries tell distinctively different stories of their entries into the United States. Of course, these works also share common themes and motifs that articulate the economic, social, and cultural struggles of individuals moving from a known community to the unknown, of losing accustomed comfort and identity, or of gaining new resources and identities.

Often these experiences are narrated as nonfiction—through autobiographies and memoirs. Sometimes these stories, told by speakers who do not have access to the English language, are preserved as oral tales. Moreover, such immigration stories are also marked by class and gender positions. The welcome enjoyed by the aristocratic and wealthy female narrator who comes to America under the protection of her diplomat husband, as described in Etsu Sugimoto's memoir *A Daughter of the Samurai,* is radically different from the hostility that meets the young peasant Filipino when he comes to work in the California farms during the Depression, as seen in Carlos Bulosan's *America Is in the Heart.* Sugimoto's story is also different from the experiences of the Japanese picture bride who, in marrying a fellow Japanese immigrant, a total stranger, enters into a life of unremitting labor, as depicted in Akemi Kikumura's *Through Harsh Winters.* In fact, Kikumura's immigrant story arguably has more in common with Bulosan's memoir than with Sugimoto's tale.

The vividness of these significant histories, whether personal or communal, is also captured in poetry and fiction, which are genres that help us imagine the complicated emotions and thoughts of immigrant characters while throwing a critical light on the social and political complexities that are causally or contextually related to the experiences represented. Some immigration stories offer more self-conscious or ironic perspectives on the United States. Shirley Geok-lin Lim's memoir excerpt from *Among the White Moon Faces* notes the ambivalence that disturbs some immigrants who, despite their choice to leave their homeland, carry a profound regret for their choice and mourn the death of their Asian selves.

The poignancy of the act of immigration and the conflicting meanings given to immigration itself can move the reader even when the author/speaker may not be educated in English and may be writing/speaking in an Asian language. The Chinese poems carved or written on the wooden walls of the detention building on Angel Island, where, from 1910 to 1940, immigrants from China were held until they could offer proof of their legitimate immigrant status, still testify, after all these intervening years, to the detainees' resentment at their treatment and their determination to overcome such injustices. Similarly, Jade Ngoc Quang Huỳnh's biographical description of the harrowing escape from Vietnam speaks eloquently to the determination of more recent immigrants to reach the shores of the United States and to their aspirations for a better life of economic and political freedom. American assimilation brings with it the potential loss of memory of an original social community, and the poems by Eugene Gloria and Christian Langworthy are both ironical and critical expressions of this interrelated immigrant experience.

As a whole, Asian American writing of the immigrant experience constitutes a powerful literary legacy that is capable of communicating the heterogeneous sensibilities and histories—including histories of colonialism, class, and gender status—of Americans who are descended from people of different Asian nations.

SAILING UNKNOWN SEAS

Etsu Sugimoto

Etsu Inagaki Sugimoto was born in Japan in 1874 and came to the United States as a young woman with her husband, who worked for the Japanese diplomatic corps. She is the author of *A Daughter of the Samurai* (1926), an autobiographical work that narrates the life of a woman raised in a traditional Samurai family who immigrates to America with her husband. Subtitled "How a daughter of feudal Japan, living hundreds of years in one generation, became a modern America," the autobiography grew out of a request by Christopher Morley, a journalist for a Philadelphia newspaper, who had asked Mrs. Sugimoto for some memories from her girlhood in Japan for his column.

In the introduction to the autobiography, Morley noted, "how startled . . . some of her knightly ancestors would be to find her putting her private thoughts on paper for all the world to see." Indeed, as one of the first Japanese immigrants to publish in English in the United States, Sugimoto was breaking the mold both as a woman and as a Japanese American. She is also the author of two novels. The first, *A Daughter of the Narikin* (1932), tells the story of a shy and protected Japanese girl who is forced into marriage by her aristocratic stepmother. Her second novel, *A Daughter of the Nohfu* (1935), portrays intergenerational conflict in a rural Japanese family. Sugimoto died in 1950.

In the following selection from *A Daughter of the Samurai* Sugimoto looks back on her first impressions of America and recalls with "surprised amusement" the difficulties of adapting to unfamiliar mores, noting that "the customs of all countries are strange to untrained eyes."

1   Another happy year I spent in school. Then I returned to Nagaoka, realizing, myself, how little I knew, but in the eyes of my friends, an educated
woman. This was an unenviable reputation—one which I knew I should
have to live down if I wanted to stand well in the eyes of my old friends during these last months before I started for my new home in America. Each
vacation I had had the same experience; for Nagaoka minds, although simple, loving, and true, were also stubborn; and no year could I begin where
I had left off the year previous. My friends all loved me and they had become
somewhat reconciled to my change of faith, but they could not help thinking, that, after all, I must be peculiar-minded to enjoy being so unlike other
women. So again I had to accommodate myself to the discomfort of being
received formally, and again patiently watch the gradual melting away of
outward reserve until I could once more reach the faithful hearts beneath.

2   But finally I found myself settled into the old life, only now with the
added excitement of my preparations for going to America.

3   As a Japanese marriage is a family matter it is not the custom for outsiders
to present gifts; but the circumstances connected with mine were so unusual
that many Nagaoka families sent large *mochi* cakes of red and white, most of
them in the shape of storks or twin love-birds—emblems of congratulation
and happy long life. Distant relatives, old retainers, and family servants, even
those married and living at some distance, remembered me with weaves of
silk and rolls of red and white *mawata*—the light, soft silk floss, so useful in
every Japanese family as interlining for cloaks and dresses and for various
delicate household purposes.

4   Most of these homely gifts were wholly inappropriate for life in America,
but they expressed so much personal interest in me and loyalty to my
father's family that I was deeply touched. And the dinners were many—most
of them from relatives—where I, always seated next to Mother, in the place
of honor, was served red rice and red snapper, head and all, and soup with
seven, nine, or eleven vegetables.

5   All this was exciting in a quiet way; but the real excitement came when
Brother, whose home was now in Tokyo, came up to be with us for my last
weeks at home. He brought a letter from Matsuo, saying that a kind
American lady, for the sake of a Japanese girl of my school in whom she was
interested, had asked Matsuo to take me to her home when I arrived, and
that we were to be married there. Mother read the letter with bowed head,
and when she looked up, I was astonished to see the shadow of tears in her
eyes. Poor Mother! Almost six years she had held, deep hidden in her heart,
the shadowy dread that had assailed her when we first heard of Matsuo's
decision to remain in America; for it was absolutely without precedent in
Japanese life that a bride should go to a husband who had no mother or
elder sister to guide and instruct the young wife in her new duties. This message was like a whisper of welcome from the thoughtful heart of a stranger;

and that the stranger was a woman brought to Mother a feeling of safe, warm comfort. Lifting the letter to her forehead, she bowed in the ordinary form of expressing thanks, but said nothing, and not one of us realized that beneath her quiet manner a flood of grateful relief was sweeping away the anxiety of years. That night, as I passed her open door, I caught the fragrance of incense. The shrine was open. Matsuo's letter had been placed within, and before it the curling incense was carrying upwards the deep thanks of a mother's heart.

6   Brother watched some of the preparations for my departure with evident disapproval.

7   "Those things are all right for a bride who is to live in Japan," he said, "but all nonsense for Etsu-bo. What will she do with a long crest-curtain and a doll festival set? Matsuo, being a merchant, will have to pay a big duty, and they're useless in America anyway."

8   At first Honorable Grandmother and Mother listened in silence, but one day Mother gently but firmly protested.

9   "They may be useless," she said. "Of Etsu-bo's future I know nothing. But now she is a Japanese bride, going from her home to her husband. It is my duty to see that she goes as well prepared as is possible, according to the custom of her family. So it is decided."

10   Brother grumbled, but it is the women in a Japanese family who decide all things in connection with the "great interior," so the preparations went on according to rule. Mother, however, conceded some things to Brother's superior knowledge of America, and the rolls of silk and crêpe-brocade which came arranged in the shape of storks, pine trees, and the many beautiful emblems for a happy life, were given to sisters and other relatives; and my doll festival set, which every girl takes with her to her husband's home, was left behind.

11   The question of my personal trousseau was so important that a family council was called. Brother's ideas were positively startling. Most of the relatives were too honest to offer guessing suggestions, and none was well enough informed to make practical ones. Matters were in a rather puzzling and still undecided state when the Tokyo uncle, whose opinion the majority of the relatives looked upon with respect, sided with Brother in favoring the American costume.

12   "Among European people," he said, "it is considered extreme discourtesy to expose the body. Even men, whose liberty is of course greater than that of women, have to wear high collars and stiff cuffs. The Japanese dress, being low in the neck and scanty of skirt, is improper for wear among the European people."

13   Since most of my relatives knew almost nothing of foreign customs my uncle's statement made a great impression. Mother looked very anxious, for this was a new aspect of the subject, but Honorable Grandmother's loyal

heart was wounded and aroused. To her, Japan was the land of the gods, and the customs of its people ought not to be criticized. Very quietly but with great dignity she protested.

14 "According to pictures," she said, "the pipe-shaped sleeves of the European costume lack grace. They are like the coats our coolies wear. It grieves me to think a time has come when my posterity are willing to humiliate themselves to the level of humble coolies."

15 Honorable Grandmother, being the most honored one in the council, her opinion carried weight, and it was finally decided to prepare Japanese dress only, leaving my European clothes to be selected after I reached America. Brother had arranged that I should travel in the care of Mr. Holmes, an English tea merchant, a business friend of my uncle's, who, with his family, was returning to Europe by way of America.

16 At last the day came when all arrangements were complete, all farewells said, and Brother and I had again started together on a trip to Tokyo. But by this time the puffing land-steamer had, step by step, advanced over, and through, the mountains, and our former journey of eight days was now reduced to eighteen hours of jolting, rattling discomfort. We did not talk much, but sometimes at large stations we would get out for a few minutes of rest and change. At Takasaki we had just returned to our seats after a brisk walk up and down the platform when Brother anxiously stuck his head out of the window.

17 "What is it?" I asked.

18 "I am looking to see if you left your wooden clogs on the platform again," he replied with the old twinkle in his eye.

19 We both laughed, and the remainder of the trip was a pleasant three hours which I like to remember.

20 In Tokyo there were more dinners of red rice and whole fish, more useless, loving gifts, more farewells with warm heart-throbs within and cool formal bows without, and then I found myself standing on the deck of a big steamer, with my brother by my side, and, on the water below, a waiting launch to take ashore the last friends of the passengers.

21 The third long, hoarse blast of the warning whistle sounded, and with an odd tightness in my throat I bent in a deep, long bow. Brother stood close to my sleeve.

22 "Little Etsu-bo," he said, with a strange tenderness in his voice. "I have been a poor brother, in whom you could not take pride; but I have never known an unselfish person—except you."

23 I saw his shadow bow, but when I lifted my head, he was in the crowd pressing towards the ship steps, his head held high and his laughing face lifted in a shout of farewell to Mr. Holmes.

24 After the first few days the voyage was pleasant, but Mrs. Holmes, who was not very strong, was ill most of the way over and her maid was busy with

the care of the baby; so I spent much time on the deck alone, either gazing quietly out over the water or reading one of several Japanese magazines that had been given me just as I started. Mr. Holmes was most kind and attentive, but I was not used to men, and was so silent that he, knowing Japanese people, must have understood; for after the first day he would see me comfortably settled in my deck-chair, then go away, leaving his own chair next to mine, vacant except for the plate of fruit or cup of tea which he would have occasionally sent to me.

25 Because of my dress and the magazine, the passengers concluded that I could not understand English; and remarks about me or about Japanese were frequently made within my hearing by persons sitting near me. They were not unkind, but it seemed discourteous to be listening to words not meant for my ears, so one morning I took an English book up to the deck with me and was reading it when a lady, walking by, paused.

26 "I see you understand English," she said pleasantly, and remained for a little chat. She must have passed the news around, for after that I not only heard no more remarks about "the quiet little Jap," but, at various times, several ladies stopped for a short conversation. My place at the table was beside Mrs. Holmes. She rarely came, but I never felt alone, for the other passengers, seeming to feel responsible for the American lady's charge, were unceasingly kind in their attentions. Indeed there was an atmosphere of free action and cheerful speech among the passengers that was as refreshing as the salty, breezy air. Everyone said "Good morning" to everyone else, friends or strangers, no one seemed to care. One day I saw two well-dressed ladies greet each other with a merry "Hello! Wonderful morning, isn't it? Let's take our constitutional together," and swinging into step, they marched off like a couple of soldier comrades. No bowing—no formal words. Everything was free and cordial. This lack of formality was very surprising, but it was most interesting, and it held a certain charm.

27 Of course I watched the dresses of these foreign ladies with the greatest interest. My uncle's remarks regarding the low neck and scanty skirt of the Japanese dress had astonished and troubled me very much, and since I was the only Japanese woman on the ship among some fifty or sixty American ladies, I felt responsible not to disgrace my nation. The Japanese dress is so made that it can be properly worn only when put on in one certain way, but I, inspired with a combination of girlish modesty and loyal patriotism, tried to pull the embroidered folds at the neck close up to my chin; and I remained seated as much as possible so my scanty skirt would not be noticed.

28 The weather was unpleasant at the beginning of the voyage, and few ladies came on deck, but it was not long before the promenading commenced, and then I began to suspect that my uncle's opinion might not be wholly correct; but it was not until an evening entertainment where there was dancing that I entirely lost faith in his judgment. There the high collar

and stiff cuffs of the gentlemen were to be seen, just as he had said; but I found that most of the ladies' dresses were neither high in the neck nor full in the skirt, and I saw many other things which mystified and shocked me. The thin waists made of lawn and dainty lace were to me most indelicate, more so, I think, unreasonable though it seemed, than even the bare neck. I have seen a Japanese servant in the midst of heavy work in a hot kitchen, with her kimono slipped down, displaying one entire shoulder; and I have seen a woman nursing her baby in the street, or a naked woman in a hotel bath, but until that evening on the steamer I had never seen a woman publicly displaying bare skin just for the purpose of having it seen. For a while I tried hard to pretend to myself that I was not embarrassed, but finally, with my cheeks flaming with shame, I slipped away and crept into my cabin berth, wondering greatly over the strange civilization of which I was so soon to be a part.

29   I have no spirit of criticism in writing this. Indeed, after years of residence in America I have so changed that I can look back with surprised amusement at my first impressions. The customs of all countries are strange to untrained eyes, and one of the most interesting mysteries of my life here is my own gradual but inevitable mental evolution. Now I can go to a dinner or a dance and watch the ladies in evening dress with pleasure. To me the scene is frequently as artistic and beautiful as a lovely painting, and I know those happy-faced women walking with the courteous gentlemen or swinging to the time of gay music are just as innocent and sweet of heart as are the gentle and hushed women of my own country over the sea.

30   My experiences in San Francisco were strange and puzzling, but delightful in their novelty. The astonishing little room at the Palace Hotel which we had no sooner entered than it began to rise upwards, finally depositing us in a large apartment where we had a view as vast as from a mountain-top; the smooth white bathtub which could be filled with hot water without fuel or delay; the locked doors everywhere, for in Japan we never had a lock; all of these strange things, combined with the bewildering sense of the *bigness* of everything, were almost overpowering.

31   This sense of the enormous size of things—wide streets, tall buildings, great trees—was also pronounced inside the hotel. The ceilings were lofty, the furniture was large, the chairs were high and the sofas were wide, with the back far from the front. Everything seemed made for a race of giants; which, after all, is not so far from the truth for that is what Americans are— a great people, with nothing cramped or repressed about them; both admirable and faulty in a giant way; with large person, generous purse, broad mind, strong heart, and free soul. My first impression has never changed.

32   We were in San Francisco only a few days, but everything was so hurried, so noisy, and so strange that my brain settled into a half-numb condition of

non-expectancy. Then something happened. So simple, so homely a thing it was, that it stands out in my memory clear and separate from all else connected with my short stay in that wonderful city. A gentle, white-haired old minister, who had lived in Japan, came to make a friendly call. After the words of greeting he unwrapped a white box and placed it in my hand.

33   "I thought you would like a bit of home after your long trip," he said. "Look inside and see what it is." I lifted the cover and what was my surprise to see real Japanese food, fresh and delicious. I must, long before, have heard my brother say that Japanese food could be obtained in America, but it had made no impression upon me, and I was as astonished as if I had expected never again to behold Japanese food.

34   I looked up gratefully, and when I saw the humorous twinkle in his eye and kindliness in every feature of his smiling face the strangeness of my surroundings melted away and there came my first throb of home-sickness; for behind the gentle smile I saw the heart of my father. Years before, just after my father's death, Ishi had taken me to the Temple of the Five Hundred Buddhas, where stood row after row of big, carved images of stone or gilded wood. Every face was gentle, calm, and peaceful, and my lonely little heart searched each one, hoping to find my father's, for he too was now a Buddha. I did not know then that a longing heart will recognize its own reflection in only a trifle; and when at last I saw a face—gentle, dignified, and with a kindly smile, I felt that it pictured my father's heart, and I was satisfied. Just so I saw my father in the face of the old man whose kind heart had prompted the homely gift. I love to remember that smile as my welcome to the strange new country, which ever after was to be linked in my heart so closely to my own.

35   During the long ride across the continent I was reminded constantly of the revolving lanterns which were so fascinating to me as a child. The rapidly changing views from the train were like the gay scenes on the lantern panels that flitted by too quickly to permit of a clear image; their very vagueness being the secret of their charm.

36   Mr. and Mrs. Holmes came as far as a large city near my future home where they placed me in charge of a lady school teacher, a friend of Mrs. Holmes. Then they said good-bye and slipped out of my life, probably for ever, but they left a memory of kindness and consideration which will remain with me always.

37   When I was whirled into the dusky station of the city of my destination, I peered rather curiously from the car window. I was not anxious. I had always been taken care of, and it did not trouble me that I was to meet one I had never known before. On the crowded platform I saw a young Japanese man, erect, alert, watching eagerly each person who stepped from the train. It was Matsuo. He wore a gray suit and a straw hat, and to me looked modern, progressive, foreign in everything except his face. Of course, he knew who I was at once but to my astonishment, his first words were, "Why did

you wear Japanese dress?" There flashed into my mind a picture of the grave faces of the family council and my grandmother's words regarding pipe-sleeves. Yet here was I in a land of pipe-sleeves, gazing upon my future husband, a pipe-sleeved man. I laugh about it now, but then I was only a lonely, loose-sleeved, reproved little girl. Matsuo's disappointment in my dress was mostly on account of a much-honored friend, Mrs. Wilson, the kind lady about whom Matsuo had written in the letter which for years was kept in Mother's shrine. With thoughtful kindness she had sent Matsuo in her carriage to meet me, and he, anxious that I should appear well in her eyes, was disgusted not to find me very up-to-date and progressive.

38   I silently took my place beside Matsuo in the shining carriage with its prancing black horses and uniformed coachman, and in absolute silence we rolled along the busy streets and up the long, sloping hill to a beautiful suburban home. I did not realize that the situation was perhaps as trying to him as to me; for I had never been so close to a man in my life, except my father, and I almost died on the trip.

39   The carriage turned into a road that circled a spacious lawn and stopped before a large gray house with a wide, many-columned porch. Outside the door stood a stately lady and a tall white-haired gentleman. The lady greeted me with outstretched hands and cordial words of welcome. I was too grateful to reply, and when I looked up into the noble, kindly face of the white-haired gentleman beside her, peace crept into my heart, for, behind his gentle smile, again I saw the heart of my father.

40   Those two good people will never know until they stand within the shining gates where heavenly knowledge clears our eyes, how much their kindness, both before and after our wedding, meant to Matsuo and to me.

41   For ten restful days I was made welcome in that beautiful home; then came the second of "The Three Inevitables"—for, in Old Japan, marriage held its place equally with birth and death. My wedding took place on a beautiful day in June. The sun shone, the soft wind murmured through the branches of the grand old trees on the lawn, the reception-room, with its treasures of art gathered from all lands, was fragrant with blossoms, and before a wonderful inlaid console table were two crossed flags—American and Japanese. There Matsuo and Etsu stood while the Christian words were spoken which made them one. By Matsuo's side was his business partner, a good kind man, and beside me stood one who ever since has proved my best and truest friend. So we were married. Everyone said it was a beautiful wedding. To me the room was filled with a blur of strange things and people, all throbbing with the spirit of a great kindness; and vaguely, mistily, I realized that there had been fulfilled a sacred vow that the gods had made long before I was born.

42   Our friend, Mrs. Wilson, was always kind to me and I have been a happy and grateful guest in her beautiful home many, many times; but my perma-

nent home was in an adjoining suburb, in a large, old-fashioned frame house set on a hill in the midst of big trees and lawns cut with winding gravel paths. The mistress of this house was a widowed relative of Mrs. Wilson, a woman in whom was united the stern, high-principled stock of New England with the gentle Virginia aristocracy. She invited us for a visit at first, because she loved Japan. But we were all so happy together that we decided not to separate; so for many years our home was there with "Mother," as we learned to call her. Close to my own mother in my heart of hearts stands my American mother—one of the noblest, sweetest women that God ever made.

43   From the love and sympathy and wisdom of this pleasant home I looked forth upon America at its best, and learned to gather with understanding and appreciation the knowledge that had been denied my poor brother in his narrow life in this same land.

DISCUSSION QUESTIONS

1. What does Sugimoto's autobiography reveal about the nature of the Japanese society in which she grew up?
2. What did the author find most unusual about American women's dresses and why?
3. In general, what were the author's impressions of America?
4. What can you infer from the fact that the author had never met Matsuo before arriving in America?
5. In small groups, discuss what you know about Japanese society today from reading, films, or knowing people who were born in Japan.

WRITING TOPICS

1. In nonfiction writing in particular, an author's tone often reflects his or her personality quite clearly. In a brief essay, reflect on what Sugimoto's tone says about her personality. Cite examples from the selection to support your views.
2. "The customs of all countries are strange to untrained eyes," according to the author. If possible, interview someone newly arrived in America or newly returned from a trip abroad. What did the person find most "foreign" at first? Write an essay based on your interview.

FROM *AMERICA IS IN THE HEART*

Carlos Bulosan

Carlos Bulosan, who was born in 1913 in the central Philippines, arrived in Seattle, Washington, at the age of seventeen. He had completed only three years of schooling in his homeland and spoke little English upon his arrival.

Immigrating at the onset of the Great Depression, he quickly realized that his beliefs in brotherhood, equality, and opportunity—ideals and values that he had learned in American schools in his homeland—would be challenged by racism directed at Filipinos, many of whom were perceived as stealing jobs from white workers. From the middle of the nineteenth century, Asian immigrants to the United States encountered much racist hostility, and many Filipinos, like other Asians who came before them, were met with intense animosity and overt suspicion. Bulosan realized that economic and social circumstances in the United States were worse than those in his native Philippines in several ways. This realization, however, did not lead Bulosan to feel defeated; instead, he sought to improve those circumstances. In Los Angeles, he organized a union of fish cannery laborers with his friend Chris Mensalves and began writing about the experiences of Filipino workers. Unfortunately, his financial status did not improve. Living in poverty, he contracted tuberculosis, underwent three lung operations, and endured a lengthy convalescence. One of the few benefits derived from this period of inactivity was the opportunity for Bulosan to read and educate himself further.

During World War II, Bulosan began to receive national recognition for his writing. *The Saturday Evening Post* picked up his essay "Freedom from Want," and other pieces appeared in prestigious and widely circulated publications, such as *The New Yorker* and *Harper's Bazaar*. His third book, *Laughter of My Father* (1944), was broadcast to American soldiers, and his autobiography, *America Is in the Heart* (1946), which literary critic Amy Ling describes as "slightly fictionalized," was acclaimed one of the fifty most important American books ever published.

By the time Bulosan died in 1956, however, he was living in poverty once again, for, Ling claims, the political climate no longer favored his type of writing and subject matter. He never returned to the Philippines and never became an American citizen.

The following selection from *America Is in the Heart* describes the dangerous and transient existence that young Filipino immigrants faced as they searched for employment and stability.

1   I began to be afraid, riding alone in the freight train. I wanted suddenly to go back to Stockton and look for a job in the tomato fields, but the train was already traveling fast. I was in flight again, away from an unknown terror that seemed to follow me everywhere. Dark flight into another place, toward other enemies. But there was a clear sky and the night was ablaze with stars. I could still see the faint haze of Stockton's lights in the distance, a halo arching above it and fading into a backdrop of darkness.

2   In the early morning the train stopped a few miles from Niles, in the midst of a wide grape field. The grapes had been harvested and the bare vines were falling to the ground. The apricot trees were leafless. Three railroad detectives jumped out of a car and ran toward the boxcars. I ran to the vineyard and hid behind a smudge pot,[1] waiting for the next train from Stockton. A few bunches of grapes still hung on the vines, so I filled my pockets and ran for the tracks when the train came. It was a freight and it stopped to pick up carloads of grapes; when it started moving again the empties were full of men.

3   I crawled to a corner of a car and fell asleep. When I awakened the train was already in San Jose. I jumped outside and found another freight going south. I swung aboard and found several hoboes drinking cans of beer. I sat and watched them sitting solemnly, as though there were no more life left in the world. They talked as though there were no happiness left, as though life had died and would not live again. I could not converse with them, and this barrier made me a stranger. I wanted to know them and to be a part of their life. I wondered what I had in common with them beside the fact that we were all on the road rolling to unknown destinations.

4   When I reached Salinas, I walked to town and went to a Mexican restau-

---

[1] *smudge pot:* a container in which oil or another fuel is burned to produce a thick smoke, usually in an orchard, to prevent the freezing of the fruit and the trees.

rant on Soledad Street. I was drinking coffee when I saw the same young girl who had disappeared[2] in the night. She was passing by with an old man. I ran to the door and called to her, but she did not hear me. I went back to my coffee wondering what would become of her.

5   I avoided the Chinese gambling houses, remembering the tragedy in Stockton.[3] Walking on the dark side of the street as though I were hunted, I returned eagerly to the freight yards. I found the hoboes sitting gloomily in the dark. I tried a few times to jump into the boxcars, but the detectives chased me away. When the freights had gone the detectives left.

6   Then an express from San Francisco came and stopped to pick up a few passengers. The hoboes darted out from the dark and ran to the rods.[4] When I realized that I was the only one left, I grabbed the rod between the coal car and the car behind it. Then the express started, gathering speed as it nosed its way through the night.

7   I almost fell several times. The strong, cold wind lashed sharply at my face. I put the crook of my arm securely about the rod, pinching myself when I feared that I was going to sleep. It was not yet autumn and the sky was clear, but the wind was bitter and sharp and cut across my face like a knife. When my arm went to sleep, I beat it to life with my fist. It was the only way I could save myself from falling to my death.

8   I was so exhausted and stiff with the cold when I reached San Luis Obispo that I could scarcely climb down. I stumbled when I reached the ground, rolling over on my stomach as though I were headless. Then I walked to town, where I found a Filipino who took me in his car to Pismo Beach. The Filipino community was a small block near the sea—a block of poolrooms, gambling houses, and little green cottages where prostitutes were doing business. At first I did not know what the cottages were, but I saw many Filipinos going into them from the gambling houses near by. Then I guessed what they were, because cottages such as these were found in every Filipino community.

9   I went into one of the cottages and sat in the warm little parlor where the Filipinos were waiting their turn to go upstairs. Some of the prostitutes were sitting awkwardly in the men's laps, wheedling them. Others were dancing cheek to cheek, swaying their hips suggestively. The Filipinos stood around whispering lustily in their dialects. The girls were scantily dressed, and one of them was nude. The nude girl put her arms around me and started cooing lasciviously.

10   I was extricated from her by the same Filipino who had taken me into

---

[2] *. . . I saw the same young girl who had disappeared . . . :* a reference to a person whom the narrator had met riding in a boxcar; the girl was sexually assaulted by some hoboes and disappeared.

[3] *tragedy in Stockton:* Earlier in the book, Bulosan relates the racially motivated killing of a Filipino and the burning of the Filipino Federation Building.

[4] *rods:* the links connecting train cars.

his car in San Luis Obispo. He came into the house and immediately took the girl upstairs. In ten minutes he was down again and asked me if I would like to ride with him to Lompoc. I had heard of the place when I was in Seattle, so naturally I was interested. We started immediately and in about two hours had passed through Santa Maria.

11   Beyond the town, at a railroad crossing, highway patrolmen stopped our car. Speaking to me in our dialect, Doro, my companion, said:

12   "Those bastards probably want to see if we have a white woman in the car."

13   "Why?" I asked him, becoming frightened.

14   "They think every Filipino is a pimp," he said. "But there are more pimps among them than among all the Filipinos in the world put together. I will kill one of these bastards someday."

15   They questioned Doro curtly, peered into the car, and told us to go on.

16   I came to know afterward that in many ways it was a crime to be a Filipino in California. I came to know that the public streets were not free to my people: we were stopped each time these vigilant patrolmen saw us driving a car. We were suspect each time we were seen with a white woman. And perhaps it was this narrowing of our life into an island, into a filthy segment of American society, that had driven Filipinos like Doro inward, hating everyone and despising all positive urgencies toward freedom.

17   When we reached the mountains to the right of the highway, we turned toward them and started climbing slowly, following the road that winds around them like a taut ribbon. We had been driving for an hour when we reached the summit, and suddenly the town of Lompoc shone like a constellation of stars in the deep valley below. We started downward, hearing the strong wind from the sea beating against the car. Then we came to the edge of the town, and church bells began ringing somewhere near a forest.

18   It was the end of the flower season, so the Filipino workers were all in town. They stood on the sidewalks and in front of Japanese stores showing their fat rolls of money to the girls. Gambling was going on in one of the old buildings, in the Mexican district, and in a café across the street Mexican girls and Filipinos were dancing. I went inside the café and sat near the counter, watching the plump girls dancing drunkenly.

19   I noticed a small Filipino sitting forlornly at one of the tables. He was smoking a cigar and spitting like a big man into an empty cigar box on the floor. When the juke box stopped playing he jumped to the counterman for some change. He put the nickels in the slot, waving graciously to the dancers although he never danced himself. Now and then a Filipino would go into the back room where the gamblers were playing cards and cursing loudly.

20   The forlorn Filipino went to the counter again and asked for change. He put all the nickels in the slot and bought several packages of cigarettes. He

threw the cigarettes on the table near the juke box and then called to the old Mexican men who were sitting around the place. The Mexicans rushed for the table, grabbing the cigarettes. The Filipino went out lighting another big cigar.

21 I followed him immediately. He walked slowly and stopped now and then to see if I was following him. There was some mysterious force in him that attracted me. When he came to a large neon sign which said Landstrom Café, he stopped and peered through the wide front window. Then he entered a side door and climbed the long stairs.

22 I opened the door quietly and entered. I heard him talking to a man in one of the rooms upstairs. When I reached the landing a hard blow fell on my head. I rolled on the floor. Then I saw him with a gun in his hand, poised to strike at my head again. Standing behind him was my brother Amado, holding a long-bladed knife.

23 I scrambled to my feet screaming: "Brother, it is me! It is Allos! Remember?"

24 My brother told his friend to stop. He came near me, walking around me suspiciously. He stepped back and folded the blade of the knife. There was some doubt in his face.

25 "I am your brother," I said again, holding back the tears in my eyes. "I am Allos! Remember the village of Mangusmana? Remember when you beat our *carabao*[5] in the rain? When you touched my head and then ran to Binalonan? Remember, Amado?" I was not only fighting for my life, but also for a childhood bond that was breaking. Frantically I searched in my mind for other remembrances of the past which might remind him of me, and re-establish a bridge between him and my childhood.

26 "Remember when I fell from the coconut tree and you were a janitor in the *presidencia*?"[6] I said. "And you brought some magazines for me to read? Then you went away to work in the sugar plantations of Bulacan?"

27 "If you are really my brother tell me the name of our mother," he said casually.

28 "Our mother's name is Meteria," I said. "That is what the people call her. But her real name is Autilia Sampayan. We used to sell salted fish and salt in the villages. Remember?"

29 My brother grabbed me affectionately and, for a long time he could not say a word. I knew, then, that he had loved my mother although he had no chance to show it to her. Yes, to him, and to me afterward, to know my mother's name was to know the password into the secrets of the past, into childhood and pleasant memories; but it was also a guiding star, a talisman, a charm that lights us to manhood and decency.

---

[5] *carabao:* buffalo.
[6] *presidencia:* city hall or main municipal building.

30 "It has been so long, Allos," Amado said at last. "I had almost forgotten you. Please forgive me, brother. . . ."

31 "My name is Alfredo," said his friend. "I nearly killed you!" He laughed guiltily, putting the gun in his pocket. "Yes, I almost killed you, Allos!"

32 My brother opened the door of their room. It was a small room, with one broken chair and a small window facing the street. Their clothes were hanging on a short rope that was strung between the door and a cracked mirror. I sat on the edge of the bed, waiting for my brother to speak. Alfredo started playing solitaire on the table, laughing whenever he cheated himself.

33 "Go out in the hall and wash your hands," said my brother. "Then we will go downstairs for something to eat. Where is your suitcase?"

34 "I don't have any—now," I said. "I lost it when I was in Seattle."

35 "Have you been in Seattle?" he asked.

36 "I have been in Alaska, too," I said. "And other places."

37 "You should have written to me," he said. "You shouldn't have come to America. But you can't go back now. You can never go back, Allos."

38 I could hear men shouting in a bar two blocks down the street. Then church bells started ringing again, and the wind from the sea carried their message to the farmhouses in the canyon near the river. I knew that as long as there was a hope for the future somewhere I would not stop trying to reach it. I looked at my brother and Alfredo and knew that I would never stay with them, to rot and perish in their world of brutality and despair. I knew that I wanted something which would ease my fear and stop my flight from dawn to dawn.

39 "Life is tough, Carlos," said my brother. "I had a good job for some time, but the depression came. I had to do something. I had to live, Carlos!"

40 I did not know what he was trying to tell me. But I noticed that he had started using my Christian name. I noticed, too, that he spoke to me in English. His English was perfect. Alfredo's English was perfect also, but his accent was still strong. Alfredo tried to speak the way my brother spoke, but his uncultured tongue twisted ridiculously about in his mouth and the words did not come out right.

41 "We are in the bootleg racket," said my brother. "Alfredo and I will make plenty of money. But it is dangerous."

42 "I like money," Alfredo said. "It is everything."

43 They spoke with cynicism, but there was a grain of wisdom in their words. We were driving a borrowed car toward a farmhouse, away from the flower fields that made Lompoc famous. We drove across a dry river and into a wide orchard, then Alfredo knocked on the door. An Italian came to the door and told us to follow him into the back yard.

44 "How many bottles do you want?" he asked my brother, starting to dig under a eucalyptus tree.

45 "I think I can sell two dozen," said Amado.

46 "The big size?" asked the Italian.

47 "The big size," Alfredo said.

48 The Italian looked at me suspiciously. When he had all the bottles ready, Amado paid him, and the Italian opened a small bottle and passed it around to us. I refused to drink, and Alfredo laughed. Then we went to the car and drove carefully to town.

49 They disappeared with the bottles, peddling their bootleg whisky in gambling houses and places of questionable reputation. They were boisterous when they entered the room, throwing their money on the bed and talking excitedly. They were disappointed when I told them that I wanted to go to Los Angeles.

50 "Don't you want to go into business with us?" Alfredo asked me.

51 "Maybe I will come back someday," I said.

52 "Well, I was hoping you would want to begin early," he said. There was a note of genuine disappointment in his voice. He put some money in my pocket. "Here is something for you to remember me by."

53 "If you would like to go to school," said my brother in parting, "just let me know. But whatever you do, Carlos, don't lose your head. Good-bye!"

54 I sat in the bus and watched them walking toward the Mexican district. I wanted to cry because my brother was no longer the person I had known in Binalonan. He was no longer the gentle, hard-working janitor in the *presidencia*. I remembered the time when he had gone to Lingayen to cook for my brother Macario! Now he had changed, and I could not understand him any more.

55 "Please, God, don't change me in America!" I said to myself, looking the other way so that I would not cry.

DISCUSSION QUESTIONS

1. Why did the narrator travel on freight trains and what were the risks involved?

2. What evidence is there of racism in this chapter from Bulosan's book?

3. What did the narrator's brother say was the reason he went into the bootleg business?

4. Explain what the narrator meant by saying that "to know my mother's name . . . was also a guiding star, a talisman, a charm that lights us to manhood and decency" (paragraph 29).

WRITING TOPICS

1. Write a brief essay telling why you think it is worthwhile to read about actual immigrant experiences.
2. The priorities of family members are seldom the same. Think about your own family and write about the differences in priorities between two members, perhaps between you and a sibling or cousin.
3. In a brief essay explore the tone of Bulosan's writing and how it contributes to the mood of this excerpt. Include passages from the reading to support your views.

FROM *EAST GOES WEST*

Younghill Kang

Younghill Kang, who was born in 1903 in Hamkyong Province in northern Korea, immigrated to the United States in 1921 with only four dollars to begin a new life. He came just three years before the passage of legislation that would bar Korean immigrants from entering the United States for approximately the next thirty years.

Kang's education, which began in Confucian and American missionary schools in Korea, was eclectic. He started in the hard sciences but quickly became interested in writing and reading. Eager to read and study English and American literature, he took classes at both Harvard and Boston University. Writing at first in Korean and Japanese, Kang began to compose in English in 1928 with the assistance of his wife, Frances Keeley, who had attended Wellesley College.

Kang worked as an editor for *Encyclopaedia Britannica* and was appointed to a lectureship at New York University. With the help of the American novelist Thomas Wolfe, his friend and colleague at NYU, Kang had *The Grass Roof* published in 1931 by Charles Scribner's Sons. Six years later, Scribner's published Kang's second major work, *East Goes West: The Making of an Oriental Yankee*. In addition, Kang traveled to Europe on a Guggenheim Award and wrote several book reviews for *The New York Times*. He died in 1972 from complications arising from a stroke.

The Asian American literary scholar Elaine Kim describes Kang as an "intensely lonely man . . . who was never afforded a permanent niche in American life." Even so, Kim, regarding Kang's work hopefully, claims that it "represents a new beginning in Asian American literature, a transition from the viewpoint of a guest or visitor . . . to the perspective of the immigrant attempting to claim a permanent place in American life."[1]

---

[1] *The Heath Anthology of American Literature*, 3rd ed., 2 vols. (Lexington: Heath, 1998) 1994.

The following excerpt from *East Goes West* explores Kang's initial reactions to New York, which was his eventual destination after a lengthy journey from Seoul to Vancouver. (J.I.)

1   From an old walled Korean city some thousand years old—Seoul—famous for poets and scholars, to New York, I did not come directly. But almost. A large steamer from the Orient landed me in Vancouver, Canada, and I traveled over three thousand miles across the American continent, a journey more than half as far as from Yokohama to Vancouver. At Halifax, straightway I took another liner. And this time for New York. It was in New York I felt I was destined really "to come out from the boat." The beginning of my new existence must be founded here. In Korea *to come out from the boat* is an idiom meaning *to be born,* as the word "pai" for "womb" is the same as "pai" for "boat"; and there is the story of a Korean humorist who had no money, but who needed to get across a river. On landing him on the other side, the ferryman asked for his money. But the Korean humorist said to the ferryman who too had just stepped out, "You wouldn't charge your brother, would you? We both came from the same boat." And so he traveled free. My only plea for a planet-ride among the white-skinned majority of this New World is the same facetious argument. I brought little money, and no prestige, as I entered a practical country with small respect for the dark side of the moon. I got in just in time, before the law against Oriental immigration was passed.

2   But New York, that magic city on rock yet ungrounded, nervous, flowing, million-hued as a dream, became, throughout the years I am recording, the vast mechanical incubator of me.

3   It was always of New York I dreamed—not Paris nor London nor Berlin nor Munich nor Vienna nor age-buried Rome. I was eighteen, green with youth, and there was some of the mystery of nature in my simple immediate response to what was for me just a name . . . like the dogged moth that directs its flight by some unfathomable law. But I said to myself, "I want neither dreams nor poetry, least of all tradition, never the full moon." Korea even in her shattered state had these. And beyond them stood waiting—death. I craved swiftness, unimpeded action, fluidity, the amorphous New. Out of action rises the dream, rises the poetry. Dream without motion is the only wasteland that can sustain nothing. So I came adoring the crescent, not the full harvest moon, with winter over the horizon and its waning to a husk.

4   "New York at last!" I heard from the passengers around me. And the information was not needed. In unearthly white and mauve, shadow of

white, the city rose, like a dream dreamed overnight, new, remorselessly new, impossibly new . . . and yet there in all the arrogant pride of rejoiced materialism. These young, slim, stately things a thousand houses high (or so it seemed to me, coming from an architecture that had never defied the earth), a tower of Babel each one, not one tower of Babel but many, a city of Babel towers, casually, easily strewn end up against the skies—they stood at the brink, close crowded, the brink of America, these Giantesses, these Fates, which were not built for a king nor a ghost nor any man's religion, but were materialized by those hard, cold, magic words—opportunity, enterprise, prosperity, success—just business words out of world-wide commerce from a land rich in natural resources. Buildings that sprang white from the rock. No earth clung to their skirts. They leaped like Athene from the mind synthetically, they spurned the earth. And there was no monument to the Machine Age like America.

5   I could not have come farther from home than this New York. Our dwellings, low, weathered, mossed, abhorring the lifeless line—the definite, the finite, the aloof—loving rondures and an upward stroke, the tilt of a roof like a boat always aware of the elements in which it is swinging—most fittingly my home was set a hemisphere apart, so far over the globe that to have gone on would have meant to go nearer not farther. How far my little grass-roofed, hill-wrapped village from this gigantic rebellion which was New York! And New York's rebellion called to me excitedly, this savagery which piled great concrete block on concrete block, topping at the last moment as in an afterthought, with crowns as delicate as pinnacled ice, this lavishness which, without prayer, pillaged coal mines and waterfalls for light, festooning the great nature severed city with diamonds of frozen electrical phenomena—it fascinated me, the Asian man, and in it I saw not Milton's Satan, but the one of Blake.[1]

6   I saw that Battery Park, if not a thing of earth, was yet a thing of dirt, as I walked about it trying to get my breath and decide what was the next step after coming from the sea. It was oddly dark and forlorn, like a little untidy room off-stage where actors might sit waiting for their cues. The shops about looked mean and low and dim. A solitary sailor stumbled past, showing neither the freedom and romance of the seas, nor the robust assurance of a native on his own shore. And the other human shadows flitting there had a stealthy and verminlike quality, a mysterious haunting corruption, suggesting the water's edge, and the meeting of foreign plague with foreign plague. I walked about the shabby little square briskly, drawing hungry lungfuls of the prowling keen March air—a Titan, he, in a titanic city—until

---

[1] *not Milton's Satan, but the one of Blake:* In John Milton's (1608–1674) *Paradise Lost,* Satan is a figure of evil, but William Blake (1757–1827) imagines Satan as a heroic figure in *The Marriage of Heaven and Hell.*

in sudden excess of elation and aggression growing suddenly too hot with life, as if to come to grips with an opponent, I took off my long coat; and sinking down on a bench, I clapped my knee and swore the oath of battle and of triumph. The first part of a wide journey was accomplished. At least that part in space. I swore to keep on. Yes, if it took a lifetime, I must get to know the West.

7   Well, mine was not the oath of battle in the militaristic sense. I was congenitally unmilitaristic. Inwoven in my fabric were the agricultural peace of Asia, the long centuries of peaceful living in united households, of seeking not the soul's good, but the blood's good, the blood's good of a happy, decorously branching family tree. In the old days the most excitement permitted to the individual man, if he got free from the struggle with beloved but ruthless and exacting elements, was poetry, the journey to Seoul, wine, and the moons that came with every season. His wife, usually older than himself and chosen by his mother and father, would be sure to know no poetry, but she would not begrudge him a feminine companion in Seoul, or even in some market place near-by—one of those childlike ladies who having bought—or more often inherited—the right to please by the loss of other social prestige, must live on gaiety, dancing, and fair calligraphy. But any wholehearted passion would have shivered too brutally the family tree. And I had done far worse. I had refused to marry my appointed bride. I had repeated that I would not marry, at the ripe age of eighteen. I had said, with more pride than Adam ever got out of sinning in Eden, that I must choose the girl, unhelped by my forefathers or the astrologers or the mountain spirits. And this rebellion against nature and fatality I had learned from the West. Small wonder I had struggled with my father over every ounce of Western learning. I had gone against his will to mission schools, those devilish cults which preach divorce in the blood, and spiritual kinships, which foster the very distortions found, says the golden-hearted Mencius,[2] in the cleverish man. I had studied in Japanese schools and it must be confessed, my studies had brought ever increased rebellion and dismay—to me as well as my father.

8   The military position of Japan—entrenched in Korea[3] in my own lifetime—forced me into dilemma: Scylla and Charybdis.[4] I was caught between—on the one hand, the heart-broken death of the old traditions irrevocably smashed not by me but by Japan (and yet I seemed to the elders to be conspiring with Japanese)—and on the other hand the zealous summary glibness of Japan, fast-Westernizing, using the Western incantations to realize her ancient fury of spirit, which Korea had always felt encroach-

---

[2] *Mencius:* Fourth-century B.C. Chinese philosopher who taught that human nature is essentially good but can be affected by one's environment.

[3] *The military position of Japan—entrenched in Korea:* Japan occupied Korea from 1910 to 1945.

[4] *Scylla and Charybdis:* Two monsters in Greek mythology. The phrase "between Scylla and Charybdis" means to be between two equal difficulties.

ing, but had snubbed in a blind disdain. Korea, a small, provincial, old-fashioned Confucian nation, hopelessly trapped by a larger, expanding one, was called to get off the earth. Death summoned. I could have renounced the scholar's dream forever (plainly scholarship had dreamed us away into ruin) and written my vengeance against Japan in martyr's blood, a blood which like that of the Tasmanians is strangely silent though to a man they wrote. Or I could take away my slip[5] cut from the roots, and try to engraft my scholar inherited kingdom upon the world's thought. But what I could not bear was the thought of futility, the futility of the martyr, or the death-stifled scholar back home. It was to that the individualist was born, the individualist, demanding life and more life, fulfilment, some answer to his thronging questions, some recognition of his death-wasted life, some anchor in thin air to bring him to earth though he seems cut off from the very roots of being.

9   And this it was—this naked individual slip—I had brought to New York.

10   "Dream tall dreams," I thought. "Such are proper to man. But they must be solid, well-planned, engineered and founded on rock."

11   Had I not reached the arena of man's fight with death? I sat there on a park bench, savoring rebellion, dreaming the Faustian dream, without knowing of Faust, seeing myself with the Eastern scholarship in one hand, the Western in the other. And as I sat it grew colder. I had thought a little of spending the night on that bench. It appealed to me to wake up here with the dawn and find myself in New York. It would not be the first night I had slept roofless in a large city. But in the inner lining of my cap, I had four dollars, all I had left, in fact, after my long gestation by boat and by train. I decided to get myself the birthday present of a room.

12   "Begin tomorrow, trouble. See if I can't have some good dream. An unpleasant dream in this dark lonely park would be bad luck."

13   Clouds over the denser uptown regions trembled with the city's man-made whiteness, a false and livid dawn light, stolen from nature. I turned my face toward the dawn as to a pillar of fire. And as I walked, steadily progressing toward the harsh curt lights and the Herculean noise, I wondered if the sight of a rainbow would be lost, the sound of thunder drowned here.

14   At last I found a hotel to my liking, neither as tall as a skyscraper—to choose such a one would not be modest the first night—and yet not a dingy one either, which would be inauspicious. The hotel had many lights inside, but not too many, not the naked glare which clashed from canyon to canyon along the outer runways of the great hive; these had a luminance more proper to honey cells and inner coffers. The fat six-foot doorman with red

---

[5] *slip:* a part of a plant cut off for grafting or planting; here, used figuratively.

face seemed an imposing sentinel. Past him, I saw inside the people walking to and fro . . . talking mysteriously, perhaps of Michelangelo,[6] but more likely of stocks and bonds. I tried to catch his eye. Always he looked past me, or without looking exactly at me, he would shake his head mournfully, directing his thumb toward a side door. But while he was engaged with one of the fortunate insiders who came outside, I went in. To me the gilded lamps, the marble floorway with its carpet of red, were luxurious and full of splendor. How gentlemanly, engaging, yet frankly businesslike, the sandy-colored hotel clerk, as I asked for a room, in my best high-school English which I had prepared to say before coming in!

15   And as I wrote my name down—Chungpa Han—in my unmistakably Oriental handwriting, which unconsciously dwelt on a stroke, or finished in a quirk that was not Western—I was elated that I had voted not to spend the night with the waifs and strays, but was enrolled there tangibly as a New Yorker.

16   I had engaged a small room for two dollars. This was half of all I had. I was satisfied. I thought I had a bargain. I had heard that all the hotels in New York cost ten and twenty dollars a night.

17   "They are worth that!" I thought, as the elevator boy danced up, a rich tobacco brown, well-formed and neatly mannered like his dress. He seized my big suitcase of brown cloth purchased in Seoul, Korea, a roomy bag, which yet carried little besides a few books, some letters of introduction and a toothbrush.

18   The elevator went zk! and up we shot. A funny cool ziffy feeling ran into my heart. It was my first elevator. Fast climb . . . I thought . . . like going to heaven. . . .

19   My room was small, white, nakedly clean, as characterless and capable as the cellophane-wrapped boxes in which American products come. The elevator boy smoothed the bed and pinched the curtains and examined the towels and looked in the wastepaper basket and picked up imaginary papers. I sat down in the chair, and crossed my legs. He stared at me dubiously. He waited. He didn't seem interested in my conversation. I asked him if he liked Shakespeare. He giggled and said coldly, "Who, suh? Me, suh? No, suh!" I know now that he was waiting for a dime. I was not sure. Besides I had nothing but bills, those four dollar bills which rested in the inner lining of my cap. I committed my first New York sin. I gave him nothing, neither then nor when I left the next morning. I am sorry. I would like to go back and make it right. I have been a waiter myself. I know the importance of tips. But I would not be able to find that bell boy now. There must be fifty thousand bell boys in New York and they never stay in the same hotel long.

---

[6] *people walking to and fro . . . talking mysteriously, perhaps of Michelangelo:* an allusion to "The Love Song of J. Alfred Prufrock" by T. S. Eliot.

Even the hotel may not have stayed. New York—its people, its buildings, its streets, are like a rushing river, the flood of which is changing all the time, so to be a New Yorker, one must feel like Heraclitus,[7] that nothing is changeless but the law of change. . . .

20   The bathroom was almost directly across from my room, beautiful, shining, glazed, so ordinary here, and yet a marvel of plumbing and utility. Even a prince in the old days could not have had such a tub. In Korea, the tubs were not of marble, nor machine-turned porcelain, but of humble intimate wood, and they were never used except for a grand occasion. Then all the water must come out from the well. In summer man bathed in streams, in winter from a great hollow gourd, a shell of the summer.

21   "But here," I thought, "a man has only to press a button. All the streams leap when he calls."

22   I let the water run—shee!—shee! as hot as I could stand it, as cold as I could stand it. I washed with soap—in my childhood, people still used an old-fashioned paste of ashes for that purpose—once more with soap, and then thoroughly with clear water. Even my hair I washed . . . everything. . . . I was washing off the dirts of the Old World that was dead, as in my country people did before they set out on a Buddhist pilgrimage. Now I had washed everything. Everything but the inside. If I could, I would have washed that as thoroughly, I suppose, and left a shell. But the inner felt the echo of the outer.

23   In my room again, I listened at the window. This incessant hum of wheels and screech of brakes . . . how different from the brawling mountain streams, the remote grass-roofed villages of Korea. . . . Korea, kingdom that was no more, taken by the little blue-clad soldiers to be a barrier against Russia, to be a continental point in Asia from which to punish Manchuria and China for their deep and stubborn resistance to the Machine Age. . . . In sheer amazement at life, I suddenly stopped at the mirror to see if I had changed, as well as my environment. For me an unusual act. In my Korean village there were mirrors, but mostly small ones, about the size of a watch, and generally with covers. Besides, the people who had mirrors usually hid them. It was thought some kind of vice to look at one's face. Some people like my uncle, the crazy poet, never properly saw themselves.

24   I have read that the Koreans are a mysterious race, from the anthropologist's viewpoint. Mixtures of several blood streams must have taken place prehistorically. Many Koreans have dark brown hair, not black—mine was black, so black as to have a blackberry's shine. Many have naturally wavy hair. Mine was quite straight, as straight as pine-needles. Koreans, especially

---

[7] *Heraclitus:* Greek philosopher who flourished around 500 B.C. who believed that all things are in constant transition and who wrote that "it is not possible to step twice into the same river."

women and young men, are often ivory and rose. My face, after the sun of the long Pacific voyage, suggested copper and brass. My undertones of the skin, too, mouth and cheek, were not at all rosy, but more plum. I was a brunette Korean. Koreans are more animated and hot-tempered than the Chinese, more robust and more solid than the Japanese, and I showed these racial traits as well. At eighteen I impressed most as being not boy but man. I needed to shave every morning for the thick growth of hair that came overnight. My limbs retained a look of extreme plasticity, as in a growing boy, or in a Gauguin painting, but with many Koreans, even grown up, they still do. In more ways than one, I looked an alien to the Machine Age and New York. One could not tell from my outside that I had lost touch with dew and stars and ghosts.

25   I tried to go to sleep, to rest baptized in the roars of Manhattan traffic, as Virgil had been in the Hellenic stream. But all my old life was passing through my brain as if I had not been able to wash out the inside at all. My eyes seemed to turn back, not forward. I saw the village where I had spent my boyhood, and where my father's father's forefather had spent his. I saw my father, responsible for the whole family, uncles and aunts and cousins every one, and I, his only son, his vehicle through time, who had made a wide parabola from him. I saw my *paksa* uncle[8] and my poet uncle and many more. . . . Yes, a synod of ancestors seemed coming to visit me, watching me disapprovingly in that high Western bed, which had renounced plain earth so literally beneath. What can you hope to find here? they said. Life, I cried. We see no life, they said. And yet they did not scold me now. Just waited, arms in sleeves, with the grave and patient wonder of the Asian in their eyes. And with a pang, I saw before me my uncle's studio, through which blew in summer the pine-laden breeze. I saw his books and the thousands of old poems in Chinese characters I knew and loved so well. Must I leave all this behind at the portals of America? . . . Couldn't they at least pass through into the world of the machines? . . . And against my will, a poem came into my head, one I had heard long ago. All in one throbbing moil it revolved, mingling in a hopeless incoherence with the foreign noises outside, of that most spectacular city so far over the rim of the world to me and yet a greater cycle in time than in space onward. It annoyed me that I could not quite rearrange the lines of this poem, nor remember the rhymes perfectly.

26   It was written in Chinese characters, but it was a Korean poem. One, I think, written by my crazy-poet uncle—although I am not quite sure. (Poetry writing then was so often anonymous. Men cared for the poem, not the fame.) It dealt with a tragedy that had happened in our province, perhaps a hundred or more years ago, yet still remembered and sung. A young

---

[8] *paksa uncle:* learned uncle.

lady of the house of Huang, or Autumn Foliage, had been suspected of unchastity. In Korea, this was such a terrible thing that the family in which it occurred would be disgraced forever, even by rumor. The young lady did the only thing possible in her environment. She gave orders for the building of a wooden coffin and said good-bye. In the wooden coffin she embarked on the sea as to the land of death. Miles away, beyond the sphere of her trouble, as if in token of true innocence, she was picked up by men of the family of Li, or Plum Blossom. She became a daughter of the Li household and married one of the sons.

27   In this poem, she speaks of herself symbolically. A leaf of the family of the Autumn Foliage floats loosely upon the sea. It is blown to rest against the branch of the white spring plum blossoms. That leaf of the yellow foliage is carried so far away that if one wishes to see her, he must ride on the back of the white crane.

28   This poem was very short, but contained in four short lines an Asian drama of fate which might have been entitled Hail and Farewell, or Autumn Saved by Spring, or Distance Bridged and Unbridgeable, or many more names besides. And the images were such that it was a poetic experience to write them in dynamic calligraphy, surrendering to the natural motion of leaves and scattering blossoms, of autumn and spring and the waves. In the end I had to rise from bed and write down the poem on paper, to get it all straightened out, before I could fall asleep in my high Western bed.

Discussion Questions

1. In paragraphs 4 and 5, the narrator contrasts New York's buildings with those of his village. How are the two architectures different?
2. The narrator says he "swore the oath of battle" (to get to know the West), but the oath was not militaristic because the "agricultural peace of Asia" was a part of him. Nevertheless, he was rebellious. What caused this rebellion and what form did it take?
3. How does the contrast between Japan and Korea at the time of his growing up help to explain the nature of the dilemma the author was forced into?
4. In small groups, discuss the advantages and disadvantages of preserving past traditions, customs, and ways of thinking.

WRITING TOPICS

1. The narrator refers to New York as "a city of Babel towers" and to the towers as Giantesses and Fates that "leaped like Athene from the mind synthetically." In a brief essay, explain what he means by all these allusions.

2. Using images gathered from online research, put together a visual and written report of how New York City would have looked circa 1921 when Kang arrived. In particular try to find illustrations of some of the places he mentions. In the written part of your report speculate about how New York must have seemed to a newly arrived immigrant from a fairly rural country.

3. A sense of place has been a prominent theme in the work of many authors, including many featured in this anthology. In a brief exploratory essay, examine how the places we grow up in shape us as people.

FROM *ISLAND*

Anonymous

In 1970 Alexander Weiss, a park ranger, discovered a number of poems in Chinese on the walls of barracks that were once part of the immigration detention center on a small island located in San Francisco Bay. The Angel Island Immigration Station, modeled after Ellis Island on the East Coast, was opened in 1910 and remained in operation for the next thirty years. It was the processing point for the 175,000 Chinese immigrants who came to the United States in the first half of the century. Chinese immigrants composed these poems while they awaited admittance to the United States.

The Chinese Exclusion Act of 1882, which was renewed in 1902 and not rescinded until 1943, prevented many Chinese immigrants from entering the country. Only those who could claim exempt status—for example, merchants, government officials, students, visitors, and those claiming American citizenship—were admitted, but not until they underwent medical examinations and interrogations that often lasted for days. After prospective immigrants were submitted to intense scrutiny, they had to wait for the results of their interviews. Those whose initial testimonies were rejected by officials often had to endure an appeals process that, in many cases, lasted up to two years. Many were deported. During periods of waiting, immigrants (many of whom did not fall into exempt categories but still wished to gain entrance) studied documents filled with information about their family and village—information that, if delivered correctly and convincingly, would assist them in the immigration process. Many also occupied their time with reading, gambling, and, of course, poetry writing.

The poems, written in the classical Chinese style, were often carved into wood and left unsigned and undated; those written in pencil or ink were eventually covered by coats of paint. References to heroic and literary figures from Chinese history and myth often fill the poems, but differences in poetic quality reflect various levels of schooling and training in composition. Some of the poems indicate a strong familiarity with literary conventions and traditions, while others demonstrate either a violation or an ignorance of the principles that guide the use of such devices as diction and rhyme.

The poets from this era of Chinese American history were mostly Cantonese villagers from the Pearl River Delta area in southern China's Guangdong Province. Their poems—many of which recount their feelings of frustration, anger, uncertainty, and loneliness—have been collected in *Island: Poetry and History of Chinese Immigrants on Angel Island, 1910–1940* (1991), edited by Him Mark Lai, Genny Lim, and Judy Yung. The following six poems illustrate the anger and frustration the immigrants felt as they waited to learn their fate. (J.I.)

8

Instead of remaining a citizen of China, I
　　willingly became an ox.
I intended to come to America to earn a
　　living.
5　The Western styled buildings are lofty; but I
　　have not the luck to live in them.
How was anyone to know that my dwelling
　　place would be a prison?

10

Just talk about going to the land of the
　　Flowery Flag[1] and my countenance fills
　　with happiness.
Not without hard work were 1,000 pieces of
5　　gold dug up and gathered together.
There were words of farewell to the parents,
　　but the throat choked up first.
There were many feelings, many tears flowing
　　face to face, when parting with the wife.

---

[1] *Flowery Flag:* a Cantonese colloquial term for the United States.

10   Waves big as mountains often astonished this traveller.
      With laws harsh as tigers,[2] I had a taste of all
          the barbarities.
      Do not forget this day when you land ashore.
15   Push yourself ahead and do not be lazy or
          idle.

By Xu from Xiangshan

30

      After leaping into prison, I cannot come out.
      From endless sorrows, tears and blood streak.
      The *jingwei*[3] bird carries gravel to fill its old
          grudge.
5   The migrating wild goose complains to the moon,
          mourning his harried life.
      When Ziqing[4] was in distant lands, who
          pitied and inquired after him?
      When Ruan Ji[5] reached the end of the road,
10   he shed futile tears.
      The scented grass and hidden orchids
          complain of withering and falling.
      When can I be allowed to rise above as I
          please?

By Li Jingbo of Taishan District

---

[2] *laws harsh as tigers:* From "Tangong" a chapter in the "Book of Rites": Confucius was passing Mt. Tai and saw a woman weeping and wailing at a grave. Confucius asked one of his disciples to ask why she was wailing so sadly. She said. "My father-in-law and my husband were killed by tigers. Now my son is also killed by a tiger." Confucius asked why she didn't leave this dangerous place. She replied that it was because there is no oppressive rule here. Confucius remarked, "Oppressive rule is surely fiercer than any tiger."

[3] *jingwei:* According to a folk tale, the daughter of the legendary Yandi, while playing in the Eastern Sea, was drowned. Her soul changed to a bird called the "jingwei," who, resenting the fact that the ocean took her life, carried pebbles in her beak from the Western Mountains and dropped them into the ocean, hoping to fill it.

[4] *Ziqing:* Another name for Su Wu (140–60 B.C.), who during the Western Han dynasty (206 B.C.–24 A.D.) was sent by the Chinese government as envoy to Xiongnu, a nomadic people north of the Chinese empire. Su Wu was detained there for nineteen years, but refused to renounce his loyalty to the Han emperor.

[5] *Ruan Ji:* Ruan Ji (210–263 A.D.), a scholar during the period of the Three Kingdoms (220–280 A.D.), was a person who enjoyed drinking and visiting mountains and streams. Often when he reached the end of the road, he would cry bitterly before turning back.

31

There are tens of thousands of poems
    composed on these walls.
They are all cries of complaint and sadness.
The day I am rid of this prison and attain
5   success,
I must remember that this chapter once
    existed.
In my daily needs, I must be frugal.
Needless extravagance leads youth to ruin.
10 All my compatriots should please be mindful.
Once you have some small gains, return
    home early.

By One From Xiangshan

34

For what reason must I sit in jail?
It is only because my country is weak and
    my family poor.
My parents wait at the door but there is no
5   news.
My wife and child wrap themselves in quilt,
    sighing with loneliness.
Even if my petition is approved and I can
    enter the country,
10 When can I return to the Mountains of Tang[6]
    with a full load?
From ancient times, those who venture out
    usually become worthless.
How many people ever return from battles?

38

Being idle in the wooden building, I opened
    a window.
The morning breeze and bright moon lingered
    together.
5 I reminisce the native village far away, cut off
    by clouds and mountains.

---

[6] *Mountains of Tang:* a Cantonese colloquial term for China.

On the little island the wailing of cold, wild
    geese can be faintly heard.
The hero who has lost his way can talk
10   meaninglessly of the sword.
The poet at the end of the road can only
    ascend a tower.
One should know that when the country is
    weak, the people's spirit dies.
15 Why else do we come to this place to be imprisoned?

DISCUSSION QUESTIONS

1. What does the reference in poem 8 to becoming an ox imply about the poet's feelings?
2. The writer of poem 10 provides a brief history of his feelings before, during, and after his journey before giving his words of advice in the last line. How might this short history be encouraging to others?
3. What do the allusions in poem 30 tell you about the poet?
4. Both the poet of number 31 and the poet of number 10 counsel others or themselves not to forget the time in prison. Why?
5. Poems 34 and 38, perhaps written by the same person, express bitterness directed at China. What adjective is used in both poems to describe China? Could the same description apply to countries from which people migrate today? Explain.
6. Many of these poems contain images of nature. What might these types of images reveal about the poets?

WRITING TOPICS

1. In a few paragraphs, express your feelings about composing and then displaying poetry as an antidote to or a protest against one's circumstances. Do you find this understandable or strange?
2. After researching the topic, write a brief history of the Angel Island Immigration Station.
3. Research and explain in a brief essay the classical style of Chinese poetry used by the poets at Angel Island.
4. Compose a five-line poem for a younger brother or sister giving advice that expresses what you have learned about life.

COMING TO AMERICA

Akemi Kikumura

Akemi Kikumura, the youngest in a family of ten girls and one boy, was born in 1944. She earned a doctorate in anthropology from the University of California, Los Angeles, and has taught Asian American studies and anthropology at UCLA and the University of Southern California. She also directed a research project, funded by the Asian American Studies Center at UCLA, that focused on rural Japanese American community life.

During her last four years at UCLA, Kikumura began to interview her mother and to record her experiences in order to assemble a family history. Kikumura says that she wanted to "close the generational and cultural gap" that she felt existed between her generation and the preceding one. Kikumura also believes that there are major differences between her and her older brothers and sisters—siblings who were educated, mostly by their parents, prior to World War II and the internment. Although Kikumura's parents were at one time strongly tied to Japan and its culture, they felt the intense shame and the "deep and irrevocable imprint" of their removal and incarceration during and after the war. Unfortunately, Akemi, as the youngest child, received less information from her parents about the Japanese language and cultural practices.

Through Harsh Winters: The Life of a Japanese Immigrant Woman (1981) is a book about her mother's life. It is the result of Kikumura's many interviews with family members and a trip to Japan to meet her parents' relatives. In the following passage from that book, Kikumura's mother recalls the harsh life of Japanese immigrants in the migrant labor camps of northern California. Note that the references to "Papa" are actually to Akemi Kikumura's father, the narrator's husband.

1   I was sick on the ship all the way to America. They fed us bread and butter. That was the first time I saw butter and just the sight of it made me sick. The ship was oppressively packed with people and the latrines were not like today's. We had to defecate into the ocean. When we stopped in Hawaii, I remember seeing funny things hanging in a store window. I never saw anything like it before. It struck me funny because the shape—they were sausages. We never ate meat before. Meat was for *yotsu* [a pejorative for Burakumin or lower-caste Japanese]. It was unheard of to eat meat.

2   About two weeks from the day we left Japan, we landed in San Francisco. From that moment on, I began to understand the world. We first went to the Aki Hotel and ate *miso shiru* (bean-paste soup), *iwashi* (sardines), and *daikon oroshi* (grated white radish). It was clean there. But when we came to Liberty (a town in northern California), the conditions were terrible. I thought America was supposed to be a beautiful, clean country, but it was dirtier than Japan.

3   We stayed at Ichikawa's boarding house. The walls were plastered with pictures from magazines, the floors were dirt, and there was only one bed. Papa said, "Well, this is it." From the window I caught a glimpse of farmers in overalls shooting guns and I thought, What an ugly place.

4   Liberty had a Japanese population of approximately 500 people, of whom very few were women. Everyone knew Papa there and they made a big fuss because he had come back with a wife. It was very rare for a man to have a wife.

5   After my initial encounter of *hakujin* (white) farmers in overalls, I rarely saw another *hakujin*. From morning to night it was just farming—no white faces. Papa would go out at night and come home very late. At first I would wait patiently for him at the boarding house. Well . . . evening glow and he still wouldn't come back. I went looking for him. He was gambling. That was the first time I saw a gambling hall—saw stacks of silver. They told me, "Pull up a chair and play." There were many women there too.

6   Many of the Issei indulged in gambling. It took care of their spare time. Papa was particularly good at gambling. When he played *hana* [a Japanese card game], he knew what everyone had in their hand. He just didn't know when to quit. He kept playing until he lost everything. Once you indulge in a life of addiction, you never quit. For Papa it became the most important thing in his life. I began to think he was incurable.

7   We moved to the country to work at Kato's labor camp. The living conditions there were even worse. When it came time to sleep . . . you know where we slept? On wooden boards cushioned with hay and partitioned by a sheet. "Here you sleep," they said. *Ma-a* . . . everyone could see us . . . a couple sleeping together—sleeping next to others!

8   From there I worked continuously. I was the cook. That was the first time I cooked, since my father's sister always prepared the meals for us in Japan. During grape season there would be around 25 men to cook for. I

was good. Everyone said my bean-paste soup was the best and they came from all around to taste it.

9   Cooking was difficult at first because American food was different. In Japan we used fish all the time but in America, Saturday meals consisted of steak (or pork chops—since it was cheap), *okazu* [slices of meat sauteed with vegetables], or hamburger meat fried with noodles and tomatoes. I experimented with an assortment of dishes because once the men ate it, they wanted new things to eat. I quickly learned how to make a variety of dishes.

10   Kato-san was a difficult man. He was the kind of person who would often caution others of their errors. Once I forgot to shut off the kitchen lamp when I went to the bathroom. He reprimanded me, telling me that I should shut it off when I wasn't using it. I remember that well. . . . I remembered everything *tanin* [nonrelatives] said. I never did it again.

11   Kato-san got himself a wife from Japan. She was the younger sister of Yamada Kumaichi (Papa's friend). That woman was so good to me. She came from Shimane-ken. I remember when she first arrived. My, was she beautiful! She looked just like Nagako of the Imperial family when she was young. I never cast my eyes on such a beautiful woman—so graceful and slender. She had one child with Kato-san and about a year later, he died.

12   That morning he was to go fishing. I made a lunch for him and brought it to him. He was dead. His wife lay sleeping with him and didn't even know he was dead. His dog, named Dick, must have known better because he barked throughout the night. The dog would fetch the paper for him each morning but that night his master had died of a heart attack in his sleep. His wife returned to Shimane-ken. During those days in the country, how could a woman get along?

13   After that, Papa's friend, Yamada Kumaichi-san, came to run the camp. He was a living Buddha. Yamada-san eventually called for a wife from Japan. This lady was short and squat—a real country hick—but what a beautiful soul. The more I got to know her, the more beautiful she became.

14   On the camp there were many little houses. There was Hanaki-san, who was there for so long: he's probably dead by now. Yamada-san's youngest brother also lived there. He was an extremely educated man but during those days, educated or not, you couldn't get a job if you were Japanese, so you helped out in the country.

15   After the grape-pruning season there was nothing to do so we would go to the asparagus camps in Stockton's Cannery Ranch. We washed and packed the asparagus into boxes for the canneries. Only Japanese did asparagus cutting. We lived in the wash house, lining up boxes and sleeping on top of them. The season lasted for three months from June through August. I remember how hard we worked . . . wearing boots all day long, stooping in the hot sun.

16   Everywhere we worked there were few married couples and the rest were single men. Those who had wives bragged. Consequently, the women without any children had many men pursuing them. A woman could take advantage of the situation and make good money. Yanagi-san did. She took up with other men because of financial problems.

17   Before Papa and I came to America the Issei were still able to secure wives through picture-bride marriages, but when that became prohibited as well as immigration to America, it left the majority of men without women. Many times men approached me and said, "Let me do it with you and I'll give you money," but I was hard—I never gave in. What an insult! I wasn't a whore. Once when Papa went to Utah to find gold, a friend of his propositioned me. "Let me do it with you," he begged. "You're crazy," I said. I told Papa when he came back. Papa was furious! That was the end of their friendship.

18   A woman couldn't show her charm to a man or he would think that she was giving him a signal to go further. And if she made him any promises she couldn't fulfill, her life was in danger. This waitress got her face badly cut with a knife because she would make promises to men that she had no intention of keeping after they had spent money on her.

19   Even false hope invited trouble. There was Ito-san, a married woman with one child, who became involved with a cook. He pleaded, "Let's get married," but she said, "How could I. I'm already married." Then he proposed to her, "Let's die together." She refused to do either with him so he shot her in the back with a pistol, then tried to take his own life only to discover there were no bullets left. He managed to find a rifle and went deep into the vineyards and shot himself. The daughter came home from school and found her mother dead.

20   After asparagus season, we returned to Liberty and I had my first child, Nesan. She was born January 1, 1924, at six in the evening. Tamura-san, the woman whose husband sold bean curd, was my midwife. In the country, doctors were not available, and when they were, either they would not treat us [Japanese] or their services were too expensive. So as a rule, the midwives substituted for doctors in delivery of the baby or the woman did it herself.

21   We made money washing and packing asparagus. We put about $2000 in the Sumitomo Bank and kept about $1000 on hand. Papa said let's go home because we had the fare and only one child. He said, "A country like America, it takes a long time to save money. We have been here one year and we have saved this much. We also have money back in Japan, so let's go home." But I didn't want to go back yet. I thought we could work just a little longer, make more money, then return home. It would have been bad to return without a lot of money. but after that time, we never had enough. No matter how much I tried to save, Papa would gamble it all away.

22   Pear picking started in Walnut Grove. I said, "Let's go." After pears came peach packing in Marysville. In Marysville the air was so stifling hot that we would arise at three in the morning and quickly pick the peaches before the sun's rays reached their peak. We lived in a vacated schoolhouse and fetched water from a well. Since there was no kitchen, we dug a hole in the earth and placed two metal bars over the hole to cook our food.

23   Apple packing came next, in Watsonville. I was the cook there. My, I did all the farm work there was to do in America . . . Papa and I and the children going from place to place. To move was easy. All I had to do was roll up the blankets and say, "Let's go," and soon after, we were gone. Issei—it was the same for all of them. They would bring their children everywhere. "*Sa-a!*" and they would wrap their children in blankets and go.

24   From Watsonville we moved on to Pismo. We stayed in a house behind a grocery store owned by a *hakujin* (white person). He felt sorry for us living in the camps and he let us live there free. It was the first time I lived in a house since coming to America. In the morning the waves would break, "Ja-a-h!" near our window. Papa would go fishing and we would dig for clams and cook them over the heat of a lamp. Oh, how delicious!

25   We worked for Masuoka-san picking peas. He planted them on the mountain's slope because they grew faster, away from the ocean fog, yet warmed from the gentle salt air. The view from the mountains was breathtaking. We would leave Nesan in the car and let her sleep while we picked peas on slopes so steep that you slipped with each step. Already my stomach bulged big with child. I worked up to the day Hana was born.

26   I remember when Hana arrived. The labor pains began late in the night. Papa drove me to the hospital in San Jose in a dilapidated Ford which barely made it over the hills. Each bump in the road sent a shock of excruciating pain. I gave birth before they had a chance to give me an enema. I stayed in the hospital for one week and came home to rest for another two.

27   I kept thinking, "I must work and go back to Japan." I was lonely—not a single relative. It might have been different had I been with someone I liked, but Papa never treated me gently. We never had conversation. We just worked and had babies.

28   Papa and I were not well suited for each other. He used to remind me that he wanted to marry his brother-in-law's daughter from a previous marriage. She was a rare beauty and a geisha, trained and quite accomplished in the arts. A person like that could have earned a living in America by teaching; Papa would have been well off. They would have been well suited to each other because Papa himself had an artist's spirit. He loved to entertain.

29   While in the company of others, Papa overflowed with laughter, but the minute he came home, he became *yakamashi* [stern, fault-finding]. At home he disciplined the children. He got angry if they used one word of English: "Use Japanese!" he admonished. "You go to school and learn English. A Japanese is no good unless he can speak Japanese." Even if I wanted to speak

English, I couldn't. He wouldn't let me. "The children will naturally learn English," he said. Therefore at home they received discipline in Japanese: the language, social graces, practical wisdom.

30 He was severe. If I sat around not taking care of the household chores after coming home from work, he would say, "Don't go to work. After the household chores are taken care of, then go to work." He believed that a woman should never be idle for one minute. In the mornings, if I didn't come to the kitchen with my hair fixed neatly, he would get angry. Or if I came with slippers, he would say, "Go back into the bedroom and fix your hair and get dressed before you come out again." After marrying Papa, I have never risen after the sun was up. Even now, past four in the morning I can't stay in bed.

31 It has been that way between Papa and me ever since we got married. He never treated me well . . . birthdays . . . presents . . . clothes . . . who ever heard of such things? If I went into town, it was because my children were sick—not to have fun. But once I got married, I never entertained the thought of divorce. As long as he brought home enough to feed the children, I didn't care. Even if he was gone for a month, I didn't complain as long as my children could eat.

DISCUSSION QUESTIONS

1. How can you account for the difference between the experiences of Kikumura and Sugimoto, whose autobiographical excerpt begins this chapter?
2. What evidence of prejudice do you find in Kikumura's memoir?
3. How can you explain the reasons for Papa's treatment of his wife and children?

WRITING TOPICS

1. The author's choice of words and the experiences she describes reveal much about her character and personality. In a brief essay, examine the author as a person and how her characteristics are revealed in this excerpt from her memoir.
2. Research the lives of migrant workers in California today. In an essay, describe how the experiences of modern migrant workers are different (or not) from Kikumura's experiences. Examine the sorts of concrete factors that Kikumura writes about, such as housing and income.

FROM *SOUTH WIND CHANGING*

Jade Ngoc Quang Huỳnh

Born in the Mekong Delta region of Vietnam in 1957, Jade Ngoc Quang Huỳnh was educated at Saigon University from 1974 until the North Vietnamese army took control of the south in 1975. After enduring a year of horrifying conditions and torture in a labor camp, he escaped and reached a refugee settlement in Thailand. In 1978, Huỳnh left Asia for the United States. He worked at factory and cleaning jobs before completing an undergraduate degree at Bennington College in Vermont and an M.F.A. at Brown University.

The following selection from *South Wind Changing* (1984) describes the Huỳnhs' horrifying journey of escape from Vietnam. (J.I.)

1   We got out from our barrels and breathed the good misty air of the pre-dawn. It was 4:30 a.m. on my watch, but it was still dark. We hung a little light on the cabin for the other boats to see, for the traffic was picking up. All of a sudden, I fell down, people shrieked. Our boat had collided with another small boat.

2   "Can't you see where you are going?" a woman's voice yelled at us.

3   "It's okay, no harm done. I'm sorry ma'am."

4   We pushed our boat away from them and turned our engine to a higher speed. At about 5:30 A.M. we arrived at the open sea. The sky was brighter but I could see light scattering from a fisherman's boat. The moist air filled my nostrils. I felt as if the light was seeping into me, showing me a new space, a new horizon. Life had just begun, maybe.

5   "Water, water leaking," a woman's voice came out from under the deck.

6   My brother and I rushed to check the situation before dark. The flashlight in his hand went to the direction of the woman calling. The children were still drunk in their sleep with the sleeping pills.

7   "Where is it?"

8   "In front here."

9   We crawled all the way to the head of the boat, moving our light slowly from spot to spot. Some water sprinkled on my face.

10 "Anh Lan, right here," I called to him.

11 He turned the light on a little hole that had a crack around it. Whenever the waves slapped outside, the water leaked and sprinkled inside. I took off my shirt and held it there.

12 "Brother, ask them if they have any wax sap left?"

13 My brother passed my message to the cabin, reporting our situation.

14 "No, we don't have any. Try to hold on till the day comes so that we can figure out what to do with it," Hanh's voice came from above the deck.

15 Both of us took turns holding the hole until daylight. Some of the children began to wake up, vomiting and crying out with their seasickness. I felt dizzy with memory in this tight, cramped place where everybody lay upon each other in their own urine, suffocated by the smell of smoke, gas, and oil.

16 "Is it okay to take some people up to the deck to get some air? We are suffocating in here!" I shouted.

17 "Okay, pull them out," someone in the cabin said.

18 We broke all the ceramic barrels and threw them into the ocean, then moved the children and women out from the compartment to get some fresh morning air. Everyone seemed to have recovered after a few minutes.

19 I let my brother hold the hole while I climbed into the cabin.

20 "Do we have any plastic cans and some nails?" I asked.

21 From the engine room beneath the cabin someone yelled out.

22 "Hold on, we found something."

23 Someone pushed up a carpenter's toolbox with wrenches, sockets, hammers, and screwdrivers. I picked it up.

24 "Don't drop it into the ocean. We desperately need it to fix our engine if it breaks."

25 "Okay," I said.

26 Hanh was our captain now. Whether he really knew where we were going, I wasn't sure.

27 "Is the compass working all right?" I asked.

28 "Yeah," Hanh said. "I guess."

29 "Which way are we going?"

30 "180 degrees east."

31 "How do you know that?"

32 "I learned from different people. Remember I have a cousin who was a captain in the southern navy."

33 "I didn't know if you were just making it up."

34 "Yes," he said, winking his clever eyes at me, his bold features looking bigger, somehow, out in the free sea air.

35   We laughed, looking at each other in appreciation.

36   "Go and fix the hole before we sink," he said.

37   The atmosphere was less tense now, even though we had a hole to take care of. I looked around the cabin to find some thing to plug it.

38   "Why don't you cut a piece of our poncho on the deck and use it?" suggested Hanh.

39   "But we cannot hold it all the time," I joked.

40   I looked at a small wooden door from the cabin, pulled a hammer out and broke off a piece of it, which I passed down to my brother.

41   We put two shirts into the hole, folded a piece of the poncho into a square over the hole, nailed it down, and hammered a piece of wood over it all. It looked okay to me, for now. We came up to the deck and put the toolbox back in the engine room.

42   The children began asking for food and water as the women started distributing our first meal at sea. The sun was red, just over the water. It looked so close. The air was clear in the high blue sky; clouds of pink, rose, orange, and red danced around the sun. The sky looked like a painting hung above the glistening water. And so our journey on the open ocean began. The waves were very gentle, the air was fresh, people in our boat started speaking all at once, lively after our meal. I saw the shoreline fade further from us. A flock of seagulls flew together in the air, gliding back and forth. In the distance, some dinghies sat on the water, fishing. The air patted lightly on my face, and I inhaled and exhaled in high spirits, enjoying my freedom at last. Two inches of mist above the water scattered, dissolved by the sunbeams that slowly began to warm us. Some of the children and women started their new day sitting along the side of the boat, searching beyond their thoughts. Maybe they were taking a last look at their homeland. It was a quiet morning except for the noise of the engine.

43   "Look, look, mama!" a child shouted, pointing a finger to the back of our boat.

44   I saw a gang of fish jumping up and down in the water, chasing us. Everyone clapped and cheered, excited.

45   "Come on, *Ong Nuoc*,[1] race with us!"

46   The louder we got, the faster the fish moved. Soon they caught up with our boat, came closer to us, the water splashing against the boat and sprinkling us. When they were ahead of us we were excited for them. Every time they went too far from our boat, they slowed down as if waiting for us, then moved on again when we got closer to them. By now the fish seemed to know me as a family member; each time I escaped, they welcomed me. "Come with us, we will escort you," they seemed to say.

---

[1] *Ong Nuoc:* old man Nuoc.

47   "We're going to have wonderful weather for at least two days," one smiling middle-aged woman said as she held a rag over the heads of the children, shielding them from the hot sun of the open deck. Our journey went on until the afternoon, when we saw a big boat appear from the distance.

48   "I think it's the government boat. It's moving toward us!" I yelled from the front deck.

49   Hanh and some others came out from the cabin to spot it if it came in our direction.

50   "Hanh, what degree have we been going for the last two hours?" I asked him as I jumped on the back cabin.

51   "350 degrees east. Never mind. Turn our boat to another direction to run away from this monster!" Hanh bellowed.

52   We lost our course from then on. But two days and one night passed without any problems. We were in the middle of nowhere and could see nothing but blue water, boundless sky, and hot sun.

53   The storm struck during the second night. The wind whistled and roared while the rain poured down harder and harder. Waves as big as a house pushed our boat from side to side; water came into our boat from the sky and from the hole I had mended, which now poured like a broken pipe. My brother and I took care of the hole, scooping the water out while the children cried and the women moaned. Hanh and Chanh tried to keep the engine running. The boat pushed against the waves. Waves pushed the boat higher, and then we'd fall into the abyss with more water gushing into our boat. Everyone struggled, but our seasickness made us weak. The kerosene lamp fell off from the side of the cabin onto the deck, broke, burst into a blaze of oil, then drowned when a big wave splattered our deck. It seemed that life was going to end at the cruel bottom of the ocean.

54   But all of a sudden the rain stopped, the howling of the wind slowed to a whine, and the waves diminished. Calm returned. Our engine stopped because too much water had flooded it. We rested there for a while, helpless. Our men began to mend the leaking hole again. We got up and cleaned away our defeat by nature. We scooped the water out, cleaned the engine, made an inventory to see what had survived. The storm had lasted for only half an hour but it seemed the night would never end. We were lost in the middle of nowhere. We moved on in the early dawn, not knowing where to go. We searched for the *Sao Mai* star[2] to locate our direction and went east. Some women and men were begging us to go back but Hanh told them to shut up. Hanh said that if he heard one more word from them he would throw them into the ocean. We lived free, or died, but would never return.

---

[2] *Sao Mai star*: evening star.

55   Another day passed. We hung a white rag as an SOS flag from the pole at the top of the cabin, hoping for a friendly rescue. We had no more food, no more water, but luckily we could squeeze our wet clothes for water, drinking water given to us by the storm. Another night passed. The hot sun came, pouring down heat as if to barbecue us. We drank our own urine to help us bear the heat and used it to dampen our clothes. The children fell down on the deck and into the bottom of the boat, where oil and excrement lay everywhere. The men lay about the boat, collapsed from exhaustion, starvation, and hopelessness. Two women who still had a little energy left collected urine. The children were groaning "Water, water." But no one responded, not even their parents now. I felt like I was walking into the sky, dizzy, wanting to move to a different place, but I couldn't move my body. I was a big rock stuck on the wood. I could comprehend everything happening around me, but I couldn't control my body. After a while, the engine stopped, out of gas. Yet even if it were running no one would have been able to steer, because nobody had any strength left.

56   We floated on the water like a ghost boat, carrying a bunch of wandering, innocent souls. I kept looking at my watch; sometimes I saw it was twelve and sometimes I saw it was two o'clock. Then our boat lurched off to one side while the water slapped harder against it. I saw a huge object appear and heard a loud noise. I was on the bottom of the deep ocean looking up at a giant on a hillside. The giant became clearer. It was a wooden boat painted red with some kind of picture on it. People stood up, looked down at us, moved away. Then another boat came, circling closer. Everything disappeared for a while. Finally, I heard people shouting in very strange voices, using a strange language. Our boat moved as if someone had jumped on it.

57   I opened my eyes and saw an old man with gray hair and skin darkened from time and hard work. His kind face looked at me sincerely, worriedly, his eyes steady. He held a teaspoon with water, putting it on my lips.

58   "*Ap nam, ap nam.*"[3] Water, I guessed.

59   I sipped it, feeling the cold energy running all over my body.

60   The old man called gently to the others. I heard people running. They surrounded me, smiling. They fed me some soup from time to time, little by little, until I could stand up and walk around.

61   A Thai fishing boat had rescued us at last. They towed our boat on the back of their boat and sent a young man to fix our engine. We scooped the water out of our boat once in a while. My brother Lan, Hanh, Chanh, and eighteen others on the boat were okay, but we had lost one child along with Chanh's mother, who had been overcome by her sickness. She had died just a few hours before we were rescued. They had already been buried in the ocean.

---

[3] *Ap nam:* [Thai] completely without water.

62   They fed us as if we were their guests. I found out that the old man was a cook, so I went to help him in the kitchen cabin. He taught me *Kawpkoon krap* (thank you) and *mai* (doesn't matter). I began to learn a new language and loved the sound of it, especially when I heard a girl's voice.

63   For two days, our group helped the fisherman sort out fish, and then we headed back to Thailand. The fisherman had already fixed our boat when we arrived in Thai territory. At sunset we bowed and said farewell to our saviors. Every one of us wept tears of appreciation and wondered when we would meet them again, since we couldn't get their address: the Thai government would punish them for helping us. The Thai captain spoke to us in broken English, saying that he couldn't take us all the way to the dock. The sky was a golden color over a tree near a small mountain range at the end of the water. Seagulls flew in the air, landed on a pole and on the deck to search for some leftover fish. They made happy sounds whenever we passed them, jumping up to another spot without hesitation, continuing their hunt. They were free to fly while we enjoyed our freedom. The water was clear but not as blue as it was farther from shore. We got back in our boat. They gave us water, food, diesel, and showed us the direction to go.

64   "There, *Chanthaburi,* go there," they shouted.

65   We held our hands together, bowing them our respectful goodbye. We started our engine. They waited until they heard our boat run, then left us. We waved until the boat disappeared. The chilly wind blew, the sun sank. Lights gleamed from here and there, far away. Black smoke came out of our engine, because it hadn't run for some time, making us cough. We moved in the direction of Chanthaburi until eleven o'clock. But it seemed we weren't getting anywhere. The stars shone restlessly and I saw that Chanthaburi was brighter than any spot I had seen in a long time. I guessed the city had more light than other surrounding areas. I saw a boat with many lights coming our way.

66   "We are safe, we have help coming!" everybody shouted happily as they stood up, looking forward to the arrival of the boat.

67   When the boat came, the crew carefully looked us over, pushing their boat closer to ours. The boat was as big as the boat that had saved us. We held the side of their boat to stop it from hitting ours, while waves shook it back and forth.

68   "Please help. We are refugees," Hanh said in English.

69   Ten young men jumped onto our boat.

70   "Police, police," one of them said.

71   I thought they were police who came to help because the group was talking in Thai and broken English. Each one of them searched each one of us. They pulled my watch off, collected all the earrings from the women and girls. They searched in every corner, in every bag, and every little spot. Something seemed funny: if they were police why weren't they in uniforms,

why did their boat carry no sign, and why were they taking our belongings? Before I could do anything the man searching me jerked a knife to my throat and yelled something to another in Thai. To our surprise, they held us hostage and we didn't know for sure what was going on. The children cried. Maybe it was a police search. They threw our utensils over to their boat, disconnected one essential part from our engine, and began to force all the men to one end of the boat, the women to the other. They turned all their lights off and I heard the three girls yell loudly for help, despair in their voices.

72   "Mama, help me, Baba, help me!"

73   The mother grasped the legs of the pirate who held her daughter, but he kicked her to the deck floor. We couldn't signal each other to fight back with our eyes, because it was dark. I shouted in Vietnamese as loud as I could.

74   "Fight for our last battle!"

75   My left hand grabbed the arm holding the knife to my throat and pushed it away while I used my right elbow to punch the chest of the false policeman with all my strength. He struggled with the pain and tried to press the knife harder into my throat but I grasped his hand with my two hands, bent down, and threw him over my head. He fell off the boat. The boat shook with our struggle and the waves, rocked from side to side as if it might capsize. I jumped in to help Hanh since with his polio he could not fight back. The pirate who held him pushed Hanh down on the floor and turned to me. He yelled something in Thai which I didn't understand, and the light from their boat turned on. Their boat was revving and gave our boat a strong push. I lost my balance and slid into the water along with others. They turned off their light and stopped crushing our boat. I swam to keep my head up for air, kept at some distance from the boat, unable to climb back on it.

76   The women and children cried out louder and louder, but who could help them? I heard the girls' voices become weaker and weaker as they struggled against the pirates. These girls were no more than seventeen years old. I was powerless and my eyes were stinging. Maybe I cried or maybe it was the salty water of the ocean, but I knew for sure that I had lost the last fight. I called out to my friends in the water to see if they were okay, but there was no response because the wind pushed the waves up and down and turned my voice into a whisper.

77   The pirates took turns holding the girls as they satisfied their animal thirsts. An hour later, I heard their boat revving louder, moving away into the dark, leaving only their laughter behind. They turned their lights on again. I swam back to our boat and got on board.

78   The women helped the three naked girls to find some clothes to wear. They were moaning, withdrawn to one spot, shaking like dying people. I saw tears drenching their faces, filled with hatred. Everyone became silent.

Hanh had a bleeding wound on his head. My brother Lan had a cut on his chest. I had a small cut on my throat. The father of one of the girls was wounded on his arm and back, but not seriously. The wounds aggravated deeper hurts in our hearts more than our bodies. We started to paddle the boat ashore, thinking about what kind of freedom we would have.

79   At 5:00 A.M. we arrived. We made more holes in our boat to make sure that, if the authorities pushed us back to sea, we wouldn't make it, and they would have to rescue us. A big wave washed our boat onto a clean beach. We got off our boat and sat on the sand, but the drunkenness of the sea stuck with us. I saw the whole world go around in my head, the palm trees along the road, houses, streetlights, and cars spun in front of me. I vomited and vomited till nothing was inside my stomach and I tasted bitterness in my mouth.

80   The police discovered us in the morning when the chill was still in the air. We were shaking with our wetness, our clothes drying on our backs. The palm tree leaves rattled in the wind, lining the street along the shore. The lights were off now. A policeman came to check our boat, looking at us very strangely, cautiously. The police isolated us in one spot, not letting anyone go anywhere. We asked for permission to go to a temple, to beg for food. People gave us some bread and soda once in a while. They tried to talk to us, seeming to feel sorry for us, but the policeman wouldn't let them.

81   A few days passed as we bathed in the ocean every day and ran around until our clothes dried under the sun. We had to wait until dark to go to the bathroom, finding an isolated spot in the sand to do our business, or pretending to swim far out in the sea and do it in the water. A policeman would beat one of us up once in awhile, for some trivial reason. The three girls were terrified of all men. They sat in a corner with the old women without speaking to anyone, always in tears; I feared they had lost their minds.

82   We were stuck there in these conditions for a month. Two more boats full of Vietnamese refugees arrived in that time. They were in good shape morally and physically. They told us that they hadn't had any problems at sea.

83   On the first day of April, a reporter with a Vietnamese wife spotted us. The wife came, spoke with us, and then devised a plan for us to escape from the police and go to a refugee camp the reporter knew of. At midnight that night three journalists came. All of us swam to the two boats anchored outside the dock. We left Chanthaburi.

84   We arrived at Leamsing Refugee Camp on the night of April 2. The police didn't let us ashore, shooting in the air to threaten us. We stayed put on the boat, anchored about fifteen meters away from the dirty mud beach. Refugees rushed to the rock shore from their huts, standing upon the hillside, welcoming us, and asking about the news from home. Some of them

identified relatives on the boat. Refugees threw bread, water, sodas, and cookies on board while the police tried to order them to go back to their shacks. It was becoming a tradition to greet new refugees, I learned.

85   "Hide any valuable things because tonight they will rob you before letting you ashore," someone in the crowd shouted to us.

86   "Where are you from?" they asked. "What is the situation at home?"

87   "Sa Dec,"[4] Hanh replied.

88   "It is horrible at home," I said.

89   "Break your engine just in case they pull you back to sea," another suggested. "Is there anybody from Phu Quoc island?"

90   We talked as if we were all relatives who hadn't seen each other for years. The refugees coached us on what to say to the police and how to fight back against intruders. Some people on the second boat gave one of the refugees a few letters to send to their loved ones in Australia; they would wait eagerly for the response.

91   We shared and enjoyed the food they had given us, celebrating our first chance to taste the air of freedom. At night we were alert on our boat and sometimes we heard pots and pans clanging, warning us of a robbery attack, but nothing happened. We were stuck on the boat as it lay at anchor for days, and then the United Nations High Commission for Refugees commissioner came to let us land.

92   On shore, we received rice, water, and several meters of plastic, which we fastened to an unfinished hut on a hillside, facing the ocean above an abandoned cemetery. This would be our place to rest, to settle for a while, and to begin our new life as a people without a country, as wandering souls who had lost their home just as surely as those lying beneath us had lost their lives. A gong sounded from the temple behind the bushes on the top of the hill. The wind hummed and whistled on bamboo leaves. Tides drew in and out, like an inner voice calling me back to the time when I was a young child, but the day went on without stopping. I sat down on the ground, inhaled the fresh air, looked further into the ocean, and wondered what was beyond.

DISCUSSION QUESTIONS

1. What qualities did the author have that enabled him to survive the journey to Thailand?

---

[4] *Sa Dec:* a village in Vietnam.

2. How can you account for the difference between the actions of the fishermen and the phony police?

Writing Topics

1. In a journal entry, write about what you hope your own response would be to a horrible situation such as that experienced by Huỳnh.
2. In a brief essay, compare Huỳnh's immigration experience with that of either Etsu Sugimoto or Akemi Kikumura. Include a discussion of how the differences in their experiences affect the manner in which they relate their tales.

TWO LIVES

Shirley Geok-lin Lim

Shirley Geok-lin Lim was born in 1944 in the historic British colony of Malacca, Malaysia. She attended the University of Malaya in her country of origin and then moved to Boston in 1969 to continue her education. She went on to earn a Ph.D. in English and American literature from Brandeis University and to study with American poet J. V. Cunningham, to whom she dedicated her first collection of poems, *Crossing the Peninsula* (1980).

An extremely prolific writer, Lim has published four additional volumes of poetry: *No Man's Grove* (1985); *Modern Secrets: New and Selected Poems* (1989); *Monsoon History* (1994), which is a retrospective selection of her work; and *What the Fortune Teller Didn't Say* (1998), her most recent collection. In addition, she has published three books of short stories and a memoir entitled *Among the White Moon Faces* (1996), which received the 1997 American Book Award.

Lim is also a visible and critically acclaimed literary scholar of Asian and Asian American literature. In collaboration with Mayumi Tsutakawa, she edited *The Forbidden Stitch: An Asian American Women's Anthology* (1990), a collection of poetry, prose, and reviews that offers a strong counterpoint to the masculinist voices of the Asian American literary community. Indeed, Lim ranks as one of the preeminent Asian American feminist scholars in the United States. She is also the author of *Writing South East/Asia in English: Against the Grain* (1994), which contains theoretical, literary, and autobiographical essays that explore literary migrancy and the experiences of the Asian diaspora.

Lim's creative and critical work reflect both her Chinese-Malaysian heritage and the social and literary landscape of the United States, of which she is now a citizen. She remains an observer of Southeast Asian life, retaining important links to the Pacific Rim's literary community, even as she gains an identity as a Californian writer. She is currently a professor of English and the chair of Women's Studies at the University of California, Santa Barbara, where she is an influential advocate of undergraduate and graduate students' pursuing both creative writing and scholarship.

"Two Lives" is an excerpt from *Among the White Moon Faces*. It examines the sense of displacement and homesickness that many immigrants experience and reflects the strong attachment to family that is a feature of traditional Chinese culture. "The Castle" referred to in the selection is a dormitory building at the university.

1 No one who has not left everything behind her—every acquaintance, tree, corner lamp post, brother, lover—understands the peculiar remorse of the resident alien. Unlike the happy immigrant who sees the United States as a vast real-estate advertisement selling a neighborly future, the person who enters the country as a registered alien is neither here nor there. Without family, house, or society, she views herself through the eyes of citizens: guest, stranger, outsider, misfit, beggar. Transient like the drunks asleep by the steps down to the subway, her bodily presence is a wraith, less than smoke among the 250 million in the nation. Were she to fall in front of the screeching wheels of the Number Four Lexington line, her death would be noted by no one, mourned by none, except if the news should arrive weeks later, twelve thousand miles away.

2 A resident alien has walked out of a community's living memory, out of social structures in which her identity is folded, like a bud in a tree, to take on the raw stinks of public bathrooms and the shapes of shadows in parks. She holds her breath as she walks through the American city counting the afternoon hours. Memory for her is a great mourning, a death of the living. The alien resident mourns even as she chooses to abandon. Her memory, like her guilt and early love, is involuntary but her choice of the United States is willful.

3 For what? She asks the question over and over again. At first, she asks it every day. Then as she begins to feel comfortable in the body of a stranger, she asks it occasionally, when the weekend stretches over the Sunday papers and the television news does not seem enough, or when the racks of dresses in the department stores fail to amuse. Finally, she forgets what it feels like not to be a stranger. She has found work that keeps her busy, or better still, tired. She has found a lover, a child, a telephone friend, the American equivalents for the opacity of her childhood. The dense solidity of Asian society becomes a thin story. At some point, she no longer considers exchanging the remote relationships that pass as American social life for those crowded rooms in Asia, the unhappy family circles. And were those rooms really that crowded, the family so intensely unhappy? . . .

4   It was the waste of time I minded most, a sludgy feeling that took over October and November. In September, almost a year after my arrival at Brandeis, Father had written to say he had been diagnosed with throat cancer. He was seeking medical care in Malacca. "Don't come home," his letter ended, "I don't want you to interrupt your studies."

5   I told no one. Food stuck in my throat whenever I thought of Father. The thought was like a fishbone, sharp and nagging. I couldn't speak of him.

6   Another short letter arrived from China without a return address. I read it over and over in the safety of my room. "I am doing well," it said. "My white blood cells have gone up, and I am feeling stronger." The small black-and-white photograph that fell out of the envelope showed that he was lying. The shirt draped over his body like a sheet over a child, although his face was old and sad.

7   For a few months, the letters came from China without a forwarding address: he was staying near the clinic in Canton, noted for its cancer cures. He wrote irregularly. Like a careful student, perhaps because he was lonely, he sent the laboratory reports on his white blood count. His letters were optimistic to begin with. The white blood-cell numbers had improved; he was enjoying this Chinese city he had never seen before, visiting parks, zoos, and museums, with a new friend also undergoing treatment at the clinic. Then a letter arrived complaining of homesickness. He wanted to be home with the family; he missed Malaysian food.

8   When Thanksgiving came, the Castle emptied out. Julie and Carol returned to Brooklyn and Missouri. On Friday I picked up a letter from my mailbox. The rice-paper-fine aerogramme rustled as I spread it out to read the ball-point print that smeared across the crumpled blue surface. It was a letter from Second Brother, and I was immediately afraid, for Second Brother had never written to me before. "We buried Father two weeks ago," he wrote.

9   I stared at the words and calculated the time. Two weeks ago, and a week for the aerogramme to cross the world to reach me in Massachusetts. It was unimaginable that Father, the source of whatever drove me, that total enveloping wretchedness of involuntary love, my eternal bond, my body's and heart's DNA, had been dead for almost a month. The world had a hole in it, it was rent, and I would never heal.

10   Maggie came knocking at my door just as I finished reading Second Brother's letter. An orphan left with a trust fund, she was slowly completing her graduate studies, while spending most of her time volunteering to help with the animals in the zoo. She wanted to know if I had had any pumpkin pie yet for Thanksgiving. Would I go with her to the cafeteria for a piece of pie? I was still holding Second Brother's blue aerogramme in my hand.

11   "My father's dead," I said to her. Why was I telling her this? Would I have said the same thing if the janitor had knocked on the door to fix the radiator? "He died three weeks ago."

12   "Oh," she said. "I'm sorry." I cold see that she was. Tall and big-boned, Maggie was deep water, quiet-spoken, all reserve.

13   I paid for my pie and coffee at the cafeteria and watched her eat. She left the crust and scraped the brown gooey filling carefully with her fork till it was all gone. My throat hurt. Then I returned alone to my room. I knew Maggie would never visit me again. I had been too painful for her.

14   At first I didn't cry. It wasn't Father's death that drove hardest at me, it was that he had been dead for more than two weeks already, and I hadn't known all that time that he had gone. "We didn't think you should come home," Second Brother wrote. The grief and the guilt lay beyond tears. Months later, in Brooklyn where I was sharing a studio apartment with Charles, the Brandeis graduate student whom I would later marry, I woke up in the middle of the night my face drenched with tears. I had wept in my sleep for Father.

15   A month after the news of Father's death, Second Brother sent me a package of papers from Father's belongings. Father had kept all my old school record books, annual school certificates of achievement, examination diplomas, yellowed letters of recommendation from high school teachers, and Malaysian citizenship documents. On an unmailed aerogramme sheet, Father had scrawled in a shaky hand, "I want you to come home now."

16   My brother also sent me a diary Father had kept in the last weeks of his life. Only a few pages were filled, and all the entries were addressed to me. In the early entries, he wrote he was hopeful he would recover, and he did not want me to return home because it was so important for me to continue my studies. In the second to last entry, he asked that I hurry home; he didn't believe he had much time left and he wanted to see me. In the very last entry, addressing me as his dear daughter, he wrote that although he knew I would do so, still he asked that I promise to take care of my brothers and sister, Peng's children. The entry was very short and the handwriting erratic. My father had willed his children to me.

17   The day I received the package, I emptied my bank account and sent the few hundred dollars in it to Peng. With it, my letter promised that I would send her as much as I could each month. For a long time, every U.S. dollar rang as precious Malaysian currency for me to remit. A ten-dollar shirt? I paid for it and guiltily counted the groceries the money could have bought for Father's family. I disapproved of my growing consumerism. The pastries that gleamed, sugar-encrusted, at Dunkin' Donuts, which I eyed longingly, would buy copybooks for my half-brothers. For the next few years, I carried my father's ghostly presence through department stores and restaurants. His sad smile was a mirage of poverty. I saw my half-siblings ragged and hungry whenever I glanced at a sales tag, and every month, I made out a bank draft to Peng and mailed it out as an exorcism.

18   An exorcism I could not explain to Charles, my American husband. How could one eat well if one's family was starving? For Chinese, eating is both material and cultural. We feed our hungry ghosts before we may feed ourselves. Ancestors are ravenous, and can die of neglect. Our fathers' children are also ourselves. The self is paltry, phantasmagoric; it leaks and slips away. It is the family, parents, siblings, cousins, that signify the meaning of the self, and beyond the family, the extended community.

19   In writing the bank drafts I remained my father's daughter, returning to Father the bargain we had made. This is the meaning of blood—to give, because you cannot eat unless the family is also eating. For years, I woke up nights, heart beating wildly. Oh Asia, that nets its children in ties of blood so binding that they cut the spirit.

DISCUSSION QUESTIONS

1. Why do you think the author titled this autobiographical chapter "Two Lives"?
2. Lim writes eloquently and at length of the illness and death of her father. Why do you think the fact of his death was made worse because she hadn't known about it for three weeks?
3. Reread the last line. How was the author's spirit cut by "ties of blood"?

WRITING TOPICS

1. In a brief essay, examine the mood of this selection and how it is conveyed through Lim's choice of words and tone. Support your views with quotations from the excerpt.
2. The author says that she "disapproved of [her] growing consumerism." Have you ever felt this same disapproval about yourself? If so, what caused the feeling? If not, what would it take for you to feel such disapproval. Speculate on these questions in a short essay.
3. Several of the authors in this chapter convey a sense of homesickness while at the same time settling into their lives in the United States. In an essay, compare Lim's yearning for her homeland and her shifting memories of her family back home in Malaysia with the experiences of another author in this chapter.

ASSIMILATION

Eugene Gloria

Eugene Gloria was born in Manila, Philippines, in 1957 and was raised in San Francisco. He was educated at San Francisco State University, Miami University of Ohio, and the University of Oregon. His poems have appeared in such publications as *Parnassus: Poetry in Review, Madison Review, Crab Orchard Review, The Asian Pacific American Journal,* and the anthology *Returning a Borrowed Tongue* (1995).

Gloria has received a Fulbright fellowship (1992), an artist grant from the San Francisco Arts Commission, and the George Bogin Memorial Award from the Poetry Society of America. His collection of poems, *Drivers at the Short-time Motel,* was selected by Yusef Komunyakaa for the 1999 National Poetry Series and will be published by Viking Penguin. He currently teaches English at Holyoke Community College.

In the following poem, Gloria uses a young boy's desire to eat the "correct" American food to exemplify how immigrants strive to fit into the new society. This theme is central to the story of those new Americans, who are "ashamed to be more different / than what my face has already betrayed."

On board the Victory Line Bus
boring down Kennon Road,[1] is the bus driver's sideline:
a Coleman chest full of cold Cokes and Sprites,
a loaf sack of sandwiches
5   wrapped in pink napkin and cellophane.
My hunger sated by thin white bread
thick with mayonnaise, diced pickles and slim slice of ham.

---

[1] *Kennon Road:* the main road to Baguio, a city in the mountain province of Northern Luzon in the Philippines.

What's mere snack for my gaunt Filipino seat mate,
was my American lunch, a habit of eating
10 shaped by boyhood shame.

Once, I believed that a meal meant at least a plate of rice
with a sauced dish like *kari kare,*[2] or *pinakbet*[3]
pungent with *bagoong.*[4]
But homeboys like us are marked
15 for not being part of the whole
in a playground full of white kids
lined on redpainted benches in the fall chill of noon—

lunch pails bright with their favorite cartoons,
and a Thermos of milk, or brown paper sacks
20 with Glad bags of chips, peeled Sunkist,
Mom's special sandwich with crisp leaf of lettuce,
and pressed turkey thick in between—
crumbed with the breakfast table bread.

I remember that first day of school,
25 my mother, with the purest intention,
took two sheets of foil hollowed with a cup of steamed rice
and a helping of last night's *caldereta.*[5] chunks of potatoes,
sliced redpeppers, and a redder sauce with beef.
And I, with hunger, could not bring myself to eat.
30 Ashamed to be more different than what my face
had already betrayed,
I hid the rice from my schoolmates.
Next morning, my mother grasped the appropriate combination:
sandwich cut in two triangles, handful of chips, fruit,
and my best broken English.
35 Weeks passed while the scattered rice—
beneath the length of that redpainted bench
blackened with the schoolyard's dirt.

---

[2] *kari kare:* oxtail and vegetable stew in peanut sauce.
[3] *pinakbet:* a stew cooked with shrimp paste, pork, eggplant, bittermelon, and okra.
[4] *bagoong:* salted shrimp paste.
[5] *caldereta:* a beef dish in spicy liver sauce.

DISCUSSION QUESTIONS

1. What prompts the speaker's reminiscences?
2. What made the speaker ashamed on his first day of school?
3. How did the speaker start to become assimilated?

WRITING TOPICS

1. Prepare an oral interpretation of this poem and present it for the class. Start by writing a short introduction that captures the audience's attention, tells the author and title, and gives any necessary background about the author. Then decide how the poem should be read, including rate, vocal quality, and volume. Determine how you will use gestures, posture, and facial expression to help create mood. Mark your script (using a copy of the poem). You will want to indicate pauses, emphasis, pronunciation of difficult words, movement, and any change of posture. These markings should help you remember how you are going to read the poem.
2. In a brief essay, discuss Gloria's tone in this poem and how it is conveyed.
3. Gloria uses concrete language to describe the texture, taste, and smell of certain Filipino foods. In an essay, analyze Gloria's use of language and how it contributes to the mood and pacing of the poem.

HOW I COULD INTERPRET THE EVENTS OF MY YOUTH, EVENTS I DO NOT REMEMBER EXCEPT IN DREAMS

Christian Langworthy

Christian Langworthy was born in 1967 in Vietnam with the name Nguyen Van Phoung. In 1975, he was adopted by American parents and came to the United States. Langworthy studied for his M.F.A. in creative writing at Columbia University under a School of Arts fellowship. His chapbook of poems, *The Geography of War,* was published by Cooper House Publishing in 1995. His poems have been anthologized in *Premonitions* (1995), *Muae* (1995), and *Watermark: Vietnamese American Poetry and Prose* (1998). He has also published in many journals, including *Mudfish, Soho Arts Magazine,* and *The Asian Pacific American Journal.*

The following poem tells of Langworthy's journey to America and the impressions the new country makes on his eight-year-old mind.

Because I was a newly adopted
    child from another country,
(a prostitute's son in a Vietnamese
    city bristling with rifles
5 and as a result of my mother's truancy
    from motherhood I was given
to nuns and locked within the confines
    of missionary walls)
I crossed the perilous South China Sea
10   and Pacific in three days
(barely surviving anti-aircraft fire)
    aboard an eight prop-engine plane.

I came to this country
    to a nine-inch carpet of snow
15 and a sure welcome by strangers
        engaged with the possibilities of parenthood.

My new beginning consisted of firsts:
    first experienced snowfall in America—
(how it was magic in a fairy tale land)
20   first toilet flushings,
(at the airport, when I flushed every
        toilet in the men's room to my new
father's delight)
        and another notable first—
25 the first cartoon I ever saw on Saturday
        morning: Bugs Bunny and Elmer Fudd,
and how there were no wounded or dead
        from the flying bullets,
and I laughed so hard I cried
30   though I did not understand their language then.

As the years of my second life progressed,
    my adopted parents tried so to be
a good father and mother and to the cinema
    we went, and I saw the children's epics:
35 Snow White and the Seven Dwarves
        and Sleeping Beauty; at home my mother read
fairy tales to me, tales like Rumpelstiltskin,
        and I learned
the false beauty of the wicked witch,
40   the castle besieged by thorns,
the terror of the kidnapped son.
        I could have told them I'd seen these tales
before, but I was too young to know the difference.

DISCUSSION QUESTIONS

1. The end of the first stanza, the middle stanza, and the beginning of the third stanza are replete with images of an idyllic childhood. By contrast, the beginning and ending of the poem are dark and disturbing. What effect does this have on your reading of the poem?

2. If, as the title suggests, the author remembers the events that occurred in Vietnam only in his dreams, how reliable do you think his memories are? Discuss in small groups.

WRITING TOPICS

1. In a brief essay, examine how the author's use of powerful verbs affects the various moods of the poem.
2. Write an essay exploring the title of the poem and how it is reflected in the poem itself.

SUMMARY WRITING TOPICS

1. What would you say are the chief factors governing whether an immigrant's initial experiences are successful? Do successful experiences have to do with class? money? language? education? laws? help from a host country? Or do they depend on an individual's own character? Discuss these questions in an essay.

2. In an essay, compare the immigration experiences of any three authors in this chapter. Consider such factors as the reason for their immigration, their journey, and their adaptation to life in the United States. Use quotions from the selections to enliven your essay.

3. In her account Etsu Sugimoto writes of her and her family's concerns about proper behavior and dress in America. Why were these concerns so important to them? Where do ideas about proper behavior and dress originate? How do the standards differ according to the occasion? For example, what marks the difference between behavior and dress at a dinner party at the White House, dinner at the house of a friend, and dinner in your own home and why? How do today's immigrants find out about "proper" American behavior and dress? Discuss in an essay.

4. Write a persuasive essay in which you argue that assimilation is or is not important and why.

5. Think back over the selections you have read in this chapter. In your journal, write about which author you admire and why.

CHAPTER TWO

ASIAN AFFILIATIONS

Much Asian American writing looks back to a time and place before entry into the United States. The authors are sometimes first-generation immigrants who are still close to the recent histories that led up to their arrival on American shores. Often these histories are painful, filled with war, conflict, poverty, and struggle. But often they are also histories of cultural achievement and pride, social standing and wealth. Many U.S.-born Asian American writers have been influenced by their families and communities to incorporate cultural practices and values drawn from Asian origins. Thus, there is often no clear demarcation between feelings and ideas attributable to an "Asian" identity and those seen as coming from an "American" identity. Instead, identities usually categorized as "nation"-bound are often deconstructed or fragmented or crossed in ways that undermine conventional notions of unitary selves.

Much of Asian American literature treats the modernist theme of individual alienation in a mass and technological society that presupposes a central individual subject attempting to make order of his or her experiences. This is seen in Meena Alexander's poem "Great Brown River," which links the naturalized universe of humanity with the freight trains that symbolize American mobility and with her South Asian ancestors, and, finally, with literature, "a whole globe seething / with words." N. V. M. Gonzalez's story "The Lives of Great Men" is told ironically through the eyes of a narrator whose brief visit to a remote island in the Philippines is itself ironically presented. The double ironies, focusing on Fidelino, who has returned from working in Hawaii to his native home with nothing but "clothes" to show for the years away, underline the historical relationship of colonized Filipinos to the United States and the recursive nature of their sojourns here.

Chitra Banerjee Divakaruni's poem "The Arranged Marriage" and Ginu Kamani's short story "The Smell" criticize the social values and customs of a society that exists in a pre-American past. Divakaruni imagines the event of her mother's arranged marriage at the age of sixteen to an unknown man whose eyes are unreadable to her. Kamani's story draws a more rebellious female character, Rani, who rejects the rigid morality that constrains her at home, as seen in her grandmother's strict vegetarianism. The injunction against eating meat figures as well in injunctions against the flesh and against sexual feelings, and these prohibitions psychologically damage those young girls who accept their grandmother's control of their appetites.

But the writings also underline certain post-modern qualities of decentered or multiple national identities, as in Theresa Hak Kyung Cha's complex collage-work *Dictee*. The excerpt here offers a fictional narrative of the violent clashes between state power and student activists pushing for democratic reform that actually did occur in Korea in the 1960s. The shifting use of first-person narrator and second-person addressee personalizes this account so as to soften the distinction between the students and the soldiers, who are also seen as brothers, albeit brothers who kill in a civil war.

Familial characters set in an Asian homeland, as in Hilary Tham's "San Chi," blur into the characters of Asian immigrants whose faces trigger memories of ancestral relationships, as in Li-Young Lee's wonderful long poem "The Cleaving," which celebrates the violence of change and the holiness of human bonds. The themes that appear in the writing of authors as different as the Filipino American Jessica Hagedorn, the Vietnamese American Nguyen Ba Trac, and the young Indian American Svati Shah are of separation from an Asian homeland, the work of memory in returning the Asian American to the past, and the celebration of these past relationships. Such writings, whether poignant or ironic, suggest something of a post-colonial context and of collective and political identities as well as individual and artistic struggles. All these selections suggest that the writers of Asian American literature are often working in the presence of memories of the Asian past and Asian cultural values.

GREAT BROWN RIVER

Meena Alexander

Meena Alexander was born in 1951 in Allahabad, India. Her family belongs to the Syrian Orthodox community in Kerala, the southernmost state of India. Alexander comes from a long political line: her maternal grandmother, whom she unfortunately never knew, was a Gandhian activist and both grandparents were involved in the struggle for Indian independence. In 1956 the family relocated to Khartoum, Sudan, when her father took a job with the Sudanese government.

After graduating from Khartoum University, Alexander earned a Ph.D. from Nottingham University in England in 1973. After graduation, she returned to India, where she published several volumes of poetry, including *The Bird's Bright Wing* (1976) and *Stone Roots* (1980). Alexander moved to New York City in 1979 with her husband, David Lelyveld. In 1988 she was a writer in residence at Columbia University's Center for American Cultural Studies, and she currently teaches at Columbia and at Hunter College of the City University of New York.

Alexander's scholarly interests include Indian and Western feminism, postcolonial studies, and British romanticism. Her body of work demonstrates a diversity of writing styles and forms; she is lyrical, analytical, political, and scholarly.

In 1989, she published a critical study entitled *Women in Romanticism: Mary Wollstonecraft, Dorothy Wordsworth , and Mary Shelley.* In addition to writing poetry, Alexander has produced a volume of memoirs entitled *Fault Lines* (1992) and the novel *Nampally Road* (1991), which deals with, among several other issues, police brutality and rape.

"Great Brown River" is taken from *The Shock of Arrival: Reflections on Postcolonial Experience* (1996), a collection of poetry and prose in which Alexander deals with the challenges faced by immigrants to America. In the poem, metaphors of the river and urban blight evoke images of Asian forebears and their influence on the present.

This river without a name
I live by:
a great brown river
flecked with foam
5 where few birds call.

There are freight cars
tethered to the trees
their metal holds
marked *Burlington Northern*
10 marked *Milwaukee.*

In the pitch black holes
between the rails,
debris of unnumbered lives,
tin cans, chipped glass
15 worn car tires,
the body of a dead hawk
its wings clapping
in a dry wind
that jars the river silt
20 batters the freight cars
till out of the blind holes
ancestors wake:

their flesh is brown
as river water,
25 sugarcane stubble,
iron bits, cut cord
laced to their skin.

Arms braced
they prevent me
30 from the musical gardens
of the rich,
well-lit fountains,

signs swaying above
this city.

35 like a child's
cut outs:
Best Flour Pilsbury,
Satin Smooth Tips,
Buy Life Insurance.

40 As they swarm into water
dragging the railroads behind,
I realize this river
will round the earth,
a whole globe seething
45 with words.
The waves are swords.

DISCUSSION QUESTIONS

1. What does the fact that the freight cars are tethered tell you about them?
2. Why do the rails and freight cars prompt the speaker's thoughts of her ancestors?
3. What can the speaker not do because of her ancestors and why?
4. In the last stanza, the great brown river takes on a metaphorical meaning. Speculate on what a river rounding the earth and seething with words might stand for.

WRITING TOPICS

1. In a short essay describe the tone of the poem and how the author achieves that tone. Cite lines from the poem to support your views.
2. Write a poem or paragraph about your cultural roots using colorful adjectives and strong verbs to express your feeling about your heritage.

THE LIVES OF GREAT MEN

N. V. M. Gonzalez

Born in the Philippines in 1915, N. V. M. Gonzalez is the son of a teacher in Romblon Province. Before taking up creative writing, Gonzalez studied law and journalism. He has been a faculty member at various universities, including the University of the Philippines and the University of Washington, where he served in both the English department and Asian American Studies.

In addition to teaching and writing fiction, Gonzalez is a journalist and a magazine editor. He has received numerous awards and recognitions throughout his literary career, including several Rockefeller grants, which have enabled him to travel and write extensively: the Commonwealth Literary Award; the Rizal Pro Patria Award; and the Republic Cultural Heritage Award. His books include *The Winds of April* (1941), *Seven Hills Away* (1947), *Children of the Ash-Covered Loam* (1954), *A Season of Grace* (1956), *The Bamboo Dancers* (1959), *Look, Stranger, on This Island Now* (1963), *Mindoro and Beyond: Twenty-One Stories* (1979), *The Father and the Maid: Essays on Filipino Life and Letters* (1991), and *The Bread of Salt and Other Stories* (1993), from which the following selection is taken.

In "The Lives of Great Men" a young Acting Credit Manager's assistant is sent on business from Manila to the rural area where his extended family lives and where he had spent time as a boy. The resulting contact serves to emphasize the distance that has come between the man and his relatives. (J.I.)

1   It was many years ago that I was in Buenavista (said our Acting Credit Manager's assistant)—one of those strokes of good fortune, you know—it was the Company that sent me over. You couldn't have thanked the Chief enough.

2   The plane ride, the two hours of grueling heat on the bus, the twelve miles by ferry to the next island—what did these difficulties matter? I had learned my three R's in Buenavista. The small barrio[1] called Hinala, now the site of the airport, was where Grandfather took us at the close of each school term. Before a gathering of his cronies, he'd make an occasion of it, showing us off as specimens of a generation better endowed than his own, a breed equipped for progress. We could be relied upon to deliver speeches or recite clever little verses in a language that neither they nor we ourselves really understood. What my cousins' performances were like I can't now exactly recall, but mine were not unremarkable. My Longfellow's "The Psalm of Life,"[2] for example, invariably won applause.

3   But the poet's homily deceived no one. If Grandfather's friends got the message, they hardly made it known. "Bravo!" they'd say, as if indeed they belonged to the *principalia*,[3] clapping their hands in the manner appropriate to members of that class. And then they'd go on with their drinking—which was *tuba*,[4] there being no libation within their means except this one provided by the ubiquitous coconut palm.

4   As might be expected, Grandfather's cronies resumed by morning the lives that Longfellow had mildly interrupted; by first light they'd set out as usual for their fish-traps or rice fields. Thus they carried on, burdened by no great faith or ideals, their every gesture showing no traces that the lives of great men had ever touched them.

5   It did not occur to me at that time that Longfellow was an irrelevance; those command performances inspired in me a terror that blocked out everything. Rescue came now and then only from Uncle Nemesio, whose promptings and encouragement did him proud as Hinala's leading citizen, being in fact the incumbent head-teacher at the barrio elementary school. In fifteen years, he would be retired from government service and, as one of Grandfather's heirs, would host many a tuba-drinking party himself.

6   My flight took hardly an hour, the palm fronds in the north wind waving a welcome as we landed. Uncle Nemesio was in the crowd to meet the plane, although hardly on my account, to be sure, for I had neither written

---

[1] *barrio*: village.
[2] *"The Psalm of Life"*: A reference to a poem by Henry Wadsworth Longfellow (1807–1882) entitled "A Psalm of Life" The title of Gonzalez's poem comes from stanza 7 of that poem: "Lives of great men all remind us / We can make our lives sublime. / And, departing, leave behind us / Footprints on the sands of time."
[3] *principalia:* in this context, a reference to the educated upper-class.
[4] *tuba:* fermented coconut juice.

him nor wired. As it turned out, he had a bad memory. Not until I had given him my nickname did the blank look in his eyes change into recognition.

7   We walked straight to his house half a kilometer from the airport, beyond the school grounds. It seemed that some festivities had been planned; a bamboo arch had been built at the school gate, and strips of colored paper fluttered from the porch eaves. Boys and girls were rigging with palm leaves the unfinished concrete fence; this consisted of slabs about two meters long and a meter high, each bearing the name of the local gentry who had been importuned into making a donation. You had a feeling that here was a cemetery where true civic-mindedness and generosity lay quietly buried.

8   The frame house where we used to stay during vacation time now lodged another family—no relation of ours, my uncle emphasized, his lips twitching as he spoke. The property had passed on, in any case, to an aunt of mine, now deceased and survived by a rather improvident son-in-law. Worse, he had no sentiments about the place whatsoever. In short, I should not expect to be put up there for the night.

9   The property directly across the street from the old place, however, was the portion that fell to Uncle Nemesio as his inheritance. In this way he came by about a hundred and fifty square meters of property, with a nipa house set off from the street by sweetsop trees.

10   The house was in reality a shack and was oddly appropriate to all concerned. My uncle, now seventy, had become shorter by three inches, it seemed to me. He had, in my aunt, who emerged from the kitchen shed holding a cooking pot in her hand, a gnomelike companion. Her faded orange dress and her long, hemp-yellow hair heightened this impression. Her eyes were deep-set and restless, like those that belonged, or so you imagined, to some figure in storyland.

11   "Fidelino is now with us. He used to work in Hawaii," Uncle Nemesio said.

12   The reference was to their son, my bachelor cousin of forty or so; he was in that airport crowd, only I hadn't recognized him.

13   "The two of them, father and son . . . that's all they do," my aunt said. "You would think that the governor, or somebody with a basketful of food or a trunkful of money, was coming to help us out."

14   The remark sounded like a familiar grudge, its point much too blunted from endless dibbling. In any case, my Uncle Nemesio had by now taken off his shirt and had climbed to a bench by the window.

15   Fastened to the post and one of the rafters, and thus held somewhat above eye level, was a small transistor radio. He devoted his attention to this object presently, turning this knob and that with great care. He became so overwhelmingly enraptured by the music, it was as though I might just as well not have arrived.

16   Except for the bench and the low center table, the room was bare. Held

down upon the table top by two square feet of glass was a spread of snap-shots, my cousin Fidelino's and, quite likely, those of his Hawaiian friends.

17   The shack itself seemed about ready to fall apart; but, quite literally, the lives of great men held it together, in defiance to all conceivable forces that bring things to naught. For here, in makeshift frames hung against the slant of the roof and the wall, was a gallery of our illustrious ones. Strands of hemp fiber, from pieces of string that held the frames in place, quivered in the wind. These pictures, doubtless, had once graced some page or maga-zine cover. Here now, at one end of the row, was a pensive Abraham Lincoln, and at the other, an amused John F. Kennedy. In a frame also all his own, a proud Manuel L. Quezon stood in white riding breeches and leather boots, in the middle of a rice paddy. A beam of mangrove wood set apart three other frames. The first was that of Elpidio Quirino, who bestowed on me an enigmatic smile. Alongside was Manuel L. Roxas in his solemn best. Yet another was a group picture of the very heroes of the nation: Jose Rizal, Marcelo H. del Pilar, and Mariano Ponce—all in heavy overcoats, so cold it must have been in Madrid during that winter of their exile.

18   My cousin Fidelino had arrived. "When we saw you," he said, "all I could think of was whether there would be fish in the fish corral." He took off the rather sporty knit shirt he had worn to the airport. "Let me go to the water this very minute." And with that he dropped out of sight.

19   I had always remembered him as a little boy who ran around as likely as not without trousers and who did not have enough stretches of beach to cover in full trot. Now he had on those dark blue dacron trousers, the cuffs folded six inches high and weighted down with sand.

20   My aunt joined us at this juncture. "Clothes are all that he brought home from Hawaii. So what do his uncles and cousins do? Here they come and they walk off with a shirt or two every time. It won't be long before he'll be as naked as before. The fish corral used to give us plenty of fish," she added, "but we are now in the wrong time of year. In two months, things could be better, though."

21   Fidelino had left without a word. I thought he might have asked me to join him, at least, and that he did not rather disturbed me. He might have wanted me to see how things were down at the beach.

22   I felt I had to go myself. The *amihan*[5] had stopped; the palm fronds hardly moved. A little to the right, on the horizon, lay Kalatong Point, reminding me of countless golden-red snappers that had often got the bet-ter of my patience. The slow oncoming twilight here could play tricks on the imagination. When the tide was down, the waterline showed markedly on the palings, creating the illusion of another horizon.

---

[5] *amihan:* fresh or clean air; an ocean breeze.

23   But I knew these waters; I knew Kalatong. The fairest of women lived there, according to legend. Kalatong trees were all of the same height, and beautiful music awaited you in the forest. On the eve of the feast of Santa Catalina, a white ship dropped anchor off the point. Exactly at the stroke of twelve, on the eve of Good Friday, you must smear your eyelids with beeswax and then hurry to the beach, for you might just see then the captain's launch heading straight for the shore. It'd be he who could take you to some country far away, where you'd make your fortune. Did Fidelino know all that?

24   He presently appeared and began wading toward the shore. For the most part the water was waist-deep, and it was not long before he proudly held up against the twilight sky, to show me, a string of wrasses and snappers.

25   "In two months, we'll have sardines and garfish here . . . a whole lot of them!"

26   We had supper soon afterwards and, too tired to do anything or go anywhere, I decided to turn in early. I did remember the bed with Fidelino's suitcases stacked beneath. A girl of ten, or thereabouts, now lay curled up on it—she must have been there all this time, only I had not noticed. The thatched wall and her sleeping mat seemed to have merged; in the darkness neither could be set apart from the other. I had been deaf to her intermittent coughing, now her efforts to clear her throat were developing into spasms. In any case, she was a presence, an identity to be accounted for.

27   "A bad cold . . . that's all," my aunt explained. "It's been a week now. She should be up and about, but she stayed too long in the sun yesterday."

28   The girl, meanwhile, had begun rolling up her mat. In a minute she had moved to the other room, the bundle too heavy-looking for her.

29   "Time for bed," my aunt now turned to Uncle Nemesio. He had been comfortable there on his bench for so long, sitting with one knee upraised, and did not seem ready to be dislodged. But slowly he rose, as obedient as a little boy.

30   "Auntie," I protested, for what she was up to dawned on me. "Let me sleep anywhere."

31   But she would not hear of it. The girl could go elsewhere—the matter was settled! The spot under the bench would be just right for her.

32   But how was I to sleep? I felt terrible over her yielding the bed. Perhaps she had done it of her own accord, perhaps not. The thatch shingles gave out a musty odor. Hordes of lice seemed to have taken possession of the sleeping mat, and I knew they had all of me to crawl over. I heard someone in the yard—Fidelino. And my aunt was chiding him gently, "Better not make any noise. You'll wake him up."

33   He was quickly gone, and it was perhaps then that I finally dropped off

to sleep, though I must have wakened later, for I thought I saw him change and leave again, now in a bright red shirt, off into the night. I might have imagined the color—I don't know. And then sometime afterward I heard some faint and melancholy music. Could this be a string band or a phonograph? Uncle Nemesio's transistor radio, perhaps?

34   Ah, the music from Kalatong forest, I said to myself, fully awake by now.

35   My aunt was in the room to fetch something. "There's a school benefit dance out there," she said, when she heard me stir. "Someone came a while ago asking about you."

36   I couldn't imagine having anything to do with a school benefit dance. "What did he want?" I asked.

37   "To know if you could join them. I said you were sound asleep. You were, weren't you? Oh, how you snored!" She gave a little laugh. "A donation for the school . . . that's what they're after. You don't go for that, I know. As to your cousin, he's one who'll not allow himself to be left out. He pledged money for an entire section of the school fence."

38   After this remark, she said nothing more. In the meantime, the distant music became one with the waves of throbbing sound that the crickets raised in the sweetsop trees.

39   The bus to the ferry landing forty kilometers away arrived about seven the next morning. It pulled up in front of a food stall across the yard from the local airline office and waited there for northbound passengers. There was only time for coffee and a piece of rice cake, which both my uncle and Fidelino declined when asked to join.

40   In Buenavista, I dispatched as quickly as I could the business I had been sent to look into and was back at the Hinala airport in good time for my flight back to Manila. My aunt had joined Uncle Nemesio at the airport to see me off; Fidelino turned up, too.

41   "People asked why you were not at the dance," he said.

42   "What excuse did you give?"

43   "You were too tired, I said."

44   And that touched me somewhat, and I thought I could pay him back in kind with some thoughtful gesture of my own. As a matter of fact, it must have been in the back of my mind for some time. "There's a good chance you might make good money here . . . if you like," I began.

45   "How?" he asked, rather puzzled.

46   "You might start a poultry farm. You could ship fresh eggs to the city every day."

47   But he laughed off the idea. "Oh, we're quite all right as it is. We really are. In two months, the fish corral will be bringing in money."

48   "If not a poultry farm, then a piggery. Something . . . anything!"

49   "Last night there was a big tide," Fidelino said. "We had a catch of five

kilos of wrasses. Off it went by the first bus this morning to Buenavista. . . . Later, there will always be income from the coconuts."

50   Yes, Grandfather's coconuts, I could have said aloud. But something made me keep it all to myself. I could also have said: After Hawaii, didn't you learn a thing or two? Have you no ambition at all? Don't you want to be better off than you are now?—But I recalled the evening before, the music from the schoolhouse, and, as if rejecting the legend of the tall trees and the white ship off Kalatong Point, I heard myself giving expression to something else. It might have been the most gross of all my thoughts.

51   "What's wrong with the girl?" I asked guardedly.

52   "Measles."

53   It was my aunt who spoke; she had overheard me. "If it's catching it that you fear," she said, "don't worry. You had it years ago. Don't you remember? You can't catch it now."

54   But, of course, I had forgotten. And once again she smiled in that gnomish way of hers. Did she know what I had been thinking? I had been mistaken, suspecting that she and Fidelino had been at odds. They had in fact been allies in good standing. Who, for instance, was the girl but a love child? Fidelino's, most naturally! How unfortunate for the girl, had Fidelino's mother—my aunt, that is—not been there to look after her while he was away in Hawaii. And who would the girl's mother be? And, if I knew, what then? Would that be knowledge that should matter?

55   The many questions in my mind could only mean one thing: they emphasized the distance that had come between us. All I could do now was to trust that I be forgiven for my coarse efforts at making contact.

56   But my remorse was shortlived. The plane had already arrived. In the ensuing commotion, I couldn't think of anything worth saying. Even small talk eluded me. All three of them—Fidelino, my uncle, and my aunt—stood at the edge of the crowd that awaited the moment of departure, and from the ramp I waved to them, much in the manner of those great ones whose photographs had appeared in newspapers and magazines. . . .

57   That pose (continued our Acting Credit Manager's assistant) I might have managed well enough then—and now might never quite live down.

Discussion Questions

1. Why did the young narrator and his cousin recite poetry or deliver speeches in front of their grandfather's cronies?

2. What is ironic about the narrator reciting this particular Longfellow poem?
3. What does the reader learn about Fidelino?
4. The narrator is acutely aware of the distance between himself and his relatives. What are the illustrations of this distance, and how does the narrator make it worse?
5. Of what importance to the story is the legend of Kalatong?
6. What is the conflict in this story?
7. What themes do you find in this story?

WRITING TOPICS

1. Write an essay in which you relate the title of the story to the plot. Is the title ironic? Recall that, in paragraph 5, the narrator says that it did not occur to him when he was a boy "that Longfellow was an irrelevance."
2. Describe the narrator's visit from Fidelino's point of view. Include his thoughts about the unexpectedness of the visit and his inner reactions to the narrator's suggestions about starting a poultry farm or a piggery, as well as other reactions he might have.

THE ARRANGED MARRIAGE

Chitra Banerjee Divakaruni

Chitra Banerjee Divakaruni, born in 1956 in Calcutta, India, claims that the challenge she faces in her poetry and fiction is "trying to bring alive, for readers of other ethnic backgrounds, the Indian—and Indian American—experience, not as something exotic and alien but as something human and shared."[1] One of her principal interests is the history of early South Asian immigrants to the United States.

Her most acclaimed work is a series of poems and poetic narratives entitled "The Yuba City Poems"; Yuba City, a town in northern California, has been the home of Punjabi farmers and their families since the early part of this century. In addition to an extensive knowledge of the histories of Indians in the United States, Divakaruni demonstrates her familiarity with classical Indian written and oral forms in much of her work. Her writing, often a melding of poetry and prose and therefore not easily classified into Western genres, contains much imagistic, nuanced, and ambiguous language.

Divakaruni was educated at Calcutta University and Wright State University in Ohio. She holds a Ph.D. in English from the University of California, Berkeley, and presently teaches creative writing at Foothill College in California. She has published three books of poetry: *Dark Like the River* (1987), *The Reason for Nasturtiums* (1990), and *Black Candle* (1991), and has edited a volume of multicultural writing entitled *Multitude: Cross-Cultural Readings for Writers* (1993). In addition, *Arranged Marriage* (1995), a collection of short stories, and *The Mistress of Spices* (1997), a novel, received a great deal of critical attention. Divakaruni was nominated twice for the Pushcart Prize and has received several other awards and recognitions, including the Barbara Deming Memorial Award and the

---

[1] From *Living in America: Poetry and Fiction by South Asian American Writers*, page 47.

Cecil Hackney Literary Award. She is also the coordinator of Maitri, a help line for South Asian women in the San Francisco Bay area.

The following poem evokes the feelings of a sixteen-year-old bride as she meets her husband for the first time at a traditional wedding ceremony. (J.I.)

The night is airless-still, as
before a storm. Behind the wedding drums,
cries of jackals from the burning grounds.
The canopy gleams, color
5 of long life, many children.
Color of bride-blood. At the entrance
the women have painted the sign
of Laxmi, goddess of wealth, have put up
a blackened pot to ward off
10 the witch who lives beyond
the *Sheora* forest and eats
young flesh.
             Guests from three villages
jostle, make marriage jokes. A long
15 conch blast for the groom's party,
men in *dhotis*[1] white as ice. Someone runs to them
with water of rose, silvered betel leaves,
piled garlands from which rise
the acrid smell of marigolds.
20 The priests confer, arrange wood and incense
for the wedding fire. The chants begin.
Through smoke, the stars
are red pinpricks, the women's voices
almost a wailing. Uncles and brothers
25 carry in the bride, her face hidden
under an edge of scarlet silk, her trembling
under the wedding jewels.
               The groom's father
produces his scales and in clenched silence
30 the dowry gold is weighed. But he smiles
and all is well again. Now it is *godbuli,*
the time of the auspicious seeing.

---

[1] *dhotis:* loincloths worn by some Indian men.

Time for you, bride of sixteen,
mother, to raise the tear-stained face
35 that I will learn so well,
to look for the first time into
your husband's opaque eyes.

DISCUSSION QUESTIONS
---

1. Who do you think is the speaker in this poem? Cite evidence from the poem to support your view.
2. Why is the bride trembling and crying?
3. How does the speaker evoke a sense of drama and anticipation?
4 What might the use of the word *opaque* to describe the groom's eyes tell you about him?
5. How do events just prior to the ceremony compare or contrast with wedding ceremonies you know about or have attended?

WRITING TOPICS
---

1. Write an essay in which you analyze the connotative language of the poem. For example, what do the words *drums, jackals, silvered,* and *garlands* connote? Many other words in the poem carry connotative meanings as well.
2. Arranged marriages have been common for centuries and are still common in many societies. Discuss the advantages and disadvantages of this custom in an essay.

FROM *DICTEE*

Theresa Hak Kyung Cha

Theresa Hak Kyung Cha, a multimedia artist whose work responds to influences as disparate as Catholicism and French film theory, was born in 1951 in the southern Korean city of Pusan. Her parents, who spent their childhood years in Manchuria in order to escape Japanese colonial rule in Korea, immigrated with their family to the United States in 1962, landing first in Hawaii and moving two years later to San Francisco. Cha received a private Catholic school education and then went on to the University of California, Berkeley, where she earned two B.A. degrees, one in art and one in comparative literature. In 1976 she went to Paris to study film theory at the Centre d'Etudes Americaine du Cinema. She then returned to Berkeley, where she earned an M.A. in art in 1977 and an M.F.A. in 1978. Cha also studied ceramics, performance art, Korean poetry, and European modernism. Her life was cut tragically short when she was murdered on November 5, 1982, only a few months after the publication of *Dictee*.

Dictee, from which the following selection is taken, is impossible to categorize in a single genre, for it includes, among other things, autobiography, journalistic accounts, religious texts, and film theory. There are sections composed in French, English, Greek, Chinese, and Korean, and several visual images—maps, photographs, anatomical diagrams—are scattered throughout. Cha named each of the nine sections of the book after one of the nine classical Greek muses and their attendant art forms.

Hyun Yi Kang, a scholar at the University of California, Irvine, describes *Dictee* as an immensely complex book that reveals Cha as an artist who is simultaneously skilled in and yet somewhat estranged from the various artistic and linguistic traditions that she spent her short life pursuing.

In the following selection the author remembers the violence of a student demonstration eighteen years before and reflects on the ongoing abuses of coercive power. Cha is probably referring to the

Spring 1980 civil unrest at Kwangju City. During these demonstra-
tions, government forces fired on students and civilians. According
to government figures, 200 people were killed. Human rights groups
put the figure at closer to 2,000. (J.I.)

1   It is 1962 eighteen years ago same month same day all over again. I am
eleven years old. Running to the front door, Mother, you are holding my
older brother pleading with him not to go out to the demonstration. You
are threatening him, you are begging to him. He has on his school uniform,
as all the other students representing their schools in the demonstration.
You are pulling at him you stand before the door. He argues with you he
pushes you away. You use all your force, all that you have. He is prepared to
join the student demonstration outside. You can hear the gun shots. They
are directed at anyone.

2   Coming home from school there are cries in all the streets. The mounting of shouts from every direction from the crowds arm in arm. The students. I saw them, older than us, men and women held to each other. They
walk into the *others* who wait in *their* uniforms. Their shouts reach a
crescendo as they approach nearer to the *other side*. Cries resisting cries to
move forward. Orders, permission to use force against the students, have
been dispatched. To be caught and beaten with sticks, and for others, shot,
remassed, and carted off. They fall they bleed they die. They are thrown into
gas into the crowd to be squelched. The police the soldiers anonymous they
duplicate themselves, multiply in number invincible they execute their role.
Further than their home further than their mother father their brother sister further than their children is the execution of their role their given identity further than their own line of blood.

3   You do not want to lose him, my brother, to be killed as the many others by now, already, you say you understand, you plead all the same they are
killing any every one. You withstand his strength you call me to run to
Uncle's house and call the tutor. Run. Run hard. Out the gate. Turn the
corner. All down hill to reach Uncle's house. I know the two German shep-
herd dogs would be guarding one at each side, chained to their house they
drag behind them barking. I must brave them, close my eyes and run
between them. I call the tutor from the yard, above the sounds of the dogs
barking. Several students look out of the windows. They are in hiding from
the street, from their homes where they are being searched for. We run back
to the house the tutor is ahead of me, when I enter the house the tutor is
standing in front of him. You cannot go out he says you cannot join the D-
e-m-o. *De. Mo.* A word, two sounds. Are you insane the tutor tells him they

are killing any student in uniform. Anybody. What will you defend yourself with he asks. You, my brother, you protest your cause, you say you are willing to die. Dying is part of it. If it must be. He hits you. The tutor slaps you and your face turns red you stand silently against the door your head falls. My brother. You are all the rest all the others are you. You fell you died you gave your life. That day. It rained. It rained for several days. It rained more and more times. After it was all over. You were heard. Your victory mixed with rain falling from the sky for many days afterwards. I head that the rain does not erase the blood fallen on the ground. I heard from the adults, the blood stains still. Year after year it rained. The stone pavement stained where you fell still remains dark.

4   Eighteen years pass. I am here for the first time in eighteen years, Mother. We left her in this memory still fresh, still new. I speak another tongue, a second tongue. This is how distant I am. From then. From that time. They take me back they have taken me back so precisely now exact to the hour to the day to the season in the smoke mist in the drizzle I turn the corner and there is no one. No one facing me. The street is rubble. I put my palm on my eyes to rub them, then I let them cry freely. Two school children with their book bags appear from nowhere with their arms around each other. Their white kerchief, their white shirt uniform, into a white residue of gas, crying.

5   I pass a second curve on the road. You soldiers appear in green. Always the green uniforms the patches of camouflage. Trees camouflage your green trucks you blend with nature the trees hide you you cannot be seen behind the guns no one sees you they have hidden you. You sit you recline on the earth next to the buses you wait hours days making visible your presence. Waiting for the false move that will conduct you to mobility to action. There is but one move, the only one and it will be false. It will be absolute. Their mistake. Your boredom waiting would not have been in vain. They will move they will have to move and you will move on them. Among them. You stand on your tanks your legs spread apart how many degrees exactly your hand on your rifle. Rifle to ground the same angle as your right leg. You wear a beret in the 90 degree sun there is no shade at the main gate you are fixed you cannot move you dare not move. You are your post you are your vow in nomine patris you work your post you are your nation defending your country from subversive infiltration from your own countrymen. Your skin scorched as dark as your uniform as you stand you don't hear. You hear nothing. You hear no one. You are hidden you see only the prey they do not see you they cannot. You who are hidden you who move in the crowds as you would in the trees you who move inside them you close your eyes to the piercing the breaking the flooding pools bath their shadow memory as they fade from you your own blood your own flesh as tides ebb, through you through and through.

DISCUSSION QUESTIONS

1. What is the effect of the author's use (or nonuse) of punctuation?
2. What is the tone of this selection?
3. What sense do you get of the author as a person? Discuss in small groups.

WRITING TOPICS

1. In a brief essay, examine the author's writing style and its effect on the tone, message, and overall impact of the selection.
2. In a journal entry, explore what you imagine to be the author's feelings on returning to the site of her brother's death.

SAN CHI

Hilary Tham

Hilary Tham was born in Malaysia in 1946. Educated in a multicultural Asian society, she married a Peace Corps volunteer and came to the United States in 1971, where she now lives in Washington, D.C., with her family. She has published four books of poetry—*No Gods Today* (1969), *Paper Boats* (1987), *Bad Names for Women* (1989), and *Tigerbone Wine* (1992)—and a memoir, *Lane with No Name* (1997). She also teaches regional creative workshops.

Tham uses Chinese myths, Asian folktales, and family stories in her poems, which are frequently humorous and satirical. In "San Chi" the ghost of a recently departed woman makes a believer of her son. "San Chi" translates literally as "third seven day"; it refers to the twenty-first day or night after death, when the ghost or spirit of a dead person returns to revisit old, familiar places before setting out to cross the Yellow River (the parallel of the Greek River Styx).

Three weeks after death, the deceased's spirit must leave the house and begin its journey to the Land of Ghosts. This night is the zenith of the ghost's power: it can commandeer a living relative for a companion on its trip. It is customary to offer substitutes of paper people.

Father saw Grandmother at midnight:
on the twenty-first day after her death.
Earlier, Mother had burned a paper man
with parasol to shade Grandmother
5   from the sun, to carry her packages
of food and money. At nightfall, her spirit
would begin the long journey

through treeless lands to the Yellow Springs.
"I never believed that nonsense," Father
10　said, "but she was here. I saw her
standing at the door to the living
room. 'Mother, is it you?' I asked."

She wore her shroud suit, grey silk
tunic and black pants she kept folded
15　in tissue paper for eighteen years.
The creases jutted from her bony frame.
Eyes like a sleepwalker, she looked
at the latest family photograph, touched
her tobacco box, her cane recliner
20　that creaked softly to her breathing
during her afternoon nap.

Looking at her recliner, Father said, "She was
saying goodbye to her things, but
she wouldn't speak to me." Mother began
25　to light incense sticks: "Had she spoken,
you would have died. Why do you think
I burned that paper man? Gods, gods,
thank you for protecting my fool."

Discussion Questions

1. What has happened in this poem?
2. What is the difference between the beliefs of the speaker's parents?
3. Who is the "fool" referred to in the last line?

Writing Topics

1. In your journal, write a few paragraphs or a poem that expresses your ideas about what happens to a spirit or soul after death.
2. In a brief essay, explore how the author's use of dialogue affects the tone or mood of the poem.

3. Though this poem is about an ephemeral visitor, the language and descriptions are fairly concrete. In an analytical essay, discuss how the author conveys the relationship between the spirit visitor and the concrete objects she left behind. Cite examples from the poem to support your views.

THE CLEAVING

Li-Young Lee

Li-Young Lee was born in 1957 in Jakarta, Indonesia. In 1951 his father and mother had moved to Jakarta from Tianjin, China, after the Communists took power and Chinese Nationalists fled to Taiwan. For nine months before his departure from China, Lee's father served as personal physician to Mao Tse-tung, the powerful chairman of the Communist Party and premier of China. In Indonesia Lee's father taught philosophy at Gamaliel University and studied Western theology and poetry. In 1959 the Lees became fugitives when President Sukarno moved to purge all Chinese resident aliens. After traveling to Macao, Hong Kong, Singapore, and Japan, the Lees immigrated to the United States in 1964. They settled in Pennsylvania, where Lee's father gained admittance to the Pittsburgh Theological Society and obtained a position as a Christian minister.

Lee attributes his love of literature in large part to his father's love of poetry. He began to write poetry during his undergraduate years at the University of Pittsburgh. He also studied at the University of Arizona and the State University of New York at Brockport. In 1986, he published his first collection of poetry, entitled *Rose*. This debut collection received New York University's Delmore Schwartz Memorial Poetry Award. Lee also received grants from the Pennsylvania Council on the Arts and the National Endowment for the Arts. His second book, *The City in Which I Love You*, from which the following poem is taken, was published in 1990 and was the 1990 Lamont Poetry Selection of the Academy of American Poets. Lee has also published a well-received memoir, *Winged Seed* (1994).

In "The Cleaving" Lee finds metaphors for human life and suffering in the sights and sounds of a butcher shop. (J.I.)

He gossips like my grandmother, this man
with my face, and I could stand
amused all afternoon
in the Hon Kee Grocery,
5 amid hanging meats he
chops: roast pork cut
from a hog hung
by nose and shoulders,
her entire skin burnt
10 crisp, flesh I know
to be sweet,
her shining
face grinning
up at ducks
15 dangling single file,
each pierced by black
hooks through breast, bill,
and steaming from a hole
stitched shut at the ass.
20 I step to the counter, recite,
and he, without even slightly
varying the rhythm of his current confession or harangue,
scribbles my order on a greasy receipt,
and chops it up quick.

25 Such a sorrowful Chinese face,
nomad, Gobi, Northern
in its boniness
clear from the high
warlike forehead
30 to the sheer edge of the jaw.
He could be my brother, but finer,
and, except for his left forearm which is engorged,
sinewy from his daily grip and
wield of a two-pound tool,
35 he's delicate, narrow-
waisted, his frame
so slight a lover, some
rough other
might break it down
40 its smooth, oily length.

In his light-handed calligraphy
on receipts and in his
moodiness, he is
a Southerner from a river-province;
45 suited for scholarship, his face poised
above an open book, he'd mumble
his favorite passages.
He could be my grandfather;
come to America to get a Western education
50 in 1917, but too homesick to study,
he sits in the park all day, reading poems
and writing letters to his mother.

He lops the head off, chops
the neck of the duck
55 into six, slits
the body
open, groin
to breast, and drains
the scalding juices,
60 then quarters the carcass
with two fast hacks of the cleaver,
old blade that has worn
into the surface of the round
foot-thick chop-block
65 a scoop that cradles precisely the curved steel.

The head, flung from the body, opens
down the middle where the butcher
cleanly halved it between
the eyes, and I
70 see, fetal-crouched
inside the skull, the homunculus,[1]
gray brain grainy
to ear.
Did this animal, after all, at the moment
75 its neck broke,
image the way his executioner
shrinks from his own death?
Is this how
I, too, recoil from my day?

---

[1] *homunculus:* a little man, or, here, what looks like a little man.

80 See how this shape
hordes itself, see how
little it is.
See its grease on the blade.
Is this how I'll be found
85 when judgement is passed, when names
are called, when crimes are tallied?
This is also how I looked before I tore my mother open.
Is this how I presided over my century, is this how
I regarded the murders?
90 This is also how I prayed.
Was it me in the Other
I prayed to when I prayed?
This too was how I slept, clutching my wife.
Was it me in the other I loved
95 when I loved another?
The butcher sees me eye this delicacy.
With a finger, he picks it
out of the skull-cradle
and offers it to me.
100 I take it gingerly between my fingers
and suck it down.
I eat my man.

The noise the body makes
when the body meets
105 the soul over the soul's ocean and penumbra[2]
is the old sound of up-and-down, in-and-out,
a lump of muscle chug-chugging blood
into the ear; a lover's
heart-shaped tongue;
110 flesh rocking flesh until flesh comes;
the butcher working
at his block and blade to marry their shapes
by violence and time;
an engine crossing,
115 re-crossing salt water, hauling
immigrants and the junk
of the poor. These
are the faces I love, the bodies

---

[2] *penumbra:* shadow.

and scents of bodies
120   for which I long
in various ways, at various times,
thirteen gathered around the redwood,
happy, talkative, voracious
at day's end,
125   eager to eat
four kinds of meat
prepared four different ways,
numerous plates and bowls of rice and vegetables,
each made by distinct affections
130   and brought to table by many hands.
Brothers and sisters by blood and design,
who sit in separate bodies of varied shapes,
we constitute a many-membered
body of love.
135   In a world of shapes
of my desires, each one here
is a shape of one of my desires, and each
is known to me and dear by virtue
of each one's unique corruption
140   of those texts, the face, the body:
that jut jaw
to gnash tendon;
that wide nose to meet the blows
a face like that invites;
145   those long eyes closing on the seen;
those thick lips
to suck the meat of animals
or recite 300 poems of the T'ang;
these teeth to bite my monosyllables;
150   these cheekbones to make
those syllables sing the soul.
Puffed or sunken
according to the life,
dark or light according
155   to the birth, straight
or humped, whole, manqué, quasi, each pleases, verging
on utter grotesquery.
All are beautiful by variety.
The soul too
160   is a debasement
of a text, but, thus, it

acquires salience,³ although a
human salience, but
inimitable, and, hence, memorable.

165 God is the text.
The soul is a corruption
and a mnemonic.⁴

A bright moment,
I hold up an old head
170 from the sea and admire the haughty
down-curved mouth
that seems to disdain
all the eyes are blind to,
including me, the eater.
175 Whole unto itself, complete
without me, yet its
shape complements the shape of my mind.
I take it as text and evidence
of the world's love for me,
180 and I feel urged to utterance,
urged to read the body of the world, urged
to say it
in human terms,
my reading a kind of eating, my eating
185 a kind of reading,
my saying a diminishment, my noise
a love-in-answer.
What is it in me would
devour the world to utter it?
190 What is it in me will not let
the world be, would eat
not just this fish,
but the one who killed it,
the butcher who cleaned it.
195 I would eat the way he
squats, the way he
reaches into the plastic tubs
and pulls out a fish, clubs it, takes it
to the sink, guts it, drops it on the weighing pan.
200 I would eat that thrash

---

³ *salience:* importance or prominence.
⁴ *mnemonic:* a device for assisting memory.

and plunge of the watery body
in the water, that liquid violence
between the man's hands,
I would eat
205   the gutless twitching on the scales,
three pounds of dumb
nerve and pulse, I would eat it all
to utter it.
The deaths at the sinks, those bodies prepared
210   for eating, I would eat,
and the standing deaths
at the counters, in the aisle,
the walking deaths in the streets,
the death-far-from-home, the death-
215   in-a-strange-land, these Chinatown
deaths, these American deaths.
I would devour this race to sing it,
this race that according to Emerson[5]
managed to preserve to a hair
220   *for three or four thousand years*
the ugliest features in the world.
I would eat these features, eat
the last three or four thousand years, every hair.
And I would eat Emerson, his transparent soul, his
225   soporific transcendence.
I would eat this head,
glazed in pepper-speckled sauce,
the cooked eyes opaque in their sockets.
I bring it to my mouth and—
230   the way I was taught, the way I've watched
others before me do—
with a stiff tongue lick out
the cheek-meat and the meat
over the armored jaw, my eating,
235   its sensual, salient nowness,
punctuating the void
from which such hunger springs and to which it proceeds.

---

[5] *Emerson:* Ralph Waldo Emerson (1803–1882) American essayist, poet, and transcendentalist, one who believes in the philosophy that emphasizes the spiritual over the material.

And what
is this
240 I excavate
with my mouth?
What is this
plated, ribbed, hinged
architecture, this *carp head,*
245 but one more
articulation of a single nothing
severally manifested?
What is my eating,
rapt as it is,
250 but another
shape of going,
my immaculate expiration?
O, nothing is so
steadfast it won't go
255 the way the body goes.
The body goes.
The body's grave,
so serious
in its dying,
260 arduous as martyrs
in that task and as
glorious. It goes
empty always
and announces its going
265 by spasms and groans, farts and sweats.

What I thought were the arms
aching *cleave,* were the knees trembling *leave.*
What I thought were the muscles
insisting *resist, persist, exist,*
270 were the pores
hissing *mist* and *waste.*
What I thought was the body humming *reside, reside,*
was the body sighing *revise, revise.*
O, the murderous deletions, the keening
275 down to nothing, the cleaving.
All of the body's revisions end
in death.
All of the body's revisions end.

Bodies eating bodies, heads eating heads,
280 we are nothing eating nothing,
and though we feast,
are filled, overfilled,
we go famished.
We gang the doors of death.
285 That is, our deaths are fed
that we may continue our daily dying,
our bodies going
down, while the plates-soon-empty
are passed around, that true
290 direction of our true prayers,
while the butcher spells
his message, manifold,
in the mortal air.
He coaxes, cleaves, brings change
295 before our very eyes, and at every
moment of our being.
As we eat we're eaten.
Else what is this
violence, this salt, this
300 passion, this heaven?

I thought the soul an airy thing.
I did not know the soul
is cleaved so that the soul might be restored.
Live wood hewn,
305 its sap springs from a sticky wound.
No seed, no egg has he
whose business calls for an axe.
In the trade of my soul's shaping,
he traffics in hews and hacks.

310 No easy thing, violence.
One of its names? Change. Change
resides in the embrace
of the effaced and the effacer,
in the covenant of the opened and the opener;
315 the axe accomplishes it on the soul's axis.
What then may I do
but cleave to what cleaves me.
I kiss the blade and eat my meat.
I thank the wielder and receive,

320 while terror spirits
    my change, sorrow also.
    The terror the butcher
    scripts in the unhealed
    air, the sorrow of his Shang
325 dynasty face,
    African face with slit eyes. He is
    my sister, this
    beautiful Bedouin, this Shulamite,
    keeper of sabbaths, diviner
330 of holy texts, this dark
    dancer, this Jew, this Asian, this one
    with the Cambodian face, Vietnamese face, this Chinese
    I daily face,
    this immigrant;
335 this man with my own face.

DISCUSSION QUESTIONS

1. Parts of this poem are fairly graphic. What effect does this have on the mood of the poem?
2. What is the theme of this poem? What particular message is Lee trying to convey? Discuss in small groups.

WRITING TOPICS

1. Like many long poems, "The Cleaving" has many moods. In a brief essay, explore those moods, citing examples from the poem to support your views.
2. Read several other poems by Li-Young Lee and write an essay examining the literary devices he seems to favor.

FROM *DOGEATERS*

Jessica Hagedorn

Jessica Tarahata Hagedorn, born in 1949 in Manila, the Philippines, moved to San Francisco with her family in 1960. From a very young age, she was encouraged to read and write. Her maternal grandfather was a writer and teacher, and her mother bought Hagedorn her first portable typewriter.

She did not opt for a formal university education but instead entered the American Conservatory Theatre, where she studied music, acting, and martial arts. When Hagedorn was in her early twenties, the poet Kenneth Rexroth, recognizing her tremendous literary talent, included her poetry in a collection entitled *Four Young Women.* In the 1970s, Hagedorn founded and wrote lyrics for the West Coast Gangster Choir, and she has created several dance, radio, and multimedia theater pieces, such as "A Nun's Story," "Holy Food," "Teenytown," and "Mango Tango."

Her literary achievements include two collections of poems and short stories, *Dangerous Music* (1979) and *Petfood and Other Tropical Apparitions* (1981). In addition to these collections, she has published two novels, *Dogeaters* (1990) and *The Gangster of Love* (1996), and has edited *Charlie Chan Is Dead* (1993), an anthology of contemporary Asian American fiction.

Dogeaters, with its extensive roster of characters, was nominated for the National Book Award in 1990. In this extremely rich novel, Hagedorn examines, with both biting humor and great sensitivity, several factions in urban Manila in the 1970s: the wealthy, the poor, the abused, the ostracized, the privileged, the politically powerful. Throughout *Dogeaters* Hagedorn references American popular culture—film, television, music, food—and demonstrates its sometimes humorous and always disturbing influence on life in the Philippines. With regard to American influence, she claims that "it was pretty clear to most of us growing up in the fifties and early sixties that what was really important, what was inevitably preferred, was the aping of our mythologized Hollywood universe. The colonization of our imagination was relentless and hard to shake off . . . . In order to be acknowledged, we had to strive to be as American as possible."

In the following excerpt, a young woman returns to the Philippines from the United States, where her mother had taken her to school, leaving her father and brother in Manila. A visit to her old house, now in decay, evokes feelings of loss and regret. (J.I.)

1 Raul writes me letters in red ink, polite letters quoting from the Scriptures and inquiring about my health. He achieves local fame as a spiritualist healer and preaches to his followers in the countryside. Erlinda and the children follow close behind, his loyal family of believers. He distances himself from the rest of the Gonzagas, who are ashamed of his newfound fundamentalist Christian ministry. Only Pucha, of all people, visits him regularly. She writes me notes on Hallmark greeting cards:

> *Oye, prima—que ba,*[1] when are you coming back? Tonyboy asked about you, I saw him at SPORTEX boy he still looks grate! I think he left his wife you dont know her shes a forinner from Austria or Australia you know he told me you really broke his heart when you left plus you never answered any of his letters, *pobrecito naman!* WOW! I saw Raul yesterday at that new apt. of his I brought him new clothes for the kids, theres so many! Erlinda's pregnant again. I didnt stay two long, he was in one of his moods you know how Raul gets. Hes always complaineing you dont write anybody and its true. Write him, okay? And send your mother my regards I hope shes not mad at me. Thanks be to God my parents are okay. Uncle Esteban had another operation, in case you didnt here. Mommie says HELLO! She and Papa had *merienda* with your father last Sunday. Mikeys getting married. AT LAST. Why dont you come to the wedding?
>
>   Love & prayers,
>   PUCHA

2 When I finally come home to Manila to visit, my father warns me not to bother visiting our old house. "You'll be disappointed. Memories are always better." Smiling apologetically, he tells me reality will diminish the grandeur of my childhood image of home. I take his picture with my new camera,

---

[1] *Oye, prima—que ba:* Listen, cousin—what are you doing?

which later falls in the swimming pool by accident. The camera is destroyed, along with my roll of film. I decide to visit our old house in Mandalayong anyway, borrowing a car from Mikey. Pucha goes with me; she loves riding around in cars and doesn't need any excuse. "After that, let's go to the Intercon Hotel and have a drink," she says, a gleam of mischief in her eyes. "Put on some makeup," she bosses me, "you look tired." I laugh. Pucha is up to her old tricks. She applies thick coats of blue eyeshadow on her heavy eyelids, studying her face in the mirror with rapt concentration.

3   My father is right. The house with its shuttered windows looks smaller than I remember, and dingy. The once lush and sprawling garden is now a forlorn landscape of rocks, weeds, and wild ferns. The bamboo grove has been cut down. "Let's go," Pucha whispers, impatient and uninterested. An old man with bright eyes introduces himself as Manong Tibo, the care-taker. He unlocks door after door for us, pulling aside cobwebs, warning us to be careful. Rotting floorboards creak under the weight of our foot-steps. "My bedroom," I say to the old man, who nods. I am overwhelmed by melancholy at the sight of the empty room. A frightened mouse dashes across the grimy tiled floor. Pucha jumps back and screams, clutching and pinching my arm. "Let's go," she pleads. "Wait outside. I'll be there soon," I say, trying to conceal my irritation. I am relieved finally to be alone, in this desolate house with only Manong for company. He studies me with his bright eyes. "You live in America?" His niece is a nurse in San Francisco, California, he tells me with pride. Someday, he hopes she'll send for him.

4   I stay another hour, walking in and out of the dusty rooms in a kind of stupor. The shutters in the windows of the kitchen, Pacita's kingdom, are hanging from their hinges. The gas stove and refrigerator are gone. "Thieves," Manong shrugs, when I ask him. Broken glass is scattered on the floor. He tells me the house will be torn down within the month and a com-plex of offices built in its place. The property and the squatters' land adjoin-ing it have been bought by the Alacran corporation, Intercoco.

5   I say good-bye and thank the old man. "See you in America!" Manong Tibo says, waving farewell. Pucha is slumped down in the front seat of the car, irritated, hot, and sweaty. "I wouldn't do this for anyone but you," she grumbles without looking at me, then peers into the rearview mirror. "Look at my makeup!" She gives me an accusing look. I slide into the driver's seat, fighting back tears. Suddenly, I grab her hand. She stares at me, puzzled. "Are you okay?" It seems an eternity, but I pull myself together. Pucha hands me her lace handkerchief, drenched in perfume. "Watch out when you blow your nose—okay, *prima*?" She teases. She squeezes my hand, uncomfortable with our display of affection. I start the car, turning to look at her before we drive away. "I really love you," I say, to her utter amaze-ment.

6   My cousin will find happiness with a man, once and for all. He is a stranger to us, a modest man from a modest family, someone we never knew in our childhood. The Gonzagas breathe a collective sigh of relief. Pucha lives with her new husband, childless and content; she never leaves Manila.

7   My *Lola*[2] Narcisa lives to be a very old woman. She is the main reason for my frequent visits to Manila; I dread not being there when she dies.

8   I return to North America. I save all Raul's letters, along with my father's cordial birthday telegrams and Pucha's gossipy notes, in a large shopping bag labeled FAMILY. I move to another city, approximately five thousand miles away from where my mother lives and paints. We talk on the phone once a week. I am anxious and restless, at home only in airports. I travel whenever I can. My belief in God remains tentative. I have long ago stopped going to church. I never marry.

9   In my recurring dream, my brother and I inhabit the translucent bodies of nocturnal moths with curved, fragile wings. We are pale green, with luminous celadon eyes, fantastic and beautiful. In dream after dream, we are drawn to the same silent tableau: a mysterious light glowing from the window of a deserted, ramshackle house. The house is sometimes perched on a rocky abyss, or on a dangerous cliff overlooking a turbulent sea. The meaning is simple and clear, I think. Raul and I embrace our destiny: we fly around in circles, we swoop and dive in effortless arcs against a barren sky, we flap and beat our wings in our futile attempts to reach what surely must be heaven.

DISCUSSION QUESTIONS

1. What are the narrator's feelings at seeing her old home?
2. How do the narrator and Pucha differ?
3. Why might traveling frequently help the narrator?
4. The narrator says her recurring dream is "simple and clear." Is it? Which of the following interpretations seem clearest to you?
   a. The ramshackle house that attracts the moths (the narrator and her brother) represents a longed-for heaven.

---

[2] *Lola:* grandmother.

b. The deserted house with the lighted window represents fear since it is located in a dangerous place, and the moths never approach it too closely.

c. Although the moths are attracted to the light in the distant house, which represents the past, they know they must continue their journey into the future.

d. The fact that the narrator dreams of flying moths is symbolic of her wish to escape her present circumstances.

WRITING TOPICS

1. In a brief essay, compare the experiences of the narrator of this selection in returning to the Philippines with those of the narrator in Gonzalez's "The Lives of Great Men." What feelings do they share? How do their memories match the reality they find?

2. As an adult, the narrator is widely separated from family members, a common situation for the immigrants you have read about thus far. Assume that you have moved far away from your family. In an essay, discuss what people in your new home could do to make you feel less lonely and what you could do as well.

THE SMELL

Ginu Kamani

Ginu Kamani was born in Bombay, India, in 1962 and came to the United States in 1976 as a teenager. After graduating with an M.A. in creative writing from the University of Colorado, Boulder, she worked for a while in film production and then went to Bombay to work for three years. She returned to the United States to become a full-time writer. Besides her first collection of short stories, *Junglee Girl* (1995), she has also published in the anthology *Our Feet Walk the Sky: Women of the South Asian Diaspora* (1993). Set in India, her stories treat sexually ambiguous characters who break out of conservative societies, and she has received much praise for presenting a "subversive" voice.

In "The Smell," meat-eating and vegetarianism are sources of contention as traditions are challenged and generations clash.

1   "Aren't you going to vomit now?" I prodded my cousin Nila.

2   "No, why should I?" She looked at me from the corner of her eye as she carefully tied my new chiffon scarf around her head. We were in the hallway right outside B.A.'s room, where she was taking her afternoon nap. The door to her room was partially open and I could see my grandmother's stout old body curled up on the narrow bed.

3   "If you don't vomit yourself, *I'll* make you." I jabbed my finger into Nila's side and she bent forward, giggling.

4   "But how can I vomit just like that? Have some sense. I can't just tell my stomach, now please vomit." Nila laughed as she whirled in front of the mirror, caressing the silky scarf from Hong Kong.

5   "You ate meat." I growled. "Now don't you want to?"

6   "When did I eat meat! I'm not like you, dirty girl. I'm a hundred percent

vegetarian." Nila's voice always rose sharply on the words *hundred percent vegetarian*. She had heard that my branch of the family ate dirty things like chicken and mutton and . . . *god-knows-what-else!*

7   In her room, B.A. stirred and smacked her lips, pulling the pillow down over her ears.

8   "I just fed you some, stupid. Now vomit."

9   "What do you mean? You gave me a . . . a . . . what do you call it . . ."

10   "Ya,[1] but you know the soft pink part in the middle? That was egg and meat. *Chicken's* egg and *cow's* meat. *Raw.*"

11   At the mention of cow's meat, Nila's throat tightened and she made a faint retching sound. She thought for a moment, then shook her head firmly.

12   "How can there be meat inside a sweet? You must be mad," she offered bravely, but already her hands were nervously massaging her throat.

13   "Did I make it? How would I know why there's meat inside a sweet! But you ate it, and I'm going to tell B.A., and she will hit you. You might as well vomit now, so there won't be any beating."

14   Nila looked around her and suddenly realized that we were standing right outside B.A.'s room. Her eyes widened and her face lengthened fearfully. She clapped her hand over her mouth, but, too late, the pink mash bubbled out of her and slithered out of her palm.

15   "Oh god! Oh god, it's coming up . . . hunnh . . . uuugggh . . . uuunnhhh . . . Mummmeeeeee!"

16   I flicked the chiffon scarf onto her shoulders, then pushed her head down and away so that I would be spared the disgusting faces she made when she vomited.

17   "Good, good, good. Mummy's little darling really knows how to make a mess!" I congratulated.

18   "Mummeeee!" she howled between waves of retching.

19   "Stop shouting. Your mummy's not here. Just stand quietly next to your precious vomit. The smell of the meat will reach B.A. soon enough and she will come out and see what a good girl you are to vomit it all out. Then she'll put you in her lap and tell you lots of stories and feed you lots of sweets and then before you know it you'll be married off to some oily-pooh. Bye!"

20   I pulled my new chiffon scarf off Nila's neck and peeped into B.A.'s room. B.A. was sitting up, confused by all the noise. She yawned, drawing in a lungful of air. Suddenly she choked, and thrust her white sari over her nose and mouth. She staggered to her feet and came barreling towards the door. I gleefully slapped Nila on her back, then skipped backward into the kitchen.

---

[1] *ya:* a colloquial form for "yes."

21   "But Rani, I don't *want* to get married. I want to play with you!" Nila sobbed, shaking off the sticky strings that hung from her hand to the floor. A second later, B.A. had a firm grip on Nila's shoulder and was bellowing for the servant to bring sawdust and a broom.

22   I ran out the other kitchen entrance, and skipped past B.A., well out of her reach. I sang out to Nila. "You silly goose, girls who don't eat meat *always* get married. Bye-bye Mrs. Oily-Pooh!"

23   Wooden buildings are good for hearing grandmothers slowly climbing up step after step, across the landing and up the next set of stairs. In a wooden house, anyone can hear where anyone else is, if you concentrate hard enough.

24   Here she comes now. I know how many steps; we all do. She groans at every four steps. Between the twelfth and thirteenth steps, she burps long, like a donkey braying. Fifteen steps to clear the landing, then onto the next set of steps. We live on the third floor. She lives on the ground floor. Every morning she climbs up those steps and landings to come and sniff for eggs.

25   Most grandmothers don't like playing games with children, but our B.A. is different. Every morning she plays this game with us. She wants to. No one forces her. She does her round every morning, like a baby or a puppy who can play games only one way.

26   As soon as we hear the first thump on the wooden steps, we move quickly to the back of the kitchen. We run into the servants' room and close the door. Then the fun begins.

27   First, the cook turns on the burner, throws a spoonful of ghee[2] into the pan and heats it on the flame.

28   *The first groan signals she has covered four steps.*

29   The ghee melts and bubbles. The cook quickly breaks the eggs on the side of the pan and pours them in. The heat of the pan sends clouds of egg steam rushing around the room, filling every corner.

30   *The donkey bray warns us that she's near the first landing. She clumps across.*

31   My brother lifts his head and pushes up his eyeglasses. He opens the packet of bread wrapped in wax paper and pulls out four slices, two for him and two for me. The eggs are fried for just a few seconds and then the cook drops the bread into the pan as well.

---

[2] *ghee:* liquid butter made from the milk of cows or buffalo.

32   *B.A. is across the first landing and on the second set of stairs.*

33   The cook presses the bread into the ghee, presses it flat until the slices have become crisp brown pancakes. We've told him that we like our eggs *on toast*, and this is the only way to make toast in the servants' room. In this way, the bread supports the eggs without getting soggy. The cook slides the fried eggs onto the fried bread and lifts the food onto our plates.

34   *B.A. crosses the second landing. She brays out of turn, and we freeze. Have we miscalculated? But it is a false alarm.*

35   My brother and I attack the eggs on toast with huge bites. Four steps up for grandma, four bites for the two of us, and the first of the eggs are gone. The windows of the room are shut to keep the breeze from blowing out the burner flame. The smell of eggs is very strong.

36   *Why don't you ever come to see me, why do you avoid me, huh? What kind of children are you, ignoring an old woman like me, why don't you come and greet me every morning, I don't take up much time in your day. All day long you play as much as you want, don't you? Is five minutes so precious that you can't stop and come see me? I don't hit you; I don't say bad things about you. I don't say anything about the fancy clothes you wear or the expensive foreign chocolates your mummy and daddy feed you. I just want you to come see me. Just touch my feet quickly and tell me some sweet things and then you can go on your way. All day long my feet hurt me, my back hurts me, my hair falls out and my stomach falls in. Do you ever stop to think that a little love would cure my pain? You only think bad thoughts about me and come to my room only when you're forced to. Is this any way to treat your old grandmother?*

37   We gobble up the remaining food. We open the windows in the servants' room. *Whoooshhh!* the breeze blows in and magically the smell of eggs is gone. My brother burps. Out comes egg smell. I hold my breath and burp even longer and harder. Out comes double-powered egg smell. *Whoooshhh!* The breeze blows it all away. I look at my brother with disappointment. It's going to be just another morning, and B.A. won't sniff out the eggs today.

38   *Kesho? Rani? Where are you my darlings? Come and touch the feet of your grandmother, you little rascals! Come to me while you're still clean, before the dirt of the whole world covers you from head to toe! Dirty rascals, playing in god knows what room with who knows what filthy people!*

39   We open the door of the servants' room with sour faces. B.A. stares at us. She has a round wrinkled face and wears round thick glasses. She is as

wide as she is tall. At her full height she is no taller than a child. She wears the same white sari every day. She is confused every day about why we are in the servants' room. She asks us with contempt:

40   *What are you doing? Who let you in there? You should be in your own room. How many times have I told your father that you shouldn't be alone with servants! I can't imagine what all goes on behind my back.*

41   The cook is already squatting over the sunken toilet inside the servants' room, scrubbing out the fried-egg pan with mud and ashes. He washes the pan in this way every day, balancing precariously over the oval porcelained opening. Water dribbles out of a rusty faucet which is connected to a thin water pipe that pokes through the ceiling. The cook is used to washing up in this way because the toilet serves as the servants' bathing area as well.

42   *You, you . . . good-for-nothing cook! How many times have I told you that the children don't belong in this part of the house? Ehh? You'll turn them into useless beggars like yourself! Have you no shame? These are children of good family.*

43   B.A. leans right into the bathroom, holding onto the door and covering her nose with the end of her sari. The cook glares at her and stands up, shaking the beads of water off the clean frying pan. B.A. shrinks back as the cook pushes past her. He snaps at her.

44   *Am I the owner of this house? Are these my children? Tie them up if you don't want them in here!*

45   B.A.'s nostrils flare in alarm. She bends forward, sniffing madly.

46   *Something is wrong here. Somebody is eating something that we do not allow in this house.*

47   B.A. can smell something like the odor of meat on the cook.

48   *It's him! He stinks of meat! Oh god, oh god, oh god! This is how we live in Bombay, suffering the sins of our servants. Kesho? Rani? Come here at once! I will say a prayer for you.*

49   B.A. pulls us close and then pushes us away. She starts sniffing again. She brushes off our school clothes to get the cook's smell off. Still she sniffs. Her lips quiver with anger and her eyes open wide. I taunt her before she can speak.

50   *Do you want me to vomit? I'll do it right now, right here. Then you can see for yourself what I've eaten. Don't you want me to?*

51   B.A. is suddenly confused by my offer. I sound too eager. There appears to be no punishment in it for me. She sighs and smiles sadly.

52   *No, no, you mustn't get yourself dirty. You have to go to school now. You must hurry down to the car, no?*

53   We nod vigorously, wave to B.A., pick up our book bags and run to the stairs. I race my brother down, laughing and pushing. He lets me win because, once again, I have challenged B.A. and won at her daily morning game.

54   On my cousin Sonia's wedding day, she couldn't stop vomiting. No one could understand what it was. Did she have a fever, were there worms in her system, had she eaten some rotten food? No, no, no, she shook her head. The vomiting kept her so busy that she couldn't even talk. Even after there was nothing left in her stomach, she kept heaving and crying.

55   Her parents went to B.A. What are we to do? This girl can hardly walk into the marriage tent. She will surely faint while the priest performs the service. How will it look? What will people think?

56   B.A. dismissed them with contempt. There is nothing wrong with Sonia, she scolded. The problem was with the *groom,* who smelled of meat!

57   B.A.'s strict training of the girls in the house had made its mark. Sonia was sensitive to the smell of strangers. B.A. telephoned the groom's house, where they were just preparing to leave. Under pressure from B.A., the groom's father admitted that his son did occasionally eat meat. B.A. tearfully announced the news.

58   Sonia lifted her aching body off the floor and stood tall and proud like a warrior queen. She lifted her hand imperially and her parents stepped back in fear. With the clear voice of conviction, Sonia shouted that under no circumstances would she marry a sinful, polluted, meat-eating man!

59   Immediately her mother started weeping. Her father's legs gave out from under him and he crumpled to the floor. Sonia stood with her hands on her hips and her legs firmly planted, daring any family member to challenge her.

60   I was thrilled! My cousin was refusing marriage! Finally, we would have a real rebel in the house. I was delirious with excitement, hopping from foot to foot and swallowing my laughter in great gulps. Sonia was my new hero.

61   But then Sonia's father called in the priest for a hurried discussion. A few phone calls were made, and within the hour, a hundred-percent-vegetarian groom was found for the bride. Sonia checked carefully with the priest, and then spoke to the vegetarian groom's parents and grandparents, friends and

neighbors, and then touched the feet of the priest and agreed that the marriage would proceed.

62   I was in shock. Sonia had betrayed me. How could she turn her back on freedom? Her warrior stance collapsed once more into the frightened nervous hunch that had always marked her posture. I blamed B.A. for making Sonia into a robot. I sat outside the marriage tent for the entire ceremony and never even saw the face of the groom.

63   Now Sonia and her husband live somewhere far away and I haven't seen my cousin since. But I hear every now and then that even with a vegetarian husband, Sonia vomits every day. She smells meat everywhere, all the time. Her husband beats her daily because she won't let him touch her. She can't get rid of the smell.

64   B.A. no longer says anything about her, in fact no one is allowed to say anything about Sonia. If B.A. finds us talking, she'll just make us vomit all the words out.

65   *Rani! Always remember, if anyone ever feeds you anything that looks, or smells, or tastes non-vegetarian, just vomit it out! Don't even think about it, just do it. You are a child still, so it will come to you naturally. Every good girl can vomit. I know, because when I was given bad food in the house of bad people, I vomited. It was very easy. I stayed clean, clean, clean. In my days in the village, it didn't happen very often. But these days, in a place like Bombay, even decent people might trick you. Eating meat is not good for women. Unnecessarily you will pollute your unborn son. You listen to your B.A. Anytime I say to you, Spit it out, you must do so automatically or you will go to hell.*

66   *Rani! Did you hear what I just said? You better stay clean, or no one is going to marry their son to you! You best listen to your B.A., or you'll end up a dried-up old hag and no one will pay any attention to you.*

67   Sometimes the cook brings home mutton kheema[3] wrapped in a banana leaf and packed in newspaper. I sit with the cook in the servants' room as he deftly scoops up the meat with pieces of white bread and gobbles down mouthful after mouthful. I draw the mutton smell into my nose with long breaths that fill me up. I exhale reluctantly. I arrange a line of the spicy ground meat along my finger so that it resembles a moist dark caterpillar. I lick at it slowly. When we have finished eating, I run my finger through the small pool of grease collected on the banana leaf and coat it thoroughly with the red oil. I spread the oil on my wrist and then go find my brother. I brush up against him "accidentally," and smear the mutton oil on his arm. My brother doesn't even know what I'm doing. I sit next to him as he does his

---

[3] *kheema:* minced meat.

homework or reads a comic book or plays with his trains. He likes my company. The aroma lingers in the air for a long time. Eventually the flies come and start bothering us. Then I grab a blanket or a towel and hug my brother tightly until the oil is wiped away. My brother doesn't know what I'm doing, but he doesn't mind because he likes this game that we play. He smells good and makes my mouth water and I am happy that I can love him in this special way.

68   *When I grow up, I will never vomit. When I grow up, I will never marry. When I grow up I will smell the meat on men and the smell will keep me hungry.*

DISCUSSION QUESTIONS

1. What is it that separates the narrator's branch of the family from her cousin Nila's branch?
2. Why do the narrator and her brother have breakfast in the servants' room?
3. What is it about the narrator that makes her thrilled that Sonia rebels at being married?
4. What do the grandmother's remarks to the cook tell you about her?
5. What do the grandmother's complaints tell you about the children in the house?

WRITING TOPICS

1. In a brief essay, describe the personality of the narrator of this piece and the devices the author uses to convey that personality. Use quotations from the story to illustrate your views.
2. Many religions, like the Hindu religion, have some prohibitions about food or require or recommend fasting at certain times. Why do you think religion concerns itself with what one does or does not eat and drink? Discuss in a small group and then summarize your discussion in a paper.

THE WHITE HORSE

Nguyen Ba Trac

Nguyen Ba Trac was born in Vietnam and came to the United States in 1974. He did postgraduate work in public administration and is now a freelance journalist in California who publishes in several Vietnamese-language newspapers. He has translated *Tears Before the Rain* (1990), an oral history of the fall of Vietnam compiled by Larry Engleman, and is the author of two collections of poetry, essays, and short stories, *A Floating Blade of Grass* and *Tales of a Refugee with Average Headaches*. His work has appeared in many Vietnamese literary journals.

In "The White Horse" an immigrant gets into difficulties with fiscal shortcomings and mounting traffic violations because he is preoccupied with haunting memories of his old life in Vietnam and the sense of loss they bring. To this man, memory is "a horse that goes where it wants to go."

1   To a country as law-abiding and orderly as America, Mr. Nguyen is not a good citizen. When it comes to income taxes, he's a mess. He doesn't file his taxes on time. He spends everything he earns, while his salary comes to him without deductions. He is enthusiastic about sending gifts to Vietnam, but when tax filing deadlines arrive, he'll be penniless. This has gone on for three years.

2   To the bank, Mr. Nguyen isn't a favored customer. Like an American consumer, he keeps an account and checkbook, but does no accounting, even simple addition or subtraction. He is routinely fined for overdrawing on his account. His name is registered in books and kept in computers that can expose those with bad credit. People whose names are in these computers can't be trusted. There's no lending to such people. No mortgages for

them. The banks send him polite letters apologizing for not wanting him as a customer.

3   To the Department of Motor Vehicles and the police, Mr. Nguyen is a careless man. In a span of three years, he has received over forty tickets for moving violations. His license has been revoked twice. In the computer, late charges on such tickets continue to multiply twice, three times the original amounts, becoming figures too large for Mr. Nguyen to deal with. The same violations keep recurring: running a red light or a stop sign. Traveling too fast or too slow on the highways.

4   Why is he such a mess?

5   To be fair, Mr. Nguyen isn't exactly someone with an antisocial attitude. He's never been indicted. He's in relatively good health. He can't really complain about his mental health. When something fun happens, he can be jovial. He knows when he's sad. Nothing extraordinary about that. If he were to feel no pain or not get burnt when he sticks his hand in a fire, well then that would be a surprise. But for a Vietnamese cast far from his family, his friends, and his homeland, mired in endless worries, remembrance, and sorrow . . . mind churning with events, questions, introspection . . . in the final analysis, this is nothing extraordinary.

6   Morning: brushes his teeth, cleans his mouth. Goes to work. Eats his lunch. An evening meal. Sleeps when night comes. Runs errands on weekends: buys the odd pieces of black fabric, some tablets, waiting until he can fill up a gift box to send home to his family, parents, brothers and sisters, wife and kids. It's not a heavy schedule, but he's always busy. Why?

7   You can't say Mr. Nguyen lives in one place. Rather, he lives in two worlds: his soul is in America, but his spirit shuttles back and forth between America and his homeland way on the other side of the globe. One moment he's sitting beneath fluorescent lights, working among various machines, the next he's walking down a Saigon alley, beneath the shade of a fish roe tree.[1] In addition, Mr. Nguyen lives in two time periods: the present and the past. He moves back and forth within his past. Sometimes he goes all the way back to a classroom in a Hanoi temple, reciting his ABCs alongside friends afflicted by eye and skin diseases. The next moment he speeds forward to a university dorm room, where he coolly whistles as he combs his hair, getting ready for a stroll in downtown Saigon.

8   Such a jumbled sense of time and space can consume his entire day.

9   You have to admit, the earth was once a massive thing. To travel once around the globe was quite an achievement. To travel with one's tent from Hanoi to Hue for the mandarin examination took three long months. But, things change. Airplanes and spaceships have shrunk the earth. Satellite photos from outer space reduce the earth to the size of an orange. Fascism and

---

[1] *fish roe tree:* the colloquial name for a particular urban shade tree in Saigon.

feudal regimes have gone out of fashion. The conflict between capitalism and communism wouldn't mean much either if the earth were attacked by aliens from Venus.

10 But even if modern technology has reduced distances . . . and no matter how fast a thought can travel . . . nothing can quite help Mr. Nguyen (as he sits behind the wheel daydreaming about his old neighborhood in the Ban Co District) to stop his car in time for a red light in America.

11 Usually, he can't make it.

12 So, the speed of a thought is really still too slow. And space is still too large. And Mr. Nguyen still has police cars chasing him with sirens screaming full blast and lights flashing, all because of ancient reasons: running a red light. Not stopping at a stop sign. Traveling too fast or too slow on the highways.

13 In America, heaven and earth are turning white.

14 The green mountains have changed to a silvery gray, and snow dots their summits. Darkness comes swiftly now. People are shopping and celebrating Christmas, but Mr. Nguyen hasn't stopped traveling back and forth between the past and present, between this and the other side of the globe.

15 The turmoil between time and space creates more complications than the damn traffic citations or bank credit.

16 In moments of solitude, people's memories burrow back into the deepest parts of a land on the other side of the globe where they were born, digging up the upheavals in history, a history either meticulously recorded or carelessly written, a history that people can begin to question only now.

17 Memory takes people back to the Highlands, the Midlands, conjuring for them the haunting calls of the Lang Son[2] rooster, even if they've never been to Lang Son before. Such memories are ephemeral. They are like the foggy image of a boat leaving the Thua Phu bank to float up the River of Perfume on a moonlit night, going upstream toward Thien Mu Pagoda, or Quan Thanh.[3] If you were to dip your hands into the water, you might imagine being able to grab hold of the costumes of the emperors from the Nguyen Dynasty, who once brought warriors from the West all the way back to Vietnam. Such memories allow you to imagine how you once meandered about on a summer night . . . to imagine you're back near the Hang Co train station, looking for that insect that is sadness, the cicada . . . or that time when you watched the Moroccan soldiers from the French Foreign Legion.

18 For Mr. Nguyen, memory and an analytical mind create such headaches. For, if memory and an analytical mind can transport him to moments of past

---

[2] *Lang Son:* a rustic town close to the Chinese border in the north of Vietnam.
[3] *Thua Phu . . . Thien Mu Pagoda . . . Quan Thanh:* Thua Phu is the name of a street; Thien Mu Pagoda is a small temple on the banks of the Perfume River a short distance southeast of Hue, the imperial city of the Nguyen kings who ruled Vietnam from 1802 to 1945; Quan Thanh is a village.

happiness, they can also fill his heart with pain. Unfortunately, thinking about the sufferings of the past doesn't help the heart to avoid being hurt.

19   Memory is a horse on an ephemeral path, but you can't stop it. It goes where it wants to go. It goes all the way back to Dalat,[4] galloping freely upon green hills in an afternoon in which the hues of sunshine are as light and thin as smoke and clouds. In such moments, all he wants is for Mrs. Nguyen to hold his hand and to go wandering with her under the sun. The horse will stretch its body to take him at great strides back to his old school. To visit his old friends. Or the graves of millions of people. To relatives North and South, people who have gone through untold seasons of separation. People in prison. People hugging their knees in reeducation camps. Men, women, children who died at sea. Bombs, land mines, traps. Russian weapons, American weapons, Japanese weapons, Czech weapons. Mongolian horses. Chinese swords and machetes dating from all dynasties.

20   Mr. Nguyen sits at work, his hands under his chin, ignoring the ringing telephone. He looks out the window and notices the arrival of the tenth winter. His memory forces him to examine himself and all his loved ones. Even acquaintances. All the people born where he was born during a season of floods, three years before millions of people died of famine. A country that for several millennia has not seen the end of suffering.

21   Memory and an analytical mind take him back to the time when the French had just arrived in Vietnam with battle ships, cannons, boots. Fortress walls falling under rockets. Vietnamese heroes calmly taking poison. His memory takes him back to Christmas seasons, when Catholics were persecuted and missionaries arrested and executed; to a time when the first Vietnamese Catholics were considered bridges for Europeans to take over and dominate Vietnam. History and politics become headaches that haunt the Vietnamese mind wherever it lives in the world.

22   It isn't right to have to deal with worries of a political nature during Christmas. All misunderstandings must end. Christmas must be a season of love and joy.

23   It is now Christmas.

24   Streets are decorated with lights and flowers. Miniature red and green light bulbs surround the windows. Each home has prepared a lovely pine tree, properly placed in the living room. Americans seriously welcome Christmas just like the Vietnamese abandon themselves to celebrate their Tet[5] festival.

---

[4] *Dalat:* a cool location in the mountains about 145 miles from Saigon; also the site of the Vietnamese Military Academy.
[5] *Tet:* the Vietnamese lunar new year.

25   The weather is clear and crisp. Bells toll, sending Mr. Nguyen back twenty-five years, when girls in white lined up in church to sing "Silent Night."

26   Mr. Nguyen tenderly remembers his first love. The girl, whose smile was bright as an apricot blossom and sweet as an orchid, had given him some fabric on Christmas Eve so that he could have a shirt made. For a seventeen-year-old boy, it was an overwhelming feeling. The girl had included a photo of Saint Theresa in a wooden frame as part of the gift.

27   These days, his heart is too old. It has grown too arid to feel the romance and saintliness of twenty-five years ago.

28   Still, the horse in his memory gallops back to that Christmas, gingerly returning him details, such as when he came home to tell his mother about the gifts. His mother said, "Then you must buy her a gift in return." His mother undid the safety pin from her pocket and took out three bills of five dong and handed them to him. He circled the shops on his bicycle but could not think of a gift for her. What could he buy her? He settled on a pair of red velvet sandals. They were small for his feet but were still a size and half larger than hers.

29   That Christmas Eve, when the bells sang out, she wore a white ao dai tunic[6] with the oversized sandals and toyed with a white scarf in her hands. She and other girls, also in white ao dai, stood solemnly on a wooden platform outside the church, looked upward, and sent their voices soaring into the sky above the city.

30   He thought then that each and every soul was lined up just as solemnly, silent as could be, listening to the song that penetrated the darkness. Listening to the gentle, joyful, echoing voices that sounded like bells from far away, swaying in the realms of ancient times.

> *In a holy night far away, a holy night long ago*
> *She stood dream-like in a quiet space,*
> *A girl in a white dress and a white scarf;*
> *A pure soul singing poetic innocence.*

31   The girl in a white dress and a white scarf with a pure soul wasn't really a saint. She moved with her parents to another province, and Mr. Nguyen never saw her again. But she remains a pure soul forever.

32   Mr. Nguyen possesses a murky understanding of the Catholic saints, except, perhaps, the saint Theresa, the one in the photo that the girl had given him in high school. His understanding of Catholicism is just as murky. Once in a while, he reads the Bible, but remembers only a romantic passage:

---

[6] *ao dai tunic:* a traditional Vietnamese costume for women, with a high collar, long sleeves, a long skirt with a high slit, and trousers that are worn under the skirt.

"Witness the bird in the wild. Without planting a seed, my father has allowed it to be properly fed. Witness the lilacs in the fields. Without weaving threads, my father has allowed them to be dressed in lovely clothes that even Solomon couldn't have."

33 When he was a child living in Hanoi, Mr. Nguyen used to stand in front of the church, watching people selling pictures of far-away Italy. Back then, printing technology in Vietnam was still rudimentary. There were pictures of floating angels or beautiful shepherds, saints with golden halos, Gothic architecture that provoked saintly emotions. Such images today continue to bring him to church during the Christmas season.

34 Mr. Nguyen's memory, a white horse raising its head to travel through golden fields and green hills, returns him to the sound of ringing bells from years past. Such bells ring out every Christmas. To tell the truth, his memory should rest there. Where there is a girl in her white dress and oversized sandals. She stands with her friends, forever looking skyward to sing for a peaceful and compassionate humanity. Such songs are always beautiful. Even if you're Muslim, Buddhist, or Hindu, or even an alien from Mars visiting the earth, you would feel peaceful inside. Who does not want such peaceful moments?

35 And if you happen to be thinking about such peaceful moments and happen to pay no attention to the stop sign, or the red light, or your account balance, then the whole business about your bad driving records, your bad credit . . . well, such a business is really a lovely quality, not something to be punished for.

Translated by Nguyen Qui Duc

DISCUSSION QUESTIONS

1. The narrator says that Mr. Nguyen lives in two worlds and two time periods. How does this affect his life?
2. Mr. Nguyen not only recalls his personal past, his memory takes him back to "the upheavals in history" in his country. Discuss why this might be so.
3. Why does Mr. Nguyen specifically remember the girl in a white dress?
4. Compare the biblical passage (Matthew 6:28) Mr. Nguyen recalls with the one you are familiar with. How is it different? the same?
5. Where, according to the narrator, should Mr. Nguyen's memory rest and why?
6. Do you think Mr. Nguyen's bank manager or a police officer who tickets him regularly would be swayed by reading this story?

WRITING TOPICS

1. Throughout the story, memory is compared to a white horse. In a paragraph or two, tell why this metaphor is appropriate and why most other animals would not be appropriate metaphors.
2. In a short essay, consider why the narrator would mention the particular Bible verse that Mr. Nguyen recalls and not another.

LUNCH VIGNETTES

Svati Shah

Svati Shah, a South Asian, was born in 1971. A social activist, she has published poetry and short stories in a number of anthologies, including *The Very Inside* (1994). In the following poem, an Americanized South Asian woman visits an ethnic restaurant seeking a connection with her heritage through the spicy traditional foods of her ancestral homeland, foods with exotic names like *puri, shak,* and *shrikhand.* She expects the proprietor to be horrified by her "shaven head / torn jeans, / nose ring," but she is welcomed and treated graciously as she sits down to "eat her culture."

        I eat my culture.
        I snarf huge bits of puri[1]
                 shak[2]
                 bhatt[3]
5   shrikhand,[4]
        and have visions of
        the restaurant keepers
        cursing in Gujarati[5]
        (words I've never heard)
10   and throwing me out
        for my shaven head
        torn jeans,
        nose ring.

---

[1] *puri:* fried bread.
[2] *shak:* a dish from the Gujarat area.
[3] *bhatt:* also spelled bhati; an Indian fried snack.
[4] *shrikhand:* a dessert usually made in the Bombay/Gujarat area.
[5] *Gujarati:* the language of Gujarat, a region of western India.

(For once) it's my prophesy left to starve
15 as the proprietor runs from
our table to the kitchen,
asks how long I'll be in town,
and graciously accepts
my accolades for his wife's cooking.

20 I eat my culture,
and remember my mother's table
feeling anglo vision
from two dearest
who never
25 bore a color standard before.

I eat my culture
till my stomach is distended.
Because I can,
I LOUDLY proclaim the event
30 "Better than sex."

I eat my culture,
making my mouth form phrases
that should be mothertongue
for brown strangers

35 who understand
despite
my
hesitant,
grammatical
40 constructs.

I eat my culture
Sometimes,
in lieu of
salty-creamy-sour-sticky-sweet
45 which began
as cumin
and turmeric flavored dishes
in her mouth
behind her mother's table
50 where, legs swinging,
she eats her culture, too.

DISCUSSION QUESTIONS

1. Why does the speaker think she will be cursed in the restaurant?
2. Is the setting India or America?
3. Who is with the speaker at her table?
4. How well does the speaker understand and speak Gujarati?
5. What is the link between the speaker and her mother?

WRITING TOPICS

1. In a brief essay, explore both the metaphorical and literal ways in which the author "eats her culture."
2. Write a descriptive paragraph telling what you would be eating if you were eating your culture.

SUMMARY WRITING TOPICS

1. If you are wholly, or in part, of Asian descent, what affiliations, if any, do you have with other Asians or Asian culture? If you are not of Asian descent, interview an Asian immigrant or someone of Asian descent who was born in America to find out what Asian affiliations he or she has. Are there connections through religion? food? holiday customs? literature? movies? music? community activities? extended family?

2. Rent some films that depict various aspects of Asian culture, view them, and write one or two reviews. For depictions of Asian life in the United States, you might look for *The Joy Luck Club,* based on Amy Tan's book; *Eat a Bowl of Tea,* based on Louis Chu's book; and *Dim Sum,* about a Chinese American family in San Francisco's Chinatown. For depictions of Asian life abroad, you might look for *A Passage to India,* about India under the Raj; *The Last Emperor,* a portrait of China's last emperor; *Gandhi; Rashomon,* a Japanese film set in medieval Japan; or the Indian trilogy about a poor country family: *Pather Panchali, Aparajito,* and *The World of Apu.* Many of these films have subtitles.

3. Choose two poems from this chapter and, in an essay, compare the authors' use of language and imagery to convey aspects of their culture.

4. The selections by Chitra Banerjee Divakaruni and Ginu Kamani are both about the efforts of children to thwart or avoid family or cultural traditions. In a brief essay, examine some of the family or cultural traditions that you are expected to follow and your own feelings about those traditions.

5. Do you think Asian immigrants have had a harder time adjusting to American society than immigrants from Cuba, Ireland, or Mexico, for example? Why or why not? Discuss in an essay. Read some accounts by immigrants from several other countries before writing.

CHAPTER THREE

STRUGGLES AND RECOGNITION

Asian Americans are sometimes negatively stereotyped as passive and apolitical, interested only in their own families and in material security. At other times, they are positively stereotyped as belonging to a "model minority," law-abiding and hardworking individuals who live in extended families that take care of each other and don't need government assistance. The history and experiences of Americans of Asian descent, however, are more complex than either of these two mirror-image stereotypes.

From the first years of their entry into United States territory, Asians have met with prejudice and discrimination. As early as 1858, California passed a law barring the entry of Chinese and "Mongolians." Americans welcomed cheap Asian labor but did not want the workers to stay on in the United States. In 1856, Chinese were recruited to help construct the Central Pacific Railroad, but they were paid less than the workers brought in from Ireland. In 1870, California passed a law forbidding the entry of Chinese, Japanese, and Mongolian women for purposes of prostitution, but the bill effectively made it difficult for women from these communities to immigrate to the United States, which hindered the development of Asian American families. Unlike immigrants from elsewhere, Asians were not permitted to become naturalized citizens, and alien land laws barred them from ownership of property on U.S. soil. Beginning in 1882, a series of exclusion laws kept the Chinese out of the United States; then the laws were expanded to exclude Japanese, Koreans, and Asian Indians. The 1924 Immigration Act denied entry to almost all Asians.

Asian Americans protested these and other overt acts of discrimination through legal appeals, strikes, community organizations, and individual struggles. This chapter focuses on the representations of such struggles for equal rights and illuminates the different responses to similar conditions of race discrimination.

Ruthanne Lum McCunn's chapter from *Thousand Pieces of Gold* tells the story of Polly Bemis, who is sold as a slave girl in China and brought to the American West in servitude. As a slave, Polly is an object to be sold and bought. In this chapter, Polly's master loses her in a gambling bet to Charlie. Polly, who has been saving her earnings to buy her freedom, is furious at finding herself again an object for exchange, but she learns from Charlie that as an immigrant from China she can never become a naturalized American and can never own land but must always remain an alien despite her skills and hard work. Polly's alien status can only be redeemed through the love of the good white American who has bought her only to free her under his protection.

Sui Sin Far's autobiographical essay offers a very different version of the relationship of the Asian woman to white men. Unlike Polly, the narrator in "Leaves from the Mental Portfolio of an Eurasian," Edith Eaton (or Sui Sin Far, the pseudonym she takes for her literary name) was born in Britain and, with a British father and Chinese mother, could pass for white in the United States. Her childhood experiences of prejudice against the Chinese, however, have made her critical of anti-Asian racism and of internalized self-hate on the part of mixed-race persons like herself. Identifying with the oppressed Chinese in the West, she rejects marriage with a young man who suggests that she deny the Asian part of her identity. For Sui Sin Far, "individuality is more than nationality," and she argues for maintaining, rather than erasing through assimilation, the significant "connecting link" between East and West that mixed-race children offer.

Carlos Bulosan's chapter from *America Is in the Heart* focuses on the contradictions in American society that confuse and complicate our response to it. Beginning with incidents of violence and hatred by white Americans against Filipinos during the time of the Great Depression, the chapter follows the movements of transient Filipinos looking for work on California farms, men who are inevitably chased out of town after town. But when a Filipino migrant worker is hurt and his companions take him to a hospital, they find "refuge and tolerance." Such contradictions bewilder the narrator, who wonders, "Why was America so kind and yet so cruel? . . . Was there no common denominator on which we could all meet?"

Such contradictory reception of Asians by white Americans is analogous to the ambiguous position in which Asian Americans frequently find themselves. Since they are seen as non-Asians by people in Asia and as non-Americans by white Americans, Asian Americans often have to struggle to make a new identity for themselves and to gain social and legal recognition for this new identity. Mitsuye Yamada's poem "Guilty on Both Counts" is an illuminating instance of such a moment of mixed identity. Visiting a relative in Japan, the poet is rejected as being an American by someone who has lost her relatives in the nuclear bombing of Hiroshima; ironically, however, in the United States, the poet is seen as Japanese and so is "blamed" for the Japanese bombing of Pearl Harbor. She is thus "guilty on both counts," caught in a lose-lose identity situation.

The particular historical situation of Japanese Americans has been explored by many writers. Some works directly address the history of internment, when about 110,000 Japanese Americans were forced to leave their homes and businesses on the West Coast after President Franklin Delano Roosevelt signed Executive Order 9066 in 1942. Many of these Japanese Americans were interned in camps in desolate areas for much of the period of the Pacific War. More than two-thirds of those interned were American-born children (nisei) of first-generation Japanese immigrants, the issei. The Supreme Court declared the internment of American citizens unconstitutional in 1944, the same year that the exclusion laws were revoked.

Instructed by this experience of internment, many Japanese Americans continue to be active in civil rights issues. Thus, Hisaye Yamamoto's short story "Wilshire Bus" is not simply a criticism of the drunk passenger's racist comments to the elderly Chinese American couple on the bus; it is also an indictment of the "moral shabbiness" of the main character, Esther, and her complicity with racism, as seen in her silence in the face of such attacks. "Wilshire Bus" depicts the rise of anti-Chinese prejudice after the end of the Pacific War, even though Chinese Americans had fought bravely for America.

In contrast, the excerpt from John Okada's novel *No-No Boy* points to the struggle for reconciliation between the United States government and Japanese Americans who refused to serve the country in protest against their internment. Ichiro, who has just been released from federal prison, recognizes that reconciliation is possible when Mr. Carrick makes a generous offer of a job that should have gone to a veteran. America's "mistake" in interning Japanese Americans should be forgiven, just as his "mistake" (which led to his prison term) in refusing to serve in the war is forgivable. Willyce Kim's poem "In This Heat" expresses another struggle, that of women against interracial male violence.

Philip Kan Gotanda's play *The Wash* also points to the transmission of painful knowledge through time. Years later, Nobu and Masi, two nisei (second-generation Japanese Americans), are still psychologically damaged by their internment experiences in the 1940s. Nobu has become sexually dysfunctional and authoritarian, while Masi recognizes that the trauma of the internment had led her to marry someone she did not love. Ironically, Nobu, in his prejudice against his daughter Judy's black husband, reproduces the kind of racial attitudes that had led to the internment of Japanese Americans. Writers such as Yamamoto and Gotanda show that no group is immune from the sickness of racism and that recognition of one's own racism is important for healing. Nobu, for example, begins to accept his mixed-race grandson once he recognizes how his rigid sense of Japanese male identity has turned his family against him.

The entry of Vietnamese as refugees into the United States after 1975 has resulted in different struggles that nevertheless echo those from an earlier era. In James Freeman's collected oral tales, the Vietnamese Americans tell stories of their frustration with an English-only society, their experiences of loneliness and isolation, their confusion with new social practices, and their hopes and fears for their future in the new country. But, as Lê Thi Diem Thúy's poem notes, ultimately the struggle of Asian Americans is to be recognized for who they are, as a piece of, as well as "so much / more" than, a particular history and place. The struggle is to be recognized as both Asian *and* American—different from and also the same as other Americans.

FROM *THOUSAND PIECES OF GOLD*

Ruthanne Lum McCunn

Ruthanne Lum McCunn was born in San Francisco's Chinatown in 1946. Her father was of Scottish descent and her mother of Chinese descent. She spent her childhood in Hong Kong and returned to the United States at age sixteen. McCunn, who left her father's home in the Midwest to attend college at San Francisco State University, currently lives in San Francisco.

Before McCunn became a full-time writer, she worked as a teacher and librarian. Her biographical novel, *Thousand Pieces of Gold* (1981), based on the story of a Chinese woman sold into slavery in America, was made into a successful film. She received the American Book Award in 1984 for her children's book, *Pie-Biter* (1983). Her second novel, *Wooden Fish Songs* (1996), tells the story of Lue Gim Gong, who immigrated from China to become a pioneer of the citrus industry in Florida. She had written two factual portraits of Lue Gim Gong earlier, in her acclaimed *Chinese-American Portraits: Personal Histories 1828–1988* (1988) and *Chinese America: History and Perspective* (1989). Much of McCunn's writing is devoted to recovering Chinese American history and to countering stereotypes of Chinese Americans prevalent in American culture.

In this excerpt from *Thousand Pieces of Gold,* Polly, the young Chinese woman who was sold into slavery in America, comes to a realization about her hopes for a future of freedom and self-reliance.

1   For Polly, Charlie's cabin with its glowing stove and two chairs pulled close, the dresser made of packing crates, and the bed they shared had always been a refuge. Now, as Charlie lit a lamp and the room flared into light, she saw it as simply another shack.

2   Charlie wrapped his arms around Polly. His belt buckle dug into her, and she felt a wave of disgust as his body quivered with the same drunken exhilaration she had detected in Hong King after a big win. But she did not move. Even if he were not her new master, she could not stop him. He was too big. Too strong.

3   "Hey, you're supposed to be happy," he said, taking Polly's face in both his hands and kissing her full on the lips.

4   She flinched.

5   "Okay, so I don't rate a hallelujah chorus, but what about a simple thank-you?" he said.

6   A thank-you? For what? For humiliating her? For forcing her to break her promise that when she left Hong King it would be as a free woman. Or for teaching her that a slave had no right to make promises, especially to herself.

7   He took the pins out of Polly's bun. Her hair rippled down her back, a sheet of black silk.

8   "Tonight I ruined a man for you."

9   "Not for me. For the game. Because you gambler."

10   "It was the only way to free you."

11   "That what you believe. Just like Jim believe I better off if I not know Hong King not sell me. Maybe Jim right. Or maybe you right. But this my life. Not Jim life. Not yours. Mine."

12   Charlie strode over to the dresser and poured himself a drink, downing it in a single swallow. "All right. What would you have done?"

13   "I shoot him," she said, knowing even as she heard the words out loud that she could never have done it, knowing that was not the point, the reason for her anger.

14   "There are more ways to kill a man than with a gun," Charlie said, setting his glass down. "Hong King's lost so much face, he'll have to leave camp. For you, for us, he's the same as a dead man."

15   Polly slumped onto the bed. Again he had not understood, had not seen beyond her words. "You could have lost," she said tiredly.

16   "I didn't."

17   "And when you play again?"

18   Charlie lifted Polly off the bed and hugged her to him. She felt the worn flannel of his shirt against her face, soft as a caress.

19   "I would never stake you," he said, his voice surprised and hurt.

20   She kept her back taut. "I your slave. You can do anything."

21   He stood back, holding her at arm's length. "I didn't win you from Hong King so you could be my slave. You're free."

22   She looked down at his arms.

23   He dropped his hold, but the marks from his grip remained, deep red purple like the bruises from Jim when he had shaken her, demanding she face a

reality neither one of them was able to confront. Rubbing the tender new bruises, she thought regretfully of the rich promise her first days with Jim had held, a promise unrealized in part because of circumstances, but more because, for all their talk, they had kept too much hidden from each other, from themselves. Was she to suffer the same loss again? And for the same reason?

24 In front of her, she could see Charlie, shoulders slumped, his head tossing back as he downed yet another drink. And in the mirror above the dresser, she could see his hands clasping bottle and glass. But she could not see his face, for he had lowered the mirror long ago to a height appropriate for her. Suddenly, all around her, Polly noticed similar instances of Charlie's thoughtful concern, the curtains nailed up to shield her from prying eyes, the second chair made smaller, the shelves and hooks lowered, and she found herself wondering if he had indeed forced the final bet to win her freedom and not the game.

25 Tonight, and the night before, she had been hurt by his apparent betrayals, angry because he could not understand her. But did she understand him? From the day she had ridden into Warrens, he had protected her, and she had accepted his help without question, as though it were her due. Now, for the first time, she asked herself why he had come to her rescue in the saloon. Had he interceded out of some strange sense of Western chivalry? Or pity? Or because he was Jim's friend. And after Jim's death, had he continued to protect her out of loyalty to Jim, or because he had come to care for her, or simply to keep her in his bed?

26 She did not even know how or why he and Jim had become friends. Like a frog at the bottom of a well, she had seen nothing beyond the small circle of blue sky that meant freedom, concentrating all her thoughts, all her energies toward piling up the gold she needed to reach it, never once considering it might be gained another way. And now she could lose that freedom which Charlie had put within her grasp, and with it, Charlie.

27 Searching for words that would clear away the misunderstandings, she began haltingly. "Charlie, sometimes I angry with you and you with me. But I know anger is only because you and I not understand, not believe the same way. Please, try understand this." She paused, waiting for acknowledgment.

28 He did not speak, but she saw his hands on bottle and glass freeze, breaking the steady drinking. Taking heart, she continued, "All my life I belong someone. My father, the bandits, Hong King. And I promise myself when I free of Hong King, I belong no man, only myself.

29 "You know I have gold I save to buy myself from Hong King. I want use that to build a house, start my own business. A boarding house like Mrs. Schultz."

30 Charlie poured another drink, gulped it. "You can't."

31 "You worry I not know how to cook? I watch Mrs. Schultz and I learn plenty quick."

32   "It's not that," he mumbled.

33   "Then what?" Polly demanded. "Because you think I not wife like Mrs. Schultz, not respectable, people say it bawdy house? You see, I show them they wrong."

34   Charlie turned to face her. "A Chinaman can't own land," he said, so softly she could barely hear him.

35   "But you say America have land for everyone. That people from all over the world come for the land. Rich. Poor. All the same. Anyone can have land. You said."

36   "Any American. You're from China."

37   She opened her mouth to shout denial, but the pain in Charlie's face told Polly his words had cost him too dearly to be negated by mere anger, and she sank silent onto the bed. She must think carefully, make sense out of Charlie's contradictions, her own confusion.

38   She knew the Chinese in Warrens did not own the stores and laundries where they worked, but she had thought that was because they planned to return to China as soon as they made enough money. Weren't the ones who came to Hong King's saloon always complaining about the loneliness of lives without wives and children, the brutish manners of white men, unfair taxes, and harsh laws? And didn't they always end their grumbling with talk of home, their eagerness to return to families left behind? But she had no family, no one to go home to.

39   Of course. That was it. Charlie didn't realize that she intended to remain in America. She would become an American and buy the land for her house. Land that would keep her free and independent always.

40   She leaped up, ran to Charlie, and crooked her arm through his. "You not understand. I never go back to China. I become American."

41   He pulled away. His fists clenched and unclenched. He took his pipe out of his pocket, rotated it in his hands, studying it, then tossed it onto the bed, and reached for the bottle.

42   Polly grabbed his arm. "What is it? What wrong?"

43   "The only way a Chinaman can become an American is to be born here."

44   She laughed. A short, bitter laugh. Here or in China, slave or free, it was the same. She needed a protector. She rubbed her hands across Charlie's back, unknotting the tight muscles. He turned. Mechanically she began unbuttoning his shirt.

45   He took her hands in his, holding them still. "Polly, I meant what I said. You're free. Let me be your China herder and build a house for you. You can do whatever you want to in it, invite anyone, refuse anyone. It's yours, I promise you." He smiled weakly. "You don't even have to have me."

46   "I . . ."

47   His fingers brushed her lips, gently silencing. "And yes, you can pay for it too."

48 She laughed, a joyous peal clear as ringing bells. Hearing it, Charlie's smile grew stronger, deepening into laughter that became one with Polly's. And suddenly, within the circle of their laughter, she felt finally, wonderfully free.

DISCUSSION QUESTIONS

1. Why has Polly felt like a slave?
2. After her initial anger at Charlie, what does Polly come to realize?
3. Even though Charlie won Polly from Hong King in a game, he says she's free. How does he prove it?

WRITING TOPICS

1. There is a certain amount of tension between Polly and Charlie in this excerpt. In an essay, analyze how McCunn creates this tension and what effect it has on the reader.
2. This is only one of several selections in this anthology about women's subjugation to men and their helplessness and resentment. Do you think men are diminished by women's freedom, and if so how? Express your views in an article that could be printed in a newspaper.

Leaves from the Mental Portfolio of an Eurasian

Sui Sin Far

Edith Maud Eaton was born in England in 1865 to a Chinese mother and an English father. Her family later settled in Quebec, where in the 1880s and 1890s she worked as a stenographer, journalist, and writer of fiction, often writing under the name Sui Sin Far, which means "water lily" in Cantonese. In 1898, she moved to the United States.

Sui Sin Far produced a collection of stories entitled *Mrs. Spring Fragrance,* nonfiction articles, autobiographical essays, and other short pieces of fiction. Her short stories are portraits of Chinese American communal and familial life in larger urban centers, such as San Francisco, Seattle, New York, and Montreal. Much of Sui Sin Far's writing was published in widely circulated journals, magazines, and newspapers, such as *The Chautauquan, Good Housekeeping,* and *The Boston Globe.* She died in 1914.

Sui Sin Far's choosing a Chinese American identity was a bold decision, for the end of the nineteenth century and the beginning of the twentieth saw intense anti-Chinese sentiment in the United States. For example, many whites responded with violence and hostility to the successes of Chinese laborers in agriculture, fishing, land reclamation, service industries, and manufacturing from the 1860s through the 1880s. The federal Chinese Exclusion Act of 1882, which was extended indefinitely in 1902, implemented restrictive measures aimed at Chinese immigrants.

Because Sui Sin Far identified herself as Chinese American, many contemporary literary scholars treat her as a Chinese American writer; however, other scholars, citing the textual moments in which she discusses issues specific to racial mixture, consider her perspective to be Eurasian.

In the following selection, the ramifications of Far's choice of identity are evidenced in several episodes describing her encounters with prejudice (the "cross of the Eurasian") in England and North America. (J.I.)

1   When I look back over the years I see myself, a little child of scarcely four years of age, walking in front of my nurse, in a green English lane, and listening to her tell another of her kind that my mother is Chinese. "Oh, Lord!" exclaims the informed. She turns around and scans me curiously from head to foot. Then the two women whisper together. Though the word "Chinese" conveys very little meaning to my mind, I feel that they are talking about my father and mother and my heart swells with indignation. When we reach home I rush to my mother and try to tell her what I have heard. I am a young child. I fail to make myself intelligible. My mother does not understand, and when the nurse declares to her, "Little Miss Sui is a story-teller," my mother slaps me.

2   Many a long year has passed over my head since that day—the day on which I first learned that I was something different and apart from other children, but though my mother has forgotten it, I have not.

3   I see myself again, a few years older. I am playing with another child in a garden. A girl passes by outside the gate. "Mamie," she cries to my companion. "I wouldn't speak to Sui if I were you. Her mamma is Chinese."

4   "I don't care," answers the little one beside me. And then to me, "Even if your mamma is Chinese, I like you better than I like Annie."

5   "But I don't like you," I answer, turning my back on her. It is my first conscious lie.

6   I am at a children's party, given by the wife of an Indian officer whose children were schoolfellows of mine. I am only six years of age, but have attended a private school for over a year, and have already learned that China is a heathen country, being civilized by England. However, for the time being, I am a merry romping child. There are quite a number of grown people present. One, a white haired old man, has his attention called to me by the hostess. He adjusts his eyeglasses and surveys me critically. "Ah, indeed!" he exclaims. "Who would have thought it at first glance. Yet now I see the difference between her and other children. What a peculiar coloring! Her mother's eyes and hair and her father's features, I presume. Very interesting little creature!"

7   I had been called from my play for the purpose of inspection. I do not return to it. For the rest of the evening I hide myself behind a hall door and refuse to show myself until it is time to go home.

8   My parents have come to America. We are in Hudson City, N.Y., and we are very poor. I am out with my brother, who is ten months older than

myself. We pass a Chinese store, the door of which is open. "Look!" says Charlie. "Those men in there are Chinese!" Eagerly I gaze into the long low room. With the exception of my mother, who is English bred with English ways and manner of dress, I have never seen a Chinese person. The two men within the store are uncouth specimens of their race, dressed in working blouses and pantaloons with queues hanging down their backs. I recoil with a sense of shock.

9   "Oh, Charlie," I cry. "Are we like that?"

10   "Well, we're Chinese and they're Chinese, too, so we must be!" returns my seven-year-old brother.

11   "Of course you are," puts in a boy who has followed us down the street, and who lives near us and has seen my mother: "Chinky, chinky, Chinaman, yellow-face, pig-tail, rat-eater." A number of other boys and several little girls join in with him.

12   "Better than you," shouts my brother, facing the crowd. He is younger and smaller than any there, and I am even more insignificant than he; but my spirit revives.

13   "I'd rather be Chinese than anything else in the world," I scream.

14   They pull my hair, they tear my clothes, they scratch my face, and all but lame my brother; but the white blood in our veins fights valiantly for the Chinese half of us. When it is all over, exhausted and bedraggled, we crawl home, and report to our mother that we have "won the battle."

15   "Are you sure?" asks my mother doubtfully.

16   "Of course. They ran from us. They were frightened," returns my brother.

17   My mother smiles with satisfaction.

18   "Do you hear?" she asks my father.

19   "Umm," he observes, raising his eyes from his paper for an instant. My childish instinct, however, tells me that he is more interested than he appears to be.

20   It is tea time, but I cannot eat. Unobserved I crawl away. I do not sleep that night. I am too excited and I ache all over. Our opponents had been so very much stronger and bigger than we. Toward morning, however, I fall into a doze from which I awake myself, shouting:

> "Sound the battle cry,
> See the foe is nigh."

21   My mother believes in sending us to Sunday school. She has been brought up in a Presbyterian college.

22   The scene of my life shifts to Eastern Canada. The sleigh which has carried us from the station stops in front of a little French Canadian hotel. Immediately we are surrounded by a number of villagers, who stare curi-

ously at my mother as my father assists her to alight from the sleigh. Their curiosity, however, is tempered with kindness, as they watch, one after another, the little black heads of my brothers and sisters and myself emerge out of the buffalo robe, which is part of the sleigh's outfit. There are six of us, four girls and two boys, the eldest, my brother, being only seven years of age. My father and mother are still in their twenties. "Les pauvres enfants," the inhabitants murmur, as they help to carry us into the hotel. Then in lower tones: "Chinoise, Chinoise."

23   For some time after our arrival, whenever we children are sent for a walk, our footsteps are dogged by a number of young French and English Canadians, who amuse themselves with speculations as to whether we, being Chinese, are susceptible to pinches and hair pulling, while older persons pause and gaze upon us, very much in the same way that I have seen people gaze upon strange animals in a menagerie. Now and then we are stopped and plied with questions as to what we eat and drink, how we go to sleep, if my mother understands what my father says to her, if we sit on chairs or squat on floors, etc., etc., etc.

24   There are many pitched battles, of course, and we seldom leave the house without being armed for conflict. My mother takes a great interest in our battles, and usually cheers us on, though I doubt whether she understands the depth of the troubled waters through which her little children wade. As to my father, peace is his motto, and he deems it wisest to be blind and deaf to many things.

25   School days are short, but memorable. I am in the same class with my brother, my sister next to me in the class below. The little girl whose desk my sister shares shrinks close against the wall as my sister takes her place. In a little while she raises her hand.

26   "Please, teacher!"

27   "Yes, Annie."

28   "May I change my seat?"

29   "No, you may not!"

30   The little girl sobs. "Why should she have to sit beside a ——"

31   Happily my sister does not seem to hear, and before long the two little girls become great friends. I have many such experiences.

32   My brother is remarkably bright; my sister next to me has a wonderful head for figures, and when only eight years of age helps my father with his night work accounts. My parents compare her with me. She is of sturdier build than I, and, as my father says, "Always has her wits about her." He thinks her more like my mother, who is very bright and interested in every little detail of practical life. My father tells me that I will never make half the woman that my mother is or that my sister will be. I am not as strong as my sisters, which makes me feel somewhat ashamed, for I am the eldest little girl, and more is expected of me. I have no organic disease, but the strength

of my feelings seems to take from me the strength of my body. I am prostrated at times with attacks of nervous sickness. The doctor says that my heart is unusually large; but in the light of the present I know that the cross of the Eurasian bore too heavily upon my childish shoulders. I usually hide my weakness from the family until I cannot stand. I do not understand myself, and I have an idea that the others will despise me for not being as strong as they. Therefore, I like to wander away alone, either by the river or in the bush. The green fields and flowing water have a charm for me. At the age of seven, as it is today, a bird on the wing is my emblem of happiness.

33 I have come from a race on my mother's side which is said to be the most stolid and insensible to feeling of all races, yet I look back over the years and see myself so keenly alive to every shade of sorrow and suffering that it is almost a pain to live.

34 If there is any trouble in the house in the way of a difference between my father and mother, or if any child is punished, how I suffer! And when harmony is restored, heaven seems to be around me. I can be sad, but I can also be glad. My mother's screams of agony when a baby is born almost drive me wild, and long after her pangs have subsided I feel them in my own body. Sometimes it is a week before I can get to sleep after such an experience.

35 A debt owing by my father fills me with shame. I feel like a criminal when I pass the creditor's door. I am only ten years old. And all the while the question of nationality perplexes my little brain. Why are we what we are? I and my brothers and sisters. Why did God make us to be hooted and stared at? Papa is English, mamma is Chinese. Why couldn't we have been either one thing or the other? Why is my mother's race despised? I look into the faces of my father and mother. Is she not every bit as dear and good as he? Why? Why? She sings us the songs she learned at her English school. She tells us tales of China. Though a child when she left her native land she remembers it well, and I am never tired of listening to the story of how she was stolen from her home. She tells us over and over again of her meeting with my father in Shanghai and the romance of their marriage. Why? Why?

36 I do not confide in my father and mother. They would not understand. How could they? He is English, she is Chinese. I am different to both of them—a stranger, though their own child. "What are we?" I ask my brother. "It doesn't matter, sissy," he responds. But it does. I love poetry, particularly heroic pieces. I also love fairy tales. Stories of everyday life do not appeal to me. I dream dreams of being great and noble; my sisters and brothers also. I glory in the idea of dying at the stake and a great genie arising from the flames and declaring to those who have scorned us: "Behold, how great and glorious and noble are the Chinese people!"

37 My sisters are apprenticed to a dressmaker; my brother is entered in an office. I tramp around and sell my father's pictures, also some lace which I make myself. My nationality, if I had only known it at that time, helps to

make sales. The ladies who are my customers call me "The Little Chinese Lace Girl." But it is a dangerous life for a very young girl. I come near to "mysteriously disappearing" many a time. The greatest temptation was in the thought of getting far away from where I was known, to where no mocking cries of "Chinese!" "Chinese!" could reach.

38   Whenever I have the opportunity I steal away to the library and read every book I can find on China and the Chinese. I learn that China is the oldest civilized nation on the face of the earth and a few other things. At eighteen years of age what troubles me is not that I am what I am, but that others are ignorant of my superiority. I am small, but my feelings are big— and great is my vanity.

39   My sisters attend dancing classes, for which they pay their own fees. In spite of covert smiles and sneers, they are glad to meet and mingle with other young folk. They are not sensitive in the sense that I am. And yet they understand. One of them tells me that she overheard a young man say to another that he would rather marry a pig than a girl with Chinese blood in her veins.

40   In course of time I too learn shorthand and take a position in an office. Like my sister, I teach myself, but, unlike my sister, I have neither the perseverance nor the ability to perfect myself. Besides, to a temperament like mine, it is torture to spend the hours in transcribing other people's thoughts. Therefore, although I can always earn a moderately good salary, I do not distinguish myself in the business world as does she.

41   When I have been working for some years I open an office of my own. The local papers patronize me and give me a number of assignments, including most of the local Chinese reporting. I meet many Chinese persons, and when they get into trouble am often called upon to fight their battles in the papers. This I enjoy. My heart leaps for joy when I read one day an article by a New York Chinese in which he declares, "The Chinese in America owe an everlasting debt of gratitude to Sui Sin Far for the bold stand she has taken in their defense."

42   The Chinaman who wrote the article seeks me out and calls upon me. He is a clever and witty man, a graduate of one of the American colleges and as well a Chinese scholar. I learn that he has an American wife and several children. I am very much interested in these children, and when I meet them my heart throbs in sympathetic tune with the tales they relate of their experiences as Eurasians. "Why did papa and mamma born us?" asks one. Why?

43   I also meet other Chinese men who compare favorably with the white men of my acquaintance in mind and heart qualities. Some of them are quite handsome. They have not as finely cut noses and as well developed chins as the white men, but they have smoother skins and their expression is more serene; their hands are better shaped and their voices softer.

44   Some little Chinese women whom I interview are very anxious to know whether I would marry a Chinaman. I do not answer No. They clap their

hands delightedly, and assure me that the Chinese are much the finest and best of all men. They are, however, a little doubtful as to whether one could be persuaded to care for me, full-blooded Chinese people having a prejudice against the half white.

45   Fundamentally, I muse, all people are the same. My mother's race is as prejudiced as my father's. Only when the whole world becomes as one family will human beings be able to see clearly and hear distinctly. I believe that some day a great part of the world will be Eurasian. I cheer myself with the thought that I am but a pioneer. A pioneer should glory in suffering.

46   "You were walking with a Chinaman yesterday," accuses an acquaintance.

47   "Yes, what of it?"

48   "You ought not to. It isn't right."

49   "No right to walk with one of my mother's people? Oh, indeed!"

50   I cannot reconcile his notion of righteousness with my own.

51   I am living in a little town away off on the north shore of a big lake. Next to me at the dinner table is the man for whom I work as a stenographer. There are also a couple of business men, a young girl and her mother.

52   Some one makes a remark about the cars full of Chinamen that passed this morning. A transcontinental railway runs through the town.

53   My employer shakes his rugged head. "Somehow or other," says he, "I cannot reconcile myself to the thought that the Chinese are humans like ourselves. They may have immortal souls, but their faces seem to be so utterly devoid of expression that I cannot help but doubt."

54   "Souls," echoes the town clerk. "Their bodies are enough for me. A Chinaman is, in my eyes, more repulsive than a black."

55   "They always give me such a creepy feeling," puts in the young girl with a laugh.

56   "I wouldn't have one in my house," declares my landlady.

57   "Now, the Japanese are different altogether. There is something bright and likeable about those men," continues Mr. K.

58   A miserable, cowardly feeling keeps me silent. I am in a Middle West town. If I declare what I am, every person in the place will hear about it the next day. The population is in the main made up of working folks with strong prejudices against my mother's countrymen. The prospect before me is not an enviable one—if I speak. I have no longer an ambition to die at the stake for the sake of demonstrating the greatness and nobleness of the Chinese people.

59   Mr. K. turns to me with a kindly smile.

60   "What makes Miss Far so quiet?" he asks.

61   "I don't suppose she finds the 'washee washee men' particularly interesting subjects of conversation," volunteers the young manager of the local bank.

62   With a great effort I raise my eyes from my plate. "Mr. K.," I say, addressing my employer, "the Chinese people may have no souls, no expression on their faces, be altogether beyond the pale of civilization, but whatever they are, I want you to understand that I am—I am a Chinese."

63   There is silence in the room for a few minutes. Then Mr. K. pushes back his plate and standing up beside me, says:

64   "I should not have spoken as I did. I know nothing whatever about the Chinese. It was pure prejudice. Forgive me!"

65   I admire Mr. K.'s moral courage in apologizing to me; he is a conscientious Christian man, but I do not remain much longer in the little town.

66   I am under a tropic sky, meeting frequently and conversing with persons who are almost as high up in the world as birth, education and money can set them. The environment is peculiar, for I am also surrounded by a race of people, the reputed descendants of Ham, the son of Noah, whose offspring, it was prophesied, should be the servants of the sons of Shem and Japheth.[1] As I am a descendant, according to the Bible, of both Shem and Japheth, I have a perfect right to set my heel upon the Ham people; but though I see others around me following out the Bible suggestion, it is not in my nature to be arrogant to any but those who seek to impress me with their superiority, which the poor black maid who has been assigned to me by the hotel certainly does not. My employer's wife takes me to task for this. "It is unnecessary," she says, "to thank a black person for service."

67   The novelty of life in the West Indian island is not without its charm. The surroundings, people, manner of living, are so entirely different from what I have been accustomed to up North that I feel as if I were "born again." Mixing with people of fashion, and yet not of them, I am not of sufficient importance to create comment or curiosity. I am busy nearly all day and often well into the night. It is not monotonous work, but it is certainly strenuous. The planters and business men of the island take me as a matter of course and treat me with kindly courtesy. Occasionally an Englishman will warn me against the "brown boys" of the island, little dreaming that I too am of the "brown people" of the earth.

68   When it begins to be whispered about the place that I am not all white, some of the "sporty" people seek my acquaintance. I am small and look much younger than my years. When, however, they discover that I am a very serious and sober-minded spinster indeed, they retire quite gracefully, leaving me a few amusing reflections.

---

[1] *Ham . . . Japheth:* Ham, Shem, and Japheth were the three sons of Noah and, according to ancient biblical writers, were the original ancestors of the three divisions of people known to these writers. At the end of Genesis 9, Noah curses Ham and condemns him or his son to serve Shem and Japheth. The mistaken idea that Ham represents the African people was at one time used to justify slavery. There is no evidence in the Bible that Ham's descendants were viewed as black.

69   One evening a card is brought to my room. It bears the name of some naval officer. I go down to my visitor, thinking he is probably some one who, having been told that I am a reporter for the local paper, has brought me an item of news. I find him lounging in an easy chair on the veranda of the hotel—a big, blond, handsome fellow, several years younger than I.

70   "You are Lieutenant——?" I inquire.

71   He bows and laughs a little. The laugh doesn't suit him somehow—and it doesn't suit me, either.

72   "If you have anything to tell me, please tell it quickly, because I'm very busy."

73   "Oh, you don't really mean that," he answers, with another silly and offensive laugh. "There's always plenty of time for good times. That's what I am here for. I saw you at the races the other day and twice at King's House. My ship will be here for —— weeks."

74   "Do you wish that noted?" I ask.

75   "Oh, no! Why—I came just because I had an idea that you might like to know me. I would like to know you. You look such a nice little body. Say, wouldn't you like to go for a sail this lovely night? I will tell you all about the sweet little Chinese girls I met when we were at Hong Kong. They're not so shy!"

76   I leave Eastern Canada for the Far West, so reduced by another attack of rheumatic fever that I only weigh eighty-four pounds. I travel on an advertising contract. It is presumed by the railway company that in some way or other I will give them full value for their transportation across the continent. I have been ordered beyond the Rockies by the doctor, who declares that I will never regain my strength in the East. Nevertheless, I am but two days in San Francisco when I start out in search of work. It is the first time that I have sought work as a stranger in a strange town. Both of the other positions away from home were secured for me by home influence. I am quite surprised to find that there is no demand for my services in San Francisco and that no one is particularly interested in me. The best I can do is to accept an offer from a railway agency to typewrite their correspondence for $5 a month. I stipulate, however, that I shall have the privilege of taking in outside work and that my hours shall be light. I am hopeful that the sale of a story or newspaper article may add to my income, and I console myself with the reflection that, considering that I still limp and bear traces of sickness, I am fortunate to secure any work at all.

77   The proprietor of one of the San Francisco papers, to whom I have a letter of introduction, suggests that I obtain some subscriptions from the people of China town, that district of the city having never been canvassed. This suggestion I carry out with enthusiasm, though I find that the Chinese merchants and people generally are inclined to regard me with suspicion. They

have been imposed upon so many times by unscrupulous white people. Another drawback—save for a few phrases, I am unacquainted with my mother tongue. How, then, can I expect these people to accept me as their own countrywoman? The Americanized Chinamen actually laugh in my face when I tell them that I am of their race. However, they are not all "doubting Thomases." Some little women discover that I have Chinese hair, color of eyes and complexion, also that I love rice and tea. This settles the matter for them—and for their husbands.

78   My Chinese instincts develop. I am no longer the little girl who shrunk against my brother at the first sight of a Chinaman. Many and many a time, when alone in a strange place, has the appearance of even a humble laundryman given me a sense of protection and made me feel quite at home. This fact of itself proves to me that prejudice can be eradicated by association.

79   I meet a half Chinese, half white girl. Her face is plastered with a thick white coat of paint and her eyelids and eyebrows are blackened so that the shape of her eyes and the whole expression of her face is changed. She was born in the East, and at the age of eighteen came West in answer to an advertisement. Living for many years among the working class, she had heard little but abuse of the Chinese. It is not difficult, in a land like California, for a half Chinese, half white girl to pass as one of Spanish or Mexican origin. This poor child does, though she lives in a nervous dread of being "discovered." She becomes engaged to a young man, but fears to tell him what she is, and only does so when compelled by a fearless American girl friend. This girl, who knows her origin, realizing that the truth sooner or later must be told, and better soon than late, advises the Eurasian to confide in the young man, assuring her that he loves her well enough not to allow her nationality to stand, a bar sinister, between them. But the Eurasian prefers to keep her secret, and only reveals it to the man who is to be her husband when driven to bay by the American girl, who declares that if the halfbreed will not tell the truth she will. When the young man hears that the girl he is engaged to has Chinese blood in her veins, he exclaims: "Oh, what will my folks say?" But that is all. Love is stronger than prejudice with him, and neither he nor she deems it necessary to inform his "folks."

80   The Americans, having for many years manifested a much higher regard for the Japanese than for the Chinese, several half Chinese young men and women, thinking to advance themselves, both in a social and business sense, pass as Japanese. They continue to be known as Eurasians; but a Japanese Eurasian does not appear in the same light as a Chinese Eurasian. The unfortunate Chinese Eurasians! Are not those who compel them to thus cringe more to be blamed than they?

81   People, however, are not all alike. I meet white men, and women, too, who are proud to mate with those who have Chinese blood in their veins,

and think it a great honor to be distinguished by the friendship of such. There are also Eurasians and Eurasians. I know of one who allowed herself to become engaged to a white man after refusing him nine times. She had discouraged him in every way possible, had warned him that she was half Chinese; that her people were poor, that every week or month she sent home a certain amount of her earnings, and that the man she married would have to do as much, if not more; also, most uncompromising truth of all, that she did not love him and never would. But the resolute and undaunted lover swore that it was a matter of indifference to him whether she was a Chinese or a Hottentot, that it would be his pleasure and privilege to allow her relations double what it was in her power to bestow, and as to not loving him—that did not matter at all. He loved her. So, because the young woman had a married mother and married sisters, who were always picking at her and gossiping over her independent manner of living, she finally consented to marry him, recording the agreement in her diary thus:

"I have promised to become the wife of —— —— on —— ——, 189—, because the world is so cruel and sneering to a single woman—and for no other reason."

82   Everything went smoothly until one day. The young man was driving a pair of beautiful horses and she was seated by his side, trying very hard to imagine herself in love with him, when a Chinese vegetable gardener's cart came rumbling along. The Chinaman was a jolly-looking individual in blue cotton blouse and pantaloons, his rakish looking hat being kept in place by a long queue which was pulled upward from his neck and wound around it. The young woman was suddenly possessed with the spirit of mischief. "Look!" she cried, indicating the Chinaman, "There's my brother. Why don't you salute him?"

83   The man's face fell a little. He sank into a pensive mood. The wicked one by his side read him like an open book.

84   "When we are married," said she, "I intend to give a Chinese party every month."

85   No answer.

86   "As there are very few aristocratic Chinese in this city, I shall fill up with the laundrymen and vegetable farmers. I don't believe in being exclusive in democratic America, do you?"

87   He hadn't a grain of humor in his composition, but a sickly smile contorted his features as he replied:

88   "You shall do just as you please, my darling. But—but—consider a moment. Wouldn't it be just a little pleasanter for us if, after we are married, we allowed it to be presumed that you were—er—Japanese? So many of my friends have inquired of me if that is not your nationality. They would be so charmed to meet a little Japanese lady."

89 "Hadn't you better oblige them by finding one?"

90 "Why—er—what do you mean?"

91 "Nothing much in particular. Only—I am getting a little tired of this," taking off his ring.

92 "You don't mean what you say! Oh, put it back, dearest! You know I would not hurt your feelings for the world!"

93 "You haven't. I'm more than pleased. But I do mean what I say."

94 That evening the "ungrateful" Chinese Eurasian diaried, among other things, the following:

> "Joy, oh, joy! I'm free once more. Never again shall I be untrue to my own heart. Never again will I allow any one to 'hound' or 'sneer' me into matrimony."

95 I secure transportation to many California points. I meet some literary people, chief among whom is the editor of the magazine who took my first Chinese stories. He and his wife give me a warm welcome to their ranch. They are broadminded people, whose interest in me is sincere and intelligent, not affected and vulgar. I also meet some funny people who advise me to "trade" upon my nationality. They tell me that if I wish to succeed in literature in America I should dress in Chinese costume, carry a fan in my hand, wear a pair of scarlet beaded slippers, live in New York, and come of high birth. Instead of making myself familiar with the Chinese Americans around me, I should discourse on my spirit acquaintance with Chinese ancestors and quote in between the "Good mornings" and "How d'ye dos" of editors.

> "Confucius, Confucius, how great is Confucius. Before Confucius, there never was Confucius, there never came Confucius," etc., etc., etc.,

or something like that, both illuminating and obscuring, don't you know. They forget, or perhaps they are not aware that the old Chinese sage taught "The way of sincerity is the way of heaven."

96 My experiences as an Eurasian never cease; but people are not now as prejudiced as they have been. In the West, too, my friends are more advanced in all lines of thought than those whom I knew in Eastern Canada—more genuine, more sincere, with less of the form of religion, but more of its spirit.

97 So I roam backward and forward across the continent. When I am East, my heart is West. When I am West, my heart is East. Before long I hope to be in China. As my life began in my father's country it may end in my mother's.

98   After all I have no nationality and am not anxious to claim any. Individuality is more than nationality. "You are you and I am I," says Confucius. I give my right hand to the Occidentals and my left to the Orientals, hoping that between them they will not utterly destroy the insignificant "connecting link." And that's all.

DISCUSSION QUESTIONS

1. The author says that as a child she had no organic diseases but that "the cross of the Eurasian bore too heavily upon my childish shoulders." What does she mean?
2. Why are the Chinese women the author interviews doubtful that she could find a Chinese man to care for her?
3. Why does Far leave the little town in the Midwest?
4. What kind of racism did Far see in the West Indies?
5. Why was the naval officer interested in Far?
6. Far writes of two women who revealed their Chinese ancestry to the white men who wanted to marry them. What was the outcome of these relationships?
7. "Individuality is more than nationality," according to Far. Do you find evidence of this belief in the world today?

WRITING TOPICS

1. In a brief essay, analyze and characterize the tone of this selection and how it affects your reading of the piece. Cite examples from the selection to support your views.
2. In a short persuasive paper, support through reasoning and examples either of the following thesis statements. The first statement is Far's.
   a. Prejudice can be eradicated by association.
   b. Mere association with people of different races or ethnicity cannot wholly eradicate prejudice.

FROM *AMERICA IS IN THE HEART*

Carlos Bulosan

Carlos Bulosan, who was born in 1913 in the central Philippines, arrived in Seattle, Washington, at the age of seventeen. He had completed only three years of schooling in his homeland and spoke little English upon his arrival.

Immigrating at the onset of the Great Depression, he quickly realized that his beliefs in brotherhood, equality, and opportunity—ideals and values that he had learned in American schools in his homeland—would be challenged by racism directed at Filipinos, many of whom were perceived as stealing jobs from white workers. From the middle of the nineteenth century, Asian immigrants to the United States encountered much racist hostility, and many Filipinos, like other Asians who came before them, were met with intense animosity and overt suspicion. Bulosan realized that economic and social circumstances in the United States were worse than those in his native Philippines in several ways. This realization, however, did not lead Bulosan to feel defeated; instead, he sought to improve these circumstances. In Los Angeles, he organized a union of fish cannery laborers with his friend Chris Mensalves and began writing about the experiences of Filipino workers. Unfortunately, his financial status did not improve. Living in poverty, he contracted tuberculosis, underwent three lung operations, and endured a lengthy convalescence. One of the few benefits derived from this period of inactivity was the opportunity for Bulosan to read and educate himself further.

During World War II, Bulosan began to receive national recognition for his writing. *The Saturday Evening Post* picked up his essay "Freedom from Want," and other pieces appeared in prestigious and widely circulated publications, such as *The New Yorker* and *Harper's Bazaar*. His third book, *Laughter of My Father* (1944), was broadcast to American soldiers, and his autobiography, *America Is in the Heart,* which literary critic Amy Ling describes as "slightly fictionalized," was acclaimed one of the fifty most important American books ever published.

By the time Bulosan died in 1956, however, he was living in poverty once again, for, Ling claims, the political climate no longer favored his type of writing and subject matter. He never returned to the Philippines and never became an American citizen.

In the following selection from *America Is in the Heart,* a young Filipino man, experiencing discrimination and brutality in the labor camps of California before World War II, wonders how America can be "so kind and yet so cruel." (J.I.)

1 It was now the year of the great hatred: the lives of Filipinos were cheaper than those of dogs. They were forcibly shoved off the streets when they showed resistance. The sentiment against them was accelerated by the marriage of a Filipino and a girl of the Caucasian race in Pasadena. The case was tried in court and many technicalities were brought in with it to degrade the lineage and character of the Filipino people.

2 Prior to the *Roldan v. The United States* case, Filipinos were considered Mongolians. Since there is a law which forbids the marriage between members of the Mongolian and Caucasian races, those who hated Filipinos wanted them to be included in this discriminatory legislation. Anthropologists and other experts maintained that the Filipinos are not Mongolians, but members of the Malayan race. It was then a simple thing for the state legislature to pass a law forbidding marriage between members of the Malayan and Caucasian races. This action was followed by neighboring states until, when the war with Japan broke out in 1941, New Mexico was the nearest place to the Pacific Coast where Filipino soldiers could marry Caucasian women.

3 This was the condition in California when José and I arrived in San Diego. I was still unaware of the vast social implications of the discrimination against Filipinos, and my ignorance had innocently brought me to the attention of white Americans. In San Diego, where I tried to get a job, I was beaten up on several occasions by restaurant and hotel proprietors. I put the blame on certain Filipinos who had behaved badly in America, who had instigated hate and discontent among their friends and followers. This misconception was generated by a confused personal reaction to dynamic social forces, but my hunger for the truth had inevitably led me to take an historical attitude. I was to understand and interpret this chaos from a collective point of view, because it was pervasive and universal.

4   From San Diego, José and I traveled by freight train to the south. We were told, when we reached the little desert town of Calipatria, that local whites were hunting Filipinos at night with shotguns. A countryman offered to take us in his loading truck to Brawley, but we decided it was too dangerous. We walked to Holtville where we found a Japanese farmer who hired us to pick winter peas.

5   It was cold at night and when morning came the fog was so thick it was tangible. But it was a safe place and it was far from the surveillance of vigilantes. Then from nearby El Centro, the center of Filipino population in the Imperial Valley, news came that a Filipino labor organizer had been found dead in a ditch.

6   I wanted to leave Holtville, but José insisted that we work through the season. I worked but made myself inconspicuous. At night I slept with a long knife under my pillow. My ears became sensitive to sounds and even my sense of smell was sharpened. I knew when rabbits were mating between the rows of peas. I knew when night birds were feasting in the melon patches.

7   One day a Filipino came to Holtville with his American wife and their child. It was blazing noon and the child was hungry. The strangers went to a little restaurant and sat down at a table. When they were refused service, they stayed on, hoping for some consideration. But it was no use. Bewildered, they walked outside; suddenly the child began to cry with hunger. The Filipino went back to the restaurant and asked if he could buy a bottle of milk for his child.

8   "It is only for my baby," he said humbly.

9   The proprietor came out from behind the counter. "For *your* baby?" he shouted.

10   "Yes, sir," said the Filipino.

11   The proprietor pushed him violently outside. "If you say *that* again in my place, I'll bash in your head!" he shouted aloud so that he would attract attention. "You damn brown monkeys have your nerve, marrying our women. Now get out of this town!"

12   "I love my wife and my child," said the Filipino desperately.

13   "*Damn* you!" The white man struck the Filipino viciously between the eyes with his fist.

14   Years of degradation came into the Filipino's face. All the fears of his life were here—in the white hand against his face. Was there no place where he could escape? Crouching like a leopard, he hurled his whole weight upon the white man, knocking him down instantly. He seized a stone the size of his fist and began smashing it into the man's face. Then the white men in the restaurant seized the small Filipino, beating him unconscious with pieces of wood and with their fists.

15   He lay inert on the road. When two deputy sheriffs came to take him away, he looked tearfully back at his wife and child.

16   I was about to go to bed when I heard unfamiliar noises outside. Quickly I reached for José's hand and whispered to him to dress. José followed me through the back door and down a narrow irrigation ditch. We crept on our bellies until we reached a wide field of tall peas, then we began running away from the town. We had not gone far when we saw our bunkhouse burning.

17   We walked all the cold, dark night toward Calexico. The next morning we met a Filipino driving a jalopy.

18   "Hop in, *Pinoys!*"[1] he said. "I'm going to Bakersfield. I'm on my way to the vineyards."

19   I ran for the car, my heart singing with relief. In the car, José went to sleep at once.

20   "My name is Frank," said the driver. "It is getting hot in Imperial Valley, so I'm running away. I hope to find work in the grape fields."

21   It was the end of spring. Soon the grapevines would be loaded with fruit. The jalopy squeaked and groaned, and once when we were entering Los Angeles, it stalled for hours. Frank tinkered and cooed over it, as though the machine were a baby.

22   I wanted to find my brother Macario, but my companions were in a hurry. In Riverside the jalopy stalled again. José ran to the nearest orange grove. In San Bernardino, where we had stopped to eat pears, José took the wheel and drove all through the night to Bakersfield.

23   We found a place on a large farm owned by a man named Arakelian. Hundreds of Filipinos were arriving from Salinas and Santa Maria, so we improvised makeshift beds under the trees. Japanese workers were also arriving from San Francisco, but they were housed in another section of the farm. I did not discover until some years afterward that this tactic was the only way in which the farmers could forestall any possible alliance between the Filipinos and the Japanese.

24   Some weeks after our work had begun rumors of trouble reached our camp. Then, on the other side of town, a Filipino labor camp was burned. My fellow workers could not explain it to me. I understood it to be a racial issue, because everywhere I went I saw white men attacking Filipinos. It was but natural for me to hate and fear the white man.

25   I was nailing some boards on a broken crate when Frank came running into the vineyard.

26   "Our camp is attacked by white men!" he said. "Let's run for our lives!"

27   "I'm going back to Los Angeles," José said.

28   "Let's go to Fresno," I insisted.

29   We jumped into Frank's jalopy and started down the dirt road toward the highway. In Fresno the old car skidded into a ditch, and when we had lifted

---

[1] *Pinoys:* Filipino-American males.

it back to the highway, it would not run any more. Frank went to a garage and sold it. I told my companions that we could take the freight train to Stockton. I knew that the figs were about ready to be picked in Lodi.

30   We ran to the freight yards, only to discover that all the boxcars were loaded. I climbed to the top of a car that was full of crates and my companions followed me. The train was already moving when I saw four detectives with blackjacks climbing up the cars. I shouted to my companions to hide. I ran to the trap door of an icebox, watching where the detectives were going.

31   José was running when they spotted him. He jumped to the other car and hid behind a trap door, but two more detectives came from the other end and grabbed him. José struggled violently and freed himself, rolling on his stomach away from his captors. On his feet again, he tried to jump to the car ahead, but his feet slipped and he fell, shouting to us for help. I saw his hands clawing frantically in the air before he disappeared.

32   I jumped out first. Frank followed me, falling upon the cinders almost simultaneously. Then we were running to José. I thought at first he was dead. One foot was cut off cleanly, but half of the other was still hanging. Frank lifted José and told him to tie my handkerchief around his foot. We carried him to the ditch.

33   "Hold his leg," Frank said, opening a knife.

34   "Right." I gripped the bleeding leg with all my might, but when Frank put the sharp blade on it, I turned my face away.

35   José jerked and moaned, then passed out. Frank chewed some tobacco and spread it on the stump to keep the blood from flowing. Then we ran to the highway and tried to hail a car, but the motorists looked at us with scorn and spat into the wind. Then an old man came along in a Ford truck and drove us to the county hospital, where a kind doctor and two nurses assured us that they would do their best for him.

36   Walking down the marble stairway of the hospital, I began to wonder at the paradox of America. José's tragedy was brought about by railroad detectives, yet he had done no harm of any consequence to the company. On the highway, again, motorists had refused to take a dying man. And yet in this hospital, among white people—Americans like those who had denied us—we had found refuge and tolerance. Why was America so kind and yet so cruel? Was there no way to simplify things in this continent so that suffering would be minimized? Was there no common denominator on which we could all meet? I was angry and confused, and wondered if I would ever understand this paradox.

DISCUSSION QUESTIONS

1. The narrator says that he was at first "unaware of the vast social impli-cations of the discrimination against Filipinos." What was the result of this ignorance and who did he at first blame for this discrimination?
2. Filipinos and Japanese were housed in different sections of one farm where the author worked "to forestall any possible alliance." What might have been the result of such an alliance?
3. What was the paradox that the narrator recognized and does it still exist in America?

WRITING TOPICS

1. Research and report on the founding of the United Farmworkers of America by Cesar Chavez. The union later merged with the United Farmworkers' Organizing Committee and became the United Farm Workers (UFW).
2. In a brief essay, compare Carlos Bulosan's experiences of racial prej-udice with those of Sui Sin Far or another author in this anthology.

GUILTY ON BOTH COUNTS

Mitsuye Yamada

Born in Kyushu, Japan, in 1923 and raised in Seattle, Washington, Mitsuye Yamada earned a bachelor's degree from New York University and a master's degree from the University of Chicago. She is an emeritus professor of English at Cypress College, where she taught for twenty years.

Yamada is the founder of Multi-Cultural Women Writers of Orange County, and she coedited an anthology of the organization's work entitled *Sowing Ti Leaves: Writings by Multi-Cultural Women* (1990). She and poet Nellie Wong are the focus of *Mitsuye and Nellie: Asian American Poets,* a documentary film that came out in 1981. Yamada was also a board member of Amnesty International, U.S.A., and has served on Amnesty International's Committee on International Development. The poetic pieces in Yamada's *Camp Notes and Other Poems* (1976) recount her experiences in an internment camp in Idaho during World War II.

In the following selection from *Desert Run: Poems and Stories* (1988), the American speaker, revisiting her birthplace in Japan after forty years, learns some ironic lessons about the perception of guilt and the gulf between cultures. (J.I.)

I glide in by Bullet Train
to my birthplace in Kyushu
after forty years
only the elevated tracks
5   that dwarf the village scene
jangle my framed memory.

I am greeted by my cousin
the country doctor
"Ma yoku kite kureta."
10 So good of you to come.
Her new clinic overlooks
a sculpted pond stocked
with fifty active koi
flashing in the sun.
15 Nurses shuffle about
in quick steps
along the outer corridors

while I
the honored guest
20 am left alone talking
with Kiichan
the family mynah bird
perched at the hallway entrance
babbling in Japanese
25 *"Moshi moshi, moshi moshi
gomen nasai, gomen nasai."*
"Kiichan, try some English.
Hello hello, excuse me excuse me."

A human voice
30 interrupts us
*"Moshi moshi
gomen nasai."*
Standing at the threshhold
is a picture of a woman
35 in a stiff kimono top and pants:
the brim of her straw hat
tied close to her head
with a blue and white towel
balanced on one hip
40 a flat bamboo basket
heavy with slender Japanese egg plants
giant cucumbers in alternate spokes
in the middle a small round watermelon.

Here is real local color
45 a rare sight in modern Japan.
I want to run for my camera
but the picture speaks
"Gomen nasai isogashii toko . . ."

Excuse me I'm sorry to bother you but . . .
50 I muster up my best American Japanese
"Iiye sonna koto ari masen"
Oh no, not at all
she places the basket at my feet
"Dozo, kore Sensei ni . . ."
55 Please, this is for the doctor.

She hesitates
her mouth a tight-lipped polite smile
aware of my grinning rudeness
I descend to my knees
60 *"Arigatoh gozai masu."*
Thank you very much.
I practice my best bow
"Arigotoh gozai masu."
I trot out my kin credentials
65 to accept her gift.
"You see, I am the doctor's cousin
visiting from America."

My cousin's voice
a soft drumroll
70 drops between us.
"Mah
how beautiful
Arigatoh
Shiro-san
75 you are
always
so generous,"
but the gift bearer's eyes
smash through our ceremonies.
80 She is gone.

"Yurushite yatte?"
Will you forgive her?
This is August
She is from Hiroshima
85 *"Tondemo nai koto dakedo . . ."*
This is outrageous but
you see . . .
her whole family . . .

I stop her with a wave of my hand.
90 I understand I say
"America demo . . ."
in America too
many people blame
me, you
95 for Pearl Harbor

She is wide-eyed.
"Nani? America demo . . ."
"What? In America too . . ."
She touches her nose
100 with her forefinger
a gesture I remember from childhood.
"Sonna koto watashiga . . . ?"
They think I . . . ?
I would do such a thing?
105 I tap my own nose facing her
"Hai, watashimo."
Yes, and me.

The Bullet Train whirs past
on elevated tracks
110 over miles of plush green rice fields
nine hours from Tokyo.

DISCUSSION QUESTIONS

1. What is the setting of the poem?
2. Why does the speaker want to photograph the visitor?
3. What is it about the speaker that makes the gift-bearer leave?
4. What causes the speaker's cousin's amazement?

WRITING TOPICS

1. In an essay discuss the use of contrast in this poem.
2. Do those who were not alive at the time of World War II but whose country killed or maimed many people have any responsibility to that country or to descendants of those people? Discuss this question in a persuasive essay.

WILSHIRE BUS

Hisaye Yamamoto

Hisaye Yamamoto was born in 1921 in Redondo Beach, California, to Japanese immigrant parents. She began writing during her teen years and continued to develop as a writer while incarcerated in a World War II internment camp in Poston, Arizona. During her internment years, she served as a reporter and columnist for the *Poston Chronicle* (the camp newspaper) and published her first fiction work, "Death Rides the Rails to Poston." She also befriended Wakako Yamauchi, who is now a prominent Japanese American playwright.

Yamamoto left camp for a brief period to work as a cook in Springfield, Massachusetts, but she returned to Arizona after learning that her brother had been killed in combat in Italy. After the war she worked as a reporter for the *Los Angeles Tribune,* an African American publication, and then moved to Staten Island to do volunteer work on a Catholic Worker rehabilitation farm. She is married to Anthony DeSoto, has five children, and lives in southern California.

Her most widely studied and anthologized story is entitled "Seventeen Syllables." In this dense short story set in pre–World War II California, Yamamoto explores the harsh agricultural life of a Japanese American family. "Seventeen Syllables" takes up several of the themes found in Yamamoto's other stories: generational and gender conflict, sexual awakening, silence and speech, economic hardship, and the pursuit of culture. Other well-known pieces by Yamamoto include "Yoneko's Earthquake," "The Legend of Miss Sasagawara," and "The Brown House." In May 1991 "Seventeen Syllables" and "Yoneko's Earthquake" were woven together to create *Hot Summer Winds,* an American Playhouse drama produced by PBS. The Before Columbus Foundation recognized Yamamoto with the American Book Award for Lifetime Achievement in 1986.

In "Wilshire Bus," taken from *Seventeen Syllables and Other Stories* (1988), Yamamoto tells the story of Esther Kuroiwa, a woman who takes a short bus ride to visit her husband, who is a patient at a military hospital. During her short trip, a white passenger verbally harasses a Chinese American couple while Esther looks on in silence. In this extremely compressed story, Yamamoto investigates the relationships between Asian Americans of different national/ethnic backgrounds, the tensions between silence and speech, and the difficulties of intervening in uncomfortable situations. (J.I.)

1   Wilshire Boulevard begins somewhere near the heart of downtown Los Angeles and, except for a few digressions scarcely worth mentioning, goes straight out to the edge of the Pacific Ocean. It is a wide boulevard and traffic on it is fairly fast. For the most part, it is bordered on either side with examples of the recent stark architecture which favors a great deal of glass. As the boulevard approaches the sea, however, the landscape becomes a bit more pastoral, so that the university and the soldiers' home there give the appearance of being huge country estates.

2   Esther Kuroiwa got to know this stretch of territory quite well while her husband Buro was in one of the hospitals at the soldiers' home. They had been married less than a year when his back, injured in the war, began troubling him again, and he was forced to take three months of treatments at Sawtelle before he was able to go back to work. During this time, Esther was permitted to visit him twice a week and she usually took the yellow bus out on Wednesdays because she did not know the first thing about driving and because her friends were not able to take her except on Sundays. She always enjoyed the long bus ride very much because her seat companions usually turned out to be amiable, and if they did not, she took vicarious pleasure in gazing out at the almost unmitigated elegance along the fabulous street.

3   It was on one of these Wednesday trips that Esther committed a grave sin of omission which caused her later to burst into tears and which caused her acute discomfort for a long time afterwards whenever something reminded her of it.

4   The man came on the bus quite early and Esther noticed him briefly as he entered because he said gaily to the driver, "You robber. All you guys do is take money from me every day, just for giving me a short lift!"

5   Handsome in a red-faced way, graying, medium of height, and dressed in a dark gray sport suit with a yellow-and-black flowered shirt, he said this in a nice, resonant, carrying voice which got the response of a scattering of titters from the bus. Esther, somewhat amused and classifying him as a somatotonic, promptly forgot about him. And since she was sitting alone in

the first regular seat, facing the back of the driver and the two front benches facing each other, she returned to looking out the window.

6   At the next stop, a considerable mass of people piled on and the last two climbing up were an elderly Oriental man and his wife. Both were neatly and somberly clothed and the woman, who wore her hair in a bun and carried a bunch of yellow and dark red chrysanthemums, came to sit with Esther. Esther turned her head to smile a greeting (well, here we are, Orientals together on a bus), but the woman was watching, with some concern, her husband who was asking directions of the driver.

7   His faint English was inflected in such a way as to make Esther decide he was probably Chinese, and she noted that he had to repeat his question several times before the driver could answer it. Then he came to sit in the seat across the aisle from his wife. It was about then that a man's voice, which Esther recognized soon as belonging to the somatotonic, began a loud monologue in the seat just behind her. It was not really a monologue, since he seemed to be addressing his seat companion, but this person was not heard to give a single answer. The man's subject was a figure in the local sporting world who had a nice fortune invested in several of the shining buildings the bus was just passing.

8   "He's as tight-fisted as they make them, as tight-fisted as they come," the man said. "Why, he wouldn't give you the sweat off his . . ." He paused here to rephrase his metaphor, ". . . wouldn't give you the sweat off his palm!"

9   And he continued in this vein, discussing the private life of the famous man so frankly that Esther knew he must be quite drunk. But she listened with interest, wondering how much of this diatribe was true, because the public legend about the famous man was emphatic about his charity. Suddenly, the woman with the chrysanthemums jerked around to get a look at the speaker and Esther felt her giving him a quick but thorough examination before she turned back around.

10   "So you don't like it?" the man inquired, and it was a moment before Esther realized that he was now directing his attention to her seat neighbor.

11   "Well, if you don't like it," he continued, "why don't you get off this bus, why don't you go back where you came from? Why don't you go back to China?"

12   Then, his voice growing jovial, as though he were certain of the support of the bus in this at least, he embroidered on this theme with a new eloquence. "Why don't you go back to China, where you can be coolies working in your bare feet out in the rice fields? You can let your pigtails grow and grow in China. Alla samee, mama, no tickee no shirtee. Ha, pretty good, no tickee no shirtee!"

13   He chortled with delight and seemed to be looking around the bus for approval. Then some memory caused him to launch on a new idea. "Or why

don't you go back to Trinidad? They got Chinks running the whole she-bang in Trinidad. Every place you go in Trinidad . . ."

14   As he talked on, Esther, pretending to look out the window, felt the tenseness in the body of the woman beside her. The only movement from her was the trembling of the chrysanthemums with the motion of the bus. Without turning her head, Esther was also aware that a man, a mild-looking man with thinning hair and glasses, on one of the front benches was smiling at the woman and shaking his head mournfully in sympathy, but she doubted whether the woman saw.

15   Esther herself, while believing herself properly annoyed with the speaker and sorry for the old couple, felt quite detached. She found herself wondering whether the man meant her in his exclusion order or whether she was identifiably Japanese. Of course, he was not sober enough to be interested in such fine distinctions, but it did matter, she decided, because she was Japanese, not Chinese, and therefore in the present case immune. Then she was startled to realize that what she was actually doing was gloating over the fact that the drunken man had specified the Chinese as the unwanted.

16   Briefly, there bobbled on her memory the face of an elderly Oriental man whom she had once seen from a streetcar on her way home from work. (This was not long after she had returned to Los Angeles from the concentration camp in Arkansas and had been lucky enough to get a clerical job with the Community Chest.) The old man was on a concrete island at Seventh and Broadway, waiting for his streetcar. She had looked down on him benignly as a fellow Oriental, from her seat by the window, then been suddenly thrown for a loop by the legend on a large lapel button on his jacket. I AM KOREAN, said the button.

17   Heat suddenly rising to her throat, she had felt angry, then desolate and betrayed. True, reason had returned to ask whether she might not, under the circumstances, have worn such a button herself. She had heard rumors of I AM CHINESE buttons. So it was true then; why not I AM KOREAN buttons, too? Wryly, she wished for an I AM JAPANESE button, just to be able to call the man's attention to it, "Look at me!" But perhaps the man didn't even read English, perhaps he had been actually threatened, perhaps it was not his doing—his solicitous children perhaps had urged him to wear the badge.

18   Trying now to make up for her moral shabbiness, she turned towards the little woman and smiled at her across the chrysanthemums, shaking her head a little to get across her message (don't pay any attention to that stupid old drunk, he doesn't know what he's saying, let's take things like this in our stride). But the woman, in turn looking at her, presented a face so impassive yet cold, and eyes so expressionless yet hostile, that Esther's overture fell quite flat.

19   Okay, okay, if that's the way you feel about it, she thought to herself. Then the bus made another stop and she heard the man proclaim ringingly,

"So clear out, all of you, and remember to take every last one of your slant-eyed pickaninnies with you!" This was his final advice as he stepped down from the middle door. The bus remained at the stop long enough for Esther to watch the man cross the street with a slightly exploring step. Then, as it started up again, the bespectacled man in front stood up to go and made a clumsy speech to the Chinese couple and possibly to Esther. "I want you to know," he said, "that we aren't all like that man. We don't all feel the way he does. We believe in an America that is a melting pot of all sorts of people. I'm originally Scotch and French myself." With that, he came over and shook the hand of the Chinese man.

20   "And you, young lady," he said to the girl behind Esther, "you deserve a Purple Heart or something for having to put up with that sitting beside you."

21   Then he, too, got off.

22   The rest of the ride was uneventful and Esther stared out the window with eyes that did not see. Getting off at last at the soldiers' home, she was aware of the Chinese couple getting off after her, but she avoided looking at them. Then, while she was walking towards Buro's hospital very quickly, there arose in her mind some words she had once read and let stick in her craw. People say, do not regard what he says, now he is in liquor. Perhaps it is the only time he ought to be regarded.

23   These words repeated themselves until her saving detachment was gone every bit and she was filled once again in her life with the infuriatingly helpless, insidiously sickening sensation of there being in the world nothing solid she could put her finger on, nothing solid she could come to grips with, nothing solid she could sink her teeth into, nothing solid.

24   When she reached Buro's room and caught sight of his welcoming face, she ran to his bed and broke into sobs that she could not control. Buro was amazed because it was hardly her first visit and she had never shown such weakness before, but solving the mystery handily, he patted her head, looked around smugly at his roommates, and asked tenderly, "What's the matter? You've been missing me a whole lot, huh?" And she, finally drying her eyes, sniffed and nodded and bravely smiled and answered him with the question, yes, weren't women silly?

DISCUSSION QUESTIONS

1. What has Esther's journey revealed to her about herself?
2. Why does she recall the man wearing the "I am Korean" button, and why was he wearing it?
3. Explain the statement that perhaps "the only time people ought to be regarded" is when they are "in liquor."
4. At the end Esther feels "once again" that there is "nothing solid." What do you think she means? When might she have felt this way before, and what has made her feel this way after the bus ride? What might it take for her to feel that there is something solid? Discuss in small groups.
5. Will Esther ever reveal her true feelings to her husband? Why or why not?

WRITING TOPICS

1. Retell this story from the point of view of the Chinese woman. How does she feel about the man's remarks? Why does she look at Esther impassively and coldly with hostile eyes? Does she somehow sense Esther's wish to distance herself?
2. In a short essay, discuss how the setting and plot of this story are linked. Consider these questions: What is the climax of the story? Where does the falling action end? What is the denouement?

FROM *No-No Boy*

John Okada

John Okada was born in Seattle, Washington, in 1923. He published only one novel, entitled *No-No Boy* (1957), before his death from a heart attack at the age of forty-seven. He and his wife, Dorothy, worked on another novel about the issei (first-generation Japanese American) immigrant experience, but this second novel never made it to press; in fact, Dorothy Okada destroyed the manuscript when she could not find a publisher that was interested in her and her husband's work.

Throughout Okada's life, writing and reading played important roles. In addition to writing fiction, he earned a degree in library studies from the University of Washington, worked at public libraries in both Seattle and Detroit, and held a position as a technical writer for Chrysler Missile Operations.

No-No Boy, the story of a young Japanese American man's return to Seattle after serving a prison sentence during World War II, went practically unnoticed by the reading public when it was first published by Charles Tuttle in 1957. In 1970 Jeffrey Chan, an Asian American literary critic and writer, discovered the novel, which had long been out of print, in a bookstore in San Francisco's Japan Town. After its "rediscovery," an excerpt from the novel appeared in *Aiiieeeee!*, an anthology of Asian American writing edited by Chan, Frank Chin, Shawn Wong, and Lawson Fusao Inada. In 1976 the novel again went to press under the auspices of the Combined Asian American Resources Project and the University of Washington Press. Since its reemergence, *No-No Boy* has received wide critical acclaim and much scholarly attention.

The title of Okada's novel refers to Japanese American men who, during World War II, gave negative responses to two questions at the end of a loyalty questionnaire entitled "Statement of United States Citizenship of Japanese Ancestry." This questionnaire was given to all Japanese Americans, aged seventeen or older, who were incarcerated in internment camps throughout the Western United States. The questions read as follows:

> No. 27. Are you willing to serve in the armed forces of the United States on combat duty wherever ordered?
> No. 28. Will you swear unqualified allegiance to the United States of America and faithfully defend the United States from any or all attack by foreign or domestic forces, and forswear any form of allegiance or obedience to the Japanese emperor, or to any other foreign government, power or organization?

Ichiro Yamada, Okada's protagonist, is a no-no boy who must contend with the repercussions of his answers to the loyalty questions, first spending time in prison and then returning to the racism of postwar Seattle. He receives much harassment from members of his own ethnic community. Okada himself was not a no-no boy; he served as a translator for the United States military and was discharged in 1946. In this excerpt, Ichiro deals with the problems that his wartime experiences pose as he tries to find employment. (J.I.)

1   Alone and feeling very much his aloneness, Ichiro drove the Oldsmobile back into the city proper and found a room in a small, clean hotel where the rates seemed reasonable. Having picked up a newspaper in the lobby, he turned to the classified section and studied the job ads. Most of them were for skilled or technical help, and only after considerable searching was he finally able to encircle with pencil three jobs which he felt he might be able to investigate with some degree of hope. Putting the paper aside, he washed, shaved, and put on a clean shirt.

2   I mustn't hesitate, he told himself. If I don't start right now and make myself look for work, I'll lose my nerve. There's no one to help me or give me courage now. All I know is that I've just got to find work.

3   With the folded paper under his arm, he walked the six blocks to the hotel which was advertising for porters. It was a big hotel with a fancy marquee that extended out to the street and, as he walked past it, he noticed a doorman stationed at the entrance. He went down to the end of the block and approached the hotel once more. He paused to light a cigarette. Then, when he saw the doorman watching, he started toward him.

4   "If it's a job you want, son, take the employee's entrance in the alley," said the doorman before he could speak.

5   He muttered his thanks a bit unsteadily and proceeded around and

through the alley. There was a sign over the door for which he was looking, and he went through it and followed other signs down the corridor to the employment office. Inside, two men and a woman, obviously other job seekers, sat at a long table filling out forms. A white-haired man in a dark suit, sitting behind a desk, looked at him and pointed to the wall. On it was another sign, a large one, instructing applicants to fill out one of the forms stacked on the long table, with pen and ink. He sat opposite the woman and studied the questions on the form. With some relief, he noted that there was nothing on the front that he couldn't adequately answer. As he turned it over, he saw the questions he couldn't answer. How was he to account for the past two years of the five for which they wanted such information as name of employer and work experience? What was he to put down as an alternative for military duty? There was no lie big enough to cover the enormity of his mistake. He put the form back on the stack and left without satisfying the questioning look on the face of the white-haired, dark-suited employment manager, because there really was nothing to be said.

6   Over a cup of coffee at a lunch counter, he examined the other two ads which he had selected for investigation. One was for a draftsman in a small, growing engineering office and the other for a helper in a bakery, the name of which he recognized as being among the larger ones. He figured that the bakery would give him a form to fill out just as the hotel had. As for the engineering office, if it wasn't a form, there would be questions. No matter how much or how long he thought about it, it seemed hopeless. Still, he could not stop. He had to keep searching until he found work. Somewhere, there was someone who would hire him without probing too deeply into his past. Wherever that someone was, it was essential that he find him.

7   Before further thought could reduce his determination to bitterness or despair or cowardice or utter discouragement, he boarded a trolley for fear that, if he took the time to walk back to the car, he would find a reason to postpone his efforts. The trolley, a trackless affair which drew its motive power from overhead wires, surged smoothly through the late morning traffic with its handful of riders.

8   It was a short ride to the new, brick structure which had recently been constructed in an area, once residential, but now giving way to the demands of a growing city. Low, flat, modern clinics and store buildings intermingled with rambling, ugly apartment houses of wood and dirt-ridden brick.

9   Striding up a path which curved between newly installed landscaping, Ichiro entered the offices of Carrick and Sons. A middle-aged woman was beating furiously upon a typewriter.

10   He waited until she finished the page and flipped it out expertly. "Mam, I . . ."

11   "Yes?" She looked up, meanwhile working a new sheet into the machine.

12   "I'm looking for a job. The one in the paper. I came about the ad."

13   "Oh, of course." Making final adjustments, she typed a couple of lines before she rose and peeked into an inner office. "Mr. Carrick seems to be out just now. He'll be back shortly. Sit down." That said, she resumed her typing.

14   He spotted some magazines on a table and started to leaf through a not-too-old issue of *Look*. He saw the pictures and read the words and turned the pages methodically without digesting any of it.

15   A muffled pounding resounded distantly through the building and he glanced at the woman, who met his gaze and smiled sheepishly. He returned to the flipping of the pages, wondering why she had smiled in that funny way, and she bent her head over the typewriter as soon as the pounding stopped and went back to work.

16   When the pounding noise came again, she muttered impatiently under her breath and went out of the room.

17   She was gone several minutes, long enough for him to get through the magazine. He was hunting through the pile of magazines in search of another when she stuck her head into the room and beckoned him to follow.

18   There was a big office beyond the door with a pile of rolled-up blueprints on a corner table and big photographs of buildings on the walls. They went through that and farther into the back, past a small kitchen and a utility room and, finally, came to stop by a stairway leading down into the basement.

19   "I told Mr. Carrick you were here. He's down there," the woman said, slightly exasperated.

20   As he started down, the same pounding began, only it was clearer now and he thought it sounded like a hammer being struck against a metal object of some kind. The object turned out to be what looked like a small hand tractor with a dozer blade in front, and a small man with unkempt gray hair was whacking away at it with a claw hammer.

21   "Mr. Carrick?" It was no use. There was too much noise, so he waited until the man threw the hammer down in disgust and straightened up with a groan.

22   "Cockeyed," the man said, rubbing both his hands vigorously over the top of his buttocks. "I guess I'll have to take her apart and do it over right." He smiled graciously. "Doesn't pay to be impatient, but seems I'll never learn. That there blade isn't quite level and I thought I could force her. I learned. Yup, I sure did. How does she look to you?"

23   "What is it?"

24   Mr. Carrick laughed, naturally and loudly, his small, round stomach shaking convulsively. "I'm Carrick and you're . . .?" He extended a soiled hand.

25   "Yamada, sir. Ichiro Yamada."

26   "Know anything about snowplows?"

27   ·"No, sir."

28   "Name's Yamada, is it?" The man pronounced the name easily.

29   "Yes, sir."

30   *"Nihongo wakarimasu ka?"*[1]

31   "Not too well."

32   "How did I say that?"

33   "You're pretty good. You speak Japanese?"

34   "No. I used to have some very good Japanese friends. They taught me a little. You know the Tanakas?"

35   He shook his head. "Probably not the ones you mean. It's a pretty common name."

36   "They used to rent from me. Fine people. Best tenants I ever had. Shame about the evacuation. You too, I suppose."

37   "Yes, sir."

38   "The Tanakas didn't come back. Settled out East someplace. Well, can't say as I blame them. What brought you back?"

39   "Folks came back."

40   "Of course. Portland's changed, hasn't it?"

41   "I'm from Seattle."

42   "That so?" He leaned over the snowplow and tinkered with the bolts holding the blade in place.

43   Thinking that spring was not far away, Ichiro ventured to ask: "Does it snow that much down·here?"

44   "How much is that?"

45   "Enough for a plow."

46   "No, it doesn't. I just felt I wanted to make one."

47   "Oh."

48   Adjusting a crescent wrench to fit the bolts, he grunted them loose and kicked the blade off. "Let's have some coffee." He rinsed off his hands at the sink and led the way up the stairs to the kitchen, where he added water to an old pot of coffee and turned on the burner.

49   "The Tanakas were fine people," he said, sitting down on a stool. In spite of his protruding belly and gray hair, he seemed a strong and energetic man. As he talked, his face had a way of displaying great feeling and exuberance. "The government made a big mistake when they shoved you people around. There was no reason for it. A big black mark in the annals of American history. I mean that. I've always been a big-mouthed, loud-talking, back-slapping American but, when that happened, I lost a little of my wind. I don't feel as proud as I used to, but, if the mistake has been made, maybe we've learned something from it. Let's hope so. We can still be the best damn nation in the world. I'm sorry things worked out the way they did."

---

[1] *Nihongo wakar imasu ka:* Do you understand Japanese?

50   It was an apology, a sincere apology from a man who had money and position and respectability, made to the Japanese who had been wronged. But it was not an apology to Ichiro and he did not know how to answer this man who might have been a friend and employer, a man who made a snowplow in a place where one had no need for a snowplow because he simply wanted one.

51   Mr. Carrick set cups on the table and poured the coffee, which was hot but weak. "When do you want to start?" he asked.

52   The question caught him unprepared. Was that all there was to it? Were there to be no questions? No inquiry about qualifications or salary or experience? He fumbled with his cup and spilled some coffee on the table.

53   "It pays two-sixty a month. Three hundred after a year."

54   "I've had two years of college engineering," he said, trying frantically to adjust himself to the unexpected turn of events.

55   "Of course. The ad was clear enough. You wouldn't have followed it up unless you thought you could qualify and, if you did, we'll soon find out. Don't worry. You'll work out. I got a feeling." He pursed his lips gingerly and sipped his coffee.

56   All he had to say was "I'll take it," and the matter would be settled. It was a stroke of good fortune such as he would never have expected. The pay was good, the employer was surely not to be equaled, and the work would be exactly what he wanted.

57   He looked at Mr. Carrick and said: "I'd like to think about it."

58   Was it disbelief or surprise that clouded the face of the man who, in his heartfelt desire to atone for the error of a big country which hadn't been quite big enough, had matter-of-factly said two-sixty a month and three hundred after a year when two hundred a month was what he had in mind when he composed the ad since a lot of draftsmen were getting less but because the one who came for the job was a Japanese and it made a difference to him? "Certainly, Ichiro. Take all the time you need."

59   And when he said that, Ichiro knew that the job did not belong to him, but to another Japanese who was equally as American as this man who was attempting in a small way to rectify the wrong he felt to be his own because he was a part of the country which, somehow, had erred in a moment of panic.

60   "I'm not a veteran," he said.

61   Mr. Carrick creased his brown, not understanding what he meant.

62   "Thanks for the coffee. I'm sorry I bothered you." He pushed himself back off the stool.

63   "Wait." His face thoughtfully grave, Mr. Carrick absently drew a clean handkerchief from his trousers pocket and ran it over the coffee which Ichiro had spilled. He straightened up quickly, saying simultaneously: "It's something I've said. God knows I wouldn't intentionally do anything to hurt you or anyone. I'm sorry. Can we try again, please?"

64   "You've no apology to make, sir. You've been very good. I want the job. The pay is tops. I might say I need the job, but it's not for me. You see, I'm not a veteran."

65   "Hell, son. What's that got to do with it? Did I ask you? Why do you keep saying that?"

66   How was he to explain? Surely he couldn't leave now without some sort of explanation. The man had it coming to him if anyone ever did. He was, above all, an honest and sincere man and he deserved an honest reply.

67   "Mr. Carrick, I'm not a veteran because I spent two years in jail for refusing the draft."

68   The man did not react with surprise or anger or incredulity. His shoulders sagged a bit and he suddenly seemed a very old man whose life's dream had been to own a snowplow and, when he had finally secured one, it was out of kilter. "I am sorry, Ichiro," he said, "sorry for you and for the causes behind the reasons which made you do what you did. It wasn't your fault, really. You know that, don't you?"

69   "I don't know, sir. I just don't know. I just know I did it."

70   "You mustn't blame yourself."

71   "I haven't much choice. Sometimes I think my mother is to blame. Sometimes I think it's bigger than her, more than her refusal to understand that I'm not like her. It didn't make sense. Not at all. First they jerked us off the Coast and put us in camps to prove to us that we weren't American enough to be trusted. Then they wanted to draft us into the army. I was bitter—mad and bitter. Still, a lot of them went in, and I didn't. You figure it out. Thanks again, sir."

72   He was in the front room and almost past the woman when Mr. Carrick caught up with him.

73   "Miss Henry," he said to the woman at the typewriter, and there was something about his manner that was calm and reassuring, "This is Mr. Yamada. He's considering the drafting job."

74   She nodded, smiling pleasantly. "You'll like it here," she said. "It's crazy, but you'll like it."

75   He walked with Ichiro to the door and drew it open. "Let me know when you decide."

76   They shook hands and Ichiro took the bus back to the hotel. He had every reason to be enormously elated and, yet, his thoughts were solemn to the point of brooding. Then, as he thought about Mr. Carrick and their conversation time and time again, its meaning for him evolved into a singularly comforting thought. There was someone who cared. Surely there were others too who understood the suffering of the small and the weak and, yes, even the seemingly treasonous, and offered a way back into the great compassionate stream of life that is America. Under the hard, tough cloak of the struggle for existence in which money and enormous white refrigerators and

shining, massive, brutally-fast cars and fine, expensive clothing had ostensibly overwhelmed the qualities of men that were good and gentle and just, there still beat a heart of kindness and patience and forgiveness. And in this moment when he thought of Mr. Carrick, the engineer with a yen for a snowplow that would probably never get used, and of what he had said, and, still more, of what he offered to do, he glimpsed the real nature of the country against which he had almost fully turned his back, and saw that its mistake was no less unforgivable than his own.

DISCUSSION QUESTIONS

1. What is your opinion of Mr. Carrick?
2. Explain why, in your opinion, Ichiro refuses to take the job offered him.
3. The word *epiphany* can mean a moment of heightened awareness or insight into a situation. What kind of epiphany did Ichiro experience?

WRITING TOPICS

1. In a brief essay, compare the conflicting and shifting emotions of Ichiro and Mr. Carrick. Discuss what you think to be their reasons for feeling as they do and how those feelings motivate them to act as they do.
2. Research and write a report on the internment of the Japanese during World War II and the reparations that were made many years later to those Japanese still living who had been sent to the relocation camps.

In This Heat

Willyce Kim

Willyce Kim was born in 1946 in Honolulu, Hawaii. She is the author of two works of fiction, *Dead Heat* (1988) and *Dancer Dawkins and the California Kid* (1985). She has published three books of poetry, *Under the Rolling Sky* (1976), *Eating Artichokes* (1972), and *Curtains of Light* (1971). Kim graduated from San Francisco College for Women in 1968 with a bachelor of arts degree in English literature. In the 1970s, she worked for the Women's Press Collective in Oakland, California. She taught for a while in Catholic elementary schools and is now a librarian in the Graduate Library of the University of California, Berkeley.

In the following poem, images of heat and darkness surround the telling of a stark tragedy.

In this heat
we gather ourselves
and hold together
day folding into night
5   we press for darkness
as if the heat
would steal away
like some errant ship,
vanquished by moon
10 and stars,
we close our eyes
the night half-swollen
with the whispers
of the day.
15 Out, across the way
a dog barks.

Yesterday,
a Chinese girl
with skin the color
20 of dragon's eyes
and hair as fine
as my beloved's
killed herself.
She answered an ad
25 in one of the dailies
and was raped
during the long interview.
No one believed her.
You know the old story.
30 Tonight I hold your
hands between my palms.
Afraid of yesterday.
Uncertain of tomorrow.
Outside the moon pales
35 against the window
as shadows lap across
the sky.
Sleep flutters
like burning incense.
40 We curl into darkness
and are gone.

DISCUSSION QUESTIONS

1. What incidents have prompted the writing of this poem?
2. What are the speaker's reactions to these incidents?
3. What is the speaker referring to in line 29?

WRITING TOPICS

1. In a brief essay, analyze the similes and metaphors in this poem, their appropriateness as well as their cultural references.

THE WASH

Philip Kan Gotanda

Philip Kan Gotanda, a sansei (third-generation Japanese American), was born in 1949 in Stockton, California. He originally planned to be a psychiatrist, but his interests in music and performance led him to playwriting. His first play, entitled *The Avocado Kid or Zen in the Art of Guacamole,* combines elements of a classic Japanese children's tale, music, dance, American popular culture, and colloquial language in an attempt to capture a "uniquely Asian American cultural aesthetic."[1] East West Players, an Asian American theater company based in Los Angeles, staged *The Avocado Kid* in 1978, and this successful initial foray into the world of drama encouraged Gotanda to pursue a career as a playwright. Other major works include *The Dream of Kitamura* (1982), *Song for a Nisei Fisherman* (1980), *Yankee Dawg You Die* (1988), *Fish Head Soup* (1991), and this anthology's selection, *The Wash* (1985).

Since his emergence as a playwright, Gotanda has also worked extensively with the Asian American Theatre Company, Northwest Asian American Theater, Pan Asian Repertory, Berkeley Repertory Theatre, and the Manhattan Theatre Club. He also holds a law degree.

In *The Wash,* a nisei (second-generation) woman leaves her husband, takes a lover, and attempts to make a new life for herself. As Michael Omi has noted, such behavior from a second-generation Japanese American woman is "unthinkable," for many wives were expected to sacrifice their own desires for the sake of husband and family. Gotanda says that in the play he wanted to demonstrate that "traditions which worked before are subject to the winds of change. I wanted to depict people struggling to live their lives after a serious

---

[1] Michael Omi, introduction to *Fish Head Soup and Other Plays,* Philip Kan Gotanda. Seattle: U. of Washington P., 1995, page xv.
[2] Ibid, page xix.

rupture in the way things are." In addition to exploring one woman's break from an unfulfilling marriage, this play serves as a commentary on gender dynamics and sexuality in nisei culture.

Note carefully the playwright's descriptions of and directions for the props, lighting, gestures, and setting, for they tell a great deal about the characters and the themes of the play. Stage directions are given from the viewpoint of the performers. Therefore, stage right is on the audience's left, stage left is on the audience's right, upstage is at the back of the stage and downstage is at the front of the set. (J.I.)

CHARACTERS

NOBU MATSUMOTO, Nisei (second-generation Japanese American), 68 years old, retired produce man. Separated from wife, Masi. Lives alone in the family house.

MASI MATSUMOTO, Nisei, 67 years old. Left Nobu. Does housework for a living. Lives in a small apartment by herself.

KIYOKO HASEGAWA, 55-ish, originally from Japan. Previously married to an American soldier. Widow. Seeing Nobu. Owns and runs a small Japanese restaurant.

SADAO NAKASOTO, Nisei, 65 years old, widower. Seeing Masi. Retired pharmacist.

MARSHA MATSUMOTO, Sansei (third-generation Japanese American), 33 years old, single. Older daughter of Nobu and Masi. Works as a dental hygienist in nearby big city.

JUDY ADAMS, Sansei, 29 years old, married to James with a baby. Younger daughter, fifth-grade teacher. Presently not working.

CHIYO FROELICH, originally from Japan, but has lived most of her adult life in the U.S. Late 40s, divorced, friend of Kiyoko. Owns and runs a small beauty salon next door to Kiyoko's restaurant.

BLACKIE, Hawaiian Nisei, 55-ish. Speaks with a thick pidgin accent. Works as the cook at Kiyoko's restaurant.

SETTING

Stage center is Nobu's place, the "old family home." Stage right is Kiyoko's restaurant. Stage left is Masi's small bedroom apartment. A clothesline runs across the upstage area. The down-stage area is used to play several scenes that take place elsewhere.

The set should be realistic but *elemental*, allowing for an underlying abstract feeling. Nobu's place is the most complete, with Masi's and Kiyoko's places more minimal, and Marsha's and Judy's places being represented by only a table and chairs.

The set as a whole must be constructed so that entrances, exits and crossovers may be easily viewed by the audience. This is because actors' movements from one area to another, both as focus action and as half-light action, are an integral part of the storytelling.

The play takes place in the present over a period of six months—July to January.

ACT ONE
SCENE 1

Nobu's place, the old family home. The kitchen is upstage. A sink, refrigerator, stove. There is a kitchen table with a pile of dirty clothes on it. On the stove, a pot of water is boiling. In the washrack there is a teapot, some dishes, chopsticks, etc. Stage left is a door that leads to the outside, the proverbial side-door entrance into the kitchen that every-one uses. Upstage right is a door leading to the hallway and bedrooms.

Down right, a TV. A long couch is angled facing it. On a long coffee table in front of the couch sits the yet undeveloped skeleton of a large kite Nobu is building. During the play, the kite becomes more and more pronounced in its construction.

The pile of dirty clothes is in a shaft of light. Lights come up to half revealing Nobu asleep lengthwise on the couch, facing the TV, a newspaper sprawled over his chest. Mouth open, snoring loudly. TV lights come up. Nobu can be seen in the flickering light of the televi-sion screen. Lights come up full. Nobu awakens with a start, news-paper falling to the floor. He pulls himself upright and just sits and stares into space for a moment, trying to awaken. Then he picks up the newspaper, tosses it in a heap on the couch. He checks to examine the progress he's making on the kite. He carefully sets the kite back on the table and shuffles over to the stove to shut the boiling water off. He gets a plate and a pair of chopsticks from the washrack, takes the two hot dogs that were cooking out of the pot and puts them on the plate. Then he gets some tea out and puts it into the teapot which he has taken from the rack. He moves to throw out the hot-dog water to boil some new water, then stops. Thinks. Proceeds to put the hot-dog water into the teapot and use it to make tea. Nobu reaches into the refrigerator and pulls out a bowl of cold rice covered over in cello-phane and a small bottle of French's mustard. He uncovers the rice, scoops some of it into a rice bowl using his chopsticks, pours hot tea over it. It starts to spill; he quickly bends down and slurps up the excess. He opens the mustard and, using his chopsticks again, shovels a healthy portion of mustard onto his hot dogs. He licks the mustard off his chopsticks. Then he carefully makes his way back to the couch with the plate of hot dogs and a bowl of rice. He sets the food down on the coffee table and begins to eat while working on the kite and watching television.

Masi enters through the side door with two large brown paper bags. She's struggling to open and close the door with both hands full. Nobu turns around and notices her but gives no greeting and makes no effort to help her. She is not upset by his actions. She appears to have no expectation for him to assist her. Masi sets both bags on the kitchen table and catches her breath.

MASI: *(Putting tomatoes and Japanese eggplant from one of the bags into refrigerator)* If you have any more dirty clothes I can take them now. Nobu? Is this everything?

NOBU: *(Not turning, eating)* Want some hot dog?

MASI: No, I ate before. Got these from Mr. Rossi. The tomatoes are soft so eat them right away. *(She gets up, folds paper bag and puts it into drawer. She knows this place well. Walks over and checks his shirt collar from behind)* No more clothes?

NOBU: *(Brushing her hand away)* No, already.

(Masi goes over to the other bag and begins unpacking the freshly washed clothes in neat piles on the kitchen table.)

MASI: I just finished cleaning Dr. Harrison's place. You should see the bathrooms. If you see the family walk down the street, they look so clean and neat. But the toilets, *kitanai* [dirty].

(Finished unpacking, Masi takes a cup out of the rack and pours herself a cup of tea. She walks over to the couch and sits down next to Nobu and watches TV. She takes a sip of tea and makes a face.)

NOBU: Hot-dog water.

(Masi decides not to drink it. She looks at the unfinished kite frame.)

MASI: You gonna fly this one? *(Picks up the kite)* Nobu, why don't you at least try a different design this—

NOBU: (*Taking kite*) My old man did it this way.

(*Masi gets up and starts to pick up the old clothes on the floor, fold them and put them in the second bag.*)

MASI: Have you talked to the kids? (*No response*) Marsha said she stopped by. (*Beat*) You know if you don't see Judy's baby soon he's going to be all grown up. Nobu?

NOBU: *No.*

(*Masi gives up trying to talk to him at all. Finishes putting old clothes into the bag.*)

MASI: No more dirty clothes, Nobu? (*Nobu shakes his head without turning away from the TV*) All right, then I'm going.

(*Masi leaves with the bag of old clothes. Nobu continues to watch TV for a few moments, then turns and stares at the door. Dim to half with the TV light illuminating Nobu. Marsha appears in a pool of light looking towards Nobu.*)

MARSHA: Dad?

(*Nobu turns to look at Marsha momentarily then back to the television. Judy appears in a pool of light, holding Timothy. Marsha fades out.*)

JUDY: Mom?

(*Masi, moving away, turns to look at Judy momentarily, then exits. Judy fades out. Lights fade on Nobu and Masi. We hear Japanese restaurant Muzak.*)

SCENE 2

Kiyoko's restaurant, afternoon, next day, upstage right. On upstage side wall there is a service window. Left of it is a swinging door that leads into kitchen. There is a small counter space with three or four small stools. Downstage there are one or two small tables with chairs.

    Lights come up. Blackie can be seen in the service window. He is taking a big swig of Budweiser. Kiyoko appears and gives him a dirty look. Blackie's been caught in the act.

KIYOKO: Blackie.

BLACKIE: It make my cooking get mo' better. (*Kiyoko stares, no response*) It make me get mo' better. (*Kiyoko continues to stare*) I'm thirsty. I wanted a beer.

KIYOKO: *(Taking bottle away)* You're always thirsty, you're always hungry. You're the cook. You're supposed to cook the food, not eat it all up. Now go wipe the tables.

(She hands him a towel and scoots him out the swinging door.)

BLACKIE: It makes my cooking get mo' better. If I feel better, my cooking get mo' better. No bull lie, yo.

KIYOKO: Your face gets red like a tomato and everything tastes like shoyu [soy sauce].

(Blackie stops and scratches his butt. Kioyko knocks his hand away.)

Don't scratch your *oshiri*. You're the cook, 'member?

(Nobu enters.)

NOBU: Kiyoko, *dō desu ka* [how are you]?

KIYOKO: *(Grabbing towel away from Blackie)* Give me that. *(Walks past Nobu, ignoring him)*

BLACKIE: Hey, brudda, you in the doghouse!

NOBU: What?

(Kiyoko finishes taking a few swipes at a tabletop.)

Kiyoko, tempura special, *onegai* [please] . . .

(Kiyoko ignores him again, moving behind the counter, wiping.)

BLACKIE: *(To Nobu)* You in the doghouse. But it going pass. *(He exits into kitchen area)*

NOBU: *(Moving to counter and seating himself)* What? What?

(Kiyoko tosses a small plate of tsukemono *[pickles] in front of him and continues to wipe around him. Nobu looks at the plate.)*

You know I don't like this kind of pickle.

KIYOKO: *(Looks at him hard, tossing towel on the counter)* I'll get your tea. *(She exits into kitchen)*

BLACKIE: *(Pokes head out of service window holding Nobu's plate in one hand)* We drop food on the floor, we pick it up. If we like you . . .*(Mimes throwing the food away) But,* if you in the doghouse . . . *(Mimes dropping food back on plate, then barks at it)*

(Blackie withdraws as Kiyoko enters with Nobu's tea.)

NOBU: *(To Kiyoko)* I like eggplant. You know that. You always give me
         eggplant pickle.
KIYOKO: *(Pouring tea)* Out of season.
NOBU: Masi brought some by yesterday with the wash.
KIYOKO: Nobu-chan, I *said* I'd do the wash for you. You gotta washing
         machine at your place. I can just come over and—
NOBU: No, no, too much trouble. I can do it myself. I don't like cucum-
         ber pickle.
KIYOKO: Nobu, how could you forget?
NOBU: I didn't. You did.
KIYOKO: I kept dropping hints . . .
NOBU: I like *eggplant.* You know that.
KIYOKO: All last week.
NOBU: Eggplant! Eggplant!
KIYOKO: *(Pause, glaring at him)* WE RAN OUT!

*(Kiyoko stomps into the kitchen. Nobu sits there stunned and very puzzled.
Blackie enters carrying a plate of food and sets it down in front of Nobu.)*

BLACKIE: Tempura special.

*(Blackie watches while sipping on a beer. Nobu is about to put a fork-load
into his mouth, then stops. Looks at food, then at Blackie. Blackie makes a
barking sound and grins. Suddenly something dawns on Nobu.)*

NOBU: Her birthday, I forgot her birthday. . .

(Cross-fade to Masi's apartment.)

SCENE 3

*Masi's place, three weeks later. Small apartment, with bedroom
downstage from main room. Sadao, seated on sofa, in a pool of light.
Masi is in half-light at counter fixing two cups of Sanka.*

SADAO: We were all sitting around in somebody's living room, when
          someone said, "How come you still wear your wedding ring?"
          They weren't being mean. That's why we were there. To ask
          those kinds of things. I didn't know what to say. Speechless.
          Then someone else said, "Sadao, you always complain about not

meeting people, not being able to start a new life—how come you still wear your ring?" I began to cry. Like a little boy. I remember thinking, "How strange I am crying in front of all these people that I don't know. And yet I feel no shame." The room was so still. All you could hear was my crying. Then I heard a tapping sound. I looked up and noticed a woman sitting across from me, slapping the sandals she was wearing against the bottom of her feet. Tap, tap, tap. . . . I said I didn't know why. It just never crossed my mind to take it off. "Why should I take the ring off?" Then one of the widows, the one who formed the group, said, "Because you're not married anymore."

(Lights come up on the rest of the apartment area. Masi wasn't quite pre-pared for Sadao's sharing such personal details and is a bit unsure how to respond. Sadao in turn fears he may have gotten a bit carried away.)

MASI: *(Bringing coffee over)* Cream? It's nondairy creamer. *(Sadao shakes head)* If you want tea?
SADAO: No, this is fine. I ran on a bit, didn't I?
MASI: No, no, it's all right. *(Pause)* It's just Sanka.
SADAO: Good. Otherwise the caffeine keeps me up all night. Have you tried decaffeinated coffee?

(Masi motions to the Sanka, unsure of what he means.)

           No, the bean. They actually make a decaffeinated bean.
MASI: No, we never did anything like that. Just instant. Yuban makes a good instant coffee. That's what I usually drink. But I don't have any since I moved over here.
SADAO: No, I've never tried it.
MASI: I'll have to get some next time I go shopping.
SADAO: They have this process they use. On the bean. I mean they don't grow a decaffeinated bean. I don't know what's worse. The caf-feine in it or the chemicals they use to get the caffeine out. *(Laughs at his own joke, gathering momentum)* I have a little grinder. A Braun? You know a Braun?

(Masi doesn't know what it is. Awkward pause.)

MASI: We never did anything like that. We just drink instant.
SADAO: I like Sanka. I have to drink it all the time. Doctor's orders. *(Imitating)* "If you drink coffee, Sadao, drink Sanka!" *(He*

laughs valiantly at his attempt at humor. Masi stares at her cup. He notices and offers a feeble explanation) Blood pressure . . .

(They both drink in silence. Suddenly Sadao remembers something.)

Oh. Excuse me. I'll be right back. I left something in the car . . . *(Sadao's voice trails off as he exits. Masi sits there uncomfortably. This isn't working out. Sadao returns with a fishing pole and reel wrapped up like presents. Nobu appears in half-light at his place watching TV, his face illuminated by the flickering screen's glow.)*

MASI: *(Surprised)* Sadao, what's this?

(Sadao holds out pole.)

           I can't.
SADAO: No, no, it's for you.
MASI: But Sadao . . .
SADAO: No, no, it's for you.
MASI: *(One hand on it)* Sadao, you shouldn't have.
SADAO: Go 'head. Open it up.
MASI: *(Takes it and begins unwrapping it)* No, I can't accept this. I don't have anything for you.

(Masi unwraps pole, which is broken down into pieces. Sadao sets reel on table and takes pole from Masi.)

SADAO: Here, let me show you. *(Puts it together)* There. *(Hands it back. Remembers reel, hands it to her)* Oh, and here's this.

(Masi now has a reel and pole in her hands. Sadao realizes she can't unwrap the reel with both hands full and takes pole away. She unwraps the reel. Sadao promptly takes it away from her and puts the pole and reel together.)

           See, it goes like this. And then you're all set to catch fish. *(Hands it back to Masi)* I told you I was going to take you. Now you can't refuse.
MASI: Yeah, but . . .
SADAO: Thought I was kidding, huh?
MASI: But this is so expensive. I know how much these things cost, 'cause of Nobu. I don't know anything about fishing. He's the fisherman. I just pack the lunch and off he goes.

SADAO: Well, this time you're going and it's lots of fun. Economical, too. You get to eat what you catch.

MASI: But you have to do all that walking.

SADAO: No, who said that? We sit on the bank and fish from there. We'll pack a good lunch—I'll make it—you bring the cards so we can play blackjack. We have to practice.

MASI: I don't play.

SADAO: That's why we have to practice so we can go to Tahoe. If there's a good game on we'll have to watch it. I'll bring my portable TV. I love the Giants.

MASI: What about fishing?

SADAO: Only if we have time. See, this is how you cast out. *(Demonstrating)* You hook your index finger around the line here. Turn the bail and . . . *(He casts)*

(Nobu, still in half-light, gets up to phone Masi. Phone rings. Masi goes over and answers it. It's Nobu. Slowly lights dim on Sadao and rest of apartment so that just Masi and Nobu are lit.)

MASI: Hello.

NOBU: You coming to pick up the clothes?

MASI: Nobu I was just there. You mean next week? Don't worry, I'll be there. I do it every week, don't I? Nobu?

NOBU: I'm not worried. You all right?

MASI: Yes, I'm all right. Did you want something? *(No response)* I got more vegetables. Do you need some more?

NOBU: No. *(Pause)* Can you bring more eggplant?

MASI: I don't have any more.

NOBU: All right, then.

MASI: I'll ask Mr. Rossi. He can always get lots more. *(Pause)* Was there something else? Did you want something?

NOBU: No.

(Pause)

MASI: Nobu, I have to go now.

NOBU: I went fishing so I got a lot of dirty clothes.

MASI: All right. Don't worry, I'll be by.

NOBU: I'm not worried.

MASI: Bye.

NOBU: Bye.

(Dim to darkness.)

SCENE 4

Kiyoko's restaurant, three weeks later, night. Kiyoko, Chiyo, Blackie are playing five-card stud. When the scene starts they each have one card down and two up. Chiyo is in the process of dealing the next card, Kiyoko to her left, Blackie to her right. Chiyo wears a poker visor. Five empty beer bottles sit in front of Blackie, who is working on a sixth. He is not drunk, though. Hawaiian music is playing on his large portable tape player.

CHIYO: *(Examining her hand)* He's got a wife. You said so yourself.

KIYOKO: They're separated.

CHIYO: He wants to get back together. I know his kind. She left him. They can't get over that. He only wants you for one thing— your "tempura." Yeah. He's over your restaurant everyday, *desho* [isn't that so]? You feeding him. He's eating up all your profits.

(Chiyo and Kiyoko notice Blackie chugging down the rest of his beer, making strange gurgling sounds. They stare.)

BLACKIE: You gotta drink beer when you're playing poker or you aren't playing poker. You're just playing cards. I don't like cards, hate cards. *(Holds up another beer)* I love poker.

KIYOKO: Nobu is a good man.

CHIYO: You like to mother him, you like that kind of thing. But you don't know about men.

KIYOKO: And you do, heh?

CHIYO: You don't get out of this restaurant of yours, I tell you, "Go out, go out." "No, I gotta work, work . . ." *(Noticing something)* Wait, wait, someone didn't ante. We only bet once, a nickel, right? *(Counting)* See. Someone didn't ante.

KIYOKO: I did.

CHIYO: So did I.

(They turn to Blackie, who's guzzling a beer.)

BLACKIE: Huh? Oh, yeah. *(Innocently tosses money in)*

CHIYO: *(Begins to deal, to Kiyoko)* Two sixes—a pair of saxophones. *(To Blackie)* A three of diamonds gives you . . . nothing. *(To self)* Eight of puppy toes to the dealer, working on a possible club flush. *(To Kiyoko)* Pair of saxes high. I just can't see myself going out with him.

KIYOKO: Nobu is an honest man. Not like that guy you've been seeing. Check.
CHIYO: Ray, his name is Ray. Blackie.
BLACKIE: *(Carefully examining his cards)* Yeah, I know.
KIYOKO: That time Blackie gave Nobu too much change. Remember? He walked all the way back from his house to return it—twenty-five cents.
CHIYO: Good investment. He gets a $4.50 combo plate free now. *(To Blackie)* Your bet.
BLACKIE: Don't rush me, don't rush me.
CHIYO: *(To Blackie)* You're queen high, working on a possible nothing. *(Motioning to her own cards)* Possible club flush here and . . . *(Pointing to Kiyoko's hand)* A pair of saxes there, possible three-of-a-kind. *(To Kiyoko)* I just think you can do better, that's all I'm saying. Besides, he's so old.
KIYOKO: I don't want to talk about it.

(Blackie finally decides to bet but Chiyo ignores him and goes right ahead.)

CHIYO: Dealer bets a nickel.
KIYOKO: He's not old.
CHIYO: Is he good in bed?
KIYOKO: He's sixty-eight years old, Chiyo. I raise you a dime.
CHIYO: So he really is old. See you and I bump you a quarter.
BLACKIE: I love it when the wahines talk dirt. *(They stare at him)* Jeez, just joking. Don't lose your coconut.

(As Blackie begins putting in the bets he missed Kiyoko and Chiyo continue on.)

KIYOKO: *(Tossing quarter in)* I call.
CHIYO: *(Starting to deal; to Kiyoko)* Nine of spades. No help there. *(To Blackie)* A trois. Oh, a pair of threes. *(To self)* And for the dealer . . . another club. Read 'em and weep. Four puppy toes looking mighty pretty. Hush, very possible. *(To Kiyoko)* Pair of saxes still high.
KIYOKO: Chiyo, you don't know him like I do. Check.

(She notices Blackie sucking on his beer.)

            He checks, too.
CHIYO: I'm just saying you could find someone else. Someone younger, more fun.

KIYOKO: *(Irritated)* You watch too many soap operas, Chiyo. Life's not like that. Men don't fall into your lap.

CHIYO: *(Upset at being lectured to)* Fifty cents. . .

BLACKIE: *(Impressed)* Fifty cents . . .

KIYOKO: *I like Nobu.* One dollar.

BLACKIE: *(In disbelief)* One dollar . . .

CHIYO: All right, all right, white hair doesn't bother me. It's no hair I can't stand. *(Tosses in dollar)* Call you. You got the three-of-kind?

KIYOKO: Pair of sixes, that's all. You got the flush?

CHIYO: Pair of eights! Hah!

(Kiyoko's disgusted. Chiyo's about to grab the pot when Blackie puts down his cards. Kiyoko and Chiyo stare in disbelief.)

BLACKIE: *(Puffing up like a rooster)* Excusez-moi's but I got three trois's.

CHIYO: Blackie . . .

(Blackie shovels the pot in. Kiyoko pushes the cards to Chiyo, who examines them skeptically.)

KIYOKO: *(To Chiyo)* Your wash. *(To Blackie)* Blackie, cut.

(Blackie cuts the shuffled deck and Kiyoko begins to deal.)

BLACKIE: *(Holding up beer)* Hate cards. *Love* poker. *(He starts to guzzle)*

KIYOKO: *(Dealing)* Today is the fifteenth, *neh* [isn't it]? *(Stops, reflecting)* Harry would have been fifty-nine this week.

(Chiyo and Blackie exchange glances. Cross fade to Nobu's place.)

SCENE 5

Nobu's place, same day as previous scene. Nobu's seated and Marsha's working in the kitchen.

NOBU: What do you mean, "Be nice to Mama"?

MARSHA: All I'm saying is, just try to be nice to her when she gets here. Say something nice about the way she looks or about her—

NOBU: I'm always nice to Mama. I'm always good to her. *(Pause)* Why the hell she has to live over there? Huh? How come Mama's got to live way over there?

(Masi enters, carrying a small paper bag.)

MARSHA: Hi Mom, come on in. *(Taking bag)* Here let me help you. Dad's already here.

MASI: *(To Nobu)* Just some leftover fruit that was in the icebox. Starting to rot so eat it right away.

(Masi and Nobu acknowledge each other awkwardly.)

MARSHA: Judy and the baby couldn't make it.

MASI: She called me.

(Nobu's expression reveals he didn't know they were coming.)

MARSHA: *(Offering explanation to Nobu)* Jimmy wasn't going to come. *(Pause)* Sit down, sit down. Dinner's almost ready in a minute. Roast beef. Dad, coffee? Tea for you, Mom?

(Marsha goes to kitchen. Silence.)

NOBU: I told her we can eat at her place. *(Beat)* She wanted to cook dinner here.

(Pause)

MASI: Her place is cozy, *neh?*

NOBU: Marsha's? Looks like the rooms back in Camp.

MASI: Nobu, the Camps were over forty years ago. At least she's clean. Not like the younger one.

(Pause)

NOBU: How you been?

MASI: All right.

NOBU: *Isogashi no* [Busy]?

MASI: No. The usual.

NOBU: I called the other night, no one answered. *(Masi doesn't offer an explanation)* How you been?

MARSHA: *(Interrupts, carrying in an ashtray)* Dad, Mom's taking a ceramics class. Judy got her to go. *(Hands him the ashtray)* She made this. *(Nobu stares at it)*

MASI: It's an ashtray.

NOBU: You don't smoke.

MASI: I'll get Daddy's coffee. *(She exits with cup)*

MARSHA: Dad, just say you like it. That's all you have to say. Just say it's nice.

NOBU: Yeah, but she doesn't smoke. Why make an ashtray if you don't smoke?

(Masi returns with a cup of coffee for Nobu and tea for herself. Marsha gives Nobu an encouraging nudge and exits into kitchen.)

              (Holding ashtray) It's a nice ashtray. Is this where you go all the time? I call in the evening. I guess that's where you must be. *(Pause)* Remember those dances they used to have in the Camps? You were a good dancer. You were. Best in the Camps.

MASI: You couldn't dance at all. You were awful.

NOBU: Remember that fellow Chester Yoshikawa? That friend of yours?

MASI: He could dance so good.

NOBU: Remember that dance you were supposed to meet me out front of the canteen? We were all going to meet there and then go to the dance together. Shig, Chester, and a couple others. Everybody else, they went on ahead. I waited and waited . . .

MASI: Nobu, that was forty years ago.

NOBU: Yeah, I know, but remember you were supposed to meet—

MASI: That's over forty years ago. How can I remember something like that?

NOBU: You didn't show up. Chester didn't show up either.

(Masi puts cream and sugar into Nobu's coffee.)

MASI: Nobu, didn't we talk about this? I'm sure we did. Probably something came up and I had to help Mama and Papa.

NOBU: Where were you, huh?

MASI: How am I supposed to remember that far back? Chester died in Italy with the rest of the 442 boys.

NOBU: Where the hell were you?

MASI: How in the hell am I supposed to remember that far back?

NOBU: *(Noticing his coffee)* *You* put the cream and sugar in. That's not mine. *(Pushes coffee away)*

MASI: That's right. *You* like to put the cream and sugar in yourself.

NOBU: I like to put it in myself.

MASI: *(Pushing the cup towards him)* It's the way you like it, the same thing.

NOBU: *(Pushes it back)* No, it's not the same thing.

MASI: All right, all right, I'll drink it myself. Here, you can drink mine. *(She shoves her tea to Nobu and grabs the coffee cup)*

NOBU: What are you doing—wait, wait.

MASI: I don't mind.

(Masi starts to raise cup, but Nobu reaches for it.)

NOBU: It's no good for you, Mama. Your blood pressure. Remember
         what Doc Takei—
MASI: *(Clinging to cup)* Who gives a damn. You make such a fuss about
         it. *Monku, monku, monku* [Kvetch, kvetch, kvetch]. *I'll* drink it.
NOBU: *(Struggling with Masi)* It's no good for you, Mama.

(Coffee spills onto table. Marsha appears with a towel.)

NOBU: *(To Masi)* Clean it up.
MASI: I'm not going to clean it up.
MARSHA: I'll clean it up.

*(While Marsha starts to wipe the table, Masi grabs Nobu's coffee cup and
exits into the kitchen.)*

MASI: I'll get him more coffee.
MARSHA: Dad.

*(Masi returns with Nobu's coffee and sets it down in front of him, turns
and quickly exits.)*

(Chasing after Masi) Mom . . .

*(Nobu is left alone with his cup of coffee. He slowly puts in the cream and
sugar himself. Raises the cup to his lips but cannot drink. Sets it back down
and stares at it. Marsha returns and sadly watches her father. Dim to darkness.)*

SCENE 6

*Masi's place, three weeks later, afternoon. Masi's at the clothesline.
Judy's visiting with Timothy.*

JUDY: I don't see how you had two of us, Mom. I need sleep. Large
         doses of it. Jimmy's so lazy sometimes. I even kick him "acci-
         dentally" when Timothy starts crying. Think he gets up to feed
         the baby?
MASI: Daddy used to.
JUDY: Used to what?
MASI: Get up at night and feed you kids.
JUDY: Dad? You're kidding.

MASI: He used to sing to you. No wonder you kids would cry.

(They laugh.)

JUDY: I saw your new phone-answering machine.
MASI: *(Proud)* Yeah. For messages.
JUDY: *(Kidding)* What? You got a new boyfriend?
MASI: Judy.
JUDY: Well, why not Mom? You moved out. It's about time you start meeting new people. Once you get a divorce you're going to have to do that anyway.
MASI: I'm not getting a divorce.
JUDY: What are you going to do? You live here, Dad's over there. . . *(No response)* You can't do that forever.
MASI: I just do his wash. That's all I do. Just his wash. *(Pause, she hangs clothes)* I think you should call Dad.
JUDY: Mom, what can I say to him? I can't talk about my husband, I can't talk about my baby. All he can talk about is how he can't show his face at Tak's barber shop because I married a *kurochan* [black].
MASI: Judy, he's not going to call you.
JUDY: That's because he might get Jimmy. *(Beat)* Can you imagine Dad trying to talk to Jimmy?

(They laugh, settle down.)

MASI: Judy. He needs you.
JUDY: Why can't he accept it? Why can't he just say, "It's okay, it's okay, Judy"? I just need him to say that much.
MASI: He can't.

(Dim to darkness.)

SCENE 7

Kiyoko's restaurant, that same evening. We hear the rhythmic pounding of fists on flesh. A pool of light comes up on Nobu and Kiyoko. Kiyoko is standing in back of Nobu pounding his back with her fists. She is massaging Nobu. This is a supreme joy for him. Kiyoko likes doing it for him.

KIYOKO: *(Not stopping)* Enough?
NOBU: *(Voice vibrating from the steady blows)* Nooo . . .

(They continue in silence, both enjoying the activity.)

KIYOKO: Enough?

NOBU: Noo . . .

KIYOKO: *(Her arms are just too tired, stopping)* Ahh . . .

NOBU: *(Stretching) Oisho* [Ahh]! Masi used to do it. Sometimes Marsha
            does it now.

KIYOKO: *(Pouring tea)* You're lucky you have children, Nobu. Especially
            daughters. Harry and I wanted children. They're good, *neh?*

*(Nobu wants to give her something but can't bring himself to do it. Makes
small talk instead.)*

NOBU: How come you take the bus? *(Kiyoko doesn't understand his com-
            ment)* You have that Honda. At your place, *desho?*

KIYOKO: Ahh. Datsun. Just to work. Just to work I take the bus. Got into
            the habit after Harry died.

*(Awkward silence. Nobu abruptly pulls out a small gift-wrapped box and
holds it out to Kiyoko.)*

NOBU: Here.

(Kiyoko is too surprised to take it.)

            Anato no tanjobi no puresento. Hayo akanesai. [Your birthday
            present. Hurry, open it.]

KIYOKO: *(Taking it) Ara!* Nobu . . . *(Opens it and holds up the earrings)*
            Nobu-chan.

NOBU: Earrings. *Inamasu Jewelry Store no neki o tōtara me ni tsuitanda
            ne.* [I was walking by Inamasu's store when I spotted them.]

KIYOKO: Mah, kirei, Nobu-chan. Tsukete mitu. [They're pretty, Nobu.
            Let me try them on.]

*(Kiyoko exits. Nobu in pool of light. Memory sequence. Masi appears in pool
of light.)*

MASI: Why don't you want me anymore? *(No response)* We don't sleep
            . . . . You know what I mean and don't give me that kind of look.
            Is it me? The way my body . . . I've seen those magazines you
            keep in the back closet with your fishing gear. I mean, it's all
            right. I'm just trying to know about us. What happened?

NOBU: Nothing. Nothing happened. What's gotten into you?

MASI: Then why don't you . . . sleep with me?

NOBU: By the time I get home from work I'm tired. I work all day long, I'm standing the whole time. I told you never to touch my fishing equipment.

MASI: What about those magazines?

NOBU: I'll throw 'em out, okay? First thing tomorrow I'll throw 'em in the trash and burn 'em. That make you feel better? *(Masi is hurt by his angry response)* Masi? *(No response)* Masi. You're pretty. You are.

MASI: Don't lie to me. I hate it when you lie to me.

NOBU: I'm not lying. *(Masi refuses to believe him)* What the hell do you expect? We got old. Not just you. Me. *Me.* Look. Look at me. You call this a catch? You still want this?

MASI: *(Quietly)* Yes. *(Nobu doesn't know what to say)* Why don't you want me?

(Memory ends. Masi withdraws into shadows. Kiyoko returns to Nobu with the earrings on. Lights come up.)

KIYOKO: *(Posing)* Nobu-chan?

NOBU: *Suteki da-nah* [Looks beautiful].

(Kiyoko attempts to embrace Nobu. It's too uncomfortable for Nobu and he gently pushes her away. Kiyoko is quite embarrassed.)

KIYOKO: How come you do that to me? *(No response)* Don't you like it?

NOBU: I like it. But I don't like it, too.

(Dim to darkness.)

SCENE 8

Masi's apartment, three weeks later. Couch has a rumpled blanket on it. Morning. Sadao is standing holding the door open for a surprised Marsha. Sadao is dressed only in pants and an undershirt. Marsha is holding a box of manju [Japanese pastry]. They have never met.

SADAO: Good morning.

MARSHA: Is my mother . . . Is Mrs. Matsumoto here?

MASI: *(Off)* Who is it?

SADAO: Come on in, please come in.

(Masi enters in a bathrobe with her hair tied up in a towel, as if just washed.)

MASI: *(Momentarily caught off guard)* Oh, hi, Marsha. Come in.

MARSHA: *(Entering hesitantly)* Hello, Mom.

MASI: This is Sadao Nakasato. *(To Sadao)* My eldest one, Marsha.

SADAO: Hello Marsha.

MARSHA: Hello.

(Awkward pause. Marsha remembers her package.)

Oh, I just thought I'd bring some *manju* by. *(Hands it to Masi)* I didn't think it was that early. Next time I guess I'll call first.

(Masi gives the package to Sadao, who sets it on the counter.)

SADAO: Hmmm, love *manju*. One of my favorites. Especially the ones with the *kinako* on top. The brown powdery stuff?

MARSHA: I meant to drop it off last night but I called and no one was here.

MASI: Oh, we got in late from fishing.

SADAO: We caught the limit.

MASI: *(Looking at phone-answering machine)* I have to remember to turn this machine on.

SADAO: In fact, Masi caught more than me.

MASI: Teamwork. I catch them and Sadao takes them off the hook. Sit down and have breakfast with us. Sit, sit.

MARSHA: That's okay, Mom.

MASI: It was so late last night, I told Sadao to sleep on the couch. So he did. He said he would cook breakfast for me in the morning. Right over there on the couch.

(Masi and Sadao are nodding to each other in agreement. Marsha doesn't move.)

SADAO: Waffles.

MASI: You sure you know how?

SADAO: I can make them, good ones. From scratch. And they're low cholesterol.

MASI: Sit down, sit down.

MARSHA: No, no, Mom. I really should be going. I'm going to stop over at the house. To see Dad, too.

MASI: Wait, wait . . . *(Wrapping up two packages of fish in newspaper)*

MARSHA: Mom, I don't want any fish.

MASI: *(Handing her a package)* Then give some to Brad. Here.

MARSHA: Mom, remember? I'm not seeing him anymore.

MASI: Then give them to Dad.

MARSHA: What do I tell him?

MASI: *(Momentary pause)* Just give it to him. No use wasting it. He can eat fish morning, noon, and night.

(Masi hustles Marsha towards the door.)

SADAO: No waffles? They're low cholesterol.

MARSHA: Uh, no thanks. Nice to meet you, Mr. Nakasato.

(Marsha pauses at the door. She and Masi exchange glances.)

       Bye, Mom. *(She exits)*

MASI: *(Calling after)* Tell Daddy I'll bring his clothes, that I've been busy. And tell him to put his old clothes in a pile where I can see it. Last time I couldn't find one of his underwear and he got mad at me. *(Closes door)* It was under the icebox.

(As Sadao rambles on, Masi seems lost in her thoughts.)

SADAO: *(Caught up in his cooking)* Everything's low cholesterol. Except for the Cool Whip. But that doesn't count because that's optional. Where's the MSG? That's my secret. My daughter gets so mad at me, "Dad, you're a pharmacist, you should know better than to use MSG." She's a health-food nut . . .

(Sadao is bending down to look in a lower cabinet for the MSG. As he disappears, Masi moves into a pool of light. Memory sequence: Nobu appears in a pool of light.)

NOBU: No, Masi, I said size eight, size eight hooks.

MASI: You told me to buy size six, not size eight. That's not what you told me.

NOBU: I get home from the store I expect you to . . . Jesus Christ . . . *(Starting to pace)* Shig, all day long ordering me around, "Do this, do that." I even gotta get up five o'clock this morning to pick up the produce 'cause his own damn son-in-law's a lazy son-of-a-bitch. And he yells at me if it don't look good in the cases. *(Mimicking)* "No, that's wrong, Nobu, that's all wrong—do it this way."

MASI: Nobu. Nobu, you didn't tell me to get size eight hooks. You told me size. . .

NOBU: I said size eight. I said size eight hooks. *(Pause)* This is my house. Masi! After I come home from that damn store—here . . . . This is *my* house.

(Silence.)

MASI: *(Quietly)* I'm sorry. I'm wrong. You said size eight hooks.

(Nobu withdraws. Lights up. Sadao gets up with the MSG.)

SADAO: You don't mind, do you? Masi? The *ajinomoto* [MSG]. Is it okay
          with you?
MASI: Yes, yes, it's fine.
SADAO: *(Aware of Masi's pensiveness)* Sometimes I add prune juice but
          then you have to go easy on the MSG. The flavor doesn't mix.
          It's mostly for medicinal reasons, though. The prune juice. But
          it really does add a nice hint of flavor to the waffles, but you
          really can't overdo it. Everything in moderation. I think these
          people got a little carried away with the MSG thing. Of course,
          I'm not running a Chinese restaurant, either, I'm just talking
          about a tiny pinch of the stuff . . .

*(During this speech, Nobu is seen lit in half-light looking at his unfinished
kite frame. As lights go to half on Sadao and Masi, Nobu is fully lit in a
pool of light. He lifts the kite above his head and begins to move it as if it
were flying . For a moment Nobu appears like a child making believe his kite
is soaring high above in the clouds. As Nobu goes to half-light, Judy is lit
carrying Timothy in front of her with a papoose carrier.)*

SCENE 9

Kiyoko and Chiyo approach Judy as she passes by carrying Timothy.

KIYOKO: You are Judy, *neh.*
JUDY: *(Cautious)* Yes?
KIYOKO: I am a friend of your father. My name is Kiyoko Hasegawa.
CHIYO: Chiyo Froelich.
KIYOKO: I run this restaurant. Hasegawa's.
CHIYO: Chiyo's Hair Salon, right next door.
JUDY: *(Still unsure)* Hi.
KIYOKO: We are having a small get-together at my place for your father.
CHIYO: A birthday party.

(They notice the baby.)

KIYOKO: Oh, hello, Timothy.
CHIYO: Nobu should see him.

(Awkward pause)

JUDY: *(Starting to leave)* It's nice meeting you. Excuse me . . .
CHIYO: *(To Kiyoko)* Show Judy your earrings. Kiyoko, show her.
KIYOKO: Chiyo.
CHIYO: He gave them to her. Your father. For her birthday.
KIYOKO: For my birthday. He comes to my restaurant almost every day.
           He likes my cooking. That's how come I know him so good.
CHIYO: *(Kidding)* He's so *mendokusai* [troublesome]. I don't like
           cucumber pickle, I like eggplant. *Monku, monku* all the time.

(Lights start to fade.)

KIYOKO: Oh, it is no trouble at all. I like to do things like that. I like to
           cook for Nobu . . .

*(Dim to darkness. Cross-fade to Nobu with kite. Masi in half-light moves
away from Sadao with the fishing pole. She begins to practice her cast.)*

SCENE 10

*Nobu puts down the kite frame. Thinks. Picks up the phone and dials
Masi. In half-light at Masi's place, Sadao is at the counter making
waffles. He hears the phone machine click on but does not answer it.
Masi is off to the side, in a pool of light, engrossed in her casting.*

NOBU: Masi? You got any . . . *(From his surprised expression we know that
           he has gotten Masi's answering machine. He doesn't know how to
           deal with it)* Masi? *(Listening to the message which finally ends)* I
           am Nobu Matsumoto. My telephone number is 751-8263. *(Not
           sure if he said his name)* I am Nobu Matsumoto.

*(He hangs up. Picks up his kite and stares at it. Masi is working on per-
fecting her casting technique, putting together all the little things that
Sadao has taught her. She goes through one complete cycle without a hitch.
Very smooth. Having done the whole thing without a mistake gives her
tremendous satisfaction. She smiles to herself. It feels good. She begins again.
Lights fade.)*

END OF ACT ONE

ACT TWO
SCENE 11

Kiyoko's restaurant, four weeks later. Surprise birthday party for Nobu. Judy stands by herself out front, picking at the food. Blackie and Marsha are in the kitchen and Kiyoko and Chiyo scurry about with last-minute preparations. Over the restaurant speakers we hear the forties tune "String of Pearls."

KIYOKO: *(Calling)* Blackie! Hurry up with the chicken teri! *(Checking the food items)* Ara! I forgot the dip. Chiyo, go talk, go talk.

(Kiyoko pushes Chiyo towards Judy, then hurries back into the kitchen as Blackie and Marsha enter, carrying more food. Marsha is holding her nose.)

CHIYO: *(To Judy in passing)* Nobu's favorite song. *(Stops momentarily, touching Judy's hair)* You come see me, I know what to do with it.

(Chiyo heads back to the kitchen as Marsha and Blackie are setting their dishes down.)

BLACKIE: If you think that stink, wait till you try my famous *hom-yu*.
MARSHA: *(Attempting to be polite)* No, really, it wasn't that bad.
BLACKIE: All Orientals gotta have stink food. It's part of our culture. Chinese, Japanese, Koreans, Filipinos—we all got one dish that is so stink. Chinese got this thing they call *ham-ha*, shrimp paste. My mudda used to cook with it. Whew! Stink like something went die.

(Chiyo enters.)

                Filipinos got fish-gut paste, *bagaoong*. Koreans, *kimchee*. Whew!
CHIYO: *(Admonishing)* Blackie.
BLACKIE: *(Ignoring Chiyo)* And us Buddhaheads eat *takuan*, the pickled horseradish. When you open up the bottle, the neighbors call to see if your toilet went explode!
CHIYO: *(Poking her head into the kitchen)* Kiyoko! He's at it again!
BLACKIE: Next time you come I make you my *hom-yu*.
MARSHA: *Hom-yu?* *(To Judy)* You know *hom-yu*?
BLACKIE: Whatsa matter? You kids live on Mars? You never heard of *hom-yu*? *Hom-yu*. Steamed pork hash. It's my specialty. Gotta have the stinky fish on top. That's the secret. Lottsa *Pake* [Chinese] places don't use that fish anymore. Know why? Too stink. Chase all the

haole [white] customers away. Take pork butt, chop it into small pieces. Four water chestnuts, chopped. Teaspoon of corn-starch—

(Kiyoko enters with dip, Chiyo trailing.)

KIYOKO: Blackie! Blackie! Go do the cake!
MARSHA: *(To Blackie)* I'll help you.
CHIYO: Kiyoko, when is he coming?
KIYOKO: *(To Marsha)* No, no . . . *(To Chiyo)* He should be on his way . . . *(To Marsha)* You shouldn't help anymore. Eat, eat. Talk to Chiyo.
MARSHA: *(Overlapping)* We met already . . .
KIYOKO: *(To Blackie)* Go, go, put the candles on the cake. No beer, either.
BLACKIE: *(Exiting, calling back to Marsha while scratching his butt)* Stinky fish. Don't forget the stinky fish . . .
KIYOKO: *(Following him out)* Don't scratch your . . . *(She remembers her guests)*

(Chiyo approaches Judy and Marsha.)

CHIYO: I've never seen her like this. She's acting like a kid back there. *(Catching her breath and looking the two daughters over)* You're Judy, *neh*, the fifth-grade teacher? And you're the dental . . .
MARSHA: *(Overlapping)* . . . hygienist, I told you earlier . . .
CHIYO: . . . hygienist—yeah, yeah you told me before. *(Quietly laughs about her mistake, calms down)* So. What do you think of the two of them? Nobu and Kiyoko?

(Awkward pause)

MARSHA: I think it's . . . good. I think it's good.

(Chiyo looks to Judy, who is silent.)

CHIYO: *(Touching Judy's hair gently)* You come see me. I know what to do with it. *(She turns and walks back towards the kitchen)*
MARSHA: Judy.
JUDY: This is stupid. What am I doing here?
MARSHA: We're doing this for Dad.
JUDY: You really think he's going to want us here? Do you?

(Kiyoko enters tentatively, followed by Chiyo.)

KIYOKO: Blackie called—Nobu's not home, so he's coming. *(To Marsha, feigning enthusiasm)* I'm so glad you could make it. Judy said you weren't sure whether you could all come or not.

MARSHA: Oh no, no. We wouldn't have missed it.

KIYOKO: Nobu-chan will be so happy you are here.

MARSHA: It was very kind of you to invite us.

KIYOKO: Oh no, no, no. I wanted all of you here. *(To Judy)* Where is the baby?

JUDY: Jimmy's home babysitting him.

CHIYO: Next time you bring him. We got plenty of room here.

KIYOKO: Yes, please, please. Next time you bring the baby and Jimmy, too. I want to get to know all of Nobu-chan's family.

BLACKIE: *(Rushing in with his ukulele)* HAYO [Hurry]! *HAYO!* THE BUGGA'S COMING! THE BUGGA'S COMING!

KIYOKO: I'll get the cake. Hide! Hide!

BLACKIE: I got the lights.

CHIYO: *(To Marsha and Judy)* Over here, over here. . .

(Darkness. Nobu enters cautiously. The lights come up abruptly, then begin a slow fade through the rest of the scene.)

ALL: SURPRISE!

(Nobu sees Judy and Marsha. He is in shock. Chiyo and Blackie lead everyone in a rousing version of "Happy Birthday" as Kiyoko enters with a birthday cake decorated with burning candles. He is attempting to appear happy, but is becoming more and more upset that his daughters are there. Lights continue their slow fade through the song, which is beginning to fall apart. Kiyoko is now standing next to Nobu holding the cake out in front of him. She senses something is wrong. The song ends with Blackie and Kiyoko mumbling the last few lyrics. Silence. Nobu's face is illuminated by the glowing candles. Nobu makes no move to blow out the candles. The moment is now uncomfortable. Kiyoko is very upset.)

KIYOKO: Nobu-chan, please.

(Pause)

JUDY: *(Irritated)* Dad.

(Nobu still refuses to blow out the candles. The moment is now extremely awkward. No one knows what to do.)

MARSHA: *(Gently)* Daddy.

(Slowly Nobu leans forward and with a forceful breath extinguishes the candles. Blackout.)

SCENE 12

Masi's place, same night. Sadao and Masi in bed. Both are propped up, Sadao intently watching TV and Masi peering at the TV over the magazine she holds in front of her. Sadao keeps switching the channels with his remote control. Each time Masi starts to settle into a program, Sadao switches the channel, causing her to jerk her head from the shock.

MASI: Sadao! *(He's busy switching channels)* Sadao?

SADAO: Hmmm?

MASI: Could you please keep it on one?

SADAO: *(Realizing what he's been doing)* Oh. I'm sorry. *(Starts switching channels again)* Which one? This one? How's this?

MASI: Fine, fine. That's fine. *(They settle into watching TV)* Sadao?

SADAO: Hmm?

MASI: I don't feel good. *(Pause)* I think something's wrong with me.

SADAO: What, what? Want me to call Doc Takei?

MASI: No, no . . .

SADAO: You have a fever? Headache? What's wrong?

MASI: No, no, nothing like that. *(Pause, thinking)* I'm too happy.

SADAO: What?

MASI: I feel . . . too happy. *(Sadao stares at her uncomprehending)* I used to feel like this as a kid, I think. But it was . . . different.

SADAO: You feel too happy?

MASI: When you're a kid you get ice cream and 'member how you used to feel? Happy, right? But then you eat it all up and it's gone, or, you eat too much of it and you throw up. But this just goes on and on.

SADAO: You mean us? *(Masi nods)* Yeah, but this is a little different than ice cream, don't you—

MASI: Of course, of course, Sadao.

SADAO: What about with Nobu? didn't you go through this with him? *(Masi shakes her head)* I mean in the beginning when you first met? When you got married?

MASI: No, it wasn't like that. *(Pause)* I think something's wrong with me. You know how they say there's no such thing as an accident?

That you really wanted it to happen and so it did? I don't think I ever really cared for Nobu. Not the way he cared for me. There was someone else who liked me in Camp. I liked him, too. I married Nobu. Something's wrong with me, huh? Now you make me feel too happy. I don't like it. It makes me . . . unhappy.

(They both laugh. Sadao reaches out and places his hand on top of hers. They exchange warm smiles.)

Was she in a lot of pain? *(Sadao doesn't follow her comment)* Your wife. Towards the end. In the hospital.

SADAO: She just slept all the time. No, not too much. After about two weeks she went into a coma and that was it. You can't tell. Cancer's like that. Mary was pretty lucky, I guess. *(Pause, thinking)* There's nothing wrong with you. Really, there isn't. *(Pause; trying to decide whether to say something or not)* You scare me. You know that? Sometimes you scare me half to death. I don't want to go through that again. I told myself, "Never, ever again." Dead is better than feeling that kind of pain. But this . . . this is . . . I don't know . . . to get a second chance . . . *(Pause)* There's nothing good about growing old. You spend most of your time taking medicine and going to the doctor so you won't die. The rest of the time you spend going to the funerals of your friends who did die, and they were taking the same medicine and seeing the same doctors so what's the use, anyway? Huh? *(Sarcastically)* The golden years . . . . Look at us. Here we are. At our age. In bed together. Not even married. Can you imagine what the kids are thinking?

MASI: We're not doing anything wrong.

SADAO: Of course, I know, I know.

MASI: We're not doing anything wrong, Sadao. We're not.

SADAO: I know. But when I really think about what we're doing . . . it embarrasses the hell out of me!

(They look at each other, then suddenly burst out laughing. They gradually calm down.)

MASI: I scare you half to death. And you . . . you make me feel so good I feel awful.

(They look at each other for a moment, then slowly reach out and embrace. Dim to darkness.)

SCENE 13

Kiyoko's restaurant, one week later. Nobu is sitting at the counter sipping sake and eating eggplant pickles. Blackie is watching him from the service window. He comes out sipping on a beer.

BLACKIE: *(Takes a big gulp)* Know why I like to drink beer? Know why? *(As Nobu looks up, he answers his own question with a loud satisfying burp)* Ahh. I like to let things out. Makes me feel good. Don't like to keep things bottled up inside. Not good for you. Give you an ulcer. Cancer. Maybe you just blow up and disappear altogether, huh. *(Laughs at his own joke. Notices Nobu isn't laughing)* That's the problem with you *katonks.* You buggas from the mainland all the time too serious. *(Nobu glances back towards the door)* No worry, no worry. Kiyoko going be back soon. Chiyo's place—yak, yak, yak. Hey, you had lots of girlfriends when you was small-kid time? *(Nobu shrugs)* Strong silent type, huh. Me? Lottsa wahines. All the time like to play with Blackie. *(Mimicking the girls)* "Blackie, darling, you're so cute . . . you're so funny . . . But I not all the time cute. I not all the time funny. How come you all the time come around here and you still got one wife?

NOBU: We're separated.

BLACKIE: So when you gonna get the divorce?

NOBU: No. *(Blackie doesn't understand)* No.

BLACKIE: What about Kiyoko? *(No response. Nobu keeps drinking)* I don't like you. I like you. I don't like you 'cause you make Kiyoko feel lousy. I like you 'cause you make her happy. Hey, she's my boss—who you think catch hell if she not feeling good? Hey, I don't like catching hell for what you do—

NOBU: It's none of your business—Kiyoko and me.

BLACKIE: None of my business? Hey, brudda, Kiyoko may be feeding your face but I'm the guy who's cooking your meals. *(Nobu stares down at his pickles)* Nobu?

NOBU: What?

BLACKIE: You like Kiyoko? *(No response)* Well, do you?

NOBU: *(Under his breath)* Yeah, I guess so.

BLACKIE: "Yeah, I guess so" what?

NOBU: *(Mumbling)* I like Kiyoko.

BLACKIE: Jesus. Talking to you *katonks* is like pulling teeth.

NOBU: I LIKE KIYOKO! I like Kiyoko.

(Blackie sips on beer while Nobu glares at him. Blackie leans forward towards Nobu and burps loudly.)

BLACKIE: Feels good, huh?

(Dim to darkness)

SCENE 14

Nobu's place one week later. Evening. Masi enters carrying the wash in a brown paper bag. She unpiles the clothes and stacks them neatly on the kitchen table. She picks up the old clothes off the floor, folds them, and puts them in the bag. As she looks up, one gets the sense that she is trying to decide whether to say hello to Nobu or just leave. She looks for a moment towards the hallway, then decides otherwise. Just as she turns and starts to make her way towards the door with the bag, Nobu enters from the hallway.

NOBU: Masi, is that you?

(Nobu realizes that she's leaving without bothering to say hello. Masi senses this and feels guilty.)

MASI: I was going. I'm a little late. I was just going to leave the clothes and go. *(As she speaks, she notices the dirty dishes on the coffee table. She puts down the bag and proceeds to clean up the mess as she continues to talk)* I didn't know you were in the back . . . *(She takes the dishes to the sink. Nobu just watches)* Nobu, why don't you wash the dishes once in a while? Clean up.

NOBU: Place is a dump anyway. *(Masi stops and looks at him. He presses point)* Place is a dump, Mama. Neighborhood's no good. Full of colored people, Mexicans . . .

MASI: *(Putting dishes in sink)* Well, move then. Move to the north side like me. I kept saying that all along. For the kids—better schools, better neighborhood. . . . Think you listen to me? *(Mimicking Nobu)* "I don't like *Hakujin*—white people make me nervous." So you don't like white people, you don't like black people, you don't like Mexicans. . . . So who do you like? Huh? *Monku, monku, monku* . . .

NOBU: *(Muttering)* I don't mind Mexicans. *(Pause)* I told Shig, "You can't keep stocking all that Japanese things when the *Nihonjins* [Japanese] are moving out of the neighborhood. You gotta sell to the Mexicans and not all that cheap crap, too, 'cause they can tell." Think Shig listens to me? He's the big store owner. The big man. If I was running the store it woulda been different. *(Pause)* And your old man said he'd get me that store.

MASI: It wasn't his fault. He didn't plan on the war, Nobu.

NOBU: He promised he could set me . . .

MASI: *(Overlapping)* It wasn't his fault.

NOBU: . . . up in business or anything else I wanted to do.

MASI: IT WASN'T HIS FAULT!

(Silence)

Who wanted to be in the relocation camps? Did you? Do you think he wanted to be in there? It broke Papa's heart. He spent his entire life building up that farm. Papa was a proud man. A very proud man. It broke his heart when he lost it.

NOBU: I'm just saying I'd run the business different. Shig is a baka [fool]. That's all I'm saying.

MASI: You're retired. Shig passed away eight years ago. The store's not even . . .

NOBU: *(Overlapping)* If all the Japanese move out you can't keep selling all that Japanese things, you can't. That's all I'm saying.

MASI: . . . there anymore. It's a cleaners.

(Silence. Masi picks up the paper bag of old clothes and starts to move towards the door. She's had enough.)

NOBU: Masi?

MASI: *(Stops)* What?

NOBU: Mr. Rossi give you any more fish?

MASI: *(Uncomfortable, lying)* No. Not lately.

(Pause)

NOBU: Mama?

MASI: Is your back bothering you, Nobu? *(No response)* Want me to *momo* [massage] it for you?

(Nobu nods. As Masi moves to put the bag down, Nobu removes his under-shirt. He seats himself. Masi begins to massage his shoulders from behind. They continue in silence. Nobu is enjoying the moment. He begins to laugh quietly to himself.)

What?

NOBU: When I started work at your papa's farm, he wanted to put me in the packing shed. I said, "No, I want to work in the fields." It was so hot, 110 degrees out there. He thought I was nuts. But I knew every day at eight in the morning and twelve noon, you and your sister would bring the water out to us.

MASI: *(Laughing as she recalls)* Nobu.

NOBU: I wanted to watch you.

MASI: You would just stand there with your cup, staring at me.

NOBU: Hell, I didn't know what to say.

MASI: You drank so much water, Lila and I thought maybe you had rabies. We used to call you "Nobu, the Mad Dog."

(They laugh.)

          Papa liked you.

NOBU: Boy, he was a tough son-of-a-bitch.

MASI: I didn't think anyone could keep up with Papa. But you could work like a horse. You and Papa. Proud. Stubborn.

(Masi massages Nobu in silence.)

NOBU: Mama? Why don't you cook me breakfast?

MASI: What?

NOBU: Cook me breakfast. I miss my hot rice and raw egg in the morning.

MASI: It's late Nobu. You have your wash. I'm not going to come all the way back over here just to cook you—

NOBU: Just breakfast. Then in the morning when we get up you can go back to your place.

(Masi stops, realizing he is asking her to spend the night. Silence. Masi does not move. Nobu stares ahead. More silence. Then, tentatively, she moves her hands forward and begins to massage him. A faint smile appears on Nobu's face. Dim to darkness.)

SCENE 15

Kiyoko's restaurant, one week later. Blackie, after hours, is seated in semidarkness, feet up on table, accompany himself on the ukulele and singing a sad Hawaiian folk song, "Manuela Boy."

BLACKIE: *(Singing)*
          Manuela Boy, my dear boy
          You no mo' hila, hila.

No mo' five cent, no mo' house
You go Aala Paka hia moe.

Mama work at the big hotel,
Brudda go to school.
Sister go with the haole boy,
Papa make his living shooting pool.

The tourist like filet mignon
And caviar it's true,
But they never lived till they went taste
Papa's Friday ole Hawaiian stew . . .

(As Blackie sings, lights up on Masi's place. Sadao stands before the door Masi has just opened. In Sadao's right hand he holds a suitcase and in his left, several fishing poles. On his head sits a fishing hat. Sadao has come to move in with Masi. For a moment they look at each other in silence. Then Masi invites him in. Sadao enters. Dim to darkness.)

SCENE 16

(Nobu's place, three days later, late afternoon. Judy has stopped by with Timothy. Judy sets the baby down on the kitchen table upstage of Nobu. Nobu turns to look at Judy, then returns to working on the kite and watching TV. This is the first time Judy has visited Nobu since their breakup over her marriage. He has never seen Timothy.)

JUDY: *(Moving down towards Nobu)* I was just driving by and I thought I'd stop in. *(No response)* You doing okay, Dad? *(Silence)* You know, Mom? I just wanted to say—

NOBU: Did he come?

JUDY: *(Exasperated)* No, he did not.

NOBU: He can come to the house now.

JUDY: "He can come to the house now"? Jesus Christ. Dad, he isn't one of your children. He doesn't need your permission. He's . . .

NOBU: *(Overlapping)* This is my house. He needs my permission.

JUDY: . . . a grown man. I don't want to fight. I didn't come here to fight with you, Dad.

NOBU: I *said* he can come—

JUDY: He won't come, he doesn't like you!

(Silence)

NOBU: Damn *kurochan* . . .

JUDY: He's black, not *kurochan*—it's black. *(Pause)* Everybody marries
         out, okay? *Sanseis* don't like *Sanseis.*

NOBU: Tak's son married a *Nihonjin,* Shig's daughter did, your cousin
         Patsy . . .

JUDY: *(Overlapping)* Okay, okay, *I* didn't, *I* didn't, all right?

NOBU: . . . did, Marsha's going to.

(Pause. Nobu looks back to Timothy.)

JUDY: But *happa* [multiracial] kids are the next generation, too.

NOBU: *No.* Japanese marry other Japanese, their kids are *Yonsei* [fourth-
         generation Japanese American]—not these damn *ainoko* [mul-
         tiracial]!

(Silence)

JUDY: You're gonna die out, you know that. You're gonna be extinct
         and nobody's gonna give a goddamn.

*(Timothy has begun to cry softly. Judy goes over and picks the baby up, try-
ing to soothe him. Composing herself, Judy decides to try one last time to say
what she came to tell her father. She walks back to Nobu, this time carrying
Timothy with her.)*

         Dad? *(No response)* Dad, you know, Mom's moving out of the
         house? I didn't put her up to it. Honest. *(Silence. Nobu stares
         straight ahead. She begins to cry)* If I did . . . I'm sorry.

*(More silence from Nobu. Judy gives up trying to talk to this man. As she
turns to leave, she notices Nobu. He is looking towards her, at Timothy.
Something in his expression makes Judy bring the baby over to Nobu. She
holds the baby out to him.)*

         Timothy. Your grandson.

*(For a moment there is hesitation. We are not sure whether Nobu is going to
take the baby. Then, Nobu reaches out and takes Timothy. Judy watches as
Nobu awkwardly holds his grandson for the first time. As Judy begins to
withdraw from the scene upstage into a pool of light, Marsha also appears
upstage in her own separate light. Nobu remains lit holding Timothy. He
begins to hum the traditional Japanese lullaby "Donguri." Marsha and
Judy watch Nobu and Timothy as they speak.)*

MARSHA: You didn't tell Dad, did you?
JUDY: No, I just brought the baby by.
MARSHA: It's going to kill him when he finds out.
JUDY: He's got that other woman.
MARSHA: Judy. (Pause) Maybe he already knows about Mom and Mr. Nakasato.
JUDY: I don't think so. I really don't think so.

(They continue to watch as Nobu begins to sing the "Donguri" song to Timothy.)

NOBU: *(Singing)*
           Donguri kor koro, koro gatte
           O ike tu hamatte, saa taihen
           Dojo o ga dette kite, kon-nichiwa
           Botchan/Timothy isshoni, asobimasho . . .

(Marsha and Judy fade out first. Nobu is left alone in pool of light singing to Timothy. As he fades out we hear the whir of a coffee grinder.)

SCENE 17

Masi's place, two days later. Masi has asked Judy and Marsha over for a talk. She has just told them that she is going over to see Nobu. She is going to tell him that she wants a divorce and to marry again. The two daughters sit uneasily while Masi is at the counter preparing coffee. Masi is trying to get the Braun grinder to work. She's getting the feel of it by pushing the button. We hear the whir of the spinning rotor blade. She's ready. Takes the plastic top off and pours the beans in, then presses the start button. Just as the grinder picks up top-speed Masi accidentally pulls the plastic top off. Beans go flying every which way pelting her face, bouncing off the cabinets. Quiet. Masi peeks from behind her hands. A couple of beans embedded in her hair fall to the counter. Masi is upset. The daughters are embarrassed. Normally, this would be a funny situation for them.

MARSHA: *(Getting up)* I'll clean it up.

(Marsha starts to pick up the beans scattered on the floor. Judy starts to giggle—it's all too ridiculous.)

JUDY: *(Trying to suppress her laughter)* I'm sorry, I'm sorry . . . *(Masi begins to laugh)* God, what a mess.

MASI: *(To Marsha)* Let it go, don't bother. I'll take care of it later.

JUDY: *(Finds a man's sock; teasing)* What's this? This belong to Mr. Nakasato?

MASI: *(Grabbing it)* Judy.

MARSHA: Why didn't you just leave sooner? You didn't have to stick around for us.

MASI: I didn't. *(Pause)* I was . . . I was scared.

MARSHA: Of Dad?

MASI: I don't know. Everything.

JUDY: Was it 'cause I kept harping on you to move out on him all those years? Is that why you left?

MARSHA: What's the difference?

JUDY: Marsha.

(Pause.)

MASI: Dad was always trying to beat me down, every little thing. "How come you can't do this, how come you can't do that"—nothing was ever right. Every time I opened my mouth I was always wrong—he was always right. He always had to be right. *(Pause)* There are things you kids don't know. I didn't want to talk about them to you, but . . . Daddy and I, we didn't sleep . . .

JUDY: *(Overlapping)* That's okay, Mom. Really, it's okay . . .

MASI: . . . together. Every time I wanted to, he would push me away. Ten, fifteen years he didn't want me. *(Pause)* We were having one of our arguments, just like always. And he was going on and on about how it was my fault this and my fault that. And I was trying to explain my side of it, when he turned on me, "Shut up, Mama. You don't know anything. You're *stupid.*" Stupid. After forty-two years of letting him be right he called me that. And I understood. He didn't even need me to make him be right anymore. He just needed me to be stupid. I was tired. I couldn't fight him anymore. He won. He finally made me feel like garbage. *(Judy and Marsha are shocked by her strong language)* That was the night I left him and came over to your place. *(Nodding towards Judy)* I like Sadao. I like Sadao very much.

(Dim to darkness)

SCENE 18

(Nobu's place, same day. "String of Pearls" can be heard playing faintly in the background. He's fixing himself in front of a small wall mirror. He adjusts the collar of his shirt and tugs at his sweater until it looks right. Nobu checks his watch. As he begins to pick up some of the scattered clothes on the floor, Masi enters. Music ends. Nobu quickly moves to the sofa. Masi goes over to the kitchen area and takes clothes out of the bag, setting them neatly on the table. She picks up the dirty clothes off the floor, folds them, and puts them into the bag. As she's doing this, Nobu gets up, shuffles over to the stove, and turns on the flame to heat some water. He stands there and watches the water heat up.)

MASI: *(Sits down on sofa)* I want to talk, Nobu.

(No response. Nobu gets tea out and pours some into pot.)

        I have something to tell you.

NOBU: *(Moving back to couch)* Want some tea?

(As Nobu sits, Masi gets up and moves towards the sink area. She gets a sponge and wipes off the tea leaves he has spilled on the counter. Nobu turns the TV on and stares at it.)

MASI: You know Dorothy and Henry's son, George?

NOBU: The pharmacist or something?

MASI: No, the lawyer one. He's the lawyer one. I went to see him. *(Turns off the stove flame)* I went to see about a divorce. About getting one. *(No response)* I want to get married again. So I went to George to see about a divorce. I wanted to tell you first so you'd know. I didn't want you to hear from someone else. I know how you hate that kind of thing. Thinking something's going on behind your back.

NOBU: Wait, wait, wait a second. . . . You want a divorce? You want to get. . . . What? What's all this?

MASI: It's the best thing, Nobu. We've been separated how long now? How long have we been living different places?

NOBU: I don't know. I never thought about it. Not too long.

MASI: Thirteen months.

NOBU: Thirteen months, who cares? I never thought about it. I don't understand, Masi.

MASI:	It's the same thing as being divorced isn't it?
NOBU:	It doesn't seem that long. You moved out of this house. It wasn't my idea. It was your idea. I never liked it.
MASI:	It doesn't matter whose idea it was. It's been over a year since we—
NOBU:	You want to get married? Yeah, I know it's been over a year, but I always thought . . . you know, that we'd—
MASI:	It's been over a year, Nobu.
NOBU:	I know! I said I know.
MASI:	I've been seeing someone. It wasn't planned or anything. It just happened.
NOBU:	What do you mean, "seeing someone"? What do you mean?
MASI:	He's very nice. A widower. He takes me fishing. He has a nice vegetable garden that he—
NOBU:	Who is he? Do I know him? Is it someone I know?
MASI:	His name is Sadao Nakasato. His wife died about two years ago. He's related to Dorothy and Henry. Nobu, it's the best thing for both of us.
NOBU:	You keep saying it's the best thing, the best thing. *(Pause)* Masi, why did you sleep with me that night?

(Silence.)

MASI:	Aren't you seeing somebody?
NOBU:	No. Not like that.
MASI:	But the kids said she's very nice. That she invited—
NOBU:	It's totally different! I'm not seeing anyone! *(Pause)* How long have you been seeing this guy? How long?
MASI:	Please, Nobu. You always get what *you* want. I always let you have your way. For once just let—
NOBU:	HOW LONG?
MASI:	About five months.
NOBU:	FIVE MONTHS! How come you never told me? Do the girls know too? The girls know! Everybody knows? Five months. FIVE DAMN MONTHS AND I DON'T KNOW!! *(He breaks the kite)*
MASI:	I asked them not to tell you.
NOBU:	Why? Why the hell not? Don't I have a right to know??
MASI:	Because I knew you'd react this way. Just like this. Yelling and screaming just like you always do.
NOBU:	Everybody in this whole damn town knows except me! How could you do this to me! Masi! HOW COULD YOU DO THIS TO ME?? *(He has her by the shoulders and is shaking her violently)*
MASI:	*(Quietly)* Are you going to hit me?

(Pause. Nobu slowly composes himself and lets her go.)

Because I want to be happy, Nobu. I have the right to be happy.

(Masi exits. Nobu is left standing alone. Dim to darkness.)

SCENE 19

Kiyoko's restaurant, same day, evening. Chiyo and Kiyoko seated at table in pool of light.

KIYOKO: Nine years. That is how long it has been. Nine years since Harry passed away. He never treated me like this. I call, I go over there. Harry never treated me like this.

CHIYO: Kiyoko. Maybe you have to stop thinking about Nobu. Hmm? Maybe . . . maybe you should give him up. *(Silence)* Kiyoko. Lots more fish in the ocean. Lots more. Go out with us. Come on.

KIYOKO: I don't do those kinds of things.

CHIYO: I'll introduce you to some new guys. Remember Ray—you met him? I've been telling him about—

KIYOKO: I don't do those kinds of things. *(Pause)* It's not easy for me, Chiyo. *(Silence)* when Harry died, right after? I started taking the bus to work. I had a car, I could drive. It was easier to drive. I took the bus. For twenty-five years you go to sleep with him, wake up next to him. He shaves while you shower, comes in from the yard all sweaty. Then he's gone. No more Harry in bed. No more the smell of aftershave in the towel you're drying off with. No more sweaty Harry coming up and hugging me. I had a car. I took the bus. I missed men's smells. I missed the smell of men. Every morning I would get up and walk to the corner to take the bus. It would be full of all these men going to work. And it would be full of all these men coming home from work. I would sit there pretending to read my magazine . . . *(Inhales, discovering the different smells)* Soap . . . just-washed skin . . . aftershave lotion . . . sweat . . .

(Lights come up to half in the restaurant. Blackie bursts through the kitchen doors holding a place of his famous hom-yu. *Brings it over and sets it down on the table which is now in a full pool of light.)*

BLACKIE: *Hom-yu! Hom-yu!*

CHIYO: *Kusai yo* [Stinky]!

KIYOKO: Blackie!

BLACKIE: I know stink. But stink goooood!

(It stinks to holy hell. Chiyo can't stand it. Kiyoko is quite moved by Blackie's gesture, though she too is having a difficult time with its odor. Blackie grins proudly. Dim to darkness.)

SCENE 20

Nobu's place, two days later. Knock at the door and Marsha enters carrying a brown paper bag. Nobu watching TV.

MARSHA: Mom asked me to drop these by and to pick up the dirty clothes. *(No response. She unpacks the newly washed clothes)* Kiyoko's been calling me. She's worried about you. She says you won't see anybody. Why don't you just talk to her, Dad?

NOBU: How come you didn't tell me? All the time you come here and you never mention it once. You. I feel so damned ashamed. How can I even show my face? All the time right under my nose. Everyone laughing at me behind my—

MARSHA: Dad, Dad, it's not like that at all. I just didn't think it was all that important to tell—

NOBU: Oh, come on! Mom told you not to tell me so she could go sneaking 'round with that son-of-a-bitch!

MARSHA: All right, all right, but it's not like that at all. No one's trying to hide anything from you and no one's laughing at you.

NOBU: *(Moving her towards the couch and pushing her down)* Sit down, sit down over here. Tell me about it. Who is he? What does he do? Tell me 'bout him! Tell me!

MARSHA: *(Seated)* What do you want me to say? Huh, Dad? They're happy. He's a nice man.

NOBU: "He's a nice man." What the hell's that supposed to mean?

MARSHA: He treats her like a very special person.

NOBU: Well, everyone does that in the beginning. In the beginning it's so easy to be—

MARSHA: She laughs. All the time she's laughing. They're like two little kids. They hold hands. Did you ever do that? I'm embarrassed to be around them. He takes her fishing. He has a little camper and they drive up to . . .

NOBU: All right, all right . . .

MARSHA: . . . Lake Berryessa and camp overnight. He teaches her how to bait the hook, cast it out, and even to tie the hook. I mean you never even took her fishing . . .

NOBU: She doesn't like fishing. I tried to take her lots of times, she wouldn't go.

MARSHA: They even dig up worms in his garden at his house. I saw them. Side by side . . .

NOBU: All right, I said.
MARSHA: . . . sitting on the ground digging up worms and putting them in a coffee can!
NOBU: *(Overlapping)* ALL RIGHT! ALL RIGHT!
MARSHA: . . . I MEAN DID YOU EVER DO THAT FOR MOM!! *(Pause)* Did you? *(Getting worked up again)* You're so . . . so stupid. You are. You're stupid. All you had to say was, "Come back. Please come back." You didn't even have to say, "I'm sorry."
NOBU: *(Overlapping)* I'm your father . . .
MARSHA: Mom would've come back. She would've. That's all you had to say. Three lousy words. "Please come back."
NOBU: *(Overlapping)* I'm your father . . .
MARSHA: You ruined everything. It's too late! YOU WRECKED EVERY-THING!! *(Pause. Composing herself)* I'm so mixed up. When I look at Mom I'm happy for her. When I think about you . . . I don't know. You have Kiyoko.
NOBU: That's not the same. I'm talking about your mama.
MARSHA: Dad, Kiyoko cares a great deal about you. She's been calling Judy and me day and night.
NOBU: She knocks on the door but I don't let her in. She's not Mama.
MARSHA: Dad. What do you want me to say? That's the way it is. I used to keep thinking you two would get back together. I couldn't imagine life any other way. But slowly I just got used to it. Mom over there and you here. Then all this happened. I mean, sometimes I can't recognize Mom anymore. . . . What do you want me to say? You'll get used to it.

(Nobu pauses, upset.)

NOBU: *(Stubbornly)* No.
MARSHA: *(Looks at her father sadly)* You'll get used to it.

(Dim to darkness.)

SCENE 21

(Judy's place, two days later. Masi is at the clothesline hanging clothes. Judy, holding Timothy, is with Masi. Nobu suddenly rushes in. Masi and Judy are surprised. Nobu appears very upset.)

MASI: Nobu . . .
JUDY: Hello, Dad . . .
NOBU: *(To Masi, ignoring Judy)* It's no good, Mama. It's no good at all.

You come home. You come home now, Mama. You come home. It's no good . . .

JUDY: *(Overlapping, trying to calm Nobu down)* Dad? Dad, take it easy . . . take it easy . . . *(Trying to get him seated)* Sit down, sit down . . .

NOBU: *(Yanking arm away from Judy)* I DON'T WANT TO SIT! I WANT MAMA TO COME HOME!

(Shocked silence.)

JUDY: *(Upset, quietly)* I'll get some coffee for you, Dad.

(Judy does not exit. Masi doesn't know what to do. She's never seen Nobu like this.)

NOBU: You come home, Mama. Just like always. You don't need to live over here. You come home. Just like always. That's the way it is . . .

MASI: *(Overlapping)* Nobu, Nobu . . . . You don't understand, Nobu. I can't come home. I can't come home anymore—

NOBU: I DON'T CARE! I DON'T CARE ABOUT ANY OF THAT STUFF, MAMA! *(Pause. Breaking down, he begins to plead)* I won't yell at you, anymore. I won't yell, I promise, Mama. I won't *monku* about the store or about your papa . . . I'm sorry . . . I'm sorry. Masi, it's no good. Please come home. Please come home . . . Please . . .

(Neither Masi nor Judy knows how to cope with this situation. Nobu continues to plead. Dim to darkness.)

SCENE 22

Lights up to Kiyoko's restaurant, one day later. Chiyo is dialing Nobu's number. A concerned Blackie stands guard next to her. Kiyoko has told them not to bother with him anymore. Kiyoko appears and watches them from the service window. She makes no attempt to stop them. In half-light, Nobu composes himself and leaves Judy's place. We follow him as he begins to make his way back home. However, he stops in front of Masi's place and stares at it. Chiyo lets the phone ring and ring. Finally she and Blackie exchange disappointed looks. At that point Kiyoko bursts in on them.

KIYOKO: How come you keep doing that? Huh? Don't phone him anymore. I told you, didn't I?

(*Blackie and Chiyo look sheepishly at Kiyoko. Kiyoko's feigned anger is very transparent to all three parties and only adds to the discomfort of the situation. As the scene darkens, Nobu arrives at his house. Nobu appears in a pool of light. He stands there for a moment in silence, still carrying some of the emotional turmoil from his previous scene with Masi. He reaches behind the sofa and pulls up a long, narrow object wrapped in cloth. As he unwraps it, we see what it is: a shotgun. Nobu sits down in the chair with the gun across his lap, staring into the darkness. As the lights do a slow fade on Nobu, the mournful wail of a* shakuhachi *[bamboo flute] is heard.*)

SCENE 23

Masi's place, one week later. Nobu stands inside with the shotgun. In half-light, Sadao is asleep in the bedroom.

NOBU: Where is he? (*Masi stares at the gun*)
MASI: He went to buy the newspaper.
NOBU: (*Notices Masi watching him cautiously*) It's not loaded. (*Pause*) At first I said, "No, no, no, I can't believe it. I can't believe it." I got so pissed off, I got my gun and drove over here. I drove around the block twenty or thirty times thinking "I'm gonna shoot this son-of-a-bitch, I'm gonna shoot him." I drove right up, rang the doorbell. No one answered. I kept ringing, ringing. . . . I went back to the car and waited. You cheated on me. How could you do that to me? I'm a good husband! I'm a good husband, Masi . . . . I kept seeing you two . The two of you together. I kept seeing that. It made me sick. I kept thinking, "I'm gonna shoot that son-of-a-bitch. I'm gonna shoot him." I waited in the car. It was three o'clock in the morning when I woke up. It was so cold in the car. You weren't back. I got worried I might catch a cold, and my back—you know how my back gets. I drove home, took a hot bath, and went to sleep. I've been sick in bed all week. I just wanted to show you. Both of you. That's why I brought it. Don't worry. It's not loaded. (*He cracks the shotgun and shows her that it is not loaded*) I just wanted to show both of you how it was, how I was feeling. But it's all right. You two. It's all right now.

(*Nobu sets the gun against the wall. Masi watches him, trying to decide if it is indeed safe.*)

MASI: Nobu.
NOBU: Yeah?
MASI: He's taking a nap. In the bedroom. He likes to do that after dinner.

NOBU: What is he? An old man or something?

MASI: He just likes to take naps. You do too.

NOBU: In front of the TV. But I don't go into the bedroom and lie down. Well, where is he? Bring him out. Don't I get to meet him?

MASI: You sure? (*She looks at him for a long while. She believes him. She turns to go wake Sadao up, then stops*) Chester Yoshikawa? That night in the Camps when I didn't show up for the dance? Chester Yoshikawa? We just talked. That's all.

(*Masi leaves for the bedroom. Nobu looks slowly around the apartment. It's Masi and yet it isn't. Nobu suddenly has no desire to meet Sadao. He doesn't want to see them together in this apartment. Nobu exits abruptly. Masi appears cautiously leading out a yawning Sadao. They look around. No Nobu. All they see is his shotgun leaning against the wall.*)

SCENE 24

Same day. Marsha and Judy appear in a pool of light far upstage. Marsha is holding a small kite and slowly moves it above Timothy, who is held by Judy. They sit in silence for a time.

JUDY: I can't believe he gave the kite to Timothy. He gets so mad if you even touch them. And he never flies them.

(*Pause*)

MARSHA: (*Moving the kite*) No. He never flies them.

(*The lights dim to half. They turn to watch the action taking place center stage.*)

SCENE 25

Two days later, darkness. The TV light comes on, lighting Nobu's face. A pool of light comes up on Nobu, seated on sofa, watching TV. No kite on the coffee table. Masi appears in another pool of light. She stands, staring pensively downstage into space. In her arms she is holding the brown paper bag of newly washed clothes. She turns and moves towards Nobu's place. As she enters the lights come up full on the house.

Masi goes over to the kitchen table and takes out the newly washed clothes, stacking them in neat piles on the table. She then proceeds to pick up the old clothes scattered on the floor and puts them in the bag. She picks up the bag and moves towards the door, then stops. She makes up her mind about something she has been struggling with for a while. Masi returns to the kitchen and leaves the bag of old clothes on the table. As she opens the door to go, Masi looks back at Nobu and watches him for a brief moment. During this whole time, Nobu has never turned around to look at Masi, though he is very aware of what is going on. Masi sadly turns and exits.

Lights dim with Nobu silently watching TV. Briefly, Nobu's face is lit by the dancing light of the television screen. At this same instant, the brown paper bag of wash on the table is illuminated by a shaft of light. Nobu's phone begins to ring. He turns to look at it. Blackout on Nobu. The wash fades into darkness. The phone continues to ring for a few moments. Then, silence.)

END OF PLAY

DISCUSSION QUESTIONS

Act One

1. What do the description of the setting and Nobu's actions at the beginning of Scene 1 tell you about him?
2. What is indicated by his short answers or silence when Masi tries to talk to him?
3. In Scene 2 what kind of mood is Kiyoko in and why?
4. What do Nobu's concerns about his food in Kiyoko's restaurant tell you about him?
5. What do you learn about Sadao in Scene 3?
6. What is Blackie's function in the play?
7. What are Chiyo's opinions about Nobu, and how close is she to the truth?
8. What is the reason for Nobu's estrangement from Judy?
9. Why does Nobu push Kiyoko away when she tries to embrace him?
10. In Scene 8, how does Marsha reveal her discomfort?
11. There is a second "memory sequence" or flashback at the end of Scene 8. (The first one was at the end of Scene 7.) How does the lighting indicate these sequences? What do these two "memory sequences" tell you about why Masi left Nobu?
12. What has Masi learned about herself by the end of Act 1?
13. What are the conflicts in the play?

Act Two

1. Who is at fault for the failure of the birthday party in Scene 11, Kiyoko or Nobu?
2. What emotions are Masi and Sadao experiencing in Scene 12 and why?
3. In literature or drama, a foil is any character who, by contrast, points up the distinctive characteristics of another. Is Blackie a foil to Nobu or is Sadao?
4. Why do you think Nobu focuses so much on the past?
5. What is Nobu's apparent acceptance of his grandson when he holds him an indication of?
6. Are Nobu's reactions to Masi's news that she wants a divorce predictable? Explain.
7. By the end of Scene 21, have your sympathies shifted from Masi to Nobu or not? Explain.
8. Why did Nobu decide not to shoot Sadao?
9. What action marks the final break between Masi and Nobu?
10. Who changes the most in this play?

WRITING TOPICS

1. Write an essay in which you contrast Sadao and Nobu.
2. Loneliness, love, racism, and estrangement are all topics in this play. Try to formulate a statement of theme based on these topics or others that you find in the play.
3. Did Nobu ever really love Masi? Explain your views in a persuasive essay.
4. The dramatic structure of a play follows the same structure found in most short stories. The exposition introduces the characters and setting and tells or implies what has happened before the opening of the play. In the rising action, the conflict is made clear. The climax is the turning point in the conflict, and the falling action, usually much shorter than the rising action, follows the climax and leads to the denouement, the final outcome of the plot. Chart the five parts of the structure of the play, showing where each part begins and ends as closely as you can.

WE CANNOT WALK IN OUR NEIGHBORHOOD

As told to James Freeman

In 1989, James Freeman, a professor of anthropology at San Jose State University, published *Hearts of Sorrow: Vietnamese American Lives,* a collection of oral histories that illuminate the lives of fourteen Vietnamese Americans. Those fourteen people, whose ages and professions vary widely, recount their experiences during the fall of South Vietnam to the Communists. Some are the survivors of prison camps, and many lost family members to the war and its aftermath. The book, arranged chronologically and thematically, explores five themes: Childhood, Youth, and Character; Sorrows of War; Sorrows of Liberation; Flight to Freedom; and America: Heartache Beneath Success. In the following excerpt, a Vietnamese family in the United States meets with kindness as well as rejection as they cope with culture shock, prejudice, and language difficulties.

1   My family arrived in America in October 1976. At that time I spoke a little English; my wife spoke none. I had not had any intention of coming to America, but since I had a relative here, the International Rescue Committee contacted the American Embassy, and we were brought into this country.

2   I remember our first misunderstanding. We saw lots of people waving to each other in greeting. My wife said, "Oh, how do they know us like a friend, that they're calling us to go over to them?" For us, the gesture signified "Come here."

3   We were sent to a place in the South where the people were quite friendly, but the climate was too cold for us in the winter, and much too hot in the summer. There were mosquitoes and flies all over. It was not pleasant.

4   Although white people were friendly with us, we saw discrimination against blacks. I asked a black friend to go with me while I visited a friend.

When he saw that I was about to enter the house of a white man, he said, "I'll stay outside and wait."

5 "Why not go inside?" I asked.

6 He replied, "My mother told me not to go to white people."

7 I tried one more time. I took a white man to a black man's house. The white man wouldn't go in. "Why?" I asked.

8 "My mother told me not to visit black people."

9 One day I went to the store and selected lots of oranges, apples, and vegetables. I had only ten dollars in my pocket. The girl at the checkout counter added up the cost of the items and said, "You owe fifteen dollars."

10 I replied, "I've only got ten, so I'll put back some oranges. Give me ten dollars' worth. Tomorrow I'll buy more."

11 A black woman standing behind me said, "Let him get everything; I'll pay the rest for him."

12 That was the first time something like that happened. I'll never forget it.

13 On another occasion, when I had moved to another state, an old man saw me buy a hamburger but nothing else at a hamburger stand. He asked, "Why did you buy only a hamburger, and nothing to drink?"

14 I replied, "I don't have enough money, only a little over a dollar."

15 The old man said, "I'll buy another hamburger for you."

16 "No, no," I said. "It's too much for me."

17 He bought me another hamburger and some orange juice. We sat down and ate together.

18 Some people are good, but others are not friendly. Where we live now, we cannot ride a bicycle, for young people shout loudly as they drive by in cars. I don't care what they say, but they startle me when they drive right behind me, pass me close by, on the narrow road, and then shout in my ear.

19 Sometimes my wife and I walk along the sidewalk. Even that we cannot do, for the young people shout out at us as they drive by. My wife feels bad when she hears this; she does not want to go out. I care about that. I say to her, "Let's drive to the park; then we can walk there." But walking nearby is better because we do not need a car.

20 My wife often feels so lonely here in America because she cannot walk near her home, for she is afraid that people will shout at her. She has friends around here, but if she wishes to visit them, she asks me to accompany her. So her behavior in America is quite different from how she lived in Vietnam, where she'd leave the house alone two, three, or four times a day, visiting the market, her parents, and her friends. She used to walk a lot and enjoyed it very much; now she fears to do it. I don't know, the old people in America are very nice, but young people are rude and destructive. At the rear of my apartment stands a large wheeled garbage bin. It is real dirty and has a bad smell that attracts lots of flies. Many people also go there to drink beer and smoke cigarettes. The manager of the apartment put up a sign to keep out

of private property; still, two to three carloads of dirty young people with long hair gather around the garbage bin; they make so much noise, even at night. Often they are drunk. They throw cans and empty bottles on the roof; the clatter is terrible. Even though the manager calls the police, these people often return. And they end the evening by urinating on the fence.

21   Although some other Vietnamese people live near here, we do not see them often. They work all day, eat, sleep, watch television, but don't go out much except to work. Like my wife, they have stopped walking in the neighborhood because the youths shout at them. In Vietnam, the old people used to walk a lot, stopping along the way at restaurants, where they would meet friends, talk, and drink coffee. Sometimes they would go fishing or swimming, and at other times they would visit friends. All of that is gone for them in America, and it is no longer possible in Vietnam either.

22   My wife says, "I feel so lonely when you and the children are away from the house." She stays home and cooks and does housework. The children too are lonely. I tell them to take the car and visit friends, but they say, "That's a waste of gas and money." They understand our situation, that with my low-paying job, which may stop at any moment, we do not have enough money to support us. A couple of my children attend one of the colleges nearby; I drive them there before going to work, and I pick them up after work. But my wife remains alone all day. For companionship, I bought her two birds in a large cage. From time to time, one of the birds sings. Because she has poor eyesight, my wife cannot watch television. Her days are long. I work five days a week. On those days, I am tired. All I want to do is relax, eat, drink, and go to sleep. On the weekends, I take her to the market, and we go to the laundromat. Sometimes we write letters to our relatives and friends. But our life is a lonely one in America. That's why lots of old people want to return to Vietnam. Religion here won't help them, that's only for a few hours on Sunday. People still remain lonely. They dream of fighting the Communists, throwing them out, and returning to live out their days peacefully in their homeland. But this is only a dream.

23   Sometimes my friends call me on the telephone. We talk about our lives here and what other people are doing. We sometimes invite one another to come by and take some food. This is different from Vietnam, where we used to just arrive at the door of our friend, and they'd invite us in. We'd say, "We've got some food ready; why don't you stay and have some." We'd travel around a lot and visit friends, more than here in America. We'd help our friends get jobs, and we'd share room, clothes, food. A friend might stay with us for months; we don't care about that. During holidays, maybe four or five people will come by and stay. That's how we do it.

24   For my wife, adjustment in America is very hard. For me and my children, adjustment is not that difficult. I had some experience in dealing with Westerners before I left Vietnam. My children are young enough to adapt

to new customs. Within three days of our arrival in America, I had enrolled them in school, within four months, they were speaking English.

25 Somewhat difficult for us was learning to cope with American food, which contains too much salt and sugar, and very peculiar seasoning. We dislike it, and I still eat mostly Vietnamese-style food. At my place of work, I eat food that I have taken from home. My daughters have learned to tolerate American food, but prefer Vietnamese.

26 Also hard for us is the speaking of English. Often we can read well, but because of our pronunciation people think we are not well educated. We find it quite difficult to ask for information over the telephone, so we may drive 20 or 30 miles to get the information. Yesterday, I tried to call a pet shop where I had bought two finches. I said to the man, "The mother bird has laid five eggs, but after they hatched, she kicked them out of her nest area, and they died. What should I do to prevent that?"

27 The men at the pet shop said, "Sorry, I cannot understand what you said."

28 I asked an American friend to call for me. He received the information and relayed it to me.

29 That's not the only language problem. One morning I was cleaning our floor with a vacuum cleaner that made a lot of noise. The people who live below us pounded on the ceiling with something. They were angry, I guess. I went next door to an American lady and asked her to explain to the people below that I was cleaning with a vacuum cleaner. She did that, and the people said it was okay.

30 In 1979, I enrolled in a technical training institute where I received nine months of instruction. I started out in one field, but a friend persuaded me to try another. It turned out I had quite a bit of skill for it, so my counselor at the institute let me switch. After completing my training, I went out to look for work. My friend, who was younger, was hired immediately; I had more difficulty, for when people saw that I was in my fifties, they were not anxious to hire me. After two months, one company offered me a job. The man who hired me said, "Take five dollars an hour."

31 I replied, "No, six."

32 "Okay," the man said. "I'll hire you."

33 In Vietnam, a man of my age would have retired. I would have been able to support my family to the end of my life. But not in America. I tell my children to work hard, because I will not be able to help them forever; one day they will be on their own. I have no security of any kind here; I must keep working as long as I have a job, and it might end at any moment.

34 I liked my job in Vietnam much more. I talked with people of a higher class, and people treated me with respect. I had three months of paid summer vacation every year. The status of my job in Vietnam was much higher than the factory labor I do here. That is very difficult, not only for me, but

for many other Vietnamese men. We have lost our country. We are making a new life in another country. We don't care about our second life in a new country, that we are lower in status. Even though it is difficult, many of us are happy because our children have a chance here. I'm at the end of my life; I'm happy simply to sacrifice for my children. I'll take any job to help them. I do know some Vietnamese people who are unable to adjust to the loss of their status.

35   I am happy that I was able to change my life and start a new job in America. At least I showed I could make the adjustment. But if you ask me what life is like for me here in America, I have to tell you: Terrible! I say that because all the money I get from my new job is gone. Almost all of it goes for rent, which is increased too much. We have no money for heating. In winter, we keep warm by wrapping blankets around ourselves, and we cover the windows with sheets. We can buy a blanket for seven dollars and use it for a year. We have no need for heat. We never use our big oven, but boil all of our food to keep down the costs. For food, we don't pay too much. If food increases in price, we decrease how much we eat. If rent increases, there is no way to decrease. Rent is a major problem for us. I have some health coverage at my place of work, but it is so inadequate that when I am ill, I try to avoid doctors and hospitals because they are so expensive. I use home remedies; my wife uses herbal medicines. That's why we are able to survive on so much less than other Americans.

36   I often wonder what will happen to my family. The future of my children is bright, for they work hard and have talent. They know they must work hard, for I will not be able to help them much longer. The work I do requires good hand-and-eye coordination. One day I will lose that. What will happen to me then? Sometimes I worry about my future; at other times I don't care.

DISCUSSION QUESTIONS

1. The narrator mentions many things that have made his and his wife's lives difficult in America. What are the effects of unfriendly people, failure to speak English or to pronounce it properly, and a low-paying job?
2. Discuss why it would be difficult to adjust to a loss of status.
3. How do you feel about the narrator's assertion that "the old people in America are very nice, but young people are rude and destructive"?
4. What did you learn about community life in Vietnam?

Writing Topics

1. What would you say to someone who complained that there were too many "foreigners" in America, that they take jobs away from Americans, and that "they" ought to learn to live like Americans or return to their home countries? Write a well-reasoned reply.

2. In an essay, compare this narrator's experiences adjusting to life in the United States with Carlos Bulosan's (from *America Is in the Heart*). Choose two or three categories in which to compare them; for instance, whose existence seems more precarious? who seems more homesick?

3. Research in periodicals or on the Internet one or two Vietnamese communities in the United States, the people's feelings about their new country, and the modes of life of the Vietnamese people in these communities, and report to the class.

SHRAPNEL SHARDS ON BLUE WATER

Lê Thi Diem Thúy

Lê Thi Diem Thúy was born in Vietnam in 1972 and grew up in Southern California. One of her short stories is included in the *Best American Essays 1997* (1997). Her work has appeared in many anthologies, including *The Very Inside* (1994), *The Arc of Love* (1995), and *Watermark: Vietnamese American Poetry and Prose* (1998). She is working on a memoir and a novel, titled *The Bodies Between Us.*

In the following poem a Vietnamese immigrant, contrasting life in the homeland with life in California—which is, after all, on the other side of the same ocean—pleads for understanding that Vietnam is not just the name of a war.

every day i beat a path to run to you
beaten into the melting snow/the telephone poles
which separate us like so many signals of slipping time
and signposts marked in another language
5 my path winds and unwinds, hurls itself toward you
until it unfurls before you
all my stories at your feet
rocking against each other like marbles
down a dirt incline
10 listen

ma took the train every morning
sunrise
from phan thiet to saigon
she arrived
15 carrying food to sell at the markets

past sunset
late every evening she carried her empty baskets
home
on the train which runs in the opposite direction
20 away from the capital
towards the still waters of the south china sea

once ba[1] bought an inflatable raft
yellow and black
he pushed it out onto a restricted part of the water
25 in southern california
after midnight
to catch fish in the dark
it crashed against the rocks
he dragged it back to the van
30 small and wet
he drove us home
our backs turned in shame
from the pacific ocean

our lives have been marked by the tide
35 everyday it surges forward
hits the rocks
strokes the sand
turns back into itself again
a fisted hand

40 know this about us
we have lived our lives
on the edge of oceans
in anticipation of
sailing into the sunrise

45 i tell you all this
to tear apart the silence
of our days and nights here

I tell you all this
to fill the void of absence
50 in our history here

---

[1] *ba:* father.

we are fragmented shards
blown here by a war no one wants to remember

in a foreign land
with an achingly familiar wound
55   our survival is dependent upon
never forgetting that vietnam is not
a word
a world
a love
60   a family
a fear
to bury

let people know
VIETNAM IS NOT A WAR

65   let people know
VIETNAM IS NOT A WAR

but a piece
of
us,
70   sister
and
we are
so much

more

Discussion Questions

1. Who is the "you" in the poem?
2. Discuss the references to seas, oceans, and sunrise.
3. To what does the speaker compare the Vietnamese or her family?
4. Why do you think the speaker is so vehement about letting people know
   that Vietnam is not something to bury and not a war?
5. What is Vietnam, according to the speaker?

WRITING TOPIC ·

1. Qui-Phiet Tran, an associate professor of English at Schreiner University in Texas, has written that in the mass media, "generally the resettlement of Vietnamese in the new land has been presented as a success story," even in Vietnam, but that "this idyllic portrayal of Vietnamese immigrants ironically finds no echo in Vietnamese American literature." Review the Vietnamese literature you have read so far in this anthology. Is Tran right, and, if so, how would you account for this discrepancy?

2. In a brief essay, analyze and characterize the mood and tone of this poem and how they are conveyed.

SUMMARY WRITING TOPICS

1: Write a persuasive essay arguing for or against the right of American citizens to refuse to serve in the military during time of war.

2: The narrators in the selections by Mitsuye Yamada, Hisaye Yamamoto, and John Okada all share a sense of guilt. In an essay, compare the experiences of these three narrators and examine whether their feelings of guilt are based on things they did or did not do or on their perceptions of themselves or how others perceive them.

3: In an essay, tell which of the selections you found most surprising and what chief thing you learned about Asian Americans in this chapter.

4: The immigration and assimilation experiences of the authors and narrators in this anthology vary widely. In an essay, compare the experiences of a nineteenth-century Chinese immigrant (as described in the selection by Ruthanne Lum McCunn) with those of a late twentieth-century Vietnamese refugee (as described to James Freeman). What similarities and differences do you find?

5: Many Asian Americans have made substantial contributions to American politics, medicine, movies, television, and the arts. Find biographical material on one of the following prominent Asian Americans and write a profile of that person: Daniel K. Inouye, Patsy Takemoto Mink, Connie Chung, Maya Lin, David Henry Hwang. Or research a well-known Asian-American whose name does not appear on this list.

CHAPTER FOUR

THE INDIVIDUAL INSIDE/
AGAINST THE ETHNIC
COMMUNITY

Although Asian Americans are often presented as homogenous and united, like all Americans they share the ideal of individualism and find themselves conflicted between the social values of their families and community, which emphasize the importance of the group, and those of U.S. society, in which the individual is primary.

Especially for native-born Asian Americans, the generation gap between parents and children may be more significant than it is for other Americans. Immigrant Asian Americans bring with them specific cultural practices from their countries of origin that their children may find strange or irrelevant. Sometimes the children no longer speak the language of their parents, or they have to serve as translators for non-English-speaking parents who find themselves disadvantaged in American society. The selections in this chapter address the many tensions that can arise in the formation of an individual identity within a community whose group identity is maintained through clearly demarcated boundaries set up by familial obligations and group-dictated conventions for behavior. The individual is thus subsumed to the greater good of the community.

Japanese Americans, because they were among the earliest to enter the United States and to become institutionally assimilated, have produced a large body of literature on this theme. The chapter from Milton Murayama's novel *All I Asking for Is My Body* focuses on one portion of this historical community—the Japanese American immigrants to Hawaii. The narrator describes a society in which family members, especially the oldest son, are obligated to subsume their interests to those of the oldest male member, the patriarch, and to honor their obligations to their parents and their younger siblings. The chapter suggests that a community in which "filial duty" is the paramount operative value creates submissive and passive individuals who are more vulnerable to economic exploitation and oppression. Thus, in their acceptance of the grandfather's debts, Tosh's family, despite their years of hard work to improve their economic standing, find themselves drastically impoverished. Tosh, the "number one son," has to sacrifice his individual dreams for mobility and a better life for his grandfather, his parents, and the many children his parents continue to have.

The individual is pitted not only against a consuming familial structure but also in the ethos of capitalist competition against other individuals in the community. Economic binds take a different turn in Toshio Mori's short story "The Chessmen." Set during the Depression, the story concerns the competition for employment between Nakagawa, a first-generation Japanese American who works in the nursery in order to support his family, and George, a second-generation Japanese American who needs a "steady job" in order to marry the girl he loves. For Mori, the economic competition between the older and the younger man, despite their common ethnic identity, illustrates "the struggle that knew no friendship, the deep stamp of self-preservation in human nature."

Asian American authors such as Wakako Yamauchi in her short story "And the Soul Shall Dance" focus on the psychological costs to the individual who holds different ideals of self, beauty, or goodness from those of the community. Mrs. Oka, ostracized by the Japanese American community and by her husband and stepdaughter for her drinking and erratic behavior, is glimpsed as an unhappy and isolated woman whose sweet voice, stately dance, and childlike delight suggest a sensitive artist trapped in an abusive, loveless marriage. Similarly, Juliet S. Kono's poem "Before Time" offers a strong criticism of the kind of ethnocentricism that teaches Asian Americans to marry "only some of our own kind" and to treat those outside their community as inferior, while the chapter from Lydia Minatoya's memoir *Talking to High Monks in the Snow* critiques the passivity and apathy of Japanese Americans who believe that they can fully assimilate into white America.

Maxine Hong Kingston's "No Name Woman," the first chapter in her award-winning memoir, *The Woman Warrior,* weaves these conflicts between the desires of the individual and the community's constraints into her story of an aunt who drowns herself and her illegitimate child after the villagers have destroyed her family home in retribution for her "crime." The chapter uses this story to open up an examination of the conflictual relationship between first-generation, or "emigrant," Chinese Americans and native-born Chinese Americans, between the narrator's dominant immigrant mother and herself. While Kingston speaks as a critical yet affiliated daughter, Genny Lim's poem, "ABCs" (referring to "American-Born Chinese") criticizes the younger generation who, accustomed to fast travel, cannot understand the immigrant experiences of the "old folk."

Lois-Ann Yamanaka's poem excerpt, written in pidgin English, imagines the voice of a parent who is violently and emotionally abusive. The parent not only controls the children's actions but also tries to control their thoughts and emotions. In contrast, Bharati Mukherjee's short story "The Management of Grief," beginning with the news of a terrorist bombing of a plane off the coast of Ireland, moves on to describe the disintegration of families and communities in the aftermath of this tragedy. At the beginning of the narrative, Mrs. Bhave, the main character and narrator, who has lost her husband and two sons, is seen by others as strong and stoical. The story follows the increasing gulf between her external show of calm and her deepening despair; the terrorist bomb has destroyed not only those on board the plane but the individuals who have lost the people they love. Rather than finding solace in her Indian community, Mrs. Bhave, desolate, returns to Canada to face her fate as an individual bereft of community.

Quang Bao's short story "Nobody Knows" picks up a common struggle in many Asian American families, the struggle to have the younger generation marry within the ethnic community, and thus continue the family line. "Nobody Knows" is a sardonically comic portrayal of such a conflict. The narrator, who is already in a "four-year relationship," wishes to share the "important things and people" in his life with his parents. But his mother and father are united in their refusal to acknowledge his personal life, which, the story suggests, does not fit into a traditional Vietnamese mold. Instead, they pressure him to marry a woman from an Asian community—this despite the failure of their own relationship. The Vietnamese American father, whose impotency and illusions of military success in Vietnam inspire little respect in the son, nonetheless continues to assert a critical authority over his life.

These narratives and poems represent some of the tensions that characterize the relationship of the individual to the larger Asian American community. Generational differences in language use, cultural values and social habits, the overbearing weight of group expectations and familial obligations, political violence between nationalist ethnics, abuse and oppressive conformity—Asian American authors take these as their themes because they constitute a significant if sometimes hidden aspect of their ethnic experience.

FROM *ALL I ASKING FOR IS MY BODY*

Milton Murayama

Milton Murayama was born in 1923 and grew up in Lahaina, Maui, on a plantation that once housed over 600 people but that no longer exists. After training at the Military Intelligence Language School at Camp Savage, Minnesota, he served as an interpreter in India and China during World War II. In 1947 he graduated from the University of Hawaii, where he studied English and philosophy, and in 1950 he earned a master's degree in Chinese and Japanese from Columbia University.

Now a resident of San Francisco, Murayama is the author of *All I Asking for Is My Body* (1959) and *Five Years on a Rock* (1994), two novels that form the first half of a tetralogy still in progress. Set in Hawaii, both novels chronicle the experiences of members of the Oyama family. In the first novel the son, Kiyoshi, a second-generation Japanese American (or nisei), struggles to define himself in the face of familial and cultural pressures. The second novel movingly recounts the story of Sawa Oyama, the mother, whose immigration from Japan to Hawaii presents her with seemingly insurmountable hardships.

The most striking feature of *All I Asking for Is My Body* is the multiple voices that Murayama creates. In order to capture the various languages that the Oyamas speak—standard English, standard Japanese, pidgin English, and pidgin Japanese—he moves adeptly among various vernaculars and languages, usually limiting the use of pidgin forms to the novel's dialogue. Kiyoshi, the narrator of the novel, tells his story in Standard English but speaks all four languages when in conversation with other characters. Critics have often praised Murayama's writing for its linguistic authenticity and its accessibility; Murayama always intended to target an audience that included and yet went beyond a Hawaiian readership.

In the excerpt below, immigrants to Hawaii are driven by filial duty as they struggle to make a life at the bottom of the economic pyramid. (J.I.)

1   On August 1, 1936, another girl was born and father must've been a little disappointed. He named her *Tsuneko* (Common child). By the end of the month he decided to quit fishing and move the family back to Kahana where he'd first arrived in 1910. Tosh was to quit high school and work in the cane fields to help support the family. It was what every number one son was expected to do. Father had done it for twelve years, turning over his entire pay to grandfather every month. Even after mother was sent for in 1915 and even after Tosh was born in 1919, father gave grandfather all of his pay. It was a model story of filial piety, which mother told over and over. Great grandfather died while grandfather was in business college, and grandfather quit school and returned to the family farm in Wakayama, Japan. He was number one son and he inherited the farm, but he wasn't any good at farming and after a couple of years, he sold the farm. He married grandmother who was a couple of years older for her dowry, and he opened a clothing store in Osaka with the dowry and money from the farm. The store kept failing and he kept borrowing money from relatives and friends till he finally went broke seven years later. By then he had a huge debt and three young sons, father being number one. But he refused to declare bankruptcy, and promised every creditor he'd pay back every cent. He looked up *Obaban,* his older sister who'd been kicked out of the family, and wrote to her in Kahana. He left his children with relatives in Japan and came to Kahana in 1902 with grandmother. Three more children were born, and father and his two brothers were sent for, and sent to work in the cane fields. When grandfather finally saved enough money to return to Japan in 1922, mother begged him to leave father and her some money. She was carrying another child, and they had nothing to live on for the next month. Grandfather wept and he begged mother not to ask. He needed every penny he'd saved. He had all the debts he had to pay back in Japan, he had a family of two girls and one boy he was taking back with him. There were the boat fare, winter clothing and a hundred unforeseen expenses after which he had to have enough to open a clothing store in Tokyo. Not only that, he asked father to pay the bill for his farewell party, which came to $300; he asked father to look after his two younger brothers. He cried, "I'll repay you. I'll send for you as soon as I'm successful! I can't ask for more filial children!" "That's why," mother would say to us,

"our minds are at peace even if he should die tomorrow. We've done our filial duty to him."

2   Moving to Kahana was a shock. The place had no indoor toilets, no private baths. It's what I hated most when I visited *Obaban* in the summer. I went with Mr. Hida of Hida Store in Pepelau, who drove there every Wednesday to deliver the orders he'd taken the week before. If I missed him, it meant I'd be stuck for a whole week. Now I was going to be stuck forever! Where I'd been only three blocks from the ocean in Pepelau, Kahana was two miles from the ocean up a pretty steep hill. In Pepelau the cane fields started beyond the plantation camps of Mill Camp, Ohia Camp, and Hau Camp, a good two miles from the center of town; in Kahana the cane fields surrounded you and they began right beyond your yard. It was like my childhood was chopped off clean.

3   In Pepelau we called the guys *bobora* (country bumpkins) who were too Japanese. In Kahana everybody was a *bobora*. Their heads looked bigger with their shorter haircuts. Most of the Japanese in Kahana had come there in the 1890's and 1900's from farming villages in Japan, and they were cut off from the world ever since. There were many different races in Pepelau, but Kahana had about one hundred Japanese families, about two hundred Filipino men, about seven Portuguese and Spanish families, and only two haoles.[1] Mr. Boyle was the principal of the Kahana Grade School, and Mr. Nelson was the overseer of Kahana. There'd been many Chinese workers before, but they left and opened stores in Pepelau and the other towns as soon as their contracts expired.

4   It was a company town with identical company houses and outhouses, and it was set up like a pyramid. At the tip was Mr. Nelson, then the Portuguese, Spanish, and nisei *lunas*[2] in their nicer-looking homes, then the identical wooden frame houses of Japanese Camp, then the more run-down Filipino Camp. There were a plantation store, a plantation mess hall for the Filipino bachelors, a plantation community bathhouse, and a plantation social hall. The *lunas* or strawbosses had their own baths and indoor toilets. There were a Catholic Church, the Japanese language school which became the Methodist Church on Sundays, a Buddhist hall, and a plantation dispensary which was open from 11 to 12 noon every working day.

5   The macadamized or "government" road ended in front of Mr. Nelson's big yard, and all the roads in camp were "plantation" roads, and the dirt was so red it stained your clothes and feet. The guys in Pepelau used to joke about how they could spot a guy from Kahana by his red feet. The place was so country they used newspaper for toilet paper, and each outhouse building was partitioned into four toilets. The rough one-by-sixteen planks used for

---

[1] *haoles:* white people.
[2] *lunas:* plantation overseers, usually of Portuguese or white descent.

the partitions did not go up to the rafters, and you could hear all the farts and everything going on in the other toilets. A three-foot-deep concrete ditch ran underneath all the toilets, and you sat back to back against a common partition with one of the other toilets. You were so close in fact you could touch the other guy's ass if you lifted the big square toilet seat. There were half a dozen rows of outhouses and the ditches under them were flushed downhill to a big concrete irrigation ditch which ran around the lower boundary of the camp, and sooner or later feces, newspaper and all ended up in the furrows of the fields below. The plantation had built pigpens along the four-foot-wide *kukai*[3] ditch, and rented them to the workers. Every family kept pigs.

6   The house we moved into, No. 173, was the last house on "Pig Pen Avenue" and next to the pigpens and ditch, and when the wind stopped blowing or when the warm Kona wind blew from the south, our house smelled like both an outhouse and a pigpen. Worse yet, the family debt was now $6,000, and the average plantation pay for forty-eight hours a week was $25 a month for adults. There was no sick pay, no holiday pay though you got off Christmas, New Year's, and one day during the County Fair in October.

7   I felt sorry for Tosh the first few months. He'd come home from the fields and collapse on the wooden floor in the parlor. A couple of times he skipped supper and bath, and slept right through in his denim work clothes covered with dust and stained with red sweat. The work clothes got so red and dirty, mother had to boil them for several hours on Saturdays. She'd done the same thing back in 1915 when she arrived from Japan.

8   "How come you bear more children than you can send to high school?" Tosh said one day when he came home from work.

9   "You *ni ga haru* (too big for your breeches). You've worked only three months and you're talking big. Look at Minoru Tanaka, Hideo Shimada, Kenji Watanabe, Toru Minami, they've been working for their parents for over ten years, and they never complain," mother said.

10   "They're dumb, that's why. They don't want to go to high school. With me it's different. I *like* school."

11   "Every child must repay his parents."

12   "How much? How long?"

13   "Your father helped grandfather for twelve years without one word of complaint."

14   "Grandfather is a thief."

15   "Don't you dare say that in front of father."

16   "He had you and father and two uncles work for him for twelve years and he took all the money and ran away to Japan."

---

[3] *kukai:* excrement.

17   "He's an honest man. He wanted to pay back all his debts. He needed all the money to open another store."

18   "That's why he lost everything. It was his retribution."

19   "Nobody could've foreseen the earthquake."

20   "So now you want us to throw away our lives to get papa out of debt."

21   "Don't worry, we won't depend on you. There's Kiyoshi to help us."

22   "That's what you get for bearing nothing but good-for-nothing girls."

23   "You've worked only three months and you're acting like a crybaby."

24   "I can think ahead, that's why. You and papa can't see beyond your noses."

25   "We'll depend on Kiyoshi."

26   They went round and round. Mother was getting stronger now and she didn't give up easy.

27   Tosh had been a boxing nut from way back. He'd gone to all of the boxing matches at the stadium behind the mill in Pepelau. He hung around the Filipino boxers and watched them train in the empty houses around Pepelau, and he always volunteered whenever they staged a match for the kids. He'd ordered a set of cloth boxing gloves from Sears Roebuck in Los Angeles when we were in Pepelau. Now he ordered a leather set, 18-ounce, and a light bag, which he installed at the back of the house. Every day after work he'd punch it and he could hit it so fast it sounded like a piece of paper caught in an electric fan. And he took me in the back yard and he practiced all the parries and counters shown in Jimmy DeForest's *How to Box* pamphlets. He'd have me lead each time, a left jab, left hook, right cross, and he'd counter. We'd go through it in slow motion first, then gradually pick up speed till he was doing it by reflex almost.

DISCUSSION QUESTIONS

1. What is your opinion of the filial duty required of the oldest son at this time in history?
2. Explain the concept of and possible reasons for the "company town" described.
3. How many different nationalities lived in Kahana and who was at the top and the bottom of the pyramid or hierarchy?
4. The narrator's mother says that "every child must repay his parents." Tosh says that his grandfather was a thief. Who is right in your opinion?

WRITING TOPICS

1. How much do children owe their parents in the society in which you live? What kind of "payment" is expected or even demanded? Examine these questions in an informal essay.
2. In a brief essay, describe Murayama's tone in this excerpt and explain how it affects you as a reader. Would you have felt differently had Murayama related these same events in a different manner?

THE CHESSMEN

Toshio Mori

Toshio Mori was born in Oakland, California, in 1910 and was raised and educated in the San Francisco Bay Area—more specifically the East Bay. Specificity of location is a critical component of Mori's writing; his well-known collection of stories entitled *Yokohama, California* (1949), now considered a foundational and abiding work of Asian American literature, is an imaginative and detailed account of the Japanese American communities in Oakland and San Leandro, mostly in the 1920s and 1930s—communities that had not yet been touched by the devastation of World War II. The collection was slated to go to press in 1941; however, its publication was delayed because of the escalation of the war and the removal of 110,000 Japanese Americans from the western United States to internment camps in the interior. Mori was interned at the Topaz Relocation Center in Utah, where he served as the camp historian. In 1949 *Yokohama, California* was finally published, but it went out of print soon after.

The history of this collection's revival and republication shares much in common with the rediscovery of John Okada's novel *No-No Boy* (a portion of which appears in this book), although Mori, unlike Okada, was able to resume his writing. In 1970 the editors of the anthology *Aiiieeeee!* found in a used-book shop a copy of *Yokohama, California*, which they bought for 25 cents. An old newspaper clipping tucked into the collection noted that Mori lived in San Leandro; after finding his name in the phone book, the four young editors, eager to establish an Asian American literary tradition, contacted Mori, then in his sixties. Mori restarted his career as a fiction writer, publishing a novel entitled *Woman from Hiroshima* in 1978 and another volume of short stories called *The Chauvinist and Other Stories* in 1979. He died in 1980.

In the following story, taken from *Yokohama, California,* friendship between young and old turns into a struggle for self-preservation. (J.I.)

◉

1   Perhaps I would have heard the news in time, but if I hadn't met the
third party of the three principals at the beginning it wouldn't have been the
same to me. By luck that day, while I was leaning on the fence resting after
a hot day's work, a young Japanese came up to me. "Hello. Where's
Hatayama's nursery?" he asked me. "I was told the place was somewhere
around here."

2   "It's a half a mile farther down," I said. I pointed out the road and told
him to go until he reached the greenhouses. That was Hatayama Nursery.
The young Japanese thanked me and went away.

3   At Hatayama Nursery I knew two men, Hatayama-san and Nakagawa-
san. They were the only men there the year around. The boss and his help.
The two managed the three greenhouses of carnations quite capably. Only
in the summer months when the carnation boxes must be lined up and filled
with new soil and the plants for the next year planted, Hatayama-san hired
additional men. Hatayama-Nakagawa combination worked beautifully. For
seven years the two men never quarreled and seldom argued with each
other. While Hatayama-san was at the flower market selling flowers to the
florists Nakagawa-san carried on at the nursery. He was wise on everything.
He attended the boiler, watered the plants, made cuttings, cut flowers and
tackled the rest of the nursery work.

4   Every once in awhile I used to visit the place and talk to these middle-
aged men. Perhaps Nakagawa-san was older than his boss. I don't know.
"Listen to him, Takeo," Hatayama-san used to tell me. "If you want to
become a good carnation grower listen to this man. He's got something. He
has many years of experience and a young man like you will learn plenty by
listening to him."

5   Nakagawa-san used to smile with these words. He talked very little. "I
don't know much," he would say. "I know very little."

6   One of the strange things about Nakagawa-san was his family life. I used
to visit him only on the weekdays. On Saturday nights and Sundays he was
in Oakland to see his family. I used to wonder how he could stand it. His
wife and three grown children lived in the city while he worked alone in the
nursery. He made his bed, washed his work clothes, swept and mopped his
bunkhouse after work hours. The only domestic work he didn't do was
cook. He ate with the Hatayamas.

7   When I'd sit and talk with him he'd talk about his family and his week-end visits.

8   "My youngest boy is now out of high school," he would tell me. "He's a smart boy but I can't send him to college."

9   "That's too bad for him," I would say. "But you're sending Tom to Cal. That's plenty."

10   "Yes," he would proudly say. "I hope he'll amount to something."

11   Nakagawa-san's only daughter worked as a domestic in an American home and helped with the upkeep of her parents' home. Often he would tell me of his children and his eyes would shine with a far-away look.

12   "Why don't you stay with the family all the time, Nakagawa-san?" I'd ask him. "Why can't you get a job in Oakland and live with your family?"

13   He would smile. "Ah, I wish I could," he'd say. "But what could an old nursery worker do in a city? I'm too old to find other jobs. No, I must remain here."

14   "It's a shame," I'd tell him.

15   "I guess we can't have everything," he'd say and smile. "I'm lucky to have this job so long."

16   Several weeks after the young man had asked about Hatayama Nursery he came to see me one night. He said his name was George Murai. "I get very lonely here," he explained to me. "I never knew a nursery could be so lonely."

17   "You're from the city, aren't you?" I asked.

18   "Oakland," he said.

19   He was a pleasant fellow. He talked a lot and was eager. "Whenever I have the time I'm going to drop in and see you. That's if you don't mind," he said. "Over at Hatayama's I don't see any young people. I'll go crazy if I don't see somebody. In Oakland I have lots of friends."

20   I brought out beer and shredded shrimp. George could take beer.

21   "How do you like the work?" I asked him.

22   "Fine," he said. "I like it. Someday I'd like to have a nursery of my own. Only I hope I get over being lonely."

23   "You'll be all right after you get used to it," I said.

24   "If I don't give up at the start I'll be all right," George said. "I don't think I'll quit. I have a girl, you see."

25   He pulled out of his wallet a candid shot of a young girl. "That's Lorraine Sakoda of Berkeley," he said. "Do you know her?"

26   I shook my head.

27   "We're crazy about each other," George said. "As soon as I find a steady job we're going to get married."

28   Before the evening was over I knew George pretty well. Several times when we mentioned friends we found them mutual. That made us feel pretty good.

29 After the first visit George Murai came often. He would tell me how the work progressed at Hatayama Nursery. It was getting busy. The carnation boxes had to be laid out evenly on the tracks. The soil had to be worked and shoveled in. The little carnation plants must be transplanted from the ground to the boxes. It was interesting to George.

30 "I'm learning everything, Takeo," he said. "Some day I'll get a nursery for myself and Lorraine."

31 When I went over to Hatayamas to see the boss as well as Nakagawa-san and George Murai, I would catch a glimpse of a new liveliness on the place. The eagerness of George Murai was something of a charm to watch. He would trot from one work to another as if he were eagerly playing a game. His shouts and laughter filled the nursery and the two men whose capering days were over would look at each other and smile. George's singing ability pleased Hatayama-san. After supper he'd ask George to sing. George knew only the modern popular songs.

32 Sometimes Nakagawa-san, George and I got together in the little house. Nakagawa-san shared the place with George. At such times George would ask question after question about carnation growing. He would ask how to get rid of red spiders; how such things as rust and spots, the menaces of the plants, could be controlled. He would press for an answer on how to take the crops at a specific period, how to avoid stem rot and root rot, what fertilizers to mix, how to take care of the cuttings. I would sit aside and listen to Nakagawa-san answer each problem patiently and thoroughly.

33 Sometimes the talk swung to Oakland. The three of us were attached to Oakland one way or another.

34 "I know your son Tom pretty well," George Murai told Nakagawa-san one night.

35 "Do you? Do you know Tom?" Nakagawa-san asked eagerly.

36 "Sure. Tom and I used to go to Tech High together," George said. "He's going to college now."

37 "Sure! Sure!" Nakagawa-san said.

38 "I know your daughter Haruyo," George said. "But I don't know Tetsuo so well."

39 Nakagawa-san nodded his head vigorously. "He's a smart boy but I can't send him to college like Tom."

40 It wasn't until I was alone with Hatayama-san one day that I began to see a change on the place. In the latter part of August Hatayama-san was usually busy hunting around for two husky men to work on the boxes. It was the time when the old plants in the greenhouses were rooted out and the boxes filled with the old soil hauled away. Then the boxes with the new carnation plants were to be hauled in. It was the beginning of heavy work in a nursery.

41 This year Hatayama-san said, "I can't afford to hire more men. Flower business has been bad. We'll have no flowers to sell until November. That's

a long way off. After the new boxes are in I'll have to lay off Murai boy."

42   "Who's going to work the boxes this year?" I asked.

43   "Murai and Nakagawa," Hatayama-san said. "They'll have to do it."

44   When the heavy work at Hatayama Nursery actually started George Murai stopped coming to see me. One afternoon when I got off early and went over there they were still out in the field. It was then I saw the struggle that knew no friendship, the deep stamp of self-preservation in human nature. Here was no flowery gesture; here were no words.

45   I stood and watched Nakagawa-san and George Murai push the truck-loads of carnation boxes one after another without resting. In the late afternoon their sweat dried and the cool wind made the going easier. It was obvious that George being young and strong could hold a stiff pace; and that he was aware that he would be laid off when the heavy work was finished. With the last opportunity to impress the boss George did his stuff.

46   I was certain that Nakagawa-san sensed the young man's purpose. He stuck grimly to the pace. All this was old stuff to him. He had been through it many times. Two men were needed to lift the boxes with the old soil and toss it deftly onto the pile so that no clump of dirt would be left sticking to the boxes. Two men were needed to carefully lift the boxes with the new plants and haul them into the greenhouses. The pace which one of the men worked up could show up the weaker and the slower partner. A man could break another man with a burst of speed maintained for several days. One would be certain to break down first. When a young man set up a fast pace and held it day after day it was something for a middle-aged man to think about.

47   Nakagawa-san straightened as if his back ached, but he was trying to conceal it. His forearms must have been shot with needle-like pains but he worked silently.

48   As I watched Nakagawa-san and George Murai heaving and pushing with all their might I lost sight of the fact that they were the friends I knew. They were like strangers on a lonely road coming face to face with fear. They looked like men with no personal lives; no interests in family life, in Oakland, in Lorraine Sakoda, in the art of plant-growing, in friendship. But there it was in front of my eyes.

49   I turned back and went home. I wondered how they could share the little shack after what was happening on the field.

50   I went over several times but each night they were so worn out with the strain of their pace they slept early. I saw them less and less. Their house was often dark and I knew they were asleep. I would then go over to see Hatayama-san.

51   "Come in, come in," he would greet me.

52   By the manner in which he talked about Nakagawa-san and George it was plain that he too had seen the struggle on the field. He would tell me

how strong and fast George was. At the rate they were going they would be finished a week ahead of the last year's schedule.

53   "Nakagawa is getting old," he would tell me of his friend. "He's getting too old for a worker."

54   "He's experienced," I would reply.

55   "Yes," he'd say, "but George is learning fast. Already he knows very much. He's been reading about the modern method of plant growing. I've already put in an electric hotbed through George's suggestion."

56   Then I knew George Murai was not so close to being fired. "Are you going to keep both of them this winter?" I asked.

57   Hatayama-san shook his head. "No. Can't afford it. I've got to let one of them go."

58   Several nights later I saw lights in their little shack and went over. George was up. He was at the sink filling the kettle with water. Nakagawa-san was in bed.

59   "What's happened, George?" I said. "Is Nakagawa-san sick?"

60   "No," George said. "He's just tired. His back aches so I'm warming it with hot water and mustard."

61   "I'll be all right tomorrow," Nakagawa-san said.

62   "You're working too hard these days, Nakagawa-san," I said. "You're straining yourself."

63   Nakagawa-san and George were silent. They looked at me as if I had accused them in one way or another.

64   Soon Nakagawa-san was back on the field. However, when I went to see how he was getting along I saw Hatayama-san out on the field with George. By the time I reached them they had pushed the truckloads of carnation boxes in and out of the greenhouses several times. George whistled when he saw me. Hatayama-san nodded his head and grinned. Something had happened to Nakagawa-san.

65   "I knew it was going to happen," Hatayama-san told me. "Nakagawa's getting too old for nursery work. His back troubles him again."

66   In the morning Nakagawa-san had stuck grimly to the work. At noon when he sat down for lunch he couldn't get up afterwards. He had to be carried to the little shack. Mrs. Hatayama applied a new plaster to his back.

67   "I've been on the job for two days. We'll finish on time," Hatayama-san said. "George's been a big help to me."

68   George looked at me and grinned.

69   When the pair resumed carting the boxes I went to see Nakagawa-san. As I entered the room he opened his eyes and smiled at me. He looked very tired. His repeated attempts to smile reminded me of his family and his pride for his sons.

70   "I'll be all right in a few days," he said eagerly. "When my back's healed I'll be like new again."

71   "Sure," I said. "You'll be all right."

72   He read to me a letter from his wife. It was filled with domestic details and his boys' activities at school. They wanted to see him soon. They missed him over the week end. They reasoned it was due to the work at the place. They missed the money too. They wanted him to be sure and bring the money for the house rent and the gas bill.

73   When I came away in the late afternoon Hatayama-san and George were washing their faces and hands back of the woodshed.

74   "How's he getting along?" Hatayama-san asked me.

75   "He says he's all right," I said.

76   "I'll go and see if he wants anything before I eat," George said.

77   George trotted off to the little shack. Hatayama-san motioned me toward the house. "At the end of this month I'm going to drop Nakagawa. I hate to see him go but I must do it," he said. "Nursery is too much for him now. I hate to see him go."

78   "Are you really going to let him go?" I asked.

79   "I'm serious. He goes." He took my arm and we went inside the house. I stayed for dinner. During the courses George talked. "Someday I want to bring my girl here and introduce her," he told Hatayama-san and me. "You'll both like her."

80   Hatayama-san chuckled. "When will you get married, my boy?"

81   George smiled. "I think I can get married right away," he said.

82   Afterwards we listened to a few Japanese records. George got out Guy Lombardo's records and we listened to them. Mrs. Hatayama brought hot tea and Japanese teacakes. When I left George accompanied me to the road. He was in a merry mood. He whistled "I Can't Give You Anything But Love."

83   We said, "So long."

84   "Be sure to come again," he said. As I walked down the road I heard his whistling for quite a distance. When the whistling stopped the chants of the crickets in the fields became loud. Across the lot from the greenhouses I saw the little shack lit by a single light, and I knew that Nakagawa-san was not yet asleep.

DISCUSSION QUESTIONS

1. How is the ending of the story foreshadowed?
2. What circumstances make it crucial that Nakagawa keep his job?
3. Is George Murai in any way to blame for Nakagawa's plight?

4. How does Mori elicit sympathy for Nakagawa?
5. Explain the title of the story.

WRITING TOPICS

1. In a brief essay, trace the sequence of cause and effect incidents in the story, and identify the climax. What starts the chain of events?
2. Predict what will happen to Nakagawa and his family in an essay, poem, or short story.

AND THE SOUL SHALL DANCE

Wakako Yamauchi

Wakako Yamauchi was born in 1924 and lived a nomadic life during her childhood years. Her parents, first-generation tenant farmers, were not eligible for citizenship and could not own land under California's Alien Land Law, so her family was forced to move often. In the 1930s Yamauchi's parents decided to end the family's itinerant existence; they ran a boardinghouse for Japanese immigrants in Oceanside, California. During World War II, the family was incarcerated at an internment camp in Poston, Arizona—the same camp in which Hisaye Yamamoto spent several of the war years. Both young women worked for the camp newspaper, the *Poston Chronicle,* but in different capacities: Yamauchi did layout and design, and Yamamoto wrote a column. Their friendship, begun during the internment, continues to the present.

After World War II, Yamauchi further developed her artistic interests by taking courses in layout design, drawing, and painting at the Otis Art Center in Los Angeles. From 1960 to 1974, she submitted short stories and drawings to the *Los Angeles Rafu Shimpo,* a Japanese American daily publication. "And the Soul Shall Dance," one of Yamauchi's most widely recognized and anthologized short stories, was selected for *Aiiieeeee!* the first anthology of Asian American writing, published in 1974.

In 1976 she finished her first play, which is based on this now famous short story and bears the same title. The play, performed first by East-West Players in Los Angeles, was nominated for Outstanding New Play of the Year by the Los Angeles Drama Critics Circle. Yamauchi has received numerous awards and recognitions, including the American Theater Critics Regional Award for Outstanding Play, the Brody Art Fund Fellowships, and several Rockefeller grants.

Although she is perhaps best known as a playwright, Yamauchi has also written pieces in other genres that have met with critical success. As literary critic Stan Yogi has pointed out, Yamauchi "por-

tray[s] the resistance of first-generation women and the consequences of their rebellions in narratives that subvert the strict cultural
codes of the issei family."[1] In addition to an exploration of gender
dynamics, Yamauchi examines intergenerational conflict, the immigrant experience, hardships in the harsh agricultural environments of
California, and burgeoning sexuality.

"And the Soul Shall Dance" is a subtle and complex tale of the
struggles of an immigrant family, the fate of the unhappy second
wife, and the acculturation of the newly arrived daughter. (J.I.)

1   It's all right to talk about it now. Most of the principals are dead, except,
of course, me and my younger brother, and possibly Kiyoko Oka, who
might be near forty-five now because, yes, I'm sure of it, she was fourteen
then. I was nine, and my brother about four, so he hardly counts. Kiyoko's
mother is dead, my father is dead, my mother is dead, and her father could
not have lasted all these years with his tremendous appetite for alcohol and
pickled chiles—those little yellow ones, so hot they could make your mouth
hurt—he'd eat them like peanuts and tears would surge from his bulging
thyroid eyes in great waves and stream down the coarse terrain of his face.

2   My father farmed then in the desert basin resolutely named Imperial
Valley, in the township called Westmorland, twenty acres of tomatoes, ten of
summer squash, or vice versa, and the Okas lived maybe a mile, mile and a
half, across an alkaline road, a stretch of greasewood, tumbleweed, and
white sand, to the south of us. We didn't hobnob much with them because,
you see, they were a childless couple and we were a family: father, mother,
daughter, and son, and we went to the Buddhist church on Sundays, where
my mother taught Japanese, and the Okas kept pretty much to themselves.
I don't mean they were unfriendly—Mr. Oka would sometimes walk over
(he rarely drove) on rainy days, all dripping wet, short and squat under a
soggy newspaper, pretending to need a plow blade or a file, and he would
spend the afternoon in our kitchen drinking sake and eating chiles with my
father. As he got drunk, his large mouth would draw down, and with the
stream of tears, he looked like a kindly weeping bullfrog.

3   Not only were they childless, impractical in an area where large families
were looked upon as labor potentials, but there was a certain strangeness
about them. I became aware of it in the summer our bathhouse burned down
and my father didn't get right down to building another, and a Japanese
without a bathhouse . . . well, Mr. Oka offered us the use of his. So every

[1] *Asian-American Women Writers* (Broomall, PA: Chelsea House, 1997) 135.

night that summer we drove to the Okas for our bath, and we came in frequent contact with Mrs. Oka, and this is where I found the strangeness.

4   Mrs. Oka was small and spare. Her clothes hung on her like loose skin, and when she walked, the skirt about her legs gave her a sort of webbed look. She was pretty in spite of the boniness and the dull calico and the barren look. I know now she couldn't have been over thirty. Her eyes were large and a little vacant, although once I saw them fill with tears—the time I insisted we take the old Victrola over and we played our Japanese records for her. Some of the songs were sad, and I imagined the nostalgia she felt, but my mother said the tears were probably from yawning or from the smoke of her cigarettes. I thought my mother resented her for not being more hospitable; indeed, never a cup of tea appeared before us, and between them the conversation of women was totally absent: the rise and fall of gentle voices, the arched eyebrows, the croon of polite surprise. But more than this, Mrs. Oka was different.

5   Obviously she was shy, but some nights she disappeared altogether. She would see us drive into her yard and then lurch from sight. She was gone all evening. Where could she have hidden in that two-room house—where in that silent desert? Some nights she would wait out our visit with enormous forbearance, quietly pushing wisps of stray hair behind her ears and waving gnats away from her great moist eyes, and some nights she moved about with nervous agitation, her khaki canvas shoes slapping loudly as she walked. And sometimes there appeared to be welts and bruises on her usually smooth brown face, and she would sit solemnly, hands on her lap, eyes large and intent on us. My mother hurried us home then: "Masako, no need to wash well. Hurry."

6   You see, being so poky, I was always last to bathe. I think the Okas bathed after we left because my mother often reminded me to keep the water clean. The routine was to lather outside the tub (there were buckets and pans and a small wooden stool), rinse off the soil and soap, and then soak in the tub of hot water and contemplate. Rivulets of perspiration would run down the scalp.

7   When my mother pushed me like this, I dispensed with ritual, rushed a bar of soap around me, and splashed about a pan of water. So hastily toweled, my wet skin trapped the clothes to me, impeding my already clumsy progress. Outside, my mother would be murmuring her many apologies and my father, I knew, would be carrying my brother whose feet were already sandy. We would hurry home.

8   I thought Mrs. Oka might be insane and I asked my mother about it, but she shook her head and smiled with her mouth drawn down and said that Mrs. Oka loved to drink. This was unusual, yes, but there were other unusual women we knew. Mrs. Naka was bought by her husband from a geisha house; Mrs. Tani was a militant Christian Scientist; Mrs. Abe, the

midwife, was occult. My mother's statement explained much: sometimes Mrs. Oka was drunk and sometimes not. Her taste for liquor and cigarettes was a step into the realm of men; unusual for a Japanese wife, but at that time, in that place, and to me, Mrs. Oka loved her sake in the way my father and Mr. Oka loved theirs, the way I loved my candy. That her psychology may have demanded this anesthetic, that she lived with something unendurable, did not occur to me. Nor did I perceive the violence of the purple welts—or the masochism that permitted her to display these wounds to us.

9   In spite of her masculine habits, Mrs. Oka was never less than a woman. She was no lady in the area of social amenities, but the feminine in her was innate and never left her. Even in her disgrace she was a small broken sparrow, slightly floppy, too slowly enunciating her few words, too carefully rolling her Bull Durham, cocking her small head and moistening the ocher tissue. Her aberration was a protest of the life assigned her; it was obstinate but unobserved, alas, unattended. "Strange" was the only concession we granted her.

10   Toward the end of summer, my mother said we could not continue bathing at the Okas'; when winter set in we'd all catch our death from the commuting, and she'd always felt dreadful about our imposition on Mrs. Oka. So my father took the corrugated tin sheets he'd found on the highway and had been saving for some other use and built our bathhouse again. Mr. Oka came to help.

11   While they raised the quivering tin walls, Mr. Oka began to talk. His voice was sharp above the low thunder of the metal sheets.

12   He told my father he had been married previously in Japan to the present Mrs. Oka's older sister. He had a child by the marriage, Kiyoko, a girl. He had left the two to come to America, intending to send for them soon, but shortly after his departure, his wife passed away from an obscure stomach ailment. At the time, the present Mrs. Oka was young and had foolishly become involved with a man of poor reputation. The family was anxious to part the lovers and conveniently arranged a marriage by proxy and sent him his dead wife's sister. Well, that was all right, after all, they were kin and it would be good for the child when she came to join them. But things didn't work out that way—year after year he postponed calling for his daughter, couldn't get the price of the fare together, and the wife . . . ahhh, the wife . . . Mr. Oka's groan was lost in the rumble of his hammering.

13   He cleared his throat. The girl was now fourteen and begging to come to America to be with her own real family. The relatives had forgotten the favor he'd done in accepting a slightly used bride, and now they tormented his daughter for being forsaken. True, he'd not sent much money, but if they knew, if they only knew how it was here.

14   "Well," he sighed, "who could be blamed? It's only right she be with me anyway."

15   "That's right," my father said.

16   "Well, I sold the horse and some other things and managed to buy a third-class ticket on the Taiyo-Maru. Kiyoko will get here the first week of September." Mr. Oka glanced toward my father, but my father was peering into a bag of nails. "I'd be much obliged to you if your wife and little girl," he rolled his eyes toward me, "would take kindly to her. She'll be lonely."

17   Kiyoko-san came in September. I was surprised to see so very nearly a woman—short, robust, buxom—the female counterpart of her father: thyroid eyes and protruding teeth, straight black hair banded impudently into two bristly shucks, Cuban heels and white socks. Mr. Oka proudly brought her to us.

18   For the first time to my recollection, he touched me; he put his fat hand on the top of my head. "Little Masako here is very smart in school. She will help you with your schoolwork, Kiyoko," he said.

19   I had so looked forward to Kiyoko-san's arrival. She would be my soul mate; in my mind I had conjured a girl of my own proportions: thin and tall but with the refinement and beauty I didn't yet possess that would surely someday come to the fore. My disappointment was keen and apparent. Kiyoko-san stepped forward shyly, then retreated with a short bow and small giggle, her fingers pressed to her mouth.

20   My mother took her away. They talked for a long time—about Japan, about enrollment in American school, the clothes Kiyoko-san would need, and where to look for the best values. As I watched them, it occurred to me that I had been deceived. This was not a child, this was a woman. The smile pressed behind her fingers, the way of her nod, so brief, like my mother when father scolded her. The face was inscrutable, but something shrank visibly, like a piece of silk in water. I was disappointed. Kiyoko-san's soul was barricaded in her unenchanting appearance and the smile she fenced behind her fingers.

21   She started school from third grade, one below me, and as it turned out, she quickly passed me by. There wasn't much I could help her with except to drill her on pronunciation—the *L* and *R* sounds. Every morning walking to our rural school: land, leg, library, loan, lot. Every afternoon returning home: ran, rabbit, rim, rinse, roll. That was the extent of our communication—friendly but not close.

22   One particularly cold November night—the wind outside was icy—I was sitting on my bed, my brother's and mine, oiling the cracks on my chapped hands by lamplight—someone rapped urgently at our door. It was Kiyoko-san; she was hysterical, she wore no wrap, her teeth were chattering, and except for the thin straw zori, her feet were bare. My mother led her to the kitchen, started a pot of tea, and gestured to my brother and me to retire. I lay very still but, because of my brother's restless tossing and my father's snoring, was unable to hear much. I was aware, though, that drunken and savage brawling had brought Kiyoko-san to us. Presently they came to the

bedroom. I feigned sleep. My mother gave Kiyoko-san a gown and pushed me over to make room for her. My mother spoke firmly: "Tomorrow you will return to them; you must not leave them again. They are your people." I could almost feel Kiyoko-san's short nod.

23   All night long I lay cramped and still, afraid to intrude into her hulking back. Two or three times her icy feet jabbed into mine and quickly retreated. In the morning I found my mother's gown neatly folded on the spare pillow. Kiyoko-san's place in bed was cold.

24   She never came to weep at our house again, but I know she cried. Her eyes were often swollen and red. She stopped much of her giggling and routinely pressed her fingers to her mouth. Our daily pronunciation drill petered off from lack of interest. She walked silently with her shoulders hunched, grasping her books with both arms, and when I spoke to her in my halting Japanese, she absently corrected my prepositions.

25   Spring comes early in the valley; in February the skies are clear though the air is still cold. By March, winds are vigorous and warm and wildflowers dot the desert floor, cockleburs are green and not yet tenacious, the sand is crusty underfoot, everywhere there is the smell of things growing, and the first tomatoes are showing green and bald.

26   As the weather changed, Kiyoko-san became noticeably more cheerful. Mr. Oka, who hated so to drive, could often be seen steering his dusty old Ford over the road that passes our house, and Kiyoko-san, sitting in front, would sometimes wave gaily to us. Mrs. Oka was never with them. I thought of these trips as the westernizing of Kiyoko-san: with a permanent wave, her straight black hair became tangles of frantic curls, between her textbooks she carried copies of *Modern Screen* and *Photoplay,* her clothes were gay with print and piping, and she bought a pair of brown suede shoes with alligator trim. I can see her now, picking her way gingerly over the white peaks of alkaline crust.

27   At first my mother watched their coming and going with vicarious pleasure. "Probably off to a picture show; the stores are all closed at this hour," she might say. Later her eyes would get distant and she would muse, "They've left her home again; Mrs. Oka is alone again."

28   Now when Kiyoko-san passed by or came in with me on her way home, my mother would ask about Mrs. Oka—how is she, how does she occupy herself these rainy days, or these windy or warm or cool days. Often the answers were polite: "Thank you, we are fine." But sometimes Kiyoko-san's upper lip would pull over her teeth, and her voice would become soft and she would say, "Always drinking and fighting." At those times my mother would invariably say, "Endure; soon you will be marrying and going away."

29   Once a young truck driver delivered crates at the Oka farm, and he dropped back to our place to tell my father that Mrs. Oka had lurched behind his truck while he was backing up and very nearly let him kill her.

Only the daughter pulling her away saved her, he said. Thoroughly unnerved, he stopped by to rest himself and talk about it. Never, never, had he seen a drunken Japanese woman. My father nodded gravely. "Yes, it's unusual," he said and drummed his knee with his fingers.

30   Evenings were longer now, and when my mother's migraines drove me from the house in unbearable self-pity, I would take walks in the desert. One night with the warm wind against me, the primrose and yellow poppies closed and fluttering, the greasewood swaying in languid orbit, I lay on the white sand beneath a shrub and tried to disappear.

31   A voice clear and sweet cut through the half-dark of the evening:

Akai kuchibiru	Red lips
Kappu ni yosete	Press against a glass
Aoi sake nomya	Drink the green wine
Kokoro ga odoru	And the soul shall dance

32   Mrs. Oka appeared to be gathering flowers. Bending, plucking, standing, searching, she added to a small bouquet she clasped. She held them away, looked at them slyly, lids lowered, demure; then in a sudden and sinuous movement, she broke into a stately dance. She stopped, gathered more flowers, and breathed deeply into them. Tossing her head, she laughed softly from her dark throat. The picture of her imagined grandeur was lost to me, but the delusion that transformed a bouquet of tattered petals and sandy leaves, and the loneliness of a desert twilight into a fantasy that brought such joy and abandon made me stir with discomfort. The sound broke Mrs. Oka's dance. Her eyes grew large and her neck tense—like a cat on prowl. She spied me in the bushes. A peculiar chill ran through me. Then abruptly and with child-like delight, she scattered the flowers around her and walked away singing:

Falling, falling, petals on a wind. . . .

33   That was the last time I saw Mrs. Oka. She died before the spring harvest. It was pneumonia. I didn't attend the funeral, but my mother said it was sad. Mrs. Oka looked peaceful, and the minister expressed the irony of the long separation of mother and child and the short-lived reunion. Hardly a year together, he said. We went to help Kiyoko-san address and stamp those black-bordered acknowledgments.

34   When harvest was over, Mr. Oka and Kiyoko-san moved out of the valley. We never heard from them or saw them again. I suppose in a large city, Mr. Oka found some sort of work, perhaps as a janitor or a dishwasher, and Kiyoko-san grew up and found someone to marry.

DISCUSSION QUESTIONS

1. What elements of setting are important in this story?
2. The narrator says that Mrs. Oka's "aberration was a protest of the life assigned her; it was obstinate but unobserved, alas, unattended." Explain this statement.
3. What is ironic about Mrs. Oka's dance at the end of the story?
4. Who is the greater victim? Kiyoko Oka or Mrs. Oka? Discuss in small groups.

WRITING TOPICS

1. Conflict in a story is the struggle between the main character and opposing forces. Does this story have a conflict? Present your views in a persuasive paper.
2. In an essay compare and contrast Mrs. Oka and her life with the narrator and her life in the excerpt from *Through Harsh Winters* by Akemi Kikumura in Chapter One.

BEFORE TIME

Juliet Kono

Juliet Sanae Kono, a Hawaiian native, was born in 1943. She was raised in Hilo during the final years before statehood, and later relocated to Honolulu. After raising her children, she returned to the University of Hawaii, where she is working on her B.A. in English. Her poetry has been published in *Bamboo Ridge, Hapa, Hawaii Review, Literary Arts Hawaii, the Paper, Malama i ka Honua,* and various other publications. She is the author of *Tsunami Years* (1995) and *Hilo Rains* (1988) and co-editor with Cathy Song of *Sister Stew* (1991).

In the following poem, the speaker lists the types that the elders say to avoid in the marriage market, haphazardly mixing together ethnic/religious stereotypes and undesirable traits or habits.

They said to marry only Japanese,
and only *some* of our own kind;
not zuzu-ben, batten, kotonk
hibakusha, eta, Uchinanchu—
5   night-soil carrier, big-rope people.
Before time, they said not to marry
keto, gaijin, haole—hair people, foreigner, white;
saila-boy, Chinee, club foot, one-thumb, glass-eye,
    hare-lip, bolinki,
10 pigeon-toe, Pologee, Uncle Joe's friend, Hawaiian,
    cane cutter, mandolin
player, night-diver, Puerto Rican, tree-climber,
    nose picker, Filipino,
thief, bartender, jintan sucker, Korean, paniolo, farmer, bearded,
15 mustachioed, Teruko's brother, daikon-leg, cane-hauler,

left-handed, right-
handed, smart-aleck, Christian, poor speller, commie, Indian,
    leper, Hakka,
cripple, drunk, flat-nose, old, Jew-pake, chicken
²⁰ fighter, pig-hunter, ice cruncher, opium
smoker, one-side-eye-brow raiser, fat,
olopop, skinny, Punti, thick-lip,
albino, kurombo.

DISCUSSION QUESTIONS

1. Who might "they" be in line 1?
2. What ideas about social class, ethnic groups, occupations, and physical characteristics and habits can you infer from this poem?
3. What word or words describe the tone of this poem?

WRITING TOPICS

1. What spoken or unspoken restrictions about your possible marriage partner exist in your family? List some of these restrictions in your journal. Are these restrictions valid in your opinion?
2. The author breaks lines in unusual ways. In a brief essay, examine how these line breaks affect your reading of the poem and why.

NO-NAME WOMAN

Maxine Hong Kingston

Born in 1940 in Stockton, California, Maxine Hong Kingston spent much of her childhood working at her parents' laundry. While washing, drying, and pressing, Kingston and her five siblings would listen to their mother "talk story," an oral tradition that is a combination of legends, folklore, ghost stories, and anecdotes. Listening to "talk stories" and reading widely and voraciously helped Kingston to develop her own skills as a storyteller. She began attending the University of California, Berkeley, in 1958, where she began to pursue writing. She originally planned to study engineering because of her capacity for mathematics, but by her second year, she changed to a major more conducive to a writing career. After graduating in 1962, she married Earl Kingston and took a teaching job in Hayward, California. In 1967, the Kingstons moved to Hawaii, where Maxine worked as a teacher.

It was during her time in Hawaii that Kingston began writing *The Woman Warrior* and *China Men,* both of which borrow from the "talk story" tradition. In both books, a young Chinese American daughter narrates the stories of her family; however, there is a difference in narrative tone. In *China Men,* the daughter is "less involved with the characters and far less concerned with relating how she feels about them"[1] but in *The Woman Warrior,* the narrator's life is inextricably linked to all the lives—both past and present—around her. These two books, conceived as an intertwining story, are classified as nonfiction, but it is clear that they push the boundaries of literary categorization through Kingston's use of multiple genres—history, anecdote, legend, cautionary tale, biography, memoir.

Both books met with instant critical acclaim. In 1976 *The Woman Warrior* won the National Book Critics Circle Award for nonfiction, and in 1980 *China Men* won a National Book Award. Encouraged

[1] Elaine Kim, *Asian-American Literature: An Introduction to the Writings and Their Social Context* (Philadelphia: Temple UP, 1984) 208.

by her successes, Kingston embarked on a novel, *Tripmaster Monkey,* which she first published in 1987. The novel is the story of Wittman Ah Sing, a fifth-generation Chinese American man who, like Kingston herself, is a Berkeley graduate and a product of the 1960s. Kingston was working on a sequel to *Tripmaster Monkey,* but the manuscript was destroyed in a fire in 1992.

The following story is the tragedy of a woman's life in the extremely male-dominated world of old China, told as a cautionary tale to a young Chinese American woman. (J.I.)

1   "You must not tell anyone," my mother said, "what I am about to tell you. In China your father had a sister who killed herself. She jumped into the family well. We say that your father has all brothers because it is as if she had never been born.

2   "In 1924 just a few days after our village celebrated seventeen hurry-up weddings—to make sure that every young man who went 'out on the road' would responsibly come home—your father and his brothers and your grandfather and his brothers and your aunt's new husband sailed for America, the Gold Mountain. It was your grandfather's last trip. Those lucky enough to get contracts waved good-bye from the decks. They fed and guarded the stowaways and helped them off in Cuba, New York, Bali, Hawaii. 'We'll meet in California next year,' they said. All of them sent money home.

3   "I remember looking at your aunt one day when she and I were dressing; I had not noticed before that she had such a protruding melon of a stomach. But I did not think, 'She's pregnant,' until she began to look like other pregnant women, her shirt pulling and the white tops of her black pants showing. She could not have been pregnant, you see, because her husband had been gone for years. No one said anything. We did not discuss it. In early summer she was ready to have the child, long after the time when it could have been possible.

4   "The village had also been counting. On the night the baby was to be born the villagers raided our house. Some were crying. Like a great saw, teeth strung with lights, files of people walked zigzag across our land, tearing the rice. Their lanterns doubled in the disturbed black water, which drained away through the broken bunds. As the villagers closed in, we could see that some of them, probably men and women we knew well, wore white masks. The people with long hair hung it over their faces. Women with short hair made it stand up on end. Some had tied white bands around their foreheads, arms, and legs.

5   "At first they threw mud and rocks at the house. Then they threw eggs and began slaughtering our stock. We could hear the animals scream their

deaths—the roosters, the pigs, a last great roar from the ox. Familiar wild heads flared in our night windows; the villagers encircled us. Some of the faces stopped to peer at us, their eyes rushing like searchlights. The hands flattened against the panes, framed heads, and left red prints.

6   "The villagers broke in the front and back doors at the same time, even though we had not locked the doors against them. Their knives dripped with the blood of our animals. They smeared blood on the doors and walls. One woman swung a chicken, whose throat she had slit, splattering blood in red arcs about her. We stood together in the middle of our house, in the family hall with the pictures and tables of the ancestors around us, and looked straight ahead.

7   "At that time the house had only two wings. When the men came back, we would build two more to enclose our courtyard and a third one to begin a second courtyard. The villagers pushed through both wings, even your grandparents' rooms, to find your aunt's, which was also mine until the men returned. From this room a new wing for one of the younger families would grow. They ripped up her clothes and shoes and broke her combs, grinding them underfoot. They tore her work from the loom. They scattered the cooking fire and rolled the new weaving in it. We could hear them in the kitchen breaking our bowls and banging the pots. They overturned the great waist-high earthenware jugs; duck eggs, pickled fruits, vegetables burst out and mixed in acrid torrents. The old woman from the next field swept a broom through the air and loosed the spirits-of-the-broom over our heads. 'Pig.' 'Ghost.' 'Pig,' they sobbed and scolded while they ruined our house.

8   "When they left, they took sugar and oranges to bless themselves. They cut pieces from the dead animals. Some of them took bowls that were not broken and clothes that were not torn. Afterward we swept up the rice and sewed it back up into sacks. But the smells from the spilled preserves lasted. Your aunt gave birth in the pigsty that night. The next morning when I went for the water, I found her and the baby plugging up the family well.

9   "Don't let your father know that I told you. He denies her. Now that you have started to menstruate, what happened to her could happen to you. Don't humiliate us. You wouldn't like to be forgotten as if you had never been born. The villagers are watchful."

10   Whenever she had to warn us about life, my mother told stories that ran like this one, a story to grow up on. She tested our strength to establish realities. Those in the emigrant generations who could not reassert brute survival died young and far from home. Those of us in the first American generations have had to figure out how the invisible world the emigrants built around our childhoods fits in solid America.

11   The emigrants confused the gods by diverting their curses, misleading them with crooked streets and false names. They must try to confuse their offspring as well, who, I suppose, threaten them in similar ways—always try-

ing to get things straight, always trying to name the unspeakable. The Chinese I know hide their names; sojourners take new names when their lives change and guard their real names with silence.

12   Chinese-Americans, when you try to understand what things in you are Chinese, how do you separate what is peculiar to childhood, to poverty, insanities, one family, your mother who marked your growing with stories, from what is Chinese? What is Chinese tradition and what is the movies?

13   If I want to learn what clothes my aunt wore, whether flashy or ordinary, I would have to begin, "Remember Father's drowned-in-the-well sister?" I cannot ask that. My mother has told me once and for all the useful parts. She will add nothing unless powered by Necessity, a riverbank that guides her life. She plants vegetable gardens rather than lawns; she carries the odd-shaped tomatoes home from the fields and eats food left for the gods.

14   Whenever we did frivolous things, we used up energy; we flew high kites. We children came up off the ground over the melting cones our parents brought home from work and the American movie on New Year's Day—*Oh, You Beautiful Doll* with Betty Grable one year, and *She Wore a Yellow Ribbon* with John Wayne another year. After the one carnival ride each, we paid in guilt; our tired father counted his change on the dark walk home.

15   Adultery is extravagance. Could people who hatch their own chicks and eat the embryos and the heads for delicacies and boil the feet in vinegar for party food, leaving only the gravel, eating even the gizzard lining—could such people engender a prodigal aunt? To be a woman, to have a daughter in starvation time was a waste enough. My aunt could not have been the lone romantic who gave up everything for sex. Women in the old China did not choose. Some man had commanded her to lie with him and be his secret evil. I wonder whether he masked himself when he joined the raid on her family.

16   Perhaps she had encountered him in the fields or on the mountain where the daughters-in-law collected fuel. Or perhaps he first noticed her in the marketplace. He was not a stranger because the village housed no strangers. She had to have dealings with him other than sex. Perhaps he worked an adjoining field, or he sold her the cloth for the dress she sewed and wore. His demand must have surprised, then terrified her. She obeyed him; she always did as she was told.

17   When the family found a young man in the next village to be her husband, she had stood tractably beside the best rooster, his proxy, and promised before they met that she would be his forever. She was lucky that he was her age and she would be the first wife, an advantage secure now. The night she first saw him, he had sex with her. Then he left for America. She had almost forgotten what he looked like. When she tried to envision him, she only saw the black and white face in the group photograph the men had had taken before leaving.

18   The other man was not, after all, much different from her husband. They both gave orders: she followed. "If you tell your family, I'll beat you. I'll kill you. Be here again next week." No one talked sex, ever. And she might have separated the rapes from the rest of living if only she did not have to buy her oil from him or gather wood in the same forest. I want her fear to have lasted just as long as rape lasted so that the fear could have been contained. No drawn-out fear. But women at sex hazarded birth and hence lifetimes. The fear did not stop but permeated everywhere. She told the man, "I think I'm pregnant." He organized the raid against her.

19   On nights when my mother and father talked about their life back home, sometimes they mentioned an "outcast table" whose business they still seemed to be settling, their voices tight. In a commensal tradition, where food is precious, the powerful older people made wrongdoers eat alone. Instead of letting them start separate new lives like the Japanese, who could become samurais and geishas, the Chinese family, faces averted but eyes glowering sideways, hung on to the offenders and fed them leftovers. My aunt must have lived in the same house as my parents and eaten at an outcast table. My mother spoke about the raid as if she had seen it, when she and my aunt, a daughter-in-law to a different household, should not have been living together at all. Daughters-in-law lived with their husbands' parents, not their own; a synonym for marriage in Chinese is "taking a daughter-in-law." Her husband's parents could have sold her, mortgaged her, stoned her. But they had sent her back to her own mother and father, a mysterious act hinting at disgraces not told me. Perhaps they had thrown her out to deflect the avengers.

20   She was the only daughter; her four brothers went with her father, husband, and uncles "out on the road" and for some years became western men. When the goods were divided among the family, three of the brothers took land, and the youngest, my father, chose an education. After my grandparents gave their daughter away to her husband's family, they had dispensed all the adventure and all the property. They expected her alone to keep the traditional ways, which her brothers, now among the barbarians, could fumble without detection. The heavy, deep-rooted women were to maintain the past against the flood, safe for returning. But the rare urge west had fixed upon our family, and so my aunt crossed boundaries not delineated in space.

21   The work of preservation demands that the feelings playing about in one's guts not be turned into action. Just watch their passing like cherry blossoms. But perhaps my aunt, my forerunner, caught in a slow life, let dreams grow and fade and after some months or years went toward what persisted. Fear at the enormities of the forbidden kept her desires delicate, wire and bone. She looked at a man because she liked the way the hair was tucked behind his ears, or she liked the question-mark line of a long torso curving at the shoulder and straight at the hip. For warm eyes or a soft voice

or a slow walk—that's all—a few hairs, a line, a brightness, a sound, a pace, she gave up family. She offered us up for a charm that vanished with tiredness, a pigtail that didn't toss when the wind died. Why, the wrong lighting could erase the dearest thing about him.

22   It could very well have been, however, that my aunt did not take subtle enjoyment of her friend, but, a wild woman, kept rollicking company. Imagining her free with sex doesn't fit, though. I don't know any women like that, or men either. Unless I see her life branching into mine, she gives me no ancestral help.

23   To sustain her being in love, she often worked at herself in the mirror, guessing at the colors and shapes that would interest him, changing them frequently in order to hit on the right combination. She wanted him to look back.

24   On a farm near the sea, a woman who tended her appearance reaped a reputation for eccentricity. All the married women blunt-cut their hair in flaps about their ears or pulled it back in tight buns. No nonsense. Neither style blew easily into heart-catching tangles. And at their weddings they displayed themselves in their long hair for the last time. "It brushed the backs of my knees," my mother tells me. "It was braided, and even so, it brushed the backs of my knees."

25   At the mirror my aunt combed individuality into her bob. A bun could have been contrived to escape into black streamers blowing in the wind or in quiet wisps about her face, but only the older women in our picture album wear buns. She brushed her hair back from her forehead, tucking the flaps behind her ears. She looped a piece of thread, knotted into a circle between her index fingers and thumbs, and ran the double strand across her forehead. When she closed her fingers as if she were making a pair of shadow geese bite, the string twisted together catching the little hairs. Then she pulled the thread away from her skin, ripping the hairs out neatly, her eyes watering from the needles of pain. Opening her fingers, she cleaned the thread, then rolled it along her hairline and the tops of her eyebrows. My mother did the same to me and my sisters and herself. I used to believe that the expression "caught by the short hairs" meant a captive held with a depilatory string. It especially hurt at the temples, but my mother said we were lucky we didn't have to have our feet bound when we were seven. Sisters used to sit on their beds and cry together, she said, as their mothers or their slaves removed the bandages for a few minutes each night and let the blood gush back into their veins.

26   Once my aunt found a freckle on her chin, at a spot that the almanac said predestined her for unhappiness. She dug it out with a hot needle and washed the wound with peroxide.

27   More attention to her looks than these pullings of hairs and pickings at spots would have caused gossip among the villagers. They owned work

clothes and good clothes, and they wore good clothes for feasting the new seasons. But since a woman combing her hair hexes beginnings, my aunt rarely found an occasion to look her best. Women looked like great sea snails—the corded wood, babies, and laundry they carried were the whorls on their backs. The Chinese did not admire a bent back; goddesses and warriors stood straight. Still there must have been a marvelous freeing of beauty when a worker laid down her burden and stretched and arched.

28   Such commonplace loveliness, however, was not enough for my aunt. She dreamed of a lover for the fifteen days of New Year's, the time for families to exchange visits, money, and food. She plied her secret comb. And sure enough she cursed the year, the family, the village, and herself.

29   Even as her hair lured her imminent lover, many other men looked at her. Uncles, cousins, nephews, brothers would have looked, too, had they been home between journeys. Perhaps they had already been restraining their curiosity, and they left, fearful that their glances, like a field of nesting birds, might be startled and caught. Poverty hurt, and that was their first reason for leaving. But another, final reason for leaving the crowded house was the never-said.

30   She may have been unusually beloved, the precious only daughter, spoiled and mirror gazing because of the affection the family lavished on her. When her husband left, they welcomed the chance to take her back from the in-laws; she could live like the little daughter for just a while longer. There are stories that my grandfather was different from other people, "crazy ever since the little Jap bayoneted him in the head." One day he brought home a baby girl, wrapped up inside his brown western-style greatcoat. He had traded one of his sons, probably my father, the youngest, for her. My grandmother made him trade back. When he finally got a daughter of his own, he doted on her. They must have all loved her, except perhaps my father, the only brother who never went back to China, having once been traded for a girl.

31   Brothers and sisters, newly men and women, had to efface their sexual color and present plain miens. Disturbing hair and eyes, a smile like no other, threatened the ideal of five generations living under one roof. To focus blurs, people shouted face to face and yelled from room to room. The immigrants I know have loud voices, unmodulated to American tones even after years away from the village where they called their friendships out across the fields. I have not been able to stop my mother's screams in public libraries or over telephones. Walking erect (knees straight, toes pointed forward, not pigeon-toed, which is Chinese-feminine) and speaking in an inaudible voice, I have tried to turn myself American-feminine. Chinese communication was loud, public. Only sick people had to whisper. But at the dinner table, where the family members came nearest one another, no one could talk, not the outcasts nor any eaters. Every word that falls from

the mouth is a coin lost. Silently they gave and accepted food with both hands. A preoccupied child who took his bowl with one hand got a sideways glare. A complete moment of total attention is due everyone alike. Children and lovers have no singularity here, but my aunt used a secret voice, a separate attentiveness.

32   She kept the man's name to herself throughout her labor and dying; she did not accuse him that he be punished with her. To save her inseminator's name she gave silent birth.

33   He may have been somebody in her own household, but intercourse with a man outside the family would have been no less abhorrent. All the village were kinsmen, and the titles shouted in loud country voices never let kinship be forgotten. Any man within visiting distance would have been neutralized as a lover—"brother," "younger brother," "older brother"— one hundred and fifteen relationship titles. Parents researched birth charts probably not so much to assure good fortune as to circumvent incest in a population that has but one hundred surnames. Everybody has eight million relatives. How useless then sexual mannerisms, how dangerous.

34   As if it came from an atavism deeper than fear, I used to add "brother" silently to boys' names. It hexed the boys, who would or would not ask me to dance, and made them less scary and as familiar and deserving of benevolence as girls.

35   But, of course, I hexed myself also—no dates. I should have stood up, both arms waving, and shouted out across libraries, "Hey, you! Love me back." I had no idea, though, how to make attraction selective, how to control its direction and magnitude. If I made myself American-pretty so that the five or six Chinese boys in the class fell in love with me, everyone else— the Caucasian, Negro, and Japanese boys—would too. Sisterliness, dignified and honorable, made much more sense.

36   Attraction eludes control so stubbornly that whole societies designed to organize relationships among people cannot keep order, not even when they bind people to one another from childhood and raise them together. Among the very poor and the wealthy, brothers married their adopted sisters, like doves. Our family allowed some romance, paying adult brides' prices and providing dowries so that their sons and daughters could marry strangers. Marriage promises to turn strangers into friendly relatives—a nation of siblings.

37   In the village structure, spirits shimmered among the live creatures, balanced and held in equilibrium by time and land. But one human being flaring up into violence could open up a black hole, a maelstrom that pulled in the sky. The frightened villagers, who depended on one another to maintain the real, went to my aunt to show her a personal, physical representation of the break she had made in the "roundness." Misallying couples snapped off the future, which was to be embodied in true offspring. The villagers pun-

ished her for acting as if she could have a private life, secret and apart from them.

38   If my aunt had betrayed the family at a time of large grain yields and peace, when many boys were born, and wings were being built on many houses, perhaps she might have escaped such severe punishment. But the men—hungry, greedy, tired of planting in dry soil—had been forced to leave the village in order to send food-money home. There were ghost plagues, bandit plagues, wars with the Japanese, floods. My Chinese brother and sister had died of an unknown sickness. Adultery, perhaps only a mistake during good times, became a crime when the village needed food.

39   The round moon cakes and round doorways, the round tables of graduated sizes that fit one roundness inside another, round windows and rice bowls—these talismans had lost their power to warn this family of the law: a family must be whole, faithfully keeping the descent line by having sons to feed the old and the dead, who in turn look after the family. The villagers came to show my aunt and her lover-in-hiding a broken house. The villagers were speeding up the circling of events because she was too shortsighted to see that her infidelity had already harmed the village, that waves of consequences would return unpredictably, sometimes in disguise, as now, to hurt her. This roundness had to be made coin-sized so that she would see its circumference: punish her at the birth of her baby. Awaken her to the inexorable. People who refused fatalism because they could invent small resources insisted on culpability. Deny accidents and wrest fault from the stars.

40   After the villagers left, their lanterns now scattering in various directions toward home, the family broke their silence and cursed her. "Aiaa, we're going to die. Death is coming. Death is coming. Look what you've done. You've killed us. Ghost! Dead ghost! Ghost! You've never been born." She ran out into the fields, far enough from the house so that she could no longer hear their voices, and pressed herself against the earth, her own land no more. When she felt the birth coming, she thought that she had been hurt. Her body seized together. "They've hurt me too much," she thought. "This is gall, and it will kill me." With forehead and knees against the earth, her body convulsed and then relaxed. She turned on her back, lay on the ground. The black well of sky and stars went out and out and out forever; her body and her complexity seemed to disappear. She was one of the stars, a bright dot in blackness, without home, without a companion, in eternal cold and silence. An agoraphobia rose in her, speeding higher and higher, bigger and bigger; she would not be able to contain it; there would be no end to fear.

41   Flayed, unprotected against space, she felt pain return, focusing her body. This pain chilled her—a cold, steady kind of surface pain. Inside, spasmodically, the other pain, the pain of the child, heated her. For hours she lay on the

ground, alternately body and space. Sometimes a vision of normal comfort obliterated reality: she saw the family in the evening gambling at the dinner table, the young people massaging their elders' backs. She saw them congratulating one another, high joy on the mornings the rice shoots came up. When these pictures burst, the stars drew yet further apart. Black space opened.

42   She got to her feet to fight better and remembered that old-fashioned women gave birth in their pigsties to fool the jealous, pain-dealing gods, who do not snatch piglets. Before the next spasms could stop her, she ran to the pigsty, each step a rushing out into emptiness. She climbed over the fence and knelt in the dirt. It was good to have a fence enclosing her, a tribal person alone.

43   Laboring, this woman who had carried her child as a foreign growth that sickened her every day, expelled it at last. She reached down to touch the hot, wet, moving mass, surely smaller than anything human, and could feel that it was human after all—fingers, toes, nails, nose. She pulled it up on to her belly, and it lay curled there, butt in the air, feet precisely tucked one under the other. She opened her loose shirt and buttoned the child inside. After resting, it squirmed and thrashed and she pushed it up to her breast. It turned its head this way and that until it found her nipple. There, it made little snuffling noises. She clenched her teeth at its preciousness, lovely as a young calf, a piglet, a little dog.

44   She may have gone to the pigsty as a last act of responsibility: she would protect this child as she had protected its father. It would look after her soul, leaving supplies on her grave. But how would this tiny child without family find her grave when there would be no marker for her anywhere, neither in the earth nor the family hall? No one would give her a family hall name. She had taken the child with her into the wastes. At its birth the two of them had felt the same raw pain of separation, a wound that only the family pressing tight could close. A child with no descent line would not soften her life but only trail after her, ghostlike, begging her to give it purpose. At dawn the villagers on the way to the fields would stand around the fence and look.

45   Full of milk, the little ghost slept. When it awoke, she hardened her breasts against the milk that crying loosens. Toward morning she picked up the baby and walked to the well.

46   Carrying the baby to the well shows loving. Otherwise abandon it. Turn its face into the mud. Mothers who love their children take them along. It was probably a girl; there is some hope of forgiveness for boys.

47   "Don't tell anyone you had an aunt. Your father does not want to hear her name. She has never been born." I have believed that sex was unspeakable and words so strong and fathers so frail that "aunt" would do my father mysterious harm. I have thought that my family, having settled among immigrants who had also been their neighbors in the ancestral land, needed

to clean their name, and a wrong word would incite the kinspeople even here. But there is more to this silence: they want me to participate in her punishment. And I have.

48 In the twenty years since I heard this story I have not asked for details nor said my aunt's name; I do not know it. People who can comfort the dead can also chase after them to hurt them further—a reverse ancestor worship. The real punishment was not the raid swiftly inflicted by the villagers, but the family's deliberately forgetting her. Her betrayal so maddened them, they saw to it that she would suffer forever, even after death. Always hungry, always needing, she would have to beg food from other ghosts, snatch and steal it from those whose living descendants give them gifts. She would have to fight the ghosts massed at crossroads for the buns a few thoughtful citizens leave to decoy her away from village and home so that the ancestral spirits could feast unharassed. At peace, they could act like gods, not ghosts, their descent lines providing them with paper suits and dresses, spirit money, paper houses, paper automobiles, chicken, meat, and rice into eternity— essences delivered up in smoke and flames, steam and incense rising from each rice bowl. In an attempt to make the Chinese care for people outside the family, Chairman Mao encourages us now to give our paper replicas to the spirits of outstanding soldiers and workers, no matter whose ancestors they may be. My aunt remains forever hungry. Goods are not distributed evenly among the dead.

49 My aunt haunts me—her ghost drawn to me because now, after fifty years of neglect, I alone devote pages of paper to her, though not origamied into houses and clothes. I do not think she always means me well. I am telling on her, and she was a spite suicide, drowning herself in the drinking water. The Chinese are always very frightened of the drowned one, whose weeping ghost, wet hair hanging and skin bloated, waits silently by the water to pull down a substitute.

DISCUSSION QUESTIONS

1. What are your initial reactions after reading this account?
2. What were the reasons for the community and family acting as they did toward the narrator's aunt?
3. Why do you think the father of the aunt's child did not suffer similar punishment?
4. The narrator says that the family wants her to participate in the punishment of her aunt. How, in fact, did she do so?

5. Traditionally, Chinese people honor their ancestors by leaving food offerings or paper replicas of other goods at their graves. By not doing so for the aunt, what did the family hope to accomplish?

WRITING TOPICS

1. The author writes that "attraction eludes control so stubbornly that whole societies designed to organize relationships among people cannot keep order." In a short paper, explain what she means, referring also to the poem "Before Time," if you wish.
2. What are the advantages and disadvantages of living in a close-knit community? If the community in which you live is close-knit, what do you like and dislike about it? If you have no experience with such a community, imagine what it would be like.
3. One of the themes of this story is how one individual's actions can affect a whole community. Write about a recent episode you know of in which one person's actions affected a whole community, perhaps yours, for bad or good.

ABCs

Genny Lim

The youngest of seven children, Genny Lim was born in 1946 and grew up in San Francisco, California. Her father, Edward, spent much of his childhood and youth in the Bay Area, but both he and Lim's mother, Lin Sun, were born in Kwantung, China. Still residing in San Francisco, Lim is the single mother of two daughters.

Lim studied liberal arts and theater at San Francisco State University and then pursued a master's degree in English with a creative writing emphasis. An accomplished playwright, poet, and multimedia artist, Lim is active in various theater and arts communities throughout the Bay Area. She started writing plays in 1978 in order to address issues of race and gender in a dramatic context. Two of her best-known plays are *Paper Angels,* which premiered in 1980 at the Asian American Theater Company, and *Bitter Cane,* which was introduced at the Bay Area Playwrights Festival in 1989. In addition, she coauthored and edited with Him Mark Lai and Judy Yung *Island: Poetry and History of Chinese Immigrants on Angel Island, 1910–1940* (1980); poems from this collection appear in this anthology.

Lim has received numerous awards and recognitions for her large and diverse body of work, including the American Book Award for *Island* and the James Wong Howe Award from the Association of Asian Pacific American Actors for *Paper Angels.*

In the following poem, "ABCs" ("American-born Chinese"), Lim points out the generation gap that is present in Chinese American culture. (J.I.)

My people talk to me
from Chinatown alleyways and
Ping Yuen[1] balconies
They stare out of doorways and fire escapes
5   between Moon Days[2] and rockets
joss sticks[3] and jesus
as if there were no difference between
hom yih[4] and hot dogs
seaweed and french fries

10   My people listen to their children
mangle the mother tongue and
give birth to blonde babies
who could care less about
Ching Ming[5] or joong[6]
15   and who think they can get on a plane and
bridge all the years, continents and oceans
which took the old folk their
whole lives to cross

DISCUSSION QUESTIONS

1. What do the ABCs usually connote and what do they connote here?
2. Why does the speaker juxtapose two types of cultural beliefs and objects?
3. What do the last four lines imply about the difference between generations?

---

[1] *Ping Yuen:* Peaceful Gardens, a housing project in San Francisco's Chinatown.
[2] *Moon Days:* days of celebrating the Moon Festival, beginning August 15, when moon cakes are eaten.
[3] *joss sticks:* slender sticks of incense burned at an altar.
[4] *hom yih:* dried, salted fish, a staple in traditional Chinese cooking.
[5] *Ching Ming:* a festival for the dead, usually celebrated on April 5, when offerings are made and graves are swept clean.
[6] *joong:* bamboo-leaf-wrapped dumplings of glutinous rice stuffed with meat or beans and peanuts.

WRITING TOPICS

1. In a short paper compare this poem with "Assimilation" by Eugene Gloria in Chapter One.
2. The speaker in the poem says that children "mangle the mother tongue." How important is one's language to one's identity? Examine this idea in an essay, taking into consideration how words shape one's view of and one's place in the world. If your first language is English, try to imagine how your sense of self would change if no one around you spoke English.

TRANSFORMATION

Lydia Minatoya

Lydia Minatoya, a Japanese American, was born in the United States in the 1950s. She has worked as a counselor and faculty member at a community college in Seattle. Her first book, a memoir titled *Talking to High Monks in the Snow,* won the 1991 PEN/Jerard Fund Award. The memoir takes the narrator/main character from upstate New York in the 1950s to an Asian journey through Japan, China, and Nepal. The geographical exploration is also an exploration of Asian identity and roots and of American identity. The memoir received glowing reviews for its sensitivity, humor, and insights into bicultural experiences.

In the following excerpt, Minatoya continues the theme of assimilation, beginning with the serious quest for a perfect "conventional name" for her new baby self. Later, the young Lydia tries to fit in when she enters school in a white American world.

1   Perhaps it begins with my naming. During her pregnancy, my mother was reading Dr. Spock. "Children need to belong," he cautioned. "An unusual name can make them the subject of ridicule." My father frowned when he heard this. He stole a worried glance at my sister. Burdened by her Japanese name, Misa played unsuspectingly on the kitchen floor.

2   The Japanese know full well the dangers of conspicuousness. "The nail that sticks out gets pounded down," cautions an old maxim. In America, Relocation was all the proof they needed.

3   And so it was, with great earnestness, my parents searched for a conventional name. They wanted me to have the full true promise of America.

4   "I will ask my colleague Froilan," said my father. "He is the smartest man I know."

5   "And he has poetic soul," said my mother, who cared about such things.

6   In due course, Father consulted Froilan. He gave Froilan his conditions for suitability.

7   "First, if possible, the full name should be alliterative," said my father. "Like Misa Minatoya." He closed his eyes and sang my sister's name. "Second, if not an alliteration, at least the name should have assonantal rhyme."

8   "Like Misa Minatoya?" said Froilan with a teasing grin.

9   "Exactly," my father intoned. He gave an emphatic nod. "Finally, most importantly, the name must be readily recognizable as conventional." He peered at Froilan with hope. "Do you have any suggestions or ideas?"

10   Froilan, whose own American child was named Ricardito, thought a while.

11   "We already have selected the name for a boy," offered my Father. "Eugene."

12   "Eugene?" wondered Froilan. "But it meets none of your conditions!"

13   "Eugene is a special case," said my father, "after Eugene, Oregon, and Eugene O'Neill. The beauty of the Pacific Northwest, the power of a great writer."

14   "I see," said Froilan, who did not but who realized that this naming business would be more complex than he had anticipated. "How about Maria?"

15   "Too common," said my father. "We want a *conventional* name, not a common one."

16   "Hmmm," said Froilan, wondering what the distinction was. He thought some more and then brightened. "Lydia!" he declared. He rhymed the name with media. "Lydia for *la bonita infanta*!"

17   And so I received my uncommon conventional name. It really did not provide the camouflage my parents had anticipated. I remained unalterably alien. For Dr. Spock had been addressing *American* families, and in those days, everyone knew all real American families were white.

18   Call it denial, but many Japanese Americans never quite understood the promise of America was not truly meant for them. They lived in horse stalls at the Santa Anita racetrack and said the Pledge of Allegiance daily. They rode to Relocation Camps under armed guard, labeled with numbered tags, and sang "The Star-Spangled Banner." They lived in deserts or swamps, ludicrously imprisoned—where would they run if they ever escaped—and formed garden clubs, and yearbook staffs, and citizen town meetings. They even elected beauty queens.

19   My mother practiced her *okoto*[1] and was featured in a recital. She taught classes in fashion design and her students mounted a show. Into exile she had carried an okoto and a sewing machine. They were her past and her future. She believed in Art and Technology.

20   My mother's camp was the third most populous city in the entire state of

---

[1] *okoto:* a stringed instrument that is plucked when played.

Wyoming. Across the barren lands, behind barbed wire, bloomed these little oases of democracy. The older generation bore the humiliation with pride. "*Kodomo no tame ni,*" they said. For the sake of the children. They thought that if their dignity was great, then their children would be spared. Call it valor. Call it bathos. Perhaps it was closer to slapstick: a sweet and bitter lunacy.

21   Call it adaptive behavior. Coming from a land swept by savage typhoons, ravaged by earthquakes and volcanoes, the Japanese have evolved a view of the world: a cooperative, stoic, almost magical way of thinking. Get along, work hard, and never quite see the things that can bring you pain. Against the tyranny of nature, of feudal lords, of wartime hysteria, the charm works equally well.

22   And so my parents gave me an American name and hoped that I could pass. They nourished me with the American dream: Opportunity, Will, Transformation.

23   When I was four and my sister was eight, Misa regularly used me as a comic foil. She would bring her playmates home from school and query me as I sat amidst the milk bottles on the front steps.

24   "What do you want to be when you grow up?" she would say. She would nudge her audience into attentiveness.

25   "A mother kitty cat!" I would enthuse. Our cat had just delivered her first litter of kittens and I was enchanted by the rasping tongue and soft mewings of motherhood.

26   "And what makes you think you can become a cat?" Misa would prompt, gesturing to her howling friends—wait for this; it gets better yet.

27   "This is America," I stoutly would declare. "I can grow up to be anything that I want."

28   My faith was unshakable. I believed. Opportunity. Will. Transformation.

29   When we lived in Albany, I always was the teachers' pet. "So tiny, so precocious, so prettily dressed!" They thought I was a living doll and this was fine with me.

30   My father knew that the effusive praise would die. He had been through this with my sister. After five years of being a perfect darling, Misa had reached the age where students were tracked by ability. Then, the anger started. Misa had tested into the advanced track. It was impossible, the community declared. Misa was forbidden entry into advanced classes as long as there were white children being placed below her. In her defense, before an angry rabble, my father made a presentation to the Board of Education.

31   But I was too young to know of this. I knew only that my teachers praised and petted me. They took me to other classes as an example. "Watch now, as Lydia demonstrates attentive behavior," they would croon as I was led to an empty desk at the head of the class. I had a routine. I would sit carefully, spreading my petticoated skirt neatly beneath me. I would pull my chair close to the desk, crossing my swinging legs at my snowy white anklets.

I would fold my hands carefully on the desk before me and stare pensively at the blackboard.

32   This routine won me few friends. The sixth-grade boys threw rocks at me. They danced around me in a tight circle, pulling at the corners of their eyes. "Ching Chong Chinaman," they chanted. But teachers loved me. When I was in first grade, a third-grade teacher went weeping to the principal. She begged to have me skipped. She was leaving to get married and wanted her turn with the dolly.

33   When we moved, the greatest shock was the knowledge that I had lost my charm. From the first, my teacher failed to notice me. But to me, it did not matter. I was in love. I watched her moods, her needs, her small vanities. I was determined to ingratiate.

34   Miss Hempstead was a shimmering vision with a small upturned nose and eyes that were kewpie doll blue. Slender as a sylph, she tripped around the classroom, all saucy in her high-heeled shoes. Whenever I looked at Miss Hempstead, I pitied the Albany teachers whom, formerly, I had adored. Poor old Miss Rosenberg. With a shiver of distaste, I recalled her loose fleshy arms, her mottled hands, the scent of lavender as she crushed me to her heavy breasts.

35   Miss Hempstead had a pet of her own. Her name was Linda Sherlock. I watched Linda closely and plotted Miss Hempstead's courtship. The key was the piano. Miss Hempstead played the piano. She fancied herself a musical star. She sang songs from Broadway revues and shaped her students' reactions. "Getting to know you," she would sing. We would smile at her in a staged manner and position ourselves obediently at her feet.

36   Miss Hempstead was famous for her ability to soothe. Each day at rest time, she played the piano and sang soporific songs. Linda Sherlock was the only child who succumbed. Routinely, Linda's head would bend and nod until she crumpled gracefully onto her folded arms. A tousled strand of blonde hair would fall across her forehead. Miss Hempstead would end her song, would gently lower the keyboard cover. She would turn toward the restive eyes of the class. "Isn't she sweetness itself!" Miss Hempstead would declare. It made me want to vomit.

37   I was growing weary. My studiousness, my attentiveness, my fastidious grooming and pert poise: all were failing me. I changed my tactics. I became a problem. Miss Hempstead sent me home with nasty notes in sealed envelopes: Lydia is a slow child, a noisy child, her presence is disruptive. My mother looked at me with surprise, "*Nani desu ka?* Are you having problems with your teacher?" But I was tenacious. I pushed harder and harder, firmly caught in the obsessive need of the scorned.

38   One day I snapped. As Miss Hempstead began to sing her wretched lullabies, my head dropped to the desk with a powerful CRACK! It lolled

there, briefly, then rolled toward the edge with a momentum that sent my entire body catapulting to the floor. Miss Hempstead's spine stretched slightly, like a cat that senses danger. Otherwise, she paid no heed. The linoleum floor was smooth and cool. It emitted a faint pleasant odor: a mixture of chalk dust and wax.

39   I began to snore heavily. The class sat electrified. There would be no drowsing today. The music went on and on. Finally, one boy could not stand it. "Miss Hempstead," he probed plaintively, "Lydia has fallen asleep on the floor!" Miss Hempstead did not turn. Her playing grew slightly strident but she did not falter.

40   I lay on the floor through rest time. I lay on the floor through math drill. I lay on the floor while my classmates scraped around me, pushing their sturdy little wooden desks into the configuration for reading circle. It was not until penmanship practice that I finally stretched and stirred. I rose like Sleeping Beauty and slipped back to my seat. I smiled enigmatically. A spell had been broken. I never again had a crush on a teacher.

DISCUSSION QUESTIONS

1. What is the Japanese view of the world, according to the author, and what is the American dream?
2. Why did the narrator's father want her to have a conventional name?
3. Did the narrator's behavior in first grade and later in school illustrate the maxim "the nail that sticks out gets pounded down" or not?
4. How was the narrator transformed?

WRITING TOPICS

1. Irony is the contrast between what appears to be and what really is. In an essay, analyze the ironies depicted in "Transformation."
2. Is the idea of the so-called American dream a valid one in your opinion, or is the whole notion a mistaken one? Defend your views in a persuasive paper.

PARTS

Lois-Ann Yamanaka

Born on the island of Molokai in 1961, Lois-Ann Yamanaka grew up on the Big Island of Hawaii. She currently lives in Honolulu with her husband and son.

Saturday Night at the Pahala Theatre, Yamanaka's first book, was selected for the Pushcart Prize XVIII, 1993. Author, artist, and critic Jessica Hagedorn acclaims Yamanaka as a "fresh new voice in poetry and prose: irreverent, sensual, street-smart, and passionate. She refuels the English language with her own brand of island music—rich in distinctive rhythms and magical insights."

In "Parts," an emotionally abusive mother tries to control her daughter's life. (J.I.)

THE BRAIN

> I get one
> splitting
> headache.
> No ask me questions
> 5 and no move.
> First one
> who breathe
> going get
> one good whack
> 10 with the fly swatter.
> You. Cook the rice.
> You. Fry some Spam.
> Open one can corn.

Everybody
15 shut up.
I work all day long,
I come home
and all you doing
is watching tv.
20 Sit down.
Shut up.
I gotta rest.

THE EYE

I
found
this letter
in your
5 panty drawer.
Did you write
all these evil things?
Looks like your
handwriting.
10 Like me read this
to Judy and her mother?
Like me call them up
come over for lunch
right now?
15 What you mean,
no, wait?
So you did
write it.
I
20 cannot believe
that so much evil
can live
in one person.
You are a evil child.
25 You are filthy.
You are a hypocrite.
Stay in your room.
Forever.

DISCUSSION QUESTIONS

1. Who is the speaker in these two parts of the same poem and who is being spoken to?
2. With whom do you sympathize most—the speaker or her listeners?

WRITING TOPICS

1. In a brief essay, characterize the tone of the narrator's voice and discuss what it conveys about the narrator's personality. Use quotations from the poem to support your views.
2. The poet has used everyday language and the first-person point of view to characterize someone. Try this technique yourself in a poem (not about your parents) that depicts a younger brother or sister or a pet on a typical day.

THE MANAGEMENT OF GRIEF

Bharati Mukherjee

One of three daughters, Bharati Mukherjee was born in Calcutta, India, in 1947. Her family belonged to the Brahmins, the highest and most privileged caste of the five-tiered social and religious structure of traditional Indian society. Her father was a renowned chemist and the owner of a successful pharmaceutical company. Throughout her childhood, Mukherjee lived in a household consisting of over thirty relatives; she often turned to literature in order to find, at least temporarily, the privacy that she felt she lacked. In 1948 Mukherjee's parents relocated the family to England, but in 1951 they moved back to Calcutta. Upon their return, her mother Bina insisted on taking up residence apart from their extended family. Although she was successful in her insistence, Bina Mukherjee often suffered verbal and physical abuse because her desire for a smaller household broke from the traditional composition and customs of Indian families.

Mukherjee's parents nurtured their daughter's love of literature and encouraged her to pursue a career as a writer. She obtained her B.A. in 1959 from the University of Calcutta and earned master's degrees both in English and in ancient Indian culture from the University of Baroda in 1961. Shortly thereafter, she received a fellowship to the Writers' Workshop at the University of Iowa. While she was doing graduate work in the United States, her father wrote to tell her that he wished to arrange a marriage between her and a Bengali man, also a Brahmin. However, she rejected the arrangement and instead married Clark Blaise after a two-week courtship. She graduated with an M.F.A. in 1963 and moved to Canada with her new husband.

Mukherjee has published several novels, including *The Tiger's Daughter* (1972), *Wife* (1975), *Jasmine* (1989), and *The Holder of the World* (1993). She also wrote *Darkness* (1985) and *The Middleman and Other Stories* (1989), two collections of short fiction; the latter won the 1988 National Book Critics Circle Award.

The following short story from *Middleman* points out the cultural gap between Indian immigrants who have lost relatives in a senseless terrorist bombing and the European social worker who tries to help them. (J.I.)

1   A woman I don't know is boiling tea the Indian way in my kitchen. There are a lot of women I don't know in my kitchen, whispering, and moving tactfully. They open doors, rummage through the pantry, and try not to ask me where things are kept. They remind me of when my sons were small, on Mother's Day or when Vikram and I were tired, and they would make big, sloppy omelets. I would lie in bed pretending I didn't hear them.

2   Dr. Sharma, the treasurer of the Indo-Canada Society, pulls me into the hallway. He wants to know if I am worried about money. His wife, who has just come up from the basement with a tray of empty cups and glasses, scolds him. "Don't bother Mrs. Bhave with mundane details." She looks so monstrously pregnant her baby must be days overdue. I tell her she shouldn't be carrying heavy things. "Shaila," she says, smiling, "this is the fifth." Then she grabs a teenager by his shirttails. He slips his Walkman off his head. He has to be one of her four children, they have the same domed and dented foreheads. "What's the official word now?" she demands. The boy slips the headphones back on. "They're acting evasive, Ma. They're saying it could be an accident or a terrorist bomb."

3   All morning, the boys have been muttering, Sikh[1] Bomb, Sikh Bomb. The men, not using the word, bow their heads in agreement. Mrs. Sharma touches her forehead at such a word. At least they've stopped talking about space debris and Russian lasers.

4   Two radios are going in the dining room. They are tuned to different stations. Someone must have brought the radios down from my boys' bedrooms. I haven't gone into their rooms since Kusum came running across the front lawn in her bathrobe. She looked so funny, I was laughing when I opened the door.

5   The big TV in the den is being whizzed through American networks and cable channels.

6   "Damn!" some man swears bitterly. "How can these preachers carry on like nothing's happened?" I want to tell him we're not that important. You look at the audience, and at the preacher in his blue robe with his beautiful white hair, the potted palm trees under a blue sky, and you know they care about nothing.

---

[1] *Sikh:* a member of the Sikh religion, a monotheistic religion of India founded in the Punjab in about 1500.

7   The phone rings and rings. Dr. Sharma's taken charge. "We're with her," he keeps saying. "Yes, yes, the doctor has given calming pills. Yes, yes, pills are having necessary effect." I wonder if pills alone explain this calm. Not peace, just a deadening quiet. I was always controlled, but never repressed. Sound can reach me, but my body is tensed, ready to scream. I hear their voices all around me. I hear my boys and Vikram cry, "Mommy, Shaila!" and their screams insulate me, like headphones.

8   The woman boiling water tells her story again and again. "I got the news first. My cousin called from Halifax before six a.m., can you imagine? He'd gotten up for prayers and his son was studying for medical exams and he heard on a rock channel that something had happened to a plane. They said first it had disappeared from the radar, like a giant eraser just reached out. His father called me, so I said to him, what do you mean, "something bad"? You mean a hijacking? And he said, *behn*,[2] there is no confirmation of anything yet, but check with your neighbors because a lot of them must be on that plane. So I called poor Kusum straightaway. I knew Kusum's husband and daughter were booked to go yesterday."

9   Kusum lives across the street from me. She and Satish had moved in less than a month ago. They said they needed a bigger place. All these people, the Sharmas and friends from the Indo-Canada Society had been there for the housewarming. Satish and Kusum made homemade tandoori on their big gas grill and even the white neighbors piled their plates high with that luridly red, charred, juicy chicken. Their younger daughter had danced, and even our boys had broken away from the Stanley Cup telecast to put in a reluctant appearance. Everyone took pictures for their albums and for the community newspapers—another of our families had made it big in Toronto—and now I wonder how many of those happy faces are gone. "Why does God give us so much if all along He intends to take it away?" Kusum asks me.

10   I nod. We sit on carpeted stairs, holding hands like children. "I never once told him that I loved him," I say. I was too much the well brought up woman. I was so well brought up I never felt comfortable calling my husband by his first name.

11   "It's all right," Kusum says. "He knew. My husband knew. They felt it. Modern young girls have to say it because what they feel is fake."

12   Kusum's daughter, Pam, runs in with an overnight case. Pam's in her McDonald's uniform. "Mummy! You have to get dressed!" Panic makes her cranky. "A reporter's on his way here."

13   "Why?"

14   "You want to talk to him in your bathrobe?" She starts to brush her mother's long hair. She's the daughter who's always in trouble. She dates

---

[2] *behn:* sister, used casually as with a close friend.

Canadian boys and hangs out in the mall, shopping for tight sweaters. The younger one, the goody-goody one according to Pam, the one with a voice so sweet that when she sang *bhajans*[3] for Ethiopian relief even a frugal man like my husband wrote out a hundred dollar check, *she* was on that plane. *She* was going to spend July and August with grandparents because Pam wouldn't go. Pam said she'd rather waitress at McDonald's.

15   "If it's a choice between Bombay and Wonderland, I'm picking Wonderland," she'd said.

16   "Leave me alone," Kusum yells. "You know what I want to do? If I didn't have to look after you, I'd hang myself."

17   Pam's young face goes blotchy with pain. "Thanks," she says, "don't let me stop you."

18   "Hush," pregnant Mrs. Sharma scolds Pam. "Leave your mother alone. Mr. Sharma will tackle the reporters and fill out the forms. He'll say what has to be said."

19   Pam stands her ground. "You think I don't know what Mummy's thinking? *Why her?* that's what. That's sick! Mummy wishes my little sister were alive and I were dead.

20   Kusum's hand in mine is trembly hot. We continue to sit on the stairs.

21   She calls before she arrives, wondering if there's anything I need. Her name is Judith Templeton and she's an appointee of the provincial government. "Multiculturalism?" I ask, and she says, "partially," but that her mandate is bigger. "I've been told you knew many of the people on the flight," she says. "Perhaps if you'd agree to help us reach the others . . .?"

22   She gives me time at least to put on tea water and pick up the mess in the front room. I have a few *samosas* from Kusum's housewarming that I could fry up, but then I think, why prolong this visit?

23   Judith Templeton is much younger than she sounded. She wears a blue suit with a white blouse and a polka dot tie. Her blond hair is cut short, her only jewelry is pearl drop earrings. Her briefcase is new and expensive looking, a gleaming cordovan leather. She sits with it across her lap. When she looks out the front windows onto the street, her contact lenses seem to float in front of her light blue eyes.

24   "What sort of help do you want from me?" I ask. She has refused the tea, out of politeness, but I insist, along with some slightly stale biscuits.

25   "I have no experience," she admits. "That is, I have an MSW and I've worked in liaison with accident victims, but I mean I have no experience with a tragedy of this scale—"

26   "Who could? I ask.

---

[3] *bhajans:* prayers.

27 "—and with the complications of culture, language, and customs. Someone mentioned that Mrs. Bhave is a pillar—because you've taken it more calmly."

28 At this, perhaps, I frown, for she reaches forward, almost to take my hand. "I hope you understand my meaning, Mrs. Bhave. There are hundreds of people in Metro directly affected, like you, and some of them speak no English. There are some widows who've never handled money or gone on a bus, and there are old parents who still haven't eaten or gone outside their bedrooms. Some houses and apartments have been looted. Some wives are still hysterical. Some husbands are in shock and profound depression. We want to help, but our hands are tied in so many ways. We have to distribute money to some people, and there are legal documents—these things can be done. We have interpreters, but we don't always have the human touch, or maybe the right human touch. We don't want to make mistakes, Mrs. Bhave, and that's why we'd like to ask you to help us."

29 "More mistakes, you mean," I say.

30 "Police matters are not in my hands," she answers.

31 "Nothing I can do will make any difference," I say. "We must all grieve in our own way."

32 "But you are coping very well. All the people said, Mrs. Bhave is the strongest person of all. Perhaps if the others could see you, talk with you, it would help them."

33 "By the standards of the people you call hysterical, I am behaving very oddly and very badly, Miss Templeton." I want to say to her, *I wish I could scream, starve, walk into Lake Ontario, jump from a bridge.* "They would not see me as a model. I do not see myself as a model."

34 I am a freak. No one who has ever known me would think of me reacting this way. This terrible calm will not go away.

35 She asks me if she may call again, after I get back from a long trip that we all must make. "Of course," I say. "Feel free to call, anytime."

36 Four days later, I find Kusum squatting on a rock overlooking a bay in Ireland. It isn't a big rock, but it juts sharply out over water. This is as close as we'll ever get to them. June breezes balloon out her sari and unpin her knee-length hair. She has the bewildered look of a sea creature whom the tides have stranded.

37 It's been one hundred hours since Kusum came stumbling and screaming across my lawn. Waiting around the hospital, we've heard many stories. The police, the diplomats, they tell us things thinking that we're strong, that knowledge is helpful to the grieving, and maybe it is. Some, I know, prefer ignorance, or their own versions. The plane broke into two, they say. Unconsciousness was instantaneous. No one suffered. My boys must have just finished their breakfasts. They loved eating on planes, they loved the

smallness of plates, knives, and forks. Last year they saved the airline salt and pepper shakers. Half an hour more and they would have made it to Heathrow.

38   Kusum says that we can't escape our fate. She says that all those people—our husbands, my boys, her girl with the nightingale voice, all those Hindus, Christians, Sikhs, Muslims, Parsis, and atheists on that plane—were fated to die together off this beautiful bay. She learned this from a swami in Toronto.

39   I have my Valium.

40   Six of us "relatives"—two widows and four widowers—choose to spend the day today by the waters instead of sitting in a hospital room and scanning photographs of the dead. That's what they call us now: relatives. I've looked through twenty-seven photos in two days. They're very kind to us, the Irish are very understanding. Sometimes understanding means freeing a tourist bus for this trip to the bay, so we can pretend to spy our loved ones through the glassiness of waves or in sunspeckled cloud shapes.

41   I could die here, too, and be content.

42   "What is that, out there?" She's standing and flapping her hands and for a moment I see a head shape bobbing in the waves. She's standing in the water, I, on the boulder. The tide is low, and a round, black, head-sized rock has just risen from the waves. She returns, her sari end dripping and ruined and her face is a twisted remnant of hope, the way mine was a hundred hours ago, still laughing but inwardly knowing that nothing but the ultimate tragedy could bring two women together at six o'clock on a Sunday morning. I watch her face sag into blankness.

43   "That water felt warm, Shaila," she says at length.

44   "You can't," I say. "We have to wait for our turn to come."

45   I haven't eaten in four days, haven't brushed my teeth.

46   "I know," she says. "I tell myself I have no right to grieve. They are in a better place than we are. My swami says I should be thrilled for them. My swami says depression is a sign of our selfishness."

47   Maybe I'm selfish. Selfishly I break away from Kusum and run, sandals slapping against stones, to the water's edge. What if my boys aren't lying pinned under the debris? What if they aren't stuck a mile below that innocent blue chop? What if, given the strong currents. . . .

48   Now I've ruined my sari, one of my best. Kusum has joined me, knee-deep in water that feels to me like a swimming pool. I could settle in the water, and my husband would take my hand and the boys would slap water in my face just to see me scream.

49   "Do you remember what good swimmers my boys were, Kusum?"

50   "I saw the medals," she says.

51   One of the widowers, Dr. Ranganathan from Montreal, walks out to us, carrying his shoes in one hand. He's an electrical engineer. Someone at the hotel mentioned his work is famous around the world, something about the

place where physics and electricity come together. He has lost a huge family, something indescribable. "With some luck," Dr. Ranganathan suggests to me, "a good swimmer could make it safely to some island. It is quite possible that there may be many, many microscopic islets scattered around."

52   "You're not just saying that?" I tell Dr. Ranganathan about Vinod, my elder son. Last hear he took diving as well.

53   "It's a parent's duty to hope," he says. "It is foolish to rule out possibilities that have not been tested. I myself have not surrendered hope."

54   Kusum is sobbing once again. "Dear lady," he says, laying his free hand on her arm, and she calms down.

55   "Vinod is how old?" he asks me. He's very careful, as we all are. *Is,* not was.

56   "Fourteen. Yesterday he was fourteen. His father and uncle were going to take him down to the Taj and give him a big birthday party. I couldn't go with them because I couldn't get two weeks off from my stupid job in June." I process bills for a travel agent. June is a big travel month.

57   Dr. Ranganathan whips the pockets of his suit jacket inside out. Squashed roses, in darkening shades of pink, float on the water. He tore the roses off creepers in somebody's garden. He didn't ask anyone if he could pluck the roses, but now there's been an article about it in the local papers. When you see an Indian person, it says, please give him or her flowers.

58   "A strong youth of fourteen," he says, "can very likely pull to safety a younger one."

59   My sons, though four years apart, were very close. Vinod wouldn't let Mithun drown. *Electrical engineering,* I think, foolishly perhaps: this man knows important secrets of the universe, things closed to me. Relief spins me lightheaded. No wonder my boys' photographs haven't turned up in the gallery of photos of the recovered dead. "Such pretty roses," I say.

60   "My wife loved pink roses. Every Friday I had to bring a bunch home. I used to say, why? After twenty odd years of marriage you're still needing proof positive of my love?" He has identified his wife and three of his children. Then others from Montreal, the lucky ones, intact families with no survivors. He chuckles as he wades back to shore. Then he swings around to ask me a question. "Mrs. Bhave, you are wanting to throw in some roses for your loved ones? I have two big ones left."

61   But I have other things to float: Vinod's pocket calculator; a half-painted model B-52 for my Mithun. They'd want them on their island. And for my husband? For him I let fall into the calm, glassy waters a poem I wrote in the hospital yesterday. Finally he'll know my feelings for him.

62   "Don't tumble, the rocks are slippery," Dr. Ranganathan cautions. He holds out a hand for me to grab.

63   Then it's time to get back on the bus, time to rush back to our waiting posts on hospital benches.

64   Kusum is one of the lucky ones. The lucky ones flew here, identified in multiplicate their loved ones, then will fly to India with the bodies for proper ceremonies. Satish is one of the few males who surfaced. The photos of faces we saw on the walls in an office at Heathrow and here in the hospital are mostly of women. Women have more body fat, a nun said to me matter-of-factly. They float better.

65   Today I was stopped by a young sailor on the street. He had loaded bodies, he'd gone into the water when—he checks my face for signs of strength—when the sharks were first spotted. I don't blush, and he breaks down. "It's all right," I say. "Thank you." I had heard about the sharks from Dr. Ranganathan. In his orderly mind, science brings understanding, it holds no terror. It is the shark's duty. For every deer there is a hunter, for every fish a fisherman.

66   The Irish are not shy; they rush to me and give me hugs and some are crying. I cannot imagine reactions like that on the streets of Toronto. Just strangers, and I am touched. Some carry flowers with them and give them to any Indian they see.

67   After lunch, a policeman I have gotten to know quite well catches hold of me. He says he thinks he has a match for Vinod. I explain what a good swimmer Vinod is.

68   "You want me with you when you look at photos?" Dr. Ranganathan walks ahead of me into the picture gallery. In these matters, he is a scientist, and I am grateful. It is a new perspective. "They have performed miracles," he says. "We are indebted to them."

69   The first day or two the policemen showed us relatives only one picture at a time; now they're in a hurry, they're eager to lay out the possibles, and even the probables.

70   The face on the photo is of a boy much like Vinod; the same intelligent eyes, the same thick brows dipping into a V. But this boy's features, even his cheeks, are puffier, wider, mushier.

71   "No." My gaze is pulled by other pictures. There are five other boys who look like Vinod.

72   The nun assigned to console me rubs the first picture with a fingertip. "When they've been in the water for a while, love, they look a little heavier." The bones under the skin are broken, they said on the first day—try to adjust your memories. It's important.

73   "It's not him. I'm his mother. I'd know."

74   "I know this one!" Dr. Ranganathan cries out suddenly from the back of the gallery. "And this one!" I think he senses that I don't want to find my boys. "They are the Kutty brothers. They were also from Montreal." I don't mean to be crying. On the contrary, I am ecstatic. My suitcase in the hotel is packed heavy with dry clothes for my boys.

75   The policeman starts to cry. "I am so sorry, I am so sorry, ma'am. I really thought we had a match."

76   With the nun ahead of us and the policeman behind, we, the unlucky ones without our children's bodies, file out of the makeshift gallery.

77   From Ireland most of us go on to India. Kusum and I take the same direct flight to Bombay, so I can help her clear customs quickly. But we have to argue with a man in uniform. He has large boils on his face. The boils swell and glow with sweat as we argue with him. He wants Kusum to wait in line and he refuses to take authority because his boss is on a tea break. But Kusum won't let her coffins out of sight, and I shan't desert her though I know that my parents, elderly and diabetic, must be waiting in a stuffy car in a scorching lot.

78   "You bastard!" I scream at the man with the popping boils. Other passengers press closer. "You think we're smuggling contraband in those coffins!"

79   Once upon a time we were well brought up women; we were dutiful wives who kept our heads veiled, our voices shy and sweet.

80   In India, I become, once again, an only child of rich, ailing parents. Old friends of the family come to pay their respects. Some are Sikh, and inwardly, involuntarily, I cringe. My parents are progressive people; they do not blame communities for a few individuals.

81   In Canada it is a different story now.

82   "Stay longer," my mother pleads. "Canada is a cold place. Why would you want to be all by yourself?" I stay.

83   Three months pass. Then another.

84   "Vikram wouldn't have wanted you to give up things!" they protest. They call my husband by the name he was born with. In Toronto he'd changed to Vik so the men he worked with at his office would find his name as easy as Rod or Chris. "You know, the dead aren't cut off from us!"

85   My grandmother, the spoiled daughter of a rich *zamindar,* shaved her head with rusty razor blades when she was widowed at sixteen. My grandfather died of childhood diabetes when he was nineteen, and she saw herself as the harbinger of bad luck. My mother grew up without parents, raised indifferently by an uncle, while her true mother slept in a hut behind the main estate house and took her food with the servants. She grew up a rationalist. My parents abhor mindless mortification.

86   The zamindar's daughter kept stubborn faith in Vedic rituals; my parents rebelled. I am trapped between two modes of knowledge. At thirty-six, I am too old to start over and too young to give up. Like my husband's spirit, I flutter between worlds.

87   Courting aphasia, we travel. We travel with our phalanx of servants and poor relatives. To hill stations and to beach resorts. We play contract bridge

in dusty gymkhana clubs. We ride stubby ponies up crumbly mountain trails. At tea dances, we let ourselves be twirled twice round the ballroom. We hit the holy spots we hadn't made time for before. In Varanasi, Kalighat, Rishikesh, Hardwar, astrologers and palmists seek me out and for a fee offer me cosmic consolations.

88   Already the widowers among us are being shown new bride candidates. They cannot resist the call of custom, the authority of their parents and older brothers. They must marry; it is the duty of a man to look after a wife. The new wives will be young widows with children, destitute but of good family. They will make loving wives, but the men will shun them. I've had calls from the men over crackling Indian telephone lines. "Save me," they say, these substantial, educated, successful men of forty. "My parents are arranging a marriage for me." In a month they will have buried one family and returned to Canada with a new bride and partial family.

89   I am comparatively lucky. No one here thinks of arranging a husband for an unlucky widow.

90   Then, on the third day of the sixth month into this odyssey, in an abandoned temple in a tiny Himalayan village, as I make my offering of flowers and sweetmeats to the god of a tribe of animists, my husband descends to me. He is squatting next to a scrawny *sadhu* in moth-eaten robes. Vikram wears the vanilla suit he wore the last time I hugged him. The sadhu tosses petals on a butter-fed flame, reciting Sanskrit mantras and sweeps his face of flies. My husband takes my hands in his.

91   *You're beautiful,* he starts. Then, *What are you doing here?*

92   *Shall I stay?* I ask. He only smiles, but already the image is fading. *You must finish alone what we started together.* No seaweed wreathes his mouth. He speaks too fast just as he used to when we were an envied family in our pink split-level. He is gone.

93   In the windowless altar room, smoky with joss sticks and clarified butter lamps, a sweaty hand gropes for my blouse. I do not shriek. The *sadhu* arranges his robe. The lamps hiss and sputter out.

94   When we come out of the temple, my mother says, "Did you feel something weird in there?"

95   My mother has no patience with ghosts, prophetic dreams, holy men, and cults.

96   "No," I lie. "Nothing."

97   But she knows that she's lost me. She knows that in days I shall be leaving.

98   Kusum's put her house up for sale. She wants to live in an ashram in Hardwar. Moving to Hardwar was her swami's idea. Her swami runs two ashrams, the one in Hardwar and another here in Toronto.

99   "Don't run away," I tell her.

100   "I'm not running away," she says. "I'm pursuing inner peace. You think you or that Ranganathan fellow are better off?"

101   Pam's left for California. She wants to do some modeling, she says. She says when she comes into her share of the insurance money she'll open a yoga-cum-aerobics studio in Hollywood. She sends me postcards so naughty I daren't leave them on the coffee table. Her mother has withdrawn from her and the world.

102   The rest of us don't lose touch, that's the point. Talk is all we have, says Dr. Ranganathan, who has also resisted his relatives and returned to Montreal and to his job, alone. He says, whom better to talk with than other relatives? We've been melted down and recast as a new tribe.

103   He calls me twice a week from Montreal. Every Wednesday night and every Saturday afternoon. He is changing jobs, going to Ottawa. But Ottawa is over a hundred miles away, and he is forced to drive two hundred and twenty miles a day. He can't bring himself to sell his house. The house is a temple, he says; the king-sized bed in the master bedroom is a shrine. He sleeps on a folding cot. A devotee.

104   There are still some hysterical relatives. Judith Templeton's list of those needing help and those who've "accepted" is in nearly perfect balance. Acceptance means you speak of your family in the past tense and you make active plans for moving ahead with your life. There are courses at Seneca and Ryerson we could be taking. Her gleaming leather briefcase is full of college catalogues and lists of cultural societies that need our help. She has done impressive work, I tell her.

105   "In the textbooks on grief management," she replies—I am her confidante, I realize, one of the few whose grief has not sprung bizarre obsessions—"there are stages to pass through: rejection, depression, acceptance, reconstruction." She has compiled a chart and finds that six months after the tragedy, none of us still reject reality, but only a handful are reconstructing. "Depressed Acceptance" is the plateau we've reached. Remarriage is a major step in reconstruction (though she's a little surprised, even shocked, over *how* quickly some of the men have taken on new families). Selling one's house and changing jobs and cities is healthy.

106   How do I tell Judith Templeton that my family surrounds me, and that like creatures in epics, they've changed shapes? She sees me as calm and accepting but worries that I have no job, no career. My closest friends are worse off than I. I cannot tell her my days, even my nights, are thrilling.

107   She asks me to help with families she can't reach at all. An elderly couple in Agincourt whose sons were killed just weeks after they had brought their parents over from a village in Punjab. From their names, I know that they are Sikh. Judith Templeton and a translator have visited them twice with offers of money for air fare to Ireland, with bank forms, power-of-attorney

forms, but they have refused to sign, or to leave their tiny apartment. Their sons' money is frozen in the bank. Their sons' investment apartments have been trashed by tenants, the furnishings sold off. The parents fear that anything they sign or any money they receive will end the company's or the country's obligations to them. They fear they are selling their sons for two airline tickets to a place they've never seen.

108   The high-rise apartment is a tower of Indians and West Indians, with a sprinkling of Orientals. The nearest bus stop kiosk is lined with women in saris. Boys practice cricket in the parking lot. Inside the building, even I wince a bit from the ferocity of onion fumes, the distinctive and immediate Indianness of frying *ghee,* but Judith Templeton maintains a steady flow of information. These poor old people are in imminent danger of losing their place and all their services.

109   I say to her, "They are Sikh. They will not open up to a Hindu woman." And what I want to add is, as much as I try not to, I stiffen now at the sight of beards and turbans. I remember a time when we all trusted each other in this new country, it was only the new country we worried about.

110   The two rooms are dark and stuffy. The lights are off, and an oil lamp sputters on the coffee table. The bent old lady has let us in, and her husband is wrapping a white turban over his oiled, hip-length hair. She immediately goes to the kitchen, and I hear the most familiar sound of an Indian home, tap water hitting and filling a teapot.

111   They have not paid their utility bills, out of fear and the inability to write a check. The telephone is gone; electricity and gas and water are soon to follow. They have told Judith their sons will provide. They are good boys, and they have always earned and looked after their parents.

112   We converse a bit in Hindi. They do not ask about the crash and I wonder if I should bring it up. If they think I am here merely as a translator, then they may feel insulted. There are thousands of Punjabi-speakers, Sikhs, in Toronto to do a better job. And so I say to the old lady, "I too have lost my sons, and my husband, in the crash."

113   Her eyes immediately fill with tears. The man mutters a few words which sound like a blessing. "God provides and God takes away," he says.

114   I want to say, but only men destroy and give back nothing. "My boys and my husband are not coming back," I say. "We have to understand that."

115   Now the old woman responds. "But who is to say? Man alone does not decide these things." To this her husband adds his agreement.

116   Judith asks about the bank papers, the release forms. With a stroke of the pen, they will have a provincial trustee to pay their bills, invest their money, send them a monthly pension.

117   "Do you know this woman?" I ask them.

118   The man raises his hand from the table, turns it over and seems to regard each finger separately before he answers, "This young lady is always coming

here, we make tea for her and she leaves papers for us to sign." His eyes scan a pile of papers in the corner of the room. "Soon we will be out of tea, then will she go away?"

119   The old lady adds, "I have asked my neighbors and no one else gets *angrezi*⁴ visitors. What have we done?"

120   "It's her job," I try to explain. "The government is worried. Soon you will have no place to stay, no lights, no gas, no water."

121   "Government will get its money. Tell her not to worry, we are honorable people."

122   I try to explain the government wishes to give money, not take. He raises his hand. "Let them take," he says. "We are accustomed to that. That is no problem."

123   "We are strong people," says the wife. "Tell her that."

124   "Who needs all this machinery?" demands the husband. "It is unhealthy, the bright lights, the cold air on a hot day, the cold food, the four gas rings. God will provide, not government."

125   "When our boys return," the mother says. Her husband sucks his teeth. "Enough talk," he says.

126   Judith breaks in. "Have you convinced them?" The snaps on her cordovan briefcase go off like firecrackers in that quiet apartment. She lays the sheaf of legal papers on the coffee table. "If they can't write their names, an X will do—I've told them that."

127   Now the old lady has shuffled to the kitchen and soon emerges with a pot of tea and two cups. "I think my bladder will go first on a job like this," Judith says to me, smiling. "If only there was some way of reaching them. Please thank her for the tea. Tell her she's very kind."

128   I nod in Judith's direction and tell them in Hindi, "She thanks you for the tea. She thinks you are being very hospitable but she doesn't have the slightest idea what it means."

129   I want to say, humor her. I want to say, my boys and my husband are with me too, more than ever. I look in the old man's eyes and I can read his stubborn, peasant's message: *I have protected this woman as best I can. She is the only person I have left. Give to me or take from me what you will, but I'll not sign for it. I will not pretend that I accept.*

130   In the car, Judith says, "You see what I'm up against? I'm sure they're lovely people, but their stubbornness and ignorance are driving me crazy. They think signing a paper is signing their sons' death warrants, don't they?"

131   I am looking out the window. I want to say, *In our culture, it is a parent's duty to hope.*

132   "Now Shaila, this next woman is a real mess. She cries day and night, and she refuses all medical help. We may have to—"

---

⁴ *angrezi:* English.

133   "Let me out at the subway," I say.

134   "I beg your pardon?" I can feel those blue eyes staring at me.

135   It would not be like her to disobey. She merely disapproves, and slows at a corner to let me out. Her voice is plaintive. "Is there anything I said? Anything I did?"

136   I could answer her suddenly in a dozen ways, but I choose not to. "Shaila? Let's talk about it," I hear, then slam the door.

137   A wife and mother begins her new life in a new country, and that life is cut short. Yet her husband tells her: Complete what we have started. We, who stayed out of politics and came halfway around the world to avoid religious and political feuding have been the first in the New World to die from it. I no longer know what we started, nor how to complete it. I write letters to the editors of local papers and to members of Parliament. Now at least they admit it was a bomb. One MP answers back, with sympathy, but with a challenge. You want to make a difference? Work on a campaign. Work on mine. Politicize the Indian voter.

138   My husband's old lawyer helps me set up a trust. Vikram was a saver and a careful investor. He had saved the boys' boarding school and college fees. I sell the pink house at four times what we paid for it and take a small apartment downtown. I am looking for a charity to support.

139   We are deep in the Toronto winter, gray skies, icy pavements. I stay indoors, watching television. I have tried to assess my situation, how best to live my life, to complete what we began so many years ago. Kusum has written me from Hardwar that her life is now serene. She has seen Satish and has heard her daughter sing again. Kusum was on a pilgrimage, passing through a village when she heard a young girl's voice, singing one of her daughter's favorite *bhajans*. She followed the music through the squalor of a Himalayan village, to a hut where a young girl, an exact replica of her daughter, was fanning coals under the kitchen fire. When she appeared, the girl cried out, "Ma!" and ran away. What did I think of that?

140   I think I can only envy her.

141   Pam didn't make it to California, but writes me from Vancouver. She works in a department store, giving make-up hints to Indian and Oriental girls. Dr. Ranganathan has given up his commute, given up his house and job, and accepted an academic position in Texas where no one knows his story and he has vowed not to tell it. He calls me now once a week.

142   I wait, I listen, and I pray, but Vikram has not returned to me. The voices and the shapes and the nights filled with visions ended abruptly several weeks ago.

143   I take it as a sign.

144   One rare, beautiful, sunny day last week, returning from a small errand on Yonge Street, I was walking through the park from the subway to my

apartment. I live equidistant from the Ontario Houses of Parliament and the University of Toronto. The day was not cold, but something in the bare trees caught my attention. I looked up from the gravel, into the branches and the clear blue sky beyond. I thought I heard the rustling of larger forms, and I waited a moment for voices. Nothing.

145   "What?" I asked.

146   Then as I stood in the path looking north to Queen's Park and west to the university, I heard the voices of my family one last time. *Your time has come,* they said. *Go, be brave.*

147   I do not know where this voyage I have begun will end. I do not know which direction I will take. I dropped the package on a park bench and started walking.

DISCUSSION QUESTIONS

1. Explain the opening situation briefly and tell who is involved.
2. How are the four stages of grief depicted in Shaila's life?
3. How do Kusum and Dr. Ranganathan eventually manage their grief?
4. What leads social worker Judith Templeton to ask for Shaila's help, and why are she and Shaila unable to deal effectively with the elderly couple from Punjab?

WRITING TOPICS

1. The narrator says that "we, who stayed out of politics and came halfway around the world to avoid religious and political feuding have been the first in the New World to die from it." Think about a current political disagreement in the United States or Canada and write about how it has affected or could affect your life.
2. Does this story have universality? That is, would it be meaningful to large numbers of people in any time or place? Discuss in an essay.
3. This story is populated with many vivid characters, both living and dead. In an essay, discuss the author's gift for characterization and what affect it has on the story. Cite examples from the story to support your views.

NOBODY KNOWS

Quang Bao

Quang Bao was born in Canh Tho, Vietnam, in 1969 and emigrated to the United States at the age of five. He earned a bachelor's degree in English from Boston University in 1991. His work has been published in *The Boston Globe, The New York Times, The Threepenny Review, The Asian American Pacific Journal,* and *Open City,* as well as in the anthologies *Watermark: Vietnamese American Poetry and Prose* (1998) and *Personals: Dreams and Nightmares from the Lives of Twenty Young Writers* (1998). He received a 1998 artist grant from the St. Botolph's Club Foundation and has just completed his first novel.

In the following story, the intergenerational battle takes a wry twist as the father, who is deaf to anyone else's needs or wishes, tries to impose his will on a son who is caught between the traditional Asian worldview and the ideals of Western society.

1   "What a lovely apartment!" my father shrieked, entering through the back door of my apartment. "Is this your room?" He deposited a duffel bag in what was actually a guest room in a two-bedroom apartment. "This is wonderful." He petted an engraved box in which I kept old letters. "Your room is clean, a bit on the small side, but nobody will know if you keep the door mostly closed." He strolled through the apartment, hands clasped behind his back, a usual disposition that marked his entrance into unfamiliar places where the possibilities for interior renovations seemed endless to him.

2   "Yeah, so, anybody who was anybody back then was there," he said, pouring himself a glass of water and walking into the living room. "I'm so glad I went. The wine had a wonderful bouquet, not a lot of cork, either." He swirled the glass around and took a sip, settling down on the living room couch.

3   During the ride back from the airport, my father was describing a reunion he had just attended in California of former military admirals from Vietnam. The affair, by his account, was no less than grand, which meant empty firing rifles mounted on the wall, a centerpiece ice sculpture of a military academy at the head table where he sat, a buffet spread of ladyfinger sandwiches, and a beautiful Vietnamese girl playing on the piano a lovely Schubert piece, or maybe Handel—whatever it was, it was definitely lovely, he thought.

4   He reminisced, dragging me through an essentially plotless evening, from A to B, feeling it necessary to go through L, M, N, and even X, first, and not necessarily in that order. When he paused for water, I spoke up, in a detached voice that seemed to come out from one of the stereo speakers. "Dad, I have something I want to confess about myself, make clear rather, while you're sitting here," I stated.

5   Quickly, but somewhat effortlessly, he set the glass down onto the glass coffee table and fell back into the sofa. He rearranged some pillows into a fortress to protect himself from wherever the conversation happened to veer next. It was as if a close relative were about to tell him, officially, that all those accounts he had been hearing about the fall of South Vietnam were true, accounts which his mind had blocked out up until now and tossed aside as rumors and the work of conspirators and journalists. Very suddenly, his face let go of its usual blank expression—he had a plan—and contorted itself into a minimally pained grimace, like that of someone who has just bitten into a rotten plum, which looked deceptively unbruised on the surface. Agitatedly, he shot up from the comfortable loveseat and fell to the floor.

6   It was like a dream, or, more accurately, I had already dreamt this scene in which I was witnessing my father's collapse, only I couldn't remember what I did next because the dream usually climaxed here. By the time I decided what to do and made it over to where he was lying, twenty-five years seemed to have passed. I fitted my hands under his armpits and flipped him onto his backside so that he lay face up. And then the phone rang.

7   "Hello, San Francisco, this is your mother calling."

8   "Mom, Dad's lying again on—"

9   "Your father tells lies all the—"

10   "He's on the living room floor," I reported.

11   "Oh, dear," my mother said, changing the telephone from one ear to the other, "just what I need."

12   Two years ago, just around the time he learned of his impotency, my father invented a habit of orchestrating fainting spells. He made very little effort to be convincing, in manner and timing, sometimes even crossing hideously clustered spaces first to avoid any superficial injury to himself on his way down.

13   "Honey, your father is getting older," my mother said. "Just finish that

Master's, give him a grandchild, and do whatever it is you keep writing about in those stories you keep sending us."

14 The stories were actually wordy, confessional letters I was mailing home regularly to my parents, who admired the "fictional sounding" aspects of the writing and the main character. They suggested sending the stories off to some well-circulated journal I had never heard of that also printed cooking recipes.

15 "They are not stories," I stressed. "They are letters, a-b-c-d-e-f-g, letters, facts about your son's l-i-f-e-s-t-y—"

16 "Where's your father now?" she broke in.

17 "He's still prostrate," I said.

18 She gasped. "I don't like all those puns and spelling games."

19 "Mother, why are you calling?"

20 "I wanted to ask your father something, but he's obviously predisposed so I won't bother," she said. "He hasn't told you anything yet?"

21 "I can't recall anything terribly newsy," I said.

22 "You and details," she said. "You're just like your—oh, honey, I've got a call on the other line. Can we talk more later?"

23 By now, a fly had landed on the bulb of my father's nose. The fly skipped and disappeared somewhere in his brownish-colored hair. I walked over and sat down perpendicularly to my father, supporting myself by leaning back on the palms of my hands. I stretched out my legs and slid my big toe underneath one of his belt loops and noticed a dry-cleaning tag still stuck to the safety pin on the inside waist of his trousers. I supposed telling your parents about the important things and people in your life outweighed the need to tell them under the ideal circumstances. To be honest, I was relishing the chance at an uninterrupted monologue and began telling my father about the four-year relationship I had been carrying on, when his eyes immediately reopened and he came to.

24 When my father was sitting back and upright on the couch, I looked at my watch (5:20 p.m.) and calculated that he had been in the apartment for approximately thirty-five minutes. He had repositioned himself safely behind an arrangement of throw pillows, the same way he was when he first entered the room.

25 "Mom just called," I said finally. "She said you were supposed to tell me something."

26 "Son, I don't know how you're going to take this," he sighed, pulling one of the pillows in closer. "Your mother and I would like you to find a wife, are considering a divorce ourselves, and, separately, I'm considering rhinoplasty."

27   The first two pieces of information had been debated, with increasing frequency and volume, over the past few years, and could hardly be considered new. The rhinoplasty, however, belonged on page one, conjuring up an image of something big and plastic that my father wanted fastened to himself.

28   "Neither of you has enough money to live apart," I pointed out. "We've done the math already. You've been together too long to separate anyway."

29   "Well, you needn't worry about the money part," he said. "The truth is that your mother doesn't know who I am anymore. She tripped over me the other day, or maybe I tripped her. Whatever. She apologized to the floor lamp, or the ottoman, or someone like that. I mean, I'm old, yes, but I'm not gone yet." He pulled his hand out from one of the pillows and scratched the stubble on his chin.

30   I'd noticed that when other men grew older, they started looking wiser. And through some generous bending of Punnet-square rules,[1] a forgivable phenotype[2] made their aged faces more interesting and complex, an unannotated, scribbled-all-over tabula rasa,[3] from which some of the most character-building experiences in life—marriage, war, death—could be downloaded on sight. My father's face seemed to have missed the wind-swept mayhem of aging. The only giveaway of his age could be located in his eyes. They were tiny, and the lids so amazingly wrinkled and overworked that I wondered if the irises could still filter the light amidst all of the erosion. With just that outstanding exception, his face looked the same as it did in a lineup photo of him at age twenty-four, a placid army cadet ready to be captured and pumped for information he didn't have.

31   I examined his nose closely. The organ was as long and rectangularish as possible, creating a visual speed bump in what would otherwise have been just an oval-shaped, trafficless layout of flesh, moles, and the normally spaced facial protuberances. I remembered when my father and I were waiting in the foyer inside the enormous three-story house of my horrific first date and how nervous I was. To prevent me from making a scene, he distracted me by trying to locate where exactly my date's bedroom was through a recreation of the entire floor plan, based on the odors he sensed coming out of different rooms. He was on a par with those who could discriminate differences in classical music or etchings. My father recognized the world only because he could smell it, and that, for him, was as close as he could get to understanding it.

---

[1] *Punnet-square rules:* a grid system for calculating heredity or genotypes.
[2] *phenotype:* the physical characteristics of an organism that are determined by genetic makeup and environment.
[3] *tabula rasa:* blank slate.

32   "Dad, why on earth do you want a new nose?" I asked.

33   "Let's talk about you," he said, pointing a finger. "In Vietnam, men your age are all married or thinking about being married. Even Truc Vanh in that famous autobiography was at least seriously considering it." My father was always making obscure-sounding cultural allusions that were virtually impossible to verify. "Find someone, that's an order. And if you can't, come home this summer and your mother and I will help. Who knows?"

34   "Help?"

35   "I know a Vietnamese couple with a young mechanical engineer daughter," he said. "She's been to Paris, like you. The family's related to Balzac, I hear."

36   "Well, that's sufficient," I said. "I'd like to marry her, but some time in between my final exams and our first child, I'd like to have an affair, preferably with a semi-younger Vietnamese woman who owns a restaurant and likes to wear high—"

37   "Don't change the subject again!" he interrupted, shooting out from behind the pillow cushions. "This is about you, not anybody else. In Vietnam, you'd be cast out of society, a stranger, an aberration . . . no twenty-five-year-old man—you'd have to get your own apartment even!" Suddenly, his eyes started jumping around the room. "I could set something up for you easily. I'm a great matchmaker! I've matchmade a whole bunch of people!"

38   "Who?" I cross-examined.

39   "At least five," he said, stretching out all five fingers on his left hand.

40   "That means ten actually, right?"

41   "Ten, even," he said, holding out the other hand. "Yes, of course, five times two is ten!"

42   "Brilliant," I said.

43   The phone rang again. He plopped back down to the sofa, and I let the answering machine pick up the call.

44   "Hi, honey, this is just Mom again," the voice said. "I want to get my two cents in before your father regains consciousness. I don't know what he's told you already but he's making up half of it and the other half he doesn't know what he's talking about, except for the fact that we would both love to marry you off and be done with the whole matter. Nobody's getting any younger around here, especially not me. This is long distance, so I won't be long, but could you just please stop telling the world about your feelings and just calm down a bit. I'm sure I speak for your father when I say that one out of seven women is Chinese, for heaven's sake, and why, I don't see how someone can't *not* find one woman with those kinds of odds. We were oppressed and everything by the Chinese, I think, but that was so long ago I can hardly remember it. I wouldn't necessarily mind—"

45   My father, having crossed the room, snatched the phone off its cradle.

46   "We're both here," he announced. "You've said enough for all of us already so why don't you just—" He paused and then covered his hand over the mouthpiece. "She wants to talk to you." I waved my hand back and forth to both of them. "You see, he doesn't even want to talk to you anymore," he said, back into the telephone. "Honestly, nagging us all to death isn't—" He abruptly stopped again, walked with the telephone into the kitchen, and shut the door for privacy.

47   Once they stopped arguing, I could overhear fragments of a ploy to get me to concede and see things their way: a newly designed house, built just down the street from my parents, with all the modern conveniences installed; inside, a twisted staircase that uncoiled eventually to the master bedroom door, half-opened to reveal a resplendently dressed bed, draped in sheets of satin, on which my new Vietnamese bride was just about to lie—"The war is over, honey, come to bed."

DISCUSSION QUESTIONS

1. Why does the narrator's father fall to the floor?
2. When did the father start "orchestrating" his fainting spells?
3. The narrator's mother is somewhat confused about words. What is her reply to her son's starting to tell her that his father is lying on the floor? What word does she mistake for *prostrate?* She says the father is "predisposed." What word should she have used instead?
4. What does the narrator finally begin to tell his father, and where is his father while he begins to talk?
5. What is rhinoplasty and why is the father's considering it bigger news than the fact that the narrator's parents want him to get married and are considering divorce?
6. How, according to the narrator, does his father recognize the world? Is this detail relevant?
7. In what tone of voice would the narrator speak paragraph 36?
8. At the end of paragraph 44, the mother doesn't get to finish her sentence. What was she going to say and how can you tell?
9. What can you conclude about communication in this family?

WRITING TOPICS

1. The author of this story is talented at writing dialogue. In fact, the story, if expanded, could be adapted into a one-act play. Try your hand at writing the opening scene of a play, perhaps based on conversations in your own family. Decide what the chief problem of the play is, who the characters are, and then start with an opening line that will get an audience's attention and hint at the chief problem.

2. Write about a time in your life when no one would listen to you. What were you trying to tell? To whom were you trying to tell it? Why didn't the person or persons listen? Did you ever get to say what you wanted to?

Summary Writing Topics

1. Considering the elements of plot and character, which story in this chapter do you find the most satisfying? Explain your choice in an essay.

2. What are the advantages and disadvantages to having strong ties to an ethnic community? If you do not have such ties, owing perhaps to the length of time your family has been in North America, would you like to feel more connected to your origins? Why or why not?

3. Group expectations are a powerful force in several selections in this chapter. What experiences have you had with group expectations? Have they conflicted with your sense of identity or reinforced that sense? Examine the expectations of family, friends, the religious community, and the school community and the effects these expectations have had on you.

4. Several of the selections in this chapter show a significant change in the life of a character because of circumstances beyond his or her control. Choose two of these selections and compare and contrast the causes and the results of these changes.

5. In an essay, compare the intergenerational conflict evident in two selections from this chapter.

CHAPTER FIVE

GENDER IDENTITIES, GENDER RELATIONSHIPS

Gender roles in traditional Asian American communities, as in most traditional societies, tend to be fixed and communally enforced. Generally, male children have been more highly valued than girls. This high esteem for males also brings with it higher economic and social expectations of sons. Daughters generally were expected to marry and to leave their natal families to become members of their husbands' families. Sons became men through marriage and through having children, especially sons. Confucianist ideas, which were dominant throughout East Asian societies, held that women were subject to the three obediences: first to fathers, then to husbands, and, if they were widowed, to sons. Relationships between the sexes were therefore heteronormative; that is, sexual relationships were socially accepted only between men and women and for purposes of marriage, while other forms (for example, concubinage) were merely tolerated.

Immigration to the United States, where the society is more permissive about sexual relationships and where conservative male and female roles are not as rigidly observed, put these social values under stress. The traditional ideal of Asian American masculinity as bound by filial and patriarchal duty can be viewed as quite different from the individualistic ethos of the American male, represented in the Marlboro Man or John Wayne cowboy archetype. Similarly, second-generation Asian American daughters may resent the restrictive qualities of the kind of femininity they are supposed to exhibit and their subordinate positions—as wives, mothers, and domestics—in the family.

The selections in this chapter illustrate both the pressures on the older generation, who are disappointed by their children's failure to maintain the traditional gender roles even as they themselves are subjected to prejudice and cultural turmoil, and the struggles of a younger generation who find themselves in between their desires for autonomy and individual happiness and their parents' expectations. The chapter from Louis Chu's *Eat a Bowl of Tea* moves between these two points of view. Although a married man, Ben Loy is still intimidated by his father, Wah Gay; their communication is limited and usually unpleasant. At the same time, Wah Gay is disappointed that Ben Loy has not been able to keep his wife faithful. In a close Chinese American community, his daughter-in-law's disgrace becomes his own. For Wah Gay, a son's duty is to provide the family with male babies. Gossip about his daughter-in-law's infidelity threatens not only his son's but his own social standing as a man.

"On Discovery," the opening chapter in Maxine Hong Kingston's book of memoirs, *China Men,* tells a different version of this fear of loss of manhood. The myth of Tang Ao vividly describes how a man is turned socially into a woman, underlining the notion that gender roles are socially constructed rather than biologically given. Tang Ao has his ears pricked and his feet bound. Costumed in women's clothing, he is forced to serve. The figure of Tang Ao also suggests the employment history of male Chinese immigrants to the United States, who were restricted by discriminatory laws to traditional "women's" work in laundries and restaurants, work that produced a public image of Chinese American men as subordinate and effeminate.

Gus Lee's chapter from his novel *China Boy* offers a realistic twist to this theme of Asian American masculinity under threat. Here, the main character is an unhappy seven-year-old Chinese American boy, who grows up in a poor mixed-race neighborhood in San Francisco. Kept out of the house every day by an unloving stepmother, he is beaten by the other children until a Latino rescuer persuades his father to send him to the YMCA for boxing lessons. The chapter focuses on this turning point in the young boy's life, when his father talks to him for the first time about his own life as a soldier. The father's telling marks the boy's first step into manhood—a manhood, the narrative suggests, that would be less restrictive than the father's, who is embarrassed by the son's tears. Similarly, Shawn Wong's chapter from his first novel, *Homebase,* tells a story about male ancestors. It narrates an encounter at Alcatraz during the Native American takeover of that island in 1969. Rainsford, the Chinese American narrator, meets an old Indian man who claims a Chinese grandfather. Through the Indian, Rainsford learns to understand the importance of a communal identity, based, the chapter suggests, on the bonds of male descendants across the generations.

This discovery of gender identity through the line of the father is not as straightforward for girls. Both Jade Snow Wong's and Jeanne Wakatsuki Houston's accounts of growing up female are critical of the gender bias in their families, where a girl is "less significant than the new son" (in Jade Snow Wong's *Fifth Chinese Daughter*) and where she is expected merely to marry someone of her own ethnicity. Wakatsuki Houston's chapter from *Farewell to Manzanar* pits the ethnic father's gender expectations against an American mainstream gender stereotype; both are viewed as sexist, for both reduce the individual female to prescriptive sexual roles, either that of modest Japanese wife or Western exotic sexual object.

Talat Abbasi's narrative illustrates the cross-cultural tensions that arise when South Asian women cross national borders. Abbasi's short story "Sari Petticoats" criticizes the main character, who abandons the traditional attributes of the good wife when she enters the United States and becomes a successful businesswoman, not so much for the loss of ethnic identity as for the loss of the ethical values of caring and giving.

The excerpt from Shawn Wong's novel *American Knees,* like Timothy Liu's poem, "Desire as the Gesture Between Us" and Vince Gotera's poem "First Mango," is a tender representation of a love relationship. In Wong's narrative of separated spouses, Raymond finally recognizes the "tensile strength and stability" of his relationship with Aurora. Cooking rice, Aurora makes a symbolic statement about her reconciliation and future domesticity with Raymond. Liu's poem captures the moment of love between lovers in the images of garden and flower, while Gotera's poem, focusing on the difficulties that a non-Filipino wife may encounter in a Filipino community, seizes on the husband's offering of the sensuous pleasures in eating a mango as a way through the senses to an appreciation of Filipino culture.

In these pieces, gender roles are presented as also culturally inflected. Asian American male characters face a crisis in their understanding of what manhood signifies when they enter into a different cultural imagination, and they look for role models to help them grow into manhood. Female characters are constrained by restrictive concepts of womanhood, and they lose crucial elements of traditional concepts of the feminine—or are in danger of losing them—when they move toward assimilation. In love or in the family, Asian Americans have to negotiate conflicting ideals of male and female identities.

FROM *EAT A BOWL OF TEA*

Louis Chu

Born in Toishan, China, in 1915, Louis Chu emigrated to the United States at the age of nine. After finishing high school in New Jersey, he earned a bachelor's degree from Upsala College, received a master's degree from New York University, and undertook post-graduate work at the New School for Social Research. Chu worked for New York City's Department of Welfare, served as the executive secretary of the Soo Yuen Benevolent Association, and hosted a radio program entitled "Chinese Festival." By the time he died in 1970, he was a prominent figure in New York's Chinatown.

In addition to his contributions to the community, Chu published *Eat a Bowl of Tea* (1961), a comic novel that revolves around the sec-ond-generation Chinese American Ben Loy and his "war bride," Mei Oi. The novel is also a commentary on Chinatown's bachelor soci-ety, which was the product of exclusionary policies that prevented Chinese wives and children from joining their husbands and fathers in the United States, and on that society's decline in the post–World War II era. Asian American literary critic Sau-ling Cynthia Wong describes the novel as "exhibiting a . . . working-class, realist 'Chinatown' sensibility," employing "a 'Chinatown English' without overtones of caricature," and providing "a narrative of community life at a critical historical moment."[1]

In the following excerpt, from *Eat a Bowl of Tea*, Ben Loy's father reacts to the distressing rumors that his daughter-in-law is "running around with another man." (J.I.)

---

[1] King-kok Cheung, ed., *An Interethnic Companion to Asian American Literature* (Cambridge: Cambridge UP, 1997) 48.

1   Shortly after his return to work, Ben Loy received a call from his father, asking him to come to see him on his day off. Ben Loy had asked his father to talk over the phone, but the elder Wang replied that the matter could not be discussed over the telephone.

2   The following Wednesday Ben Loy steeled himself for the ordeal of meeting his father. He had always dreaded talking to the old man; for there existed a stern relationship between a Chinese father and his son. The prevailing practice is for neither to speak to the other unless he has to. As he walked toward the Money Come Club, the thought foremost on his mind was to get out of his father's place as soon as possible. Perhaps his father had another of those letters from his mother. What could a letter from Lau Shee contain? The usual things: "Need more money, send more home." Or: "What is Ben Loy and Lee Shee waiting for? I'm getting old. I want a grandchild before I close my eyes . . ."

3   When he tried the door, it was locked. He took a quarter from his pocket and knocked on the glass panel. Tap . . . tap . . . tap. There was no movement within. Then he put his nose against the glass, and he could see the silhouette of his father in the darkened interior hurrying to open the door.

4   "Come in," the elder Wang greeted.

5   "Did I wake you up?" Ben Loy stepped inside.

6   "No, I woke up a long time ago. I didn't bother to get up. I was reading the papers in bed." The father fiddled with the belt of his bathrobe. "Sit down. I'll be with you in a moment."

7   Even with the 100-watt bulb burning in the middle of the room directly above the mah-jong table, the room looked dingy. To Ben Loy, having just come in from the sunlight, the room was like a dimly-lit tunnel. As the minutes ticked by, he began to discern the various objects in the room. He felt a dampness coursing through his body. This he attributed to his unfamiliarity with the place. This was really the first time he had sat in the room. Previously he had been in and out, like a mailman. He wrinkled his nose. "It's like a dungeon," he said to himself. Only an old man like his father could stand a shut-in dingy place like this. It seemed a long time before Wah Gay came out.

8   "Ben Loy," he began slowly, taking a seat almost opposite from his son. "I've heard some very distressing news. Do you have any idea what it is?"

9   "No," he replied sulkily.

10   "I've heard from reliable sources that Ah Sow is running around with another man. Is that true?" His voice was stern but his manner was not unpleasant. He placed his palms on his lap and leaned forward. "I want to listen to the truth."

11   The question exploded on Ben Loy like ten thousand firecrackers. It took him several seconds to recover from the shock. "This is the first time I've heard of it," he said nervously but defiantly. He pursed his lips. His first

reaction was to dash out of the place, but he changed his mind and waited.

12   "It is your business to find out!" Wah Gay raised his voice, jumping to his feet. "She's *your* wife, not mine." He gestured vigorously with his hands. "It's a disgrace. Maybe you feel no shame, but I do!" He started pacing the floor. He whirled and faced his son. "People will say Wang Wah Gay's daughter-in-law is running around. They don't say *your* wife is running around!"

13   "Where did you get the news from?" demanded Ben Loy, not knowing what else to say. "It's all a lie," he added weakly.

14   "I hope it is," Wah Gay growled. "I hope it is. But when people talk like that, it's my business to find out!"

15   "People can say anything they want," retorted the son.

16   "But why should people say such a thing if it's not true?" the father demanded impatiently, clenching his fists. "Can you tell me that?"

17   "How should I know?" Ben Loy shot back. "I have no control over other people's mouths."

18   "No, but you can find out if it's true or not." Wah Gay shook a finger at his son. "People just don't talk for nothing. There must be a reason." He paused for an answer, but there was none. "Some people are stupid, but they are stupid only to a degree," continued the exasperated father. "Not like you. Unless your wife is no good, people don't say she's no good!"

19   Ben Loy stormed out of the club house and slammed the door behind him.

20   "Wow your mother," Wah Gay shouted after him, his face red and his veins bulging with anger. "You think because you can open and shut your eye lids, you're a human being? You dead boy!" He rushed up to the door and flipped the latch on the lock. "Sonavabitch!" His whole body shook with rage. Foolish. How foolish it was to get this no good dead son to this country in the first place! Should have left him in the village to work the fields . . .

21   The end of the world came crashing down upon the shoulders of Wah Gay. He saw in his son a renegade. A no good loafer. A stupid, useless youth. A son who would disgrace his own father. He had lost his one and only son. He and his wife had lived for the boy. The hopes of grandparenthood were just emerging over the horizon and they could see in their future many grandchildren. Wah Gay had enjoyed thoroughly the pleasant task of writing to his wife Lau Shee, informing her that Ah Sow was at last with child. This, he assumed, had only been the first of such missives. For indeed, in America, with the best possible nutrition, babies would come as regularly as the harvest. Lau Shee would announce proudly to their cousins in the village: Our Ben Loy has another son. And then there would be celebrations. There would be thanksgiving at the temples for Mei Oi's mother. Tiny feet and tiny voices would come in to see Grandpa . . .

22   But this beautiful picture was only a dream, a dream mirrored in the subconscious fantasy of the man. A mirror shattered by the alleged scandal of Ben Loy's wife. A mirror shattered and irreparable. The destruction of a beautiful picture. Wah Gay sighed an agonizing sigh, alone and to himself. What was there for him to do? Ben Loy had denied any wrong-doing by his wife. If Ben Loy did not care, why should the old man care?

23   The private meeting with Chuck Ting flooded his mind. But how could he stop it? He had just tried . . . with Ben Loy. What about Lee Shee? Could he talk to her? No. That would be out of the question. She is much closer to her husband than to her father-in-law. But the old man would be the first to feel the brunt of scandal-talk. Once this hushed whispering burst into lively coffee shop topics, where could an old-timer like Wah Gay hide? Get out of town? He would have to! The father-in-law gets out of town because the daughter-in-law misbehaves. What a farce that would make. One would think the father-in-law was a party to this misconduct.

24   If he hadn't sunk such deep roots in New York, Wah Gay would find it easier to pull up his stakes and disappear. After more than forty years in the community, a sudden uprooting would be bound to have repercussions. If he were to go elsewhere, say Boston or Washington, D.C., he had many friends there too. How could he face them? Through his membership in the Ping On Tong, he had made many contacts with out-of-town delegates when they came to New York for their conventions. Frequently these friends had come in and played mah-jong at his club house. They had sipped coffee together. Now when he needed to get out of town, the choice of site for his exile became agonizingly difficult. What would he say to his friends if they should ask him: Why did you leave New York after so many years? His type of business demanded a large enough city to have a number of mah-jong players. True, he could always go back to the restaurant business, but he was not yet ready for such a drastic move. At his age he would consider that only as a last resort. The prospect of returning to manual labor made the old man shake his head, more in shame than in self-pity. He had worked hard and long to leave the drudgery of the restaurant business for the semi-retirement of the mah-jong game. Returning to it now would be humiliating.

25   To write to his wife, Lau Shee, informing her of what had happened to her daughter-in-law, would be an insurmountable task. What words could he compose that would not bring tears and heartache to the recipient? That his own son is the wearer of a *green hat*? The mere words *green hat* would strike terror and shame to anyone capable of human emotions. Like typhoid or polio.

26   His head spun with pains. Big pains. As big as a boulder. Now this boulder came tumbling out of the sky, like an exhausted satellite, and crash-landed on Wah Gay's head. The basement club house suddenly was dark and empty.

Discussion Questions

1. The word *shame* occurs several times in this excerpt. What does the fact that Wah Gay is feeling shame tell you about traditional Chinese families?
2. Who is Wah Gay most worried about? His son? his wife? his daughter-in-law? himself?
3. Wah Gay feels that his son is a "renegade," a "son who would disgrace his father." What has Ben Loy done?
4. This excerpt is told from two points of view. Whose point of view would you like to read next?

Writing Topics

1. In a brief essay, analyze the personalities of Wah Gay and Ben Loy as presented in this excerpt and explore how the author conveys those personalities.
2. Write the letter that Wah Gay will write to his wife after he has learned about Ben Loy's wife's rumored behavior.

ON DISCOVERY

Maxine Hong Kingston

Born in 1940 in Stockton, California, Maxine Hong Kingston spent much of her childhood working at her parents' laundry. While washing, drying, and pressing, Kingston and her five siblings would listen to their mother "talk story," an oral tradition that is a combination of legends, folklore, ghost stories, and anecdotes. Listening to "talk stories" and reading widely and voraciously helped Kingston to develop her own skills as a storyteller. She began attending the University of California, Berkeley, in 1958, where she began to pursue writing. She originally planned to study engineering because of her capacity for mathematics, but by her second year, she changed to a major more conducive to a writing career. After graduating in 1962, she married Earl Kingston and took a teaching job in Hayward, California. In 1967, the Kingstons moved to Hawaii, where Maxine worked as a teacher.

It was during her time in Hawaii that Kingston began writing *The Woman Warrior* and *China Men,* both of which borrow from the "talk story" tradition. In both books, a young Chinese American daughter narrates the stories of her family; however, there is a difference in narrative tone. In *China Men,* the daughter is "less involved with the characters and far less concerned with relating how she feels about them"[1] but in *The Woman Warrior,* the narrator's life is inextricably linked to all the lives—both past and present—around her. These two books, conceived as an intertwining story, are classified as nonfiction, but it is clear that they push the boundaries of literary categorization through Kingston's use of multiple genres—history, anecdote, legend, cautionary tale, biography, memoir.

Both books met with instant critical acclaim. In 1976 *The Woman Warrior* won the National Book Critics Circle Award for nonfiction, and in 1980 *China Men* won a National Book Award. Encouraged by her successes, Kingston embarked on a novel, *Tripmaster*

---

[1] Elaine Kim, *Asian-American Literature: An Introduction to the Writings and Their Social Context* (Philadelphia: Temple UP, 1984) 208.

Monkey, which she first published in 1987. The novel is the story of Wittman Ah Sing, a fifth-generation Chinese American man who, like Kingston herself, is a Berkeley graduate and a product of the 1960s. Kingston was working on a sequel to *Tripmaster Monkey,* but the manuscript was destroyed in a fire in 1992.

The following tale, from *China Men,* is a fantasy in which the tables are turned on a hapless male sojourner in the Land of Women. (J.I.)

1   Once upon a time, a man, named Tang Ao, looking for the Gold Mountain, crossed an ocean, and came upon the Land of Women. The women immediately captured him, not on guard against ladies. When they asked Tang Ao to come along, he followed; if he had had male companions, he would've winked over his shoulder.

2   "We have to prepare you to meet the queen," the women said. They locked him in a canopied apartment equipped with pots of makeup, mirrors, and a woman's clothes. "Let us help you off with your armor and boots," said the women. They slipped his coat off his shoulders, pulled it down his arms, and shackled his wrists behind him. The women who kneeled to take off his shoes chained his ankles together.

3   A door opened, and he expected to meet his match, but it was only two old women with sewing boxes in their hands. "The less you struggle, the less it'll hurt," one said, squinting a bright eye as she threaded her needle. Two captors sat on him while another held his head. He felt an old woman's dry fingers trace his ear; the long nail on her little finger scraped his neck. "What are you doing?" he asked. "Sewing your lips together," she joked, blackening needles in a candle flame. The ones who sat on him bounced with laughter. But the old women did not sew his lips together. They pulled his earlobes taut and jabbed a needle through each of them. They had to poke and probe before puncturing the layers of skin correctly, the hole in the front of the lobe in line with the one in back, the layers of skin sliding about so. They worked the needle through—a last jerk for the needle's wide eye ("needle's nose" in Chinese). They strung his raw flesh with silk threads; he could feel the fibers.

4   The women who sat on him turned to direct their attention to his feet. They bent his toes so far backward that his arched foot cracked. The old ladies squeezed each foot and broke many tiny bones along the sides. They gathered his toes, toes over and under one another like a knot of ginger root. Tang Ao wept with pain. As they wound the bandages tight and tighter around his feet, the women sang footbinding songs to distract him: "Use aloe for binding feet and not for scholars."

5   During the months of a season, they fed him on women's food: the tea was thick with white chrysanthemums and stirred the cool female winds

inside his body; chicken wings made his hair shine; vinegar soup improved his womb. They drew the loops of thread through the scabs that grew daily over the holes in his earlobes. One day they inserted gold hoops. Every night they unbound his feet, but his veins had shrunk, and the blood pumping through them hurt so much, he begged to have his feet re-wrapped tight. They forced him to wash his used bandages, which were embroidered with flowers and smelled of rot and cheese. He hung the bandages up to dry, streamers that drooped and draped wall to wall. He felt embarrassed; the wrappings were like underwear, and they were his.

6   One day his attendants changed his gold hoops to jade studs and strapped his feet into shoes that curved like bridges. They plucked out each hair on his face, powdered him white, painted his eyebrows like a moth's wings, painted his cheeks and lips red. He served a meal at the queen's court. His hips swayed and his shoulders swiveled because of his shaped feet. "She's pretty, don't you agree?" the diners said, smacking their lips at his dainty feet as he bent to put dishes before them.

7   In the Women's Land there are no taxes and no wars. Some scholars say that the country was discovered during the reign of Empress Wu (A.D. 694–705), and some say earlier than that, A.D. 441, and it was in North America.

DISCUSSION QUESTIONS

1. What do the first four words tell you about this selection?
2. Why did the women do what they did to Tang Ao?
3. A fable is a brief tale told to illustrate a moral, and this selection resembles a fable in many ways. In a small group, discuss a possible moral for "On Discovery."
4. Would you call this a feminist tale? Why or why not? First define what feminism means to you.

WRITING TOPICS

1. In a brief persuasive essay, discuss what you think Kingston's message is in this selection and whether she succeeds in conveying it forcefully.
2. Try your hand at writing a fable (like Kingston's) in which a common practice or situation is turned around.

HECTOR PUEBLO

Augustus Samuel Mein-Sun (Gus) Lee

Born in 1946, Augustus Samuel Mein-Sun (Gus) Lee attended West Point and the law school at the University of California, Davis. He has enjoyed a long and highly visible career in law, serving as an Army Command Judge Advocate; a Deputy District Attorney in Sacramento, California; and the Deputy Director of the California District Attorneys Association. He is presently the Senior Executive for Legal Education Competence for the California State Bar. In addition to his work in law, he has published three books: *China Boy* (1991), *Honor and Duty* (1994), and *Tiger's Tail* (1996).

China Boy, from which the following selection is taken, is semi-autobiographical in nature. The setting of the novel is San Francisco in the 1950s, a place significantly different from the Shanghai that the protagonist's family left for a life in the United States. Kai Ting, with a father struggling to support his family and with sisters attempting to adapt to American life, must try to make sense of life in an impoverished and ethnically diverse area in San Francisco.

1   Salvation arrived near the middle of my first term on the street. It happened during my worst beating.

2   Little Aaron Williams was five and twice my size. Blessed with a roundness of body and limb, a breadth of chest and shoulders, he presented like a thoroughbred fighter, but fought like a dray horse. He had been scuffed a couple times in his first fights and had cried too loudly. His stock on the street was down, and he was itching for an opportunity to redeem it. That was my job.

3   As he looked at me, Aaron must have thought: Here come Chicken Little!

4   I cannot remember what stimulated the event, but I was in the middle of a routine panicked run and somehow, as I faced the motor traffic on the bad corner of Fulton and Masonic, Toussaint's urgings broke through, and I got tired of flight.

5   I felt my buddy's handshake, and I stopped. I stuck a fist in Little Aaron's face. I think the surprise of it exceeded the hurt, but he cried like a stuck pig while I shook my wounded hand, marveling at the fact that I had somehow won. I had avoided a pounding. I should have said, Not so fast, hotdog . . .

6   Anita Mae Williams was a tall and swift-limbed ten-year-old. She was beautiful, with a smile that tugged at the hearts of boys and a careful, watchful grace amplified by an elegant swan's neck that suggested unattainable royalty and wonderful, confusing, mesmerizing girlhood. She also had a sincere right cross. She was responsible for raising her baby brother Aaron. There were a lot of kids with that responsibility on the block. Janie was one of them, and these young girls shared in common the fact they were serious about it.

7   When Anita Mae Williams found out that the China Boy had punched out her Little Aaron, she tracked me down. Later, when I discovered Western literature, I recognized in Inspector Javert the steadfast resolution of Anita Mae when she put me in her cross hairs.

8   I was on my return leg from Fremont, hustling down the clutter of McAllister, just past the drunks at the Double Olive Bar. I was stupidly smelling the fries at the door to the Eatery and wondering how angry Rupert the cook might be when she got me.

9   "Flies," I said, hesitantly. Fl-ries. Uh, fl—"

10   Anita knocked me down and wasted me from the Reliance Market, on Lyon, all the way to Cutty's Garage on Central. She was stripping the skin from her knuckles, but all she could see was her baby brother's cut lip. I tried not to cry and then she hit me square in the nose. I hurt enough to scream, startling the winos and causing one of them to drop his paper-sacked Tokay on the street with a wet explosion of cheap glass and bad grapes. "Aww, shoot!" he complained.

11   This was a serious licking and it worsened when she tired of chasing me and picked me up, stuffing me into a square metal garbage can, the likes of which once adorned the streets of San Francisco. She began punching me methodically in the face, her grunts of effort so ugly, so unlike her delicate, angelic face.

12   I was hurt past crying, and I could sense in Anita's blows the momentary hesitation that all people feel when they are about to kill someone. She kept hitting my forehead, and penumbra replaced myopia, and my arms fell away, no longer offering interference.

13   A Mexican mechanic named Hector stopped it.

14   "Hey, girl," he said. "Park yo' fists! Boy don have no *sangre,* no blood

lef fo' you. You made yo' point. You keep swingin, he gonna fo'get why you hate him. You bein a *pendeja*,[1] chica."

15   Anita nodded, not knowing the foreign word but recognizing the truth. I knew it had stopped but the pain seemed to worsen. I tried to thank him but my lip was split, and a dislodged late baby tooth impeded articulate expression. I couldn't crawl out of the can. His rescue allowed me to sob and cry weakly, all I had left.

16   Hector extracted me from the steel box, which was like pulling a barbed fishhook, and took me into Cutty's rest room and cleaned me up, using fresh oil rags. The rags turned heavy with blood. My cheek was swollen like I had misplaced a tennis ball. My ears rang off and on like a broken telephone deep in my cranium and my lips began to swell toward Sutro Heights. Every now and again I sat down involuntarily. In the middle of all this I got the hiccups, and as he gave me a glass of water I tried to look for waves inside it, half cross-eyed. I began to laugh hysterically.

17   "Sorry I cly," I said to the world.

18   I felt safe in the garage. It smelled of dead grease. My blood was on his hands, on his T-shirt, and on his floor. He was not angry. Nor was Joe Cutty when he pulled out the engine from an old truck and walked over to inspect my body damage. I kept trying to wipe up the drops of blood on his concrete floor.

19   "Man, oh man," he said. "Don't sweat that. This here's a garage, not an officers' club. That cheek could use a stitch. You gonna live, son?"

20   "Ah could sew that rip up," said a third man. It was Tom Molineaux, a small, wiry, jumpy sort of person who had just graduated from Polytechnic High. He called wrenches "spanners" and liked to spin them like batons. He was always eager to do what Joe called the "garbage details." He always was in a rush, working fast. He had received his draft notice for Korea.

21   "No, no," said Joe Cutty. "That'd hurt more'n the tear."

22   I was ready to move in.

23   "Hector. Who pounded this boy?" asked Cutty.

24   "Anita Mae," he said. "*Hombre*,[2] she was plenty P-O'd!" There was a silence. A girl had just trashed a boy on McAllister. Wonders would never cease.

25   "Why she screw wif you so bad, chico?" asked Hector.

26   "Hit bruddah," I squeaked.

27   "She hit her brother?" asked Tom Molineaux.

28   I shook my head, and it hurt. I pointed at me. The men nodded. They knew that Anita Mae really watched out for Aaron.

---

[1] *pendeja:* fool.
[2] *Hombre:* man.

29 "When yo' daddy come home, *niño?*"[3] asked Hector.

30 "Six," I said.

31 "Yo momma expec' you home now?"

32 I shrugged my shoulders and he nodded. Hector went into the office and came out with a stack of *Argosy* magazines and some Donald Duck comics. I smiled and he smiled.

33 I was reading about Huey, Louie, and Dewey's Woodchuck Guide and the Magic Flying Radish while Hector pulled chains, banged tools, hummed Navy tunes; Joe cranked ratchets; and Tom moved around the garage like a zephyr.

34 Then Anita Mae said, "Hey. I'm sorry, China Boy. Doncha be hittin my Little Aaron no mo'."

35 I nearly jumped out of my socks. I was afraid of talking to her. I nodded, my throat jammed, all the hurts in my head, mouth, and stomach coming back, with the hiccups. Her knuckles were skinned from tagging my face. I started to cry and she shook her head, her drop earrings bobbing, catching the fading light from the open garage doors. She walked off on her long legs.

36 Later, when I was twelve, and driven by blind ambition, and she was fifteen, and knew better, I asked her to marry me. She laughed in a deep rich woman's tone that made rejection both interesting and bearable.

37 Hector Pueblo was from Guadalajara, making him an outsider as well to the main culture of the Handle. He spoke blackgang Navy and black street with a Hispanic panache. He had been an unemployed carpenter until Joe Cutty hired him.

38 Cutty was huge, formed from a template that would have served two normal adults. He had a round face made jovial by bright, almost boyish eyes and eyebrows ridiculously small for a man his size. His biceps were as big as his head.

39 Joe Henry Cutty was like most of the men in the Panhandle. He had returned from the war, relieved to be alive and unsure about the future. With his savings, bolstered by intelligent poker play across the breadth of the Pacific, he managed to buy the garage from a redneck who viewed the black migration into California as the end of the free world. The seller had said to him. "Glad you're not like them other ones. I can trust *you.*"

40 Cutty smiled his slow smile that expressed no joy. He then lowered his offer to the owner by half, and the man took it, cursing himself and the black nation.

41 "Bastards trying ta get a good deal. Can you believe that?" the seller muttered to his god.

---

[3] *niño:* child, young one.

42   Cutty hired Hector after seeing his tattoos. Both of them had been Navy machinists. In Lingayen Gulf in 1944, their carrier groups had fought next to each other, and that had cemented it. Hector was heavily muscled with long arms and big, high-knuckled hands that caught sharp and hot metal surfaces and absorbed grease. He and Joe Cutty were top mechanics, artisans with wrenches, and they smelled like engines on a hot summer day.

43   "*Joven*,"[4] said Hector. "C'mon. We gonna hump dis hill, go to your home." He pulled me out of the deep couch, and kept his hand on my back as we trudged up Central to my house.

44   "Lissen. Say *tío*. It mean 'uncle.' You unnerstan'?"

45   "*Tío*," I said.

46   "*Joven*. You call me Tió Hector, hokay?"

47   I nodded. "Uncle" was *dababa*. Now I had two uncles. He and Uncle Shim did not resemble each other very much, and looking carefully at Hector while we climbed the hill did not change the perception.

48   Edna did not want to let Hector or me in the house. My father opened the door. He knew Hector and invited him in. Father and Edna looked at my face and my clothing. Hector, wearing a nice Navy khaki shirt, jumped right in.

49   "Missa Ting. Yo' boy, he need lesson in *boxeo*, in *pugilato*, fists. I see him tussle, and ees *ugly*." Hector glanced at Edna, licking his lip nervously.

50   "He's *muy rápido*, you know, bery quick. Black boy get in his face and firs' t'ree punches, firs' kick, yo' boy go lik' dis an lik' dat, no touch." Hector twisted his upper body, his arms up.

51   "But his eyes, dey get *muy grande* and he take to feet an try to run home. Den dey take him down and dey beat him."

52   He looked down at me and rubbed my hair with his hand. He looked at me. I smiled, but only halfway; Edna did not like Hector, his shirt, his speech, or the hair-rubbing. Beatings were okay in our family, but touching was taboo.

53   "Now wors ting, dis boy tink," pointing at me, "ees cryin. Ain't bad, cryin." Hector could see that Stepmother Edna was not buying it.

54   "*Los jóvenes*, de children, dey cry. Ees natural. You know, dey say, 'Cry Lika Baby'?" Hector smiled engagingly at Edna, a great, shining, teeth-gleaming, Cesar Romero, Gilbert Roland heart-warmer.

55   My father grinned. I smiled.

56   Edna's face said: No sale, you common laborer.

57   "Hokay. Not fightin, dot's bad news," Hector said forcefully and directly to my father, making my guts jump. I had a feeling our house confused him. He was not alone.

58   "Chinee boy gotta fisticuff, maybe mo' dan odder kids. He stand out,

---

4 *Joven:* youth.

bery big-time. Yo'll better tell him dot, cuz cryin ain't de problem. *Boxeo, dot* de problem."

59   My father's face was impassive, but I felt grand relief. The reality of my life had come before him.

60   "Thank you," my father said, and I tried to keep my face passive, too.

61   Hector was trying to figure out Edna, whose stern disapproval was patent in the hallway. Hector's advice regarding the saving of my life did not belong in this house, either. His tattoos and muscled arms also felt out of place, and he put them behind him. I think he liked my father, because he said, "Missa Ting. I teach yo' boy *un poco.*[5] But firs', you sen him to de Y.M.C.A. Dey teach him de basics, *las reglas.*[6] De boy, he can come to Cutty's to learn. But, no way he come to hide." His arms were out, and I watched them, fascinated. He made a fist and cocked his right arm up, a gesture of strength and defiance.

62   "Den, I teach him *street*," and he pumped it. His biceps bulged; the long muscles in his forearm popping. Edna glided out of the entryway and Hector ignored her. I breathed again.

63   The Y.M.C.A. cost twelve dollars every two months. At first, Stepmother Edna balked. But she realized that further beatings could result in medical bills. She had just discovered that we were not only poor, but very poor. She had restated her position that she did not want me in the house between school and dinner, or during sunlight on weekends. Six dollars a month. An investment in childcare.

64   Hector said good-bye. My father pointed to the old round leather hassock. I sat down and he turned on a table lamp. The hassock had once been green and red and was now a uniform brown. He cleared his throat. We had the best talk of my life to date.

65   "I was in Chinese Army," he said in a gruff voice, looking out the window, toward China, his posture militarily erect, shoulders square.

66   "We lost to *Gungtsetang*, the communists. To the Red political chief, Mao Tse-tung. Very smart man. He reached the peasants, and they went to him, like fish to sea. We lost to the Red generals, Chu Teh and Lin Piao, who fought like Sun-tzu, master of war.

67   "That's why we're here. We did not fight so well." The pain on my father's face was profound. His features did not move, but his eyes looked so vacantly sad, so ineffably alone. It was a war he needed to win and could not afford to lose.

68   "Your mother missed home." He coughed a little, squaring his shoulders to the window, filling his small, dark pipe with Edgeworth, a prize in wartime China. Sometimes I thought that the Nationalist Army had fought

---

[5] *un poco:* a little.
[6] *las reglas:* the rules.

the war for Virginia tobacco. He lit the pipe, his own shadow playing on the walls, and he slipped into Songhai.

69   "In a way, the war goes on. The Reds might still be kicked out, and we could return to Kiangsu, where everyone but you was born. The Nationalists, my old army, are not a lot better than the Reds, but they won't kill *us*. I don't want to go back. I am American. But it might be better for you."

70   Better for me. Father, talking to me in our true tongue, talking about Mother. Oh, Mah-mee. I wanted him to keep talking, to never stop. Drunk on his words, intoxicated with the communication. He was talking about somehow returning to China. But I was having a hard time figuring out how to be black, how to be American. Now I had to learn to be Chinese? To go to China now, with our mother dead.

71   Here I had Toussaint, and Titus McGovern and Alvin Sharpes. I had Toussaint's momma, who hugged me, spoke to me with laughter in her voice, and had sung to me. A number of other women on the block were likewise kind, wiping my blood with white hankies. Hector had just saved my life, and he and Joe Cutty had great coin on the street. Reverend Jones always smiled at me, welcoming me to his church. I was not sure that I would be so lucky on the streets of Shanghai, trying to get by as a cultural Chinese. I could hardly speak Songhai anymore. The idea of backtracking on the Chinese tongues made me ill.

72   I, of course, in my eclectic upbringing, would have an opportunity to try that, as well.

73   "When you are older," he said, "I can teach you to use a gun and to knife-fight. To patrol and ambush, call in artillery fire. Military combat." He chuckled, an unusual sound. "But these are things the Army will teach you."

74   He shook his head. "But I am not expert at fighting with my fists." He unlocked a drawer in his desk. He pulled out a huge gun, snugged inside a light tan shoulder holster. He untied the restraining straps, the dust rising softly in the lamplight.

75   He looked so strong, so handsome, his jaw square, shoulders broad, the scar on his temple pronounced, his eyes far away, thinking, seeing memories, touching China and his former world.

76   The gun came out of the holster, complaining against the leather. It was a Government Colt Super .38 on a .45 frame. It looked heavily used, with the dark bluing worn away down to cold steel around the trigger housing and the hammer. It fit in his muscular hand like a big Thorson wrench in Hector's grip. I smelled the light oil on it. Given to him by Na-men Schwartzhedd after the Japanese invasion, it had become a talisman, an invitation to fight the enemy and survive, to find new life in the New World, to become one with the gun and with the country that had forged it from the hardest elements in the earth.

77   Jennifer Sung-ah had told me stories about Father during the Run. So I

knew this gun had been inside his peasant jacket on the Yangtze River road, when he had found Mother and my sisters at the edge of Free China, when he had lowered his recently injured forehead to rest it against my mother's face, nine years ago.

78   "I know you," he had said to Mother that day in 1944. "You don't give up. You would never give up."

79   He snapped the action, locking it open and removing the well-worn magazine, verifying that it was empty by inserting his little finger into the breech. I was nervous, looking at it. This gun had killed people.

80   "When you go in the Army, this will be yours. This is not to be touched until then. I am showing this to you, because weapons are for war, for death. Never confuse this with *wu-shu*."

81   I didn't know that I was going in the Army. I thought they gave you a gun, which was the only reason I could think of for joining.

82   He frowned at me, releasing the lock, which made the slide snap shut with a startling metallic punch. He locked the magazine into the butt of the handle, slid the weapon into the holster, and put it away.

83   "You have been beaten badly. Children expect parents to fix things. But you need boxing, to stand on your own.

84   "My older brother Han was a good boxer. The Chinese invented boxing, *wu-shu,* and are the best at it, a secret foreigners do not know. Chinese boxers are almost like magic, they are so good.

85   "Uncle Han's nose was broken and our mother stopped his lessons, and mine before they began. Han is a very handsome man, like a movie actor, and Mother feared for his looks. I am sorry you have never met my brother. Uncle Han and I. We, we were not friends. But I am his Younger Brother, and always will be, regardless of what I do. You have not met your grandfather, grandmother. Your aunts. The tutors. The cooks, servants."

86   "Where Han Dababa now?" I asked.

87   "Aahh," he sighed quietly, like dying seltzer bubbles. There had been no word about Uncle Han at all. He, and Da-ma, my aunt, and Round Pearl, Mother's servant, Wang the fish cook, Chief Tutor Luke, the Hanlin master, Tutor Tang, and the horsemaster Yip, and Jamie's wetnurse, Sweet Plum, all were lost in the distant haze of invasion and the Chinese revolution. Gung-Gung, of course, had been terminally reeducated. But Father missed the staff of his family more than the management. His father had treated him like yesterday's newspaper.

88   He went to the kitchen, where he blindly rattled in the cupboards. The kitchen smelled of sauerkraut and scrapple, a flat, cerealed, pork Pennsylvania Dutch sausage that Edna was trying to sell to our palates.

89   I was intoxicated with the information he had provided me, and my bruises were forgotten. I felt shaky, shuddering in emotion, electrified by his communication.

90   My father, his other life, a big gun in our house, a boxing uncle named Han, a nation of fighting Chinese, the Army. Was I to join his Kuomintang Army, or the U.S. Army, which was taking so many men from the neighborhood for Korea?

91   *Wu-shu.* Fighting talent, or fight arts, something like that. Something deep in my shallow years, so mysterious in my utter simplicity, so ancient in my youth, connected to a distant land and long-dead ancestors. Deep racial memory. *Wu-shu* was magical fighting. Combat by ghost warriors, faster than dreams, stronger than concrete, war using wind, iron, and fire.

92   From the kitchen, where the intense bare bulb cast light that was both too bright and insufficient, he said, "I am going to send you to the Y, the Young Men's Christian Association. I think my wife will agree."

93   I coughed, and said, softly, "Ba-Ba. Stepma Edna is my ma-ma? And Janie's ma-ma? *Real* ma-ma?"

94   Silence came from the kitchen. He approached me, looking down. I looked up. "She thinks of you as stepchildren," he said. "But you must give her the respect that you would give your mother."

95   "Stepma Edna want me go Y.M.C.A.?" I asked.

96   "I think so," he said. "The Y will teach you to fight, how to protect yourself. I want you to try very hard and learn. It will probably hurt.

97   "It was the same for me. At St. John's College, and Taoping Academy, I was eighteen when I started learning about the ways of the West." He switched to English, clearing his throat.

98   "See here. America. It has the answers." His shoulders hunched and he made a huge fist, banging into the open palm of the other hand. "It has *the answers!*" His voice rang passionately through the apartment, and I knew that Edna and Janie were listening, from different levels in the house.

99   He looked up at me. More quietly, he said. "If you are very good—terrific, terrific, good—you can make application to West Point, someday, to make us proud. I will find Major Na-men, and ask his advice. He is West Pointer. Maybe he help get you in. It is something, the only thing, I pray for."

100   Father *praying?* Praying for me to be an American *ping*—a soldier. A small, white ivory figure on a dark teak Chinese chessboard. My heart pounded.

101   "Where Major Na-men, Father?" I asked.

102   "He is in Korea. Ahh. How I worry about him." Father's face said everything, with all the articulation Mother had used. And I knew, with sweeping, insightful clarity, that Father would have been long in Korea, with his true comrade, fighting the Reds, laughing at death, if he had not had children. Or a dying wife. Or a new one. That his family was a barrier to a greater destiny. He was passing time with us, while greater events marched past his window.

103   More solemn shadows flared as he lit his pipe, the sound of the drawing air strained and high.

104   Our magical talk was over. I found myself crying helplessly. This was so hard, crying in front of him, but his words, his sharing, his interest, the weight of his own loss caused by me, were more than I could bear. My shoulders shaking, my arms trembling uselessly by my side, I snorted and snuffled as I tried to stop myself.

105   My crying discomforted him. I sensed that he wanted me to shake his hand and say thank you in a manful way, and not turn into a quivering, protoplasmic blubber of tears.

106   I thought of my mother. He had said "us." I stood and left the room, going to the place in the hallway where her portrait had hung until Edna had removed it. I closed my wet eyes and mentally drew in every detail of her face and smiled when I reached her mouth.

DISCUSSION QUESTIONS

1. What kind of neighborhood does the narrator live in?
2. In Cutty's garage, the narrator says that he was ready to move in. What makes him feel this way?
3. The narrator and protagonist have several antagonists in this chapter. Who or what are they?
4. Where does this excerpt show the conflict between the narrator and his stepmother?
5. Why does his father's talk about his life in the Chinese Army and other things both relieve and astonish the narrator, and what is his final reaction?

WRITING TOPICS

1. Gus Lee describes Cutty's garage, the men who work there, and the smells and sights, and actions in great detail. Reread these descriptions and then describe a place you know well in similar detail. You might describe a kitchen, a restaurant, a small shop or store, a gym, or your own favorite place to be. Try to use some vivid similes and metaphors.
2. In an essay, analyze the methods the author uses to characterize Hector Pueblo, and tell what makes him a likable character.

FROM *HOMEBASE*

Shawn Wong

Shawn Wong, born in Oakland, California, in 1949 and raised in nearby Berkeley, has been a highly visible and outspoken member of the Asian-American literary community for several decades. A second-generation Chinese-American whose father was fond of literature, Wong was educated in the San Francisco Bay area, where he earned a bachelor's degree in English literature from the University of California, Berkeley, and a master's degree from San Francisco State University. He has had teaching appointments at several institutions in northern California, including Mills College and the University of California, Santa Cruz, and is presently the chair of the English Department at the University of Washington.

Wong was an active voice in civil rights campus politics and the Asian American movement of the late 1960s and early 1970s, and in collaboration with Frank Chin, Lawson Fusao Inada, and Jeffrey Paul Chan, he edited *Aiiieeeee!* (1974) and *The Big Aiiieeeee!* (1991), both of which remain extremely influential and controversial anthologies of Asian-American literature (the two volumes emphasize Chinese-American and Japanese-American works). He and his co-editors are often called "the four horsemen of Asian American literature" by admirers and detractors alike.

Wong also co-edited the *Before Columbus Foundation Fiction/Poetry Anthology: Selections from the American Book Awards, 1980–1990* and has received numerous awards, including a National Endowment for the Arts creative writing fellowship. Although he also writes poetry, Wong is best known for his two novels: *Homebase* (1979) and *American Knees* (1995).

In the following excerpt from *Homebase*, a young Chinese American participating in the Native American protest at Alcatraz Island in San Francisco Bay engages in a dialogue that raises questions of racial identity, home, and belonging. (J.I.)

1   My grandfather's island is Angel Island. It was there that he almost died and that makes it his island.

2   There are two islands in San Francisco Bay which contain ruined buildings with doors four inches thick. The islands are Alcatraz[1] and Angel Island. Alcatraz is a National Park and Angel Island is a California State Park. Both were places of great sadness and great pain.

3   During Christmas 1969, an Indian man in whom I saw my grandfather showed me my grandfather's face.

4   I am inclined to believe in ghosts because islands in California are places of waiting and the waiting is what destroys people.

5   I saw the man that Christmas while I was leaning on a four-inch-thick door that led to an isolation cell. I was facing out into the main corridor of the cell block on Alcatraz. Behind me, inside the isolation cell, were two women sleeping in sleeping bags laid on top of newspapers on the concrete floor. I was shivering and felt cold and damp all over. The cold moved in on me through the concrete and the salt air etched its way through my skin, attacking my bones until they ached. Each night for the last three nights I woke up and wandered into the corridor to sit near a kerosene lantern with a few others believing light had something to do with warmth. And each night I noticed the old man sitting against a wall between cell doors. He was smoking as usual. We never spoke. As I seated myself on a piece of newspaper, he stood up and walked over to me and stood over me holding his enormous wool jacket in his hand.

6   "You know, people say I look Chinese," he said.

7   I nodded a little trying to shake off the shivers. He held out his jacket.

8   "Oh, ah, no. I've got a jacket on. You probably need it."

9   "Take it off and sit on it and put this one on."

10   I did what he said and he sat down next to me. I moved over to make room on the newspaper. Both of us leaned against the wall and faced out into the corridor as we spoke. The jacket was about ten sizes too big and smelled of cigarettes.

11   "People say I look Chinese," he repeated.

12   I looked at him in the dim light. He did look Chinese. "Where are you from?" I asked.

13   "Acoma."

14   "Lots of Chinese in New Mexico?"

15   He started laughing and lit up another cigarette. "Where are you from?"

16   "Berkeley."

17   "Where are you from originally?"

18   "Berkeley."

19   "How long you been here?"

---

[1] *Alcatraz:* a former federal penitentiary.

20   "Three days."

21   "No. How long you been in the United States?"

22   "All my life."

23   "You mean you ain't born in China?"

24   "What do you mean? Don't I look like I come from Gallup?"

25   "You ain't Navajo. You Chinese. You like me."

26   "You ain't Chinese, though."

27   "My ancestors came from China thirty thousand years ago and settled in Acoma Pueblo."

28   "Is that why you look Chinese?"

29   "Naw, my grandfather was Chinese."

30   "Your grandfather was Chinese?" I turned to look at the old man and tore our newspaper.

31   "He wandered into New Mexico and married a widow before anyone knew he was Chinese." He crushed his cigarette into the floor and smiled to himself. I was looking at his face more closely. He started chuckling then turned to me. "You pretty lucky"—he pointed into the room I was sleeping in —"to sleep in isolation with two women."

32   "Oh, they're just friends from school."

33   "That one, Sandy, the Nez Percé, looks Japanese."

34   "Yeah, me and your grandfather . . ."

35   "What does she call you?"

36   "What do you mean?"

37   "What's your name?"

38   "Rainsford."

39   "Rainsford?"

40   "That's my name. Rainsford."

41   "Sounds like the name of a town."

42   "It was. My great-grandfather lived there."

43   "It was in California?"

44   "Did you ever hear of it?"

45   He appeared to think carefully for a while. Then he said, "We used to call it Ah-Caht-Cho."

46   "Ah-Caht-Cho? What does that mean?"

47   "What are you doing here?" he said.

48   "Huh?"

49   "What are you doing here? This isn't your battle or your land."

50   "I'm part of this land too."

51   "You should be out looking for your place, your home. This is a part of mine." He paused for a moment to take another cigarette out. He couldn't find a match and put the cigarette back into the pack. "If you came here because of the two women, then you're as smart as my grandfather. But you got your own land to find."

52   "But I live here."

53   "That's what I mean. This is your country. Go out and make yourself at home." The man chuckled to himself. Then took a breath like he was going to let me in on the joke, but he only chuckled again. "You know what my grandfather did for a living?"

54   "The Chinese one?"

55   "Yes."

56   "Railroad worker? Miner?"

57   "No. He was a bone collector."

58   "A what?"

59   "A bone collector."

60   "He collected bones?"

61   As the old man nodded he looked in the direction of a young man carrying a rifle and walking toward us. As he came nearer the old man asked him for a light. He stopped and drew out a small box of matches and tossed them to the old man saying, "Here's a whole box. Keep warm. Merry Christmas."

62   "You said your Chinese grandfather collected bones. What kind of bones?"

63   "Chinese bones, of course."

64   " . . . of Chinese?"

65   "Yes."

66   "Yes?"

67   The old man nodded his head again. Then he said, "Haven't you ever heard of the bone collectors?"

68   I shook my head.

69   "You know what a tong is?"

70   "Yeah."

71   "You sure you're Chinese?"

72   "I'm as Chinese as your grandfather."

73   Well, in my grandfather's days the tongs hired men like him to travel around looking for the bones of dead Chinamen so that the tong could send them back to China."

74   "What was your grandfather doing in New Mexico?"

75   "There was some Chinamen there . . . a graveyard somewhere and my grandfather went around asking people who might have known them, you know, known their names. Probably some Indian bones got sent back to China by mistake." He laughed and brought a hand down on my shoulder.

76   "Well, you Indians came from China thirty thousand years ago."

77   "Yes, you might be right." He took a drag off his cigarette and then crushed it out on the floor in front of us. He looked up and pointed at the walls, "Look at this. These things we've painted on the walls, claiming this piece of land." He paused for a moment. I was feeling warm now, even tired

and drowsy. "It's funny how people write on walls. Most times it's a desperate and lonely job. Look inside some of these cells."

78　　I was letting him talk, his deep voice almost making the air warm and dry.

79　　"There's an island," he said, "next to this one, you know, where they used to keep prisoners of war and Chinese. Some of the buildings are still standing. I wonder what's written on those walls."

80　　"Chinese were kept on Angel Island?"

81　　"You didn't know that? I'm more Chinese than you are. I said before you got to find your own land, you know, where your people have been. Like Angel Island, like Rainsford, California."

82　　"Where is Rainsford, California? Do you know where in the Sierra?"

83　　"You better get some sleep now. We'll talk tomorrow."

84　　I went to bed and forgot to take off his jacket. When I went back to the door, he was gone. I laid it out like a blanket over me. I slept soundly. I dreamed my father and I were walking through a forest of redwood trees. I talked like my father, I laughed like him, I smelled like him. And I knew then that I was only my father's son, that he was Grandfather's son and Grandfather was Great-Grandfather's son and that night we were all the same man.

85　　I dreamed all this underneath the wool jacket, not knowing the old man had made up the name "Ah-Caht-Cho" after someone's nighttime sneeze that echoed in the cell block while we were talking.

86　　It was barely light out when he came to get his jacket. He woke me with a gentle nudge. "Rainsford," he said, while lifting the weight of his jacket off me. When I opened my eyes, be bent over to look me in the face. "Rainsford, an island is the saddest kind of land there is."

DISCUSSION QUESTIONS

1. How are the narrator and the Indian man similar in their viewpoints about islands and in their appearance?
2. The Indian tells the narrator, "You should be out looking for your place, your home." He also says, "This is your country. Go out and make yourself at home." Then he chuckles. Why do you think he chuckles?
3. How does the narrator come to feel kinship with his father and grandfather?
4. Why does Angel Island become important to the narrator?

WRITING TOPICS

1. Place figures prominently in several selections in this anthology—notably in "The Lives of Great Men" and the excerpt from *Dogeaters* in Chapter Two, in "The Management of Grief" in Chapter Four, and in this selection. In an informal essay, tell about a place that has importance for a previous generation in your family, whether you have been there or not. If you have been there, you might describe it and its importance. If you have not, you might tell what you know about it from family stories and how you imagine it to be.

2. Most of the story in this selection is told through dialogue. In an analytical essay, explore Wong's use of dialogue and what effect it has on your reading of this material.

FORGIVENESS FROM HEAVEN

Jade Snow Wong

Born in 1919 and raised in a poverty-stricken section of San Francisco's Chinatown, Jade Snow Wong was determined, despite her parents' wishes, to pursue a university education after graduating from high school as class valedictorian. She earned enough money as a cook and housekeeper to attend San Francisco Junior College, from which she graduated with highest honors, and she won a scholarship that enabled her to attend Mills College, from which she graduated once again with highest distinction. During World War II she worked for the War Production Board and wrote an essay on absenteeism, which won a National Congressional Award.

Her first book, the best-selling and critically acclaimed *Fifth Chinese Daughter,* was published in 1950 and has been translated into several languages, including Chinese, Japanese, German, Urdu, and Burmese. This autobiographical work details, among other things, Wong's perceptions of the tensions between Chinese and American cultures; the difficulties of yielding to paternal and Chinese cultural authority; and the racial myths that allow Chinese Americans to be stereotyped. Her second book, *No Chinese Stranger,* was published in 1975 and is an account of her life after the publication of *Fifth Chinese Daughter.* In addition to these longer works, Wong also contributed pieces to such publications as *Holiday, Horn Book Magazine,* and the *San Francisco Examiner.* In acknowledgment of her years of literary achievement, Mills College granted Wong an honorary doctorate of humane letters in 1976. Her creativity does not end at the literary, however, for Wong is also recognized as a potter and sculptor whose pieces can be found in collections at both the Museum of Modern Art and the Metropolitan Museum of Art in New York City.

In the following excerpt from *Fifth Chinese Daughter,* young Jade Snow comes to a sobering realization after a joyous celebration of the birth of her baby brother. (J.I.)

1   For the first time in Jade Snow's memory Mama was confined to bed. Jade Snow thought she must be very ill indeed, for all her food had to be brought to her, while Grandmother took over the household duties and meal preparations. Female relatives, including aunts, cousins, and older sisters, came to visit Mama in her close and dimly lit bedroom. But no one seemed particularly worried over her condition; for some reason, her illness appeared quite acceptable.

2   During the hours when Jade Snow was not at school, she had to remain with Mama, and whenever Mama wanted anything, she went to tell Daddy or Grandmother. But she did not seem to want much; even her meals were quite simple, since she desired only rice and a special steamed dried vegetable from China, which was chopped fine and mixed with peanut oil. Staying quietly with Mama became so tedious that company was very welcome, for Jade Snow would then seize upon the temporary distraction to edge slowly out through the door.

3   This enforced vigil continued for days, until one night Jade Snow and Jade Precious Stone were awakened from sleep by a great deal of confused noise, a mixture of clattering pans and excited chatter. This unusual activity came from Mama's bedroom, which was separated from the girls' by a folding partition. Through the cracks in the partition, Jade Snow could see a bright light sifting into their bedroom.

4   The two sisters consulted with each other in whispers—somehow the situation called for whispers. Jade Precious Stone asked from the depths of her bed: "Shall we get up and see what is going on?"

5   Jade Snow listened a moment longer—it really was strange—some woman was talking to Daddy, and it was not Mama! She seemed to speak with authority; moreover, she was decisively giving orders!

6   Jade Snow cautioned her younger sister: "You had better stay in bed because you catch cold easily, and I'll find out what is happening. Perhaps Mama is getting worse."

7   Jade Snow was not able to see anything through the cracks, but she called to Daddy for reassurance.

8   Daddy answered, "We do not need you; go back to sleep."

9   Jade Precious Stone called out, "I heard him too, come back to bed."

10 For a little while the two sisters continued to whisper their perplexity, but soon fell asleep despite their troubled wondering.

11 The next morning, Jade Snow went in to see Mama to ask what she would like for breakfast. First she started to ask, "What was all the noise last night . . . ," but she was arrested in her questioning by astonishment, for Mama had in bed with her a very small baby. It did not look like any other baby that Jade Snow remembered, for this one had a red, red face, no hair, tightly shut eyes, and tightly clenched fists.

12 "Mama! Who left this? While you are sick, must you care for a baby too?"

13   But she saw that Mama did not look so sick as yesterday, at least not sick the same way. She was very tired-looking, it was true. At the same time, though, the tenseness of the last few days was now gone. It was replaced by an expression of serene happiness.

14   Mama explained, "The lady doctor whom you may have heard last night brought this baby. I feel much better now and I can take care of him. He is your brother and his name will be 'Forgiveness from Heaven.' "

15   "But where did the lady doctor get 'Forgiveness from Heaven'?"

16   "I guess I have not yet told you where babies come from. They are roasted at the hospital ovens. There are three kinds of babies. When they are nearly done, they are white foreign babies. When they bake a little longer, they become golden Chinese babies. Sometimes they are left in too long, and they become black babies!"

17   Jade Snow turned over this information in her mind, and concluded that it was quite reasonable. Then she looked at her little brother critically. He appeared more red than golden, but seemed basically Chinese. "Good thing he was done just right," she thought.

18   On her way to school that morning, she met one of Daddy's seamstresses coming to work. She stopped Jade Snow with "Did the baby come last night and is it a girl or a boy?"

19   Imagine that! How did she know? She could not have heard the noise last night; she had not seen the baby in Mama's room this morning. It was very odd that she should ask such a question.

20   "Yes, we have a baby done just right, and his name is Forgiveness from Heaven. He is my baby brother, so he must be a boy."

21   After school Jade Snow returned home to find all the women of their family gathered. Everybody was talking at once, sitting around in the dining room, and of course the talk was centered around Forgiveness from Heaven. For once, Daddy was sitting idle during working hours, but he never looked happier.

22   Oldest Sister Jade Swallow said, "Baby has the largest ears in the family, and they are close to his head too."

23   Then, catching Jade Snow's puzzled expression, she explained, "You know, the larger the ears, the longer one will live; and the closer to one's head, the more they indicate success in life. A person whose ears stick out has genuine cause for worry; he has 'wind-catchers'! A person whose ears are undersized is not supposed to live long. If you don't believe me, look at the ears of old people, and study the lives of those with 'wind-catcher' ears."

24   They continued to discuss the baby.

25   "He has Grandmother's beautiful mouth."

26   "He has a well-rounded nose, which means material prosperity."

27   "His face finishes nicely at the chin; that means he will have good fortune in later life."

28   "A nice high brow means great intelligence."

29   Daddy added his opinion, "At last we have the happiness of another son to carry on the Wong name. We must have a fine celebration when his age reaches a full month. In the meantime, to announce the good news we shall send out red eggs to our friends and invite them to come here to taste pickled pigs' feet."

30   For days afterward, there was great bustle in the household to prepare the announcements. With Grandmother and older sisters, Jade Snow helped to dye eggs red. They took case after case of clean white hens' eggs, and boiled them in giant kettles. Into the boiling water they dropped red printed rice paper imported from China. The dissolving red dye turned the eggs pale pink, then a deeper pink, and at last they were ready to be lifted out and drained.

31   Big baskets of fresh-killed chickens were delivered to the house, and these were gently simmered in water until they were just done. Then hot boiled peanut oil was brushed on their plump bodies as they hung to cool. This was the favorite Chinese way of cooking chicken.

32   Paper bags were filled with the delicious announcements, to be distributed to relatives and friends. Each bag contained some red eggs, a section of chicken, and some slices of pickled white ginger root.

33   Cooking in the kitchen at the same time were big kettles containing at least fifty pounds of pigs' feet, simmering until tender in black Chinese vinegar and ginger root. Every visitor who arrived to call on Mama tasted some of this "Pigs'-Feet Vinegar." Even the lady doctor liked it. She said that the calcium dissolved in the vinegar was very nutritious. Afterward, whenever Jade Snow smelled this particular brew in Chinatown, she knew that someone was celebrating the coming of a new baby.

34   In a week Mama was up and about again. A new baby meant much work. There were many diapers to wash. Mama took care of these in big buckets in the bathtub. She said they were fortunate in having an automatic hot-water heater, since most other families in Chinatown had to boil their water. Baby brother cried to be fed all the time, it seemed to Jade Snow, even in the middle of the night.

35   As the end of a full month approached, Forgiveness from Heaven lost his redness, and became more interesting. Great preparations were now begun for the important celebration. A baby was not supposed to be taken out before this month had passed.

36   Daddy wanted the feast held at his factory and home, on the second floor. The older sisters bought many bundles of crepe paper in red, white, and blue, and cut it into two-inch widths, unraveling long streamers which were fastened along the ceiling from one end of the store to the other. Long tables were constructed by placing planks over sawhorses. Extra dozens of bowls, chopsticks, and glasses for the occasion were also delivered to the house.

37   Daddy had an additional stove installed, and not a burner remained idle, as ducks, chickens, squabs, pork and beef were all cooked each in its own

best way with appropriate spices, seasonings and vegetables. Aunts and female cousins helped with the cooking. It was the happiest work they had ever done; even Jade Snow had fun trying to help. Laughter, excitement, and anticipation made light work of the activities.

38   Then came the party! On Daddy's side, his first cousin, who was like a brother to him, came with his wife, son and daughter-in-law, daughter and son-in-law, and all his numerous grandchildren. Other cousins and nephews of Daddy's were also there. On Mother's side, her brothers and Grandmother were there. Many friends, some of Daddy's employees, as well as others that Jade Snow did not know, also came, until she lost count of their numbers.

39   Those who drank were offered Chinese spirits, and those who did not, like the women, had sparkling apple cider, which was an imitation champagne always served at Chinatown's celebrations or feast occasions.

40   The arriving guests first greeted Mama and Forgiveness from Heaven, making a great deal of fuss over the baby, and each gave him a present of money, wrapped in red paper for good luck. At the age of one month, Forgiveness from Heaven had a good start toward his bank account.

41   The dramatic high light of the evening was unexpectedly provided by Third Uncle on Mother's side, who drank too much rice wine and became violent. He started to become quarrelsome, broke some dishes, and finally let fly a few wild punches. At that point, Daddy and one of his cousins took some rope and tied his hands behind him, led him downstairs, and left him on the floor to sober up. Then they returned and the fun went on. No one seemed to be bothered by Third Uncle's behavior. They commented that he often became violent after drinking.

42   The Wong family had never before seen such merrymaking, and Jade Snow enjoyed all the excitement. Just one remark she had heard, however, marred the perfect celebration, and remained in her mind as she lay in bed after the guests had departed. It was something she had overheard one of her older sisters say to the other while she was helping them twist the crepe-paper hangings.

43   "This joyfulness springs only from the fact that the child is at last a son, after three daughters born in the fifteen years between Blessing from Heaven and him. When Jade Precious Stone was born before him, the house was quiet. There was no such display."

44   Under the comfortable warmth of her covers, Jade Snow turned over restlessly, trying to grasp the full meaning of that remark. Forgiveness from Heaven, because he was a brother, was more important to Mama and Daddy than dear baby sister Precious Stone, who was only a girl. But even more uncomfortable was the realization that she herself was a girl and, like her younger sister, unalterably less significant than the new son in their family.

DISCUSSION QUESTIONS

1. What do you think of Jade Snow's mother's explanation of where babies come from?
2. What did you find most interesting about Chinese customs at the time of the author's childhood?
3. What has Jade Snow come to realize about her position in the family by the end of this account?
4. What is the effect of the author's use of her name instead of "I" in relating her autobiography?

WRITING TOPICS

1. Though this excerpt is autobiographical, the author writes about herself in the third person (referring to "Jade Snow" rather than using "I"). In an essay, discuss this use of the third person and what effect it has on the mood, tone, and force of this memoir.
2. As shown in this excerpt, it has been common in Chinese culture to prefer sons over daughters. In a brief essay, compare this Chinese phenomenon with other cultures you are familiar with and speculate on the reasons for it.

FROM *FAREWELL TO MANZANAR*

Jeanne Wakatsuki Houston and James D. Houston

Jeanne Wakatsuki Houston, born in 1934, considers herself a "late-comer" to the literary scene, due in part to a more traditional Japanese upbringing that encouraged women to be domestic and silent. She earned an undergraduate degree from San Jose State University and pursued graduate work at both San Francisco State University and the Sorbonne. In addition, she received a U.S.-Japan creative arts fellowship, which enabled her to work on her first novel while living in Japan, and the Wonder Woman Award, which is given to women over forty who have made eminent contributions to "the pursuit of truth and positive social change."

Wakatsuki Houston's husband, James D. Houston, born in 1933, is a visiting professor of literature at the University of California and the author of five novels, including *Love Life* (1985) and *Continental Drift* (1978). His shorter pieces have appeared in *The New Yorker, The New York Times, Best of the West,* and *Rolling Stone.* He has been the recipient of a National Endowment for the Arts grant and an American Book Award from the Before Columbus Foundation for a nonfiction work entitled *Californians: Searching for the Golden State* (1982).

Wakatsuki Houston and her husband coauthored the book *Farewell to Manzanar* (1973), the story of her family before, during, and after World War II. The majority of the narrative recounts the experiences of Wakatsuki Houston's family inside Manzanar, one of the ten internment camps in which West Coast Japanese Americans were incarcerated throughout the early 1940s. When the Houstons embarked on this emotional project, Wakatsuki Houston said, "I began to make connections I had previously been afraid to see. It had taken me twenty-five years to reach the point where I could talk openly about Manzanar." What she describes here is a common phenomenon among those Japanese Americans who lived through the internment: a long self-imposed silence that serves to cover up the shame of the incarceration.

In the following excerpt, which takes place after the camp experience, Wakatsuki Houston, in her desire to fit into American society,
becomes caught up in the high school "carnival queen" competition,
an ambition that is opposed by her stern, traditional Japanese father.
(J.I.)

1   That bow was from the world I wanted out of, while the strutting,
sequined partnership I had with Radine was exactly how I wanted my life to
go. My path through the next few years can be traced by its relationship to
hers. It was a classic situation.

2   In many ways we had started even. Poor whites from west Texas, her
family was so badly off sometimes she'd come to school with no lunch and
no money and we would split whatever I had brought along. At the same
time we were both getting all this attention together with the drum and
bugle corps. After three years at our junior high school, in a ghetto neighborhood that included many Asians, Blacks, Mexicans, and other white
migrants from the south, we had ended up close to being social equals.

3   We stayed best friends until we moved to Long Beach Polytechnic. There
everything changed. Our paths diverged. She was asked to join high school
sororities. The question of whether or not I should be asked was never even
raised. The boys I had crushes on would not ask me out. They would flirt
with me in the hallways or meet me after school, but they would ask Radine
to the dances, or someone like Radine, someone they could safely be *seen*
with. Meanwhile she graduated from baton twirler to song girl, a much
more prestigious position in those days. It was unthinkable for a Nisei to be
a song girl. Even choosing me as majorette created problems.

4   The band teacher knew I had more experience than anyone else com-
peting that year. He told me so. But he was afraid to use me. He had to go
speak to the board about it, and to some of the parents, to see if it was
allowable for an Oriental to represent the high school in such a visible way.
It had never happened before. I was told that this inquiry was being made,
and my reaction was the same as when I tried to join the Girl Scouts. I was
apologetic for imposing such a burden on those who had to decide. When
they finally assented, I was grateful. After all, I was the first Oriental
majorette they'd ever had. Even if my once enviable role now seemed
vaguely second-rate, still I determined to try twice as hard to prove they'd
made the right choice.

5   This sort of treatment did not discourage me. I was used to it. I expected
it, a condition of life. What demoralized me was watching Radine's success.
We had shared everything, including all the values I'd learned from the world

I wanted into, not only standards of achievement but ideas about how a girl should look and dress and talk and act, and ideas of male beauty—which was why so many of the boys I liked were Caucasian. Because I so feared never being asked, I often simply made myself unavailable for certain kinds of dates. If one of them had asked, of course, I would have been mortified. That would mean coming to Cabrillo Homes to pick me up, and the very thought of one of his daughters dating a Caucasian would have started Papa raving. He would have chased the fellow across the grass. This was my dilemma. Easy enough as it was to adopt white American values, I still had a Japanese father to frighten my boyfriends and a Japanese face to thwart my social goals.

6   I never wanted to change my face or to be someone other than myself. What I wanted was the kind of acceptance that seemed to come so easily to Radine. To this day I have a recurring dream, which fills me each time with a terrible sense of loss and desolation. I see a young, beautifully blond and blue-eyed high school girl moving through a room full of others her own age, much admired by everyone, men and women both, myself included, as I watch through a window. I feel no malice toward this girl. I don't even envy her. Watching, I am simply emptied, and in the dream I want to cry out, because she is something I can never be, some possibility in my life that can never be fulfilled.

7   It is a schoolgirl's dream, one I tell my waking self I've long since outgrown. Yet it persists. Once or twice a year she will be there, the boyfriend-surrounded queen who passed me by. Surely her example spurred me on to pursue what now seems ludicrous, but at the time was the height of my post-Manzanar ambitions.

8   It didn't happen in Long Beach. There I felt defeated. I watched Radine's rise, and I knew I could never compete with that. Gradually I lost interest in school and began hanging around on the streets. I would probably have dropped out for good, but it was just about this time that Papa decided to go back into farming and finally moved us out of Cabrillo Homes.

9   A few months earlier he had almost killed himself on a combination of whiskey and some red wine made by an Italian drinking buddy of his. He had been tippling steadily for two days, when he started vomiting blood from his mouth and nose. It sobered him up permanently. He never touched alcohol again. After that he pulled himself together, and when the chance came along to lease and sharecrop a hundred acres from a big strawberry grower up north in Santa Clara Valley, he took it. That's where he stayed until he died, raising premium berries, outside of San Jose.

10   I was a senior when we moved. In those days, 1951, San Jose was a large town, but not yet a city. Coming from a big high school in southern California gave me some kind of shine, I suppose. It was a chance to start over, and I made the most of it. By the spring of that year, when it came time to elect the annual carnival queen from the graduating seniors, my

homeroom chose me. I was among fifteen girls nominated to walk out for inspection by the assembled student body on voting day.

11   I knew I couldn't beat the other contestants at their own game, that is, look like a bobbysoxer. Yet neither could I look too Japanese-y. I decided to go exotic, with a flower-print sarong, black hair loose and a hibiscus flower behind my ear. When I walked barefooted out onto the varnished gymnasium floor, between the filled bleachers, the howls and whistles from the boys were double what had greeted any of the other girls. It sounded like some winning basket had just been made in the game against our oldest rivals.

12   It was pretty clear what the outcome would be, but ballots still had to be cast and counted. The next afternoon I was standing outside my Spanish class when Leonard Rodriguez, who sat next to me, came hurrying down the hall with a revolutionary's fire in his eye. He helped out each day in the administration office. He had just overheard some teachers and a couple of secretaries counting up the votes.

13   "They're trying to stuff the ballot box," he whispered loudly. "They're fudging on the tally. They're afraid to have a Japanese girl be queen. They've never had one before. They're afraid of what some of the parents will say."

He was pleased he had caught them, and more pleased to be telling this to me, as if some long-held suspicion of conspiracy had finally been confirmed. I shared it with him. Whether this was true or not, I was prepared to believe that teachers would stuff the ballot box to keep me from being queen. For that reason I couldn't afford to get my hopes up.

14   I said, "So what?"

15   He leaned toward me eagerly, with final proof. "They want Lois Carson to be queen. I heard them say so."

16   If applause were any measure, Lois Carson wasn't even in the running. She was too slim and elegant for beauty contests. But her father had contributed a lot to the school. He was on the board of trustees. She was blond, blue-eyed. At that point her name might as well have been Radine. I was ready to capitulate without a groan.

17   "If she doesn't make carnival queen this year," Leonard went on smugly, "she'll never be queen of anything anywhere else for the rest of her life."

18   "Let her have it then, if she wants it so much."

19   "No! We can't do that! *You* can't do that!"

20   I could do that very easily. I wasn't going to be caught caring about this, or needing it, the way I had needed the majorette position. I already sensed, though I couldn't have said why, that I would lose either way, no matter how it turned out. My face was indifferent.

21   "How can I stop them from fudging," I said, "if that's what they want to do?"

22   He hesitated. He looked around. He set his brown face. My champion. "You can't," he said. "But I can."

23   He turned and hurried away toward the office. The next morning he told me he had gone in there and "raised holy hell," threatened to break this news to the student body and make the whole thing more trouble than it would ever be worth. An hour later the announcement came over the intercom that I had been chosen. I didn't believe it. I couldn't let myself believe it. But, for the classmates who had nominated me, I had to look overjoyed. I glanced across at Leonard and he winked, shouting and whooping now with all the others.

24   At home that evening, when I brought this news, no one whooped. Papa was furious. I had not told them I was running for queen. There was no use mentioning it until I had something to mention. He asked me what I had worn at the tryouts. I told him.

25   "No wonder those *hakajin*[1] boys vote for you!" he shouted. "It is just like those majorette clothes you wear in the street. Showing off your body. Is that the kind of queen you want to be?"

26   I didn't say anything. When Papa lectured, you listened. If anyone spoke up it would be Mama, trying to mediate.

27   "Ko," she said now, "these things are important to Jeannie. She is . . ."

28   "Important? I'll tell you what is important. Modesty is important. A graceful body is important. You don't show your legs all the time. You don't walk around like this."

29   He did an imitation of a girl's walk, with shoulders straight, an assertive stride, and lips pulled back in a baboon's grin. I started to laugh.

30   "Don't laugh! This is not funny. You become this kind of woman and what Japanese boy is going to marry you? Tell me that. You put on tight clothes and walk around like Jean Harlow and the *hakajin* boys make you the queen. And pretty soon you end up marrying a *hakajin* boy . . ."

31   He broke off. He could think of no worse end result. He began to stomp back and forth across the floor, while Mama looked at me cautiously, with a glance that said, "Be patient, wait him out. After he has spoken his piece, you and I can talk sensibly."

32   He saw this and turned on her. "Hey! How come your daughter is seventeen years old and if you put a sack over her face you couldn't tell she was Japanese from anybody else on the street?"

33   "Ko," Mama said quietly. "Jeannie's in high school now. Next year she's going to go to college. She's learning other things . . ."

34   "Listen to me. It's not too late for her to learn Japanese ways of movement. The Buddhist church in San Jose gives odori class twice a week. Jeannie, I want you to phone the teacher and tell her you are going to start taking lessons. Mama has kimonos you can wear. She can show you things

---

[1] *hakajin:* a variation on *hakujin*—Caucasians.

too. She used to know all the dances. We have pictures somewhere. Mama, what happened to all those pictures?"

35   I had seen them, photos of Mama when she lived in Spokane, twelve years old and her round face blanched with rice powder. I remember the afternoon I spent with the incomprehensible old geisha at Manzanar.

36   "Papa," I complained.

37   "Don't make faces. You want to be the carnival queen? I tell you what. I'll make a deal with you. You can be the queen if you start odori lessons at the Buddhist church as soon as school is out."

38   He stood there, hands on hips, glaring at me, and not at all satisfied with this ultimatum. It was far too late for odori classes to have any effect on me and Papa knew this. But he owed it to himself to make one more show of resistance. When I signed up, a few weeks later, I lasted about ten lessons. The teacher herself sent me away. I smiled too much and couldn't break the habit. Like a majorette before the ever-shifting sidewalk crowd, I smiled during performances, and in Japanese dancing that is equivalent to a concert violinist walking onstage in a bathing suit.

39   Papa didn't mention my queenship again. He just glared at me from time to time, with great distaste, as if I had betrayed him. Yet in that glare I sometimes detected a flicker of approval, as if this streak of independence, this refusal to be shaped by him reflected his own obstinance. At least, these glances seemed to say, she has inherited *that*.

40   Mama, of course, was very proud. She took charge and helped me pick out the dress I would wear for the coronation. We drove to San Jose and spent an afternoon in the shops downtown. She could take time for such things now that Papa was working again. This was one of the few days she and I ever spent together, just the two of us, and it confirmed something I'd felt since early childhood. In her quiet way, she had always supported me, alongside of or underneath Papa's demands and expectations. Now she wanted for me the same thing I thought I wanted. Acceptance, in her eyes, was simply another means for survival.

41   Her support and Papa's resistance had one point in common: too much exposure was unbecoming. All the other girls—my four attendants—were going strapless. Mama wouldn't allow this. By the time we finished shopping, I had begun to agree with her. When she picked out a frilly ball gown that covered almost everything and buried my legs under layers of ruffles, I thought it was absolutely right. I had used a low-cut sarong to win the contest. But once chosen I would be a white-gowned figure out of *Gone With the Wind;* I would be respectable.

42   On coronation night the gym was lit like a church, with bleachers in half-dark and a throne at one end, flooded brightly from the ceiling. The throne was made of plywood, its back shaped in a fleur-de-lis all covered with pur-

ple taffeta that shone like oily water under moonlight. Bed sheets were spread to simulate a wide, white carpet the length of the gym, from the throne of the door of the girls' locker room where, with my attendants, we waited for the PA system to give us our musical cue.

43   Lois Carson, the trustee's daughter, was one of them. She wore a very expensive strapless gown and a huge orchid corsage. Her pool-browned shoulders glowed in the harsh bulb light above the lockers.

44   "Oh Jeannie," she had said, as we took off our coats. "What a marvelous idea!"

45   I looked at her inquisitively.

46   "The high *neck*," she explained, studying my dress. "You look so . . . *sedate*. Just perfect for a queen."

47   As the other girls arrived, she made sure they all agreed with this. "Don't you *wish* you'd thought of it," she would say. And then to me, during a silence she felt obliged to fill, "I just *love* Chinese food." The others exclaimed that they too loved Chinese food, and we talked about recipes and restaurants until the music faded in:

> *Girl of my dreams, I love you,*
> *Honest I do,*
> *You are so sweet.*

48   It swelled during the opening bars to cover all other sounds in the gym. I stepped out into blue light that covered the first sheet, walking very slowly, like you do at weddings, carrying against the white bodice of my gown a bouquet of pink carnations.

49   A burst of applause resounded beneath the music, politely enthusiastic, followed by a steady murmur. The gym was packed, and the lights were intense. Suddenly it was too hot out there. I imagined that they were all murmuring about my dress. They saw the girls behind me staring at it. The throne seemed blocks away, and now the dress was stifling me. I had never before worn such an outfit, it was not at all what I should have on. I wanted my sarong. But then thought, NO. That would have been worse. Papa had been right about the sarong. Maybe he was right about everything. What was I doing out there anyway, trying to be a carnival queen? The teachers who'd counted the votes certainly didn't think it was such a good idea. Neither did the trustees. The students wanted me though. Their votes proved that. I kept walking my processional walk, thinking of all the kids who had voted for me, not wanting to let them down, although in a way I already had. It wasn't the girl in this old-fashioned dress they had voted for. But if not her, who *had* they voted for? Somebody I wanted to be. And wasn't. Who was I then? According to the big wall speakers now saxophoning through the gym, I was the girl of somebody's dream:

Since you've been gone, dear,
Life don't seem the same.
Please come back again . . .

50   I looked ahead at the throne. It was even further away, a purple carriage receding as I approached. I glanced back. My four attendants seemed tiny. Had they stopped back there? Afterward there would be a little reception in one of the classrooms, punch and cookies under fluorescent tubes. Later, at Lois Carson's house, there'd be a more intimate, less public gathering, which I'd overheard a mention of but wouldn't be invited to. Champagne in the foothills. Oyster dip. I wanted to laugh. I wanted to cry. I wanted to be ten years old again, so I could believe in princesses and queens. It was too late. Too late to be an odori dancer for Papa, too late to be this kind of heroine. I wanted the carnival to end so I could go somewhere private, climb out of my stuffy dress, and cool off. But all eyes were on me. It was too late now not to follow this make-believe carpet to its plywood finale, and I did not yet know of any truer destination.

DISCUSSION QUESTIONS

1. What part does Leonard Rodriguez play in the narrative?
2. What is the worst thing that could happen to Jeanne according to her father?
3. Why does Jeanne want to be homecoming queen?
4. How can you account for the difference between Jeanne's parents' reactions to her being chosen homecoming queen?
5. Why does Lois Carson make the remark about Chinese food?
6. What is the narrator's feeling about being queen at the end of the excerpt?

WRITING TOPICS

1. In a brief essay, discuss the tone of this excerpt, how it is conveyed by the author, and what effect it has on the reader.
2. In a journal entry, consider who are the villains in this excerpt and who are the heroes and why.

SARI PETTICOATS

Talat Abbasi

Talat Abbasi was born in Pakistan and came to the United States in the 1970s. She has published in *Ascent, Feminist Studies, and Short Story International Seedling Series* and in the anthology *The Forbidden Stitch: An Asian American Women's Anthology* (1989).

In the following story, the ambitious and assertive female character is contrasted with her fearful and indecisive spouse. She wholeheartedly embraces the American ideals of competitiveness, individuality, and striving, while he remains grounded in the values of traditional South Asian society. Abbasi implicitly criticizes the woman's failure to help the ex-husband, who has returned to Lahore, because it demonstrates the woman's loss of the ethical values of caring and giving.

1   I received a letter from my ex-husband. My almost late ex-husband because he says he's dying. Not that it'll affect me at all since I'm hard as iron. Imagine a house burning, everything turns to ashes. The fire escape alone remains standing. That's me. He's always envied me this quality because he himself is sensitive. That's why he's dying before his time. It's not his kidneys, lungs, liver, that's killing him. It's his heart. It palpitates so. He feels everything. Felt it when I said six years ago, "All right go!" He didn't mind the parting. But there's a standard way of doing these things. Tears and pleading on my part, firm refusal on his. Instead, I took the initiative away from him as if I were the man. And it's not as though I'm an American woman born and bred. Not that he knows anything about American women or any other for that matter because he's a decent man.

2   And it's this tendency to forget I'm a woman that brought down all our misfortunes upon us. A tendency he detected in me even when he was living in my father's house as the orphan nephew who had to be fed and

clothed and educated. Being a decent man he's grateful, though it was all done out of a sense of duty, not affection. He sensed that. A nuisance, a poor relation. He was only ten and I was sixteen when he was orphaned. Suddenly they both died in an accident, his parents, sitting together in a horse-drawn *tonga*[1] on a stormy winter night in Lahore. The truck driver said how could he see the *tonga* when there wasn't even a lantern dangling from it? That wasn't true because they found the shattered lantern by the three bodies. The *tongawallah*[2] died too. Four if you count the horse which had to be shot later. What chance does a *tonga* have against a truck?

3   . . . a question he asked himself throughout the period of our marriage— a rhetorical question of course, because he always knew the answer. But he was fatalistic, so he agreed to marry me. Now they all tell him he never should have, but how could he have said no? Consider the scene. My father lay on his death bed. I lay on the shelf. He pretended not to see. But then from his death bed my father begged. She's twenty-five, he called out. The anguish in that cry. In all decency then, the offer had to be made. How was he to know that my father would survive another ten years and run through his fortune himself? Or that when he brought me down from shelf to bed he'd turn the other way. Dark, shapeless and hairy. He slept for years on his left side and dreamt of buffaloes.

4   Still, he was young then. He came to America with such high hopes thinking that the streets were paved with gold. He discovered that the street in Brooklyn where we lived was riddled with bullets instead. He's sure to this day those were bullet holes. So he stayed in the studio. About the size of a servant's quarter at home, without a bathroom, rats, roaches, flies, even mosquitoes, everything the lower classes there are used to. Plus neighbors worse than ever he'd imagined, junkies all, he was sure. While I, having nothing to fear from bullets, lost no time, jumped on a subway to seek my fortune, got off at a station chosen at random. There I stood astonished. Naturally. Because Jackson Heights in New York City is like the smell of sandalwood coming from an apple tree. My senses whirled even faster than the *saris* on high-heeled *chappals*.[3] Oiled plaits swung like pendulums against bare midriffs. Gold earrings tinkled, glass bangles jingled. Netted beards and saffron turbans. Hindi, Urdu, Punjabi, Bengali, English, too, in thick accents. And of course the smell of sandalwood. Then suddenly the spinning stopped and in my head I clearly heard a whirring sound.

5   And imagine his amazement when peeping anxiously through the window (where in his waking hours he kept constant watch with the blinds drawn down, of course) he saw me come home that same evening. I was lug-

---

[1] *tonga:* a carriage drawn by horses.
[2] *tongawallah:* the driver of a tonga.
[3] *chappals:* sandals.

ging a sewing machine which I proceeded to open as soon as I entered. Without a word of explanation I sat down cross-legged (a common tailor sitting by a roadside sewing *shalwars*[4] for laborers immediately came to his sensitive mind) and started sewing *sari* petticoats. He paced the floor for months exclaiming tragically, "A Master's in Persian poetry from Punjab University is sewing sari petticoats!" I could not see the tragedy for the dollar bills which Sardarji of Sari Mahal paid me regularly. But the green of the dollar bills which I flaunted at him so shamelessly made him so bilious he had to leave the country, went back to Lahore. There, he writes, it's all patronage and he's discovered he isn't a landowner's son. We're first cousins he reminds me in the next sentence. That's a relationship which can never be severed. Americanized as I am, that's surely something I still understand. The doctor's bills, he repeats . . .

6   Two thousand four hundred *rupees*,[5] two thousand—I drum my fingers on my mahogany desk and look out of the picture window. It's not all that much he's asking. He doesn't know how my view's improved since I bought out Sardarji. I can see every one of the tall ships which will pass by today on the East River on their way to Miss Liberty to celebrate her centenary. I've waited all week for this moment. But now it's here all I can hear is hooves and wheels clattering down cobbled streets, the *tonga* and the truck. How I love that bit! The stroke of genius I can't resist! Perhaps I shouldn't, but my weakness is still poetry. So I give in, take out my check book. Besides, suppose he's really dying. It's true about the first cousin anyway. And, as he points out, two thousand four hundred *rupees* at twelve *rupees* to the dollar equals only two hundred dollars. I pick up my pen then put it down immediately. He's not dying, it's a lie! The *rupee* is seventeen to the dollar in the black market. Over my dead body.

7   "Come and see," calls out my neighbor from her balcony.

8   I step out. It is indeed a fantastic sight, the East River. It's filled with *tongas*.

9   I go in and take out my calculator. At seventeen to the dollar two thousand four hundred *rupees* equal . . .

---

[4] *shalwars:* loose pantaloons.
[5] *rupees:* Indian currency.

DISCUSSION QUESTIONS

1. What words would you use to characterize the narrator?
2. Why was the narrator's age an impetus to getting married?
3. The narrator says she has a "tendency to forget she's a woman" and that "brought down all our misfortune." What was the specific result of this memory lapse and why?
4. Why did the expectations of the narrator's ex-husband come to nothing?
5. What has caused the narrator to see an East River filled with tongas?

WRITING TOPICS

1. How would you characterize the tone of this selection? Discuss in an essay.
2. In his letter, the ex-husband says that the narrator has become "Americanized," with the implication that she has changed. In an essay, explain what you think it means to be Americanized.

FROM *AMERICAN KNEES*

Shawn Wong

Shawn Wong, born in Oakland, California, in 1949 and raised in nearby Berkeley, has been a highly visible and outspoken member of the Asian-American literary community for several decades. A second-generation Chinese-American whose father was fond of literature, Wong was educated in the San Francisco Bay area, where he earned a bachelor's degree in English literature from the University of California, Berkeley, and a master's degree from San Francisco State University. He has had teaching appointments at several institutions in northern California, including Mills College and the University of California, Santa Cruz, and is presently the chair of the English Department at the University of Washington.

Wong was an active voice in civil rights campus politics and the Asian American movement of the late 1960s and early 1970s, and in collaboration with Frank Chin, Lawson Fusao Inada, and Jeffrey Paul Chan, he edited *Aiiieeeee!* (1974) and *The Big Aiiieeeee!* (1991), both of which remain extremely influential and controversial anthologies of Asian-American literature (the two volumes emphasize Chinese-American and Japanese-American works). He and his co-editors are often called "the four horsemen of Asian American literature" by admirers and detractors alike.

Wong also co-edited the *Before Columbus Foundation Fiction/Poetry Anthology: Selections from the American Book Awards, 1980–1990* and has received numerous awards, including a National Endowment for the Arts creative writing fellowship Although he also writes poetry, Wong is best known for his two novels: *Homebase* (1979) and *American Knees* (1995).

In the following excerpt from *American Knees,* Raymond, who likes to use engineering terms metaphorically, reflects that generations of Chinese tradition resulted in something like "redundant compression strength," and during a move to new quarters he comes to recognize the "tensile strength and stability" of his relationship with his separated spouse, Aurora.

1   Wood wanted to help Raymond buy a house instead of a condominium. He didn't consider a glorified apartment to be a safe investment.

2   "I'll give you the down payment on a house. A house will appreciate faster, and it's got room for a family. You can have a garden."

3   "You're rushing it a little, Dad. Aurora and I are still sorting things out."

4   "You've moved out of your apartment, haven't you?"

5   "Well, yes, until I find something to buy."

6   "I don't see you living here, so I'm assuming you're back living with her."

7   "Well, yes."

8   "Well? Get married, have some children. Name one of them Grace for me."

9   Raymond looked up to be sure his father was teasing and it wasn't really Chinese family pressure at work. "OK, Dad; we'll have five girls and name them all Grace, as long as it keeps you on this side of the globe."

10   Raymond reached for one of his father's engineering manuals. He had taken to reading them. He liked the vocabulary and even used some of the words on the job, adapting the jargon to his new management of minority affairs. Stress. Equilibrium. Stability. Fatigue. Tensile strength. The more he read, the more he came to understand that his father was not so much traditionally Chinese as he was a typical engineer who measured the world as a structure and applied the principles of building to families, lovers, dreams. Old buildings built of unreinforced bricks and mortar had a lot of what was defined as compression strength, but in an earthquake they couldn't withstand the shaking. They were low on tensile strength. Generations and generations of Chinese tradition must result in something Raymond decided was "redundant compression strength." He didn't know if he was using the terms correctly, but philosophically they made sense to him. Maybe the tensile strength and stability his father recognized in Raymond's relationship with Aurora allowed him to relinquish the project of building a "real" Chinese family with a "real" Chinese wife of his own.

11   Aurora cleaned her apartment, without knowing if she was making room for Raymond or not. She picked up magazines and stacked them on the coffee table. She emptied a dresser drawer onto the bed and began to sort her T-shirts, socks, and tights, then left them and went into the bathroom, where she began to rearrange the medicine cabinet. She consolidated a shelf of cos-

metics. She inspected several tubes of lipstick, applied one to her lips and wiped it off, then drew stripes with the others on the back of her hand. She set four of them aside to give to Brenda. She examined the expiration dates on pill bottles and threw away those that had expired. She threw away sample bottles and tubes of creams, lotions, makeup. She returned to the living room and took the magazines off the coffee table and threw them away. In the bedroom, she tackled the socks and tights with new intensity, throwing away the socks with no mates and the tights with holes. She sorted through the dresser drawers and consolidated her clothes until there were two empty drawers, then folded the discards into neat piles for her sister or Goodwill.

12   When the apartment was clean, Aurora sat down at her desk and began to sort through photos and contact sheets. She started a folder for old news photos. Then there were her own: black-and-white vacation shots of gargoyles, architectural details from buildings in Paris, white ocean foam and black lava formations from Hawaii, Brenda's leg and foot in a tide pool. At the bottom of the pile she found photos of her life with Raymond—the unmade bed, his clothes on the chairs, the kitchen table for two, and an obscure silhouette of him behind the opaque glass of the shower. There was another photo of uncooked grains of rice scattered across the tile of the kitchen floor, and she remembered it was taken the day Raymond left. The rice bag had broken in her hand. Would a viewer see in the quality of the light the helplessness and despair of the moment? Was it apparent that the rice stayed on the floor overnight? That the woman outside the frame of the photo who spilled the rice left it on the floor and went to bed hungry?

13   "I thought we were going out to dinner," said Raymond.

14   "We are," Aurora replied. "I like the smell of rice cooking in the apartment."

15   Raymond's father transplants a forty-year-old *bonsai* pine from his house to theirs. Aurora inherits a pair of goat-skin garden gloves. Perhaps they are too young to be found visiting formal gardens in Vienna, marveling at the blossoms, writing down the Latin names of the plants, and searching for the source of an isolated fragrance in a botanical garden. They are thrilled to discover the fragrance in the garden is hidden by planting an aromatic herb at the base of hedges. It is their passion. "Do we have this same light at home?" they wonder. He holds her by the elbow, urging her down a narrow pathway of stepping stones where he hears the sound of water. Crossing an arched footbridge that spans a narrow reflecting pool, she is separated from him momentarily. He looks at a map to see where they are. He thinks about the woman he loves—the one who is embedded in the heart and life lines of his palms, the one who makes love to him on a tiny bed, the one who is similar to a character on the page of a book he is reading, the one who lives in a city filled with roses, the one who sends him a picture of herself cuddling

an infant she calls her niece, the one who speaks to him from the wrinkled pages of an old letter he is rereading which says how much their friendship borders her life, or, in another letter, how much she loves him and wishes things could have been different. He wishes he could mark his life at each of these points so that he could come back later with the memory and the knowledge of how to occupy the heart in order to find solutions, discover a sense of place, reach home, explain his love.

16   He crosses the bridge between them.

DISCUSSION QUESTIONS

1. What does Raymond infer has made his father give up the idea of his building a " 'real' Chinese family with a 'real' Chinese wife"?
2. How can you tell that Aurora's and Raymond's relationship has been somewhat rocky in the past?
3. Is Aurora the one Raymond loves? Explain.
4. What will it take, if anything, for Aurora and Raymond to be permanently happy together?

WRITING TOPICS

1. The words and ideas having to do with structures make up a motif that runs through this excerpt. In an essay, discuss what they contribute to the narrative.

DESIRE AS THE GESTURE BETWEEN US

Timothy Liu

Timothy Liu (Liu Ti Mo) was born in San Jose, California, in 1965. Named after the famous Chinese poet Hsu Chi, he was raised by immigrant parents from mainland China. His poems have appeared in many anthologies, including *Premonitions*. Liu is the author of a book of poems, *Vox Angelica* (1992), and teaches at Cornell College in Iowa. He has also lived in Hong Kong, Utah, and Texas.

In the poem below, Liu explores the ambiguous nature of the love relationship.

One moment we lie in a meadow
listening to the wind, and the next
we are lost in a forest

of fallen needles. Even when birds
5   are out of sight, I cannot stop
the singing. It's late summer

and I walk into the coldest room
of the house. You wait in the garden,
break an iris off its stalk

10   then set it in a bowl of water.
In that quiet, the space between us
changes into music. An ant

emerges from the flower's chamber,
inching its way to the petal's edge
15   then turns back. You look at me

but I no longer can hear your voice
as I take the flower and thrust it
all the way into my mouth

DISCUSSION QUESTIONS

1. Are singing and music appropriate metaphors for feelings of love and desire?
2. Note that the poet writes of listening, singing, quiet, music, and not hearing, but he does not mention touching. Do you find this emphasis on sound or lack of it effective? Why or why not?
3. How do the speaker's emotions affect his actions?

WRITING TOPICS

1. Liu's poem is very visual—it is easy to picture in your mind everything he describes. In a brief essay, analyze how he achieves that visual quality and how it affects your reading of the poem.
2. How a poet breaks the lines of a poem has a profound impact on the rhythm and pace of a poem. Try your hand at changing some of Liu's line breaks and write a brief analysis of what effect your changes had.

FIRST MANGO

Vince Gotera

Vince Gotera was born in San Francisco 1952 but lived for several years in the Philippines as a child. He received a B.A. from Stanford University, an M.A. from San Francisco State University, and an M.F.A. and Ph.D. from Indiana University. He currently directs the creative writing program at the University of Northern Iowa. Gotera has won an Academy of American Poets Prize, the Mary Roberts Rinehart Award in Poetry, the Felix Pollak Poetry Prize (awarded by the University of Wisconsin at Madison), and a Creative Writing Fellowship from the National Endowment for the Arts.

Gotera's first book of poems, *Dragonfly,* appeared in 1994. He has published poems in journals such as *Ploughshares, Amerasia, Kenyon Review, Caliban,* and *Seattle Review,* and also in the important collections of Asian American poetry *The Open Boat: Poems from Asian America* (1993) and *Premonitions: The Kaya Anthology of New Asian North American Poetry* (1995). He is a well-known critic of the literature of the Vietnam War and the author of a critical study, *Radical Visions: Poetry by Vietnam Veterans* (1994).

In "First Mango" Gotera wonders how his betrothed will react to his unusual family.

For Mary Ann
Remember that June before our wedding we spent
in San Francisco? That first morning you woke
to my brother in silver sequins singing like
Diana Ross? What must have gone through your mind?
5   What kind of people were you marrying into?
My father who laughed a lot but was schizophrenic.
My stepmom who'd tried, they say, to stab him in the back
with scissors. Love may be blind, but not *stone* blind.

Then, one Sunday we bought at the corner market
10   one perfectly ripened red-gold mango.
How carefully I slit the skin with my penknife
. . . rivers of yellow juice, the furry seed . . .
then sliced the golden half-moons into quadrangles,
open petals. Your first bite of our sweet life.

DISCUSSION QUESTIONS

1. What is the speaker's state of mind?
2. How do the two stanzas relate to each other?
3. Expand on the aptness of the image of the mango as a symbol for the relationship between the speaker and his fiancée.

WRITING TOPICS

1. In an essay, characterize what you find to be the mood of "First Mango" and explore how the author establishes that mood. Cite words or lines from the poem to support your views.

SUMMARY WRITING TOPICS

1. In a brief essay, analyze the relationship between fathers and their children as presented in at least two selections from this chapter.
2. Both Jade Snow Wong and Jeanne Wakatsuki Houston experience moments (or episodes) in which they realize certain facts about their lives and how they will be shaped by their gender and/or ethnicity. In an essay, explore and compare these moments of revelation and how they affected the authors.
3. In an essay, analyze and compare the imagery in Timothy Liu's "Desire as the Gesture Between Us" and Vince Gotera's "First Mango." Which author do you think is more successful in painting a picture in your mind? Cite lines from the poems to support your views.
4. Talat Abbasi paints a grimmer picture of male-female love relationships than do Timothy Liu and Vince Gotera. In an exploratory essay, speculate on possible reasons for this difference.
5. Recall the parents in "Hector Pueblo" and the excerpt from *Farewell to Manzanar.* Which ones had the best parenting skills in your opinion? Support your views in a paper.

CHAPTER SIX

PARENTS AND CHILDREN

A great deal of Asian American writing focuses on relations between parents and children. Historically, because of the language barriers that faced immigrant Asian Americans, it is the American-born, second-generation sons and daughters whose point of view prevails in these works. As early as 1944, Pardee Lowe's autobiographical *Father and Glorious Descendant* gave American readers the character of a dominant father who serves as the metonymic figure for a strong, cohesive ethnic community. The son's perspective is that of the native informant, whose narrative celebrates the father and his ethnic community while observing the tensions between an old-world patriarch and the new-world scion, who has to negotiate between the sometimes conflicting demands of old and new worlds.

Of course, while second-generation children often reject their parents' social expectations, immigrant parents are not simply flat representations of static societies. They are also themselves individuals who had broken away from their original communities in moving to America. Thus, the American-born Asian American writers portray complex parental characters who are themselves double figures.

"Best Quality," a chapter in Amy Tan's well-received novel *The Joy Luck Club,* also offers a mixed message on the relations between mothers and daughters. Describing a Chinese New Year dinner in which the narrator, a freelance copywriter, is humiliated by Waverly, the accountant daughter of her mother's "longtime friends," the story gradually reveals the daughter's complex feelings of wariness and dependence. She observes her mother's resistance and vulnerability; for example, in the mother's interaction with the tenants whom she is unsuccessfully trying to dislodge. The story contrasts the selfish absorption of the guests with the mother's silent generosity and sacrifice; while her guests feast on the crabs, she accepts the bad one and goes without. For the daughter, the mother's gift of the jade pendant symbolizes her esteem for the daughter, and her desire for the daughter to understand her own value, her "life's importance."

When parents are celebrated in a universalizing manner as stable centers to the child's emotional life, these loving attributes are contextualized in cultural specifics. For example, in Eric Chock's poem to his father, the image is of a strong working-class father, whose presence in his son's life serves as a grounding influence. Chock sees his father building a house and a wall of stones with his own hands. The poem suggests the father's sacrifice of his desires in order to establish a stable foundation for the son and points to the son's dreams as a continuation of the father's own abandoned desires. A Hawaiian poet, Chock has filled his poem with images that are both universal and specific to Hawaii—images of black rock, fish, harbor, and orchids.

Paternal figures also dominate David Mura's and Jaime Jacinto's poems. Mura's "Gardens We Have Left" is set in the present. In a moment of tenderness between the poet-father and his young daughter, the father thinks about the racism that will face her someday, and he is reminded of his own father's history—the tragic history of Japanese Americans who were chased out of California during the Pacific War. Just as Mura's poem enlarges the relation between son and father to include the adult son's relationship with his daughter, so Jacinto in his poem treats the grandfather as a primal relation in the extended family. The coming of spring reminds the poet of his "father's father." Seen through the eyes of the child, the grandfather is not so much a pathetic as a mysterious figure, coaxing "pale green sprouts" from his well-tended garden—a figure the adult evokes as a symbol of ancient familial bonds.

Li-Young Lee's poem "The Gift" is also a retrospective narrative that imagines the paternal figure in a mythic light. The poet recalls an incident when his father pulls a metal splinter out of his seven-year-old palm while distracting the child by reciting a story. The father is presented almost as a godlike figure who heals the sick and raises the dead, and the poet traces the continuity between his father and himself as he lifts a splinter out of his wife's thumb.

Another perspective on father-son relations is seen in Frank Chin's *Donald Duk*. The twelve-year-old protagonist resents his stern father and hates his comical name. He rejects all things Chinese until he becomes an unwilling participant in the Chinese New Year celebration in San Francisco's Chinatown. Aided by dreams of the Chinese railroad workers of the nineteenth century who built the Central Pacific railroad, he comes to terms with his heritage.

Jeff Tagami's and Cathy Song's poems treat the relationships of Asian Americans and their mothers. The mother in Tagami's poem, like the parents in Chock's and Mura's poems, is from the working class. The poem focuses on the love and tenderness between son and mother as they pick apples in an orchard. Despite their fear for each other's safety, in sharing the work with his mother the son achieves a kind of epiphany, a recognition or experience of full emotional learning. Song's poem, "The Youngest Daughter," is more critical of these mother-child ties. The poem is narrated from the point of view of the youngest daughter who, in the absence of the daughters-in-law who serve as caretakers in the traditional Japanese family, is expected to remain unmarried in order to care for her parents. It imagines the daughter's ambivalent feelings toward her aged mother. Its details draw a domestic scene between a neurasthenic woman in her thirties and her elderly mother. Just as the daughter cares for the mother by giving her a bath, so the mother cares for the daughter in preparing a meal for her. This intimate supportive scene is, however, simply a sham. In the last four lines, the poem suggests the daughter's resentment at her entrapment in this traditional familial role. Even as the daughter toasts the mother's health, the image of the thousand cranes—an East Asian symbol for longevity—flying up in a sudden breeze ironically intimates her desire for the mother's demise and her own escape.

Like Song's poem, Wakako Yamauchi's short story, "So What; Who Cares?" focuses on a domestic scene between a caregiver daughter and an aged mother but reverses the point of view. Told through the consciousness of the old woman, who resents what she sees as her daughter's neglect, the narrative juxtaposes present and past through the use of flashbacks. The mother's life had been irrevocably changed during the internment period. After her husband volunteered to serve in the army and died in battle in France, she decided to devote herself to her family and her baby girl. But she is haunted by the memory of an unnamed man whose advances she had rejected. The flashbacks suggest that the mother's silence is a form of withdrawal from an unsatisfying world, but when she breaks the silence, prompted by her memory, she surprises her daughter and breaks through their emotional constraints.

Many of the poems and stories in this chapter suggest that mother-daughter relationships are prone to conflict and tensions, perhaps because the identities of mothers and daughters, as women, are not as clearly differentiated as the identities of mothers and sons. The daughter's desire for separation from the mother may be as strongly felt as the son's, but it is also complicated by gender identification. While males look to their father for role models, daughters sometimes are compelled to deny their similarities to their mothers. Janice Mirikitani's poem, "Breaking Tradition," told through a mother's voice, treats this knotty theme directly. Just as the poet's daughter "denies she is like me," so the poet must "deny I am like my mother." Watching her daughter "breaking tradition," the poet ironically sees the daughter as a "mirror" of herself at a younger age.

In Lan Samantha Chang's short narrative, "The Eve of the Spirit Festival," the two daughters have very different relationships with their father. The older, Emily, rejects the father after their mother's death. As an immigrant from China, he faces discrimination and never achieves the level of success he deserves. Emily has only contempt for his incompetence and lack of social power and leaves home as soon as she can. The younger daughter, Claudia, who narrates the story, remains with Baba, although she knows that Emily is his favorite daughter. Years later, the sisters meet after the father's funeral, when in a final act of rebellion Emily has her hair cut short. But Emily's nightmare sighting of her father's ghost later that night acknowledges that, despite her attempts to break free of Baba's influence, the father's love for her will link her to him psychologically in a way that Claudia will never experience.

As we can see in these selections, parent-child relationships are not merely signified in a set of themes but are also explored in patterns of narrative strategies, points of view, plots, characters, voices, and language choices. Who the center of consciousness is in the poem or story affects the flow of identity for the reader. The stylistic registers given to the speakers tell us whether the parents are non-English-speaking immigrants or bilingual, and whether the children differ vastly from their parents in cultural attitudes and values. What is seldom in doubt is the central significance of the parent-child relationship in these works, illuminating the primary social role that families play in Asian American communities.

BEST QUALITY

Amy Tan

Amy Tan, who was born in Oakland, California, in 1952, like several other writers in this volume, did not think that she was clearly destined to make writing a central part of her life. Her parents, who immigrated to the United States from China in the 1940s, wished her to practice medicine, and throughout her childhood and adolescence, Tan thought that she would eventually become a physician. After the deaths of her father and her brother, who had developed brain cancer, Tan's mother moved the family to Europe in order to escape the tragedies that they had encountered in the United States. While living abroad, Tan rebelled against her mother, whose standards she felt she could not meet.

Tan graduated from high school in Switzerland and returned to the United States in 1969, where she entered Linfield College in Oregon. While in Oregon, she began to prepare for medical school but quickly decided to pursue literature instead, much to the disappointment of her mother. She transferred to San Jose State University and received bachelor's degrees in linguistics and English. In 1974 she earned an M.A. in linguistics. After two years in a Ph.D. program at the University of California, Berkeley, Tan decided to quit graduate school in order to work with disabled children. After four years in this line of work, she became a freelance writer, composing speeches for businesspeople in the computer technology industry. This work made her extremely unhappy, so she began to read fiction voraciously again and joined a writer's group, whose members gave her much encouragement to pursue creative writing. In 1985, she completed her first story, "Rules of the Game," which would grow into her first novel, *The Joy Luck Club* (1989). This novel became a best-seller and was adapted for the big screen; the film, directed by Wayne Wang, became an instant success. Her second and third books, *The Kitchen God's Wife* (1991) and *The Hundred Secret Senses* (1995), also met with popular acclaim.

In the following excerpt from *The Joy Luck Club,* Tan explores the problems of miscommunication between Chinese mothers and their American-born daughters. The focus is on food and its rituals, which is the way "Chinese mothers show their love for their children." (J.l)

1   Five months ago, after a crab dinner celebrating Chinese New Year, my mother gave me my "life's importance," a jade pendant on a gold chain. The pendant was not a piece of jewelry I would have chosen for myself. It was almost the size of my little finger, a mottled green and white color, intricately carved. To me, the whole effect looked wrong: too large, too green, too garishly ornate. I stuffed the necklace in my lacquer box and forgot about it.

2   But these days, I think about my life's importance. I wonder what it means, because my mother died three months ago, six days before my thirty-sixth birthday. And she's the only person I could have asked, to tell me about life's importance, to help me understand my grief.

3   I now wear that pendant every day. I think the carvings mean something, because shapes and details, which I never seem to notice until after they're pointed out to me, always mean something to Chinese people. I know I could ask Auntie Lindo, Auntie An-mei, or other Chinese friends, but I also know they would tell me a meaning that is different from what my mother intended. What if they tell me this curving line branching into three oval shapes is a pomegranate and that my mother was wishing me fertility and posterity? What if my mother really meant the carvings were a branch of pears to give me purity and honesty? Or ten-thousand-year droplets from the magic mountain, giving me my life's direction and a thousand years of fame and immortality?

4   And because I think about this all the time, I always notice other people wearing these same jade pendants—not the flat rectangular medallions or the round white ones with holes in the middle but ones like mine, a two-inch oblong of bright apple green. It's as though we were all sworn to the same secret covenant, so secret we don't even know what we belong to. Last weekend, for example, I saw a bartender wearing one. As I fingered mine, I asked him, "Where'd you get yours?"

5   "My mother gave it to me," he said.

6   I asked him why, which is a nosy question that only one Chinese person can ask another; in a crowd of Caucasians, two Chinese people are already like family.

7   "She gave it to me after I got divorced. I guess my mother's telling me I'm still worth something."

8   And I knew by the wonder in his voice that he had no idea what the pendant really meant.

9   At last year's Chinese New Year dinner, my mother had cooked eleven crabs, one crab for each person, plus an extra. She and I had bought them on Stockton Street in Chinatown. We had walked down the steep hill from my parents' flat, which was actually the first floor of a six-unit building they owned on Leavenworth near California. Their place was only six blocks from where I worked as a copywriter for a small ad agency, so two or three times a week I would drop by after work. My mother always had enough food to insist that I stay for dinner.

10   That year, Chinese New Year fell on a Thursday, so I got off work early to help my mother shop. My mother was seventy-one, but she still walked briskly along, her small body straight and purposeful, carrying a colorful flowery plastic bag. I dragged the metal shopping cart behind.

11   Every time I went with her to Chinatown, she pointed out other Chinese women her age. "Hong Kong ladies," she said, eyeing two finely dressed women in long, dark mink coats and perfect black hairdos. "Cantonese, village people," she whispered as we passed women in knitted caps, bent over in layers of padded tops and men's vests. And my mother—wearing light-blue polyester pants, a red sweater, and a child's green down jacket—she didn't look like anybody else. She had come here in 1949, at the end of a long journey that started in Kweilin in 1944; she had gone north to Chungking, where she met my father, and then they went southeast to Shanghai and fled farther south to Hong Kong, where the boat departed for San Francisco. My mother came from many different directions.

12   And now she was huffing complaints in rhythm to her walk downhill. "Even you don't want them, you stuck," she said. She was fuming again about the tenants who lived on the second floor. Two years ago, she had tried to evict them on the pretext that relatives from China were coming to live there. But the couple saw through her ruse to get around rent control. They said they wouldn't budge until she produced the relatives. And after that I had to listen to her recount every new injustice this couple inflicted on her.

13   My mother said the gray-haired man put too many bags in the garbage cans: "Cost me extra."

14   And the woman, a very elegant artist type with blond hair, had supposedly painted the apartment in terrible red and green colors. "Awful," moaned my mother. "And they take bath, two three times every day. Running the water, running, running, running, never stop!"

15   "Last week," she said, growing angrier at each step, "the *waigoren* accuse me." She referred to all Caucasians as *waigoren,* foreigners. "They say I put poison in a fish, kill that cat."

16   "What cat?" I asked, even though I knew exactly which one she was talking about. I had seen that cat many times. It was a big one-eared tom with gray stripes who had learned to jump on the outside sill of my mother's kitchen window. My mother would stand on her tiptoes and bang the kitchen window to scare the cat away. And the cat would stand his ground, hissing back in response to her shouts.

17   "That cat always raising his tail to put a stink on my door," complained my mother.

18   I once saw her chase him from her stairwell with a pot of boiling water. I was tempted to ask if she really had put poison in a fish, but I had learned never to take sides against my mother.

19   "So what happened to that cat?" I asked.

20   "That cat gone! Disappear!" She threw her hands in the air and smiled, looking pleased for a moment before the scowl came back. "And that man, he raise his hand like this, show me his ugly fist and call me worst Fukien landlady. I not from Fukien. Hunh! He know nothing!" she said, satisfied she had put him in his place.

21   On Stockton Street, we wandered from one fish store to another, looking for the liveliest crabs.

22   "Don't get a dead one," warned my mother in Chinese. "Even a beggar won't eat a dead one."

23   I poked the crabs with a pencil to see how feisty they were. If a crab grabbed on, I lifted it out and into a plastic sack. I lifted one crab this way, only to find one of its legs had been clamped onto by another crab. In the brief tug-of-war, my crab lost a limb.

24   "Put it back," whispered my mother. "A missing leg is a bad sign on Chinese New Year."

25   But a man in white smock came up to us. He started talking loudly to my mother in Cantonese, and my mother, who spoke Cantonese so poorly it sounded just like her Mandarin, was talking loudly back, pointing to the crab and its missing leg. And after more sharp words, that crab and its leg were put into our sack.

26   "Doesn't matter," said my mother. "This number eleven, extra one."

27   Back home, my mother unwrapped the crabs from their newspaper liners and then dumped them into a sinkful of cold water. She brought out her old wooden board and cleaver, then chopped the ginger and scallions, and poured soy sauce and sesame oil into a shallow dish. The kitchen smelled of wet newspapers and Chinese fragrances.

28   Then, one by one, she grabbed the crabs by their back, hoisted them out of the sink and shook them dry and awake. The crabs flexed their legs in midair between sink and stove. She stacked the crabs in a multileveled steamer that sat over two burners on the stove, put a lid on top, and lit the burners. I couldn't bear to watch so I went into the dining room.

29   When I was eight, I had played with a crab my mother had brought home for my birthday dinner. I had poked it, and jumped back every time its claws reached out. And I determined that the crab and I had come to a great understanding when it finally heaved itself up and walked clear across the counter. But before I could even decide what to name my new pet, my mother had dropped it into a pot of cold water and placed it on the tall stove. I had watched with growing dread, as the water heated up and the pot began to clatter with this crab trying to tap his way out of his own hot soup. To this day, I remember that crab screaming as he thrust one bright red claw out over the side of the bubbling pot. It must have been my own voice, because now I know, of course, that crabs have no vocal cords. And I also try to convince myself that they don't have enough brains to know the difference between a hot bath and a slow death.

30   For our New Year celebration, my mother had invited her longtime friends Lindo and Tin Jong. Without even asking, my mother knew that meant including the Jongs' children: their son Vincent, who was thirty-eight years old and still living at home, and their daughter, Waverly, who was around my age. Vincent called to see if he could also bring his girlfriend, Lisa Lum. Waverly said she would bring her new fiancé, Rich Schields, who, like Waverly, was a tax attorney at Price Waterhouse. And she added that Shoshana, her four-year-old daughter from a previous marriage, wanted to know if my parents had a VCR so she could watch *Pinocchio,* just in case she got bored. My mother also reminded me to invite Mr. Chong, my old piano teacher, who still lived three blocks away at our old apartment.

31   Including my mother, father, and me, that made eleven people. But my mother had counted only ten, because to her way of thinking Shoshana was just a child and didn't count, at least not as far as crabs were concerned. She hadn't considered that Waverly might not think the same way.

32   When the platter of steaming crabs was passed around, Waverly was first and she picked the best crab, the brightest, the plumpest, and put it on her daughter's plate. And then she picked the next best for Rich and another good one for herself. And because she had learned this skill, of choosing the best, from her mother, it was only natural that her mother knew how to pick the next-best ones for her husband, her son, his girlfriend, and herself. And my mother, of course, considered the four remaining crabs and gave the one that looked the best to Old Chong, because he was nearly ninety and deserved that kind of respect, and then she picked another good one for my father. That left two on the platter: a large crab with a faded orange color, and number eleven, which had the torn-off leg.

33   My mother shook the platter in front of me. "Take it, already cold," said my mother.

34   I was not too fond of crab, ever since I saw my birthday crab boiled alive, but I knew I could not refuse. That's the way Chinese mothers show they love their children, not through hugs and kisses but with stern offerings of steamed dumplings, duck's gizzards, and crab.

35   I thought I was doing the right thing, taking the crab with the missing leg. But my mother cried, "No! No! Big one, you eat it. I cannot finish."

36   I remember the hungry sounds everybody else was making—cracking the shells, sucking the crab meat out, scraping out tidbits with the ends of chopsticks—and my mother's quiet plate. I was the only one who noticed her prying open the shell, sniffing the crab's body and then getting up to go to the kitchen, plate in hand. She returned, without the crab, but with more bowls of soy sauce, ginger, and scallions.

37   And then as stomachs filled, everybody started talking at once.

38   "Suynan!" called Auntie Lindo to my mother. "Why you wear that color?" Auntie Lindo gestured with a crab leg to my mother's red sweater.

39   "How can you wear this color anymore? Too young!" she scolded.

40   My mother acted as though this were a compliment. "Emporium Capwell," she said. "Nineteen dollar. Cheaper than knit it myself."

41   Auntie Lindo nodded her head, as if the color were worth this price. And then she pointed her crab leg toward her future son-in-law, Rich, and said, "See how this one doesn't know how to eat Chinese food."

42   "Crab isn't Chinese," said Waverly in her complaining voice. It was amazing how Waverly still sounded the way she did twenty-five years ago, when we were ten and she had announced to me in that same voice, "You aren't a genius like me."

43   Auntie Lindo looked at her daughter with exasperation. "How do you know what is Chinese, what is not Chinese?" And then she turned to Rich and said with much authority, "Why you are not eating the best part?"

44   And I saw Rich smiling back, with amusement, and not humility, showing in his face. He had the same coloring as the crab on his plate: reddish hair, pale cream skin, and large dots of orange freckles. While he smirked, Auntie Lindo demonstrated the proper technique, poking her chopstick into the orange spongy part: "You have to dig in here, get this out. The brain is most tastiest, you try."

45   Waverly and Rich grimaced at each other, united in disgust. I heard Vincent and Lisa whisper to each other, "Gross," and then they snickered too.

46   Uncle Tin started laughing to himself, to let us know he also had a private joke. Judging by his preamble of snorts and leg slaps, I figured he must have practiced this joke many times: "I tell my daughter, Hey, why be poor? Marry rich!" He laughed loudly and then nudged Lisa, who was sitting next to him. "Hey, don't you get it? Look what happen. She gonna marry this guy here. Rich. 'Cause I tell her to, *marry Rich.*"

47 "When *are* you guys getting married?" asked Vincent.

48 "I should ask you the same thing," said Waverly. Lisa looked embarrassed when Vincent ignored the question.

49 "Mum, I don't *like* crab!" whined Shoshana.

50 "Nice haircut," Waverly said to me from across the table.

51 "Thanks. David always does a great job."

52 "You mean you still go to that guy on Howard Street?" Waverly asked, arching one eyebrow. "Aren't you afraid?"

53 I could sense the danger, but I said it anyway: "What do you mean, afraid? He's always very good."

54 "I mean, he *is* gay," Waverly said. "He could have AIDS. And he is cutting your hair, which is like cutting a living tissue. Maybe I'm being paranoid, being a mother, but you just can't be too safe these days. . . ."

55 And I sat there feeling as if my hair were coated with disease.

56 "You should go see my guy," said Waverly. "Mr. Rory. He does fabulous work, although he probably charges more than you're used to."

57 I felt like screaming. She could be so sneaky with her insults. Every time I asked her the simplest of tax questions, for example, she could turn the conversation around and make it seem as if I were too cheap to pay for her legal advice.

58 She'd say things like, "I really don't like to talk about important tax matters except in my office. I mean, what if you say something casual over lunch and I give you some casual advice. And then you follow it, and it's wrong because you didn't give me the full information. I'd feel terrible. And you would too, wouldn't you?"

59 At that crab dinner, I was so mad about what she said about my hair that I wanted to embarrass her, to reveal in front of everybody how petty she was. So I decided to confront her about the free-lance work I'd done for her firm, eight pages of brochure copy on its tax services. The firm was now more than thirty days late in paying my invoice.

60 "Maybe I could afford Mr. Rory's prices if someone's firm paid me on time," I said with a teasing grin. And I was pleased to see Waverly's reaction. She was genuinely flustered, speechless.

61 I couldn't resist rubbing it in: "I think it's pretty ironic that a big accounting firm can't even pay its own bills on time. I mean, really, Waverly, what kind of place are you working for?"

62 Her face was dark and quiet.

63 "Hey, hey, you girls, no more fighting!" said my father, as if Waverly and I were still children arguing over tricycles and crayon colors.

64 "That's right, we don't want to talk about this now," said Waverly quietly.

65 "So how do you think the Giants are going to do?" said Vincent, trying to be funny. Nobody laughed.

66   I wasn't about to let her slip away this time. "Well, every time I call you on the phone, you can't talk about it then either," I said.

67   Waverly looked at Rich, who shrugged his shoulders. She turned back to me and sighed.

68   "Listen, June, I don't know how to tell you this. That stuff you wrote, well, the firm decided it was unacceptable."

69   "You're lying. You said it was great."

70   Waverly sighed again. "I know I did. I didn't want to hurt your feelings. I was trying to see if we could fix it somehow. But it won't work."

71   And just like that, I was starting to flail, tossed without warning into deep water, drowning and desperate. "Most copy needs fine-tuning," I said. "It's . . . normal not to be perfect the first time. I should have explained the process better."

72   "June, I really don't think . . ."

73   "Rewrites are free. I'm just as concerned about making it perfect as you are."

74   Waverly acted as if she didn't even hear me. "I'm trying to convince them to at least pay you for some of your time. I know you put a lot of work into it. . . . I owe you at least that for even suggesting you do it."

75   "Just tell me what they want changed. I'll call you next week so we can go over it, line by line." ·

76   "June—I can't," Waverly said with cool finality. "It's just not . . . sophisticated. I'm sure what you write for your other clients is *wonderful*. But we're a big firm. We need somebody who understands that . . . our style." She said this touching her hand to her chest, as if she were referring to *her* style.

77   Then she laughed in a lighthearted way. "I mean, really, June." And then she started speaking in a deep television-announcer voice: "*Three* benefits, *three* needs, *three* reasons to buy . . . Satisfaction *guaranteed* . . . for today's and tomorrow's tax needs . . ."

78   She said this in such a funny way that everybody thought it was a good joke and laughed. And then, to make matters worse, I heard my mother saying to Waverly: "True, cannot teach style. June not sophisticate like you. Must be born this way."

79   I was surprised at myself, how humiliated I felt. I had been outsmarted by Waverly once again, and now betrayed by my own mother. I was smiling so hard my lower lip was twitching from the strain. I tried to find something else to concentrate on, and I remember picking up my plate, and then Mr. Chong's, as if I were clearing the table, and seeing so sharply through my tears the chips on the edges of these old plates, wondering why my mother didn't use the new set I had bought her five years ago.

80   The table was littered with crab carcasses. Waverly and Rich lit cigarettes and put a crab shell between them for an ashtray. Shoshana had wandered

over to the piano and was banging notes out with a crab claw in each hand. Mr. Chong, who had grown totally deaf over the years, watched Shoshana and applauded: "Bravo! Bravo!" And except for his strange shouts, nobody said a word. My mother went to the kitchen and returned with a plate of oranges sliced into wedges. My father poked at the remnants of his crab. Vincent cleared his throat, twice, and then patted Lisa's hand.

81   It was Auntie Lindo who finally spoke: "Waverly, you let her try again. You make her do too fast first time. Of course she cannot get it right."

82   I could hear my mother eating an orange slice. She was the only person I knew who crunched oranges, making it sound as if she were eating crisp apples instead. The sound of it was worse than gnashing teeth.

83   "Good one take time," continued Auntie Lindo, nodding her head in agreement with herself.

84   "Put in lotta action," advised Uncle Tin. "Lotta action, boy, that's what I like. Hey, that's all you need, make it right."

85   "Probably not," I said, and smiled before carrying the plates to the sink.

86   That was the night, in the kitchen, that I realized I was no better than who I was. I was a copywriter. I worked for a small ad agency. I promised every new client, "We can provide the sizzle for the meat." The sizzle always boiled down to "Three Benefits, Three Needs, Three Reasons to Buy." The meat was always coaxial cable, T-1 multiplexers, protocol converters, and the like. I was very good at what I did, succeeding at something small like that.

87   I turned on the water to wash the dishes. And I no longer felt angry at Waverly. I felt tired and foolish, as if I had been running to escape someone chasing me, only to look behind and discover there was no one there.

88   I picked up my mother's plate, the one she had carried into the kitchen at the start of the dinner. The crab was untouched. I lifted the shell and smelled the crab. Maybe it was because I didn't like crab in the first place. I couldn't tell what was wrong with it.

89   After everybody left, my mother joined me in the kitchen. I was putting dishes away. She put water on for more tea and sat down at the small kitchen table. I waited for her to chastise me.

90   "Good dinner, Ma," I said politely.

91   "Not so good," she said, jabbing at her mouth with a toothpick.

92   "What happened to your crab? Why'd you throw it away?"

93   "Not so good," she said again. "That crab die. Even a beggar don't want it."

94   "How could you tell? I didn't smell anything wrong."

95   "Can tell even before cook!" She was standing now, looking out the kitchen window into the night. "I shake that crab before cook. His legs—droopy. His mouth—wide open, already like a dead person."

96   "Why'd you cook it if you knew it was already dead?"

97 "I thought . . . maybe only just die. Maybe taste not too bad. But I can smell, dead taste, not firm."

98 "What if someone else had picked that crab?"

99 My mother looked at me and smiled. "Only *you* pick that crab. Nobody else take it. I already know this. Everybody else want best quality. You thinking different."

100 She said it in a way as if this were proof—proof of something good. She always said things that didn't make any sense, that sounded both good and bad at the same time.

101 I was putting away the last of the chipped plates and then I remembered something else. "Ma, why don't you ever use those new dishes I bought you? If you didn't like them, you should have told me. I could have changed the pattern."

102 "Of course, I like," she said, irritated. "Sometime I think something is so good, I want to save it. Then I forget I save it."

103 And then, as if she had just now remembered, she unhooked the clasp of her gold necklace and took it off, wadding the chain and the jade pendant in her palm. She grabbed my hand and put the necklace in my palm, then shut my fingers around it.

104 "No, Ma," I protested. "I can't take this."

105 "*Nala, nala*"—Take it, take it—she said, as if she were scolding me. And then she continued in Chinese. "For a long time, I wanted to give you this necklace. See, I wore this on my skin, so when you put it on your skin, then you know my meaning. This is your life's importance."

106 I looked at the necklace, the pendant with the light green jade. I wanted to give it back. I didn't want to accept it. And yet I also felt as if I had already swallowed it.

107 "You're giving this to me only because of what happened tonight," I finally said.

108 "What happen?"

109 "What Waverly said. What everybody said."

110 "Tss! Why you listen to her? Why you want to follow behind her, chasing her words? She is like this crab." My mother poked a shell in the garbage can. "Always walking sideways, moving crooked. You can make your legs go the other way."

111 I put her necklace on. It felt cool.

112 "Not so good, this jade," she said matter-of-factly, touching the pendant, and then she added in Chinese: "This is young jade. It is a very light color now, but if you wear it every day it will become more green."

113 My father hasn't eaten well since my mother died. So I am here, in the kitchen, to cook him dinner. I'm slicing tofu. I've decided to make him a spicy bean-curd dish. My mother used to tell me how hot things restore the

spirit and health. But I'm making this mostly because I know my father loves this dish and I know how to cook it. I like the smell of it: ginger, scallions, and a red chili sauce that tickles my nose the minute I open the jar.

114 Above me, I hear the old pipes shake into action with a *thunk!* and then the water running in my sink dwindles to a trickle. One of the tenants upstairs must be taking a shower. I remember my mother complaining: "Even you don't want them, you stuck." And now I know what she meant.

115 As I rinse the tofu in the sink, I am startled by a dark mass that appears suddenly at the window. It's the one-eared tomcat from upstairs. He's balancing on the sill, rubbing his flank against the window.

116 My mother didn't kill that damn cat after all, and I'm relieved. And then I see this cat rubbing more vigorously on the window and he starts to raise his tail.

117 "Get away from there!" I shout, and slap my hand on the window three times. But the cat just narrows his eyes, flattens his one ear, and hisses back at me.

DISCUSSION QUESTIONS

1. What do you learn from the exposition of the story (the background material at the beginning)?
2. What kind of person is Waverly and on what do you base your response?
3. Waverly says the narrator's advertising copy is not sophisticated, and the narrator's mother agrees that her daughter is not a sophisticate. Later the mother says, "Everybody else want best quality. You thinking different." Is her mother insulting her or complimenting her?
4. The narrator loses her anger at Waverly. Why?
5. To what does the mother compare Waverly?
6. Do you think the narrator will ever know her "life's importance"? Why or why not?
7. How do the final four paragraphs tie together some of the ideas in the story?

WRITING TOPICS

1. In a brief essay, discuss what you see as the success or failure of characterization in this story. How well or poorly drawn do you think the characters are? Cite examples from the story to support your views.
2. June's mother says at one point, "Only *you* pick that crab. Nobody else take it. I already know this. Everybody else want best quality. You thinking different." In your journal, speculate on what the mother meant by this comment and on what it says about June as a person.

POEM FOR MY FATHER

Eric Chock

Eric Chock, born in 1950, currently coordinates and teaches in the Hawaiian Poets in the Schools program in Honolulu, Hawaii. His first book of poems, *Ten Thousand Wishes,* is now out of print. His second book of poems, *Last Days Here,* appeared in 1989. Chock is the editor or coeditor of several anthologies, including *The Best of Bamboo Ridge* (1986), *Small Kid Time Hawaii* (1981), and *Talk Story: An Anthology of Hawaii's Local Writers* (1978). An active member of the Hawaiian literary community, Chock has served on the board of directors of the Hawaii Literary Arts Council and the Honolulu City Commission on Culture and the Arts.

In the following poem, the father builds a "wall of dreams" for his son, crafting the lava stones and thinking of fish in the sea and orchids in the hair of women.

I lie dreaming
when my father comes to me and says,
I hope you write a book someday.
He thinks I waste my time,
5   but outside, he spends hours over stones,
gauging the size and shape a rock will take
to fill a space,
to make a wall of dreams around our home.
In the house he built with his own hands
10   I wish for the lure that catches all fish
or girls with hair like long moss in the river.
His thoughts are just as far and old
as the lava chips like flint off his hammer,
and he sees the mold of dreams

15   taking shape in his hands.
His eyes see across orchids on the wall,
into black rock, down to the sea,
and he remembers the harbor full of fish,
orchids in the hair of women thirty years before
20   he thought of me, this home, these stone walls.
Some rocks fit perfectly, slipping into place
with light taps of his hammer.
He thinks of me inside
and takes a big slice of stone,
25   and pounds it into the ground
to make the corner of the wall.
I cannot wake until I bring
the fish and the girl home.

DISCUSSION QUESTIONS

1. Two objects of desire are equated here. What are they?
2. What are the father's dreams and memories?
3. What will the son have to do to fulfill his father's dreams for him?

WRITING TOPICS

1. In a brief essay, analyze the contrasting images in this poem and what they tell you about the father and the son.

THE GIFT

Li-Young Lee

Li-Young Lee was born in 1957 in Jakarta, Indonesia. In 1951 his father and mother had moved to Jakarta from Tianjin, China, after the Communists took power and Chinese Nationalists fled to Taiwan. For nine months before his departure from China, Lee's father served as personal physician to Mao Tse-tung, the powerful Chairman of the Communist Party and Premier of China. In Indonesia Lee's father taught philosophy at Gamaliel University and studied Western theology and poetry. In 1959 the Lees became fugitives when President Sukarno moved to purge all Chinese resident aliens. After traveling to Macao, Hong Kong, Singapore, and Japan, the Lees immigrated to the United States in 1964. They settled in Pennsylvania, where Lee's father gained admittance to the Pittsburgh Theological Society and obtained a position as a Christian minister.

Lee attributes his love of literature in large part to his father's love of poetry. He began to write poetry during his undergraduate years at the University of Pittsburgh. He also studied at the University of Arizona and the State University of New York at Brockport. In 1986, he published his first collection of poetry, entitled *Rose*. This debut collection received New York University's Delmore Schwartz Memorial Poetry Award. Lee also received grants from the Pennsylvania Council on the Arts and the National Endowment for the Arts. His second book, *The City in Which I Love You,* from which the following poem is taken, was published in 1990 and was the 1990 Lamont Poetry Selection of the Academy of American Poets. Lee has also published a well-received memoir, *Winged Seed* (1994).

In "The Gift" a man remembers a moment from his boyhood when his father performs a small service that is full of greater meaning. (J.I.)

To pull the metal splinter from my palm
my father recited a story in a low voice.
I watched his lovely face and not the blade.
Before the story ended, he'd removed
5   the iron sliver I thought I'd die from.

I can't remember the tale,
but hear his voice still, a well
of dark water, a prayer.
And I recall his hands,
10   two measures of tenderness
he laid against my face,
the flames of discipline
he raised above my head.

Had you entered that afternoon
15   you would have thought you saw a man
planting something in a boy's palm,
a silver tear, a tiny flame.
Had you followed that boy
you would have arrived here,
20   where I bend over my wife's right hand.

Look how I shave her thumbnail down
so carefully she feels no pain.
Watch as I lift the splinter out.
I was seven when my father
25   took my hand like this,
and I did not hold that shard
between my fingers and think,
Metal that will bury me,
christen it Little Assassin,
30   Ore Going Deep for My Heart.
And I did not lift up my wound and cry,
Death visited here!
I did what a child does
when he's given something to keep.
35   I kissed my father.

DISCUSSION QUESTIONS

1. How did the father distract his son while he removed the iron sliver?
2. What was the gift of the title?
3. How have the father's actions been repeated?
4. Describe the tone of the poem.

WRITING TOPICS

1. In a brief essay, discuss what you think is the mood of this poem and how it is conveyed.
2. In this poem, as in Amy Tan's "Best Quality," a parent gives a child a gift. In an essay, compare the gifts given in these two selections and speculate on the meaning these gifts will have to the recipients.

FROM *DONALD DUK*

Frank Chin

Frank Chin was born in 1940 in San Francisco. His plays, *The Chickencoop Chinaman* and *The Year of the Dragon,* were first performed at the American Place Theater in New York in 1972 and 1974. He is a founding director of the Combined Asian American Resources Project, coeditor of *Aiiieeeee!* (1975), an influential pioneering anthology of Asian American literature, and coeditor of *The Big Aiiieeeee!* (1991), a sequel to the first anthology. He is also the author of a collection of short stories, *The Chinaman Pacific & Frisco R. R. Co.* (1988), which received the American Book Award, and a novel, *Donald Duk* (1991). He lives in California, and has lectured all over the United States and internationally. Chin is a controversial author, and his critical work has had as strong an impact on Asian American cultural productions as his creative writing.

In his first novel, *Donald Duk,* the main character, Donald, is a young boy living in Chinatown. His best friend, Arnold Azalea, comes to stay with him for a few days. In trying to introduce Arnold to his family and ethnic community, Donald finds that he himself is ignorant about much of his community's culture and history. This chapter, written in a mixture of fantasy and realism, incorporates characters from Chinese classics such as *The Three Kingdoms, The Water Margin,* and *Monkey's Journey to the West* and more contemporary narratives that have Chinese-American characters from American popular culture, such as Charlie Chan. Donald's fantasy is chiefly peopled with male heroes who are legendary Chinese warriors and tough guys. The chapter ends with Donald and Arnold discovering that, in the history book they find in the library, the history of the construction of the Central Pacific Railroad does not include any reference to the twelve hundred Chinese laborers who helped build it. When Donald complains to his father about this, the father tells him, "You gotta keep the history yourself or lose it forever, boy."

1 Donald Duk dreams he's sleeping at night and wakes up dreaming, and wakes up from that dream into another, and wakes up into the real.

2 Morning in San Francisco Chinatown. The clammy milky light before dawn collects in the tissue paper skins of Dad's model planes hanging from the ceiling, and they glow like Chinese lanterns. Pieces of the balsa wood skeleton of the P-26A Donald is building to replace the one he still remembers burning over Chinatown lay assembled and pinned to the plans laid out on his worktable. The planes seem to move as he passes the doorway to the dining room. He feels like he's still a character in his dream and expects to wake up just one more time. Is this another dream when he sees the girl his age with the staff at the White Crane Club? No. It's a tubby boy with glasses and braces.

3 On the way home, at a trot with Arnold Azalea, Donald Duk does not feel all here. There is a peculiar silly stillness about Chinatown. He walks home by streets and through alleys he does not usually walk. Everything is closed this early in the morning. Cold darkness inside every shop. Cold light. A book and magazine store is open in an alley.

4 Strange. The lights are on bright. The doors are open. A Chinese woman wearing a buttoned-up sweater sits on a high stool behind a cash register. A lookout for a gambling den? No. The gamblers go home before first light. They are all asleep and dreaming, not to wake up till noon or later.

5 No one is surprised Donald Duk and Arnold Azalea step inside to browse this early in the morning. A cat pads between the rows of books. Donald Duk faces a wall of softbound multi-volume sets of comic books telling the stories of *The Three Kingdoms,* and *The Water Margin, Monkey's Journey to the West, The Seven Women Generals of the Yang Family* and other heroic tales with bows and arrows, swords and slings, spears and horses. Donald Duk slides open the box reading *Characters in Water Margin Playing Cards. Made in Shanghai, China.* Two full decks of cards inside. One with red backs. One with blue backs. Full-length portraits of the characters of the popular novel are on the playing card faces. Each deck has four suits with ace, king, queen, jack, two through ten, and three jokers. One of the red jokers is the man who stopped Lee Kuey from throwing a battle axe through Donald Duk. The peach-colored robe. The long trailing feathers, like the long trailing pheasant feathers on the headdresses of Aztec warriors on the calendars in Mexican restaurants. "Arnold! Come here! Here he is."

6 "Who?"

7 "The Timely Rain, he called himself," Donald takes the red joker to the woman knitting behind the cash register. "Can you tell me who this is?" he asks.

8 The woman glances at the card. "Why, that's Soong Gong. So, who did you think it was?"

9 "Who is Soong Gong?"

10   "Who is Soong Gong?" the woman laughs. "Come on, boy!"

11   The door behind the cash register opens. A medium tall man in a black three-piece suit and a black hat steps into the doorway. He slips a coiled black bullwhip over his shoulder. He focuses his eyes on Donald Duk, and Donald Duk doesn't like it. He feels himself coming apart being seen by this man.

12   "Come on, Ah-Bok, people here don't wear hats anymore. And that bullwhip. I'm surprised they let you on the plane with such a terrible thing," the woman says.

13   The man with the bullwhip yawns and slips a large round gold pocket-watch out of his vest pocket, and drops it back in. "I'm a detective sergeant of the Honolulu Police Department. People on the plane are happy I carry my bullwhip, and my gun too, by dammit."

14   "Watch your language in front of this boy, Charlie. *Wuhay!* He doesn't know who Soong Gong is."

15   "What's that you say?" and the bullwhip snaps his eyes on Donald Duk again. Donald Duk shows the card to Sgt. Bullwhip and asks, "Who's this? She says his name is Soong Gong. I think he's called the Timely Rain. So who is he?"

16   "He's the leader of 108 outlaws. Name Soong Gong. Nickname him: Timely Rain. Don't you know that, boy? Every boy and girl knows that. Why don't you? You some kind of dimwit? Everything a little foggy to you?"

17   Donald Duk shows Sgt. Bullwhip from Honolulu the card showing the dark naked man with a battle axe in each hand. "Who's this?"

18   "Why, that's Lee Kuey. They call him the Black Tornado, because he is ugly, bad-tempered and cuts through fighting men like a buzzsaw. This guy is crazy in the cabeza.[1] He kills as many of his friends by accident as bad guys. But he's so good at it, understand me? You never heard of him? So why do you ask?"

19   "Where are you from, boy?" the woman asks. "You a Chinatown kid?"

20   "Yeah . . ."

21   "How come you don't know these guys?" the woman asks, buttoning her buttons again. "Do you know who this old man is?"

22   "No."

23   "This is Charlie Chan."

24   "Charlie Chan?" Donald Duk asks and looks at the man without looking into the man's eyes. "He's not fat enough to be Charlie Chan."

25   "The real Charlie Chan," the woman says. "His family name is Chang. In Hawaii they call him Chang Apana."

26   "Sergeant Chang Apana," Bullwhip says.

---

[1] *cabeza:* colloquialism meaning *head,* from "caboose."

27   "He's famous just famous for keeping the peace on Hotel Street in the twenties. Aren't you, Ah-Bok?"

28   "I keep the peace at the baseball too," Bullwhip says. "Get him a copy of that poster picture of 108 outlaws." He points at the characters appearing lined up on the banks of a river or lake as the woman unrolls the poster. "There, you see, here's Soong Gong. And here's the Black Tornado. Ugly fella, huh! Stupid too. Loyal. Righteous too. Bad combination."

29   "That's just the way I saw them!" Donald Duk says. The 108 outlaws are lined up on the riverbank the way they were on the edge of the cloud. He pulls money out of his pocket to buy the poster, but Bullwhip won't let the woman roll the poster up and wrap it. "See here, this one. Sagacious Lowe. Wanted murderer becomes this Buddhist monk. Eats meat. Drinks booze. Beats people up. Breaks statues of Buddha up. Too devout to live in a monastery. Ha ha. And this one's Tiger Killer Jung. One by one all these fella join up with Soong Gong in the Water Margin. This is the one guy who is not jealous. He give you a helping hand in good times or bad times. When I'm a kid like you, I daydream someday someone from Leongshan Marsh— that one Marvelous Traveler—find me and say, *The Timely Rain says he is man no talent, but he's seen lots of war. He longtime admire your bravery. Soong Gong asks you to join him and his gang of outlaw heroes in Leongshan Marsh. Before you lie. Before you betray. Before you sell out* . . . But you grow up. You sell out. You lie. Just a little bit, maybe you cheat on your wife, no good, and think it is just little bit, but too much to ever expect the Marvelous Traveler to come up with that message from the Timely Rain . . ."

30   "If you're the real Charlie Chan, how do you solve murder mysteries?"

31   "I got my bullwhip."

32   "For solving murders?"

33   "And for crowd control too," Sgt. Bullwhip says.

34   Donald Duk and Arnold Azalea are the only people in the huge marble reading room of the main library. "Here it is!" Donald Duk whispers.

35   "Me too," Arnold says, reading from a book on top of a pile of closed books, "I found it too. *Thursday, April 29, 1869.*"

36   Donald Duk reads from the book on top of his stack of closed books, "Listen to this: *Each man in Strobridge's astonishing team of tracklayers had lifted 125 tons of iron in the course of the day. The consumption of materials was even more impressive, 25,800 ties, 3,520 rails, 28,160 spikes, 14,800 bolts* . . ."

37   "Wow," Arnold whispers.

38   "Listen to this: *As soon as the epic day's work was done, Jim Campbell, who later became a division superintendent for the C.P., ran a locomotive over the new track at forty miles an hour to prove the record-breaking feat was a sound job as well.* Does it say anything about Kwan in any of your books?"

39   "I don't see anything yet," Arnold says.

40 "Look at this: *At rails' end stood eight burly Irishmen, armed with heavy track tongs. Their names were Michael Shay, Patrick Joyce, Michael Kennedy, Thomas Daily, George Elliot, Michael Sullivan, Edward Killeen, and Fred McNamara.* Not one Chinese name. We set the record and not one of our names. Not one word about our last crosstie." Donald Duk whispers in the library.

41 And while working on his model P-26A Peashooter at home, he says, "We made history. Twelve hundred Chinese. And they don't even put the name of our foreman in the books about the railroad."

42 "So what?" Dad asks.

43 Donald Duk doesn't say a word back.

44 Dad catches Donald Duk's eye. "What're you look at me that way for? Fix your face."

45 "Didn't you hear what I said?" Donald Duk asks.

46 "They don't want our names in their history books. So what? You're surprised. If we don't write our history, why should they, huh?"

47 "It's not fair."

48 "Fair? What's fair? History is war, not sport! You think if you are a real good boy for them, do what they do, like what they like, get good grades in their schools, they will take care of you forever? Do you believe that? You're dreaming, boy. That is faith, sincere belief in the goodness of others and none of your own. That's mysticism. You believe in the goodness of others to cover your butt, you're good for nothing. So, don't expect me to get mad or be surprised the *bokgwai*[2] never told our history in any of their books you happen to read in the library, looking for yourself. You gotta keep the history yourself or lose it forever, boy. That's the mandate of heaven."

DISCUSSION QUESTIONS

1. How does Chinatown appear in this story? Does it seem like the kind of Chinatown you have visited in a big city?
2. What do all the Chinese heroes described in the chapter have in common?
3. According to Donald's father, how is history written? Do you agree with this assessment?
4. Explain why the contributions of Chinese in the United States may not be included in the official history of the country.

---

[2] *bokgwai:* white ghost (for a white American).

WRITING TOPICS

1. Is there a difference between legend or myth and history? How are they different? How might they be the same? Explore these questions in a brief essay.
2. What kinds of heroes did you have when you were twelve or thirteen? Have your heroes changed as you have grown older? Write a short essay on the significance of one particular heroic figure on how you think and live.

LABOR OF LOVE

Jeff Tagami

Jeff Tagami was born in Watsonville, California. He currently lives in San Francisco with his family. His first book of poems, *October Light,* appeared in 1990. His poetry appeared in *The United States of Poetry* (1996), a richly illustrated anthology of modern American poets that was a companion volume to a PBS series. Tagami also coedited *Without Names,* a collection of poetry by Bay Area Filipino American writers (1997), and co-translated the chapbook *This Wanting to Sing: Asian American Poets in South America* (1988).

In the following poem, the tender and caring relationship of mother and son is brought out in their concern for each other as they go about the labor of picking apples.

    When my mother and I
    entered the orchard
    with our ladders,
    the morning moisture wet everything—
5   the leaves, the apples, the dust
    that fell on them all night.
    And then that dust became mud
    which stuck to our hands
    and dried when the sun came out.
10 The boss who stopped by earlier
    in his jeep reminded us
    to take your time, so as not to bruise
    the apples they call Golden Delicious.
    How you must, with great care,
15 gently rock them into the bin
    as if putting a sleeping child to bed.
    "It's like a labor of love," he said.

Because the apples were the same color
as the leaves, a light green,
20 picking was slow, having to reach
into a clump of leaves, blindly
until we felt the smooth globe.
"Come on out, little darlings,"
my mother called to them
25 as though they were hiding.
I suggested she stick with the short
ladder, to pick, only, the ones
hanging low. From above,
I could keep an eye on her,
30 making sure she planted
her ladder firmly in the soft earth,
asking her, politely, to empty
her bag before it got too full.

It was when I ran out
35 of ladder and I had to climb
into the tree that I began singing,
hoping this would ease my fear
and my mother's fear for me.
"Careful," she said, "careful."
40 I began singing her favorite song.
I'm in the Mood for Love,
until I had to stop and ask
her for the right words, coaxing
her, finally, to sing along, her sweet
45 voice lifting above the scant chattering
of birds in the canyon.

Over the canyon,
a jetliner lazily headed west.
Nothing between it and me
50 but blue sky
and my black hand poking
from the tops of trees and waving,
there being so much love
in my heart and heaven
55 in my eyes.

DISCUSSION QUESTIONS

1. How does the speaker show his concern for his mother?
2. What has made the speaker so happy?
3. Explain the connection between the title and the poem itself.
4. How does the organization of the poem suit the topic? In thinking about this question, ask yourself how the poem would have been affected if it had begun with the last stanza.

WRITING TOPICS

1. "Labor of Love" is a very visual poem. In an essay, examine the images Tagami uses and how they work together to paint the scene. Cite words or lines from the poem to support your analysis.
2. In a brief essay, write about a time when you performed a labor of love—either because you enjoyed the labor, such as raking, washing a car, or painting, for example—or because you labored beside someone you loved, or both.

THE YOUNGEST DAUGHTER

Cathy Song

Born in 1955 in Honolulu, Hawaii, to a Chinese mother and a Korean father, Cathy Song received her formal education in the northeastern United States. She graduated from Wellesley College in 1977 and went on to earn an M.A. in creative writing from Boston University in 1981. She also attended the Advanced Poetry Workshop conducted by Kathleen Spivak. Her poems have appeared in several literary publications, including *Bamboo Ridge, The Greenfield Review,* and *Asian-Pacific Literature. Picture Bride* (1983), her first book of poetry, was chosen from among 625 entries to win the Yale Series of Younger Poets in 1983. In the wake of such a prestigious award, Song began to receive much wider attention and critical acclaim.

Literary critic and poet Shirley Geok-lin Lim describes many of the thirty-one poems found in *Picture Bride* as "autobiographical, portrait-like and heavily regional and ethnic in thrust." Among Song's major concerns in this collection are familial relationships, generational ties, the female voice, and the complexities of sexuality. Richard Hugo, who selected Song's manuscript as the winner in the Yale Series competition, points out the visual quality of her poetry— indeed, a few poems are named after paintings by Georgia O'Keeffe—and several present the "floating world" of Utamaro, a nineteenth-century Japanese woodblock artist. Song's second volume of poems, *Frameless Windows, Squares of Light,* appeared in 1988. In this collection, she takes up issues involving the family once again, "plumbing," according to Lim, "domestic relations between child and parent, sister and brother, mother and child."

"The Youngest Daughter," is a revealing portrait of mother-daughter relationships, showing the dependency of old age and the burden of filial obligation. (J.I.)

The sky has been dark
for many years.
My skin has become as damp
and pale as rice paper
5   and feels the way
mother's used to before the drying sun
parched it out there in the fields.

Lately, when I touch myself,
my hands react as if
10   I had just touched something
hot enough to burn.
My skin, aspirin-colored,
tingles with migraine. Mother
has been massaging the left side of my face
15   especially in the evenings
when it flares up.

This morning
her breathing was graveled,
her voice gruff with affection
20   when I took her into the bath.
She was in a good humor,
making jokes about her great breasts,
floating in the milky water
like two walruses,
25   flaccid and whiskered around the nipples.
I scrubbed them with a sour taste
in my mouth, thinking:
six children and an old man
have sucked from these brown nipples.

30   I was almost tender
when I came to the blue bruises
that freckle her body,
places where she has been injecting insulin
for thirty years, ever since
35   I can remember. I soaped her slowly,
she sighed deeply, her eyes closed.

In the afternoons
when she has rested,
she prepares our ritual of tea and rice,

40 garnished with a shred of gingered fish,
a slice of pickled turnip,
a token for my white body.
We eat in the familiar silence.
She knows I am not to be trusted,
45 even now planning my escape.
As I toast to her health
with the tea she has poured,
a thousand cranes curtain the window,
fly up in a sudden breeze.

DISCUSSION QUESTIONS

1. What are the mother's and daughter's attitudes toward each other?
2. Why would the youngest daughter be at home still?
3. What is the mood of the poem, and how is it achieved?
4. Why might the speaker be planning her escape?

WRITING TOPICS

1. Is the daughter right to think of escape? In a paragraph or two, write a convincing argument expressing your point of view.
2. In this poem, which consists chiefly of domestic details, at least one image symbolizes desire for escape. What is it? Working in small groups, make lists of other things you can think of that could represent the idea of escape.
3. This poem effectively conveys mundane details of daily life. Choose another poem in this anthology that does the same and, in an essay, compare how the two authors make the ordinary memorable through their use of language.

SO WHAT; WHO CARES?

Wakako Yamauchi

Wakako Yamauchi was born in 1924 and lived a nomadic life during her childhood years. Her parents, first-generation tenant farmers, were not eligible for citizenship because of the Naturalization Act, and they could not own land under California's Alien Land Law, so her family was forced to move often. In the 1930s Yamauchi's parents decided to end the family's itinerant existence; they ran a boarding-house for Japanese immigrants in Oceanside, California. During World War II, the family was incarcerated in an internment camp in Poston, Arizona—the same camp in which Hisaye Yamamoto, another well-known Japanese-American writer, spent several of the war years. Both young women worked for the camp newspaper, the *Poston Chronicle,* but in different capacities: Yamauchi did layout and design, and Yamamoto wrote a column. Their friendship, begun during the internment, continues to the present.

After World War II, Yamauchi further developed her artistic interests by taking courses in layout design, drawing, and painting at the Otis Art Center in Los Angeles. From 1960 to 1974, she submitted short stories and drawings to the *Los Angeles Rafu Shimpo,* a Japanese American daily publication. "And the Soul Shall Dance," one of Yamauchi's most widely recognized and anthologized short stories, was selected for *Aiiieeeee!* the first anthology of Asian American writing, published in 1974.

In 1976 she finished her first play, which is based on this now famous short story and bears the same title. The play, performed first by East-West Players in Los Angeles, was nominated for Outstanding New Play of the Year by the Los Angeles Drama Critics Circle. Yamauchi has received numerous awards and recognitions, including the American Theater Critics Regional Award for Outstanding Play, the Brody Art Fund Fellowships, and several Rockefeller grants.

Although she is perhaps best known as a playwright, Yamauchi has also written pieces in other genres that have met with critical success. As literary critic Stan Yogi has pointed out, Yamauchi "portray[s] the resistance of first-generation women and the consequences of their rebellions in narratives that subvert the strict cultural codes of the issei family."[1] In addition to an exploration of gender dynamics, Yamauchi examines intergenerational conflict, the immigrant experience, hardships in the harsh agricultural environments of California, and burgeoning sexuality.

"So What; Who Cares?" is written from the point of view of an elderly parent and presents a picture of filial obligation grudgingly served. (J.I.)

1   Close your mouth when you chew," she says.
2   I close my mouth. Hunh!
3   She reaches across the table to wipe my chin. I rear back and grab her arm.
4   "There's gravy on your chin, Ma!" she says loudly.
5   "Shhh . . ." I hiss. She thinks because I don't talk, I can't hear. In spite of myself, a tear sneaks down my face.
6   "What are you crying about now?" She is exasperated. "Those are the very things you taught me: 'Close your mouth, please, and thank you,' all that. Remember?"
7   She dabs my cheek with the same napkin (I smell the food on it) and spoons mashed potato into a puddle of gravy. I shake my head. "Just one more bite," she coos, making up for the other, harsh words. I open my mouth.

8   I can feed myself. Most of the time I insist on it, but I'm slow and she often glances at her watch, sometimes taking the fork from me, like now, and I must swallow half-masticated food to accommodate her—especially on holidays when she comes with my dinner and rushes back to serve her family. I'd rather go to her house to eat—I can still walk, I can take a bus—but she never invites me. I depress her husband. His mother died a few years ago in a convalescent home, and why should he do for me what he never did for his mother? Oh, he gave her money and things; she had the woolliest lap robe in the ward, they say, the grandest slippers, but who cares about that? I know. Not much gets past me.

9   And it doesn't matter to me either, but it's the children I miss—the girls. I like to hear their silly chatter, the giggling. Soon their words will grow too clever, their eyes will change, their thoughts will turn to designer labels.

---

[1] *Asian-American Women Writers* (Broomall, PA: Chelsea House, 1997) 135.

They live in a storybook world now, where princesses don't die, only sleep—no wrinkled faces, no gnarled fingers, no stroke to remind them of reality. No pyorrhea.

10 She takes me to her dentist, but my teeth are going anyway. That's why she brings me dinner every night. I can cook; I can putter around, but she's afraid I'll die of malnutrition with the rice gruel I keep cooking. It's easy. It goes down fast. But what's my hurry?

11 "How's the food? Good?" she asks sweetly.

12 I nod. Juicy dark meat—she always remembers I prefer dark—finely sliced and crushed with a fork—tender garden peas, also crushed, a wedge of cranberry jelly, a mound of mashed potato with a crater of gravy, dark and smooth, like I taught her, a tablespoon of dressing—not my favorite—she knows me well. "A devoted daughter," one of her friends said. They think I'm deaf.

13 She didn't bring dessert. Maybe she didn't want to cut into the meringue (her meringues are famous). Her husband may have told her to let the kids have the first pieces. Like Joe always said: "Let the baby have the first piece."

14 I'd almost forgotten, he died so long ago. What would he think of me now—so old and gap-toothed. He wouldn't like me. "Straighten up," he'd say. "Put on some lipstick; wear something pretty; go to a hairdresser." He liked pretty. Everything had to be pretty and smell nice. He wouldn't have liked growing old.

15 He died in the Vosges Mountains, Joe, in beautiful France. He saw some awful things there: torn bodies, ruined villages, broken families—not pretty or nice smelling.

16 He loved the baby. He said, "If I don't come back, promise you won't let her forget me."

17 "You won't die," I said.

18 "If I do, will you marry again?"

19 "No," I said. "If I marry again, she'll forget you. And I would too."

20 I have anyway. And she has. And I've grown old enough to be your mother, Joe, plus you should see her now.

21 I didn't get a chance to love you, you know. I was five years out of high school and sitting up there on the farm sorting tomatoes every spring. When you asked, it seemed like a good idea to marry. Then the baby came and the war and the awful relocation camps—the price of being a Japanese in America. Then you left with the volunteers, returned once on a furlough, and never came back.

22 There were lots of handsome guys in camp, and lots of cute girls. A widow with a baby didn't have a chance. The smart people got out as soon

as possible and pursued careers. They became nurses, engineers, secretaries, some even doctors. Me, I stayed the whole four years. It was easier that way, with my father and little sister helping with the baby. My mother died the first year we were there. With a lot of pain—she had ulcers.

23 I was old then already, a mother of a baby, a gold-star wife and nothing more. I was never young.

24 Except that once.

25 He came in while my father and sister were at a camp movie or some-place—I don't remember. He waited until he saw them leave. He lived in another block, a stranger. Well, not really. I'd seen him once or twice at the canteen. He had smiled at me. He was older, a Kibei, born in America, edu-cated in Japan. He spoke mostly Japanese. He knocked and opened the door at the same time. I didn't know what to do—what to say. The baby cried and he picked her up. "*Yoshi-yoshi*," he crooned. Then he put her in my arms and left.

26 I lied. I had seen him often. I've told myself so many variations of the story, I can't separate fact from fiction anymore. At the camp talent shows he sang romantic Japanese songs of longing and loneliness. He was not good looking, not very tall, but his arms were strong and his eyes—they looked through you, past your fluttering heart, and all the way down to you-know-where. And when he finally came to see me, I didn't know what to do. Then the baby cried and he sang to her and he left. The only time a man came near me the whole four years. I've clung to this memory through four decades, embellishing it, stripping it to its bone, and putting on the flesh again.

27 He's probably dead now anyway. Everyone is dead: my mother, father, my little sister. I loved her so much. She died before she could fall in love and marry. I had looked forward to it like a mother might; I could share her excitement, I could be happy too. But she died. It was harder to take than Joe's death. I don't know why. I lived with her longer, maybe; I loved her more, maybe. It nearly broke my heart. It broke Pop's, because he didn't live long after that. Everyone was gone then, Joe's parents had returned to Japan with the repatriates (they didn't want Joe to volunteer), and it was just the baby and me. Sometimes in my dreams it all comes back with a suffo-cating longing. Then I wake up and see it's just another day.

28 She efficiently slides the leftovers into one large dish and sets it in the refrigerator. "I put it here, Mom," she says. "Tomorrow you'll set it in the microwave. One minute—no more. Okay? And you'll have a nice turkey dinner again."

29 That means she won't be coming tomorrow. A four-day holiday. Maybe they're going on a trip. That's okay; that's good. I'm glad she's doing for her girls what I couldn't do for her.

30   She was a latchkey kid. By the time we were released from camp, she was in school. I had to go to work. I tied the key on colored ribbons to match her dress. Maybe it's one of those traumas that haunt you later in life, but at the time, she didn't seem to mind. She grew up fast, learning to start dinner, learning to mend and sew her own clothes.

31   She was proud of her competence. She joined every school activity. She got a part-time job—maybe to keep from coming home to an empty apartment. It seems so sad to me now, I want to grab her and say, "I couldn't help it, Baby, forgive me." But she wouldn't like that. She hates tears. She won't let herself cry, and she won't forgive anyone who does.

32   She went to college and got a good job as a legal secretary. That's where she met Fred—a lawyer. She made me take a night course in typing and insisted I apply for civil service. She made me quit my sewing job so I stopped embarrassing her with the lint in my hair and threads on my clothes. It got so you couldn't tell who was the mother and who was the child. Even before the stroke. But I was lucky. I got disability and a pension of sorts.

33   What's she doing now? Running water? But I took a bath yesterday. Oh. She's not coming tomorrow, that's why. She doesn't like me to bathe when she's not here. She's afraid I'll have a stroke and drown, and she'll come by the next day or the day after that and find me in the cold water, face down, my hair floating, the soap all soft and gummy.

34   I want her to say it: "I'm not coming tomorrow," so I shake my head.

35   "You have to take your bath today; I'm not coming by tomorrow," she says. She gets a fresh towel and my change of underwear and hands it to me.

36   Homely underwear. They don't hardly make these anymore. They look like they come from a Salvation Army bin or some cleric's dusty drawer. She thinks I like these no-nonsense kind and goes to considerable lengths to find them.

37   I never had pretty underwear. Joe was appalled when he first saw them. "I thought girls wore pretty things," he said. Not on a farm, they don't. He later bought some lacy rayon things for me. It took a lot of courage to go into the lingerie department, but he did it. It takes a lot of courage to go to war to be shot or to shoot someone. He did that too, and someone shot him.

38   They sent him home a few years after the war ended, when we were already used to not having him around. We buried him in a short Buddhist ceremony in the little cemetery on Normandy Avenue.

39   When she was little she used to say, "Mama, tell me about him," and I would tell her she was Daddy's little honey and that he called her lots of sweet names (he could not call me), and I told her of some incidents that grew worn and changed with each telling. She would laugh with delight. "More! More!" she'd scream.

40   We used to take flowers regularly. She would romp around the mounds and pick other people's flowers and bring them to his headstone. "This is for you, Daddy," she'd say happily. All the people who loved her were buried there or in some other graveyard. She hadn't known any of them, and so she didn't really miss them.

41   As she grew older, she stopped wanting to go to the cemetery, and after a while, when I told those old stories she started saying, "I don't remember that." We went less and less, and toward the end, we even quit the Memorial Day thing.

42   We have forgotten you, Joe. That's the way it is when there is no one around to remember. When I am gone, we will all be forgotten. There'll be no one left to remember how young we were, how handsome, and those . . . well, they're stupid stories anyway. No one laughed at them.

43   The water's too cool for my taste. The bottom of the tub stays cold and I can't warm up. I like my bath hot—the way we always had it, even when we had to draw water from a well and heat it with the desert sage and chaparral. She forgot Mr. Bubbles; the bubbles prevent a ring from forming around the tub. Not that I'm ever that dirty. How dirty can you get moving from bed to TV to table to bath?

44   "I forgot the bubbles," she screams from the kitchen. She is washing the dishes. She comes to the bathroom door. "Did you hear me?" she asks. I rap on the wall. "Put the bubbles in," she says. I rap again. What's the use of wasting my voice on idle words? The things I want to say, she won't hear. "I don't remember," she'll say, or, "Not that story again," and she'll look at her husband.

45   I run the hot water.

46   "Not too hot," she calls. "I don't want you to faint in there."

47   They say drowning is a pleasant way to go. They say that at the end there is such a feeling of euphoria. Maybe it's like going back to the uterus. They say all dying is that way. There's this wonderful light and feeling of joy, and you see the forms of all those you love who have preceded you. I will see my mother and father and my little sister—I love her still—and Joe. I'd be older than all of them. What fun is that? And him.

48   I should have done it the night he came over. The baby cried and he held her and began to sing. He drew me close (what a leaping in my heart), and we put her to bed. He said, "Let's go to bed too."

49   "I can't," I said.

50   "Why?" he asked.

51   "I don't know."

52   "Don't you want me to?" He ended the sentence with a preposition.

53   "No," I lied.

54   "Well, then, we won't." He put his hands up. "Good-bye," he said and left.

55   No, he didn't. He stayed and kissed me and we made love and it was the most wonderful . . . "Wonderful, wonderful," is that the only word I know? He said good-bye and left.

56   I came out of the bathroom and she says, "Did you hear me?"

57   What did she say? "Wonderful, wonderful . . ." No, *I* said that. I shrug.

58   She holds vitamin pills in front of me. "You didn't take them yesterday, did you? I want you to take them while I watch." She gives me a glass of water. I hesitate. "Please?" she asks. She wants me to live longer.

59   I swallow them down.

60   "I don't know why I have to keep reminding you," she says. "I swear, you're worse than the girls. At least the girls . . ."

61   I should have done it. I should have let him do it.

62   "At least the girls . . ."

63   Or did I? Did we do it?

64   ". . . will answer me. At least they do that. I'm not saying . . ."

65   Did I forget? Could I have forgotten such a thing?

66   "They don't always mind, but at least they answer me. Here I don't know if you hear me or not."

67   Naw, I wouldn't have forgotten. Would it have changed my life? I should have. I should have.

68   "Between you and the girls and Fred pulling me apart . . . I don't know what I did to deserve it."

69   Naw. But it's something to remember. At least. "At least it's something to . . ." I blurt it aloud. It comes out aloud.

70   "What?" She's stunned. "What did you say?"

71   I clamp my mouth. Close the gate.

72   " 'At least,' you said. 'At least.' "

73   "So what?" I say.

74   She shakes me. "You can talk!" she screams.

75   "So what?" I say. She heaves great humps of dry tears. "What's the use of talking? There's nothing to say anymore." Aloud. Well, that's not exactly true, but that's the way it came out. The truth is, there's nothing anyone wants to hear anymore.

76   "Mom," she says. She is breathless and almost embraces me but instead veers to the closet. Can't lose your head at a time like this, you know. She riffles through my clothes and brings out a skirt and shirt. She pushed them toward me. "Get dressed," she says, "the girls will want to see you."

77   She wipes her eyes with the sleeve of my shirt.

DISCUSSION QUESTIONS

1. What has caused the mother's dependency?
2. Stream-of-consciousness is a technique used to provide characterization. The term refers both to the organization of thoughts and to the content of those thoughts. For example, note how the mother's thoughts are connected in paragraph 9, which ends with "pyorrhea" and leads to paragraph 10 in which she thinks about the dentist and cooking rice gruel. What starts her thinking about her husband Joe in paragraph 13?
3. When does the mother first realize that her daughter won't be coming the next day and what thoughts does this realization prompt?
4. Find another place in the story where the present prompts the mother's thoughts of the past.
5. How did World War II affect the mother's life?
6. How does the daughter feel about her mother?
7. What is the climax of the story?

WRITING TOPICS

1. In an analytical essay, discuss how the characterization of the mother makes her a realistic character. Consider physical description, personality traits, the content of her thoughts, and her diction.
2. In a brief essay, compare the mother-daughter relationship in this selection and in Cathy Song's "The Youngest Daughter."

BREAKING TRADITION

Janice Mirikitani

Janice Mirikitani, a sansei (third-generation Japanese American), was born in Stockton, California, in 1942. She expends her creative and intellectual energies in several activities: in addition to being a highly visible poet, she is a political activist, a teacher, a dancer, and an editor. She earned an undergraduate degree from the University of California, Los Angeles, and pursued an M.A. in creative writing at San Francisco State University. In addition, Mirikitani has been the program director of the Glide Church/Urban Center since 1967 and the director of the Glide Theater Group. She also serves as the editor of several publications, including *Aion, Third World Women, Time to Greez! Incantations from the Third World,* and *AYUMI.* Her major publications are *Awake in the River* (1978) and *Shedding Silence* (1987).

Literary critic and poet Shirley Geok-lin Lim points out that much of Mirikitani's work "seeks defiantly to break the stereotypes of Asian Americans prevalent in mainstream American culture."[1] In some of her work Mirikitani explicitly explores issues of sexuality and there-fore contests the stereotype of the Asian or Asian American woman as demure and reticent. Other poems deal with the Japanese American community's experiences during World War II; Mirikitani's family, like thousands of other Japanese American families in the western United States, were forced into concentration camps during this dark period of American history. In a poem titled "Breaking Silence," for example, the poet intersperses portions of her mother's testimony before the Commission on Wartime Relocation and Internment with stanzas that celebrate the courage required to speak out against injustice.

In "Breaking Tradition," which is from *Shedding Silence,* a nisei

---

[1] *The Heath Anthology of American Literature,* third edition. (Boston: Heath, 1998) 2989.

(second-generation Japanese American) woman reflects on her mother's struggles with the dislocation of immigration and contrasts her own attempts at self-assertion and assimilation with those of her own daughter. (J.I.)

My daughter denies she is like me,
her secretive eyes avoid mine.
　　She reveals the hatreds of womanhood
　　already veiled behind music and smoke and telephones.
5　I want to tell her about the empty room
　　of myself.
　　This room we lock ourselves in
　　where whispers live like fungus,
　　giggles about small breasts and cellulite,
10　where we confine ourselves to jealousies,
　　bedridden by menstruation.
　　This waiting room where we feel our hands
　　are useless, dead speechless clamps
　　that need hospitals and forceps and kitchens
15　and plugs and ironing boards to make them useful.
　　I deny I am like my mother. I remember why:
　　She kept her room neat with silence,
　　defiance smothered in requirements to be otonashii,[1]
　　passion and loudness wrapped in an obi,
20　her steps confined to ceremony,
　　the weight of her sacrifice she carried like
　　a fetus. Guilt passed on in our bones.
　　I want to break tradition—unlock this room
　　where women dress in the dark.
25　Discover the lies my mother told me.
　　The lies that we are small and powerless
　　that our possibilities must be compressed
　　to the size of pearls, displayed only as
　　passive chokers, charms around our neck.
30　Break Tradition.
　　I want to tell my daughter of this room
　　of myself
　　filled with tears of shakuhachi,[2]

---

[1] *otonashii:* quiet, serene.
[2] *shakuhachi:* a flutelike wind instrument.

the light in my hands,
35 poems about madness,
the music of yellow guitars,
sounds shaken from barbed wire and
goodbyes and miracles of survival.

My daughter denies she is like me
40 her secretive eyes are walls of smoke
and music and telephones.
her pouting ruby lips, her skirts
swaying to salsa, Madonna and the Stones.
her thighs displayed in carnivals of color.
45 I do not know the contents of her room.
She mirrors my aging.

She is breaking tradition.

DISCUSSION QUESTIONS

1. What does it mean to break tradition?
2. Why doesn't the speaker want to be like her mother?
3. Has the speaker broken tradition?
4. Are the speaker and her daughter alike?

WRITING TOPICS

1. A strong motif of imprisonment runs through this poem. In a short essay, examine some of the words and images that contribute to this motif.
2. The speaker uses the metaphor of an empty room to describe herself. Reexamine what is in that room (lines 7–15) and then, in a paragraph, imagine what might fill that empty room instead.
3. From what you have read so far in this anthology, do you think that the concept of tradition in Japanese, Chinese, and Korean society is, for the most part, repressive and inhibiting, or is it a source of comfort, providing a sense of connection to one's roots? Examine this question in an essay.

GARDENS WE HAVE LEFT

David Mura

David Mura, a third-generation Japanese American, was born in 1952, in Illinois. His first book of poetry, *After We Lost Our Way* (1989), was selected by Gerald Stern as a winner of the National Poetry Series Contest. He is also the author of *Turning Japanese: Memoirs of a Sansei* (1991), which has won the Oakland PEN Josephine Miles Book Award, and *A Male Grief: Notes on Pornography and Addiction* (1987). His most recent book of poems is *The Colors of Desire* (1995).

Mura has used different mediums—such as poetry, creative nonfiction, and drama—to produce and perform two multimedia performance pieces, *Relocations: Images from Sansei* and *The Colors of Desire*. The recipient of numerous fellowships, including the U.S.–Japan Creative Arts Exchange Fellowship, N.E.A. Literature Fellowship, and a McKnight Playwright's Center Advancement Grant, he also won a Discovery/*The Nation* Award. Mura earned his B.A. from Grinnell College and did graduate work at the University of Minnesota. He has taught at the University of Minnesota, the Loft, St. Olaf College, and the University of Oregon, and has served as the artistic director of the Asian American Renaissance Conference. He lives in Minneapolis.

In the following poem, Mura uses the images of an interlude in a late-summer garden with his daughter Samantha to connect to a memory of his own father. (J.I.)

As Sam fingers lumps of tofu on her tray,
I sizzle onions in oil, *shoyu*,[1] rice wine,
toss noodles, ginger, sugar, *shitake*,[2]

shoots of bamboo and chrysanthemum leaves.
5   Before the beef, veined with fat, thin as gauze,
I stir what for years I could not love.

(As a child, I shunned *mochi*,[3] *futomaki*,[4]
loved hot dogs, baseball, the GI John Wayne.
Now my *hashi*[5] hauls up steaming *sukiyaki*.[6])

10   Later I take Sam out back, dressed in her *happi*,[7]
and hum to her a nursery ditty
on the devil digging tatties with his shovel.

Yanking drooping petunias, scattering petals
like a cyclone, she tramples through the garden.
15   Soon she's crumbling parsley, mint, basil,

vines blackened dry as ash; now she splatters
tomatoes, half-caved in, shriveling with rot.
If this were August, I'd shout and stop her,

but since it's autumn, the clouds burnished, cool,
20   I let it spill from her, some giggle caught
from you, how her spine stoops and curls

like yours as you weed, trowel or clip flowers.
The air darkens, milky galaxies pour over us.
As I pick her up, Sam points, "Star . . . star . . . star . . ."

25   Feeling her weight, I think how someone
someday will call her *gook,* as surely as
this taste of ginger breathing on my tongue;

---

[1] *shoyu:* soy sauce.
[2] *shitake:* a kind of mushroom.
[3] *mochi:* a rice flour cake noted for its extreme stickiness and usually prepared for the new year.
[4] *futomaki:* a type of sushi.
[5] *hashi:* chopsticks.
[6] *sukiyaki:* a meat and vegetable stew that is usually prepared at the table.
[7] *happi:* a short kimono or jacket.

how the other day at this wedding, you
were matron of honor, and the priest greeted
30   you: "Oh, I've heard so much about you.

You must have such a large heart, it's so
generous of you to adopt this child . . ."
Suddenly, I envision—why would I want to

see this?—a white sheet descending, mapping
35   the body of my father, his dark leathery face
almost blue, like a baby before the slap

that shuttles its howl out to the world.
The sheet washes him from sight, the way
surf sucks up footprints from the shore—

40   Who will tell our daughter about the dark
gardener's boy who swam the Venice surf,
who never returned to L.A. after the war?

A late moth, a few crickets. I hear you call
us, the skin on our bodies, warm at last.
45   A man holds his child, sees his father laid

out in the sleep of his death. The wind
brushes his face. And then, it's his child's hand.

DISCUSSION QUESTIONS

1. This poem encompasses the present, the future, and the past of a family. What events take place in the present?
2. What do the speaker's food preferences tell you about him?
3. Who is the "you" in the poem?
4. What may the priest's remark reveal about the speaker's family?
5. What happened to the speaker's father, and why would the speaker think of his father as he holds his daughter?

WRITING TOPICS

1. In a brief essay, explore the sensory details the author uses in this poem and discuss what they contribute to the poem. Cite examples from the poem to support your views.
2. In a brief essay, discuss the tone or mood of this poem and how it is conveyed.

THE EVE OF THE SPIRIT FESTIVAL

Lan Samantha Chang

Lan Samantha Chang graduated from the Iowa Writers' Workshop and is a former Wallace Stegner Fellow at Stanford University, where she now teaches creative writing. She is the recipient of a number of fellowships, and her stories have appeared in many journals, including *The Atlantic Monthly* and *Story,* and in anthologies such as *The Best American Short Stories 1994* and *The Best American Short Stories 1996.* Her first collection of stories, *Hunger,* came out in 1999.

In "The Eve of the Spirit Festival," Emily, the eldest of two sisters, blames her father for the mother's death and resents his attempts to be like his American colleagues. The younger sister, Claudia, senses that despite his clashes with his elder daughter, the father loves Emily more.

1   After the Buddhist ceremony, when our mother's spirit had been chanted to a safe passage and her body cremated, Emily and I sat silently on our living room carpet. She held me in her arms, her long hair stuck to our wet faces. We sat as stiffly as temple gods except for the angry thump of my sister's heart against my cheek.

2   Finally she spoke. "It's Baba's fault," she said. "The American doctors would have fixed her."

3   I was six years old—I only knew that our father and mother had decided against an operation. And I had privately agreed, imagining the doctors tearing a hole in her body. As I thought of this, and other things, I felt a violent sob pass through me.

4   "Don't cry, Baby," Emily whispered. "You're okay." I felt my tears dry to salt, my throat lock shut.

5   Then our father walked into the room.

6   He and Emily had become quite close in the past few months. Emily was eleven, old enough to visit my mother when it had become clear that the hospital was the only option. But now she refused to acknowledge him.

7   "First daughter—" he began.

8   "Go away, Baba," Emily said. Her voice shook. She put her hand on the back of my head and turned me away from him also. The evening sun glowed garnet red through the dark tent of her hair.

9   "You said she would get better," I heard her say. "Now you're burning paper money for her ghost. What good will that do?"

10   "I am sorry," our father said.

11   "I don't care."

12   Her voice burned. I squirmed beneath her hand, but she wouldn't let me look. It was between her and Baba. I watched his black wingtip shoes retreat to the door. When he had gone, Emily let go of me. I sat up and looked at her; something had changed. Not in the lovely outlines of her face—our mother's face—but in her eyes, shadow-black, lost in unforgiveness.

13   They say the dead return to us. But we never saw our mother again, although we kept a kind of emptiness waiting in case she might come back. I listened always, seeking her voice, the lost thread of a conversation I'd been too young to have with her. Emily rarely mentioned our mother, and soon my memories faded. I could not picture her. I saw only Emily's angry face, the late sun streaking red through her dark hair.

14   After the traditional forty-nine-day mourning period, Baba didn't set foot in the Buddhist temple. It was as if he had listened to Emily: what good did it do? Instead he focused on earthly ambitions, his research at the lab.

15   At that time he aspired beyond the position of lab instructor to the rank of associate professor, and he often invited his American colleagues over for "drinks." After our mother died, Emily and I were recruited to help. As we went about our tasks, we would sometimes catch a glimpse of our father standing in the corner, watching the American men and studying to become one.

16   But he couldn't get it right—our parties had an air of cultural confusion. We served potato chips on lacquered trays; Chinese landscapes burned against watercolors of the Statue of Liberty, the Empire State Building.

17   Nor were Emily or I capable of helping him. I was still a child, and Emily didn't care. She had grown beyond us; she stalked around in blue jeans, seething with fury at everything to do with him.

18   "I hate this," she said, fiercely ripping another rag from a pair of old pajama bottoms. "Entertaining these jerks is a waste of time." Some chemists from Texas were visiting his department and he had invited them over for cocktails.

19   "I can finish it," I said. "You just need to do the parts I can't reach."

20   "It's not the dusting," she said. "It's the way he acts around them. 'Herro, herro! Hi Blad, hi Warry! Let me take your coat! Howsa Giants game?' " she mimicked. "If he were smart he wouldn't invite people over on football afternoons in the first place."

21   "What do you mean?" I said, worried that something was wrong. Brad Delmonte was my father's boss. I had noticed Baba reading the sports page that morning—something he rarely did.

22   "Oh, forget it," Emily said. I felt as if she and I were utterly separate. Then she smiled. "You've got oil on your glasses, Claudia."

23   Baba walked in carrying two bottles of wine. "They should arrive in half an hour," he said, looking at his watch. "They won't be early. Americans are never early."

24   Emily looked up. "I'm going to Jodie's house," she said.

25   Baba frowned and straightened his tie. "I want you to stay while they're here. We might need something from the kitchen."

26   "Claudia can get it for them."

27   "She's barely tall enough to reach the cabinets."

28   Emily stood up, clenched her dustcloth. "I don't care," she said. "I hate meeting those men."

29   "They're successful American scientists. You'd be better off with them instead of running around with your teenage friends, these sloppy kids, these rich white kids who dress like beggars."

30   "You're nuts, Dad," Emily said—she had begun addressing him the way an American child does. "You're nuts if you think these bosses of yours are ever going to do anything for you or any of us." And she threw her dustcloth, hard, into our New York Giants wastebasket.

31   "Speak to me with respect."

32   "You don't deserve it!"

33   "You are staying in this apartment! That is an order!"

34   "I wish you'd died instead of Mama!" Emily cried, and ran out of the room. She darted past our father, her long braid flying behind her. He stared at her, his expression oddly slack, the way it had been in the weeks after the funeral. He stepped toward her, reached hesitantly at her flying braid, but she turned and saw him, cried out as if he had struck her. His hands dropped to his sides.

35   Emily refused to leave our room. Otherwise that party was like so many others. The guests arrived late and left early. They talked about buying new cars and the Dallas Cowboys. I served pretzels and salted nuts. Baba walked around emptying ashtrays and refilling drinks. I noticed that the other men also wore vests and ties, but that the uniform looked somehow different on my slighter, darker father.

36   "Cute little daughter you have there," said Baba's boss. He was a large bearded smoker with a sandy voice. He didn't bend down to look at me or the ashtray that I raised toward his big square hand.

37   I went into our room and found Emily sitting on one of our unmade twin beds. It was dusk. Through the window the dull winter sun had almost disappeared. She didn't look up when I came in, but after a moment she spoke.

38   "I'm going to leave," she said. "As soon as I turn eighteen, I'm going to leave home and never come back!" She burst into tears. I reached for her shoulder but her thin, heaving body frightened me. She seemed too grown up to be comforted. I thought about the breasts swelling beneath the sweater. Her body had become a foreign place.

39   Perhaps Emily had warned me that she would someday leave in order to start me off on my own. I found myself avoiding her, as though her impending desertion would matter less if I deserted her first. I discovered a place to hide while she and my father fought, in the living room behind a painted screen. I would read a novel or look out the window. Sometimes they forgot about me—from the next room I would hear one of them break off an argument and say, "Where did Claudia go?" "I don't know," the other would reply. After a silence, they would start again.

40   One of these fights stands out in my memory. I must have been ten or eleven years old. It was the fourteenth day of the seventh lunar month: the eve of Guijie, the Chinese Spirit Festival, when the living are required to appease and provide for the ghosts of their ancestors. To the believing, the earth was thick with gathering spirits; it was safest to stay indoors and burn incense.

41   I seldom thought about the Chinese calendar, but every year on Guijie I wondered about my mother's ghost. Where was it? Would it still recognize me? How would I know when I saw it? I wanted to ask Baba, but I didn't dare. Baba had an odd attitude toward Guijie. On one hand, he had eschewed all Chinese customs since my mother's death. He was a scientist, he said; he scorned the traditional tales of unsatisfied spirits roaming the earth.

42   But I cannot remember a time when I was not made aware, in some way, of Guijie's fluctuating lunar date. That year the eve of the Spirit Festival fell on a Thursday, usually his night out with the men from his department. Emily and I waited for him to leave, but he sat on the couch, calmly reading the *New York Times*.

43   Around seven o'clock, Emily began to fidget. She had a date that night and had counted on my father's absence. She spent half an hour washing and combing her hair, trying to make up her mind. Finally she asked me to give her a trim. I knew she'd decided to go out.

44   "Just a little," she said. "The ends are scraggly." We spread some newspapers on the living room floor. Emily stood in the middle of the papers with her hair combed down her back, thick and glossy, black as ink. It hadn't really

been cut since she was born. Since my mother's death I had taken over the task of giving it the periodic touchup.

45 I hovered behind her with the shears, searching for the scraggly ends, but there were none.

46 My father looked up from his newspaper. "What are you doing that for? You can't go out tonight," he said.

47 "I have a date."

48 My father put down his newspaper. I threw the shears onto a chair and fled to my refuge behind the screen.

49 Through a slit over the hinge I caught a glimpse of Emily near the foyer, slender in her denim jacket, her black hair flooding down her back, her delicate features contorted with anger. My father's hair was disheveled, his hands clenched at his sides. The newspapers had scattered over the floor.

50 "Dressing up in boys' clothes, with paint on your face—"

51 "This is nothing! My going out on a few dates is nothing! You don't know what the hell you're talking about!"

52 "Don't shout." My father shook his finger. "Everyone in the building will hear you."

53 Emily raised her voice. "Who the hell cares? You're such a coward, you care more about what other people think than how I feel!"

54 "Acting like a loose woman in front of everybody, a streetwalker!"

55 The floor shook under my sister's stamp. Though I'd covered my ears, I could hear her crying. The door slammed, and her footfalls vanished down the stairs.

56 Things were quiet for a minute. Then I heard my father walk toward my corner. My heart thumped with fear—usually he let me alone. I had to look up when I heard him move the screen away. He knelt down next to me. His hair was streaked with gray, and his glasses needed cleaning.

57 "What are you doing?" he asked.

58 I shook my head, nothing.

59 After a minute I asked him, "Is Guijie why you didn't go play bridge tonight, Baba?"

60 "No, Claudia," he said. He always called me by my American name. This formality, I thought, was an indication of how distant he felt from me. "I stopped playing bridge last week."

61 "Why?" We both looked toward the window, where beyond our reflections the Hudson River flowed in the darkness.

62 "It's not important," he said.

63 "Okay."

64 But he didn't leave. "I'm getting old," he said after a moment. "Someone ten years younger was just promoted over me. I'm not going to try to keep up with them anymore."

65 It was the closest he had ever come to confiding in me. After a few more

minutes he stood up and went into the kitchen. The newspapers rustled under his feet. For almost half an hour I heard him fumbling through the kitchen cabinets, looking for something he'd probably put there years ago. Eventually he came out, carrying a small brass urn and some matches. When Emily returned home after midnight, the apartment still smelled of the incense he had burned to protect her while she was gone.

66   My father loved Emily more. I knew this in my bones: it was why I stayed at home every night and wore no makeup, why I studied hard and got good grades, why I eventually went to college at Columbia, right up the street. Jealously I guarded my small allotment of praise, clutching it like a pocket of precious stones. Emily snuck out of the apartment late at night; she wore high-heeled sandals with patched blue jeans; she twisted her long hair into graceful, complex loops and braids that belied respectability. She smelled of lipstick and perfume. So certain she was of my father's love. His anger was a part of it. I knew nothing I could ever do would anger him that way.

67   When Emily turned eighteen and did leave home, a part of my father disappeared. I wondered sometimes, where did it go? Did she take it with her? What secret charm had she carried with her as she vanished down the tunnel to the jet that would take her to college in California, steadily and without looking back, while my father and I watched silently from the window at the gate? The apartment afterward became quite still—it was only the two of us, mourning and dreaming through pale blue winter afternoons and silent evenings.

68   Emily called me, usually late at night after my father had gone to sleep. She sent me pictures of herself and people I didn't know, smiling on the sunny Berkeley campus. Sometimes after my father and I ate our simple meals or TV dinners I would go into our old room, where I had kept both of our twin beds, and take out Emily's pictures, trying to imagine what she must have been feeling, studying her expression and her swinging hair. But I always stared the longest at a postcard she'd sent me one winter break from northern New Mexico, a professional photo of a powerful, vast blue sky over faraway pink and sandy-beige mesas. The clarity and cleanness fascinated me. In a place like that, I thought, there would be nothing to search for, no reason to hide.

69   After college, she went to work at a bank in San Francisco. I saw her once when she flew to Manhattan on business. She skipped a meeting to have lunch with me. She wore an elegant gray suit and had pinned up her hair.

70   "How's Dad?" she said. I looked around, slightly alarmed. We were sitting in a bistro on the East Side, but I somehow thought he might overhear us.

71   "He's okay," I said. "We don't talk very much. Why don't you come home and see him?"

72 Emily stared at her water glass. "I don't think so."

73 "He misses you."

74 "I know. I don't want to hear about it."

75 "You hardly ever call him."

76 "There's nothing to talk about. Don't tell him you saw me, promise?"

77 "Okay."

78 During my junior year at Columbia, my father suffered a stroke. He was fifty-nine years old, and he was still working as a lab instructor in the chemistry department. One evening in early fall I came home from a class and found him on the floor near the kitchen telephone. He was wearing his usual vest and tie. I called the hospital and sat down next to him. His wire-rimmed glasses lay on the floor a foot away. One half of his face was frozen, the other half lined with sudden age and pain.

79 "They said they'll be right here," I said. "It won't be very long." I couldn't tell how much he understood. I smoothed his vest and straightened his tie. I folded his glasses. I knew he wouldn't like it if the ambulance workers saw him in a state of dishevelment. "I'm sure they'll be here soon," I said.

80 We waited. Then I noticed he was trying to tell me something. A line of spittle ran from the left side of his mouth. I leaned closer. After a while I made out his words: "Tell Emily," he said.

81 The ambulance arrived as I picked up the telephone to call California. That evening, at the hospital, what was remaining of my father left the earth.

82 Emily insisted that we not hold a Buddhist cremation ceremony. "I never want to think about that stuff again," she said. "Plus, all of his friends are Americans. I don't know who would come, except for us." She had reached New York the morning after his death. Her eyes were vague and her fingernails bitten down.

83 On the third day we scattered his ashes in the river. Afterward we held a small memorial service for his friends from work. We didn't talk much as we straightened the living room and dusted the furniture. It took almost three hours. The place was a mess. We hadn't had a party in years.

84 It was a cloudy afternoon, and the Hudson looked dull and sluggish from the living room window. I noticed that although she had not wanted a Buddhist ceremony, Emily had dressed in black and white according to Chinese mourning custom. I had asked the department secretary to put up a sign on the bulletin board. Eleven people came; they drank five bottles of wine. Two of his Chinese students stood in the corner, eating cheese and crackers.

85 Brad Delmonte, paunchy and no longer smoking, attached himself to Emily. "I remember when you were just a little girl," I heard him say as I walked by with the extra crackers.

86 "I don't remember you," she said.

87   "You're still a cute little thing." She bumped his arm, and he spilled his drink.

88   Afterward we sat on the couch and surveyed the cluttered coffee table. It was past seven but we didn't talk about dinner.

89   "I'm glad they came," I said.

90   "I hate them," Emily looked at her fingernails. Her voice shook. "I don't know whom I hate more, them or him—for taking it."

91   "It doesn't matter anymore," I said.

92   "I suppose."

93   We watched the room grow dark.

94   "Do you know what?" Emily said. "It's the eve of the fifteenth day of the seventh lunar month."

95   "How do you know?" During college I had grown completely unaware of the lunar calendar.

96   "One of those chemistry nerds from China told me this afternoon."

97   I wanted to laugh, but instead felt myself make a strange whimpering sound, squeezed out from my tight and hollow chest.

98   "Remember the time Dad and I had that big fight?" she said. "You know that now, in my grownup life, I don't fight with anyone? I never had problems with anybody except him."

99   "No one cared about you as much as he did," I said.

100   "I don't want to hear about it." Her voice began to shake again. "He was a pain, and you know it. He got so strict after Mama died. It wasn't all my fault."

101   "I'm sorry," I said. But I was so angry with her that I felt my face turn red, my cheeks tingle in the dark. She'd considered our father a nerd as well, had squandered his love with such thoughtlessness that I could scarcely breathe to think about it. It seemed impossibly unfair that she had memories of my mother, as well. Carefully I waited for my feelings to go away. Emily, I thought, was all I had.

102   But as I sat, a vision distilled before my eyes: the soft baked shades, the great blue sky of New Mexico. I realized that after graduation I could go wherever I wanted. Somewhere a secret, rusty door swung open and filled my mind with sweet freedom, fearful coolness.

103   "I want to do something," I said.

104   "Like what?"

105   "I don't know." Then I got an idea. "Emily, why don't I give you a haircut?"

106   We found newspapers and spread them on the floor. We turned on the lamps and moved the coffee table out of the way, took the wineglasses to the sink. Emily went to the bathroom, and I searched for the shears a long time before I found them in the kitchen. I glimpsed the incense urn in a cabinet and quickly shut the door. When I returned to the living room, it smelled

of shampoo. Emily was standing in the middle of the papers with her wet hair down her back, staring at herself in the reflection from the window. The lamplight cast circles under her eyes.

107 "I had a dream last night," she said. "I was walking down the street. I felt a tug. He was trying to reach me, trying to pull my hair."

108 "I'll just give you a trim," I said.

109 "No," she said. "Why don't you cut it?

110 "What do you mean?" I snapped a two-inch lock off the side. Emily looked down at the hair on the newspapers. "I'm serious," she said. "Cut my hair. I want to see two feet of hair on the floor."

111 "Emily, you don't know what you're saying." I said. But a strange, weightless feeling had come over me. I placed the scissors at the nape of her neck. "How about it?" I asked, and my voice sounded low and odd.

112 "*I don't care.*" An echo of the past. I cut. The shears went *snack*. A long black lock of hair hit the newspapers by my feet.

113 The Chinese say that our hair and our bodies are given to us from our ancestors, gifts that should not be tampered with. My mother herself had never done this. But after the first few moments I enjoyed myself, pressing the thick black locks through the shears, heavy against my thumb. Emily's hair slipped to the floor around us, rich and beautiful, lying in long graceful arcs over my shoes. She stood perfectly still, staring out the window. The Hudson River flowed behind our reflections, bearing my father's ashes through the night.

114 When I was finished, the back of her neck gleamed clean and white under a precise shining cap. "You missed your calling," Emily said. "You want me to do yours?"

115 My hair, browner and scragglier, had never been past my shoulders. I had always kept it short, figuring the ancestors wouldn't be offended by my tampering with a lesser gift. "No," I said. "But you should take a shower. Some of those small bits will probably itch."

116 "It's already ten o'clock," she said. "We should go to sleep soon anyway." Satisfied, she glanced at the mirror in the foyer. "I look like a completely different person," she said. She left to take her shower. I wrapped up her hair in the newspapers and went into the kitchen. I stood next to the sink for a long time before throwing the bundle away.

117 The past sees through all attempts at disguise. That night I was awakened by a wrenching scream. I gasped and stiffened, grabbing a handful of blanket.

118 "*Claudia,*" Emily cried from the other bed. "Claudia, wake up!"

119 "What is it?"

120 "I saw Baba." She hadn't called our father Baba in years. "Over there, by the door. Did you see him?"

121   "No," I said. "I didn't see anything." My bones felt frozen in place. After a moment I opened my eyes. The full moon shone through the window, bathing our room in silver and shadow. I heard my sister sob and then fall silent. I looked carefully at the door, but I noticed nothing.

122   Then I understood that his ghost would never visit me. I was, one might say, the lucky daughter. But I lay awake until morning, waiting; part of me is waiting still.

DISCUSSION QUESTIONS

1. What are the conflicts in this story?
2. What kind of relationship does the narrator, Claudia, have with her sister?
3. Why didn't Emily want to help entertain her father's visitors?
4. Describe Claudia, referring to passages in the story to support your description.
5. Of what significance is the title of the story?
6. The narrator feels that Emily squandered her father's love. What does she mean?

WRITING TOPICS

1. With which of the two sisters do you sympathize most? In a paper, explain reasons for your choice.
2. In an essay tell how the first-person point of view of this story affects the style (diction, imagery, syntax, and organization).

VISITATION

Jaime Jacinto

Jamie Jacinto was born in 1954 and grew up in San Francisco. He received a B.A. from the University of California, Santa Cruz, where he studied under William Everson and George Hitchcock. He has completed an M.A. in TEFL (teaching English as a foreign language) and is working on his first book of poems. Jacinto's poetry has been anthologized in *Dissident Song* (1991) and *Premonitions* (1995), and he coedited *Without Names,* a collection of poetry by Bay Area Filipino American writers (1997).

In "Visitation," the approaching spring brings memories of the poet's ancient grandfather, whose ties to the earth seemed almost mystical to the poet's young former self.

It is spring today
and I think of him
kneeling beside me
this companion
5 who was my father's father,
who appeared one day
and stayed with us,
never to leave the house—
all day dressed in pajamas
10 shuffling in his slippers
down the back stairs
to the garden where we'd watch him
bunching the dead leaves
tamping the pulpy soil
15 flicking the hollow shells of dead beetles.
He would tend his garden

day by day, little by little
brushing away the loose earth,
the soggy crumbs of moss
20　until his fingers found
what they had wanted.
From a fist full of black earth—
the pale green sprouts
more delicate than morning light.
25　Now years later when I'm nearly asleep
listening to the slow movements
of animals, the rustle of leaves
where their paws might fall,
he returns, ancient, waving
30　his leathery hands,
knuckles nicked by thorns.
I hear him whispering
our names, and the night breeze passes
over us with the first sliver of moonlight.

DISCUSSION QUESTIONS

1. Even though the speaker remembers his grandfather as an old man, what words indicate that his grandfather was still active?
2. Is this a poem about a ghost or about a strong, sharp memory?

WRITING TOPICS

1. Both this poem and Li-Young Lee's "The Gift" recollect interactions with older relatives (in Jacinto's case, his grandfather; in Lee's, his father). In a brief essay, compare the tone of the two poems. What emotions seem most prevalent in each?

Summary Writing Topics

1. Both Cathy Song's "The Youngest Daughter" and Wakako Yamauchi's "So What; Who Cares?" deal with daughters taking care of their aging mothers. In an essay, compare the impact of the selections and how their genres (one is a poem; one is a story) contribute to that impact. Is one more effective than the other because of its genre?

2. The selections by Amy Tan and Janice Mirikitani explore the passing on of traditions and personality traits from mothers to daughters. The Tan selection is told from the daughter's viewpoint, while the Mirikitani poem is narrated by the mother. In an essay, explore the similarities and differences the daughters in these selections show as they either fight against or embrace their mothers' heritage.

3. For the most part, the relationships between sons and parents in the selections in this chapter are less troubled than the relationships between daughters and parents. In an essay, explore this phenomenon, citing examples from several selections, and speculate on its cause.

4. In a personal essay, choose one selection from this chapter in which the parent-child relationship most closely resembles your own relationship with a parent. Describe the similarities and what effect the selection had on you as you read it.

5. In an analytical essay, compare the tone of three of the poems in this chapter. Cite words and lines from the poems to illustrate how the authors' choice of words and line breaks affects the tone and mood.

CHAPTER SEVEN

AMERICAN PLACE AND DISPLACEMENT

As immigrants from the Asian continent whose presence in U.S. society was historically unwelcome, Asian Americans share a history of struggles to overcome exclusion. The struggle was not only political but social, as their cultural beliefs and customs were and are excluded from everyday American life. These struggles mark the sensibility of many Asian American writers in a distinctive manner. Their works not only look back to an original non-American homeland, as seen in the selections in Chapter Two, but are expressive of the difficult process of change and displacement, as individuals evolve their consciousness, adjust, adapt (or fail to do so), resist, critique, or question both their exclusion from and their assimilation into American society.

There is no one given approach to the complex experiences of socialization and the formation of individual and collective identities. Each Asian American author, each Asian American work, offers a different perspective and a different story, and as readers we may have very different responses to these works. Marilyn Chin's "We Are Americans Now, We Live in the Tundra" is a semihumorous poem that wryly observes the cultural disjunctures that Chinese Americans experience in the United States. The poem's speaker, now living in San Francisco, can only imagine China through a sentimental haze. China is no longer a lived reality but an extinct memory. Chinese Americans, now culturally constituted as American citizens, share an American culture that is logical, urban, and mobile. Ironically, although the Chinese had historically been fearful of all things Western, Chinese Americans are now inhabitants of this cultural and territorial construct known as the West.

The first chapter of Kim Ronyoung's novel *Clay Walls* offers a similar theme on the displacement of immigrant Korean Americans who lost their original high social positions when they entered the United States. Haesu, a high-born (*yangban*) woman in Korea, is forced to clean the toilet of a white woman when she attempts to find work as a domestic in the United States. Haesu sees Mrs. Randolph as a *sangnyun*, or low-class person, and quits her job. Her husband, who is from the lower class in Korea, does not share her distaste for such "demeaning work," and her best friend Clara is determined to "get used to America," a process that includes imitating the culture that Hollywood movies sell. These displacements of class and culture will eventually wreck Haesu's marriage and destroy Clara.

Wendy Law-Yone's novel *The Coffin Tree* describes the culture shock of such displacement: "awkward as the astronauts' first steps in the atmosphere of the moon." Moving from a nontechnological rural society to New York, the refugee brother and sister from Burma receive no help from the man whom their father had claimed had received funds for them. Facing winter for the first time, the sister finds a job, then loses it, and the brother falls ill and becomes more isolated. Social displacement has severe psychological consequences, and America, often mythologized as the land of milk and honey, is for many Asian immigrants a terrifying and fearful place of suffering.

David Wong Louie's story also has a couple as its major characters. Like Haesu in *Clay Walls*, Mrs. Chow is a proud and sensitive woman who dislikes the way her employer, a widow, treats her. Her husband is a less imaginative and less adventurous character who accepts his lowly position in U.S. society. The story suggests that resistant characters like Mrs. Chow are the rightful descendants of pioneering Chinese Americans. The story offers a moment of epiphany when Mrs. Chow wraps her arms around a little girl on a carnival ride. At this moment, when she becomes "anchored by another's being," she recognizes her relationship to another person in the United States, and her vision changes from "the land on the other side"—China—to America. Significantly, it is also the moment when she begins to show her husband that she can read and speak English fluently.

Bienvenido Santos's "Scent of Apples," told from the point of view of a visiting professor from the Philippines, focuses on the emotional and economic condition of exile in its characterization of an immigrant farmer from the Philippines. The narrator is introduced to Fabia's faithful wife, Ruth, a white woman who is just "like our own Filipino women." Living in the Midwest, and perhaps even more economically deprived than he had been in the Philippines, Fabia is nostalgic for a homeland he has not seen in twenty years. The narrator views Fabia as a lost spirit, whose yearning for his homeland is captured in his idealization of the Filipino woman, and whose American wife and son offer a tentative balance to his inner desolation.

Lan Cao's *Monkey Bridge* brings a new Asian American community into view. The story is told from the point of view of a Vietnamese American woman, and the chapter excerpted here imagines the relationship between the Americanized daughter and her mother, whose Vietnamese cultural self "became undone in our new life." The daughter narrates the reversal of roles as the mother fails to adjust to the new language and the strange social interactions. The story is not a simple retelling of an immigrant experience but lays out a specific complicated position for immigrants from Vietnam, a country whose role in the history of the United States' unsuccessful military adventures in Southeast Asia is significant for the immigrants' uneasy and ambivalent relationship to the American nation. To the Vietnamese American characters in the novel, America's promise of freedom is therefore both a serious ideal and an ironic one, not to be trusted, composed of "promises, real and hypothesized, . . . made as extravagantly as they could be broken."

M. Evelina Galang's short story, "Our Fathers," is also a daughter's story, only this time the author portrays a daughter's loving relationship with her father, Danilo. Tessa's curiosity about her grandparents in the Philippines is part of a familial intimacy that, despite the displacement of the characters to the United States, remains grounded in a larger communal setting. Like her father, Tessa is looking forward to the family's being reunited in the United States. Instead, the grandfather's death sends the father back to the Philippines for the funeral. Both Danila's grief when he first hears the news and Tessa's grief when she views a video of the funeral underline the theme of a double rupture. The generational break is compounded by the communal break, which Tessa begins to understand as she views the scene of the crowd of mourning Filipino relatives in the video. In their American life, the story suggests, Filipino communal or extended-family relationships become reduced to images in pictures, and even the closeness of an American family life does not compensate for that loss.

Poet Marilyn Chin and novelist Gish Jen, both born in 1955, share a desire to develop strong female voices in their respective literary genres. The title character in Jen's *Mona in the Promised Land,* for instance, befuddles her parents with her strong will and wisecracking wit. The female speakers in Chin's poetry, although usually more serious in tone, share with Jen's heroines a confidence, verbal agility, and active imagination that topple the stereotype of the silent, passive Chinese-American woman.

Helen and Ralph, the two Chinese American immigrants in Gish Jen's novel *Typical American* have been cheated out of their business by Ralph's partner, Grover, and have just come through a crisis in their marriage. Ralph adopts a puppy, which the family names Grover, and spends his time training it. The chapter presents Ralph's relationship with the dog as a displacement of his anxiety over his financial precariousness. His mastery over

Grover the dog allows Ralph to overcome the feelings of inadequacy that had been stirred by his failure in dealing with Grover the business partner. The chapter humorously portrays owning a dog as a therapeutic form of American socialization that makes Ralph a more successful man in his relationships with his wife and daughters.

The last prose narrative offers a very different version of the Asian American diasporic experience. The passage from *My Own Country*, Abraham Verghese's memoir, introduces us to a more recent Asian American community, composed of members from groups who have earlier emigrated from an original national territory. The narrator's parents, for example, had emigrated from Ethiopia from India, and in coming to the United States after completing his medical degree in India, the narrator finds himself reproducing his parents' diasporic, or wandering and unsettled, condition. In contrast to the Filipino American stories, *My Own Country* does not construct an original homeland to which its characters can imagine returning. Instead, the memoir draws a picture of diasporic professionals—in this case, foreign medical workers—who share a cosmopolitan consciousness even as they look for employment all over the United States. Abraham, as both the storyteller and the major character, offers a fascinating report of a newly emerging subcommunity of South Asian doctors who are attempting to preserve their cultural and religious identity at the same time that they are being assimilated into mainstream U.S. society.

"Dreamhouse," by R. Zamora Linmark, is a short story that encapsulates many of the themes that organize the chapters in this anthology. Set in Hawaii, the narrative action focuses on the separation between rich and poor, Americans of Asian descent and white Americans. Four children, whose names imply their different ethnic identities, are selling chocolates door-to-door to raise funds to send the narrator/main character to summer camp. Their quest brings them through a mixed neighborhood when, with only three boxes left to sell, they arrive at the largest, richest-looking house on the street, a house in which they know one of their white schoolmates lives. The children are disillusioned when they discover that their schoolmate's family has deliberately refused to open the door to them. While the story marks the four friends as nonwhite and poor, it also contrasts their supportive companionship with the isolated and aloof society of the rich white family. It suggests that wealth and white privilege, in the image of the dreamhouse, may be viewed as desirable attributes, but they also isolate and imprison subjects in their individual selfishness.

The three poems in this second half of the chapter, Diana Chang's "Foreign Ways," Linh Dinh's "The Dead," and Eric Chock's "Chinese Fireworks Banned in Hawaii," treat issues of identity, place, and displacement. Chang's poem notes that even a shift in place and language—moving to China and speaking Mandarin—does not make a Chinese out of a Chinese

American. The emphasis in her poem is on the subjectivity, the interior feeling of *who* one is, of the Asian American individual whose Americanness is "betrayed" or revealed by her voice and physical movements. "The Dead" makes a similar observation, this time of Vietnamese who now live in California but who have carried their histories and memories with them to their new country. These Vietnamese "selves," supposedly dead in the United States, "are not dead" although they may have changed their names. In fact, the poem notes ironically, the survivors of the war in Vietnam continue to relive their traumatic histories, "to dig up the dead . . . shoot them again." "The Dead" makes a point about the role of traumatic memories in a Vietnamese American community that remains obsessed with its military past.

Eric Chock's poem makes a counterpoint about the loss of ethnic cultural practices in the United States and the necessity of resisting the loss of this specific history. Taking the banning of Chinese New Year fireworks in Hawaii in 1987 as its occasion, the poem creates a detailed celebratory picture of a family reunion that also suggests a larger celebratory history of Chinese Hawaiians living in Honolulu: "the collected smoke of our consciousness / floats over Honolulu, as it has / each year for the last century." The fireworks form part of Chinese cultural practices handed down through the generations, which have now become part of Hawaiian culture. The ban, however, places this Chinese Hawaiian culture in jeopardy; it is now "history," rather than part of a living social relation.

These selections exhibit the range of particular imaginations that fill Asian Americans' works; whether humorous, ironic, pathetic, tragic, critical, or celebratory, Asian American writers try to find their place in U.S. history and society. Finding one's place may also result in finding that one has been displaced. Knowledge of belonging is crucially related to acknowledging where we do not belong, and both knowledges are not static; they change and mutate as our subjectivities and identities undergo historical and personal transformation. Whether it is American place, no-place, another national place, or multiple places that make up our memories and our comfort zones, these selections always remind us that we have to read with specific national ethnic contexts in mind.

WE ARE AMERICANS NOW, WE LIVE IN THE TUNDRA

Marilyn Chin

Marilyn Chin was born in Hong Kong in 1955 and raised in Portland, Oregon. She studied ancient Chinese literature at the University of Massachusetts, Amherst; earned an M.F.A. from the University of Iowa; and received a Stegner Fellowship from Stanford. Chin has published two collections of poetry—*Dwarf Bamboo* (1987) and *The Phoenix Gone, the Terrace Empty* (1994)—and other poems have appeared in *The Iowa Review, Ploughshares, The Kenyon Review,* and *Parnassus: Poetry in Review.* In addition to several awards and recognitions, Chin has been an artist in residence at Yaddo, the MacDowell Colony, the Virginia Center for the Creative Arts, and the Djerassi Foundation. She currently teaches creative writing at San Diego State University.

In several poems, Chin explores what it means to be a Chinese American woman who experiences the pull of both Chinese and non-Chinese cultures, the pressures of assimilation, the conflicts of gender and sexuality, and the tensions between generations. In much of her work, Chin examines these issues with a powerful and often self-reflective voice that still allows at times for a certain ambiguity.

In the following poem, images of old-country plants and animals are evoked to contrast East and West. The failure of the pandas to reproduce in the alien Western zoo speaks to the sense of separation and loss felt by their human counterparts. (J.I.)

Today in hazy San Francisco, I face seaward
Toward China, a giant begonia—

Pink, fragrant, bitten
By verdigris and insects. I sing her

5   A blues song; even a Chinese girl gets the blues,
Her reticence is black and blue.

Let's sing about the extinct
Bengal tigers, about giant Pandas—

"Ling Ling loves Xing Xing[1] . . . yet,
10   We will not mate. We are

Not impotent, we are important.
We blame the environment, we blame the zoo!"

What shall we plant for the future?
Bamboo, sasagrass, coconut palms? No!

15   Legumes, wheat, maize, old swines
To milk the new.

We are Americans now, we live in the tundra
Of the logical, a sea of cities, a wood of cars.

Farewell my ancestors:
20   Hirsute Taoists, failed scholars, farewell

My wetnurse who feared and loathed the Catholics,
Who called out:

Now that the half-men have occupied Canton
Hide your daughters, lock your doors!

---

[1] *Ling Ling loves Xing Xing:* two pandas brought to the Washington D.C. zoo from China in the hope that they would mate.

DISCUSSION QUESTIONS

1. Why is the speaker blue?
2. What is the metaphor for China, and why does the speaker say it is "bitten / By verdigris and insects"?
3. Why does the speaker contrast the plants in stanzas 7 and 8?
4. What does the phrase "tundra / Of the logical" convey about America?

WRITING TOPICS

1. In a brief essay, explore the metaphors in this poem and what they contribute to the overall effect.

FROM *CLAY WALLS*

Kim Ronyoung

Kim Ronyoung (Gloria Hahn) was born in Los Angeles in 1926 and died in 1987. For the first nineteen years of her life, she lived in a Korean community. Her parents had immigrated to the United States from North Korea. Her mother was from the educated upper class and her father from a farming family, social details that she included in her semi-autobiographical novel, *Clay Walls*. She married a Korean American surgeon, moved away and "assimilated" to a predominantly white upper-class society, and raised her children, while earning a degree in Far Eastern Art and Culture. She was diagnosed with cancer at the age of fifty and began writing *Clay Walls* then. It was published in 1987, just before her death, by the Permanent Press in New York, and was re-issued in 1990 by the University of Washington Press. It is read widely as an immigrant novel and as a historical narrative testifying to the travails of first-generation Korean Americans torn between their loyalties to their homeland, which was still fighting Japanese imperialism in Asia, and their emergent identities in the United States, where their children were rapidly undergoing acculturation.

In the following excerpt, Haesu, after a clash with her employer, quits her menial job. Seething with resentment over the reversal of her station, she goes straight to her friend Clara, who is doing her best to become Americanized as soon as possible.

1   "You've missed a spot," Mrs. Randolph said, pointing. "Dirty." Haesu had been holding her breath. She let it out with a cough.

2   Mrs. Randolph shook her finger at the incriminating stain. "Look," she demanded, then made scrubbing motions in the air. "You clean."

3   Haesu nodded. She took in another breath and held it as she rubbed away the offensive stain.

4   "Th-at's better," Mrs. Randolph nodded with approval. "Good. Clean. Very good. Do that every week," she said, scrubbing the air again. She smiled at Haesu and left the room.

5   Haesu spat into the toilet and threw the rag into the bucket. "*Sangnyun!*" she muttered to herself. "*Sangnyun, sangnyun, sangnyun!*" she sputtered aloud. She did not know the English equivalent for "low woman," but she did know how to say, "I quit" and later said it to Mrs. Randolph. The woman looked at her in disbelief.

6   "I don't understand. We were getting on so well. I . . ." Mrs. Randolph pointed to herself "teach you." She pointed at Haesu. "You do good. Why you say, 'I quit'?"

7   "Toilet make me sick."

8   "That's part of the job."

9   "No job. No toilet. Not me. I go home." Haesu held out her hand, palm up to receive her pay.

10 Mrs. Randolph stiffened as she backed away from Haesu's outstretched hands. "Oo-oh no. You're supposed to give me adequate notice. I'm not obligated to pay you anything."

11 They were words not in Haesu's vocabulary. Perhaps she had not made herself clear. Haesu raised her hand higher.

12 Mrs. Randolph tightened her lips. "So you're going to be difficult. I'm very disappointed in you, Haesu, but I'm going to be fair." She motioned Haesu to stay put and left the room.

13 Haesu sighed with relief and put down her hand. She knew that Mrs. Randolph's purse was on top of the dresser in the bedroom; the woman had gone to get the money. As she waited, Haesu looked around. It was a beautiful room. She had thought so when she first agreed to take the job. Later, when she ran the vacuum over the carpet, she had admired the peach-like pinks and the varying shades of blues of the flowing Persian pattern. She felt an affinity with the design. Perhaps what some historians say is true, that sometime in the distant past Hittites were in Korea. She ran her fingers over the surface of the table. The mahogany wood still glowed warmly from her earlier care. She had not minded dusting the furniture. It was cleaning the toilet she could not stand.

14 Mrs. Randolph returned carrying a coin purse. She gestured for Haesu to hold out her hand, then emptied the contents of the purse into the outstretched palm. The coins barely added up to one dollar. Haesu held up two fingers of her other hand.

15 Mrs. Randolph gave a laugh. "No. You quit. Two dollars only if you were permanent." She shook her head; it was final.

16 Carefully, so as not to scratch the surface, Haesu placed the coins on the table. She picked up a dime. "Car fare," she explained.

17 Mrs. Randolph glared at Haesu. She began to fume. "Why you insolent yellow . . ."

18 Haesu knew they were words she would not want translated. She turned on her heels and walked out.

19 The dime clinked lightly as it fell to the bottom of the coin box. Haesu found a seat by the window. She would put her mind to the scenes that passed before her and forget the woman. She enjoyed her rides on streetcars, becoming familiar with the foreign land without suffering the embarrassment of having to speak its language. In three months, she had learned more about America from the seat of streetcars than from anywhere else.

20 The ride from Bunker Hill to Temple Street was all too brief for her. Only a few minutes separated the mansions of well-to-do Americans from the plain wood-framed houses of the ghettos. But it might as well be a hundred years, she thought. Her country's history went back thousands of years but no one in America seemed to care. To her dismay, few Americans knew where Korea was. This was 1920. The United States was supposed to be a modern country. Yet to Americans, Koreans were "oriental," the same as Chinese, Japanese, or Filipino.

21 As shops began to come into view, Haesu leaned forward to see the merchandise in the windows. In front of the Five and Ten-cent Store, children were selling lemonade. A discarded crate and hand-scrawled signs indicated they were in business. Charmed, Haesu smiled and waved at the children. When she recognized the shops near her stop, she pulled the cord to signal the conductor she wanted off.

22 Clara's house was several blocks away. Although the rambling Victorian was really the meeting house of the National Association of Koreans, Haesu thought of it as Clara's. It was because of Clara that Haesu and her husband, Chun, were given a room, a room usually reserved for visiting Korean dignitaries. It was because of Clara that Mr. Yim, her husband, had agreed to make an exception to the rule.

23 The front door was open. Rudy Vallee's tremulous voice filtered through the screendoor. Clara was practicing the foxtrot again. Haesu stepped out of her shoes and carried them into the house.

24 "I quit my job," she announced, loud enough to be heard over the Victrola.

25 Clara stopped dancing and took the needle off the record. "But you've just started," she said.

26 Haesu set her shoes on the floor and plopped into the sofa. "It was horrible. That *sangnyun* stood over me while I worked. I had to practically wipe my face on her filthy toilet to satisfy her."

27 "Oh, *Onni,* how terrible," Clara said, looking as if she had swallowed something distasteful.

28 The expression on Clara's face made Haesu laugh. "Onni," older sister. The honorific title further softened her anger. "The work wasn't hard. I could have done it," Haesu said confidently. "I have to admit the *sangnyun* has good

taste. Beautiful furniture. Carpets this thick." She indicated the thickness with her forefinger and thumb. "Such lovely patterns. Like the twining tendrils on old Korean chests. Do you think we have Persian blood in us?"

29 Clara laughed. "I wouldn't know. You're the one who always says you're one hundred percent Korean."

30 "I am. But I'm talking about way back. Long, long ago. It would be fun to know." She absent-mindedly picked up one of the round velvet pillows Clara kept on the sofa and ran her hand over it, smoothing down the nap of the fabric. "What difference does it make now?" she said with a sigh. "What difference does it make who our ancestors were? I don't have a job."

31 "A lot of difference, *Onni*. Your ancestors were *yangbans*. No one can ever deny that. Everyone knows that children of aristocrats are not supposed to clean toilets," Clara declared.

32 Haesu tossed the pillow aside with such force that it bounced off the sofa onto the floor. "Then what am I doing here?"

33 Clara picked up the pillow and brushed it off. "How many times are you going to ask me that? You're here . . ."

34 "Living with you and Mr. Yim because Chun and I can't afford a place of our own," Haesu said.

35 "Why do you let that bother you? Mr. Yim and I don't mind. We want you here." Clara sat down next to Haesu and slipped her arm into Haesu's. "You're like a sister to me. If you were in my place, you would do the same."

36 Haesu looked earnestly into Clara's eyes. "I would, that's true. We had such fun in Korea, laughing at everything, worrying about nothing."

37 "It will be that way again. We haven't been here long enough. I've only been here a year and you've hardly had time to unpack. We'll get used to America." Clara leaped from her seat and pulled at Haesu's arm. "Put on your shoes and let's do the foxtrot. I think I'm getting it."

38 Laughing as she pulled away, Haesu protested, "No, no. I can't do that kind of dance."

39 "Yes you can. Just loosen up. You act like an old lady, Haesu. You act like you're eighty not twenty." Clara put Rudy Vallee on again and began dancing around the parlor, gliding effortlessly on the linoleum rug.

40 Haesu drew her feet onto the sofa out of Clara's way. She reached for the cushion and held it in her lap. Clara's enthusiasm amused her. It also puzzled her. Rudy Vallee stirred nothing in Haesu to make her want to dance.

41 Haesu stood at the screendoor waiting for Chun. Since Monday she had been thinking about what she would say to her husband. She knew what she would not say to him. At dinner on Monday, when Haesu had explained to Mr. Yim why she had quit her job, Clara had chimed in with, "It's so hard here. Haesu's right. We had such fun in Korea, laughing at everything, worrying about nothing."

42 Mr. Yim's jaw had dropped, the *kimchee* he held in his chopsticks falling onto his rice, causing a momentary lapse in his usual courtly manners. "Laughing at everything and worrying about nothing?" he had said incredulously. "Then, tell me, what are we doing here?" While Haesu and Clara had searched for an answer, Mr. Yim had sardonically added, "As I recall, no one I knew was laughing at Japanese atrocities. Everyone I knew was worrying about persecution." Haesu had shrunk with embarrassment. Mr. Yim was a Korean patriot who had suffered torture in a Japanese prison, and was now forced to live in exile to escape death. "How thoughtless of me," she had replied. "Please forgive me."

43 Up until two weeks ago Haesu walked with Chun to Clara's house on Thursdays. Chun had found them work as live-in domestics. But Haesu could not bear being summoned by the persistent ringing of a bell and, after two months, had quit. Chun had insisted upon staying on, choosing the security of room and board and five dollars a month. Haesu now saw him only on his days-off.

44 As soon as she recognized his slight build and flat-footed gait, she flung open the screendoor and walked out to meet him.

45 Chun did not stop for her. She had to turn around and walk alongside him, matching her steps to his. "I quit my job," she said.

46 "Let's talk about it later," he said, speeding up. "I have to go to the bathroom. The damn food makes me sick." He hopped up the front steps and disappeared into the house.

47 Later that night, when they were alone in their room, Haesu told her husband the details of her quitting.

48 "You'll get used to the work," he said.

49 "Never! I'll never get used to cleaning someone else's filth."

50 "It takes two minutes to clean a toilet. It won't kill you," he said as he climbed into bed.

51 Haesu felt the heat rise to her cheeks. "I'll never understand how you do it, how you can remain mute while someone orders you to come here, go there, do this, do that . . . like you were some trained animal. They call you a houseboy. A twenty-five year old man being called 'boy.' "

52 "They can call me what they want. I don't put the words in their mouths. The work is easy. Work for pay. There's no problem as long as they don't lay a hand on me. Just a job, Haesu. Work for pay."

53 "Cheap pay and demeaning work," she said.

54 Chun shrugged his shoulders. "No work, no pay. No money, no house, no food, no nothing. It's as simple as that."

55 "That's not good enough for me and I won't disgrace my family by resorting to menial labor," she whispered hoarsely, keeping her voice down as her anger rose. She was obliged to maintain the peace of her host's home.

56   "I haven't met a *yangban* yet who thought any work was good enough for him. Me? I'm just a farmer's son. Any work is good enough for me. Isn't that right?" He pulled the covers over him.

57   "I don't want to talk about that now. I have an idea. Are you listening? Riding home on the streetcar, I saw these little stands where people were selling things. Nothing big and fancy. Little things. Standing in the sun selling . . . things. It didn't seem like hard work. Why can't we do something like that? Are you listening?" She shook his shoulders.

58   Chun snorted. "You? Selling things? Out in the sun where all the Koreans can see you?"

59   Haesu pulled the blanket from his shoulders. "I don't care about that. All I care about is that we be our own boss. Can't you see that? No one will tell us what to do."

60   Chun pulled the blanket from her. "Let a man get some sleep, will you?" He covered himself then turned his back to her.

61   Haesu walked over to his side of the bed. She leaned over him and put her lips close to his ears. She spoke softly. "I will never work for anyone. Do you hear me, Chun? I'll never clean someone else's filth. Never! You'll never make enough money as a houseboy to support us. Do you hear me, Chun? As soon as we make enough money, we are going back to Korea. We don't belong here. Just tell me, what are we doing here?" She really had laughed at everything and worried about nothing in Korea; a daughter protected from the world by her parents, groomed in seclusion for marriage.

62   Chun's answer was a series of rattled breaths followed by deep snores.

DISCUSSION QUESTIONS

1. Why is Mrs. Randolph angry, and is she justified in being so?
2. Are you most in sympathy with Haesu's views about work or with her husband's?
3. What seems to account for the differences in their attitudes?
4. How has Clara adjusted to her new life in America?
5. The narrator is surprised that in 1920 few Americans know anything about Korea. Does this surprise you? Why or why not?

WRITING TOPICS

1. Though this is a fairly brief excerpt, the personalities of Haesu, Clara, Mr. Yim, and Chun are readily discerned. In a brief essay, explore how Ronyoung's use of characterization results in these distinct personalities.
2. Mr. Yim refers to Japanese atrocities and persecution. Research the relations between Korea and Japan in the early twentieth century and write a brief outline of events.

FROM *THE COFFIN TREE*

Wendy Law-Yone

Wendy Law-Yone was born in Mandalay, Burma, in 1947 to a Eurasian mother and a Chinese-Burmese father. She lived in Rangoon until she was twenty, when she married an American journalist living in Southeast Asia. She came to the United States in 1973 and now lives in Washington, D.C., with her second husband and two children. Law-Yone graduated from Eckert College in St. Petersburg, Florida, in 1975. She has been an editor and freelance writer since the late 1960s and has studied several languages. *The Coffin Tree*, published in 1983, is her first novel. She won a National Endowment for the Arts fellowship for her second novel, *Irrawaddy Tango* (1987).

In the following selection, from *The Coffin Tree,* the narrator recalls the struggles she and her brother endured upon their arrival in New York. (J.I.)

1   Even when times were hard, the life we left behind had run along a groove cut by tradition, familiarity, and habit. But arriving in New York, my brother and I fell out of that groove, and finding our footing was nearly as awkward as the astronauts' first steps in the atmosphere of the moon.

2   We landed in America three months after they landed on the moon and watched the event on a giant television screen that hung above the maze of cosmetics and costume jewelry in a Fifth Avenue store. It was our first American department store, but the visit was short-lived. After several runs of the moon footage we had wandered into the women's shoe department, where we tried to beat down the price of a pair of sandals, bazaar-style.

3   "How much are these?"

4   "Twenty-five dollars."

5   "I'll give you seventeen."

6 "Excuse me?"

7 "All right, twenty."

8 The saleswoman began to treat us like morons, shouting, "Twenty-five! Twenty-five! Twenty-five!" Red-faced, we abandoned the sandals and the store.

9 We had arrived with two bags of lightweight clothing and five hundred dollars in cash. In his message instructing us to leave the country, Father had said we should get in touch with Morrison, a friend who lived in New York, and explain our circumstances. He would give us what help we needed. In the meantime, he would be sending us more money in Morrison's care to tide us over our first few months.

10 But contacting this man was harder than we had imagined. The letter we wrote him came back ten days later marked: MOVED, ADDRESS UNKNOWN. We didn't have a telephone number, and when we looked through the directory there were enough Morrisons to make us despair.

11 We must have called fifty different numbers before reaching the one that seemed likeliest. But we couldn't be certain, because it was a recording.

12 The voice bore a promising resemblance to what we remembered of Morrison's. But how to make sense out of the recording? Was it a joke or a trick or a code? So we took turns redialing and hanging up with each beep.

13 In those early days it seemed as if we had been thrown into a colossal obstacle course where machinery, gadgetry, and mystery of one sort or another stood in our way at every turn. All around us, hordes of people were buzzing through those same obstacles without a second thought: waiting for the right buses, running down the right entrances to the subways, dropping the right change into the right slots, not even needing to look up from their papers to get off at the right stops, pushing the right buttons on elevators, giving their orders at restaurants and cafeterias in the right voices, the right words. We had had glimpses of these marvels in the movies back home, but seeing an elevator on film is inadequate preparation for stepping into one for the first time without getting crushed by the heavy, ineluctable doors, and then recovering in time to press the right button.

14 We kept calling the number with the recording for weeks, though prevented by an inexpressible shyness from saying a word. And when at last a real voice answered, we hung up again—from habit. But when we plucked up the nerve to call back, the miraculous happened. We had found our Morrison.

15 It wasn't quite the exchange we'd expected. Instead of offering to pick us up immediately and take us back to his home, he invited us to dinner— and on a day that was three weeks away. From that brief exchange, we should have guessed that Morrison knew nothing of Father's promised funds. But we couldn't be sure. Maybe he thought it improper to raise the subject over the telephone. (We came from a purse-proud society where talk

of money had its own rules of decorum.) Maybe he was waiting till we met in person. We would just have to wait.

16   But the dinner invitation brought its own set of worries. What would we wear? What would we talk about? What subjects should we try to evade, for fear of revealing our ignorance about things that concerned our still unsorted past, our shaky present, our even shakier future?

17   By lucky accident we had managed to find a run-down but reasonably priced hotel on the Upper West Side. The desk clerk there, who had advised us on other matters, told us that the best bargains for clothing could be found along Orchard and Mulberry streets, so we walked up and down those blocks, combing through the racks for clothes both affordable and appropriate. Years later, I came across a cartoon that reminded me of our bumbling stabs at presentability. It showed a cloddish-looking fellow in a folksy costume and a belled cap, holding a tambourine and saying, "And now I will sing you a song of my country."

18   So must we have seemed when we arrived at the Morrisons' Park Avenue address. Shan in his shiny suit that drooped at the shoulders, I in my lime green dress with shoes to match—a pair of bumpkins singing a song of our country.

19   When I was growing up, Morrison had been an occasional visitor, always arriving crumpled and sweaty from the long ride in from the airport, but full of laughter and loaded with presents. Now, on his turf, he greeted us at the door with brisk handshakes—not the exuberant embraces we were used to. Admittedly, five years had passed since we had seen him last. He had been a bachelor then, a ruddy-faced man in safari shirts with a startlingly loud laugh. Now, in his dark suit, he was older and paler and far from uproarious.

20   I heard other voices in the room beyond and discovered with a sinking heart that we were not the only guests. Mrs. Morrison came forward to greet us. She held out the tips of her fingers as if expecting them to be kissed. She was very thin, with broad, freckled shoulders that jutted out above a strapless black dress. Her eyes were sunken and seemed to require an effort to stay open, her cheeks were hollow, her smile hinted at disappointment. She led us across several Persian carpets into the living room. The introductions made, she promptly turned her back on us and resumed the conversation we had apparently interrupted, which had to do with the difficulty of flying in fresh salmon from Alaska.

21   Morrison seemed at a loss for words. We were faces out of a past he didn't appear eager to recall. Perhaps he no longer wished to dabble in the politics of our country. Perhaps he had seen the writing on the wall when, after the long summer he spent in Father's rebel camp, he returned to the United States to raise funds for the cause, only to raise a shipment of used grade-school texts for the children of the rebel villages.

22   Whatever the reasons, he seemed almost as ill-at-ease at his own dinner table as we were, sitting there in our chintzy clothes, while the Japanese butler smirked at our hesitations over the linen and silver. Unequal to the level and pace of conversation, we remained mute, regretting the mistake of our presence there.

23   We made our escape as soon as we could, refusing a cab with the excuse that we preferred to walk. The coats we still couldn't afford we claimed to have left at home. ("No, no, we like the cold!"—we who had grown up in tropical heat.)

24   Outside, we shivered in the autumn wind and walked with bowed heads all the thirty blocks home.

25   The next day we steeled ourselves to make the odious telephone call asking about the money Father was supposed to have sent. It fell to me, the younger, the brasher of the two, to call. The indecency of asking for money (though rightfully ours) would be mitigated, we agreed, coming from me.

26   It was such a simple question: Had the Morrisons by chance received some money from Father? And yet it took some twelve hours of hesitation and argument to make that call. It took repeated rehearsals of that single line for me to collect the nerve.

27   Over the telephone, and without the appeasement of her tired smile, Mrs. Morrison's voice had the unfaltering resonance of a radio announcer. It was the Voice of America. I managed to deliver my well-rehearsed query. On the other end, there was a pause, and then a deep breath.

28   "You know, my dear," she said, her voice taking on the coziness of a nanny reading a bedtime story, "Mr. Morrison and I have not been involved with your part of the world for many years now. We've had no contact, financial or otherwise. We certainly know nothing about these funds from your father. Surely you don't think we'd be sitting on it if we had it? Now, we know it isn't easy for you and your brother here, so far away from home. You come from a proud family, it must be hard for you to ask for help. But I personally believe it is always better to speak openly and directly. Why not come right out and say you need money? Then maybe we could work something out."

29   I could think of no other response than to drop the phone. "I told you we shouldn't have asked," I said to Shan, blaming him for the humiliation.

30   When I told him what had happened, he bit his lip in anger. It was at moments like these that Father's spirit seemed to possess his face. Otherwise, they were not really alike at all.

31   Father was not a tall man, but he had no need for height. He carried himself with the assurance of a natural bully. All his expressions—the way he lifted his chin, the way he moved his mouth—spelt braggadocio. From a distance, his small hooded eyes seemed set in a humorous slant, but up close they flashed every kind of threat. His head was too big for his body, but even

this disproportion was right. It had the logic of a mythic creature: the head of a lion on the body of a buck.

32   Shan was half a head taller than Father, but it was a smaller, more delicate head. He had Father's thick lips, which could curl up with similar bravado, but on the whole his features were set on a feminine scale, which robbed him of the forceful look.

33   My aunts used to say about Shan, "Look at those lovely long lashes. All that thick curly hair. He should have been a girl."

34   "Bloody stupid woman," Shan said now, still smarting from Mrs. Morrison's insult. "Just like that woman at the train station."

35   I had heard the story before: how when he was a boy—this was after he had come south—he had seen, at a train station, a beggar woman dragging herself about on her hands. She was not only crippled but crazed, and had attracted, like some zoo animal, a small audience that threw things at her: coins, nuts, bottle caps, sticks, and stones. The trick she performed was to dart at the flying debris, catch it in mid-air, and, after a quick appraisal, tuck it into her ragged bodice. When the object turned out to be a bottle cap rather than a coin, she spat and hissed, her shoulders swaying with the taut movements of a cobra poised to strike.

36   Suddenly, distracted by a new face, the beggar turned her back on the crowd. At the edge of the platform close to the trains, a white woman as tall as a man was sitting on a pile of suitcases.

37   The beggar moved toward her, scraping the ground as she went with a broken razor blade. The woman with the suitcases began to notice the approaching cripple with her mysterious scrapings and looked this way and that, uneasily.

38   The beggar kept scratching away, until she reached the woman's feet. There she deposited the little mound of dirt she had scraped along, with a flourish that betokened an extravagant gift. Flustered, the white woman reached into her purse, threw a folded money bill at the beggar, and hurriedly dragged her bags toward the train.

39   The beggar had made no move to pick up the money; but as the tall woman threw her suitcases up onto one of the cars and climbed in, she bounded after her, racing on her hands, and, shouting out a string of vile abuse, flung the note at the woman's back.

40   "Stupid foreigners," Shan said. "They think money is everything."

41   "We're the foreigners now," I reminded him. "We're the men on the moon."

42   We moved to a cheaper place—a certain Hotel Macy on Broadway near Times Square. In the narrow lobby we rubbed shoulders with its floating clientele of junkies, pimps, and whores. The air was so thick with marijuana that the sweet fumes clung to our clothes.

43   But our room was a double with a four-burner gas range, utensils

included. We cooked whatever went on sale at the corner grocery store: dented cans of string beans or mushroom soup; a head of discolored cabbage; a packet of lentils. But the mainstay was rice: We had a pot of it daily as a base for the meager toppings. Occasionally, when hot dogs went on sale, there would be meat on the table: one sausage per meal, diced small, heavily camouflaged with curry powder and garlic, and mixed in with the rice.

44   Money was dwindling, but sometimes, walking past a cafeteria, we stopped to study the menus pasted to the window and broke down under the assault of the greasy, oniony odors. Inside, we attacked our $1.25 specials of meat loaf with savage concentration, resuming talk only when the last smudge of gravy had disappeared—and then regretting our haste.

45   The wonder of our first snow! We stood at the corner of Lexington and Twenty-third and held out our palms to the falling snowflakes—the way we beckoned to the pigeons back home.

46   Then came the rush of the crippling cold: the piercing air, the wind lashing through our cheap, foam-lined loden coats, our aching toes inside the rubber boots, the fear for our fingers and ears. We wanted never to leave our garlicky, overheated room.

47   Working in tandem out of fear and insecurity, we went as a pair in search of work, one of us waiting outside while the other was interviewed. We were so poorly prepared for the tests of survival in a changed habitat that we started out with blind ambition—blind to our own limitations.

48   At first we circled the want ads in the *Times*'s clerical and sales columns, but after the repeated rejections, we lowered our sights until we sank to the grind of washing dishes and waiting on tables at any restaurant that would hire us as a pair.

49   Christmas came with its frantic commercial festivity. Dazzled by the window displays of opulence such as occurred only in dreams, we could walk along, on our days off, for hours at a time and almost forget the cold.

50   On Christmas Eve, we stayed in our room and listened to the drama of two streetwalkers quarreling outside and two men ending an affair in the room next door.

51   In the drawer of the rusty cabinet under the kitchen sink, Shan found a roll of green insulating tape ("insulting tape," he read in his careless way), which he cut into strips and stuck to the window in a Christmas tree design of inverted V's.

52   The next morning, three lumpy packages wrapped in aluminum foil awaited me on the windowsill: a hairbrush, a pair of woolen tights, and a knitted cap.

53   A rough calculation of how much those three items had cost made me tremble: There was a week's worth of groceries. I said, "We can't eat these. Why did you do it?"

54   I may as well have wiped my feet on his presents.

55   "So we'll starve," he said and began to peel off the green tape from the window. "But at least one of us won't freeze."

56   I went into the bathroom, where I stood over the sink for a long time, washing my face again and again until I had composed myself.

57   "What's the matter?" he asked, noticing my red eyes.

58   "Nothing. I got soap in my eyes."

59   We pretended all was well. I brushed my hair with the new brush, put on the tights and the cap, and suggested a walk through the snow.

60   Lying across a sidewalk was a scraggly pine tree still draped with tinsel and stiff with sprayed-on snow. Underneath its branches, we found a portable typewriter in a boxy case and carried it home. The *q* was missing and the spacing erratic, but the carriage was sound.

61   I bought a typing manual and tapped out the lessons in the evenings. Shan memorized the keyboard. With two fingers, he could make better time than I, but he soon tired of the exercise and went to bed early, while I continued to pick out my lessons at night.

62   Braver now, I left him in our room one afternoon and went to a succession of interviews that would take several hours. By then it would be dark, so we arranged to meet at six in the evening, at a halfway point, and from there to walk home together.

63   Snow was coming down in a drizzle scarcely distinguishable from rain when I stood at the corner where we were to meet. Although Christmas was past, a Salvation Army Santa Claus stamped his fireman's boots in the gray slush and shook a bell, first in one hand, then in the other. The store window behind me was festooned with plastic sandals that seemed crafted out of colored glass. Six o'clock had passed without any sign of Shan. Another half hour went by. I walked up and down the block, stopping under the lamp lights to look up at the insects of snow swarming around the light.

64   I wanted to find a telephone booth but was afraid of missing him. At seven o'clock, finally, I took the risk and went to call the "hotel." The front desk rang our room. No answer. I ran back to my spot, fearing he had come and gone, waited another ten minutes, then ran back to the phone booth again. Still no answer. Distraught, I rushed back to the corner and, looking down the street, saw him at last. He was hurrying through the crowds, a halo of ice around his forehead.

65   "What happened? I've been going crazy!" My teeth were chattering from cold and relief.

66   "I fell asleep. I don't know what's wrong with me."

67   We started down the street back toward the hotel. "Asleep! How could you sleep for so long, leaving me out in the cold like that? I almost called the police."

68   "Police!" He looked at me fearfully. "Don't ever start anything with the police in this country. They do what they want. Say you're driving along in

a car and they stop you? If you don't freeze at once, they blow your head off."

69 I stopped him. He was out of breath and incoherent. "What's the matter? You look sick."

70 "I don't know," he said, puzzled himself. "I slept as if I died."

71 That day marked a new pattern for him of chronic tiredness and drowsiness.

72 Weeks later, one of my countless interviews bore fruit. The new job paid a pittance, but it required nothing more than sorting mail and operating a Xerox machine. And from the coffee room I could smuggle out packets of hot chocolate, dried milk, coffee, tea, sugar, and Saltine crackers.

73 At home, it was I who consumed most of it. Shan's appetite had fallen off. Complaining of aches and chills that came and went erratically, he scarcely left his bed. One night I was awakened by a pounding beside me: his whole bed was electrified and throbbing from the violence of his chill. I covered him with a heap of bedsheets and blankets and both our coats, but he continued to shiver and babble.

74 The next morning his temperature had dropped, but he could barely stand up by himself.

75 He had been so drenched in sweat during the night that I had spread newspapers over the damp sheets. But the papers, too, were soon soaked through and in the end I had stripped the sheets and soaked them in the bathtub. They were lying now in water that was gray with newsprint.

76 There was no place to hang the sheets out to dry, so after wringing them out, I carried them to work in plastic bags.

77 On the way, I decided it was time to tap our last emergency reserve. I unscrewed the pearls from my ears and stopped off at a pawnshop, where in return for the earrings I walked away with a ticket and twenty-five dollars in cash.

78 It was the briefest of transactions—and it covered the cost of a physician's house call.

79 I was already late for work, and by the time I had made the calls to locate a doctor, the morning was almost gone while the office mail was still unsorted. I rushed through the pile as best I could and left at lunchtime with my plastic bags of wet sheets, heading for the nearest laundromat.

80 While the sheets were in the washer, I called home and learned that the doctor had come and gone. The provisional diagnosis was, as we had suspected, malaria.

81 I left the clothes in the washer, took the subway home to pick up the prescription the doctor had written, rushed back to the laundromat to throw the sheets into the dryer, and went to fill the prescription at a drugstore. When I returned to the laundromat, the sheets had been taken out of the

dryer and were lying on the table, still damp. The plastic bags were gone, so I folded the sheets hurriedly and raced back to the office.

82   As luck determined, I walked into the same elevator as the office manager, who took in the sheets with an inquiring glance but said nothing. When I reached my desk in the mailroom, I found a note asking to see me in his office.

83   All that rushing around had made me absentminded: I carried the pile of bedsheets in with me.

84   "Let me get to the point," he said. "Are you holding another job?"

85   I opened my mouth to speak and found myself dissolving from a stammer into a chuckle.

86   "You may think because we are a friendly group here that we have time for games," he went on. "If so, you have the wrong impression. I've been watching you and I've noticed, a number of us have noticed, that you've been coming in late, taking long lunches, and generally, well, falling down on the job.

87   "I can't tell you how disappointed I am. You came in here with no credentials to speak of, and I hired you on faith. Faith, yes, and because I sensed there was more to you than meets the eye. I had a feeling about you. I hoped you'd be a kind of iron butterfly. Now I hate to say this, but you've turned out to be just a butterfly, flitting in and out. I can't understand it. You're a bright girl, basically, and I know that most Oriental people are honest and hardworking. I've seen many others who've come here from your part of the world—real go-getters, starting from scratch and making it. But you've got to want to be somebody. You've got to have values. I can't teach you commitment. You've got to be committed yourself."

88   His voice dropped. "I'm sorry. You don't cut the mustard. I'm afraid we're going to have to let you go."

89   I stood up and gathered the damp sheets. "If I don't cut the mustard, why are you afraid?" I said, light-headed with defiance.

90   The office manager reddened. "It's an expression," he said. "Someday, when your English is better, you'll understand it."

91   I called Shan to tell him I'd be home early. He assumed I was simply taking the afternoon off.

92   "I'll make dinner," he said. "I feel much better. Just tell me what to cook."

93   I hadn't eaten all day and was limp with hunger, but hesitant about letting him cook. "Are you sure?"

94   "Shoooooer," he said playfully, to let me know he was in good spirits.

95   I could smell the garlic the minute I walked through the door of the lobby at the Hotel Macy. The cloud thickened with each flight of stairs I climbed. Shan answered my knock with a ladle in his hand. "It's all done," he said. "You can eat. But I think I put a little too much garlic in it."

96   I opened the pot of curried mushroom soup and reeled. Beside the stove, the bottle of garlic powder lay open, its perforated top by its side. I saw that the powder level had gone down almost an inch since I'd last used it.

97   "I was shaking the garlic powder and the top fell into the soup," he explained.

98   "Never mind," I said. "Let's eat."

99   "You eat," he said. "I already ate."

100   "I've already eaten," I corrected him churlishly as I piled my dish with rice and topped it with the gummy soup.

101   I took my first mouthful and gagged. The garlic had the potency of ammonia. I set the plate down. "I can't eat this. A dog can't eat this."

102   "There's nothing else," he said in a small voice. "I'll make you hot chocolate."

103   "I'm sick of hot chocolate," I said. "I'm sick of crackers. I just wanted rice and soup. I've been starving."

104   "I'm sorry," he said. "Really sorry. I know how hungry you are."

105   "I lost the job," I told him.

106   "What? Why?"

107   "I didn't cut the mustard."

108   "What mustard."

109   "You see? Our English just isn't good enough."

110   I picked up the plate again and took a deep breath. Barely chewing the mouthfuls of rice, I swallowed the food until I gagged again.

111   "This is so horrible," I burst out, spraying a mouthful of rice onto the floor.

112   He took my plate away and knelt beside me. "I'm feeling better now," he said. "Soon I'll get a job and we'll be all right. Wait and see."

113   And he started to pick up the grains of rice from the floor, saying, "This place has enough rats already."

DISCUSSION QUESTIONS

1. The narrator and her brother had to overcome many handicaps, but they also had some advantages that helped them survive. What were the handicaps and what enabled them to overcome them?
2. The narrator and her brother were timid about contacting Mr. Morrison and then embarrassed, puzzled, and angry at the Morrisons. Why?
3. Shan has frightening ideas about the police. How right is he?
4. What, in your opinion, might have prevented the narrator from being fired?

5. Shan once said that "stupid foreigners" think "money is everything." And his sister reminds him that now they are foreigners. How important is money in America, and is the importance of money the same or different in other countries of the world? Discuss in a small group.

WRITING TOPICS

1. This excerpt covers the first several months after the narrator's arrival in the United States. In a brief essay, discuss what changes she seems to undergo as she becomes more accustomed to her new home.
2. How would you describe the tone of this excerpt? Does it seem appropriate for the events that are related? Consider these questions in a journal entry.

Displacement

David Wong Louie

David Wong Louie was born in Rockville Center, New York, in 1954. He attended Vassar College and the University of Iowa and began publishing in Midwestern and Western literary magazines such as *The Iowa Review, Kansas Quarterly, Ploughshares, and Quarry West*. He is the recipient of a fellowship from the National Endowment for the Arts and has been a fellow at the McDowell Colony and Yaddo. His stories have been anthologized in *The Best American Short Stories 1989* and *The Big Aiiieeeee!: An Anthology of Chinese American and Japanese American Literature* (1992). Louie's collection of short stories, *Pangs of Love* (1991), received the *Ploughshares* John C. Zacharis First Book Award and the *Los Angeles Times* Art Seidenbaum Award for First Fiction in 1991. He also coedited *Dissident Song: A Contemporary Asian American Anthology* (1991). Louie, who has taught at Vassar College and at the University of California, Los Angeles, is presently completing his first novel.

Louie's parents owned a Chinese laundry in a Long Island suburb, and Louie's short stories reflect that marginalized labor force as well as the conflicts and tensions between Chinese immigrants and a United States mainstream, chiefly white, population that neither understands nor appreciates them.

In the following story, Mrs. Chow, a Chinese woman from an upper-class background, struggles to adapt to the white American world. She and her husband are employed as domestics by a selfish and demanding elderly invalid. Mrs. Chow had been a promising artist in Hong Kong, but her talents and abilities are frustrated by servitude. Yet she believes that "her imagination would return . . . once she was away from that house."

1   Mrs. Chow heard the widow. She tried reading faster but kept stumbling over the same lines. She thought perhaps she was misreading them: "There comes, then, finally, the prospect of atomic war. If the war is ever to be carried to China, common sense tells us only atomic weapons could promise maximum loss with minimum damage."

2   When she heard the widow's wheelchair, she tossed the copy of *Life* down on the couch, afraid she might be found out. The year was 1952.

3   Outside the kitchen, Chow was lathering the windows. He worked a soft brush in a circular motion. Inside, the widow was accusing Mrs. Chow of stealing her cookies. The widow had a handful of them clutched to her chest and brought one down hard against the table. She was counting. Chow waved, but Mrs. Chow only shook her head. He soaped up the last pane and disappeared.

4   Standing accused, Mrs. Chow wondered if this was what it was like when her parents faced the liberators who had come to reclaim her family's property in the name of the People. She imagined her mother's response to them: "What people? All of my servants are clothed and decently fed."

5   The widow swept the cookies off the table as if they were a canasta trick won. She started counting again. Mrs. Chow and the widow had played out this scene many times before. As on other occasions, she didn't give the old woman the satisfaction of a plea, guilty or otherwise.

6   Mrs. Chow ignored the widow's busy blue hands. She fixed her gaze on the woman's milky eyes instead. Sight resided at the peripheries. Mornings, before she prepared the tub, emptied the piss pot, or fried the breakfast meat, Mrs. Chow cradled the widow's oily scalp and applied the yellow drops that preserved what vision was left in the cold, heaven-directed eyes.

7   "Is she watching?" said the widow. She tilted her big gray head sideways; a few degrees in any direction Mrs. Chow became a blur. In happier days, Mrs. Chow might have positioned herself just right or left of center, neatly within a line of sight.

8   Mrs. Chow was thirty-five years old. After a decade-long separation from her husband, she finally had entered the United States in 1950 under the joint auspices of the War Brides and Refugee Relief acts. She would agree she was a bride, but not a refugee, even though the Red Army had confiscated her home and turned it into a technical school. During the trouble, she was away safely studying in Hong Kong. Her parents, with all their wealth, could've easily escaped, but they were confident a few well-placed bribes among the Red hooligans would put an end to the foolishness. Mrs. Chow assumed her parents now were dead. She had seen pictures in *Life* of minor landlords tried and executed for lesser crimes against the People.

9   The widow's fondness for calling Mrs. Chow a thief began soon after the

old woman broke her hip. At first, Mrs. Chow blamed the widow's madness on pain displacement. She had read in a textbook that a malady in one part of the body could show up as a pain in another locale—sick kidneys, for instance, might surface as a mouthful of sore gums. The bad hip had weakened the widow's brain function. Mrs. Chow wanted to believe the crazy spells weren't the widow's fault, just as a baby soiling its diapers can't be blamed. But even a mother grows weary of changing them.

10 "I live with a thief under my roof," the widow said to the kitchen. "I could tell her to stop, but why waste my breath? She's too dumb to understand me anyway."

11 When the widow was released from the hospital, she returned to the house with a live-in nurse. Soon afterward her daughter paid a visit, and the widow told her she didn't want the nurse around anymore. "She can do me," the widow said, pointing in Mrs. Chow's direction. "She won't cost a cent. Besides, I don't like being touched that way by a person who knows what she's touching," she said of the nurse.

12 Nobody, not even her husband, knew, but Mrs. Chow spoke a passable though highly accented English she had learned in British schools. Her teachers in Hong Kong always said that if she had the language when she came to the States, she'd be treated better than other immigrants. Chow couldn't have agreed more. Once she arrived, he started to teach her everything he knew in English. But that amounted to very little, considering he had been here for more than ten years. And what he had mastered came out crudely and strangely twisted. His phrases, built from a vocabulary of deference and accommodation, irritated Mrs. Chow for the way they resembled the obsequious blabber of her servants back home.

13 The Chows had been hired ostensibly to drive the widow to her canasta club, to clean the house, to do the shopping, and, since the bad hip, to oversee her personal hygiene. In return they lived rent-free upstairs in the rooms where the widow's children grew up, three tiny bedrooms and a large bath. Plenty of space, it would seem, except the widow wouldn't allow them to clear out her children's old furniture and toys and things that pressed up against their new life together.

14 On weekends and Tuesday afternoons, Chow borrowed the widow's tools and gardened for spending money. Friday nights, after they dropped the widow off at the canasta club, the Chows dined at Ming's and then went to the amusement park at the beach boardwalk. First and last, they got in line to ride the Milky Way. On the day the Immigration authorities finally let Mrs. Chow go, before she even saw her new home, Chow took his bride to the boardwalk. He wanted to impress her with her new country. All that machinery, brainwork, and labor done for the sake of fun. He never tried the roller coaster before she arrived; he saved it for her. After that very first time he realized he was much happier with his feet on the ground. But not Mrs.

Chow. Oh, this speed, this thrust at the sky, this UP! Oh, this raging, clattering, pushy country! So big! And since that first ride she looked forward to Friday nights and the wind whipping through her hair, stinging her eyes, blowing away the top layers of dailiness. On the longest, most dangerous descent, her dry mouth would open to a silent O and she would thrust up her arms as if she could fly away.

15   Some nights as the Chows waited in line, a gang of toughs out on a strut, trussed in denim and combs, would stop and visit: MacArthur, they said, will drain the Pacific; the H-bomb will wipe Korea clean of Commies; the Chows were to blame for Pearl Harbor; the Chows, they claimed, were Red Chinese spies. On occasion, overextending his skimpy English, Chow mounted a defense: he had served in the U.S. Army; his citizenship was blessed by the Department of War; he was a member of the American Legion. The toughs would laugh at the way he talked; Mrs. Chow cringed at his habit of addressing them as "sirs."

16   "Get out, get out!" the widow said. She brought her fist down on the table. Cookies broke, fell to the floor.

17   "Yes, missus," said Mrs. Chow, thinking how she'd have to clean up the mess.

18   The widow, whose great-great-great-grandfather had been a central figure within the faction advocating Washington's coronation, was eighty-six years old. Each day, Mrs. Chow dispensed medications that kept her alive. At times, though, Mrs. Chow wondered if the widow would notice if she were handed an extra blue pill or one less red.

19   Mrs. Chow filled an enamel-coated washbasin with warm water from the tap. "What's she doing?" said the widow. "Stealing my water now, is she?" Ever since Mrs. Chow first came into her service, the widow, with the exception of her hip, had avoided serious illness. But how she had aged: her ears were enlarged; the opalescence in her eyes had spread; her hands worked as if they were chipped from glass. Some nights, as she and her husband lay awake in their twin-size bed, Mrs. Chow would imagine old age as green liquid that seeped into a person's tissues, where it coagulated and, with time, crumbled, caving in the cheeks and the breasts it had once supported. In the dark she fretted that fluids from the widow's old body had taken refuge in her youthful cells. On such nights she reached for Chow, touched him through the cool top sheet, and was comforted by the fit of her fingers in the shallows between his ribs.

20   Mrs. Chow knelt at the foot of the wheelchair and set the washbasin on the floor. The widow laughed. "Where did my little thief go?" She laughed again, her eyes closing, her head dropping to her shoulder. "Now she's after my water. Better see if the tap's still there." Mrs. Chow abruptly swung aside the wheelchair's footrests and slipped off the widow's matted cloth slippers and dunked her puffy blue feet into the water. It was the widow's naptime,

and her physician had prescribed a warm footbath to stimulate circulation before she could be put to bed; otherwise, in her sleep, her blood might settle comfortably in her toes.

21   Chow was talking long distance to the widow's daughter in Texas. Earlier, the widow had told the daughter that the Chows were threatening again to leave. She apologized for her mother's latest spell of wildness. "Humor her," the daughter said. "She must've had another one of her little strokes."

22   Later, Mrs. Chow told her husband she wanted to leave the widow. "My fingers," she said, snapping off the rubber gloves the magazine ads claimed would guarantee her beautiful hands into the next century. "I wasn't made for such work."

23   When she was a girl, her parents had sent her to a Christian school in Hong Kong for training in Western-style art. The authorities agreed she was talented. As expected, she excelled there. Her portrait of the King[1] was chosen to hang in the school cafeteria. When the colonial Minister of Education on a tour of the school saw her painting, he requested a sitting with the gifted young artist.

24   A date was set. The rumors said a successful sitting would bring her the ultimate fame: a trip to London to paint the royal family. But a month before the great day she refused to do the Minister's portrait. She gave no reason; in fact, she stopped talking. The school administration was embarrassed, and her parents were furious. It was great scandal; a mere child from a country at the edge of revolution but medieval in its affection for authority had snubbed the mighty British colonizers. She was sent home. Her parents first appealed to family pride; then they scolded and threatened her. She hid from them in a wardrobe, where her mother found her holding her fingers over lighted matches.

25   The great day came and went, no more momentous than the hundreds that had preceded it. That night her father apologized to the world for raising such a child. With a bamboo cane he struck her outstretched hand—heaven help her if she let it fall one inch—and as her bones were young and still pliant, they didn't fracture or break, thus multiplying the blows she had to endure.

26   "Who'd want you now?" her mother said. Her parents sent her to live with a servant family. She could return to her parents' home when she was invited. On those rare occasions, she refused to go. Many years passed before she met Chow, who had come on the grounds of their estate seeking work. They were married on the condition he take her far away. He left for America, promising to send for her when he had saved enough money for

---

[1] *the King:* the King of England; at the time, Hong Kong was under British rule.

her passage. She returned to Hong Kong and worked as a secretary. Later she studied at the university.

27   Now as she talked about leaving the widow, it wasn't the chores or the old woman that she gave as the reason, though in the past she had complained the widow was a nuisance, an infantile brat born of an unwelcomed union. This time she said she had a project in mind, a great canvas of a yet undetermined subject. But that would come. Her imagination would return, she said, once she was away from that house.

28   It was the morning of a late-spring day. A silvery light filtered through the wall of eucalyptus and warmed the dew on the widow's roof, striking the plums and acacia, irises and lilies, in such a way that, blended with the heavy air and the noise of a thousand birds, one sensed the universe wasn't so vast, so cold, or so angry, and even Mrs. Chow suspected that it might be a loving thing.

29   Mrs. Chow had finished her morning chores. She was in the bathroom rinsing the smell of bacon from her hands. She couldn't wash deep enough, however, to rid her fingertips of perfumes from the widow's lotions and creams, which, over the course of months, had seeped indelibly into the whorls. But today her failure was less maddening. Today she was confident the odors would eventually fade. She could afford to be patient. They were going to interview for an apartment of their very own.

30   "Is that new?" Chow asked, pointing to the camisole his wife had on. He adjusted his necktie against the starched collar of a white short-sleeved shirt, which billowed out from baggy, seersucker slacks. His hair was slicked back with fragrant pomade.

31   "I think it's the daughter's," said Mrs. Chow. "She won't miss it." Mrs. Chow smoothed the silk undershirt against her stomach. She guessed the shirt was as old as she was; the daughter probably had worn it in her teens. Narrow at the hips and the bust, it fit Mrs. Chow nicely. Such a slight figure, she believed, wasn't fit for labor.

32   Chow saw no reason to leave the widow's estate. He had found his wife what he thought was the ideal home, certainly not as grand as her parents' place, but one she'd feel comfortable in. Why move, he argued, when there were no approaching armies, no floods, no one telling them to go? Mrs. Chow understood. It was just that he was very Chinese, and very peasant. Sometimes she would tease him. If the early Chinese sojourners who came to America were all Chows, she would say, the railroad wouldn't have been constructed, and Ohio would be all we know of California.

33   The Chows were riding in the widow's green Buick. As they approached the apartment building, Mrs. Chow reapplied lipstick to her mouth.

34   It was a modern two-story stucco building, painted pink, surrounded by asphalt, with aluminum windows and a flat roof that met the sky like an

engineer's level. Because friends of theirs lived in the apartment in question, the Chows were already familiar with its layout. They went to the manager's house at the rear of the property. Here the grounds were also asphalt. Very contemporary, no greenery anywhere. The closest things to trees were the clothesline's posts and crossbars.

35 The manager's house was a tiny replica of the main building. Chow knocked at the screen door. A radio was on and the smell of baking rushed through the wire mesh. An orange-colored cat came to the door, followed by a girl. "I'm Velvet," she said. "This is High Noon." She gave the cat's tail a tug. "My mother did this to me," said Velvet, picking at clumps of her hair, ragged as tossed salad; someone apparently had cut it while the girl was in motion. She had gray, almost colorless eyes, which, taken with her hair, gave her the appearance of agitated smoke. She threw a wicked look at the room behind her.

36 A large woman emerged from the back room carrying a basket of laundry. She wasn't fat, but large in the way horses are large. Her face was round and pink, with fierce little eyes and hair the color of olive oil and dripping wet. Her arms were thick and white, like soft tusks of ivory.

37 "It's the people from China," Velvet said.

38 The big woman nodded. "Open her up," she told the girl. "It's okay."

39 The front room was a mess, littered with evidence of frantic living. This was, perhaps, entropy[2] in its final stages. The Chows sat on the couch. From all around her Mrs. Chow sensed a slow creep: the low ceiling seemed to be sinking, cat hairs clung to clothing, a fine spray from the fish tank moistened her bare arm.

40 No one said anything. It was as if they were sitting in a hospital waiting room. The girl watched the Chows. The large woman stared at a green radio at her elbow broadcasting news about the war in Korea. Every so often she looked suspiciously up at the Chows. "You know me," she said abruptly. "I'm Remora Cass."

41 On her left, suspended in a swing, was the biggest, ugliest baby Mrs. Chow had ever seen. It was dozing, arms dangling, great melon head flung so far back that it appeared to be all nostrils and chins. "A pig-boy," Mrs. Chow said in Chinese. Velvet jabbed two fingers into the baby's rubbery cheeks. Then she sprang back from the swing and executed a feral dance, all elbows and knees. She seemed incapable of holding her body still

42 She caught Mrs. Chow's eye. "This is Ed," she said. "He has no hair."

43 Mrs. Chow nodded.

44 "Quit," said Remora Cass, swatting at the girl as if she were a fly. Then the big woman looked Mrs. Chow in the eyes and said, "I know what you're thinking, and you're right. There's not a baby in the state bigger than Ed;

---

[2] *entropy:* the steady disorganization of a system or society.

eight pounds twelve ounces at birth and he doubled that inside a month," She stopped, bringing her palms heavily down on her knees, and shook her wet head. "You don't understand me, do you?"

45   Mrs. Chow was watching Velvet.

46   "Quit that!" Remora Cass slapped the girl's hand away from the baby's face.

47   "Times like this I'd say it's a blessing my Aunt Eleanor's deaf," said Remora Cass. "I've gotten pretty good with sign language." From her over-stuffed chair she repeated in pantomime what she had said about the baby.

48   Velvet mimicked her mother's generous, sweeping movements. When Remora Cass caught sight of her, she added a left jab at the girl's head to her repertoire of gestures. Velvet slipped the punch with practiced ease. But the blow struck the swing set. Everyone tensed. Ed flapped his arms and went on sleeping. "Leave us alone," said Remora Cass, "before I really get mad."

49   The girl chased down the cat and skipped toward the door. "I'm bored anyway," she said.

50   Remora Cass asked the Chows questions, first about jobs and pets. Then she moved on to matters of politics and patriotism. "What's your feeling about the Red Chinese in Korea?"

51   A standard question. "Terrible," said Chow, giving his standard answer. "I'm sorry. Too much trouble."

52   Mrs. Chow sat by quietly. She admired Chow's effort. She had studied the language, but he did the talking; she wanted to move, but he had to plead their case; it was his kin back home who benefited from the new regime, but he had to bad-mouth it.

53   Remora Cass asked about children.

54   "No, no, no," Chow said, answering as his friend Bok had coached him. His face was slightly flushed from the question. Chow wanted children, many children. But whenever he discussed the matter with his wife, she answered that she already had one, meaning the old woman, of course, and that was enough.

55   "Tell your wife later," the manager said, "what I'm about to tell you now. I don't care what jobs you do, just so long as you have them. What I say goes for the landlady. I'm willing to take a risk on you. Be nice to have nice quiet folks up there like Rikki and Bok. Rent paid up, I can live with anyone. Besides, I'm real partial to Chinese take-out. I know we'll do just right."

56   The baby moaned, rolling its head from side to side. His mother stared at him as if in all the world there were just the two of them.

57   Velvet came in holding a beach ball. She returned to her place beside the swing and started to hop, alternating legs, with the beach ball held to her head. "She must be in some kind of pain," Mrs. Chow said to her husband.

58   The girl mimicked the Chinese she heard. Mrs. Chow glared at Velvet as if she were the widow during one of her spells. The look froze the girl, standing on one leg. Then she said, "Can Ed come out to play?"

59   Chow took hold of his wife's hand and squeezed it the way he did to brace himself before the roller coaster's forward plunge. Then in a single, well-rehearsed motion, Remora Cass swept off her slipper and punched at the girl. Velvet masterfully sidestepped the slipper and let the beach ball fly. The slipper caught the swing set; the beach ball bounced off Ed's lap.

60   The collisions released charged particles into the air that seemed to hold everyone in a momentary state of paralysis. The baby's eyes peeled open, and he blinked at the ceiling. Soon his distended belly started rippling. He cried until he turned purple, then devoted his energy to maintaining that hue. Mrs. Chow had never heard anything as harrowing. She visualized his cry as large cubes forcing their way into her ears.

61   Remora Cass picked Ed up and bounced on the balls of her feet. "You better start running," she said to Velvet, who was already on her way out the door.

62   Remora Cass half smiled at the Chows over the baby's shoulder. "He'll quiet down sooner or later," she said.

63   Growing up, Mrs. Chow had been the youngest of five girls. She'd had to endure the mothering of her sisters, who, at an early age, were already in training for their future roles. Each married in her teens, plucked in turn by a Portuguese, a German, a Brit, and a New Yorker. They had many babies. But Mrs. Chow thought little of her sisters' example. Even when her parents made life unbearable, she never indulged in the hope that a man—foreign or domestic—or a child could save her from her unhappiness.

64   From the kitchen Remora Cass called Mrs. Chow. The big woman was busy with her baking. The baby was slung over her shoulder. "Let's try something," she said as she transferred the screaming Ed into Mrs. Chow's arms.

65   Ed was a difficult package. Not only was he heavy and hot and sweaty but he spat and squirmed like a sack of kittens. She tried to think of how it was done. She tried to think of how a baby was held. She remembered Romanesque Madonnas cradling their gentlemanly babies in art history textbooks. If she could get his head up by hers, that would be a start.

66   Remora Cass told Mrs. Chow to try bouncing and showed her what she meant. "Makes him think he's still inside," she said. Ed emitted a long, sustained wail, then settled into a bout of hiccups. "You have a nice touch with him. He won't do that for just anyone."

67   As the baby quieted, a pain rolled from the heel of Mrs. Chow's brain, down through her pelvis, to a southern terminus at the backs of her knees. She couldn't blame the baby entirely for her discomfort. He wanted only to escape; animal instinct told him to leap from danger.

68   She was the one better equipped to escape. She imagined invading soldiers murdering livestock and planting flags in the soil of her ancestral estate,
as if it were itself a little nation; they make history by the slaughter of generations of her family; they discover her in the wardrobe, striking matches;
they ask where she has hidden her children, and she tells them there are
none; they say, good, they'll save ammunition, but also too bad, so young
and never to know the pleasure of children (even if they'd have to murder
them). Perhaps this would be the subject of her painting, a non-representa-
tional canvas that hinted at a world without light. Perhaps—

69   Ed interrupted her thought. He had developed a new trick. "Woop,
woop, woop," he went, thrusting his pelvis against her sternum in the manner of an adult male in the act of mating. She called for Chow.

70   Remora Cass slid a cookie sheet into the oven and swept Ed off Mrs.
Chow's shoulder and then stuck a bottle of baby formula into his mouth.
He drained it instantly. "You do have a way with him," said Remora Cass.

71   They walked into the front room. The baby was sleepy and dripping curds
on his mother's shoulder. Under the swing High Noon, the cat, was licking
the nipple of an abandoned bottle. "Scat!" she said. "Now where's my wash
gone to?" she asked the room. "What's she up to now?" She scanned the little room, big feet planted in the deep brown shag carpet, hands on her beefy
hips, baby slung over her shoulder like a pelt. "Velvet—" she started. That
was all. Her jaw locked, her gums gleamed, her eyes rolled into her skull. Her
head flopped backward as if at the back of her neck there was a great hinge.
Then she yawned, and the walls seemed to shake.

72   Remora Cass rubbed her eyes. "I'm bushed," she said.

73   Mrs. Chow went over to the screen door. Chow and the girl were at
the clothesline. Except for their hands and legs, they were hidden behind
a bed sheet. The girl's feet were in constant motion. From the basket her
hands picked up pieces of laundry that Chow's hands then clipped to the
line.

74   "Her daddy's hardly ever here," Remora Case said. "Works all hours, he
does. Has to." She patted Ed on the back, then rubbed her eyes again.
"Looks like Velvet's found a friend. She won't do that with anyone. You two
are naturals with my two. You should get you some of your own." She
looked over at Mrs. Chow and laughed. "Maybe it's best you didn't get
that. Here." She set the baby on Mrs. Chow's shoulder. "This is what it's
like when they're sleeping."

75   Before leaving, the Chows went to look at Rikki and Bok's apartment.
They climbed up the stairs. No one was home. Rikki and Bok had barely
started to pack. Bok's naked man, surrounded by an assortment of spears
and arrows, was still hanging on the living-room wall. Bok had paid good
money for the photograph: an aboriginal gent stares into the camera; he's

smiling, his teeth are good and large, and in his palms he's holding his sex out like a prize eel.

76   Mrs. Chow looked at the photograph for as long as it was discreetly possible before she averted her eyes and made her usual remark about Bok's tastes. Beyond the building's edge she saw the manager's cottage, bleached white in the sun. Outside the front door Remora Cass sat in a folding chair, her eyes shut, her pie-tin face turned up to catch the rays, while Velvet, her feet anchored to the asphalt, rolled her mother's hair in pink curlers. Between the big woman's legs the baby lay in a wicker basket. He was quietly rocking from side to side. Remora Cass's chest rose and fell in the rhythm of sleep.

77   Driving home, they passed the boardwalk, and Mrs. Chow asked if they might stop.

78   Chow refused to ride the roller coaster in the daytime, no matter how much Mrs. Chow teased. It was hard enough at night, when the heights from which the cars fell were lit by a few rows of bulbs. As he handed her an orange ticket, Chow said, "A drunk doesn't look in mirrors."

79   The Milky Way clattered into the terminus. After she boarded the ride, she watched Chow, who had wandered from the loading platform and was standing beside a popcorn wagon, looking up at a billboard. His hands were deep in the pockets of his trousers, his legs crossed at the shins. That had been his pose, the brim of his hat low on his brow, as he waited for her finally to pass through the gates of Immigration.

80   "Go on," an old woman said. "You'll be glad you did." The old woman nudged her young charge toward the empty seat in Mrs. Chow's car. "Go on, she won't bite." The girl looked back at the old woman. "Grandmuthther!" she said, and then reluctantly climbed in beside Mrs. Chow.

81   Once the attendant strapped the girl in, she turned from her grandmother and stared at her new companion. The machine jerked away from the platform. They were climbing the first ascent when Mrs. Chow snuck a look at the girl. She was met by the clearest eyes she had ever known, eyes that didn't shy from the encounter. The girl's pupils, despite the bright sun, were fully dilated, stretched with fear. Now that she had Mrs. Chow's attention, she turned her gaze slowly toward the vertical track ahead. Mrs. Chow looked beyond the summit to the empty blue sky.

82   Within seconds they tumbled through that plane and plunged downward, the cars flung suddenly left and right, centrifugal force throwing Mrs. Chow against the girl's rigid body. She was surprised by Chow's absence.

83   It's gravity that makes the stomach fly, that causes the liver to flutter; it's the body catching up with the speed of falling. Until today, she had never known such sensations. Today there was a weightiness at her core, like a hard, concentrated pull inward, as if an incision had been made and a fist-sized magnet embedded.

84   Her arms flew up, two weak wings cutting the rush of wind. But it wasn't the old sensation this time, not the familiar embrace of the whole fleeting continent, but a grasp at something once there, now lost.

85   Chow had moved into position to see the riders' faces as they careened down the steepest stretch of track. Whenever he was up there with her, his eyes were clenched and his scream so wild and his grip on his life so tenuous that he never noticed her expression. At the top of the rise the cars seemed to stop momentarily, but then up and over, tumbling down, at what appeared, from his safe vantage point, a surprisingly slow speed. Arms shot up, the machine whooshed past him, preceded a split second earlier by the riders' collective scream. And for the first time Chow thought he heard her, she who loved this torture so, scream too.

86   As she was whipped skyward once more, her arms were wrapped around the little girl. Not in flight, not soaring, but anchored by another's being, as her parents stood against the liberators to protect their land.

87   Some curves, a gentle dip, one last sharp bend, and the ride rumbled to rest. The girl's breath was warm against Mrs. Chow's neck. For a moment longer she held on to the girl, whose small ribs were as thin as paintbrushes.

88   The Chows walked to the edge of the platform. He looked up at the billboard he had noticed earlier. It was a picture of an American woman with bright red hair, large red lips, and a slightly upturned nose; a fur was draped around her neck, pearls cut across her throat.

89   "What do you suppose they're selling?" he asked.

90   His wife pointed at the billboard. She read aloud what was printed there: "No other home permanent wave looks, feels, behaves so much like naturally curly hair."

91   She then gave a quick translation and asked what he thought of her curling her hair.

92   He made no reply. For some time now he couldn't lift his eyes from her.

93   "I won't do it," she said, "but what do you say?"

94   She turned away from him and stared a long time at the face on the billboard and then at the beach on the other side of the boardwalk and at the ocean, the Pacific Ocean, and at the horizon where all lines of sight converge, before she realized the land on the other side wouldn't come into view.

DISCUSSION QUESTIONS

1. What is the difference in background between Mr. and Mrs. Chow, and what kind of relationship do they have?
2. How important are the settings in this story?
3. Has Mrs. Chow entirely given up her artistic ambitions? Explain.
4. As Mrs. Chow rides the roller coaster at the end of the story, she wraps her arms around the little girl and she continues to hold onto her for a moment after the ride has ended. What does this tell you about Mrs. Chow?
5. How would you describe the structure of the plot?

WRITING TOPICS

1. Discuss the title of the story in an essay.
2. In an essay discuss how the tone of the story might have changed if it had been told from Mr. Chow's point of view.
3. Mrs. Chow believes that her imagination will return once she is able to leave the widow's house and she will be able to start a "great canvas." What kind of atmosphere is needed to nurture imagination and creativity? Discuss your ideas in an informal essay.

SCENT OF APPLES

Bienvenido Santos

Bienvenido Santos was born in 1911 in Manila and was educated in public schools and at the University of the Philippines. Coming to the United States in 1941, he spent the years of the Second World War pursuing an advanced education at American universities—the University of Illinois, Harvard, and Columbia. The United States government called upon Santos to tour the country in order to give lectures on Filipino culture and to meet other Filipinos. At first he was known as a storyteller who could describe, with great affection and charm, the "simple folk" of his homeland; but after coming into contact with so many lonely and disillusioned Filipinos in the United States, an awareness of his own isolation grew. This was especially true as he endured a long separation from his wife and three daughters during the war years and during the postwar decades, when he was a resident author on Midwestern campuses. According to scholar Leonard Casper, in much of Santos's fiction a compulsion to belong and to connect raises "images of departure and provisional return, of loss and attempted recovery."[1] Indeed, Santos explores feelings of displacement, flight, and loneliness throughout most of his fiction.

Although six collections of his writings have been published in the Philippines, *Scent of Apples* (1979), from which the following selection is taken, is the first volume of his work to appear in the United States. In the following excerpt, Santos is lecturing in southwestern Michigan—apple-growing country—when he takes a side trip to the hardscrabble farm of a Filipino immigrant with mournful memories of the homeland. (J.I.)

---

[1] Introduction to *Scent of Apples*, pages xi–xii.

1   When I arrived in Kalamazoo it was October and the war[1] was still on. Gold and silver stars hung on pennants above silent windows of white and brick-red cottages. In a backyard an old man burned leaves and twigs while a gray-haired woman sat on the porch, her red hands quiet on her lap, watching the smoke rising above the elms, both of them thinking the same thought perhaps, about a tall, grinning boy with blue eyes and flying hair, who went out to war: where could he be now this month when leaves were turning into gold and the fragrance of gathered apples was in the wind?

2   It was a cold night when I left my room at the hotel for a usual speaking engagement. I walked but a little way. A heavy wind coming up from Lake Michigan was icy on the face. It felt like winter straying early in the northern woodlands. Under the lampposts the leaves shone like bronze. And they rolled on the pavements like the ghost feet of a thousand autumns long dead, long before the boys left for faraway lands without great icy winds and promise of winter early in the air, lands without apple trees, *the singing and the gold!*

3   It was the same night I met Celestino Fabia, "just a Filipino farmer" as he called himself, who had a farm about thirty miles east of Kalamazoo.

4   "You came all that way on a night like this just to hear me talk?" I asked.

5   "I've seen no Filipino for so many years now," he answered quickly. "So when I saw your name in the papers where it says you come from the Islands and that you're going to talk, I come right away."

6   Earlier that night I had addressed a college crowd, mostly women. It appeared that they wanted me to talk about my country, they wanted me to tell them things about it because my country had become a lost country.[2] Everywhere in the land the enemy stalked. Over it a great silence hung, and their boys were there, unheard from, or they were on their way to some little known island on the Pacific, young boys all, hardly men, thinking of harvest moons and smell of forest fire.

7   It was not hard talking about our own people. I knew them well and I loved them. And they seemed so far away during those terrible years that I must have spoken of them with a little fervor, a little nostalgia.

8   In the open forum that followed, the audience wanted to know whether there was much difference between our women and the American women. I tried to answer the question as best as I could, saying, among other things, that I did not know that much about American women, except that they looked friendly, but differences or similarities in inner qualities such as naturally belonged to the heart or to the mind, I could only speak about with vagueness.

---

[1] *the war:* World War II.

[2] *my country had become a lost country:* Japan invaded the Philippines in 1942 with the fall of Bataan; Filipinos living in the United States could not return home until the end of the war in the Pacific in 1945.

9   While I was trying to explain away the fact that it was not easy to make comparisons, a man rose from the rear of the hall, wanting to say something. In the distance, he looked slight and old and very brown. Even before he spoke, I knew that he was, like me, a Filipino.

10   "I'm a Filipino," he began, loud and clear, in a voice that seemed used to wide open spaces, "I'm just a Filipino farmer out in the country." He waved his hand toward the door. "I left the Philippines more than twenty years ago and have never been back. Never will perhaps. I want to find out, sir, are our Filipino women the same like they were twenty years ago?"

11   As he sat down, the hall filled with voices, hushed and intrigued. I weighed my answer carefully. I did not want to tell a lie yet I did not want to say anything that would seem platitudinous, insincere. But more important than these considerations, it seemed to me that moment as I looked towards my countryman, I must give him an answer that would not make him so unhappy. Surely, all these years, he must have held on to certain ideals, certain beliefs, even illusions peculiar to the exile.

12   "First," I said as the voices gradually died down and every eye seemed upon me, "First, tell me what our women were like twenty years ago."

13   The man stood to answer. "Yes," he said, "you're too young . . . Twenty years ago our women were nice, they were modest, they wore their hair long, they dressed proper and went for no monkey business. They were natural, they went to church regular, and they were faithful." He had spoken slowly, and now in what seemed like an afterthought, added, "It's the men who ain't."

14   Now I knew what I was going to say.

15   "Well," I began, "it will interest you to know that our women have changed—but definitely! The change, however, has been on the outside only. Inside, here," pointing to the heart, "they are the same as they were twenty years ago. God-fearing, faithful, modest, and *nice*."

16   The man was visibly moved. "I'm very happy, sir," he said, in the manner of one who, having stakes on the land, had found no cause to regret one's sentimental investment.

17   After this, everything that was said and done in that hall that night seemed like an anti-climax, and later, as we walked outside, he gave me his name and told me of his farm thirty miles east of the city.

18   We had stopped at the main entrance to the hotel lobby. We had not talked very much on the way. As a matter of fact, we were never alone. Kindly American friends talked to us, asked us questions, said goodnight. So now I asked him whether he cared to step into the lobby with me and talk.

19   "No, thank you," he said, "you are tired. And I don't want to stay out too late."

20   "Yes, you live very far."

21   "I got a car," he said, "besides . . ."

22   Now he smiled, he truly smiled. All night I had been watching his face and I wondered when he was going to smile.

23   "Will you do me a favor, please," he continued smiling almost sweetly. "I want you to have dinner with my family out in the country. I'd call for you tomorrow afternoon, then drive you back. Will that be all right?"

24   "Of course," I said. "I'd love to meet your family." I was leaving Kalamazoo for Muncie, Indiana, in two days. There was plenty of time.

25   "You will make my wife very happy," he said.

26   "You flatter me."

27   "Honest. She'll be very happy. Ruth is a country girl and hasn't met many Filipinos. I mean Filipinos younger than I, cleaner looking. We're just poor farmer folk, you know, and we don't get to town very often. Roger, that's my boy, he goes to school in town. A bus takes him early in the morning and he's back in the afternoon. He's nice boy."

28   "I bet he is," I agreed. "I've seen the children of some of the boys by their American wives and the boys are tall, taller than the father, and very good looking."

29   "Roger, he'd be tall. You'll like him."

30   Then he said goodbye and I waved to him as he disappeared in the darkness.

31   The next day he came, at about three in the afternoon. There was a mild, ineffectual sun shining, and it was not too cold. He was wearing an old brown tweed jacket and worsted trousers to match. His shoes were polished, and although the green of his tie seemed faded, a colored shirt hardly accentuated it. He looked younger than he appeared the night before now that he was clean shaven and seemed ready to go to a party. He was grinning as we met.

32   "Oh, Ruth can't believe it. She can't believe it," he kept repeating as he led me to his car—a nondescript thing in faded black that had known better days and many hands. "I says to her, I'm bringing you a first class Filipino, and she says, aw, go away, quit kidding, there's no such thing as first class Filipino. But Roger, that's my boy, he believed me immediately. What's he like, daddy, he asks. Oh, you will see, I says, he's first class. Like you daddy? No, no, I laugh at him, your daddy ain't first class. Aw, but you are, daddy, he says. So you can see what a nice boy he is, so innocent. Then Ruth starts griping about the house, but the house is a mess, she says. True it's a mess, it's always a mess, but you don't mind, do you? We're poor folks, you know."

33   The trip seemed interminable. We passed through narrow lanes and disappeared into thickets, and came out on barren land overgrown with weeds in places. All around were dead leaves and dry earth. In the distance were apple trees.

34   "Aren't those apple trees?" I asked wanting to be sure.

35   "Yes, those are apple trees," he replied. "Do you like apples? I got lots of 'em. I got an apple orchard, I'll show you."

36   All the beauty of the afternoon seemed in the distance, on the hills, in the dull soft sky.

37   "Those trees are beautiful on the hills," I said.

38   "Autumn's a lovely season. The trees are getting ready to die, and they show their colors, proud-like."

39   "No such thing in our own country," I said.

40   That remark seemed unkind, I realized later. It touched him off on a long deserted tangent, but ever there perhaps. How many times did the lonely mind take unpleasant detours away from the familiar winding lanes towards home for fear of this, the remembered hurt, the long lost youth, the grim shadows of the years; how many times indeed, only the exile knows.

41   It was a rugged road we were travelling and the car made so much noise that I could not hear everything he said, but I understood him. He was telling his story for the first time in many years. He was remembering his own youth. He was thinking of home. In these odd moments there seemed no cause for fear no cause at all, no pain. That would come later. In the night perhaps. Or lonely on the farm under the apple trees.

42   *In this old Visayan town, the streets are narrow and dirty and strewn with coral shells. You have been there? You could not have missed our house, it was the biggest in town, one of the oldest, ours was a big family. The house stood right on the edge of the street. A door opened heavily and you enter a dark hall leading to the stairs. There is the smell of chickens roosting on the low-topped walls, there is the familiar sound they make and you grope your way up a massive staircase, the bannisters smooth upon the trembling hand. Such nights, they are no better than the days, windows are closed against the sun; they close heavily.*

43   *Mother sits in her corner looking very white and sick. This was her world, her domain. In all these years, I cannot remember the sound of her voice. Father was different. He moved about. He shouted. He ranted. He lived in the past and talked of honor as though it were the only thing.*

44   *I was born in that house. I grew up there into a pampered brat. I was mean. One day I broke their hearts. I saw mother cry wordlessly as father heaped his curses upon me and drove me out of the house, the gate closing heavily after me. And my brothers and sisters took up my father's hate for me and multiplied it numberless times in their own broken hearts. I was no good.*

45   *But sometimes, you know, I miss that house, the roosting chickens on the low-topped walls. I miss my brothers and sisters, Mother sitting in her chair, looking like a pale ghost in a corner of the room. I would remember the great live posts, massive tree trunks from the forests. Leafy plants grew on the sides, buds pointing downwards, wilted and died before they could become flowers. As they fell on the floor, father bent to pick them and throw them out into the coral streets. His hands were strong. I have kissed these hands . . . many times, many times.*

46 Finally we rounded a deep curve and suddenly came upon a shanty, all but ready to crumble in a heap on the ground, its plastered walls were rotting away, the floor was hardly a foot from the ground. I thought of the cottages of the poor colored folk in the south, the hovels of the poor everywhere in the land. This one stood all by itself as though by common consent all the folk that used to live here had decided to stay away, despising it, ashamed of it. Even the lovely season could not color it with beauty.

47 A dog barked loudly as we approached. A fat blonde woman stood at the door with a little boy by her side. Roger seemed newly scrubbed. He hardly took his eyes off me. Ruth had a clean apron around her shapeless waist. Now as she shook my hands in sincere delight I noticed shamefacedly (that I should notice) how rough her hands, how coarse and red with labor, how ugly! She was no longer young and her smile was pathetic.

48 As we stepped inside and the door closed behind us, immediately I was aware of the familiar scent of apples. The room was bare except for a few ancient pieces of second-hand furniture. In the middle of the room stood a stove to keep the family warm in winter. The walls were bare. Over the dining table hung a lamp yet unlighted.

49 Ruth got busy with the drinks. She kept coming in and out of a rear room that must have been the kitchen and soon the table was heavy with food, fried chicken legs and rice, and green peas and corn on the ear. Even as we ate, Ruth kept standing, and going to the kitchen for more food. Roger ate like a little gentleman.

50 "Isn't he nice looking?" his father asked.

51 "You are a handsome boy, Roger," I said.

52 The boy smiled at me. "You look like Daddy," he said.

53 Afterwards I noticed an old picture leaning on the top of a dresser and stood to pick it up. It was yellow and soiled with many fingerings. The faded figure of a woman in Philippine dress could yet be distinguished although the face had become a blur.

54 "Your . . ." I began.

55 "I don't know who she is," Fabia hastened to say. "I picked that picture many years ago in a room on La Salle Street in Chicago. I have often wondered who she is."

56 "The face wasn't a blur in the beginning?"

57 "Oh, no. It was a young face and good."

58 Ruth came with a plate full of apples.

59 "Ah," I cried, picking out a ripe one. "I've been thinking where all the scent of apples came from. The room is full of it."

60 "I'll show you," said Fabia.

61 He showed me a backroom, not very big. It was half-full of apples.

62 "Every day," he explained. "I take some of them to town to sell to the groceries. Prices have been low. I've been losing on the trips."

63   "These apples will spoil," I said.

64   "We'll feed them to the pigs."

65   Then he showed me around the farm. It was twilight now and the apple trees stood bare against a glowing western sky. In apple blossom time it must be lovely here, I thought. But what about wintertime?

66   One day, according to Fabia, a few years ago, before Roger was born, he had an attack of acute appendicitis. It was deep winter. The snow lay heavy everywhere. Ruth was pregnant and none too well herself. At first she did not know what to do. She bundled him in warm clothing and put him on a cot near the stove. She shoveled the snow from their front door and practically carried the suffering man on her shoulders, dragging him through the newly made path towards the road where they waited for the U.S. Mail car to pass. Meanwhile snowflakes poured all over them and she kept rubbing the man's arms and legs as she herself nearly froze to death.

67   "Go back to the house, Ruth!" her husband cried, "you'll freeze to death."

68   But she clung to him wordlessly. Even as she massaged his arms and legs, her tears rolled down her cheeks. "I won't leave you. I won't leave you," she repeated.

69   Finally the U.S. Mail car arrived. The mailman, who knew them well, helped them board the car, and, without stopping on his usual route, took the sick man and his wife direct to the nearest hospital.

70   Ruth stayed in the hospital with Fabia. She slept in a corridor outside the patients' ward and in the day time helped in scrubbing the floor and washing the dishes and cleaning the men's things. They didn't have enough money and Ruth was willing to work like a slave.

71   "Ruth's a nice girl," said Fabia, "like our own Filipino women."

72   Before nightfall, he took me back to the hotel. Ruth and Roger stood at the door holding hands and smiling at me. From inside the room of the shanty, a low light flickered. I had a last glimpse of the apple trees in the orchard under the darkened sky as Fabia backed up the car. And soon we were on our way back to town. The dog had started barking. We could hear it for some time, until finally, we could not hear it anymore, and all was darkness around us, except where the head lamps revealed a stretch of road leading somewhere.

73   Fabia did not talk this time. I didn't seem to have anything to say myself. But when finally we came to the hotel and I got down, Fabia said, "Well, I guess I won't be seeing you again."

74   It was dimly lighted in front of the hotel and I could hardly see Fabia's face. Without getting off the car, he moved to where I had sat, and I saw him extend his hand. I gripped it.

75   "Tell Ruth and Roger," I said, "I love them."

76   He dropped my hand quickly. "They'll be waiting for me now," he said.

77   "Look," I said, not knowing why I said it, "one of these days, very soon, I hope, I'll be going home. I could go to your town."

78   "No," he said softly, sounding very much defeated but brave, "Thanks a lot. But, you see, nobody would remember me now."

79   Then he started the car, and as it moved away, he waved his hand.

80   "Goodbye," I said, waving back into the darkness. And suddenly the night was cold like winter straying early in these northern woodlands.

81   I hurried inside. There was a train the next morning that left for Muncie, Indiana, at a quarter after eight.

Discussion Questions

1. Has Fabia's economic condition improved or deteriorated as a result of his immigration to the United States? Offer evidence for your response.
2. Is Fabia satisfied with his new life in the United States? If you answer no, what appears to be missing for Fabia? If yes, what does he find satisfaction in?
3. At the lecture Fabia remarks that the women in the Philippines were faithful but the men were not. What do you think this remark suggests about the differences in the relationships between men and women in the United States and the Philippines?
4. What is the mood of this story and how is it achieved?
5. How does Ruth compare with Filipino women according to Fabia?
6. What do the narrator's reactions to Fabia tell you about the narrator?

Writing Topics

1. In a brief essay, discuss what you think is the theme of this story. Cite evidence from the story to support your views.
2. Decide what you think is the strongest feature of this story: plot, characterization, dialogue, theme, or something else. In an essay, analyze that feature and why it is successful.

FROM *MONKEY BRIDGE*

Lan Cao

Lan Cao was born in Saigon, Vietnam, in 1961, and left that country for the United States in 1975. She is a graduate of Mount Holyoke College (1983) and Yale University Law School (1987). She received a Ford Foundation fellowship in 1991 and is currently a professor of international law at Brooklyn Law School.

Cao is the coeditor of *Everything You Need to Know About Asian Americans* (1996) and has written many articles in the field of Asian American Studies. Her first novel, *Monkey Bridge* (1997), received much critical attention. The term "monkey bridge" refers to a bridge made of flimsy bamboo that spans perilous terrain. Such treacherous bridges were used by Vietnamese peasants for centuries. The novel makes use of Vietnamese myth, history, and dreams to tell both a typical American immigrant story and a darker tale of a mother's revenge.

[1]   "Connecticut is not the safest place in America," my mother had insisted stubbornly. Since she left Vietnam on April 30, 1975, she had spent four months at Fort Chaffee, an Arkansas army camp used as a refugee-resettlement center, and we were trying to decide on a place to live. It did not matter that I was already settled in Connecticut with Uncle Michael and Aunt Mary. The paraphernalia of trust that coaxed my mother to Northern Virginia consisted of a Catholic church willing to sponsor us, but, most important of all, Virginia beckoned because it was a mere thirty minutes away from Washington, D.C., capital of the United States and of the Free World. "In war," she said, "the capital of any country is like the king in a game of chess. It's what you protect first and foremost, because it's the most precious. The same way you intuitively bring your arms to shield your face. The way a mother lion embraces its cubs in the folds of its own body."

2   She did not notice that we had left the age of guerrilla warfare. That, in a nuclear age, Washington, D.C., and its vicinity would probably be the first target of an intercontinental ballistic missile launched by the Soviet Union was not a possibility she had truly considered.

3   And so it was that on our first night in Virginia, six months or so after I had entered the United States, my mother whispered, "This is now the safest place in the world." From our bed, with my mother by my side, I could see the moon etched against our windowpane, fat and full of milk, clinging with great expectations to the sanctuary of the lavender-blue sky. It hardly mattered that all around us ghosts of a different war lingered, the Battle of Fredericksburg, the Battle of Bull Run, Confederate victories secured by Robert E. Lee's Army of Northern Virginia.

4   There was nothing to be afraid of. My mother and I were looking at a country in love with itself, beckoning us to feel the same. We'd cross the rough edges of the war into this lustrous new territory that faced the heart of the nation's capital. We were on a flabby mattress, in an empty but uncursed apartment, waiting for tomorrow to arrive.

5   "You can lose a country. But no one, no war can take away your education," my mother reassured me as we lay together in bed. "You will have the best education in America," she whispered.

6   Years later, that was the hook I had used to trick my mother into my idea of college, American-style. Every serious student in America embarked on a four-year quest, to be taught by a master teacher at a college far away from home, I had explained. It was the equivalent of a martial artist leaving her village to study kung fu at the Shaolin Temple, I would say, or even Siddhartha Gautama[1] going away to seek enlightenment under the bo tree. It was as prestigious as a local scholar being admitted to the mandarin rank at the emperor's court. And although she did not do it with grace, she believed me. Bit by bit, I tricked her into believing the reason I wanted to leave was to attend college, not to flee from a phantom world that could no longer offer comfort or sanctuary.

7   I discovered soon after my arrival in Falls Church that everything, even the simple business of shopping the American way, unsettled my mother's nerves. From the outside, it had been an ordinary building that held no promises or threats beyond four walls anchored to a concrete parking lot. But inside, the A & P brimmed with unexpected abundance. Built-in metal stands overflowed with giant oranges and grapefruits meticulously arranged into a pyramid. Columns of canned vegetables and fruits stood among multiple shelves as people well rehearsed to the demands of modern shopping meandered through the fluorescent aisles. I remembered the sharp chilled

---

[1] *Siddhartha Gautama:* the original name of the prince who eventually received enlightenment and became the Buddha.

air against my face, the way the hydraulic door made a sucking sound as it closed behind.

8   My first week in Connecticut with Uncle Michael and Aunt Mary, I thought Aunt Mary was a genius shopper. She appeared to have the sixth sense of a bat and could identify, record, and register every item on sale. She was skilled in the art of coupon shopping—in the American version of Vietnamese haggling, the civil and acceptable mode of getting the customers to think they had gotten a good deal.

9   The day after I arrived in Farmington, Aunt Mary navigated the cart— and me—through aisles, numbered and categorized, crammed with jars and cardboard boxes, and plucked from them the precise product to match the coupons she carried. I had been astonished that day that the wide range of choices did not disrupt her plan. We had a schedule, I discovered, which Aunt Mary mapped out on a yellow pad, and which we followed, checking off item after item. She called it the science of shopping, the ability to resist the temptations of dazzling packaging. By the time we were through, our cart would be filled to the rim with cans of Coke, the kinds with flip-up caps that made can openers obsolete, in family-size cartons. We had chicken and meat sealed in tight, odorless packages, priced and weighed. We had fruits so beautifully polished and waxed they looked artificial. And for me, we had mangoes and papayas that were still hard and green but which Aunt Mary had handed to me like rare jewels from a now extinct land.

10   But my mother did not appreciate the exacting orderliness of the A & P. She could not give in to the precision of previously weighed and packaged food, the bloodlessness of beef slabs in translucent wrappers, the absence of carcasses and pigs' heads. In Saigon, we had only outdoor markets. "Sky markets," they were called, vast, prosperous expanses in the middle of the city where barrels of live crabs and yellow carps and booths of ducks and geese would be stacked side by side with cardboard stands of expensive silk fabric from Hong Kong. It was always noisy there—a voluptuous mix of animal and human sounds that the air itself had assimilated and held. The sharp acrid smell of gutters choked by the monsoon rain. The unambiguous odor of dried horse dung that lingered in the atmosphere, partially camouflaged by the fat, heavy scent of guavas and bananas.

11   My mother knew the vendors and even the shoppers by name and would take me from stall to stall to expose me to her skills. They were all addicted to each other's oddities. My mother would feign indifference and they would inevitably call out to her. She would heed their call and they would immediately retreat into sudden apathy. They knew my mother's slick bargaining skills, and she, in turn, knew how to navigate with grace through their extravagant prices and rehearsed huffiness. Theirs had been a mating dance, a match of wills.

12 Toward the center of the market, a man with a spotted boa constrictor coiled around his neck stood and watched day after day over an unruly hodgepodge of hand-dyed cotton shirts, handkerchiefs, and swatches of white muslin; funerals were big business in Vietnam. To the side, in giant paper bags slit with round openings, were canaries and hummingbirds which my mother bought, one hundred at a time, and freed, one by one, into our garden; it was a good deed designed to generate positive karma[2] for the family. My mother, like the country itself, was obsessed with karma. In fact, the Vietnamese word for "please," as in "could you please," means literally "to make good karma." "Could you please pass the butter" becomes "Please make good karma and pass me the butter." My mother would cup each bird in her hand and set it on my head. It was her way of immersing me in a well-spring of karmic charm, and in that swift moment of delight when the bird's wings spread over my head as it contemplated flight, I believed life itself was utterly beautiful and blessed.

13 Every morning, we drifted from stack to stack, vendor to vendor. There were no road maps to follow—tables full of black market Prell and Colgate were pocketed among vegetable stands one day and jars of medicinal herbs the next. The market was randomly organized, and only the mighty and experienced like my mother could navigate its patternless paths.

14 But with a sense of neither drama nor calamity, my mother's ability to navigate and decipher simply became undone in our new life. She preferred the improvisation of haggling to the conventional certainty of discount coupons, the primordial messiness and fishmongers' stink of the open-air market to the aroma-free order of individually wrapped fillets.

15 Now, a mere three and a half years or so after her last call to the sky market, the dreadful truth was simply this: we were going through life in reverse, and I was the one who would help my mother through the hard scrutiny of ordinary suburban life. I would have to forgo the luxury of adolescent experiments and temper tantrums, so that I could scoop my mother out of harm's way and give her sanctuary. Now, when we stepped into the exterior world, I was the one who told my mother what was acceptable or unacceptable behavior.

16 All children of immigrant parents have experienced these moments. When it first occurs, when the parent first reveals the behavior of a child, is a defining moment. Of course, all children eventually watch their parents' astonishing return to the vulnerability of childhood, but for us the process begins much earlier than expected.

17 "We don't have to pay the moment we decide to buy the pork. We can put as much as we want in the cart and pay only once, at the checkout

---

[2] *karma:* In Hinduism and Buddhism, the force generated by people's actions that determines their destiny in their next life.

counter." It took a few moments' hesitation for my mother to succumb to the peculiarity of my explanation.

18   And even though I hesitated to take on the responsibility, I had no other choice. It was not a simple process, the manner in which my mother relinquished motherhood. The shift in status occurred not just in the world but in the safety of our home as well, and it became most obvious when we entered the realm of language. I was like Kiki, my pet bird in Saigon, tongue untwisted and sloughed of its rough and thick exterior. According to my mother, feeding the bird crushed red peppers had caused it to shed its tongue in successive layers and allowed it to speak the language of humans.

19   Every morning during that month of February 1975, while my mother paced the streets of Saigon and witnessed the country's preparation for imminent defeat, I followed Aunt Mary around the house, collecting words like a beggar gathering rain with an earthen pan. She opened her mouth, and out came a constellation of gorgeous sounds. Each word she uttered was a round stone, with the smoothness of something that had been rubbed and polished by the waves of a warm summer beach. She could swim straight through her syllables. On days when we studied together, I almost convinced myself that we would continue that way forever, playing with the movement of sound itself. I would listen as she tried to inspire me into replicating the "th" sound with the seductive powers of her voice. "Slip the tip of your tongue between your front teeth and pull it back real quick," she would coax and coax. Together, she and I sketched the English language, its curious cadence and rhythm, into the receptive Farmington landscape. Only with Aunt Mary and Uncle Michael could I give myself an inheritance my parents never gave me: the gift of language. The story of English was nothing less than the poetry of sound and motion. To this day, Aunt Mary's voice remains my standard for perfection.

20   My superior English meant that, unlike my mother and Mrs. Bay, I knew the difference between "cough" and "enough," "bough" and "through," "trough" and "thorough," "dough" and "fought." Once I made it past the fourth or fifth week in Connecticut, the new language Uncle Michael and Aunt Mary were teaching me began gathering momentum, like tumbleweed in a storm. This was my realization: we have only to let one thing go—the language we think in, or the composition of our dream, the grass roots clinging underneath its rocks—and all at once everything goes. It had astonished me, the ease with which continents shift and planets change course, the casual way in which the earth goes about shedding the laborious folds of its memories. Suddenly, out of that difficult space between here and there, English revealed itself to me with the ease of thread unspooled. I began to understand the levity and weight of its sentences. First base, second base, home run. New terminologies were not difficult to master, and gradually the possibility of perfection began edging its way into my life. How did those numerous

Chinatowns and Little Italys sustain the will to maintain a distance, the desire to inhabit the edge and margin of American life? A mere eight weeks into Farmington, and the American Dream was exerting a sly but seductive pull.

21 By the time I left Farmington to be with my mother, I had already created for myself a different, more sacred tongue. Khe Sanh, the Tet Offensive, the Ho Chi Minh Trail—a history as imperfect as my once obviously imperfect English—these were things that had rushed me into the American melting pot. And when I saw my mother again, I was no longer the same person she used to know. Inside my new tongue, my real tongue, was an astonishing new power. For my mother and her Vietnamese neighbors, I became the keeper of the word, the only one with access to the lightworld. Like Adam, I had the God-given right to name all the fowls of the air and all the beasts of the field.

22 The right to name, I quickly discovered, also meant the right to stand guard over language and the right to claim unadulterated authority. Here was a language with an ocean's quiet mystery, and it would be up to me to render its vastness comprehensible to the newcomers around me. My language skill, my ability to decipher the nuances of American life, was what held us firmly in place, night after night, in our Falls Church living room. The ease with which I could fabricate wholly new plot lines from TV made the temptation to invent especially difficult to resist.

23 And since my mother couldn't understand half of what anyone was saying, television watching, for me, was translating and more. This, roughly, was how things went in our living room:

24 The Bionic Woman had just finished rescuing a young girl, approximately my age, from drowning in a lake where she'd gone swimming against her mother's wishes. Once out of harm's way, Jaime made the girl promise she'd be more careful next time and listen to her mother.

25 Translation: the Bionic Woman rescued the girl from drowning in the lake, but commended her for her magnificent deeds, since the girl had heroically jumped into the water to rescue a prized police dog.

26 "Where's the dog?" my mother would ask. "I don't see him."

27 "He's not there anymore, they took him to the vet right away. Remember?" I sighed deeply.

28 "Oh," my mother said. "It's strange. Strong girl, Bionic Woman."

29 The dog that I convinced her existed on the television screen was no more confusing than the many small reversals in logic and the new identities we experienced her first few months in America.

30 "I can take you in this aisle," a store clerk offered as she unlocked a new register to accommodate the long line of customers. She gestured us to "come over here" with an upturned index finger, a disdainful hook we Vietnamese use to summon dogs and other domestic creatures. My mother did not understand the ambiguity of American hand gestures. In Vietnam, we said "Come

here" to humans differently, with our palm up and all four fingers waved in unison—the way people over here waved goodbye. A typical Vietnamese signal beckoning someone to "come here" would prompt, in the United States, a "goodbye," a response completely opposite from the one desired.

31   "Even the store clerks look down on us," my mother grumbled as we walked home. This was a truth I was only beginning to realize: it was not the enormous or momentous event, but the gradual suggestion of irrevocable and protracted change that threw us off balance and made us know in no uncertain terms that we would not be returning to the familiarity of our former lives.

32   It was, in many ways, a lesson in what was required to sustain a new identity: it all had to do with being able to adopt a different posture, to reach deep enough into the folds of the earth to relocate one's roots and bend one's body in a new direction, pretending at the same time that the world was the same now as it had been the day before. I strove for the ability to realign my eyes, to shift with a shifting world and convince both myself and the rest of the world into thinking that, if the earth moved and I moved along with it, that motion, however agitated, would be undetectable. The process, which was as surprising as a river reversing course and flowing upstream, was easier said than done.

33   All of Little Saigon maneuvered to pull the experiment off. The obsession with optical illusion was something I might have learned from my mother's friends. It became something of a community endeavor, the compulsion to deceive. Mrs. Bay, whose name translated literally into "Mrs. Seven," since she was the seventh child in her family, gave herself a new birthday the day she applied for her Social Security card, for no other reason than that she no longer wanted to be associated with the Year of the Rat. Her husband, who had died years before, had been born in the Year of the Cat. Spurred by the ease with which all of us could produce new identities, Mrs. Bay made herself two years younger and became, in one easy revolutionary twist, a tiger toying with a domesticated pet. "When I see him again in the next life, I will be the boss," she said, laughing. "That crazy old cat will expect to see a rat, but he'll see a tiger instead." In their new shadow warfare, Mrs. Bay would resurrect old battles she had once fought against her husband and rewrite the endings.

34   Like all of us who made up the refugee community, Little Saigon too was preoccupied with the possibility of astrological and historical revisions. It was as if the refugee portion of Falls Church decided that it would simply stretch its limbs, lean into the wind, and heave itself in a new, untried direction. Little Saigon was the still-tender, broken-off part of the old, old world, and over here, so far away from the old country, our ghosts could roam unattached to the old personalities we once inhabited. There was an odd element of righteousness in this transformation. Out of the ruins came a clat-

ter of new personalities. A bar girl who once worked at Saigon's Queen Bee, a nightclub frequented by American soldiers, acquired a past as a virtuous Confucian teacher from a small village in a distant province. Here, in the vehemently anti-Vietcong refugee community, draft dodgers and ordinary foot soldiers could become decorated veterans of battlefields as famous as Kontum and Pleiku and Xuan Loc. It was the Vietnamese version of the American Dream; a new spin, the Vietnam spin, to the old immigrant faith in the future. Not only could we become anything we wanted to be in America, we could change what we had once been in Vietnam. Rebirthing the past, we called it, claiming what had once been a power reserved only for gods and other immortal beings.

35   The absence of documentation was not surprising. Even those with identification papers burned them before any authority could see. There was, after all, something awesome about a truly uncluttered beginning, the complete absence of identity, of history.

36   "Tell the Americans you couldn't have brought anything with you," Mrs. Bay advised her friends. "Who could have thought to bring birth certificates and photo identifications?" One after another, we were all taking leave of our old lives and sharing our liars' wisdom.

37   "Tell the teachers your daughter was a fifth-grader in Saigon, even if she was only in third grade—steal a few extra years for your daughter, why not. Better yet, tell them your son was in the eighth grade, even if he was really in the tenth. That way, when he surpasses his eighth-grade classmates with his tenth-grade skills, they will think he is especially gifted," Mrs. Bay told them.

38   There was other advice as well. From my mother I discovered the importance of maintaining a silence.

39   "Keep what you see behind your eyes, and save what you think under your tongue. Let your thoughts glow from within. Hide your true self," my mother warned, her arms like iron scaffolding clasping me tight. " 'Sage,' " she said, "is a Sanskrit term for 'silent one.' " My mother had already begun to see me, even as early as our first year in Virginia, as somebody volatile and unreliable, an outsider with inside information—someone whose tongue had to be perpetually checked and contained.

40   But there were real reasons why not hiding our true selves would have been unthinkable, why shape-shifting had been so important even by ordinary standards. America had rendered us invisible and at the same time awfully conspicuous. We would have to relinquish not just the little truths—the year of our birth, where we once worked and went to school—but also the bigger picture as well.

41   "We're guests in this country. And good guests don't upset their hosts," I had been told. I was not ignorant of history. We would have to go through the motions and float harmlessly as permanent guests, with no more impact on our surroundings than the mild, leisurely pace of an ordinary day. We

would have to make ourselves innocuous and present to the outside world a mild, freeze-dried version of history.

42   After all, there was a difference, especially in 1975, between being a mere foreigner and a Vietnamese. Foreigner was quaint, but Vietnamese was trouble. Once, not long ago, Vietnam was just a country. But in America, Vietnam meant war, antipathies. I didn't want to parade an unpleasant American experience in America.

43   Even without papers and identifications, all of us in Little Saigon had left too long a trail of history to erase. Ours, after all, was an inescapable history that continued to be dissected and remodeled by a slew of commentators and experts months after April 1975. Against a clenched and complicated landscape, the picture continued to be played and replayed, glowering from the curved glass pane of the television set, a silent rage that careened through the buzzing darkness of our new lives.

44   In the rectangle of a room where the television stood, months after the actual collapse of South Vietnam, my mother and I watched the slow-motion disintegration of our country through the ice-white lens of an American camera. Lolloping streaks of fire crisscrossed bruised, purple skies, and from a balcony a white bedsheet tied to the end of a pole—the universal symbol of surrender—swayed gently in the breeze, a shadowy presence as strange and surreal as a funeral dress. Even through the glass screen of the television set, we were not immune from the infection that accompanied the imminence of doom. The sad, savage end was in sight, played and replayed slowly, with the pace and rhythm of a second hand, brooding notch by notch across the stark face of the impassive screen.

45   A South Vietnamese colonel, someone reported, had shot himself in front of the war memorial my mother believed to be a bad omen. Minutes before the South's surrender, the colonel, dressed in full uniform and decked in medals, had walked up the steps leading to the black statue, faced the National Assembly, saluted, and shot himself. I could almost hear the dusky, purple skies of Saigon, bloated as usual with the animal cries of bats and stray cats gorging on garbage and the indefatigable roar of motorcycle engines defying the curfew, and then suddenly the quick rat-tat-tat of the colonel's pistol, quick and clean, like the sound of a monk's clapping palms.

46   History was being catalogued here, the missed opportunities, blunders, and outright mistakes. Interesting stories were emerging, the commentators noted—America's elaborate determination, for instance, to keep all plans for the final evacuation a secret from the local population.

47   Weeks before the final American departure, while plans were being worked and reworked, it had apparently been clear that the giant tamarind tree in the parking lot of the United States Embassy would have to be cut down to make room for the final evacuation. To fell the tree would have

provoked a national panic—the tamarind tree had become a symbol of American protection, its branches, looming implacably from the embassy compounds, a reassuring reminder of American commitment to South Vietnam. The tree must have struck the ambassador as infinitely connected to history, and he had denied urgent requests that it be chopped down. There would be no panic while he was in charge. Something could still happen at the last minute—emergency aid from the United States, perhaps. But the marines under his command must have known better. They noted the width of the tamarind's torso, the way its branches spread haphazardly across the length of the parking lot. Outside the embassy compounds, Saigon was still struggling to fill its lungs with air. But inside, in the darkness of night, the men surreptitiously sawed through part of the massive trunk, and when the ambassador finally allowed it, all they had to do was topple it, simply and quietly, and with nothing but the weight and force of their bodies.

48 Already the story was being repeated as standard history. My mother continued to gaze at me to provide her with a plausible translation. "Are they saying anything important?" she whispered. Her undramatic transformation from mother to child could still be a surprise, even though I was beginning to believe that that aspect of her had always been there, like a stackable chair permanently folded inside her body. I reached over and stroked my mother's shoulders. We were in a new, immovable world, fortified by its proximity to Washington, D.C. From now on, our future lay in the capital of the Free World, our new home, where promises, real and hypothesized, would be made as extravagantly as they could be broken.

Discussion Questions

1. Why was the narrator's mother uncomfortable in the A & P?
2. The narrator says that "when the parent first reveals the behavior of a child, it is a defining moment." What does she mean and what was the most obvious illustration of this?
3. What makes the English words the narrator mentions in paragraph 20 so difficult for foreign speakers?
4. Why did the narrator's mother misinterpret the checkout clerk's gesture in the grocery store?
5. The Vietnamese in Little Saigon reinvented past histories. Why?
6. The narrator says the Vietnamese in America were both invisible and conspicuous. Explain this remark.

7. How were the Vietnamese in America made to confront their history and the "sad end" of the conflict in Vietnam?
8. What is ironic about the last sentence?

WRITING TOPICS

1. In an essay, characterize the tone of this selection and how the author conveys it.
2. Getting accustomed to a different way of shopping would seem to be a fairly simple transition for an immigrant, yet the narrator's mother in this selection is particularly overwhelmed by an American grocery store. In a journal entry, consider what you think would be your greatest challenges in moving to a new country with a different language and customs.

OUR FATHERS

M. Evelina Galang

Born in 1961 in Pennsylvania, M. Evelina Galang was raised in Illinois and Wisconsin. She now lives in Virginia, where she teaches creative writing at Old Dominion University. Her first book, *Her Wild American Self* (1996), according to author Marjorie Sandor, is a "witty and defiant stance against the stereotyping of Asian women. She strips away every form of category and limitation she discovers and delivers an honest, generous, and deeply felt celebration of the Filipina American experience."

In the following selection, a young girl longs for a relationship with her faraway grandparents as her immigrant family struggles to cope with adjusting to a new culture. (J.I.)

1 Tessa Villa carried a picture of her grandparents in a little hemp purse around her neck. Brown-toned and porous, scalloped at the edges, it seemed to defy the passing of time. She'd stare at the photo for hours, running her finger up and down her *lolo*'s[1] face, rubbing the picture to life, wondering which eye was the blind one. He wore dark glasses. Her father, Danilo, told her it was because one eye didn't work. Tessa focused on the lenses, hoping to see beyond the black-brown tint. She was concentrating, hoping to see the eyes behind them.

2 "You'll burn a hole into that picture, Tessa," her father told her. "Go help Mommy set the table."

3 It was dusk and they were surrounded by almost night. In their house, they conserved energy because Daddy said so. There were pockets of light in their home, in the kitchen where Tessa's mom worked, in the family room above her father's easy chair and over their dinner table, there was light,

---

[1] *lolo:* grandfather; *lola* is grandmother.

golden and safe. Danilo was reading the paper, listening to the six o'clock news and his daughter at once.

4   "Why does he wear sun glasses?" Tessa touched *Lolo*'s face, imagining what it would be like to lift the glasses. He stood at attention in a suit woven of shiny silk threads. His tie was dark, like the pomade-greased flat top of his hair. And if she squinted just right, Tessa could see her father in *Lolo*, his cheek bones sticking out above a slender face, his eyes black and strong beneath the tinted glass. Everything about *Lolo*'s expression, everything about his posture was serious.

5   Close to him stood her *lola*, dressed in a fancy gown, long and stiff and covered with embroidered flowers. Along the dress gleamed little clusters of pearls, like tiny bunches of grapes, opalescent bundles of fruit. Her sleeves were starched and high above her shoulder like butterfly wings. Her long black hair was pulled back into a stately bun. And propped on her nose, ready to slide off her face, sat a pair of rhinestone cat-eye glasses. Regular glasses.

6   "Why does *Lola* let him wear sun glasses?" They were clearly indoors.

7   "You know why, Tessa." Danilo turned a page and seeing the opportunity, Tessa crawled under the paper and into his lap.

8   "How did he lose his eye?" she asked as she pulled his face towards hers.

9   Resting her hands on the walls of his enormous face, she watched his expression. Her father was a handsome man. She knew it and all her friends said so too. "Did he look like you when he was young? I mean, except for the blind eye?" Tessa held onto Danilo firmly, waiting for him to tell her the story when David and Tony charged into the room.

10   "Tessa!" they shrieked. "Mom wants you to help her."

11   "Why can't you?" she asked them.

12   "We're boys!"

13   Danilo scooted her off his lap, and told her to help her mother in the kitchen. "We'll talk more later," he told her. "Or you know, what? You can ask him yourself, when he gets to the States."

14   She sighed, placing the photo back into her purse. "Okay, okay," she mumbled. "But when is he getting here?"

15   "Soon."

16   At dinner that night, she wondered about *Lolo*. She knew that during World War II he had been in the army. Maybe Japanese soldiers took his eye out in a fight. Maybe he had saved her father's barrio from destruction. Or maybe it was during a cock fight.

17   Her father liked to paint. All over their home, he painted oils of fantastic birds—red, orange, yellow raging birds. They were always suspended in mid-air, stunned and frozen. She remembered that her father used to sneak off to bet on these wild birds. He was always talking about getting caught

by his dad. Maybe, she thought, *Lolo* found him in a cock ring when he was supposed to be in school. Maybe he grabbed her father's collar, just as a rooster flew right into his face. Maybe *Lolo* had saved him, and lived.

18   "Tessa," her mother said, "I asked you to pass the rice to Tony, okay, *hija?*"[2]

19   "Sorry."

20   "I don't know about this girl, Daddy," her mother continued as she brushed her hand over her daughter's forehead. "Her head is always someplace else."

21   "I know what you mean, Nora," her father agreed. "She must get that from you, ha?"

22   "Sorry, Mom," she said again as she fingered the picture in her purse. She knew that photo so well, she knew where their faces were, could feel where the glasses interrupted the flow of his face. She was certain he had lost his eye heroically.

23   Her best friend, Carmen Hernandez, was always going to her Nana's and Poppa's house. She'd leave Tessa for entire weekends, which Tessa hated. She was always so bored when Carmen was gone. But then Carmen would bring back cookies and Mexican candy, piñatas and other new toys. Her Nana and Poppa were always giving Carmen presents. "It's their job," she told Tessa. "It's what grandparents do."

24   "I know," Tessa said. "You don't have to tell me."

25   "Too bad you don't have a nana and poppa."

26   "I have 'em. They just live in the Philippine Islands."

27   One Saturday, Carmen brought Tessa with her. The two girls spent most of Saturday morning sitting in a tree branch, spying on Nana. "She looks so young," Tessa whispered. She watched Nana pull a rack of cookies out of the oven, watched her springy head of black curls bob as she moved, watched as Nana puckered up her red lips and blew onto the hot tray.

28   "It's because she got married when she was thirteen," Carmen answered. She drew her legs close to her chest, hugging them. "That's how they do it in Mexico."

29   "Wow, I don't know when my *lola* married *Lolo*. But it must have been early too. She had seventeen babies, you know. Three of them died in the war." She pulled out the photo and showed it to Carmen. "Can you believe someone this pretty could have seventeen babies?"

30   "What war was that?" Carmen's pigtails were falling out of their red rubber bands.

31   "You know, World War II."

---

[2] *hija:* daughter.

32   Carmen took the photo from her and squinted at it hard. "Too bad you've never met your nana and poppa, huh?"

33   She nodded her head and thought of her neighbor Charlie. Sometimes, Tessa sat at her bedroom window, watching Charlie with his grandkids. He liked building them things—forts, boats, wagons. Some afternoons he sat with them under his tree, telling stories about Poland, telling ridiculous jokes and riddles. It seemed no matter what Charlie said, they were always giggling and tickling and yelling. She thought they were so lucky.

34   Tessa and David were lying with their faces to the floor, waiting for Tony to come from the bedroom. Their dad was so mad. While he was in the garage and their mother was napping, they played. Now they were waiting to get it. David and Tessa lay with their bare bums to the sky. Tony was already crying and he hadn't even taken his pants down yet.

35   They had turned the kitchen table into an altar, pushed it up against the wall and smeared blue and red tempera paint on the windows to make them look like stained glass. They took the white bread from its narrow plastic bag and pressed it flat with bottles. Then they cut perfect little circles out of them with scissors. They made Holy Communion. David played the part of the priest, Tessa the lady in church and Tony acted like an altar boy. The crusts were brushed off their makeshift altar onto the linoleum floor and the glass they had used to press the bread was also tossed to the floor. It had shattered like a giant church chime, splintered all over the floor and summoned their dad back into the house.

36   Now, they were waiting to get it. Danilo strutted around the family room, whacking his leather belt across his hand. He snapped and they shuddered. Tessa could hear Tony and she knew his face was red and blubbery. She could feel her bottom tense up every time Danilo cracked his belt.

37   "Tony," his father warned him, "pull your pants down. Now."

38   He cried and screamed, but eventually he pushed his pants to his ankles. Tessa peeked out of the cracks of her fingers, tasted the salt from them and started to giggle. Tony had pulled his pants down, alright, but he also had on ten pairs of underwear. She could see her father grinning, but still he scolded Tony.

39   How many times have I told you kids not to be so wild?" WHACK! It was only the air. "Why do you mess the house like this? Can't your mommy get any sleep?" ZAM! He slapped the carpet next to Tessa. "Tony, you take all the pants off and join your brother and sister." He slashed the air with the belt, an old trick for their father, the disciplinarian. Tony screamed as though he'd been hit.

40   They were scared. And they cried. But he never spanked them. He hit the carpet around them, his hand, snapping the belt on belt, but he never hit them. He scared them and they promised to be good children forever more.

41 Tessa loved the weekends. On Sundays, after Mass, Tessa's parents, Danilo and Nora Villa always brought them to the county park. On this day, she felt the sun beating down on their metallic green station wagon and the hot air smothering them, invading the spaces between them. Tony and David leaned against the vinyl backs of the front seat, with their noses buried into their father's ear. They were singing the jingle to their favorite fast food place. "Such a hap hap happy place . . ." She thought they were annoying, as always.

42 "Come on, Tessa," David said, nudging her. "Sing and maybe Dad'll get the hint."

43 "That is so stupid," she told him. She socked him in the arm and he sang even louder.

44 "Settle down, kids," Danilo said. "When your *lolo* and *lola* come you're going to have to learn to be quiet."

45 "How?" Tony asked.

46 "What your dad means," Nora explained, "is that your grandparents aren't used to small children. You'll make them dizzy."

47 "That seems weird," Tessa jumped in. "I mean they had seventeen babies."

48 The station wagon entered the park, driving into a sea of Sunday people. Tessa could hear the twinkling of an ice cream truck some place on the grounds, the waves crashing on the manmade lake, and she wriggled in her seat. She couldn't wait to get out of the car. "So, are *Lolo* and *Lola* coming soon?" she asked. "Every week you say they're coming."

49 "That's because we've been saving to bring them here," Danilo said. "So my mom and dad can see this life too."

50 He pulled the wagon's nose into a diagonal of cars. Looking out, Tessa saw people walking without pattern, surrounding their car and screaming to people on the other side of the park.

51 They settled under an oak tree, not far from the lake and ate Kentucky Fried Chicken and cold rice on paper plates. After lunch, their father took a ball of string, some left over rice, the Sunday paper, and a few tree branches and created a cartoon kite. He sculpted a "T" with the two sticks, held them together with a piece of string. He covered the frame with paper. The rice worked as glue, held the newspaper together like buttons on a coat, kept the corners of the kite square.

52 "This is how we made kites when I was a boy," he told them. Tessa watched her father's hands. They were long and dark. He worked quickly like a magic man.

53 "Your dad taught you," Tessa said. "Right? *Lolo.* Because they didn't have glue in your town and your dad showed you how to use rice for glue, right?"

54 "And he showed you how to make boats too," David said. Danilo took a couple of grains of rice and smeared them into the newspaper. He folded another piece over that and pressed.

55   When Tessa and the boys grew tired of the kite, Danilo built them a boat out of the travel section, and hats from fashion. "Look, Ma," Tessa said, as she ran to her mother who sat under a tree, reading a book. She waved the paper toys in Nora's face, fanning a tiny breeze up. Tessa's bangs flew from her face, her hot, sweaty face. The sun had flushed her pink and her hair was damp. "You have *pawis*,"[3] Nora said as she brushed the perspiration from her daughter's face. "I know," Tessa told her. Meanwhile, Danilo folded the rest of the paper into birds and animals that lived in a jungle on their picnic table. With magical words, he made the animals live and suddenly Tessa and the boys were the elephant, they were the tiger, the monkey. They acted like animals flying kites. They were the kites flying like birds, zipping across the light blue space, the sky.

56   On Friday night, the Villas threw a dinner party. They invited Carmen's parents, Uncle Tommy, Auntie Baby and Dr. Santos and his mother. She had just arrived from the Philippines and Tessa could not stop following her about. She was pretending Mrs. Santos was her grandmother's best friend, or better yet, that she was her grandmother. Mrs. Santos wore her hair exactly as her *lola* did in the photo. All night, the old woman sat quietly in a corner, away from the action, speaking occasionally, nodding to those who could not speak her language. Smiling always.

57   Tessa approached her and looked into her eyes. She took Mrs. Santos' hand and brought it to her forehead. When Tessa looked up, she saw the old woman giggling. Mrs. Santos pulled Tessa's face towards hers and pressed her pink powdered cheek next to Tessa's. Her face was full of soft wrinkles that wrapped itself in rings the way trees make rings in the passing of time.

58   "She knows how to make *mano?*"[4] Dr. Santos shouted. "That's amazing that a child from this country knows how to make *mano*." He reached down to pat Tessa's head. "Good for you, *hija*. It's good to see kids still respecting their elders."

59   "She's practicing for her own *lola*," Danilo said. "Aren't you, sweetheart?" Tessa beamed, stood tall. Yes, she thought, I am.

60   Carmen, Tony, David and Tessa sat in the kitchen, eating at the children's table. They were low to the ground, in a world of their own as the grown-ups whizzed about them, talking at once, laughing at everything, hearing absolutely nothing.

61   From where she sat, she could see slips hanging from skirts, high heels piercing the toes of leather shoes and pant legs being hoisted as they took

---

[3] *pawis*: sweat.
[4] *mano*: a gesture of respect for one's elders; a younger person takes an older person's hand and places the back of the hand against his or her forehead.

their places in the dining room next door. She watched Mrs. Santos shuffle her old feet under the table. Her legs were brown and bare. She wore straw slippers, embroidered with bright flowers like the hemp purse Tessa wore around her neck.

62   "Leave me alone," Carmen said as she pulled her hand away from David. "Just eat your own food."

63   "Shhht," Tessa warned them. Standing from the table, she motioned Carmen to follow. They crouched their bodies so low, they felt invisible, tiny like mice shooting from behind the china cabinet.

64   The listened to the low garble of conversation filter out of the adult mouths, teetering in the air like bubbles in a cartoon strip.

65   "They talk weird," Carmen whispered.

66   "That's their accent, dummy," Tessa whispered back. "Your nana has one too, you know."

67   "Not like that she doesn't."

68   The grown-ups sit at a rectangular table, Tessa's parents on either end, their guests between them, evenly spaced with elbows at their sides. There was no shoving. Danilo's voice loomed out above the others.

69   "When I was a boy," he said gesturing to himself. "I wanted to see MacArthur talk at Rizal Square for myself. So I told my mother I was going to school and instead, I hitchhiked my way there."

70   "How old were you, Danilo?" Carmen's mother asked.

71   "Old enough to know better," said Auntie Baby .

72   "A black American soldier picked me up in his jeep. I gave him a few cigarettes and he drove me to Rizal."

73   "This is the kind of talk I want to keep away from the children," Nora said.

74   Tessa turned to Carmen and whispered, "I love that story. He never gets in trouble either . . ."

75   "Better we tell the kids than my folks tell them—they'd make it sound so much worse."

76   Dr. Santos leaned back in his chair, lit up a cigarette. "Are they coming soon?" he asked. The doctor was round. He had a round head, round eyes and a mouth like a golf hole. He had stocky little fingers with a belly to match. Tessa noted that all his roundness was puffed with her mother's cooking.

77   "They should be left alone," said Uncle Tommy. "They should live out their days back home, where they're comfortable. Where they are respected." Uncle Tommy rocked forward as he spoke. Tessa thought of the nights the three Villa siblings sat at their kitchen table arguing. Uncle Tommy would turn red in the face, would sway like a tree in a storm with every point he made. He didn't want his mom and dad to come here. Auntie Baby spoke as loudly as Uncle Tommy. Only she was trying to mediate

because, as always, Danilo was the loudest. His voice would cover all the noise, the shouting and he would punctuate his sentences by pounding his heavy fists on the table. Auntie Baby always ended up crying.

78   "Life's hard back there," Danilo answered. "You know we've finally gotten ourselves settled. My work, the house, and Nora and the kids."

79   "I still think it's unfair," said Uncle Tommy. "What makes you think Mommy and Daddy want to come here?"

80   "Are the papers ready?" Dr. Santos wanted to know. He blew smoke out of his mouth, puffed like a train so that the rings linked together and floated to the ceiling.

81   "I've been told they should be in order by the end of the month," Danilo answered.

82   Finally, a date, a commitment, Tessa thought. Something to look forward to. Her father would never give her a date, but his friends? In a month she would have a *lola* and *lolo* like Carmen's.

83   That Monday, around six o'clock, the phone rang. Sitting in the dark, Tessa watched *I Love Lucy* on channel thirteen. She could hear her mother in the kitchen. She could hear the lights sizzling with grease, vegetables spinning and slipping across the surface of her hot frying pan, water gurgling to a boil and a fan swirling relentlessly above the stove. She patted her tummy and thought of how hungry she was. David and Tony raced up and down stairs, reenacting that day's *Batman* episode. Every time they ran past her, she screamed at them and rolled her eyes. What babies. The phone kept ringing, but no one answered it. They were all busy.

84   The Villa house seemed to vibrate with sound no one heard. Maybe because noise was a part of their house, like air and electricity and dust, noise was always there. They ignored it. Except Tessa, she heard everything. Even though Ricky Ricardo stood before her in a light box, crooning "Babaloo," she still heard the motor of the garage door as it rose. She felt her father's footsteps as he entered their home. She even heard the phone ringing, but she didn't answer it. She heard Danilo squawk a kiss onto Nora's lips. Then he answered the phone.

85   She heard everything, except her father's conversation. But then, she was more concerned with how funny Lucy was tonight. Still, she felt weird. For once, her father's voice wasn't booming into the phone. Usually it carried above all the noise and that voice was Tessa's comfort. It was how she knew she was home.

86   She turned from the TV and saw his silhouette. His long body bent, his chin falling softly onto his chest. He spoke in an almost whisper. She strained her eyes to see the expression of his face, but it was too dark. She couldn't tell what he was speaking of, but she knew it was something awful.

87   He placed the phone back into its cradle and walked into the family

room. Without taking off his overcoat, he sat down on the brown leather recliner and slowly folded his legs under himself.

88   Tessa had never seen her father cry. Her mother came into the room and quietly he told her that his father had died. In his sleep, he died. She leaned over him, held him the way she holds Tony or David when they've fallen. She rocked his body as the sobbing grew louder.

89   David and Tony ran into the room, still garbed in blue and red capes. Silently they stood next to Tessa and watched. The house was quiet except for her father's cries. The children looked at each other and then their parents. The only thing they knew was to be quiet.

90   Later that night, Nora tried to feed them, but they couldn't eat. The sound of their father crying bothered Tessa, made her feel sick. He was still sitting in the family room, rocking. Dinner grew cold and no one could eat.

91   All night long, their father curled up in his chair and wept. Wrapping his arms around himself he rolled in the arms of that recliner. Cooing, he chanted, "My daddy, my daddy, my daddy." He didn't know it, but Tony, David and Tessa kept him company. From the top of the stairs they watched over him. Tessa thought he looked different, like someone else, a stranger maybe. He rocked from side to side and rubbed his eyes. His face was red like Tony's when he was hurt. Sometimes he whimpered soft and low, other times that night he howled and pounded his fists into the arms of the chair, uttering words Tessa didn't understand. She thought he might be going mad.

92   Tessa was nervous, her stomach was tight and as her parents moved about, she kept looking over her shoulder at her dad. She was worried. Danilo had gone to the Philippines and when he came back he brought with him all kinds of Filipino cookies and candy—little pastries in shapes of boats with icing doodles, candied tamarind fruit rolled in sugar and even a few bamboo toys and tops. These things Tessa loved. He also brought with him a movie of *Lolo*'s funeral. She had never been to a funeral and was not sure what to expect.

93   Tessa and the boys sat in a row on their shag carpet. Above the doorway, between the kitchen and family room, Nora had hung a bed sheet, creating a makeshift screen.

94   "Ready?" Danilo asked as he finished threading the projector.

95   Their mother leaned over and flipped off the lights. Tessa grabbed Tony's hand, squeezed it. Nobody spoke, only the click-click-purr of the projector could be heard. For a moment, they were suspended in black, not knowing what to expect. Not knowing if they should be curious or scared or sad.

96   She glanced at her father again and thought she saw him crying, then she turned to the wall and saw. On the sheet before her, they carried *Lolo* above

their heads, proceeding slowly along the unpaved streets of Danilo's barrio. Gliding before his casket was a statue of the Blessed Virgin. Her skin, white and veiled in porcelain, adorned with bright flowers, looked soft against the grain of the super-eight camera. The mourners were lined up ten across and one mile long. People of his town. Heads bowed up and down the lines, while women pulled black lace over their heads, rubbing their beads and whispering something Tessa couldn't hear. Amid the crowd were pockets of umbrellas, shutting out the sun, the light. The camera skipped back and forth and back, in search of her father, her *lola,* the rest of her aunts and uncles. It looked for cousins Tessa had never met. But everyone was in black, or hidden behind their darkest pair of sun glasses and Tessa could not find one familiar face. Every now and then, a jagged movement towards the camera suggested a wave, a recognition of some kind. And each time the camera nodded back politely.

97   Tessa closed her eyes quickly. She rubbed. And when she opened them wide and round, she focused on the coffin, floating above the people. Gently they placed it down. They opened it. A plate of glass upon the casket separated him from them. Tessa could see his face, slightly ashen and green, somewhat older than her photo, but as defined and striking as she had pictured *Lolo.* He lay in a bed of flowers, the same kind that dressed Mary's statue. The sun glasses were gone. His eyes were closed. And it didn't matter that one eye was blind, but Tessa still wanted to know, which one?

98   For a moment, the camera was still and the crowd appeared to be hushed. Tessa was still searching for her grandmother, she knew *Lola* must be near. After the silence, there was a fluttering motion at the head of the casket. Tessa leaned forward, trying somehow to slip into the scene, crawl onto the sheet on the wall. She found her *lola* and she wanted to go to her. Her arms, draped in a long black veil, shooed them away, fluttering about them like the ruffled feathers of an angry, wild bird. *Lola*'s fists, clenched at the edges of her black veil, flying about like ruffled feathers of an angry, wild bird. She used her body to cover the glass plate, to keep from the good-bye. Tessa thought she heard her sobbing. *Lola* wouldn't let anyone put their arms on her. She let no one get between her and her husband.

99   Now in their family room, Tessa reached for her father and placed her arms around his neck. She could no longer keep from crying. "So many people," she whispered to him. And from her hemp purse, she pulled out a picture, showed him. She let him touch it, rub it to life like a genie lamp, like a wish waiting to come true. She offered her photo to him so he could make it come to life, bringing *Lolo* to them, the way she always did.

DISCUSSION QUESTIONS

1. Tessa daydreams a lot about her grandparents, particularly her grandfather. Why?
2. Why do you think the author includes the episode of the "spanking"? Could it have been omitted without changing the story?
3. Cite by appropriate paragraph numbers evidence that reveals the narrator's father to be creative.
4. Summarize Tessa's attitude toward her father.
5. Is this a successful story in your opinion? Explain.

WRITING TOPICS

1. This story is told from a child's point of view. In a brief essay, consider whether this narrator is reliable. Cite evidence from the story to support your views.

A MAN OF STEEL

Gish Jen

Gish Jen was born in 1955 on Long Island, New York. Like other Asian American writers in this anthology—for example, Philip Kan Gotanda, Maxine Hong Kingston, and Amy Tan—she received a strong formal education in various disciplines. Having pursued both English and a premed course of study, she earned a bachelor's degree from Harvard University in 1977 and went on to Stanford Business School in 1979. In the early 1980s, she attended the Iowa Writers' Workshop, where she earned an M.F.A. Between business school and her M.F.A. program, she taught English to coal-mining engineers in Shandung, China. The pursuit of education seems to have been greatly emphasized in Jen's family even before her generation; her parents, who immigrated separately to the United States from Shanghai, underwent rigorous academic training in China, her mother in educational psychology and her father in engineering.

Having focused her creative and intellectual energies on writing, Jen has published widely. In her first novel, *Typical American* (1991), she examines, through the character of Ralph Chang and his family, the myth of the American Dream and the considerable influence that Chinese culture exerts on Chinese Americans in pursuit of that dream. Her second novel, *Mona in the Promised Land* (1996), explores the experiences of teenager Mona Chang, whose family moves to Scarshill, New York, where the Chinese are considered "the new Jews." Jen's shorter fiction has appeared in publications such as *Best American Short Stories 1988*, *The Atlantic Monthly,* and *The New Yorker*. Writing with wit and humor, Jen has risen to national prominence and has enjoyed much critical acclaim.

In the following excerpt, Mona's family, which, "like bamboo . . . bent but did not break," copes with the arrival of a lively puppy. (J.I.)

1   All through the closing of the store, Helen and Ralph agreed on everything. They agreed who should hang the sign, and when, and what the sign should say. They agreed on what to tell the employees, and what to tell the neighbors, and what to tell Chuck. If being married was a matter of becoming one, they had finally achieved what in better times they could not. Even their moods seemed to meld together, so that when one of them was dispirited, the other also drooped; and if Helen grew philosophical, Ralph found himself stretching his neck and clearing his throat, as perspective and clarity irradiated his mind. "*Every river has its own course,*" Helen reflected. "*It is not for people to try to change destiny.*"

2   Ralph shrugged, antiphonal. "*Can't always make money, sometimes have to lose.*"

3   Like bamboo, they bent but did not break, agreeing as they did that, despite their difficulties, they were the luckiest people in the world, having each other, and the children—a family anyone would envy, even if there were no boys. How fast Callie and Mona had grown! It was hard to believe they were both in school already, much less that they could jump rope, and say the rosary, and play the piano. They were taking ballet lessons; Mona wanted to be a ballerina. Callie wanted to be a saint. Ralph and Helen talked again about having more children; two sons would be perfect. Even without the sons, though, how much luckier they were than Grover! How empty his life! They agreed they wouldn't change places with him for the world. "For a million dollars," Ralph said. They agreed that there was something the matter with Grover. "*With his head,*" Ralph said. Helen said that she had read articles about people like him in magazines. "*His family probably didn't take very good care of him,*" she said. "*He was like a child, in need of attention.*"

4   "*Not like a grown man,*" Ralph said.

5   "*People like that will do anything,*" Helen said.

6   "*If I ever see him again, I'll kill him,*" Ralph said.

7   That is, until Helen said, "*I feel sorry for Grover.*"

8   Then Ralph's anger was transformed, and he realized that he felt sorry for Grover too. "*That man, he has no family. All he has is his empire, and so much money, he doesn't know how to spend it.*" He shook his head.

9   It was a kind of sympathy he had begun to feel for almost anyone—not only bums, and orphans, and dogs with porcupine quills in their snouts, but also people he might at another time have envied. Presidents of corporations, state governors, movie stars—people he didn't know but nonetheless understood to be lonely, and afraid of failure. How much wiser he was than they! He talked to their pictures in Helen's magazines, explaining the nature of life difficulties—how matters that one day seemed material, and hard with importance, could the next day simply vaporize. "*You'd be surprised,*" he told them, "*I've never had such a peaceful mind as I have now. After a hundred smeltings, I indeed have become steel.*"

10   Sometimes he drove by the building, just to feel how dispassionately he could look upon it. What self-control he'd achieved! He was Confucius. He was Buddha. He was his idling car motor as he looked, looked, looked—observing with some satisfaction how almost impossible it was to tell from the outside of the building that inside it was collapsing. There was that one letter missing, and the framing bulged slightly out of kilter, but overall, it looked as solid as ever. It was not a building to sag pathetically. It was firm in adversity, especially the well-designed addition, which showed no cracks at all.

11   If only he could separate his part of the building from the part that came from Grover!

12   But, of course, he couldn't. He accepted this with an equanimity so complete that he had to get out of the car and go for a walk. He paced. Was it fair, what Grover had done? Was it right?

13   He thought how sorry he felt for Grover, stuck with his hollow victories. He thought of Grover letting Chuck in on a little scheme he'd come up with: "How about we tell him I've been thrown in the slammer . . ."

14   Ralph calmly paced faster. Just around the block, swinging his arms with nonchalant vehemence. It was a gray day, the clouds so low and heavy and ready to rain that they begged, Ralph thought, to be punched. How sorry for Grover he felt! How sorry, sorry, sorry! His sympathy was like one of those clouds in the even blue of his calmness—that's how sorry he felt, so sorry, and sorry, and sorry. What was this frenzy of sorriness? He felt so sorry that he gave a dollar to a panhandler, so sorry that, tears leaking from his eyes, he found himself holding a door for a woman with two shopping bags and a stroller. And when he came upon a couple trying to give away a box of snarling puppies, he felt so sorry that, quick, before it rained and the box got soggy, he picked out the noisiest tough of the litter as a present for the girls.

15   "*A dog*?" said Helen, at home. "*Now we really are* Americanized."

16   Ears back, the puppy yapped furiously at her, baring his teeth as though he'd been assigned the kitchen cabinets to defend with his life. He was a shorthaired dog, gray with black and brown spots—to call him nondescript would be a kindness. He had a flat, triangular head like a crocodile's, and his legs were strangely spindly; they looked as though they were not his legs at all, but a charitable donation from a relative with a spare set.

17   "*I felt sorry for him*," explained Ralph.

18   Helen frowned. "*Your sister got a cat not long ago. Did I tell you? Two of them, actually.*"

19   "*This has nothing to do with that*," he insisted. "*This is a present for the girls.*"

20   But the girls were terrified of the dog, who, growing more and more excited, barked and lunged at Callie, and nipped Mona's socks.

21   "Stop!" yelled Ralph, trying to catch him.

22   "He bites," wailed Mona.

23   "And goes *xu-xu*," said Callie, observing the several yellow pools dotting the kitchen floor.

24   "Can you bring him back?" asked Helen.

25   The dog, still yelping, was circling the girls, who huddled together in the middle of the room. Ralph chased after him. "Come here, dog! Come here!"

26   "Go away," yelled Callie. "Shoo!"

27   "How come he doesn't bite *you?*" Mona cried. "How come he bit *me?*"

28   "Because you're the smallest," explained Callie.

29   "How come he doesn't run after Dad?"

30   "Because I'm not afraid of him." Ralph ordered, sternly, in a deep voice, "Stop."

31   The dog looked up, cocking his head. His tongue lolled, long and unnatural, out the side of his mouth.

32   Actually Ralph felt leery of the dog too, but because the girls were watching, he picked him up. The dog yelped some more, then licked Ralph's hand and panted before struggling away.

33   "Please give him back," Helen begged.

34   By the next morning, though, the girls had decided the dog was cute. Ralph came down to breakfast to discover that Helen and they had reinstalled some old baby gates; also they had set out newspapers for the dog to go *xu-xu* on, and put out a plate of food. His claws, clattering across the linoleum, sounded like mah-jongg tiles in play.

35   "He licked me!" said Mona. "We're friends!"

36   "We're going to call him Daddy," said Callie. "After you."

37   Mona tittered.

38   "Girls!" admonished Helen. "We're going to find him a nice name."

39   "No, Daddy, Daddy," sang the girls. "We want to name him Daddy."

40   "No," said Ralph firmly; and just as it had worked on the dog, it worked on his daughters.

41   Momentarily, at least. "How about Uncle Grover?" Callie piped up then. "Can we name him Uncle Grover?"

42   "He's not your uncle."

43   "He used to be."

44   "He's not anymore."

45   "Anyway," said Helen, "those are people, and this is a dog."

46   "How about—" The girls thought. "How about—"

47   "Grover," mused Ralph.

48   "Grover!" the girls shrieked. "We'll name him Grover!"

49   Grover wagged his spotted tail, lifted his flat head and, sidestepping the newspaper, went *xu-xu* again.

50   "He needs," said Ralph sternly, "to be trained."

51   Ralph had never heard of taking a dog to school, but Helen said that was exactly how dogs got trained in America, so he signed up for a class. It was good to have to be someplace every once in a while, and though he did not like the way the dogs nuzzled each other—such familiarity! it was obscene—he took intense pleasure in the classes themselves. Who would've believed people could reach an understanding with dogs? Ralph burst with pride when Grover was paper-trained; and when he'd shrunk the paper down and moved it successfully outside, he felt such a profound sense of accomplishment that all his organs seemed to relax and settle. He had been having some trouble with his stomach; Helen thought he was swallowing air, but it felt more like fire. Anyway, his appetite now seemed to be returning to him, and eating more put the flames out.

52   Ralph taught Grover to sit, and to sit and stay longer than any other dog in the class. Teaching him to stop straining maniacally on the leash was harder, but Ralph kept at it like a man who knew what he wanted, and after a while it was sheer joy to take Grover out for a walk. Particularly as Grover never bit anyone, but often looked as though he might; so that Arthur Smith, for one, was much more respectful when Ralph ran into him. A few months before, he'd asked what Ralph was going to do with the restaurant, and when Ralph answered, "We have so many buyers, we have to consider which to choose," he'd more or less snickered. "I had me a business once too," he said. Now he unsquinted his eyes and unbunched his mouth and edged away, and he wasn't the only one. In general, Ralph did not have to talk to people for as long as he used to, unless they had dogs; and then, as the dogs socialized, he could chat dog-owner style. He'd learned all the things he should say in dog training class—What kind of dog is that? How old is he? What's her name? It was easy.

53   With Grover, he patrolled the neighborhood calmly, like a man of steel. This gave him time to evaluate different people's grass and bushes and cars, and to ponder. "*What are we going to do?*" Helen had asked a hundred times. Meaning, Ralph knew, what was *he* going to do.

54   "*Do?*" he joked. Of course, he realized they had to do something. Why else would he spend so much time walking around with the dog?

55   "*We have to do something,*" she said.

56   "*Don't worry,*" he told her. "*Relax. You'll see. 'Dying ashes will burn again.' We'll 'rise again from the East Mountain.' Believe me.*" He hadn't been able to tell her about Grover's pretending to be away when he was not; even so, she wasn't sleeping very well, he'd noticed. "*I'm investigating possibilities,*" he said. "*I have a feeling we may be wrong about the taxes. Maybe we can still cheat some.*"

57   "*How can we still cheat? What do you mean, don't worry?*" She didn't seem any more able to have faith than to sleep. "*Are you doing anything?*"

58   "*Sure. I have ideas.*"

59   "*What kind of ideas?*"

60   Since when did she cross-examine him? He didn't like her tone; he thought he ought to train her the way he had Grover. Step one, remain unfazed. "*Well, for instance, maybe we should take the addition off. Take the beam back out.*"

61   "*You said before you didn't think that would work.*"

62   He hesitated, then smiled. Unfazed. Watching the fire from a distant bank. "*I'm joking.*"

63   She had no faith. To Ralph's mind, that was the main problem. Just when he was thinking for example, that maybe he should call up Old Chao and find out what was going on at school, Helen spoiled his initiative, saying, "*If you want to sign up to teach some summer courses, you'd better call right away. They're doing assignments now.*"

64   "*How do you know?*"

65   Helen blushed violently. "*Janis told me,*" she said, though it was not Janis, actually, to whom she'd spoken, but Theresa.

66   "*Janis told you? Janis? And what did you tell Janis?*"

67   "*Nothing.*" True enough.

68   "*Nothing?*" Ralph glared at her. "*And what is she going to tell Old Chao? Did you think of that?*"

69   "*I didn't.*"

70   "*You didn't? But I think you did. You must have.*"

71   Helen blushed again.

72   "*I know,*" said Ralph. "*You think I don't know? You think I'm like Grover here, I know nothing? I know.*"

73   "*You can't just walk around training Grover forever.*"

74   She showed him the bankbook then, and again the next day, and again a few days after that, trying to provoke a response.

75   But it didn't work. "*You think I don't know?*" said Ralph. "*I know.*"

Discussion Questions

1. Why does Ralph feel wiser than the people he used to envy?
2. Why does his feeling sorry for everyone and everything seem to make Ralph feel better?
3. What does Ralph's taking so much interest in the dog tell you about him?
4. What is Helen worried about?
5. Is Ralph being truthful with himself?

WRITING TOPICS

1. What role does the extensive use of dialogue play in this selection? How does it affect your reading? Explain in a brief essay.

FOREIGN WAYS

Diana Chang

Diana Chang was born in New York City in 1934. She was taken to live in China at the age of eight months, but the family returned to the United States after the Communist revolution of 1949. Chang began writing poems while an undergraduate at Barnard College, New York, where she later taught creative writing.

The author of six novels, Chang is also a well-published poet and a painter whose work has been exhibited. Her drawings and paintings are included in the collections of James Brooks and Betty Friedan, among other collectors. Her first novel, *The Frontiers of Love*, appeared in 1956 to much acclaim; it was reissued by the University of Washington Press in 1994. Among her books of poetry are *The Horizon Is Definitely Speaking* (1982), *What Mattisse Is After* (1984), and *The Mind's Amazement* (1998).

In the following poem, Chang reflects on the subtle traits that mark a person as "foreign."

If I were in China this minute
and running after a friend
spied across from the hotel
I was staying at

waving to him, say
5   calling his name in Mandarin
Still they'd know me—

the body giving the person away
betrays a mind
of its own—

10

my voice from Duluth
my lope with its prairie air

DISCUSSION QUESTIONS

1. How has the speaker become an American?
2. Would the speaker seem a foreigner in China?

WRITING TOPICS

1. How would you characterize the tone of this poem? Does the author seem wistful? resigned? amused? Describe the tone in a journal entry and speculate on what it reflects about the author.

FROM *MY OWN COUNTRY*

Abraham Verghese

Abraham Verghese was born in 1955 in Addis Ababa, Ethiopia, where his parents were immigrants from India. He graduated from Madras Medical College in Madras, India, in 1979. Since coming to the United States Verghese has held several professorships at medical schools and administrative posts in hospitals. Verghese was a James Michener fellow at the University of Iowa Writers' Workshop in 1991–1992 and has published widely in *The New Yorker, Granta, Story*, as well as in many medical journals.

In 1985, Verghese was a successful practitioner in Johnson City, Tennessee, when he encountered his first cases of AIDS. His memoir, *My Own Country: A Doctor's Story of a Town and Its People in the Age of AIDS* (1994), testifies to the ways in which this epidemic has affected American society and to the poignant narratives obscured by the medical crisis.

In the following excerpt, a young doctor from India joins a network of fellow newcomers trying to establish themselves in American medicine. His experiences as a new resident are made more grueling than usual by his status as an immigrant.

1   When my parents tell me the story of their arrival in Ethiopia—the tough times in India, the struggle to get a college education, the word of mouth from friends about jobs overseas, the letters of inquiry to "relatives" abroad, the establishment of a base, the accumulation of a nest egg, the consolidation of resources by marriage, the help and support extended to their younger cousins and more distant "relatives" who wrote asking for advice— I understand the migration of Indians to South Africa, Uganda, Kenya, Tanzania, Mozambique, Mauritius, Aden, Ethiopia. And the next wave on

to Birmingham, Bristol, London and Toronto. And to Flushing, Jersey City, Chicago, San Jose, Houston and even Johnson City, Tennessee.

2 In their herald migration, my parents individually and then together reenacted the peregrination of an entire race. Like ontogeny repeating phylogeny—the gills and one-chamber heart of a human fetus in the first trimester reenacting man's evolution from amphibians—they presaged their own subsequent wanderings and those of their children.

3 During the hiatus in my medical education, while I worked as an orderly in America and before I went to India to finish medical school, I had seen from the vantage of a hospital worker the signs of urban rot in Newark, Elizabeth, Jersey City, Trenton and New York. The (insured) middle class continued to flee farther out to the suburbs where chic, glass-fronted hospitals complete with birthing suites and nouvelle cuisine popped up on the freeway like Scandinavian furniture franchises.

4 Meanwhile, the once grand county hospitals were sliding inexorably, like the cities themselves, into critical states. Understaffing, underfunding, the old stories. Their patients had become the uninsured and indigent whose problems revolved around drug addiction and trauma. In the emergency rooms of these fading institutions, bodies were pressed together like so many sheep. Old people languished on stretchers shunted into hallways and corridors while beleaguered nurses attempted some form of triage.

5 An inevitable accompaniment to this scene of a city hospital under siege was the sight of foreign physicians. The names of these doctors—names like Srivastava, Patel, Khan, Iqbal, Hussein, Venkateswara, Menon—bore no resemblance to those of the patients being served or the physicians who supervised them.

6 City and county hospitals were the traditional postgraduate training grounds for foreign medical graduates: hospitals like Cook County Hospital in Chicago, Nassau County and Kings County in New York and dozens of others across the country counted on foreign interns and residents for manpower, particularly in internal medicine.

7 By the time I completed medical school in India and returned stateside, a few of my seniors from my medical school in India had begun internships at county hospitals across America. Through them and through their friends and their friends' friends, an employment network extended across the country. With a few phone calls, I could establish for any city which hospital to apply to, which hospital to not bother with because they never took foreign graduates, and which hospital took foreign graduates for the first year, used them for scut work, but never promoted them to the second year—the infamous "pyramid" residencies. And the network invariably provided me with the name of someone to stay with.

8 At hospitals that took foreign physicians the work was grueling, the con-

ditions appalling—but only by American standards—and the supervision and teaching often minimal because of the sheer volume of work. This was particularly true in hospitals that were not university-affiliated. The scut work—wheeling the patient down to x-ray, drawing blood, starting intravenous drips, putting in Foley catheters, doing ECGs—was endless and the every-other-night-call schedule was brutal.

9   As I crisscrossed the country, in search of a residency slot, by way of Greyhound, sleeping on friends' couches (or on their beds if they were on call), I was amazed by the number and variety of foreign interns and residents I met in these hospitals. I overheard snatches of Urdu, Tagalog, Hindi, Tamil, Spanish, Portuguese, Farsi and Arabic. Some hospitals were largely Indian in flavor, others largely Filipino. Still others were predominantly Latin or East European.

10   In the cafeteria of a hospital in a less-desirable section of Los Angeles, a hospital at which I was interviewing, I took my tray over to a table where an Indian physician sat. She had the handsome Aryan features of a Parsi or a Kashmiri. I thought she might be from Bombay or Chandigarh or Delhi— the other end of the country from where my parents were born. But when she spoke I was bowled over: from her lips emerged the purest Birmingham cockney! (I recognized this accent easily: as a ten-year-old I had spent a year in Birmingham while my father was there on sabbatical.)

11   She told me her family had fled Uganda and settled in Britain when she was a young girl. She had never seen India, neither had her parents. Her family had been in Uganda for two generations. She had gone to medical school in Leeds and then come to the States. When I told her I was born in Ethiopia, she tried her Swahili on me and I my Amharic on her. Neither of us got very far with that and so we retreated to English.

12   The England she reminisced about was vastly different from my memory of it. The Asians, she said, now had pubs of their own in Asian strongholds like Wembley and Southall. These hybrid establishments served *tandoori* chicken, *pakodas* and *samoosas*[1] to be washed down with pints of the finest British bitter. And the music and dance were likely to be "bhangara-disco"— an electronic rendering of Punjabi and Gujarati folk music. The youth, most of whom, like her, had never been to India, had taken up the music of Lata Mangeshkar, Mukesh or Mohammed Rafi—old playback singers for Hindu movies.

13   Before she left to return to the wards, she paged a fellow intern, a Zachariah Mathen. From his name I knew he was a Christian-Indian like me. Zachariah took me around the hospital and as a matter of course offered me his apartment and car keys. "Make my home your home! Explore the City of Angels," he said.

---

[1] *tandoori chicken, pakodas and samoosas:* traditional Indian dishes.

14   Some hospitals, like Coney Island Hospital in New York, sent contracts to graduating medical students in India who had been recommended by their seniors. Come July, the seniors were dispatched to Kennedy to pick up the new blood fresh off Air-India, bring them to Coney Island and orient them. The cultural adjustment was simple: the reassuring scents of green chili and frying *papads*[2] wafted down the corridor of the house-staff quarters. Indian sari stores, Indian restaurants and Indian grocery stores abounded—some even delivered. The latest Hindi blockbuster starring Amitabh or Dimple could be rented in Queens on bootleg video within days of its debut in Delhi or Poona. And the faces of the physicians on the wards were those that one might have seen on the platform in Victoria Station, Bombay.

15   The few *American* interns and residents I saw in the various hospitals I visited were graduates of the "offshore' or Caribbean schools in places like Antigua, St. Lucia, Montserrat or Grenada. These schools existed solely for Americans who could not make it into U.S. medical schools.

16   Now that I had returned to America with my medical degree, a certain perverseness and contrariness made me want to buck this system. What was the point in coming to America to train if I wound up in a little Bombay or a little Manila? In India I had met Rajani Chacko, a lovely sloe-eyed account executive working for a leading advertising agency. After a whirlwind courtship, we were now newlyweds. I was loath to bring her to an urban war-zone, to an apartment where she would have to be alone for long periods of time while I worked as an intern.

17   Through a relative who was on the faculty, I heard of a new medical school: East Tennessee State University. It had started a residency program in internal medicine. As residents we would rotate through the Mountain Home Veterans Administration Medical Center (the "VA")—a veritable town within the town of Johnson City—as well as the adjacent Johnson City Medical Center (the "Miracle Center"), a community hospital. This rural setting in the foothills of the Smoky Mountains, in the shadow of the Appalachian Trail, seemed a beautiful place to bring my bride.

18   During my internship and residency in Johnson City, I moonlighted on free weekends in small emergency rooms (ERs) on the Tennessee-Virginia border. I pulled sixty-hour shifts—Friday evening to Monday morning—in places like Mountain City, Tazewell, Grundy, Norton, Pound, Lebanon and the Lonesome Pine Hospital in Big Stone Gap, Virginia. These hospitals had anywhere from twenty to forty beds, two-bed intensive care units, and the ambience of a mom-and-pop grocery store.

19   The ER nurses were on a first-name basis with every patient that came in. The ambulance drivers rarely resorted to the "forty-three-year-old-white-

---

[2] *papads:* fried, spiced flat crackers.

male-with-chest-pain-unrelieved-by-nitroglycerin" jargon. One was more apt to hear on the scanner that "Louise Tipton over on Choctaw Hollow says Old Freddy's smothering something awful and we better get over there right away, 'cause it's worse than the last time when he came in and Doc Patel put him on the breathing machine."

20   If I was lucky, no more than eighteen to thirty patients came through the ER in twenty-four hours. The drive up through the mountains was breathtaking, the staff exceptionally friendly, and the cafeteria food free and plentiful.

21   The patients were earthy and appreciative and spoke a brand of English that made diagnosis a special challenge. Who knew that "fireballs in the ovarus" meant uterine fibroids, or that "smiling mighty Jesus" meant spinal meningitis? Or that "roaches in the liver" meant cirrhosis? Soon, "high blood" (hypertension), "low blood" (anemia) and "bad blood" (syphilis) became part of my own vocabulary as I obtained a patient's medical history.

22   It was at one of these small hospitals that I met Essie, an affectionate woman with pretty doll's eyes, a generous bosom and dimples deep enough to get lost in. Essie worked as a lab technician. Like so many of the other hospital staff, she was from the area and, except for a brief sojourn in Kingsport, Tennessee, had lived her entire life there. The tiny communities nestled in the hollows and connected to each other by narrow mountain roads provided a security that made city life difficult to contemplate. Her parents and her brother and cousins all lived within a mile of each other.

23   "I know one day I might *have* to leave. Say if the jobs around here dry up. But I can't imagine living anywhere else."

24   This attitude made jobs precious. One was apt to encounter people whose first job was also their only job and they had worked at it for twenty years or more.

25   Of course, not everyone felt the same way. Many of the young felt confined by the little towns and had moved at least to the Tri-Cities area (Johnson City, Kingsport, Bristol) or even farther afield to Knoxville, Atlanta, Charlotte or Memphis.

26   Essie's brother, Gordon, was a case in point. It seemed he couldn't wait to leave their small town. She said he had moved to Kingsport as soon as he finished high school. Shortly thereafter he moved to Atlanta. Then, after a year in Atlanta, Gordon had vanished from the face of the earth.

27   The small hospital where I moonlighted the most had an on-call room leading off the ER corridor. There I could read, sleep, or watch TV till a patient signed in. Or I could come out to the nurses' station and shoot the breeze with the ER clerk, with the nurses, with Essie, and with "J.D."—the part-time security guard and self-styled entrepreneur.

28   J.D., Essie and the rest of the gang took it on themselves to not only feed me but also expand my Appalachian folk lexicon and coach me on the right way to "talk country." I was a quick study.

29   It became a challenge for them to find food that I would not eat. I enjoyed corn pone. I tolerated hominy grits. But I loved homemade biscuits, a great improvement on "whopping" biscuits—the frozen kind you whopped on the refrigerator door to open. I graduated to poke salad and tasted "dry-land-fish" (fried mushrooms) and ramps—an oniony tuber that you excreted in your sweat glands for weeks after. I tried and liked squirrel stew. Baked possum in a collar of sweet potatoes looked better than it tasted, while 'coon looked and tasted wonderful.

30   In return for the incredible hospitality and the culinary treats, I would sometimes relent and crack the ER staff up with my mimicry of the regional accents of India. The nuances that differentiated a Punjabi accent from a Madras accent from a Gujarati accent were appreciated by the ER folk. The staff physicians in the tiny community hospitals that served the scattered mining towns of southwest Virginia, east Tennessee and Kentucky were predominantly from India or the Philippines with a smattering of Pakistanis, Koreans and Palestinians.

31   The few white M.D.s and D.O.s around, it seemed to me, were near retirement or else were serving out a National Health Service commitment. It was evidently difficult to entice young American medical school graduates into these isolated and often depressed rural areas where reimbursement depended heavily on the health of the coal mines and on being willing to have a large proportion of Medicaid patients in the practice.

32   Meanwhile, year by year, more foreign physicians, recruited by the same word-of-mouth that brings fresh blood to the newspaper kiosks, motels, gas stations, taxi fleets, restaurants and wholesale groceries of America, were completing their training in American urban war-zones and moving into these rural havens.

33   The foreign doctors—with some glaring exceptions—were well received. They developed reputations as sound physicians. Though they were friendly, the majority chose not to integrate with the community except at a superficial level. They retained many of their foreign customs, the women wore saris, they were very protective of their children, and most of their socialization was with each other. In the corner of the kitchen or in a separate *puja* room[3] would be a collection of Hindu icons: invariably Lakshmi (the goddess of wealth) and Ganesha. Also Muruga, Venkateswara, Sai Baba, Durga, according to taste. Once a day the incense and the oil lamp would be lit, the silver bell rung and burning camphor waved around the idols. And at least once a year the family would travel to the Hindu temple in Nashville to do a more elaborate *puja* or *mahabhishekam*.[4]

---

[3] *puja room:* a room set aside for family worship.
[4] *mahabhishekam:* Hindu religious rituals.

34   The effect of having so many foreign doctors in one area was at times comical. I had once tried to reach Dr. Patel, a cardiologist, to see a tough old lady in the ER whose heart failure was not yielding to my diuretics and cardiotonics. I called his house and his wife told me he was at "Urology Patel's" house, and when I called there I learned he and "Pulmonary Patel" had gone to "Gastroenterology Patel's" house. Gastroenterology Patel's teen-age daughter, a first-generation Indian-American, told me in a perfect Appalachian accent that she "reckoned they're over at the Mehta's playing rummy," which they were.

35   Rajani and I, perhaps because we were of a younger generation, traveled easily between these two worlds: the parochial world of Indians in America, and the secular world of east Tennessee. For the Indian parties, Rajani wore a sari and we completely immersed ourselves in a familiar and affectionate culture in which we had our definite place as the juniormost couple; but at night we could don jeans and boots and go line dancing at the Sea Horse on West Walnut or listen to blues at the Down Home.

Discussion Questions

1. The narrator recounts the differences between suburban and city or county hospitals. What were these differences?
2. What astonished him about the Indian doctor he met in the cafeteria?
3. Why did the narrator want to go to Tennessee?
4. What were some of the things the narrator learned in and around Johnson City?
5. The narrator says that he and his wife "traveled easily between these two worlds: the parochial world of Indians in America and the secular world of east Tennessee." He admits that the reason for this ease may have been because they were of a younger generation, but what else about the narrator made this ease possible in the Tennessee world?

Writing Topics

1. According to Verghese, he and his wife were able to move between two worlds: "the parochial world of Indians in America, and the secular world of east Tennessee." In an essay, compare Verghese's situation to that of an author in this chapter who seemed isolated in his or her new community and speculate on the reasons for their different experiences.

DREAMHOUSE

R. Zamora Linmark

R. Zamora Linmark was born in Manila, the Philippines, in 1970. He studied at the University of Hawaii, Manoa, and took creative writing classes with the Detroit-born poet Faye Kicknosway, who influenced his style. Linmark has worked toward a master's degree in creative writing, and his first book, *Rolling the R's,* a collection of short stories and poems, appeared in 1995. His work is set in Kalihi, Honolulu, an urban area with a large Filipino community, both local-born and immigrant. He lives in Honolulu, Hawaii, and has published his work in a number of important anthologies, including *Charlie Chan Is Dead* (1993) and *Into the Fire: Asian American Prose* (1996).

The excerpt below, from *Rolling the R's,* follows three children selling candy door-to-door as they confront the gulf between the haves and the have-nots.

1   I saw Steve Johnson's house for the first time last week. Florante, Mai-Lan, and Loata were helping me sell Jewel chocolate-covered almonds, the kind that came in a box with a two-dollar coupon from Pizza Hut wrapped around it. I needed to sell sixty boxes so I could go to Camp Erdman and participate in the Junior Police Officer's annual get-together.

2   After we nearly covered the entire valley and got the same response of sorry-just-bought-one, I told them I'd try once more before calling it quits. I walked to the nearest house and knocked. A fat lady wearing glasses so thick they made her eyes look twenty-times bigger than the actual size, answered the door. I pulled out a box of Jewel's and was about to ask her if she wanted to buy some when she interrupted, "Too late. Just bought a case the other day. Too late."

3   We did an about-face and started to head back to my house when Mai-Lan came up with the idea of going to the far end of the valley where peo-

ple like Steve Johnson live. "I'm sure we can sell everything in less than a minute," she said. "Yeah," Florante said, "maybe you might even win an AM-FM headset."

4   It took us almost an hour's walk to reach the road that became narrower and narrower as the houses got bigger and bigger. The first doors we knocked on were all owned by Filipinos like Nelson Ariola's and Alan Vicente's families. We sold over twenty boxes in less than thirty minutes.

5   We ran excitedly through the next couple blocks where the houses began to look more like a dream than wooden structures. Like Judy-Ann Kunishige's tea house in the middle of a lighted lily pond. Or Mr. and Mrs. Bernard Chun's indoor swimming pool with a jacuzzi. We sold only ten boxes and it took us more than an hour's wait for them to decide. Only the Chuns didn't hesitate because we are always spending our allowance in their store.

6   Mai-Lan counted the number of boxes sold. "Fifty-seven," she said. "Three more to go," Florante subtracted. "And one house left," I added. "That's o.k. We still have a chance," Loata said pointing across the field to the biggest house in the valley. It seemed so far from us that it didn't look like a part of the valley. Or the valley didn't belong to it.

7   With the sweltering heat on our backs, we trudged across the field littered by gravel, broken bottles, and thorny weeds. We stopped in front of the gate and read the wooden sign drilled through the iron bars. Stenciled in fancy letterings were "No Trespassing" next to "Visitors, Please Ring Buzzer."

8   Loata rang the buzzer and we waited while Mai-Lan and Florante pressed their faces against the bars that barricaded the house. "It's so beautiful and so quiet like a museum," she said. "Miniature rolling hills and Hollywood cars," he said. "A fountain of Cupid in the center of a pool," she said. "A walkway that unfolds like a wedding gown," he said. "It's a dreamhouse," she said. Loata pushed the button once more and did not let go. "Like Iolani Palace with department store windows," he said.

9   "It looks like Dillingham Prison," Loata blurted, finally releasing his finger off the buzzer. "I don't think anyone's home," I said. "But his parents' cars are there," he argued, "there's gotta be someone home." "Maybe they don't want to buy any chocolate," I said.

10   I did an about-face and started to walk back home when Florante shouted, "Look, there's Steve and his mom and dad." I turned around and saw the three of them standing behind the giant window. Like breathing mannequins on display. Steve and his mother smiling blankly, and his father blowing out smoke from the cigarette clipped between his fingers. Loata pressed the buzzer and we waited, our faces pushing against the bars.

11   But not one of them budged. They stood there posing like a Sears family portrait. We continued watching them until Steve's mother walked out

of the picture and all we saw were bodies disappearing behind closing drapes. We stood there for I don't know how long, staring at the dream-house that was as far away as the hour it took us to get there and see them pretend that we were never there.

Discussion Questions

1. Why do you think the Johnsons pretended that the four young people weren't there?
2. What aspect of this story is most important in your opinion—plot, setting, or character?
3. In small groups discuss what you think is the theme of this story.

Writing Topics

1. In a brief essay, describe the plot progression and pacing in this story, identifying various key points (such as the climax and the resolution) along the way. How does this progression affect the tension in the story?
2. Imagine that you are one of the four children walking away from the big house. In a journal entry, describe your feelings at this point. What would you say to your friends as you returned home?

THE DEAD

Linh Dinh

Linh Dinh was born in Saigon in 1963 and came to the United States in 1975. He is the editor and translator of the anthology *Night, Again: Contemporary Fiction from Vietnam* (1996) and has a collection of short stories, *Fake House,* appearing soon. He has published short stories, poems, and translations in many journals, including *Sulfur, American Poetry Review, Kenyon Review,* and *Manoa,* and he received a Pew Fellowship for poetry in 1993. In the following poem, "The Dead," Dinh questions the ultimate success of assimilation.

The nine-year-old hockey puck
Bounced from the fender of an olive truck
Now bounces a leather ball on his forehead.
The old lady who scrounged potted meat
5 From foreign men lying in a mortar pit
Now sells gold jewelry in Santa Barbara.
The dead are not dead but wave at pretty strangers
From their pick-up trucks on Bolsa Avenue.
They sit at Formica tables smoking discount cigarettes.
10 Some have dyed their hair, changed their names to Bill,
But the living, some of them, like to dig up the dead,
Dress them in native costumes, shoot them again,
Watch their bodies rise in slow motion.

DISCUSSION QUESTIONS

1. What can you infer about why "the dead" are not dead?
2. Why would these characters have changed names and dyed their hair?
3. What kind of people want to shoot them again?

WRITING TOPICS

1. "The Dead" is a tight, compact poem. In an essay, analyze how the author achieves these qualities. Is it the word choice? the line breaks?
2. Line 12 in the poem suggests that it is easier to hate people who don't look or dress the way you do than to hate those who resemble you in looks and dress. Examine your own feelings about this suggestion and write about these feelings in your journal.

CHINESE FIREWORKS BANNED IN HAWAII

Eric Chock

Eric Chock, born in 1950, currently coordinates and teaches in the Hawaiian Poets in the Schools program in Honolulu, Hawaii. His first book of poems, *Ten Thousand Wishes,* is now out of print. His second book of poems, *Last Days Here,* appeared in 1989. Chock is the editor or coeditor of several anthologies, including *The Best of Bamboo Ridge* (1986), *Small Kid Time Hawaii* (1981), and *Talk Story: An Anthology of Hawaii's Local Writers* (1978). An active member of the Hawaiian literary community, Chock has served on the board of directors of the Hawaii Literary Arts Council and the Honolulu City Commission on Culture and the Arts. In the following poem, Chock evokes the old ways that are cherished by a Chinese family in Hawaii, even as these traditions are becoming history.

for Uncle Wongie, 1987

Almost midnight, and the aunties
are wiping the dinner dishes
back to their shelves,
cousins eat jook[1] from the huge vat
5 in the kitchen, and small fingers
help to mix the clicking ocean
of mah jong tiles, so the uncles can play
through another round of seasons.
And you put down your whiskey
10 and go outside to find your long bamboo pole
so Uncle Al can help you tie on

---

[1] *jook:* rice porridge.

a ten foot string of good luck,
red as the raw fish we want
on our plates every New Year's.
15 As you hang this fish over the railing
Uncle Al walks down the steps
and with his cigarette lighter
ignites it and jumps out of the way.
You lean back and jam the pole
20 into the bottom of your guts,
waving it across the sky,
whipping sparks of light from its tail,
your face in a laughing Buddha smile
as you trace your name in the stars
25 the way we teach our kids to do
with their sparklers.
This is the family picture
that never gets taken, everyone
drawn from dishes and food and games
30 and frozen at the sound
of 10,000 wishes filling our bodies
and sparkling our eyes.
You play the fish till its head explodes
into a silence that echoes,
35 scattering red scales to remind us of spirits
that live with us in Hawaii.
Then, as we clap and cheer,
the collected smoke of our consciousness
floats over Honolulu, as it has
40 each year for the last century.
But tonight, as we leave,
Ghislaine stuffs her styrofoam tea cup
full of red paper from the ground.
This is going to be history, she says.
45 Let's take some home.

DISCUSSION QUESTIONS

1. Who is the "you" in the poem?
2. What is the family celebrating?
3. Who might the spirits be (lines 35–36)?
4. What is the meaning of the next-to-last line?

WRITING TOPICS

1. Write an analytical essay about whatever aspect of the poem strikes you most (for example, the imagery, the syntax, and so on). Cite words or lines from the poem to support your views.
2. With the end of Chinese fireworks, a part of the culture of the Chinese in Hawaii has been lost. Write about a part of your culture that has disappeared, perhaps because of the death of older family members, lack of interest on the part of the present generation, or for some other reason. You may have to question older family members.

SUMMARY WRITING TOPICS

1. In a short essay, tell which selection in this chapter best conveys the disappointments felt by immigrants to America and tell why you chose this selection. Which selection best conveys the success of an immigrant? Give reasons for your opinion.

2. Both the excerpt from Kim Ronyoung's *Clay Walls* and the excerpt from Wendy Law-Yone's *The Coffin Tree* explore the protagonists' difficult adjustment to life in the United States. Ronyoung's excerpt is third person, while Law-Yone's is in first person. In an essay, analyze what effect this difference has on the impact of the selections.

3. Some of the authors in this chapter tell about a feeling of not belonging. What are some factors that contribute to this feeling, both in this chapter and in your own experience? Write about these factors and this feeling in a journal entry.

4. Choose three poems from this chapter. In an analytical essay, compare the authors' use of language and imagery. Cite words and lines from the poems to support your views.

5. Consider the protagonists in three or four of the prose selections of this chapter. Which seem to be most comfortable in their new homes and which seem to feel most displaced? Citing evidence from the selections, explore the protagonists' "at-homeness" in an essay.

CHAPTER EIGHT

LANGUAGE AND VISION

The final chapter focuses on a central concern and theme in Asian American writing, that of language. To Asian American authors, language is often an obsessive theme. They are concerned not simply with the divide between English and a historical mother tongue, but with the place of language in the art of crafting narrative or poetry or drama. The struggle to speak and master English as a new language, the experience of moving out of an original mother tongue into an alien second language, is sometimes viewed as painful and emotionally debilitating for the recent immigrant. The process of adjusting to living in a different language world is not always successful. The second-language speaker may be humiliated, isolated, or silenced by the mockery or lack of empathetic understanding of native speakers of English. Or English may be viewed as the means by which immigrants and their children can succeed in U.S. social institutions such as churches, schools, and professions. In the push for economic mobility and social acceptance, some Asian American families abandon their original language. Even without such a deliberate decision to give up the first language, American-born Asian Americans become acculturated, and as generations pass the language of their ancestors is easily forgotten.

For the artist, language is not merely a means of communication, a tool for some other end; the thing itself is valued for its intrinsic qualities. These qualities may include aesthetic attributes and/or attributes related to dimensions of spirituality. That is, language becomes not only the theme of the poem or short story but also the meaning of the work itself. The language of the work becomes inseparable from what it is saying, or the qualities of harmony, imagery, vividness, surprise, playfulness, musicality, and dissonance become themselves what is most significant and valuable about the work.

Myung Mi Kim's poem "Into Such Assembly" begins with a brief re-creation of the process of acquiring citizenship that immigrants undergo, emphasizing the importance of English in the United States. The poem is composed of fragments of scenes, memories, thoughts, and images, which are juxtaposed or organized in what appears to be a random order that suggests the disjointedness of the immigrant experience. The speaker in the poem remembers pastoral scenes from her Korean past and contrasts these happy memories with the taunts thrown at Koreans living in America. These sharply conflicted images are embedded in a larger meditation on the experience of learning English, presented on the level of physical difficulty, and emotional loss, as the immigrant's Korean identity dissolves into the conglomerate that is American society.

Extending this theme, "Modern Secrets," Shirley Geok-lin Lim's title poem for one of her books of poetry, imagines a speaker who is multilingual, not simply in the sense that she knows many languages but as a condition of her existence. The speaker dreams in Chinese, but in her everyday American life, English dominates. Chinese, therefore, becomes associated with a childhood past and a part of the speaker's self that is hidden from American view.

While Kim's and Lim's poems illuminate the identity issues that recent Asian immigrants face, which are integral to the unequal relationship between their original Asian language and English, "The Stubborn Twig," Monica Sone's narrative about growing up in the 1930s in Seattle, reminds us that the experience of living in two languages has historical validity for all Asian American communities. The chapter, from *Nisei Daughter* (that is, "second-generation Japanese American" daughter), focuses on a young girl's experiences in Nihon Gakko, the Japanese-language school. The noisy tomboy Kazuko finds herself changing her personality; in Japanese school she becomes a little Japanese girl with a small, timid voice. Sone shows how language helps shape a cultural self, so that learning Japanese also means becoming conscious of a driving spirit of strict discipline. Finally, however, Kazuko resists such discipline, for her busy American everyday life remains her reality.

In the final chapter of Chang Rae-Lee's novel *Native Speaker*, the author celebrates the multiplicity of languages found in American cities. Lee's New York is a city of words, which includes all kinds of communicative codes. While the narrator praises New York's multiethnic and multilingual social ethos—Korean, Spanish, Hasidic, German, Vietnamese, Italian, and so forth—he suggests that English is a significant influence in uniting this multicultural spectrum. As speech teacher to ESL students, the narrator's wife, Lelia, shows us that foreign-language speakers should not be afraid of learning English and that there is a place for "all the lovely and native languages . . . of who we are." That is, the relationship between English and an immigrant's native language need not be one of conflict, domination, and loss but of inclusion. The seven final selections underline this observation about the English language.

Many Asian American poets and prose writers view English as a wonderfully rich and complex language capable of expressing subtle emotions and thoughts. For example, Jessica Hagedorn's "Sorcery" insists that we read it for its playful language as much as for what the language is saying. Using colloquial or informal language, the poem begins by talking about people whose beauty can overwhelm others, but it soon moves on to talking about other types of beauty. Beauty is a dangerous form of power; and words, being "the most common/instruments of/illusion," have the power to make people dance and never stop.

The last selections in the chapter also treat the topic of language, whether in the obvious form of reading or listening to words, or as a means of evoking or imagining a vision of a way of life or a kind of community. The final chapter in Maxine Hong Kingston's *China Men* is aptly titled "On Listening," for it reverses the role of the author of the memoir from writer to listener. Here the author is the ignorant person who must listen to the stories told by younger Asians and Asian Americans or who must watch the young men who listen. This short chapter encapsulates many legends, myths, and talk stories on the adventures of Chinese people as they migrate all over the globe, forming a diasporic community that finds its identity in imagination, through listening to each other's stories.

Li-Young Lee's tender poem "My Father, in Heaven, Is Reading Out Loud" imagines his dead father, now in heaven, very much as he was in life. To the poet, the father is a powerful, godlike figure, whose emphasis on reading, religion, and books resulted in a complicated mixture of positive and negative influences. The son believes he is a remarkable disappointment to his father, and the profound sense of failure, of never being able to achieve what his father wanted of him, marks his sensitivity to the mysterious and unknown.

In "Yellow Light," Garrett Hongo offers a dense portrait of a multicultural Los Angeles neighborhood through the characterization of a woman returning home from shopping for groceries. The poem is full of precise details carefully chosen to illuminate working-class urban life, while the poem places these ordinary scenes among lyrical passages that suggest the overarching presence of a beautiful natural world, that yellow light "that covers everything . . . in sight."

The last two poems, "Finding the Center" and "A Theory About Dancing," offer visions of community and intimations of the relationship between art and individual existence. Lawson Fusao Inada's poem asserts a brotherhood between different ethnic groups based on living in a common space, on sharing work and play. The center of California (and by extension, of America) is where children and neighbors share good dirt as equals.

Diana Chang's poem focuses on the individual as artist to suggest something about how individuals must live their lives. Using the dancer to represent the human, you, the poem repeats its mantra: "You can't dance / in the past." The present is where art and life happen.

Language and vision are inseparable achievements in literature. Asian American writers are perhaps more burdened by their consciousness of English as one language among many others and their realization that the use of English may lead to their forgetting the home cultures that are transmitted through a different mother tongue. But many of these writers also celebrate the power and beauty both of English and of language itself, and their writing insists that how the words are crafted is as significant as what those words say.

INTO SUCH ASSEMBLY

Myung Mi Kim

Myung Mi Kim was born in 1957. A poet of Korean descent, she received an M.F.A. from the University of Iowa. Her poems were first anthologized in the award-winning collection *The Forbidden Stitch: An Asian American Women's Anthology* (1989), and her first book of poems, *Under Flag,* appeared in 1991. Her work has appeared in many journals and anthologies since then, including *The Open Boat* (1993) and *Premonitions* (1995). She is now teaching creative writing at San Francisco State University.

"Into Such Assembly," like many of Kim's poems, explores the problems of living in two languages and cultures simultaneously and expresses the struggle against racial, gender, and linguistic discrimination.

1.

Can you read and write English? Yes_____. No_____.
Write down the following sentences in English as I dictate them.
     There is a dog in the road.
     It is raining.
5   Do you renounce allegiance to any other country but this?
Now tell me, who is the president of the United States?
You will all stand now. Raise your right hands.

Cable car rides over swan flecked ponds
Red lacquer chests in our slateblue house
10 Chrysanthemums trailing bloom after bloom
Ivory, russet, pale yellow petals crushed
Between fingers, that green smell, if jade would smell

So-Sah's thatched roofs shading miso[1] hung to dry—
Sweet potatoes grow on the rock choked side of the mountain
15   The other, the pine wet green side of the mountain
Hides a lush clearing where we picnic and sing:
    Sung-Bul-Sah, geep eun bahm ae[2]

Neither, neither

Who is mother tongue, who is father country?

2.

Do they have trees in Korea? Do the children eat out of garbage cans?

We had a dalmatian
We rode the train on weekends from Seoul to So-Sah where we grew
    grapes

We ate on the patio surrounded by dahlias

5   Over there, ass is cheap—those girls live to make you happy

Over there, we had a slateblue house with a flat roof where
I made many snowmen, over there

No, "th," "th," put your tongue against the roof of your mouth,
lean slightly against the back of the top teeth, then bring your
10   bottom teeth up to barely touch your tongue and breathe out, and
you should feel the tongue vibrating, "th," "th," look in the mirror,
that's better

And with distance traveled, as part of it

How often when it rains here does it rain there?

15   One gives over to a language and then

What was given, given over?

---

[1] *miso:* a stiff paste consisting of soybeans, rice or barley, and salt and used in making soups and sauces.
[2] *Sung-Bul-Sah, geep eun bahm ae:* "Deep into the night in Sung-Bul-Sah temple," the words of a well-known Korean song.

3.

The rain eats into most anything

And when we had been scattered over the face of the earth
We could not speak to one another[3]

The creek rises, the rain-fed current rises

5   Color given up, sap given up
Weeds branches groves what they make as one

This rain gouging already gouged valleys
And they fill, fill, flow over

What gives way losing gulch, mesa, peak, state, nation

10   Land, ocean dissolving
The continent and the peninsula, the peninsula and the continent
Of one piece sweeping

One table laden with one crumb
Every mouthful off a spoon whole

15   Each drop strewn into such assembly

DISCUSSION QUESTIONS

1. Where is the speaker now living, and where has the speaker lived
   before?
2. What is happening in the first stanza?
3. What is the setting of stanza 2 and to what senses do the images appeal?
4. What do you think lies behind the speaker's questions in the last line of
   stanza 1?
5. The speaker presents an alternative view of her former homeland rather
   than responding directly to the question and comment in lines 1 and 5
   of stanza 2. What kind of picture of her former life does she present?

---

[3] *And . . . to one another:* An echo of the biblical story of Babel when the Lord scattered the peoples and confused their tongues. (Genesis 11: 1–9)

6. What is happening in lines 8–12 of stanza 2?
7. Tell in your own words what the speaker is wondering about in lines 15–16 of stanza 2.
8. In line 19 of stanza 1 the speaker asks a question. Speculate about why the words *mother* and *father* are traditionally used to describe one's native language and country. Why not *father tongue* and *mother country?*

WRITING TOPICS

1. In an essay, analyze the effect of the author's repetition of words and phrases. What purpose might such repetition serve? Cite words and phrases from the poem to support your views.

MODERN SECRETS

Shirley Geok-lin Lim

Shirley Geok-lin Lim was born in 1944 in the historic British colony of Malacca, Malaysia. She attended the University of Malaya in her country of origin and then moved to Boston in 1969 to continue her education. She went on to earn a Ph.D. in English and American literature from Brandeis University and to study with American poet J. V. Cunningham, to whom she dedicated her first collection of poems, *Crossing the Peninsula* (1980).

An extremely prolific writer, Lim has published four additional volumes of poetry: *No Man's Grove* (1985); *Modern Secrets: New and Selected Poems* (1989); *Monsoon History* (1994), which is a retrospective selection of her work; and *What the Fortune Teller Didn't Say* (1998), her most recent collection. In addition, she has published three books of short stories and a memoir entitled *Among the White Moon Faces* (1996), which received the 1997 American Book Award.

Lim is also a visible and critically acclaimed scholar of Asian and Asian American literature. In collaboration with Mayumi Tsutakawa, she edited *The Forbidden Stitch: An Asian American Women's Anthology* (1990), a collection of poetry, prose, and reviews that offers a strong counterpoint to the masculinist voices of the Asian American literary community. Lim ranks as one of the preeminent Asian American feminist scholars in the United States. She is also the author of *Writing South East/Asia in English: Against the Grain* (1994), which contains theoretical, literary, and autobiographical essays that explore literary migrancy and the experiences of the Asian diaspora.

Lim's creative and critical work reflect both her Chinese-Malaysian heritage and the social and literary landscape of the United States, of which she is now a citizen. She remains an observer of Southeast Asian life, retaining important links to the Pacific Rim's literary community, even as she gains an identity as a

California writer. She is currently a professor of English and the chair of women's studies at the University of California, Santa Barbara, where she is an influential advocate of undergraduate and graduate students' pursuing both creative writing and scholarship.

The following poem, "Modern Secrets," evokes the dual personae present in a bilingual and bicultural person. (J.I.)

Last night I dreamt in Chinese.
Eating Yankee shredded wheat
I said it in English
To a friend who answered
5   In monosyllables:
All of which I understood.

The dream shrank to its fiction.
I had understood its end
Many years ago. The sallow child
10   Ate rice from its ricebowl
And hides still in the cupboard
With the china and tea-leaves.

DISCUSSION QUESTIONS

1. What is the secret to which the poem alludes?
2. What is suggested by the phrase "Eating Yankee shredded wheat"? What else could be absorbed by such a diet?

WRITING TOPICS

1. In a brief essay, explore the meaning of the title of this poem and how its meaning is revealed by the poem itself.

THE STUBBORN TWIG

Monica Sone

Monica Sone was born in 1919, at a hotel in Seattle's Pioneer Square District. She studied at Hanover College in Indiana and received a master's degree in clinical psychology from Western Reserve University in Cleveland, Ohio. She lives in Canton, Ohio, with her family. Her autobiography, *Nisei Daughter,* was first published in 1953, a few years after the end of the Pacific War with Japan. It was the first life story told from the point of view of a second-generation Japanese American woman, and it followed upon the publishing success of *Fifth Chinese Daughter* by Jade Snow Wong, which received much critical attention as the story of a second-generation Chinese American woman. *Nisei Daughter* was reprinted in 1979 by the University of Washington Press, and continues to be read both as a historical document of the experiences of Japanese Americans during the history of internment and as a lively narrative of a character who has to negotiate across cultures to arrive at a positive acceptance of her bicultural identity.

In this selection from *Nisei Daughter,* young Japanese American children are subjected to the rigid discipline of the Nihon Gakko, where they attend classes in Japanese language and culture after their regular American grammar-school day. (J.I.)

1   The inevitable, dreaded first day at Nihon Gakko arrived. Henry and I were dumped into a taxicab, screaming and kicking against the injustice of it all. When the cab stopped in front of a large, square gray-frame building, Mother pried us loose, though we clung to the cab door like barnacles. She half carried us up the hill. We kept up our horrendous shrieking and wailing, right to the school entrance. Then a man burst out of the door. His face seemed to have been carved out of granite and with turned-down mouth and

nostrils flaring with disapproval, his black marble eyes crushed us into a quivering silence. This was Mr. Ohashi, the school principal, who had come out to investigate the abominable, un-Japanesey noise on the school premises.

2   Mother bowed deeply and murmured, "I place them in your hands."

3   He bowed stiffly to Mother, then fastened his eyes on Henry and me and again bowed slowly and deliberately. In our haste to return the bow, we nodded our heads. With icy disdain, he snapped, "That is not an *ojigi*."[1] He bent forward with well-oiled precision. "Bow from the waist, like this."

4   I wondered, if Mr. Ohashi had the nerve to criticize us in front of Mother, what more he would do in her absence.

5   School was already in session and the hallway was empty and cold. Mr. Ohashi walked briskly ahead, opened a door, and Henry was whisked inside with Mother. I caught a glimpse of little boys and girls sitting erect, their books held upright on the desks.

6   As I waited alone out in the hall, I felt a tingling sensation. This was the moment for escape. I would run and run and run. I would be lost for days so that when Father and Mother finally found me, they would be too happy ever to force me back to Nihon Gakko. But Mr. Ohashi was too cunning for me. He must have read my thoughts, for the door suddenly opened, and he and Mother came out. He bowed formally again, "*Sah*,[2] this way," and stalked off.

7   My will completely dissolved, I followed as in a terrible nightmare. Mother took my hand and smiled warmly, "Don't look so sad, Ka-chan. You'll find it a lot of fun when you get used to it."

8   I was ushered into a brightly lighted room which seemed ten times as brilliant with the dazzling battery of shining black eyes turned in my direction. I was introduced to Yasuda-sensei, a full-faced woman with a large, ballooning figure. She wore a long, shapeless cotton print smock with streaks of chalk powder down the front. She spoke kindly to me, but with a kindness that one usually reserves for a dull-witted child. She enunciated slowly and loudly, "What is your name?"

9   I whispered, "Kazuko," hoping she would lower her voice. I felt that our conversation should not be carried on in such a blatant manner.

10   "*Kazuko-san desuka?*"[3] she repeated loudly. "You may sit over there." She pointed to an empty seat in the rear and I walked down an endless aisle between rows of piercing black eyes.

11   "Kazuko-san, why don't you remove your hat and coat and hang them up behind you?"

12   A wave of tittering broke out. With burning face, I rose from my seat and struggled out of my coat.

---

[1] *ojigi:* a formal bow to an audience.
[2] *sah:* okay.
[3] *desuka:* Isn't it?

13   When Mother followed Mr. Ohashi out of the room, my throat began to tighten and tears flooded up again. I did not notice that Yasuda-sensei was standing beside me. Ignoring my snuffling, she handed me a book opened to the first page. I saw a blurred drawing of one huge, staring eye. Right above it was a black squiggly mark, resembling the arabic figure one with a bar across the middle. Yasuda-sensei was up in front again, reading aloud, "*Meh!*" That was "eye." As we turned the pages, there were pictures of a long, austere nose, its print reading "*hana,*" an ear was called "*mi-mi,*" and a wide anemic-looking mouth, "*ku-chi.*" Soon I was chanting at the top of my voice with the rest of the class, "*Meh! Hana! Mi-mi! Ku-chi!*"

14   Gradually I yielded to my double dose of schooling. Nihon Gakko was so different from grammar school I found myself switching my personality back and forth daily like a chameleon. At Bailey Gatzert School I was a jumping, screaming, roustabout Yankee, but at the stroke of three when the school bell rang and doors burst open everywhere, spewing out pupils like jelly beans from a broken bag, I suddenly became a modest, faltering, earnest little Japanese girl with a small, timid voice. I trudged down a steep hill and climbed up another steep hill to Nihon Gakko with other black-haired boys and girls. On the playground, we behaved cautiously. Whenever we spied a teacher within bowing distance, we hissed at each other to stop the game, put our feet neatly together, slid our hands down to our knees and bowed slowly and sanctimoniouly. In just the proper, moderate tone, putting in every ounce of respect, we chanted, "*Konichi-wa, sensei.* Good day."

15   For an hour and a half each day, we were put through our paces. At the beginning of each class hour, Yasuda-sensei punched a little bell on her desk. We stood up by our seats, at strict attention. Another "ping!" We all bowed to her in unison while she returned the bow solemnly. With the third "ping!" we sat down together.

16   There was *yomi-kata* time when individual students were called upon to read the day's lesson, clear and loud. The first time I recited I stood and read with swelling pride the lesson which I had prepared the night before. I mouthed each word carefully and paused for the proper length of time at the end of each sentence. Suddenly Yasuda-sensei stopped me.

17   "Kazuko-san!"

18   I looked up at her confused, wondering what mistakes I had made.

19   "You are holding your book in one hand," she accused me. Indeed, I was. I did not see the need of using two hands to support a thin book which I could balance with two fingers.

20   "Use both hands!" she commanded me.

21   Then she peered at me. "And are you leaning against your desk?" Yes, I was, slightly. "Stand up straight!"

22   "*Hai!*[4] Yes, ma'am!"

23   I learned that I could stumble all around in my lessons without ruffling sensei's nerves, but it was a personal insult to her if I displayed sloppy posture. I must stand up like a soldier, hold the book high in the air with both hands, and keep my feet still.

24   We recited the Japanese alphabet aloud, fifty-one letters, over and over again. "Ah, ee, oo, eh, *OH!* Kah, kee, koo, keh, *KOH!* Sah, shi, soo, seh, *SOH!*" We developed a catchy little rhythm, coming down hard on the last syllable of each line. We wound up the drill with an ear-shattering, triumphant, "Lah, lee, loo, leh, *LOH!* WAH, EE, OO, EH, OH! UN!"

25   Yasuda-sensei would look suspiciously at us. Our recital sounded a shade too hearty, a shade too rhythmic. It lacked something . . . possibly restraint and respect.

26   During *kaki-kata* hour, I doubled up over my desk and painfully drew out the *kata-kanas,* simplified Japanese ideographs, similar to English block printing. With clenched teeth and perspiring hands, I accentuated and emphasized, delicately nuanced and tapered off lines and curves.

27   At five-thirty, Yasuda-sensei rang the bell on her desk again. "Ping!" We stood up. "Ping!" We bowed. "Ping!" We vanished from the room like magic, except for one row of students whose turn it was to do *otohban,* washing blackboards, sweeping the floor, and dusting the desks. Under sensei's vigilant eyes, the chore felt like a convict's hard labor.

28   As time went on, I began to suspect that there was much more to Nihon Gakko than learning the Japanese language. There was a driving spirit of strict discipline behind it all which reached out and weighed heavily upon each pupil's consciousness. That force emanated from the principal's office.

29   Before Mr. Ohashi came to America, he had been a zealous student of the Ogasawara Shiko Saho, a form of social conduct dreamed up by a Mr. Ogasawara. Mr. Ohashi himself had written a book on etiquette in Japan. He was the Oriental male counterpart of Emily Post. Thus Mr. Ohashi arrived in America with the perfect bow tucked under his waist and a facial expression cemented into perfect samurai control. He came with a smoldering ambition to pass on this knowledge to the tender Japanese saplings born on foreign soil. The school-teachers caught fire, too, and dedicated themselves to us with a vengeance. It was not enough to learn the language. We must talk and walk and sit and bow in the best Japanese tradition.

30   As far as I was concerned, Mr. Ohashi's superior standard boiled down to one thing. The model child is one with deep *rigor mortis* . . . no noise, no trouble, no back talk.

31   We understood too well what Mr. Ohashi wanted of us. He yearned and wished more than anything else that somehow he could mold all of us into

---

⁴ *Hai:* yes.

Genji Yamadas. Genji was a classmate whom we detested thoroughly. He was born in Seattle, but his parents had sent him to Japan at an early age for a period of good, old-fashioned education. He returned home a stranger among us with stiff mannerisms and an arrogant attitude. Genji boasted that he could lick anyone, one husky fellow or ten little ones, and he did, time and time again. He was an expert at judo.

32   Genji was a handsome boy with huge, lustrous dark eyes, a noble patrician nose, jet crew-cut setting off a flawless, fair complexion looking every bit the son of a samurai. He sat aloof at his desk and paid strict attention to sensei. He was the top student scholastically. He read fluently and perfectly. His handwriting was a beautiful picture of bold, masculine strokes and curves. What gnawed at us more than anything else was that he stood up as straight as a bamboo tree and never lost rigid control of his arms or legs. His bow was snappy and brisk and he always answered "*Hai!*" to everything that sensei said to him, ringing crisp and clear with respect. Every time Mr. Ohashi came into our room for a surprise visit to see if we were under control, he would stop at Genji's desk for a brief chat. Mr. Ohashi's eyes betrayed a glow of pride as he spoke to Genji, who sat up erect, eyes staring respectfully ahead. All we could make out of the conversation was Genji's sharp staccato barks, "*Hai! . . . Hai! . . . Hai!*"

33   This was the response sublime to Mr. Ohashi. It was real man to man talk. Whenever Mr. Ohashi approached us, we froze in our seats. Instead of snapping into attention like Genji, we wilted and sagged. Mr. Ohashi said we were more like "*konyaku,*" a colorless, gelatinous Japanese food. If a boy fidgeted too nervously under Mr. Ohashi's stare, a vivid red stain rose from the back of Mr. Ohashi's neck until it reached his temple and then there was a sharp explosion like the crack of a whip. "*Keo-tsuke!* Attention!" It made us all leap in our seats, each one of us feeling terribly guilty for being such an inadequate Japanese.

34   I asked Mother, "Why is Mr. Ohashi so angry all the time? He always looks as if he had just bitten into a green persimmon. I've never seen him smile."

35   Mother said, "I guess Mr. Ohashi is the old-fashioned schoolmaster. I know he's strict, but he means well. Your father and I received harsher discipline than that in Japan . . . not only from schoolteachers, but from our own parents."

36   "Yes, I know, Mama." I leaned against her knees as she sat on the old leather davenport, mending our clothes. I thought Father and Mother were still wonderful, even if they had packed me off to Nihon Gakko. "Mrs. Matsui is so strict with her children, too. She thinks you spoil us." I giggled, and reassured her quickly, "But I don't think you spoil us at all."

37   Mrs. Matsui was ten years older than Mother, and had known Mother's father in Japan. Therefore she felt it was her duty to look after Mother's progress in this foreign country. Like a sharp-eyed hawk, she picked out

Mother's weaknesses. Why did Mother find it necessary to stay up late every night to read and write poetry? She should be resting her body for the next day's work. Each time Mrs. Matsui called, Mother was on tenterhooks, wishing desperately for some sort of remote control over our behavior. It was impossible for us to remember the endless little things we must not do in front of Mrs. Matsui. We must not laugh out loud and show our teeth, or chatter in front of guests, or interrupt adult conversation, or cross our knees while seated, or ask for a piece of candy, or squirm in our seats.

38   I knew I could never come up to Yaeko, Mrs. Matsui's only daughter. She was a few years older than I, and plump and vicious like her mother. Yaeko would sit quietly beside her mother, knees together, dress pulled down modestly over the ankles, hands folded demurely in her lap, and eyes fixed dully on the floor. Whenever Mother gave her a magazine to look at, Yaeko would bow graciously. "*Arigato gazai masu.*"[5] And she would stare politely at one picture for a long, long time, turn a page so slowly and quietly that I felt like tearing into her and rattling the paper for her. But whenever we were given permission to play outside, Yaeko became a different person. She would look at me scornfully, "Let's not play jacks again! It's baby stuff. Don't you have some good magazines to read . . . like *True Love?*"

39   I did not have *True Love* magazines. So we played an ill-tempered game of jacks at which time she would cheat, pinch and jar my elbows whenever she felt I was taking too long.

40   Mrs. Matsui thought Mother's relationship with her children was chaotic. She clucked sympathetically at Mother, "Do they still call you 'Mama' and 'Papa'?"

41   "Oh, yes," Mother smiled to hide her annoyance. "You know how it is. That's all they've ever heard around here. In fact, my husband I have been corrupted, too. We call each other 'Mama' and 'Papa.' It just seems natural in our environment."

42   Mrs. Matsui drew herself up stiffly. "I taught my young ones to say 'Otoh-san' and 'Okah-san' from the very beginning."

43   "That's wonderful, Mrs. Matsui, but I'm afraid it's too late for us."

44   "Such a pity! You really ought to be more firm with them, too, Itoi-san. When I say 'no,' my children know I mean it. Whenever I feel they're getting out of hand, my husband and I take steps."

45   Mother looked interested.

46   "We give '*okyu*' quite often." Mrs. Matsui folded her hands neatly together. *Okyu* was an old-country method of discipline, a painful and lasting punishment of applying a burning punk on a child's bare back. "Believe me, after *okyu*, we don't have trouble for a long, long time."

---

[5] *Arigato gazai masu:* Thank you very much.

47   Henry, Kenji, Sumiko and I eyed each other nervously. We wished Mrs. Matsui would stop talking about such things to Mother.

48   Mr. Ohashi and Mrs. Matsui thought they could work on me and gradually mold me into an ideal Japanese *ojoh-san*, a refined young maiden who is quiet, pure in thought, polite, serene, and self-controlled. They made little headway, for I was too much the child of Skidrow. As far as I was concerned, Nihon Gakko was a total loss. I could not use my Japanese on the people at the hotel. Bowing was practical only at Nihon Gakko. If I were to bow to the hotel patrons, they would have laughed in my face. Therefore promptly at five-thirty every day, I shed Nihon Gakko and returned with relief to an environment which was the only real one to me. Life was too urgent, too exciting, too colorful for me to be sitting quietly in the parlor and contemplating a spray of chrysanthemums in a bowl as a cousin of mine might be doing in Osaka.

Discussion Questions

1. What was Mr. Ohashi's background and mission in life?
2. The narrator found that she was switching her personality "back and forth daily like a chameleon." How did her behavior reflect this?
3. Why did the narrator and her classmates detest Genji Yamada?
4. How was Yaeko Matsui affected by her mother's training?
5. What instances do you find that suggest that Mr. Ohashi and Mrs. Matsui valued conformity?
6. To what does the title of this selection refer?

Writing Topics

1. In a brief essay, discuss the author's skill at characterization and which characters you find particularly well realized. Cite examples from the excerpt to support your views.
2. When is conformity a good thing and when is it a bad thing? Consider this question in a journal entry.

FROM *NATIVE SPEAKER*

Chang-rae Lee

Chang-rae Lee was born in 1965 in Seoul, South Korea. He studied at Yale University and received his M.F.A. at the University of Oregon in 1993. His first novel, *Native Speaker*, was published (when he was twenty-nine years old) in 1995 to much acclaim. According to reviewers, *Native Speaker* is a lyrical, mysterious, and nuanced novel. It tells the story of Henry Park, the son of a first-generation Korean American grocer in New York, whose work as an industrial spy begins to have negative effects on his emotional life and marriage. Lee has taught at the University of Oregon and is currently working on a second novel.

This excerpt from *Native Speaker* follows Henry and his wife, an ESL teacher, as they experience the many languages and cultures of an American metropolis.

1   This is a city of words.

2   We live here. In the street the shouting is in a language we hardly know. The strangest chorale. We pass by the throngs of mongers, carefully nodding and heeding the signs. Everyone sounds angry and theatrical. Completely out of time. They want you to buy something or hawk what you have, or else shove off. The constant cry is that you belong here, or you make yourself belong, or you must go.

3   Most of my days begin the same. In the morning I go out in the street and I search for them. I rarely need to go far. I look for the rises of steam from pushcarts. I look for old-model vans painted in matte, their tires always bald. I look for rusty hand trucks and hasty corner displays, and then down tenement alleys strung with fancy laundry and in the half-soaped windows of basement stores. I stop in the doorways of every smoke shop and deli and grocer I can find. They are all here, the shades of skin I know, all the mouths

of bad teeth, the speaking that is too loud, the cooking smells, body smells, the English, and then the phrases of English, their grunts of it to get by.

4   Once inside, I flip through magazines, slowly choose a piece of fruit, a candy. The store will grow quiet. The man or woman at the register is suspicious of my lingering, and then murmurs to the back, in a tone they want me to understand and in a language I won't, to their brother or their wife. A face appears from a curtain, staring at me. I finally decide on something, put my money on the counter. I look back and the face is gone.

5   My father, I know, would have chased someone like me right out, stamping his broom, saying, *What you do? Buy or go, buy or go!*

6   I used to love to walk these streets of Flushing[1] with Lelia and Mitt, bring them back here on Sunday trips during the summer. We would eat cold buckwheat noodles at a Korean restaurant near the subway station and then go browsing in the big Korean groceries, not corner vegetable stands like my father's but real supermarkets with every kind of Asian food. Mitt always marveled at the long wall of glassed-door refrigerators stacked full with gallon jars of five kinds of kimchee, and even he noticed that if a customer took one down the space was almost immediately filled with another. *The kimchee museum,* he'd say, with appropriate awe. Then, Lelia would stray off to the butcher's section, Mitt to the candies. I always went to the back, to the magazine section, and although I couldn't read the Korean well I'd pretend anyway, just as I did when I was a boy, flipping the pages from right to left, my finger scanning vertically the way my father read. Eventually I'd hear Lelia's voice, calling to both of us, calling the only English to be heard that day in the store, and we would meet again at the register with what we wanted, the three of us, looking like a family accident, gathering on the counter the most serendipitous pile. We got looks. Later, after he died, I'd try it again, ride the train with Lelia to the same restaurant and store, but in the end we would separately wander the aisles not looking for anything, except at the last moment, when we finally encountered each other, who was not him.

7   Still I love it here. I love these streets lined with big American sedans and livery cars and vans. I love the early morning storefronts opening up one by one, shopkeepers talking as they crank their awnings down. I love how the Spanish disco thumps out from windows, and how the people propped halfway out still jiggle and dance in the sill and frame. I follow the strolling Saturday families of brightly wrapped Hindus and then the black-clad Hasidim, and step into all the old churches that were once German and then Korean, and are now Vietnamese. And I love the brief Queens sunlight at the end of the day, the warm lamp always reaching through the westward tops of that magnificent city.

---

[1] *Flushing:* a section in northern Queens (a borough of New York City) on western Long Island.

8   When I am ready, I will flag a taxi and have the driver take only side streets for the three miles to John Kwang's house, going the long way past the big mansions near the water of the Sound, where my mother once said she would like to live if we were rich enough. She wanted for us to stay in Queens, where all her friends were and she could speak her language in the street. But my father told her they wouldn't let us live there for any amount of money. All those movie stars and bankers and rich old Italians. *They'll burn us out*, he warned her, laughing, *when they smell what you cook in a house.*

9   Once, I get inside the Kwang house again. I call the realtor whose name is on the sign outside and we tour the place. As she keys the door she asks what I do and I tell her I am between jobs. She smiles. She still carefully shows me the parlor, the large country kitchen, the formal dining room, all six of the bedrooms, two of them masters. I look out to the street from the study at the top of the stairs. We go down to the basement, still equipped with office partitions. When we're done she asks if I'm interested and I point out that she hasn't yet mentioned who used to live in such a grand place.

10   Foreigners, she says. They went back to their country.

11   By the time I reach home again Lelia is usually finishing up with her last students. I'll come out of the elevator and see her bidding them goodbye outside our door. She'll kiss them if they want. They reach up with both arms and wait for her to bend down. The parent will thank her and they pass by me quickly to catch the elevator. Then she is leaning in the empty door-way, arms akimbo, almost standing in the way I would glimpse her when I left her countless times before, her figure steeled, allowing. She wouldn't say goodbye.

12   Now, I am always coming back inside. We play this game in which I am her long-term guest. Permanently visiting. That she likes me okay and bears my presence, but who can know for how long? I step inside and walk to the bedroom and lie down and close my eyes. She follows me and says that this is her room. I usually sleep on the couch.

13   Usually? I murmur.

14   Yes, she says, her voice suddenly closer, hot to the ear, and she's already on me.

15   After a few hours of lying around and joking and making funny sounds she'll get up and drift off to the other end of the apartment. It's a happy distance. She'll prepare some lessons or read. Maybe practice in a hand mirror being the Tongue Lady, to make sure she's doing it right for the kids.

16   I make whatever is easy for dinner, tonight a Korean dish of soup and steamed rice. I scoop the rice into deep bowls and ladle in the broth and bring them over to where she is working. We eat by the open windows. She likes the spicy soup, but she can't understand why I only seem to make it on

the hottest, muggiest nights. It's a practice of my mother's, I tell her, how if you sweat and suffer a boiling soup in the heat you'll feel that much cooler when you're done.

17 I don't know, Lelia says, wiping her brow with her sleeve. But she eats the whole thing.

18 She has been on her visits around the city. The city hires people like her to work with summer students whose schools don't have speech facilities, or not enough of them. She brings her gear in two rolling plastic suitcases and goes to work. Today she has two schools, both in Manhattan. One of the schools is on the Lower East Side, which can be rough, even the seven- or eight-year-olds will carry knives or sharp tools like awls.

19 We decide that I should go with her. Besides, I've been an assistant before. Luckily, the school officials we check in with don't seem to care. They greet her and then look at me and don't ask questions. They can figure I am part of her materials, the day's curriculum. Show and tell.

20 Lelia usually doesn't like this kind of work, even though it pays well, mostly because there are too many students in a class for her to make much difference. There are at least twenty anxious faces. It's really a form of day care, ESL-style. We do what we can. We spend the first half hour figuring out who is who and what they speak. We have everyone say aloud his or her full name. When we finally start the gig, she ends up giving a kind of multimedia show for them, three active hours of video and mouth models and recorded sounds. They love it. She uses buck-toothed puppets with big mouths, scary masks, makes the talk unserious and fun.

21 I like my job. I wear a green rubber hood and act in my role as the Speech Monster. I play it well. I gobble up kids but I cower when anyone repeats the day's secret phrase, which Lelia has them practice earlier. Today the phrase is *Gently down the stream*. It's hard for some of them to say, but it helps that they can remember the melody of the song we've already taught them, and so they singsong it to me, to slay me, subdue me, this very first of their lyrics.

22 Lelia doesn't attempt any other speech work. The kids are mostly just foreign language speakers, anyway, and she thinks it's better with their high number and kind to give them some laughs and then read a tall tale in her gentlest, queerest voice. It doesn't matter what they understand. She wants them to know that there is nothing to fear, she wants to offer up a pale white woman horsing with the language to show them it's fine to mess it all up.

23 At the end of the session we bid each kid goodbye. Many freelancers rotate in these weekly assignments, and we probably won't see them again this summer. I take off my mask and we both hug and kiss each one. When I embrace them, half pick them up, they are just that size I will forever know, that very weight so wondrous to me, and awful. I tell them I will miss them. They don't quite know how to respond. I put them down. I sense that some

of them gaze up at me for a moment longer, some wonder in their looks as they check again that my voice moves in time with my mouth, truly belongs to my face.

24   Lelia gives each one a sticker. She uses the class list to write their names inside the sunburst-shaped badge. Everybody, she says, has been a good citizen. She will say the name, quickly write on the sticker, and then have me press it to each of their chests as they leave. It is a line of quiet faces. I take them down in my head. Now, she calls out each one as best as she can, taking care of every last pitch and accent, and I hear her speaking a dozen lovely and native languages, calling all the difficult names of who we are.

DISCUSSION QUESTIONS

1. The narrator says that New York is a city of words. How does he illustrate what he means?
2. The narrator seems particularly touched by the vulnerability of the children Lelia works with. In small groups, discuss possible reasons for this.

WRITING TOPICS

1. Chang-rae Lee's prose writing has certain poetic qualities. In an analytical essay, identify some of these qualities (citing examples from the selection) and explore what effect this poetic prose has on you as a reader.

SORCERY

Jessica Hagedorn

Jessica Tarahata Hagedorn, born in 1949 in Manila, the Philippines, moved to San Francisco with her family in 1960. From a very young age, she was encouraged to read and write. Her maternal grandfather was a writer and teacher, and her mother bought Hagedorn her first portable typewriter.

She did not opt for a formal university education but instead entered the American Conservatory Theatre, where she studied music, acting, and martial arts. When Hagedorn was in her early twenties, the poet Kenneth Rexroth, recognizing her literary talent, included her poetry in a collection entitled *Four Young Women*. In the 1970s, Hagedorn founded and wrote lyrics for the West Coast Gangster Choir, and she has created several dance, radio, and multimedia theater pieces, such as "A Nun's Story," "Holy Food," "Teenytown," and "Mango Tango."

Her literary achievements include two collections of poems and short stories, *Dangerous Music* (1979) and *Petfood and Other Tropical Apparitions* (1981). In addition to these collections, she has published two novels, *Dogeaters* (1990) and *The Gangster of Love* (1996), and has edited *Charlie Chan Is Dead* (1993), an anthology of contemporary Asian American fiction.

Dogeaters, with its extensive roster of characters, was nominated for the National Book Award in 1990. In this extremely rich novel, Hagedorn examines, with both biting humor and great sensitivity, several factions in urban Manila in the 1970s: the wealthy, the poor, the abused, the ostracized, the privileged, the politically powerful. Throughout *Dogeaters,* Hagedorn references American popular culture—film, television, music, food—and demonstrates its sometimes humorous and always disturbing influence on life in the Philippines. With regard to American influence, she claims that "it was pretty clear to most of us growing up in the fifties and early sixties that what was really important, what was inevitably preferred, was the aping of our mythologized Hollywood universe. The colonization of our imagination was relentless and hard to shake off . . . In order to be acknowledged, we had to strive to be as American as possible."[1]

"Sorcery" portrays the ambivalent attitude of the speaker toward beauty—human physical beauty as well as the beauty of artistic expression. (J.I.)

there are some people i know
whose beauty
is a crime.
who make you so crazy
5 you don't know
whether to throw yourself
at them
or kill them.
which makes
10 for permanent madness.
which could be
bad for you.
you better be on the lookout
for such circumstances.

15 stay away
from the night.
they most likely lurk
in corners of the room
where they think
20 they being inconspicuous
but they so beautiful
an aura
gives them away.

stay away
25 from the day.
they most likely
be walking
down the street
when you least

---

[1] Introduction to *Charlie Chan Is Dead* (New York: Penguin, 1993) xxiii.

30   expect it
trying to look
ordinary
but they so fine
they break your heart
35   by making you dream
of other possibilities.

stay away
from crazy music.
they most likely
40   be creating it.
cuz when you're that beautiful
you can't help
putting it out there.
everyone knows
45   how dangerous
that can get.

stay away
from magic shows.
especially those
50   involving words.
words are very
tricky things.
everyone knows
words
55   the most common
instruments of
illusion.

they most likely
be saying them,
60   breathing poems
so rhythmic
you can't help
but dance.
and once
65   you start dancing
to words
you might never
stop.

DISCUSSION QUESTIONS

1. What is sorcery and why would the author use it as a title for this poem?
2. According to the speaker, what might happen if one encounters beautiful people? How should one avoid these people?
3. In small groups, discuss the imagery in this poem. Which images seem particularly striking and why?

WRITING TOPICS

1. In a brief essay, describe the tone of this poem and how it is conveyed. Cite words and lines from the poem to support your views.
2. In an essay, analyze the rhythm and pacing of this poem. What effect do they have on the reading of the poem?

ON LISTENING

Maxine Hong Kingston

Born in 1940 in Stockton, California, Maxine Hong Kingston spent much of her childhood working at her parents' laundry. While washing, drying, and pressing, Kingston and her five siblings would listen to their mother "talk story," an oral tradition that is a combination of legends, folklore, ghost stories, and anecdotes. Listening to "talk stories" and reading widely and voraciously helped Kingston to develop her own skills as a storyteller. She began attending the University of California, Berkeley, in 1958, where she began to pursue writing. She originally planned to study engineering because of her capacity for mathematics, but by her second year, she changed to a major more conducive to a writing career. After graduating in 1962, she married Earl Kingston and took a teaching job in Hayward, California. In 1967, the Kingstons moved to Hawaii, where Maxine worked as a teacher.

It was during her time in Hawaii that Kingston began writing *The Woman Warrior* and *China Men,* both of which borrow from the "talk story" tradition. In both books, a young Chinese American daughter narrates the stories of her family; however, there is a difference in narrative tone. In *China Men,* the daughter is "less involved with the characters and far less concerned with relating how she feels about them"[1] but in *The Woman Warrior,* the narrator's life is inextricably linked to all the lives—both past and present—around her. These two books, conceived as an intertwining story, are classified as nonfiction, but it is clear that they push the boundaries of literary categorization through Kingston's use of multiple genres—history, anecdote, legend, cautionary tale, biography, memoir.

Both books met with instant critical acclaim. In 1976 *The Woman Warrior* won the National Book Critics Circle Award for nonfiction,

---

[1] Elaine Kim, *Asian-American Literature: An Introduction to the Writings and Their Social Context.* (Philadelphia: Temple UP, 1984) 208.

and in 1980 *China Men* won a National Book Award. Encouraged by her successes, Kingston embarked on a novel, *Tripmaster Monkey,* which she first published in 1987. The novel is the story of Wittman Ah Sing, a fifth-generation Chinese American man who, like Kingston herself, is a Berkeley graduate and a product of the 1960s. Kingston was working on a sequel to *Tripmaster Monkey,* but the manuscript was destroyed in a fire in 1992.

The following excerpt from *China Men* delivers a wry comment on the elasticity of myth and legend, and the difficulties caused by miscommunication. (J.I.)

1   At a party, I met a Filipino scholar, who asked, "Do you know the Chinese came to the Philippines to look for the Gold Mountain?"

2   "No," I said. "I know hardly anything about the Philippines."

3   "They came in a ship in March of 1603," he said. "Three great mandarins landed at the Bay of Manila. The Filipinos were amazed to see them riding in ivory and gold chairs. They were higher class than the thirty thousand Chinese who were already living in Luzon. They had with them a Chinese in chains, who was to show them where to look for a gold needle in a mountain."

4   It was past midnight, or it was his accent, but I could not hear if he was saying that looking for the Gold Mountain was like looking for a needle in a haystack. "No. No," he said. "A gold needle." To sew the sails, was it? A compass needle, was it? "The mandarins asked for more ships, which they would fill with gold, some to give to the Filipino king, some to take back to the Queen of Spain, and some for the Emperor of China."

5   A group of Chinese Americans were gathering around the Filipino scholar. "Oh, yes," said a young man, "a Chinese monk went to Mexico looking for that mountain too, and either he came there with Cortez, or it was before that."

6   "And the Filipino king," continued the Filipino, "who had met conquistadores and knew about seven cities of gold and a fountain of youth, sent them to the town of Cabit."

7   "And they went to Weaversville, California," said another. "And in Weaversville, Cantonese laborers built a replica of their village in China."

8   "No, no," said someone else. "The way I heard it was that some cowboys saw mandarins floating over California in a hot-air balloon, which had come all the way from China."

9   "Now, these Chinese who were looking for the gold needle," I reminded the Filipino man, "what happened after they got to Cabit?"

10 "They sailed up a river farther and farther inland." And they built roads and railroads and cities on their way to this mountain. They filled swamps. They had children. "And on a certain mountain they sifted rocks and dirt looking for a gold needle. They asked the man in chains where the gold was, and he said that all they saw was gold."

11 Because I didn't hear everything, I asked him to repeat the story, and what he seemed to say again was "They found a gold needle in a mountain. They filled a basket with dirt to take with them back to China."

12 "Do you mean the Filipinos tricked them?" I asked. "What were they doing in Spain?"

13 "I'll write it down in a letter, and mail it to you," he said, and went on to something else.

14 Good. Now I could watch the young men who listen.

Discussion Questions

1. What was the result of the narrator's not listening?
2. Why do you think the Chinese Americans interrupted the Filipino scholar?
3. What does this selection convey about communication?
4. What is the significance of including speakers from many geographical regions? What does this suggest about "Chinese" identity in the United States?
5. What is the narrator telling us about her role as a storyteller?

Writing Topics

1. In a brief essay, examine what you think is the theme of "On Listening" and why Kingston chose to convey her message in the way she did.

MY FATHER, IN HEAVEN,
IS READING OUT LOUD

Li-Young Lee

Li-Young Lee was born in 1957 in Jakarta, Indonesia. In 1951 his father and mother had moved to Jakarta from Tianjin, China, after the Communists took power and Chinese Nationalists fled to Taiwan. For nine months before his departure from China, Lee's father served as personal physician to Mao Tse-tung, the powerful Chairman of the Communist Party and Premier of China. In Indonesia Lee's father taught philosophy at Gamaliel University and studied Western theology and poetry. In 1959 the Lees became fugitives when President Sukarno moved to purge all Chinese resident aliens. After traveling to Macao, Hong Kong, Singapore, and Japan, the Lees immigrated to the United States in 1964. They settled in Pennsylvania, where Lee's father gained admittance to the Pittsburgh Theological Society and obtained a position as a Christian minister.

Lee attributes his love of literature in large part to his father's love of poetry. He began to write poetry during his undergraduate years at the University of Pittsburgh. He also studied at the University of Arizona and the State University of New York at Brockport. In 1986, he published his first collection of poetry, entitled *Rose*. This debut collection received New York University's Delmore Schwartz Memorial Poetry Award. Lee also received grants from the Pennsylvania Council on the Arts and the National Endowment for the Arts. His second book, *The City in Which I Love You*, from which the following poem is taken, was published in 1990 and was the 1990 Lamont Poetry Selection of the Academy of American Poets. Lee has also published a well-received memoir, *Winged Seed* (1994).

In this poem Lee reflects in maturity on his father's character and circumstances and recalls the impact the elder man had on his own younger self.

My father, in heaven, is reading out loud
to himself Psalms or news. Now he ponders what
he's read. No. He is listening for the sound
of children in the yard. Was that laughing
5 or crying? So much depends upon the
answer, for either he will go on reading,
or he'll run to save a child's day from grief.
As it is in heaven, so it was on earth.

Because my father walked the earth with a grave,
10 determined rhythm, my shoulders ached
from his gaze. Because my father's shoulders
ached from the pulling of oars, my life now moves
with a powerful back-and-forth rhythm:
nostalgia, speculation. Because he
15 made me recite a book a month, I forget
everything as soon as I read it. And knowledge
never comes but while I'm mid-stride a flight
of stairs, or lost a moment on some avenue.

A remarkable disappointment to him,
20 I am like anyone who arrives late
in the millennium and is unable
to stay to the end of days. The world's
beginnings are obscure to me, its outcomes
inaccessible. I don't understand
25 the source of starlight, or starlight's destinations.
And already another year slides out
of balance. But I don't disparage scholars;
my father was one and I loved him,
who packed his books once, and all of our belongings,
30 then sat down to await instruction
from his god, yes, but also from a radio.
At the doorway, I watched, and I suddenly
knew he was one like me, who got my learning
under a lintel; he was one of the powerless,
35 to whom knowledge came while he sat among
suitcases, boxes, old newspapers, string.

He did not decide peace or war, home or exile,
escape by land or escape by sea.
He waited merely, as always someone
40 waits, far, near, here, hereafter, to find out:
is it praise or lament hidden in the next moment?

Discussion Questions

1. Explain how the speaker's father has affected the speaker's present life, according to stanza 2.
2. Why was the speaker a disappointment to his father?
3. What kind of instruction might the father have been waiting for?
4. In line 34 the speaker says that his father "was one of the powerless." How is this idea borne out in the last stanza?
5. How does the last line echo the thoughts in the first stanza?
6. Why do you think the speaker envisions his father as reading out loud in heaven?

Writing Topics

1. In an analytical essay, compare this poem with the two other Lee poems in this anthology, "The Gift" and "The Cleaving." What poetic devices does he seem to favor? Cite words and lines from the poems to support your views.
2. The speaker says that for him knowledge comes "when I'm mid-stride a flight of stairs, or lost a moment on some avenue." Recall a time when you had a sudden insight or an understanding when you weren't really thinking about anything in particular. Write about that time in your journal.

YELLOW LIGHT

Garrett Hongo

Garrett Hongo was born in 1951 in Volcano, Hawaii, but moved throughout his childhood, first to other places in Hawaii, then to California's San Fernando Valley, and finally to Gardena, a community in south Los Angeles with a large Japanese American population. He attended Pomona College, and after graduation he traveled throughout Japan on a Thomas J. Watson fellowship. Upon his return to the United States, Hongo began graduate work at the University of Michigan, where he studied with several poets, including Philip Levine and Donald Hall. While in Michigan, Hongo won the Hopwood Prize for Poetry. Moving back to the West Coast, he completed an M.F.A. at the University of California, Irvine, and later took an academic position at the University of Missouri. He currently teaches creative writing at the University of Oregon.

Hongo's list of recognitions and awards is extensive: in addition to the Hopwood Prize, he claims a Guggenheim Fellowship, two NEA grants, the Pushcart Prize, the Wesleyan University Press poetry competition, and the Lamont Poetry Selection for 1987 by the Academy of American Poets. Hongo collaborated on his first collection of poems, *The Buddha Bandits Down Highway 99* (1978), with Lawson Fusao Inada, who is also featured in this anthology, and Alan Chong Lau. *Yellow Light* followed in 1982. In 1988 *The River of Heaven,* his third collection, earned the praise of many critics and was named as a finalist for the Pulitzer Prize in poetry. Literary critic Amy Ling describes his poetry as filled with "striking images and unexpected, luminous lines" and further claims that he "has a special talent for close observation, an eye for the telling detail, and an ability to make the mundane beautiful."[1] He very often takes up issues of origin in his poetry, exploring ethnic identities, poetic inspiration, and the culture and history of Japan and Hawaii.

---

[1] *The Heath Anthology of American Literature,* third edition. (Boston: Heath, 1998) 2798.

In "Yellow Light" Hongo points out the persistence of natural beauty amid the mundane realities of barrio life. (J.I.)

One arm hooked around the frayed strap
of a tar-black patent-leather purse,
the other cradling something for dinner:
fresh bunches of spinach from a J-Town *yaoya*,[1]
5 sides of split Spanish mackerel from Alviso's,
maybe a loaf of Langendorf; she steps
off the hissing bus at Olympic and Fig,
begins the three-block climb up the hill,
passing gangs of schoolboys playing war,
10 Japs against Japs, Chicanas chalking sidewalks
with the holy double-yoked crosses of hopscotch,
and the Korean grocer's wife out for a stroll
around this neighborhood of Hawaiian apartments
just starting to steam with cooking
15 and the anger of young couples coming home
from work, yelling at kids, flicking on
TV sets for the Wednesday Night Fights.

If it were May, hydrangeas and jacaranda
flowers in the streetside trees would be
20 blooming through the smog of late spring.
Wisteria in Masuda's front yard would be
shaking out the long tresses of its purple hair.
Maybe mosquitoes, moths, a few orange butterflies
settling on the lattice of monkey flowers
25 tangled in chain-link fences by the trash.

But this is October, and Los Angeles
seethes like a billboard under twilight.
From used-car lots and the movie houses uptown,
long silver sticks of light probe the sky.
30 From the Miracle Mile, whole freeways away,
a brilliant fluorescence breaks out
and makes war with the dim squares

---

[1] *yaoya:* grocer.

of yellow kitchen light winking on
in all the side streets of the Barrio.
35 She climbs up the two flights of flagstone
stairs to 201-B, the spikes of her high heels
clicking like kitchen knives on a cutting board,
props the groceries against the door,
fishes through memo pads, a compact,
40 empty packs of chewing gum, and finds her keys.

The moon then, cruising from behind
a screen of eucalyptus across the street,
covers everything, everything in sight,
in a heavy light like yellow onions.

DISCUSSION QUESTIONS

1. This poem is a portrait of ordinary events and ordinary scenes in a Los
   Angeles neighborhood. Which parts of the portrait are seen and heard
   from afar, from a middle distance, and close up?
2. What time of day is depicted?
3. The poet has conveyed two seasons in the poem. How does he do so?
4. What are the moods or atmospheres of the scenes described?
5. Are the similes in lines 37 and 44 appropriate in your opinion? Why or
   why not?

WRITING TOPICS

1. Hongo achieves a great energy in this poem through the use of active,
   muscular verbs. In an analytical essay, explore Hongo's choice of verbs
   and what impact they have on the reading of the poem. Which word
   choices in particular seem to give the poem life? Cite words and lines
   from the poem to support your views.

FINDING THE CENTER

Lawson Fusao Inada

Lawson Fusao Inada, born in 1938 in Fresno, California, has been a major part of the Asian American literary community for the last thirty years. He spent much of his childhood, which coincided with World War II, interned in camps in Arkansas and Colorado. His debut collection, *Before the War: Poems as They Happened* (1971), was the first book of poetry to be written and published by an Asian American. In the mid-1970s he collaborated with Garrett Kaoru Hongo, whose work is also found in this anthology, and Alan Chong Lau to produce *The Buddha Bandits Down Highway 99*, published in 1978. His latest collection, *Drawing the Line: Poems*, was released in 1997.

Inada also has made significant contributions to Asian American literary criticism; with Jeffrey Paul Chan, Frank Chin, and Shawn Wong, he compiled and edited two anthologies of prose and poetry, *Aiiieeeee!* (1976) and *The Big Aiiieeeee!* (1991). In addition to receiving several awards and recognitions, including two fellowships from the National Endowment for the Arts, Inada has read his poetry at the White House and has served as a member of the Commission on Racism and Bias in Education for the National Council of Teachers of English. The Los Angeles Public Schools and Visual Communications made a film based on his life, entitled *I Told You So*. He is presently an English professor of creative writing at Southern Oregon State College and lives with his wife and two sons in Ashland, Oregon.

Inada's poetry takes up several themes found in the poetry of other Japanese Americans—the internment, the war, life in California towns. However, Ishmael Reed, an American novelist and poet who was born in the same year as Inada, also points out African American influences in his poems, especially the power of jazz and blues music. Inada studied the bass for a time and spent much time listening to important musicians, including Miles Davis and John Coltrane, at clubs in the San Francisco Bay Area.

In "Finding the Center" two young boys are not at all surprised to find that the "good dirt" of their youthful games has attracted official attention. (J.I.)

Charles and I had played there all along.
It was dirt. Good dirt. It made good
gardens—tomatoes, squash, peppers, corn.
It made good mud. It made good mounds
5   around the orange tree, the cactus,
for rivers and roads and boats and cars
living life in the valleys and mountains.

That was about it, for now—
Mama Gomez was calling us in for supper—
10 but tonight, if we were good, or lucky,
she would feed us sweet tortillas
and the crunchiest iced tea
as we sat on the porch, watching
moths meet the moon, fluttering stars,
15 and whatever else was doing on C Street.

Yes, it was a good life, on good dirt—
dirt to be smoothed over for marbles
mañana, and as we worked the earth
for our bright little spheres,
20 we looked for all the world like farmers.
Two kids, neighbors, an industrious lot.

That is why it didn't surprise us
when the dirt was finally discovered.
And, oh, the attention it got.
25 It was even, as they say, "in the paper"—
politicians and surveyors going loco,
placing a plaque in the Gomez yard.

And what the plaque said, we already knew.
It was obvious, and if they had asked
30 me or Charles or the Gomez family,
we could have saved them a lot of money:

"You're standing on it:
This dirt
Is the exact
35   Geographical
Center
Of the State
of
California!"

DISCUSSION QUESTIONS

1. What does the poem suggest about the speaker, who is a Japanese American, and his attitude toward Americans of other ethnic identities, such as Charles Gomez?
2. What can you infer of the age of the "two kids" whose activities are described in the poem?
3. Why does the speaker call the dirt good? What is it good for?
4. Did the event the poem describes—politicians and surveyors placing a plaque recognizing the dirt where the two kids played as "the exact geographical center" of California—actually happen? If it is a fantasy, or even if you believe it did happen, what is the symbolic significance of a center?

WRITING TOPICS

1. In a brief essay, analyze the tone of this poem and how it is conveyed.
2. Write a few paragraphs exploring the title of the poem. Is its meaning as straightforward as it seems or is there another "center" to which the author is referring?

A THEORY ABOUT DANCING

Diana Chang

Diana Chang was born in New York City in 1934. She was taken to live in China at the age of eight months, but the family returned to the United States after the Communist revolution of 1949. Chang began writing poems while an undergraduate at Barnard College in New York, where she later taught creative writing.

The author of six novels, Chang is also a well-published poet and a painter whose work has been exhibited. Her drawings and paintings are included in the collections of James Brooks and Betty Friedan, among other collectors. Her first novel, *The Frontiers of Love,* appeared in 1956 to much acclaim; it was reissued by the University of Washington Press in 1994. Among her books of poetry are *The Horizon Is Definitely Speaking* (1982), *What Mattisse Is After* (1984), and *The Mind's Amazement* (1998).

In "A Theory About Dancing," Chang shows that dancing must be done "in the present tense." (J.I.)

You can't dance
    in the past

It all happens here,
    now,
5   in the bone

The body sculpts time,
    calligraphy

in the first person,
    arms reaching,
10   ecstasy traveling

You can't dance
in the past

and the future's
a swooping lift
15   residing in air

How the beat
balances
on its vanishing

Dancing dances
20   in the present tense

It all happens here,
now,
in the bone

DISCUSSION QUESTIONS

1. Why can't one dance in the past?
2. What does it mean for the body to sculpt time?
3. Explain how this theory about dancing can apply to life itself.

WRITING TOPICS

1. Chang uses line breaks and staggered indents to great effect in this poem. In a brief essay, analyze Chang's use of these devices and the effect they have on the pace and rhythm of the poem.

SUMMARY WRITING TOPICS

1. In an essay, analyze the tone and mood of Lim's "Modern Secrets," Lee's "My Father, in Heaven, Is Reading Out Loud," and Garrett Hongo's "Yellow Light." Cite lines and words from the poems to support your views.

2. Reread the three Maxine Hong Kingston selections in this anthology, "No Name Woman," "On Discovery," and "On Listening." Write a brief essay on what you can discern of Kingston's personality and politics after reading these selections.

3. Assume that you can interview two of the authors in this chapter. Which two would you choose and why? Write reasons for your choices and then write several questions that you would like to ask each author.

4. Nobel Prize–winning poet Derek Walcott wrote, "To change your language you must change your life." Comment on this statement in a brief essay, citing examples from readings in this chapter to support your views.

5. Which selection in this chapter resonates most with you? Which seems to speak truths about your own life? Explore these questions in a personal essay.

ACKNOWLEDGMENTS

Abbasi, Talat. "Sari Petticoats" by Talat Abbasi is reprinted by permission of the publisher from *The Forbidden Stitch: An Asian American Women's Anthology,* © 1989 (Calyx Books).

Alexander, Meena. "Great Brown River" by Meena Alexander from *The Shock of Arrival: Reflections on Postcolonial Experience.* Copyright © 1996 by Meena Alexander. Reprinted by permission of the author.

Bao, Quang. "Nobody Knows" by Quang Bao, reprinted from *The Threepenny Review* (Fall 1995). Copyright © 1995 by Quang Bao. Reprinted by permission of the author.

Bulosan, Carlos. Excerpts from *America Is in the Heart: A Personal History* by Carlos Bulosan, copyright 1946 by Harcourt, Inc., reprinted by permission of the publisher.

Cao, Lan. From *Monkey Bridge* by Lan Cao. Copyright © 1997 by Lan Cao. Used by permission of Viking Penguin, a division of Penguin Putnam Inc.

Cha, Theresa Hak Kyung. From *Dictee* by Theresa Hak Kyung Cha. Reprinted by permission of the University of California, Berkeley Art Museum; gift of the Theresa Hak Kyung Cha Memorial Foundation.

Chang, Diana. "A Theory About Dancing" from *The Mind's Amazement* by Diana Chang, © 1998 by Diana Chang. Reprinted by permission of the author. "Foreign Ways" by Diana Chang, copyrighted and reprinted by permission of the author.

Chang, Lan Samantha. "The Eve of the Spirit Festival" by Lan Samantha Chang. Reprinted from *Prairie Schooner* by permission of the University of Nebraska Press. Copyright 1995 University of Nebraska Press.

Chin, Frank. From *Donald Duk* by Frank Chin. Copyright © 1991 by Frank Chin. Reprinted by permission of Coffee House Press.

Chin, Marilyn. From *Dwarf Bamboo* by Marilyn Chin, The Greenfield Review Press, Greenfield Center, New York. Reprinted by permission.

Chock, Eric. "Poem for My Father" and "Chinese Fireworks Banned in Hawaii" from *Last Days Here* (Bamboo Ridge Press, 1989). Copyright by Eric Chock. Reprinted by permission.

Chu, Louis. From *Eat a Bowl of Tea* by Louis Chu. Copyright © 1961 by Louis Chu. Published by arrangement with Carol Publishing Group. A Lyle Stuart book.

Divakaruni, Chitra. "The Arranged Marriage" is reprinted by permission of the publisher from *Black Candle* by Chitra Divakaruni, © 1991 (Calyx Books).

Far, Sui Sin. "Leaves from the Mental Portfolio of an Eurasian" from *Mrs. Spring Fragrance and Other Writings* by Sui Sin Far.

Freeman, James. Excerpts from "We Cannot Walk in our Neighborhood" reprinted from *Hearts of Sorrow: Vietnamese-American Lives* by James M. Freeman with the permission of the publishers, Stanford University Press. © 1989 by the Board of Trustees of the Leland Stanford Junior University.

Galang, M. Evelina. From *Her Wild American Self* by M. Evelina Galang. Copyright © 1996 by M. Evelina Galang. Reprinted by permission of Coffee House Press.

Gloria, Eugene. "Assimilation" by Eugene Gloria. Reprinted by permission of the author.

Gonzales, N. V. M. From *The Bread of Salt and Other Stories* by N. V. M. Gonzalez. Copyright © 1993 by N. V. M. Gonzalez. Reprinted by permission of the University of Washington Press.

Gotanda, Philip Kan. *The Wash* by Philip Kan Gotanda, © 1984, 1987 by Philip Kan Gotanda. Reprinted by permission. All inquiries regarding rights to Dramatist's Play Service.

Gotera, Vince. "First Mango" by Vince Gotera first appeared in *Returning a Borrowed Tongue*, ed. Nick Carbo, Coffee House Press. Copyright © 1995. Reprinted by permission of the author.

Hagedorn, Jessica. "Sorcery," from *Danger and Beauty* by Jessica Hagedorn. Copyright © 1993 by Jessica Hagedorn. Used by permission of Viking Penguin, a division of Penguin Putnam Inc. From *Dogeaters* by Jessica Hagedorn. Copyright © 1990 by Jessica Hagedorn. Reprinted by permission of Pantheon Books, a division of Random House, Inc.

Hongo, Garrett Kaoru. "Yellow Light" from *Yellow Light* by Garrett Kaoru Hongo, © 1982 by Garrett Kaoru Hongo, Wesleyan University Press by permission of University Press of New England.

Houston, James D. and Jeanne Wakatsuki. Excerpts from *Farewell to Manzanar* by James D. and Jeanne Wakatsuki Houston. Copyright © 1973 by James D. Houston. Reprinted by permission of Houghton Mifflin Co. All rights reserved.

Huỳnh, Jade Ngoc Quang. Excerpt copyright 1994 by Jade Ngoc Quang Huỳnh. Reprinted from *South Wind Changing* with the permission of Graywolf Press, Saint Paul, Minnesota.

Inada, Lawson Fusao. "Finding the Center" from *Legends from Camp* by Lawson Fusao Inada. Copyright © 1993 by Lawson Fusao Inada. Reprinted by permission of Coffee House Press.

Jacinto, Jaime. "Visitation" by Jaime Jacinto. Reprinted by permission of the author.

Jen, Gish. "A Man of Steel" from *Typical American*. Copyright © by Gish Jen. Reprinted by permission of Houghton Mifflin Co. All rights reserved.

Kamani, Ginu. From *Junglee Girl* by Ginu Kamani. © 1995 by Ginu Kamani. Reprinted by permission.

Kang, Younghill. From *East Goes West* by Younghill Kang. Copyright © 1937, 1965, 1997 by Christopher Kang.

Kikumura, Akemi. Reprinted by permission of the publisher from *Through Harsh Winters* by Akemi Kikumura. Copyright © 1981 by Chandler & Sharp Publishers, Inc. All rights reserved.

Kim, Myung Mi. "Into Such Assembly" from *Under Flag* by Myung Mi Kim, Kelsey St. Press, First edition 1991, Second edition 1998. Reprinted by permission.

Kim Ronyoung. Reprinted with permission from *Clay Walls* by Kim Ronyoung, published by The Permanent Press, Sag Harbor, NY 11963.

Kim, Willyce. "In This Heat" by Willyce Kim. Copyright © 1986 by Willyce Kim. Reprinted by permission of the author.

Kingston, Maxine Hong. From *The Woman Warrior* by Maxine Hong Kingston. Copyright © 1975, 1976 by Maxine Hong Kingston. Reprinted by permission of Alfred A. Knopf, Inc. From *China Men* by Maxine Hong Kingston. Copyright © 1980 by Maxine Hong Kingston. Reprinted by permission of Alfred A. Knopf, Inc.

Kono, Juliet. "Before Time" by Juliet S. Kono. Used by permission of the author.

Lai, Him Mark. From *Island: Poetry and History of Chinese Immigrants on Angel Island, 1910–1940* by Him Mark Lai, Genny Lim and Judy Yung, University of Washington Press. Copyright © 1980 by the HOC DOI (History of Chinese Detained on Island) Project. Reprinted by permission of the University of Washington Press.

Langworthy, Christian. "How I Could Interpret the Events of My Youth, Events I Do Not Remember Except in My Dreams" by Christian Langworthy. Used by permission of the author.

Law-Yone, Wendy. From *The Coffin Tree* by Wendy Law-Yone. Copyright © 1983 by Wendy Law-Yone. Reprinted by permission of Alfred A. Knopf, Inc.

Lee, Chang-Rae. From *Native Speaker* by Chang-Rae Lee. Copyright © 1995 by Chang-Rae Lee. Used by permission of Putnam Berkley, a division of Penguin Putnam Inc.

Lee, Gus. "Hector Pueblo" from *China Boy* by Gus Lee, published by the Penguin Group. Copyright © 1991 by Augustus S. M. S. Lee.

Lee, Li-Young. "The Cleaving" and "My Father in Heaven is Reading Out Loud" by Li-Young Lee, copyright © 1990 by Li-Young Lee. Reprinted from *The City in Which I Love You* with the permission of BOA Editions, Ltd., 260 East Ave., Rochester, NY 14604. "The Gift," copyright © 1990 by Li-Young Lee. Reprinted from *Rose* with the permission of BOA Editions, Ltd., 260 East Ave., Rochester, NY 14604.

Lê Thi Diem Thúy. "Shrapnel Shards on Blue Water" by Lê Thi Diem Thúy from *The Very Inside*, edited by Sharon Lim-Hing. Published in 1994 by Sister Vision Press, Toronto. Reprinted by permission of the publisher.

Lim, Genny. "ABCs" from *Winter Place* by Genny Lim, © 1989 by Genny Lim. Reprinted by permission of the author.

Lim, Shirley Geok-lin. Reprinted by permission of The Feminist Press at The City University of New York, from Shirley Geok-lin Lim, *Among the White Moon Faces: An Asian-American Memoir of Homelands* (New York: The Feminist Press at The City University of New York, 1996). Copyright © 1996 by Shirley Geok-lin Lim. "Modern Secrets" from *Modern Secrets* by Shirley Geok-lin Lim. Copyright © 1989 by Shirley Geok-lin Lim. Used by permission from the author.

Linh Dinh. "The Dead" by Linh Dinh, as appeared in *Watermark: Vietnamese American Poetry & Prose,* published by Asian American Writers' Workshop.

Linmark, R. Zamora. "Dreamhouse" by R. Zamora Linmark, first appeared in *Into the Fire,* The Greenfield Review Press, Greenfield Center, NY. Reprinted by permission.

Liu, Timothy. "Desire as the Gesture Between Us" by Timothy Liu, first appeared in *Burnt Offerings* (Copper Canyon Press, 1995). Copyright © 1995 by Timothy Liu. Reprinted by permission of the author.

Louie, David Wong. From *Pangs of Love & Other Stories* by David Wong Louie. Copyright © 1991 by David Wong Louie. Reprinted by permission of Alfred A. Knopf, Inc.

McCunn, Ruthanne Lum. From *Thousand Pieces of Gold* by Ruthanne Lum McCunn. © 1981 by Ruthanne Lum McCunn. Reprinted by permission of Beacon Press, Boston.

Minatoya, Lydia Yuri. "Transformation" from *Talking to High Monks in the Snow* by Lydia Minatoya. Copyright © 1992 by Lydia Minatoya. Reprinted by permission of HarperCollins Publishers, Inc.

Mirikitani, Janice. Excerpted from *Shedding Silence* by Janice Mirikitani, © 1987. Reprinted by permission of Celestial Arts, Berkeley, CA.

Mori, Toshio. From *Yokohama, California* by Toshio Mori. Reprinted by permission of Caxton Press, a division of The Caxton Printers Ltd., Coldwell, Idaho.

Mukherjee, Bharati. "The Management of Grief" from *The Middleman and Other Stories* by Bharati Mukherjee. Copyright © 1988 by Bharati Mukherjee. Used by permission of Grove/Atlantic, Inc.

Mura, David. From *The Colors of Desire* by David Mura. Copyright © 1994 by David Mura. Used by permission of Doubleday, a division of Random House, Inc.

Murayama, Milton. Excerpt from *All I Asking for Is My Body* by Milton Murayama. Reprinted by permission of the University of Hawaii Press.

Nguyen Ba Trac. "The White Horse" by Nguyen Ba Trac, translated by Nguyen Qui Duc. Reprinted by permission.

Okada, John. From *No-No Boy* by John Okada, University of Washington Press. Copyright © 1976 Dorothy Okada. Reprinted by permission of the University of Washington Press.

Santos, Bienvenido. From *Scent of Apples* by Bienvenido N. Santos. Copyright © 1955, 1967 by Bienvenido N. Santos. Reprinted by permission of the University of Washington Press.

Shah, Svati. "Lunch Vignettes" by Svati Shah from *The Very Inside*, edited by Sharon Lim-Hing. Published in 1994 by Sister Vision Press, Toronto. Reprinted by permission of the publisher.

Sone, Monica. From *Nisei Daughter* by Monica Sone. Copyright © 1953 by Monica Sone; copyright © renewed 1981 by Monica Sone. By permission of Little, Brown and Company.

Song, Cathy. "The Youngest Daughter" from *Picture Bride* by Cathy Song, Yale University Press. Copyright 1983. Used by permission of the publisher.

Sugimoto, Etsu. "Sailing the Unknown Seas" from *A Daughter of the Samurai* by Etsu Sugimoto.

Tagami, Jeff. "Labor of Love" from *October Light* by Jeff Tagami. Reprinted by permission of the author.

Tan, Amy. From *The Joy Luck Club* by Amy Tan, published by G. P. Putnam's Sons. Copyright © 1989 by Amy Tan.

Tham, Hilary. "San Chi" from *Bad Names for Women* by Hilary Tham, The Word Works, Inc., Washington D.C., 1989. Reprinted by permission.

Verghese, Abraham. Reprinted with the permission of Simon & Schuster, Inc., from *My Own Country* by Abraham Verghese. Copyright © 1994 by Abraham Verghese.

Wong, Jade Snow. From *Fifth Chinese Daughter* by Jade Snow Wong. Copyright © 1945 by Jade Snow Wong. Reprinted by permission of the University of Washington Press.

Wong, Shawn. Reprinted with permission of Simon & Schuster, Inc., from *American Knees* by Shawn Wong. Copyright © 1995 by Shawn Wong. From *Homebase* by Shawn Wong. Copyright © 1979, 1991 by Shawn Hsu Wong. Used by permission of Dutton Signet, a division of Penguin Putnam Inc.

Yamada, Mitsuye. From *Desert Run: Poems and Stories* by Mitsuye Yamada, copyright © 1988 by Mitsuye Yamada. Reprinted by permission of Rutgers University Press.

Yamamoto, Hisaye. *Seventeen Syllables and Other Stories*, copyright © 1988 by Hisaye Yamamoto. Originally published in Pacific Citizen, 1950. Reprinted by permission of Rutgers University Press.

Yamanaka, Lois-Ann. From *Saturday Night at the Pahala Theatre*. Copyright © 1993 by Lois-Ann Yamanaka. Published by Bamboo Ridge Press. First published in *Bamboo Ridge: The Hawaii Writer's Quarterly*. Reprinted by permission of Susan Bergholz Literary Services, New York. All rights reserved.

Yamauchi, Wakako. "And the Soul Shall Dance" and "So What; Who Cares?" reprinted, by permission of The Feminist Press at The City University of New York, from Wakako Yamauchi, *Songs My Mother Taught Me: Stories, Plays, and Memoir*, edited by Garrett Hongo (New York: The Feminist Press at The City University of New York, 1994). Copyright © 1994 by Wakako Yamauchi.

AUTHOR-TITLE INDEX